ANCIENT INDIAN TRADITION & MYTHOLOGY

Translated by

A BOARD OF SCHOLARS

Edited by

G.P. Bhatt

VOLUME 38

ANCIENT INDIAN TRADITION AND MYTHOLOGY

Mahāpurāṇas *Translated into English*
Gen. Ed. Dr. G.C. TRIPATHI
Founder Eds. LATE J.L. SHASTRI and LATE G.P. BHATT

PUBLISHED VOLUMES

Vols. 1-4	ŚIVA PURĀṆA *Tr.* J.L. Shastri
Vols. 5-6	LIṄGA PURĀṆA *Tr.* J.L. Shastri
Vols. 7-11	BHĀGAVATA PURĀṆA *Tr.* G.V. Tagare
Vols. 12-14	GARUḌA PURĀṆA *Tr.* J.L. Shastri
Vols. 15-19	NĀRADA PURĀṆA *Tr.* G.V. Tagare
Vols. 20-21	KŪRMA PURĀṆA *Tr.* G.V. Tagare
Vols. 22-26	BRAHMĀṆḌA PURĀṆA *Tr.* G.V. Tagare
Vols. 27-30	AGNI PURĀṆA *Tr.* N. Gangadharan
Vols. 31-32	VARĀHA PURĀṆA *Tr.* S. Venkitasubramonia Iyer
Vols. 33-36	BRAHMA PURĀṆA *Tr.* J.L. Shastri
Vols. 37-38	VĀYU PURĀṆA *Tr.* G.V. Tagare
Vols. 39-48	PADMA PURĀṆA *Tr.* N.A. Deshpande
Vols. 49-71	SKANDA PURĀṆA *Ed.* G.P. Bhatt, *Tr. & Annot.* Shridhar Balooni & Pratosh Panda
Vols. 72-73	VĀMANA PURĀṆA *Tr. & Annot.* R.S. Shiva Ganesha Murthy
Vols. 74-76	GAṆEŚA PURĀṆA *Tr. & Annot.* Greg Bailey
Vols. 77-82	BRAHMAVAIVARTA PURĀṆA *Tr. & Annot.* G.P. Bhatt

PURĀṆAS UNDER PREPARATION

Viṣṇu Purāṇa • Harivaṃśa Purāṇa • Bhaviṣya Purāṇa • Matsya Purāṇa • Devī Bhāgavata Purāṇa • Kālika Purāṇa • Mārkaṇḍeya Purāṇa • Viṣṇudharmottara Purāṇa

THE VĀYU PURĀṆA

PART- II

Section 3 : Anuṣaṅga, and
Section 4 : Upasaṁhāra

Translated and annotated by
G.V. TAGARE

MOTILAL BANARSIDASS PUBLISHERS
PRIVATE LIMITED • DELHI

2nd Reprint : ***Delhi, 2018***
First Edition: Delhi, 1988

ISBN: 978-81-208-0455-5

MOTILAL BANARSIDASS
41 U.A. Bungalow Road, Jawahar Nagar, Delhi 110 007
1 B, Jyoti Studio Compound, Kennedy Bridge, Nana Chowk, Mumbai 400 007
120 Royapettah High Road, Mylapore, Chennai 600 004
236, 9th Main III Block, Jayanagar, Bengaluru 560 011
8 Camac Street, Kolkata 700 017
Ashok Rajpath, Patna 800 004
Chowk, Varanasi 221 001

UNESCO COLLECTION OF REPRESENTATIVE WORKS—*Indian Series*
This book has been accepted in the Indian Translation Series of the UNESCO Collection of Representative Works, jointly sponsored by the United Nations Educational, Scientific and Cultural Organization (UNESCO) and the Government of India

MLBD Cataloging-in-Publication Data
The Vāyu Puraṇa (Part-II)
Translated and Annotated by
G.V. Tagare
Includes Notes
ISBN: 978-81-208-0455-5
I. Hinduism II. Purana III. Padma
IV. Tagare, G.V.

Printed in India

by RP Jain at NAB Printing Unit,
A-44, Naraina Industrial Area, Phase I, New Delhi–110028
and published by JP Jain for Motilal Banarsidass Publishers (P) Ltd,
41 U.A. Bungalow Road, Jawahar Nagar, Delhi-110007

PUBLISHER'S NOTE

The purest gems lie hidden in the bottom of the ocean or in the depth of rocks. One has to dive into the ocean or delve into the rocks to find them out. Similarly, truth lies concealed in the language which with the passage of time has become obsolete. Man has to learn that language before he discovers that truth.

But he has neither the means nor the leisure to embark on that course. We have, therefore, planned to help him acquire knowledge by an easier course. We have started the series of Ancient Indian Tradition and Mythology in English Translation. Our goal is to universalize knowledge through the most popular international medium of expression. The publication of the Purāṇas in English Translation is a step towards that goal.

PREFACE

This thirty-eighth volume in the series on *Ancient Indian Tradition and Mythology* constitutes the second part (*Uttarārdha*) of the Vāyu Purāṇa in English translation comprising the last two of the four sections (*Pādas*) into which the Purāṇa is divided, viz. (1) *Prakriyā*, (2) *Upodghāta*, (3) *Anuṣaṅga* and (4) *Upasaṁhāra*.

This part contains in all fifty chapters, out of which the first three really belong to the second section ie. the *Upodghāta Pāda* of the first part or *Pūrvārdha*, which appear to have wantonly sneaked into this part. The redactors of the Purāṇa should have made these three chapters the last three of the Pūrvārdha which would in that case have 64 chapters instead of the present 61, not a big difference really, rather than transfer them to the second part, to which they have no special logical affinity.

The explanation of this anomaly is not far to seek. As Dr. Tagare has pointed out in his Introduction to Part I, the original Vāyu Purāṇa ended with chapter 41 of the *Uttarārdha* which contains the *Phalaśruti* i.e. merit of listening to the Purāṇa as well as the *Avabhṛtha* or the valedictory bath taken at the completion of a ritual undertaking, followed by a line of teachers who received and transmitted the text of the Purāṇa. From this it is obvious that chapters 42-50 of the *Uttarārdha* are later additions and not a genuine part of the Purāṇa. Apparently some zealous advocate of the Gayātīrtha which is the subject of these chapters included them in the Purāṇa at a later stage to impart sanctity to his cherished subject and an authoritative character to Gayā pilgrimage, at the same time introducing in the text a fake division into *Pūrvārdha* and *Uttarārdha* over and above the original four sections and making the two parts as two almost exact halves by the spliting and transfer of the three chapters of the *Upodghāta Pāda*, without caring for the anomaly that would thus result, in order to give to the later addition an appearance of genuineness. This would look like a most plausible explanation.

As a matter of fact fact, even the older division of the text into four sections does not appear to be quite relevant and logical as the distribution of the chapters under these four major heads does not follow any logical pattern. In view of this one could wish that someone bring out a new edition of the Purāṇa with only 102 chapters (61 of Part I & 41 of Part II) re-numbered from 1 to 102 without these artificial divisions along with the last nine chapters in the form of one or rather two Appendices.

Among the topics included in the contents of this part two have obviously received special prominence, viz. the Śrāddha cult and the glorification of Gayā. But of the total 50 chapters 12, from 10 to 21, are related to the former, which constitute slightly less than one-fourth of the whole. The last seven chapters, approximately one-seventh of the whole, have been devoted to Gayā as a great sacred place and related legends as well as the rules and procedure to be observed during the pilgrimage to Gayā. The importance of this portion is amply shown by the fact that it has to a great extent influenced the later Tīrtha literature, notably *Tirthacintāmaṇi* and *Tristhalisetu.*

The project of this series was envisaged in 1970 by the late Lala Sundar Lal Jain of Messrs. Motilal Banarsidass. Thirty-eight volumes of the series, including the present one, have so far been published and others are in progress. Complete sets of eleven major Purāṇas, viz. *Agni*, *Bhāgavata*, *Brahma*, *Brahmāṇḍa*, *Garuḍa*, *Kūrma*, *Liṅga*, *Nārada*, *Śiva*, *Varāha* and *Vāyu* are now available in English to the lovers of ancient Indian wisdom.

It is our pleasant duty to put on record our sincere thanks to Dr. R.N. Dandekar and the UNESCO authorities for their kind encouragement and valuable help which render this work more useful than it would otherwise have been. We are extremely grateful to Dr. G.V. Tagare for translating the text. We are also thankful to all those who have been helpful in our project.

—*Editor*

CONTENTS

ABBREVIATIONS

Common and self-evident abbreviations such as Ch(s)—Chapter(s), p—page, pp—pages, V—Verse, VV—Verses, Ftn—footnote, Hist. Ind. Philo.—History of Indian Philosophy are not included in this list.

ABORI	*Annals of the Bhandarkar Oriental Research Institute*, Poona
AGP	S. M. Ali's *The Geography of Purāṇas*, PPH, New Delhi, 1973
AIHT	*Ancient Indian Historical Tradition*, F. E. Pargiter, Motilal Banarsidass (MLBD), Delhi
AITM	*Ancient Indian Tradition and Mythology* Series, MLBD, Delhi
AP	*Agni Purāṇa*, Guru Mandal Edition (GM), Calcutta, 1957
Arch.S.Rep.	Archaeological Survey Report
AV	*Atharva Veda*, Svādhyāya Mandal, Aundh
Bd. P.	*Brahmāṇḍa Purāṇa*, MLBD, Delhi 1973
BG	*Bhagavadgītā*
Bh. P.	*Bhāgavata Purāṇa*, Bhagavat Vidyapeeth, Ahmedabad
Br.	*Brāhmaṇa* (preceded by name such as Śatapatha)
BS. P.	*Bhaviṣya Purāṇa*, Vishnu Shastri Bapat, Wai
BV. P.	*Brahma Vaivarta Purāṇa*, GM, 1955-57
CC	*Caturvarga Cintāmaṇi* by Hemādri
CVS	*Caraṇa Vyūha Sūtra* by Śaunaka, Com. by Mahidāsa
DB	*Devī Bhāgavata*, GM, 1960-61
De or GDAMI	*The Geographical Dictionary of Ancient and Mediaeval India*, N. L. De, Oriental Reprint, Delhi, 1971
Dh. S.	*Dharma Sūtra* (preceded by the author's name such as Gautama)
ERE	*Encyclopaedia of Religion and Ethics* by Hastings
GP	*Garuḍa Purāṇa*, ed. R. S. Bhattacharya, Chowkhamba, Varanasi, 1964

GS	*Gṛhya Sūtra* (preceded by the name of the author such as Āpastamba)
HD	*History of Dharma Śāstra*, P. V. Kane, G. O. S.
IA	*The Indian Antiquary*
IHQ	*The Indian Historical Quarterly*
JP	*Purāṇa* (Journal of the Kashiraj Trust), Varanasi
KA	*Kauṭilya Arthaśāstra*
KP	*Kūrma Purāṇa*, Veṅkaṭeśvara Press Edn., Bombay; also Kashiraj Trust Edn., Varanasi, 1971
LP	*Liṅga Purāṇa*, GM, 1960; also MLBD, Delhi, 1981
Manu.	*Manusmṛti*
Mbh.	*Mahābhārata*, Gītā Press, Gorakhpur, VS 2014
MkP	*Mārkaṇḍeya Purāṇa*
MN	*Mahābhārata Nāmānukramaṇī*, Gītā Press, Gorakhpur, VS 2016
MtP	*Matsya Purāṇa*, GM, 1954
MW	Monier Williams' *Sanskrit-English Dictionary*, MLBD, Delhi, 1976
NP	*Nāradīya* or *Nārada Purāṇa*, Veṅkaṭeśvara Press, Bombay
PCK	*Bhāratavarṣīya Prācīna Caritrakośa*, Siddheshwar Shastri, Poona, 1968
Pd.P.	*Padma Purāṇa*, GM, 1957-59
PE	*Purāṇic Encyclopaedia*, V. Mani, English version, MLBD, Delhi, 1975
PR or PRHRC	*Puranic Records on Hindu Rites and Customs*, R. C. Hazra, Calcutta, 1948
ṚV	*Ṛg-Veda*, Svādhyāya Mandal, Aundh
Śat.Br.	*Śatapatha Brāhmaṇa*
SC or SMC	*Smṛti Candrikā* by Devanna Bhaṭṭa
SEP	*Studies in Epics and Purāṇas*, A.D. Pusalkar, Bharatiya Vidya Bhavan (BVB), Bombay

VĀYU PURĀṆA

PART II

CHAPTER ONE

Manvantaras : The Milking of the Earth

Obeisance to Śrī gaṇeśa

Śāṁśapāyana said :

1. I wish to know precisely the order of Manvantaras[1] and all the respective deities pertaining to the different Manvantaras.

Sūta said :

2. Listen to and understand as I recount succinctly and in detail, the Manvantaras which have gone and which are yet to come.

3. The first Manu was Svāyaṁbhuva and then there was Svārociṣa Manu. Thereafter the Manus were Auttama, Tāmasa,

---

1 Manvantara is a period during which a Manu presides over the world. It (the period) consists of seventyone cycles of four yugas (*catur-yugī*) or one-fourteenth part of god Brahmā's day. In other words there are fourteen Manus in one day of Brahmā at the end of which there is *Pralaya* (Dissolution) of the universe. Every Manu has his special set of gods, Indra, an incarnation of Viṣṇu, seven sages (*saptarṣis*). Thus in the 1st Manvantara, Svāyaṁbhuva (the son of god Brahmā) was the presiding Manu, Yāmas were the gods, Yajña, the incarnation of Viṣṇu officiated as Indra and the group of seven sages consisted of Marīci, Atri, Aṅgiras, Pulaha, Kratu, Pulastya and Vasiṣṭha. In every Manvantara, though the set of these functionaries is different, they have got the same powers, functions and the same tenure.

The description of Manvantaras is one of the five essential characteristics of a Purāṇa. Thus we find Purāṇas like Bh. P. VIII.1.29, NP. I.40.17-37, VP. III chs. 1 and 2, KP.I.51, Bd. P. I.2.36 describing various Manvantaras.

Raivata and Cākṣuṣa. These six Manus have already passed away. I shall explain the eight future Manus.[1]

4. They are the five Sāvarṇas, Raucya, Bhautya and Vaivasvata. I shall explain them after Vaivasvata Manu.

5. Know the five Manus who have passed away to be Mānavas. The Manvantara of Svāyaṁbhuva Manu which has already passed has been described by me.

6. Henceforth, I shall describe briefly the activity of creation by Svārociṣa, the second Manu of noble soul.[2]

7. In the Svārociṣa Manvantara, there were the Devas called Tuṣitas and the learned scholars called Pārāvatas. Only these two are remembered as the groups of Devas.

8. They were born of Tuṣitā as the sons of Kratu, the Svārociṣa (Manu). The Pārāvatas and the remaining ones—these two *Gaṇas* (groups) consist of twelve each. (Thus) all these Devas together are remembered as *chandajas* and they are twenty-four (in number).

9-10. Dhaivasyaśa, Vāmānya, Gopā, Devāyata, lord Aja, the powerful lord Duroṇa, Āpa of powerful arms, the vigorous Mahaujas, Cikitvān, Nibhṛta, Vīryavān, and Aṁśa: these were the sons of Kratu. They were then the imbibers of Soma.

11-13. Lord Pracetas, Viśvedeva, Samañja who was well known, Ajihma the suppressor of enemies, Ajihmāna and Mahīyāna endowed with learning, the blessed Aja and Uṣa, Yavīya of great strength, Hotṛ and Yajvā were the Pārāvatas of great exploit. These all were the deities who functioned in the Svārociṣa Manvantara.

14. At that time these twenty-four Devatās (deities) were the imbibers of Soma. Their Indra (ruler and leader) was Vaidha who was world-famous.

15-16. The *Saptarṣis* (the Seven Sages) were Ūrja the son of Vasiṣṭha, Staṁbha the son of Kaśyapa, Droṇa the son of Bhṛgu,

1. There are some variations in the names of future Manus in some Purāṇas. Our Purāṇa gives some different names (such as Raucya and Bhautya) of future Manus.

2. Verses 6-22 enumerate and describe the functionaries (gods, Indra etc.) during the second Manvantara.

Ṛṣabha the son of Aṅgiras, Dattātri the son of Pulastya, Niścala the son of Atri, and Dhāvān the son of Pulaha.

17-18. Caitra, Kaviruta, Kṛtānta, Ravi, Bṛhat, Guha, Nava and Śubha[1]: these nine are rememberd as the sons of Svārociṣa Manu who established his race. They have been enumerated in the Purāṇa. Such is the second Manvantara.

19. The Seven Sages, Manu, Devas and Pitṛs—these four constitute the root (and foundation) of a Manvantara. All the subjects are subsidiary to them.

20. Deities are the sons of Sages, Pitṛs are the sons of Devas and the Sages are the sons of Devas—This is the conclusion of the *Śāstras* (Scriptures).

21. Kṣatriyas and Vaiśyas were born of Manu and Brāhmaṇas were born of the Seven Sages. Thus the Manvantara has been described in brief, not in details.

22. The detailed description of the Svārociṣa Manvantara should be understood through (that of) Svāyaṁbhuva Manvantara. It is impossible to describe it in detail even in hundreds of years, since the progenies are many in every family and they are oft-repeated.

23. The Manvantara of Auttama is the third among the Manvantaras.[2] There are five *Gaṇas*. I shall recount them. Understand them.

24. The Devas are Sudhāmans, Vaśavartins, Pratardanas, Śivas, and Satyas. Each of these groups (*Gaṇas*) consists of twelve (Devas).

25. The names of the twelve constituting Sudhāmans are Satya, Dhṛti, Dama, Dānta, Kṣama, Kṣāma, Dhṛti (Dhvani—Bd.P.), Śuci, Īṣa, Ūrjas, Jyeṣṭha and Vapuṣmān the twelfth.

26. The Vaṁśakarin Devas (Vaśavartins) were Sahasradhāra, Viśvātman, Śamitāra, Bṛhadvasu, Viśvadhā, Viśvakarmā Manasvanta, Virāḍ. Yaśas, Jyotis, Vibhāvya and Kīrtimān.

27-28. Pramardana (Pratardana) gods are glorified. They are[3]—Avadhya, Arati, Lord Vasu, Dhiṣṇya, Vivasvasu (Vibhā-

---

1. As per A.

2. Verses 23-36 describe the Auttama or Uttama's Manvantara. As noted in v. 36 the activities of creation etc. are the same as in the previous Manvantara.

3. The reading *anyānārādhito devo* 'God not worshipped by others' is meaningless, as this is a list of Pratardana gods.—'*Pramardana*' in the text is an

vasu in Bd.P.) Dinakratu (Vitta and Kratu in Bd.P.), Sudharmā, Dhṛtavarmā, Yaśasvina (Yaśasvija in Bd.P.) and Ketumān[1].

29-30. Haṁsa, Svara, Ahihā, Pratardana, Yaśaskara, Sudāna Vasudāna, Sumañjasa, Viṣa, Jantuvāhyati, Suvitta and Sunaya—these are to be known as Śivas. They are the twelve other gods worthy of partaking their share in sacrifice.

31-33. Understand the names of those constituting the Satya category of Devas, as agreed (by sages of yore). They are Dikpati, Vākpati, Viśva, Śaṁbhu, Svamṛḍīka, Adhipa, Varcodhas, Muhyasarvaśa (?), Vāsava, Sādāśva, Kṣema and Ānanda. These are those sacrifice-worthy other twelve (Devas) famous as Satyas. These are the deities who lived in the Manvantara of Auttama.

34-35. Aja, Paraśu, Divya, Divyauṣadhi, Naya, the unequalled Devānuja, Mahotsāha, Auśija, Vinīta, Suketu, Sumitra, Subala and Śuci—these thirteen were the noble-souled sons of the Manu Auttama. These were the progenitors of the race of Kṣatriyas and made them flourish. Such is the third Manvantara.

36. The activity of creation etc. in the course of the Auttama Manvantara has been explained through (that of) Svārociṣa Manvantara. Now listen and understand the creation etc. in the Tāmasa Manvantara in detail and in the proper order.

37. In the fourth period of Manvantara[2] of the Manu Tāmasa, the Gaṇas were four, viz. Satyas, Svarūpas, Sudhīs and Haris.

38. In the Manvantara of Tāmasa, the gardsons of Pulastya (manifested themselves). Each of these Devagaṇas consisted of twentyfive (gods).

---

obvious misprint, for *Pratardana* is mentioned in v. 24 above. Verses 26ff. give the list of the twelve gods in each set or class (*gaṇa*) of Devas. The reading in our text does not satisfy the condition of giving twelve gods in the Pratardana class. Hence the reading from a corresponding verse in Bd. P. (I.2.36. 30b) viz. *avadhyo' varatir devo* is accepted here.

1. If Vitta, Kratu and Rathormi from the readings in Bd. P. is accepted, the list will have twelve names (the expected number of this group of Devas).

2. Verses 37-43 deal with Tāmasa Manvantara.

39. The hundred *Indriyas* (sense-organs) and the eighth Tamas (Darkness) which the top-most sages who value truth as life, enunciate, are remembered as the Devas in that Manvantara.

40. Śibi the lord of (great) exploit, was the Indra of those Devas. O excellent ones, understand the seven sages of that Manvantara.

41-42. Harṣa, the son of Kavi; Pṛthu, the son of Kaśyapa; Agni, the son of Atri; Jyotirdhāman, the son of Bhṛgu; Vanapīṭha, the son of Pulaha, Gotra, the son of Vasiṣṭha; and Caitra, the son of Pulastya were the (seven) sages in the Tāmasa Manvantara.

43. Janughaṇḍa, Śānti, Nara, Khyāti, Bhaya, Priyabhṛtya, Avakṣi, Pṛṣṭaloḍhā, Dṛḍhodyata, Ṛta and Ṛtabandhu were the sons of Tāmasa Manu.

44. In the fifth cycle of Manvantara of Cāriṣṇava Manu,[1] the groups of Devatās are well enumerated. Understand them.

45. Amṛtābha, Ābhūtarajas, Vikuṇṭha and Sumedhas were the auspicious sons of Cariṣṇu alias Vasiṣṭha, the Prajāpati. Their shining and glorious Gaṇas were fourteen and four (i.e. eighteen) (or fourteen for each of the four Gaṇas).

46-47. Svatra (Svapna in A.), Vipra, Agnibhās, Pratyetiṣṭha, Amṛta, Sumati, Vāvirāva, Vācinoda, Srava, Pravirāśī, Vāda and Prāśa were the fourteen (?) Amṛtābhas remembered as the *devas* in the Cāriṣṇava Manvantara.

48-49. Mati, Sumati, Ṛta, Satya, Āvṛti,[2] Vivṛti, Mada, Vinaya, Jetā, Jiṣṇu, Sahas, Dyutimān and Sravasa—these are the names of Ābhūtarajas Gaṇas as (they) know.

50. Vṛṣa, Bhettā,[3] Jaya, Bhīma, Śuci, Dānta, Yaśa, Dama, Nātha, Vidvān, Ajeya, Kṛśa, Gaura and Dhruva are glorified as Vikuṇṭhas. Uunderstand the Sumedhas.

---

1. Verses 44-55 describe the fifth Manvantara which the text calls Cāriṣṇava i.e. of Manu Cariṣṇu but calls the same Manu as Raivata in verses 54, 55 and 56. Manus from Svārociṣa to Raivata belonged to the lineage of Priyavrata.

2. Bd.P. ibid v. 56 adds '*Edhana*' here and makes up the number fourteen.

3. Reading in Bd. P. accepted to make up the number (14).

51-52. Medhā, Medhātithi, Satyamedhā, Pṛśnimedhā, Alpamedhā, Bhūyomedhā and others (?), the lord Dīptimedhā, Yaśomedhā, Sthiramedhā, Sarvamedhā, Aśvamedhā, Pratimedhā, Medhāvān and Medhahārtā are glorified as Sumedhas.

53-54. Vibhu of well known exploits and manliness was their Indra. Then the (seven) sages in the fifth Manvantara of Raivata Manu were: Vedabāhu, son (descedant) of Pulastya; the sage called Yaju, the son of Kaśyapa; Hiraṇyaromā, son of Aṅgiras; Vedaśrī, son of Bhṛgu; Ūrdhvabāhu, son of Vasiṣṭha; Parjanya, son of Pulaha; and Satyanetra, son of Atri.

55. Mahāpurāṇasambhāvya, Pratyaṅgaparahā, Śuci, Balabandhu, Nirāmitra, Ketubhṛṅga and Dṛḍhavrata were the sons of Cariṣṇava. Such is the fifth Manvantara.

56. Svārocisa, Auttama, Tāmasa and Raivatas—these four Manus belong to the family of Priyavrata.

57. In the sixth cycle of Cākṣuṣa Manvantara[1] the Devas are remembered as consisting of five Gaṇas (classes), viz. Ādyas, Prasūtas, Bhāvyas, the heaven-dwelling Pṛthukas and the Lekhas of great dignity.

58. This creation of heaven-dwellers is mentioned in accordance with the names of their mothers. The Gaṇas of those Devas are the great-grandsons of Āraṇya, the Prajāpati, the son of Atri. Each of these groups is remembered as comprising of eight Devas.

59. Antarikṣa, Vasu, Haya, Atithi, Priyavrata, Śrotā, Mantā and Sumantā—these are glorified as Ādyas.

60. Śyenabhadra, Paśya, Pathyanetra of great fame, Sumanas, Suvetas, Raivata, Supracetas and Dyuti of great prowess—these are mentioned as Prasūtas.

61. Vijaya, Sujaya, Mana, Udyāna, Sumati, Supari, Vijñāta and Arthapati—these Devas are remembered as Bhāvyas. Now listen and understand the Pṛthuka gods.

62. Ajiṣṭa, the Lord Śākyana, Vānapṛṣṭha, Śaṅkara, Satyadhṛṣṇu, Viṣṇu, Vijaya and the highly blessed Ajita are the heaven-dwelling Pṛthukas.

1. Verses 57-69 describe the Cākṣuṣa Manvantara.

63-64. I shall now describe Lekhas. Understand as I recount them. Manojava, Praghāsa, Pracetas of great fame, Vāta, Dhruvakṣiti, Adbhuta of great virility, Avana and Bṛhaspati are glorified as Lekhas.

65-66. Manojava of great virility and prowess became their Indra then. The seven sages in the Cākṣuṣa Manvantara were: Unnata, son (descendant) of Bhṛgu; Haviṣmān, son of Aṅgiras; Sudhāman, son of Kaśyapa; Virajas, son of Vasiṣṭha; Atimāna, son of Pulastya; Sahiṣṇu, son of Pulaha, and Madhura, descendant of Atri.

67-68. Ūru, Pūru, Śatadyumna, Tapasvin, Satyavāk, Kṛti, Agniṣṭut, Atirātra and Sudyumna—these nine and the tenth one Abhimanyu; these were the sons of Cākṣuṣa Manu born of Nādvalī. Such is the sixth Manvantara.

69. O Brāmaṇas, the creation of that noble soul is explained through (that of) Vaivasvata Manvantara and it has been explained by me in detail and in the proper order.

The sages requested :

70. The successors and heirs of Cākṣuṣa Manu were born in the family of Kaśyapa. Please mention (enumerate) to us all those others who were born in his family.

Sūta said :

71. It behoves you to hear the creative activity of Cākṣuṣa Manu in brief. Pṛthu, the valorous son of Vena, was born in his family.

72. Other Prajāpatis and Dakṣa, son of Pracetas, too were born (of that family). Atri, the Prajāpati, adopted Uttānapāda as his son.

73-74. The son of Dakṣaka, the Prajāpati, became a king. He was given in adoption to Atri for some reason by Svāyaṁbhuva Manu after the advent of the sixth (Manvantara). O Brāhmaṇas, having reached the future Manvantara Cākṣuṣa, I shall now explain it by way of introduction.

75. The very clever daughter of Dharma and his wife Lakṣmī, the lady of sparkling smiles named Sunṛtā (Sunīti), the lady who could produce wealth, bore to Uttānapāda a son named Dhruva and became his auspicious mother.

76. Uttānapāda begot of her Dhruva, Kīrtimān, Ayasmān and Vasu and also two daughters of sparkling smiles, Manasvinī and Svarā. Their sons have been already mentioned.

77. The valorous Dhruva, praying for (desirous of) extensive fame, performed penance for ten thousand divine years observing fast.

78-79. In the first Tretāyuga, he (Dhruva), the grandson of Svāyaṁbhuva Manu, controlled himself by means of Yoga in his desire to win great fame. The delighted Brahmā granted him the excellent abode among luminaries. It is pleasing and lasting till the final dissolution of the Universe. It is devoid of setting and rising.

80. On seeing his unlimited glory and greatness, Uśanas, the preceptor of Daityas and Asuras, sang this *Śloka* (verse).

81. "How wonderful is the prowess of his penance ! How commendable is his learning ! Wonderful is his *Huta* (Holy rite) that the seven sages have kept Dhruva above themselves. The firmament depends on Dhruva. He is the controller and the lord of the firmament".

82. Bhūmi bore to Dhruva two kings (as sons), viz. Puṣṭi and Bhavya. The powerful lord Puṣṭi told his shadow, "Be a woman".

83. At his truthful utterance, the shadow of divine body became a woman immediately. She was bedecked in divine ornaments.

84. Puṣṭi begot of his Chāyā five sinless sons, viz. Prācīnagarbha, Vṛṣaka, Vṛka, Vṛkala and Dhṛti.

85. The wife of Prācīnagarbha named Bhūvarcā gave birth to a son who became a king by the name of Udāradhī. In his previous birth, he had been Indra.

86. He used to take food but once at the end of every thousand years. Thus the lord secured Indra-hood which lasted a Manvantara.

87. Bhadrā bore to Udāradhī the son Divañjaya. Varāṅgī bore to Divañjaya the son Ripu, the conqueror of foes.

88. From Ripu, Bṛhatī, bore a son Cākṣuṣa endowed with all types of brilliance. Cākṣuṣa begot Manu of Puṣkariṇī, a descendant of Varuṇa and the daughter of the noble-souled Prajāpati Araṇya.

89. O blessed one, Manu begot ten auspicious sons of Nadvalā, the daughter of Vairāja, the Prajāpati.

90. The sons of Manu and Nadvalā were Ūru, Pūru, Śatadyumna, Tapasvin, Satyavāk, Kavi, Agniṣṭut, Atirātra and Sudyumna—these nine as well as the tenth son Abhimanyu.

91. Āgneyī bore to Ūru six sons of great brilliance, viz. Aṅga, Sumanas, Svāti, Kratu, Aṅgiras and Śiva.

92. To Aṅga, Sunīthā bore a single child Vena. Due to the misdemeanour of Vena, there was a great indignant commotion.

93. For the sake of progeny, the sages (churned) his right hand. When the hand of Vena was pressed, a great king was born. The royal descendant of Vena was glorified as Pṛthu.

94. Pṛthu, the son of Vena, was the foremost of Kṣatriyas. He was born with a bow and a coat of mail. He appeared blazing with his splendour. He protected all the worlds.

95. He was the first among kings who had been crowned in the Rājasūya sacrifice. He was the ruler of the Earth. In order to eulogise him, the clever Sūta and Māgadha (Bards) were born.

96-97. For the sake of his subjects desirous of livelihood the Earth in the form of a cow was milked, yielding all sorts of plants, along with the Devas, groups of Sages, Pitṛs, Dānavas, Gandharvas, Apsaras-s, all Puṇyajanas, creepers and mountains.

98. Being milked in different vessels, the Earth (*Vasundharā*—that which contains rich deposits) yielded milk as much as they desired. Thereby, he sustained the world.

The sages said :

99-100. O highly intelligent one, narrate in detail the story of the birth of Pṛthu and how the Earth (*Vasundharā*) was milked formerly by that noble-souled (king) along with Devas, serpents, Brāhmaṇas, Sages, Yakṣas, Gandharvas and Apsaras-s.

101. To us who solicit (the information) describe their special forms of vessels, the milker, the milk and the different calves (used for milking).

102. Please mention everything to us, for what reason the hand of Vena was pressed formerly by the infuriated sages.

Sūta said :

103. O Brāhmaṇas, I shall describe the origin of Pṛthu, the son of Vena. O excellent Brāhmaṇas, listen attentively with minds purified by austerities.

104. I shall not describe this holy narrative to an impure person, nor to a sinful one, nor to one who is not a disciple, nor to one who is malevolent and never to (by no means to) one who does not observe holy rites.

105-106. This story is conducive to fame, longevity and attainment of heaven. It is holy and on a par with the Vedas. It is esoteric as the sages, have said. He who is not malicious shall hear it. The man who recounts this narrative of the birth of Pṛthu, the son of Vena, to Brāhmaṇas after bowing to them shall not bewail errors of commission and omission. This king (i.e. Pṛthu) was a defender of faith. He was equal to Atri.

107. The Prajāpati named Aṅga was born in the family of Atri. Vena was his son. He was not very pious or faithful.

108. The Prajāpati was born of Sunīthā, the daughter of Mṛtyu. Vena was the son of the daughter of Kāla. Hence on account of the (hereditary) evil trait of his maternal grandfather, Vena (was cruel).

109. He turned his back on Dharma; he indulged in covetousness as he pleased. He established institutions devoid of Dharma (Virtue and Piety).

110. Disregarding the Vedas and Śāstras he was engrossed in sinful and evil activities. While he reigned the subjects were devoid of Vedic study and utterance of Vaṣaṭkāras. The deities did not partake of the sacrificial offerings nor did they drink the Soma juice.

111. "No Yajña should be performed. No offerings should be oblated to fire". This was the cruel, solemn declaration of that Prajāpati when his (utter) ruin was imminent.

112. He proclaimed : "In all sacrifices, I deserve to be offered sacrifice (sacrificial oblations) and worship, by all twice-born castes. Yajñas should be performed unto me. I should be invoked while (performing) Homas."

113. When he crossed the limits of decency, when he took up an improper stand, Marīci and other great sages told him:

114-115. "We are going to be initiated (into a rite lasting) for many hundreds of years. O Vena, do not perform unrighteous acts. This is not the eternal Dharma. In the (family of the God of) Death you are undoubtedly born as a Prajāpati. It has been promised by you formerly: 'I shall protect the subjects.'" While they talked thus, Vena spoke to the Brahmarṣis:

116-118. The evil-minded but eloquent Vena laughingly said thus : "Who else is the creator of Dharma ? Whose words are needed by me ? Who is there on the Earth equal to me in prowess, learning, penance and truthfulness ? You all know precisely that I am inferior to none, that I am a noble soul. I am the source of origin of all the worlds and particularly of all *Dharmas*. If I wish I can burn the entire Earth or make it flooded with water. I can create it or swallow (annihilate) it. No doubts or suspicions need be entertained in this matter."

119. When the king Vena who was utterly deluded by stubbornness and sense of false prestige, could not be dissuaded, the great sages became infuriated.

120. They caught hold of that mighty one even as he was dazzling like fire. Highly infuriated, they twisted and churned his left hand.

121-123. O Brāhmaṇas, from his hand that was being twisted and churned, a man black in colour and very short in stature, was born. Formerly it was heard so (by us). He was agitated in all his sense-organs. Frightened, he stood there with palms joined in reverence. On seeing him confused and dejected, (the sages) said: "*Niṣīda* (Sit down). He, of infinite valour, became the founder of the dynasty of Niṣādas (a hill tribe). He created *Dhivaras* too (the fishermen) born of the sins and defects of Vena.

124. All those others (hill tribes) residing on the Vindhya mountains such as Tuṁburas, Tuvaras and Khasas and persons interested in evil actions were born of the sins of Vena.

125. Becoming indignant again, the great sages pressed and churned the right hand of Vena in great fury as though it were the *Araṇi* (a pice of wood used to kindle sacred fire by attrition).

126. From the splendid brilliance originating from the pressure exerted on the right hand, Pṛthu was born. Since he

was born of the big (*Pṛthu*) hand (palm) he was called Pṛthu.[1] He was dazzling with the brilliance of his body like the Fire-god.

127. He wielded the primordial bow of loud report, named Ājagava. Then he took up the arrows and the coat of mail of great lustre for the sake of protection.

128. When he was born, all the living beings became highly delighted. When the great king was born, Vena went to heaven.

129. Due to the birth of that intelligent noble-souled son, he (Vena) was (elevated as) a *Rājarṣi* (a royal sage). The tiger among men (Pṛthu) then protected him from the hell called *Put* (by being born as a son).

130. All the rivers and oceans brought gems and jewels and came there. They crowned the son of Vena as the king. With a great royal kingdom, he became an Emperor of great splendour.

131. That Emperor was coronated by the Devas, the sons of Aṅgiras. The valorous son of Vena, Pṛthu, became the first king and a great Emperor.

132. The subjects who had been antagonised by his father were won over by him. Hence thanks to his *Anurāga* (love and affection) he got the name *Rājā* (king).

133. When he rushed against the ocean, the waters stood steady and motionless, and mountains crumbled before him. He never experienced the breakage of his banner.

134. The Earth yielded food-grains without being cultivated. All edible things were achieved on mere thought. Cows yielded whatever one desired. Honey was obtained in every leaf-cup (cluster of flowers ?)

135. At that time, in the auspicious Yajña of Pitāmaha, the highly intelligent Sūta was born of *suti* (the extraction of Soma juice) on the day intended for the extraction of Soma juice. The intelligent Māgadha was also born in the same great Yajña.

---

1. Our text gives a number of popular etymologies, *vide* that of Niṣāda (in v. 123) and of Pṛthu here.

136. With the *Havis* of Indra the *Havis* of Bṛhaspati got mixed. The offering was made to Indra by the Devas and thereby Sūta was born.[1]

137. The *Havya* offering of the preceptor which was mingled with that meant for the disciple, was over-powered by the disciple's *Havis*. On account of the (mingling) activity of the lower and the upper, a mixed caste came into being.

138. A Sūta (charioteer) is begot of a Brāhmaṇas lady by a Kṣatriya who belongs to an inferior caste. Hence Sūta is proclaimed to have rites of the latter (Kṣattriya) one.

139. It is the middle type of Dharma of a Sūta, viz. that of Kṣattriyas. (He has these duties:) looking after and maintenance of chariots, elephants, horses. Practice of medicine is (his) lowliest of duties.

140. Both of them (Sūta and Māgadha) were called there by the Devas and Sages for eulogising Pṛthu. All the sages said to them: "May this king be eulogised. This is a befitting activity of yours. He is also a person deserving praise".

141-142. Then Sūta and Māgadha told all the sages: "We shall propitiate the Devas and the sages with our activities. We do not know the performances, characteristics and reputation of this (Pṛthu) king. Wherefore, O Brāhmaṇas, can we eulogise this brilliant king?"

143. They were enjoined by the sages :"Let him be eulogised by his future activities. He has control over his sense organs. He is always engaged in charitable rites. He is truthful, endowed with knowledge. He is munificent and is never defeated in battles.

144. Sūta and Māgadha eulogised him by composing songs about the past achievements of the powerful king Pṛthu.

145. At the end of the eulogy, the delighted Pṛthu, the lord of the subjects, gave the land of Anūpa to Sūta and Magadha to Māgadha.

146. Ever since, all the kings are eulogised by Sūtas

1. Verses 136-146 explain how and why the mixed class called sūta came into existence and the duties assigned to that caste. The relation between Māgadha and the land called Magadha is understandable but not that between Sūta and Anūpa (South Malwa).

and Māgadhas. They are awakened by Sūtas, Māgadhas and Bandis (Bards) with benedictory songs.

147. On seeing him (King Pṛthu), the subjects were extremely pleased. The great sages told (them) : "Let this protector of men (King), the son of Vena, be the bestower of livelihood to you".

148-149. Then the subjects hurried and flocked round (literally) the blessed son of Vena saying, "As per promise of the great sages you make arrangements for our livelihood. On being hustled by the subjects, the powerful (king Pṛthu), with the desire to perform what was beneficent to the subjects, took up his bow and arrows and rushed at *Vasudhā* (the Earth). Being afraid of being hit, the Earth assumed the form of a cow and fled.

150. Taking up his bow, Pṛthu ran in pursuit of the fleeing Earth. Frightened of the son of Vena, she (the Earth) ran to Brahmaloka and other worlds (but finally) saw in front of her the son of Vena holding the bow lifted up.

151. He had his splendour brightened up by the blazing arrows and shafts. He was of never failing (power) and endowed with great Yogic power. He was invincible even to the Devas. He could not be thwarted by anyone.

152. The goddess (Earth) who is always worthy of being worshipped by the three worlds, could not get succour (from elsewhere) and so yielded to the son of Vena with palms joined in reverence.

153. She spoke to the son of Vena : "O king, you are not aware of the sin inherent in killing a lady. How are you going to sustain the subjects without me.

154. O most excellent of all kings, but for me the subjects will be ruined. O king, all the worlds rest in me. The whole universe is sustained by me.

155. O protector of the Earth, if you wish to do what is beneficial to the subjects, it does not behove you to kill me. Pay heed to my words.

156. All undertakings become fruitful if they are begun with proper means. O king, even after killing me, you will not be competent to protect and look after the subjects.

157. O extremely refulgent one, I shall become the producer of food. Refrain from fury. They say that females are not to be killed even from among the hundreds of lower animal species. O protector of the Earth, in consideration of this, it does not behove you to forsake Dharma".

158. On hearing these various statements the noble-minded king of righteous soul, restrained his anger and spoke thus to (the Earth) :

159. "If any one destroys a single life or many, whether his own or anyone else's and for the sake of one, he attains enough sin.

160. O auspicious lady, when many attain happiness, if one man is killed there is no great or small sin.

161. O Earth (repository of wealth), if you do not act according to my instructions which are conducive to the welfare of the Universe, I will kill you for the cause of the subjects.

162. If you turn your face (disobey) against my behest, I shall presently kill you with an (single) arrow. After proclaiming myself (as their Lord), I shall sustain the subjects.

163. Hence, O excellent lady, foremost among the upholders of virtue paying heed to my words will enliven the subjects perpetually. There is no doubt about it that you are competent to do so.

164. Be my daughter. This is the great and excellent step (in the circumstances). O furious-looking lady, I control you for the sake of (establishing) piety".

165. Thus admonished, the chaste lady, the Earth, spoke to the son of Vena in reply: "O king, undoubtedly I shall carry out this thus.

166. O excellent one among the upholders of virtue, give me a calf so that can give milk out of affection. Make me flat-surfaced and level everywhere so that I can spread everywhere the flowing milk."

167. With the tip of his bow the son of Vena pushed away the heaps of rocks everywhere. The hills were raised up by him.

168-169. In the past Manvantaras the Earth was rugged and uneven. Naturally some parts were even and some uneven. In the course of the previous creations, there was no demarcation of cities and villages, as the Earth was uneven and rugged.

170. In the Cākṣuṣa Manvantara there were no plants, no breeding of cows, no cultivation and no trade routes. All these occurred in the Vaivasvata Manvantara.

171. Wherever there was evenness (plain ground) the subjects always occupied it.

172. The diet cansisted of fruits and roots. Since the reign of the son of Vena all these things appeared in this world.

173. When the medicinal herbs were destroyed, lord Pṛthu made Cākṣuṣa Manu the calf, and with great difficulty milked with his own hand, the Earth (in the form of a cow)[1] and produced plants.

174. Food grains and plants were milked by the son of Vena from the Earth-goddess after making Cākṣuṣa Manu the calf and the bare ground the vessel. The subjects always maintained themselves with that food.

175-176. The Earth (The holder of treasures)was eulogised by the sages and milked again. Their calf was Soma (the Moon) and the milker (milkman) was Bṛhaspati. The vessel was Gāyatrī and other (Vedic) metres. Their milk was penance and the eternal Brahman.

177. Again (the Earth was) eulogised by the groups of Devas led by Purandara after taking up a golden vessel and Amṛta (Nectar) was milked by them. The Devas led by Indra sustained themselves with that alone.

178. The Earth was eulogised by the *Nāgas* (Serpents) and milked. Poison was the milk, Vāsuki the son of Kadru, was the milkman, on behalf of those highly powerful serpents.

179. O excellent Brāhmaṇas, the fierce, huge-bodied and

1. The story of Pṛthu and his milking of the Earth is a Purāṇic presentation of the Vedic conception of milking of the Virāj cow. The *Virāj Sūkta* (AV. VIII.10) forms the basis of this Purāṇic legend. The Purāṇic legend asserts the right of sages (public leaders) to remove a wilful tyrant.

This Pṛthu is a Vedic king and is recorded to have worshipped the Aśvins in his sacrificial chamber (AV. XX.140.5). The milking of Virāj cow by Pṛthu with the earth as a milking pail and Vaivasvata Manu as a calf is mentioned in AV. VIII.10.24. But in our Purāṇa Cākṣuṣa Manu is made the calf. See v. 174.

This episode is depicted in various Purāṇas as in Mbh Śānti, 59.98-128, Bh. P. IV.18, Mt. P. 10.1-35, Bd. P. 12.36.177-202.

excessively aggressive ones among the Nāgas and Sarpas sustain themselves with that alone. That is their diet and sustenance. Their conduct and prowess were in accordance with that.

180. After making themselves invisible, the Earth was milked again by the Yakṣas and Puṇyajanas. They had made Vaiśravaṇa (Kubera) the calf. It was an unbaked vessel that they milked into.

181. The milker was Jatunābha, the father of Maṇivara. He possessed great strength and excessive splendour. He had full self-control. He was the son of a Yakṣa. The great sage said that they sustained themselves with that milk.

182. The Earth was milked again by Rākṣasas and Piśācas. Their milkman was Kubera endowed with the knowledge of Brahman.

183. The calf was the powerful Sumālī. Blood was the milk yielded. It was a vessel of skull that the Rākṣasas milked into by being invisible. All the Rākṣasas sustain themselves with that milk.

184. In the vessel of lotus (leaves) the Earth was milked again by Gandharvas and the groups of Apsaras-s. They made Citraratha the calf, and pure scents was the yield.

185. Viśvāvasu who was the pure son of a sage and who was the very powerful king of Gandharvas and who was a noble soul resembling the sun was their milkman.

186. The goddess Earth was eulogised and milked again by the mountains. The yield was the medicinal herbs in embodied form and various kinds of precious stones.

187. Mt. Himavān was their calf. The great mountain Meru was the milkman.[1] The mountain itself was the vessel. With that the mountain was stabilised.

188. The Earth-goddess was eulogised and milked again by the trees and creepers. They took the leafy cup of Palāśa as the vessel. The milk yielded was the ability to grow after being cut.

189. The mountain in full bloom was *Kāmadhuk* (the milkman of what is desired). Plakṣa tree was the calf. The Earth (was thus) the yielder of all desires, the benefactress of all living beings and very famous.

---

1. Kālidāsa echoes this in *Kumāra-saṁbhava* I.2.

190. Such is the Earth (*Vasundharā*) (the possessor of riches) who became the *Dhātrī* (nurse), *Vidhātrī* (the creative agent), and Dhāraṇī (the support). We have heard that it was milked for the welfare of all the people by Pṛthu. It became the foundation of the world consisting of the mobile and the immobile beings and its source of origin.

CHAPTER TWO

The Dynasty of Pṛthu

Sūta said :

1. It is reported that the Earth extended to the oceans as its limit. It is called *Vasudhā*, because it holds riches (*Vasu*—wealth, *Dhārayate*—holds).

2-3. Formerly the earth was covered with the fat of Madhu and Kaiṭabha. Hence the Earth extending to the oceans became famous as *Medinī* (*Medas*—fat). Since the intelligent son of Vena, king Pṛthu, adopted her as his daughter, she is called *Pṛthivī*.[1]

4. The division of this famous, beautiful Earth was formerly made by King Pṛthu. The Earth consisting of a series of towns and mines (of various natural products) and populated by people of four castes was protected by that intelligent king.

5. That excellent king, the son of Vena, had such prowess. He was worthy of being bowed to and worshipped by all living beings.

6. Being ancient and born of Brahman, Pṛthu alone is worthy of being offered obeisance by Brāhmaṇas of great dignity (and fortune) who were experts in the Vedas and their *Aṅgas* (ancillary subjects).

7. The primordial king Pṛthu, the valorous son of Vena, should be bowed to by the excessively blessed kings who seek great fame.

---

1. As in v. 190 of the previous chapter, etymologies of other names of the Earth are given here.

8. Only Pṛthu, the first maker of men, should be bowed to by the warriors also seek victory in battle.

9. The warrior who, after glorifying Pṛthu, proceeds to the battlefield, returns safely from the terrible battle and attains glorious fame.

10. The saintly king Pṛthu, the excessively renowned one, should be bowed to by the Vaiśyas, strictly adhering to the avocation and duties of Vaiśyas, as it was he who gave them livelihood and sustenance.

11. These different calves and milkers, milk and the vessels all have been described by me in the proper order.

12. At the very outset the Earth was milked by the noble-shouled Brahmā after making Vāyu the calf.[1] The vessel was the surface of the Earth and the yield, the seeds.

13. Then in the early Svāyaṁbhuva Manvantara, the Earth was milked by Agnīdhra[2] after making Svāyaṁbhuva Manu the calf.

14. Formerly, when Svārociṣa was Manu, the Earth was milked by the intelligent Caitra, after making Svārociṣa Manu the calf. The yield consisted of plants and foodgrains.

15. In the Auttama Manvantara, the Earth was milked by the most excellent and intelligent Devabhuja, after making the Manu Uttama the calf. The yield consisted of all foodgrains.

16. Again in the fifth Manvantara, viz. the Tāmasa Manvantara the Earth was milked by Balabandhu after making Tāmasa Manu the calf.

17. When the Manvantara of lord Cāriṣṇava Manu arrived, the Earth was milked by Purāṇa after making Cāriṣṇava Manu the calf.

18. When the Cākṣuṣa Manvantara arrived, the Earth was again milked by Purāṇa, after making Cākṣuṣa Manu the calf.

---

1. Verses 12-20 give the list of persons who "milked" the earth in each Manvantara. Each 'milking' shows in a way the advancement of human civilization.

2. Bd. P. I.2-37 reads *Sarva-sasyāni caiva hi* "all types of foodgrains were the milky yield". Here *grīṣma* probably stands for Agnīdhra. But the milky yield is not mentioned in our text.

19. When the Cākṣuṣa Manvantara elapsed and Vaivasvata Manvantara arrived, the Earth was again milked by the son of Vena, as narrated by me to you.

20. Formerly in the previous Manvantaras the Earth was milked by the Devas and others, by human beings as well as by the Bhūtas (living beings or goblins) and others.

21. Thus the Devas should be known in all the past and present Manvantaras. Now listen to the sons of Pṛthu.

22. Two valorous sons, Antardhi and Pālin were born to Pṛthu. Śikhaṇḍinī bore to Antardhāna (Antardhi) the son Havirdhāna.

23. Dhiṣaṇā, the daughter of Agni, bore to Havirdhāna six sons, viz. Prācīnabarhis, Śukra, Gaya, Kṛṣṇa, Vraja and Ajina.

24. The holy lord Prācīnabarhis was a great Prajāpati. Thanks to his strength, learning, penance and prowess, he was the sole Emperor of the Earth. The tips of his Kuśa grasses pointed to the east by frequent use in Yajñas. Hence he is called Prācīnabarhis.[1]

25. That lord duly married Savarṇā, the daughter of the ocean, far beyond the extensive darkness. From the Prajāpati the daughter of the ocean, Savarṇā, bore the ten sons of Prācīnabarhis.

26. All of them are named Pracetas. They were masters of the science of archery. Performing rtghteous actions (in close association) without being separated, they performed great penance for ten thousand years lying in the waters of the ocean.

27. While the Pracetas were performing penance on the Earth the trees not being properly cared for covered the earth resulting in the decline and ruin of the subjects.

28. When (the firmament) was obstructed in the Cākṣuṣa Manvantara, wind could not blow. The sky was covered with trees. The subjects could not (carry their activities) for ten thousand years.

29. On realising it by means of their power of penance, all

1. Cf Bd. P. 1.2.37.25—an etymology to explain the significance of the king's name.

the Pracetas, endowed with Yogic power, became infuriated and created wind and fire from their mouths.

30. Vāyu uprooted those trees and dried them up. The fierce fire burned them. Thus the destruction of trees took place.

31. Learning of the destruction of the trees (and when only) a few trees survived, king Soma (the Moon-god) approached these Pracetas and spoke to them:

32. "O kings, O sons of Prācīnabarhis, give up your anger after considering the benefits conferred (by flourishing trees) for the continuance of the worlds.

33. The trees will grow on the Earth. May the fire and the wind calm down. This jewel of a girl of fair complexion is the daughter of the trees.

34. Knowing this future (contingency), she has been nurtured (and brought up) by me with my rays. She is named Mārisā and is created by the trees themselves. May she, nurtured in the womb of the moon*, be your wife.

35. By means of a moiety of your splendour as well as a moiety of my splendour, the learned Prajāpati named Dakṣa will be born of her.

36. He, of fiery splendour, shall again develop the subjects and protect the Earth almost burnt by the fire of your brilliance."

37. Then, at the instance of Soma (the Moon-god) those Pracetas curbed their fury and accepted righteously from the trees (their daughter) Māriṣā as their wife.

38-39. They then impregnated Māriṣā mentally. Dakṣa the Prajāpati was born of Māriṣā and the ten Pracetas. He possessed great splendour and virility, thanks to the part of Soma. At first Dakṣa created progeny by mental process and subsequently by means of sexual intercourse.

40. After creating the immboile beings, mobile beings, bipeds and quadrupeds mentally, Dakṣa created women (daughters) thereafter.

41. He gave ten (of his daughters) to Dharma, thirteen to Kaśyapa and twenty-seven engaged in the movement of time (i.e. the twenty-seven constellations) to the moon.

---

*i.e. 'by rays of the moon' (as stated in v. 34a).

42. After giving these (daughters) to them he gave four other daughters to Ariṣṭanemi, two to Bāhuputra, two to Aṅgiras and one daughter to Kṛśāśva. Now know their progeny.

43. By this time, the sixth Manvantara of Cākṣuṣa Manu ceases giving place to the seventh Manvantara of the Prajāpati Vaivasvata Manu.

44. In them (the daughters of Dakṣa) Devas, birds, cows, serpents, Daityas, Dānavas, Gandharvas, Apsaras-s and other classes of beings were born.

45. The creation of the earlier ones was due to thought, sight and touch. Thenceforth, the subjects in this world were born of sexual intercourse.[1]

The sages said :

46-48. The auspicious birth of Devas, Dānavas, Celestial Sages and the noble-souled Dakṣa has been narrated by you before. It was mentioned by you (before) that Dakṣa, the Prajāpati, was born of Prāṇa. How did he who had great penance subsequently attain the status of the son of Pracetas? O Sūta, it behoves you to clarify this doubt of ours. He was the son of the daughter of Soma. How did he become his (Soma's) father-in-law?

Sūta said :

49. O excellent ones, birth and dissolution (death) occur perpetually among living beings. The sages and those men who are endowed with learning are not deluded in this matter.

50. O Brāhmaṇas, Dakṣa and others are born in every Yuga. They undergo subsequent death too. A learned man is not confused in this matter.

51. O excellent Brāhmaṇas, formerly there was neither seniority nor juniority among them. Penance alone was considered weightier and prowess was the basis thereof.

52. He who comprehends this creation of the mobile and the immobile beings in Cākṣuṣa Manvantara passes his life-span fully and is honoured in the heavenly region (after it).

1. This is the main difference between the previous six Manvantaras and the present one. With this chapter closes the description of the Cākṣuṣa Manvantara.

53. This creation of Cākṣuṣa Manu has been succinctly narrated. Thus these six cycles of creation, in the form of Manvantaras have elapsed. They have the Svāyaṁbhuva Manvantara as their first one and the Cākṣuṣa Manvantara as the last one. They have been briefly narrated in the proper sequence.

54. O excellent Brāhmaṇas, these creations have been narrated in accordance with my understanding. The details of these creations should be known through the creation in the Vaivasvata Manvantara.

55. All the creations of Vivasvān are endless and non-different (from other Manvantaras) in the matter of states of health, duration of life, virtue, love and wealth. He who reads this without malice attains these attributes.

56. Now I shall describe the creative activity of the current noble-souled Vaivasvata Manu succinctly and in detail (as the case may be). Listen and understand even as I recount.

CHAPTER THREE

Vaivasvata Manvantara: The Mārīca Creation

Sūta continued :

1. In the seventh cycle called Vaivasvata Manvantara, the Devas and the great sages were born of Kaśyapa, son of Marīci.[1]

2. The eight groups of Devas are remembered as follows: (1) Ādityas, (2) Vasus, (3) Rudras, (4) Sādhyas (5) Viśvedevas (6) Maruts, (7) Bhṛgus and (8) Aṅgiras-s.

3. (Among them) Ādityas, Maruts and Rudras are to be known as the sons of Kaśyapa. The three groups, viz. Sādhyas, Vasus and Viśvedevas are the sons of Dharma.

4. Lord Bhārgava was born of Bhṛgu and Aṅgirā was the son of Aṅgiras. In this Vaivasvata Manvantara, those Devas are

1. Hence the title of the chapter 'Mārīca creation'.

perpetually *Chandajas* (born according to their own will or born of Vedic *chandas*?).

5. The current auspicious creation should be known as that of the descendants of Marīci. Their present brilliant Indra is Mahābala by name.

6. All the Indras in the different Manvantaras whether of the past or future or those who exist now should be known as having equal characteristics.

7. All of them are the lords of past, present and future objects, thousand-eyed and Purandara (destroyers of the cities of enemies). All of them are bountiful, crested (wearers of crowns with crests). They hold thunderbolt in the hand. All performed hundred sacrifices and all possessed hundreds of attributes.

8. They establish themselves after excelling all the living beings in the three worlds, whether weak or mobile, for various reasons such as Dharma (Piety) etc.

9. I shall explain everything as to how they are the lords of the past, present and future by means of splendour, penance, intellect, strength, learning and exploits; how they have become powerful; listen and understand even as I recount.

10. Three worlds have been remembered by the Brāhmaṇas as *Bhūta*, *Bhavya* and *Bhaviṣya*.[1] They are respectively remembered as follows: *Bhūrloka* or the Earth, *Bhuvarloka* or the firmament and *Bhavya* or the heaven. I shall explain how they have been accomplished.

11-12. This was uttered at the outset by Brahmā who was desirous of sons and who was meditating. The word "*Bhūḥ*" was uttered in the beginning and this *Bhūrloka* took shape. The root *Bhū* is remembered in the sense of *Sattā* (existence) as also *Loka Darśana* (visibility to the people). Since it existed and was visible it became *Bhūrloka*, hence this first *Loka* is remembered as *Bhūḥ*, because it existed.

13. When this (world) had taken shape, the second word, "*Bhavat*" was uttered again by Brahmā. That which is about to take shape in the immediate future time is indicated by the word "*Bhavat*".

---

1. Verses 10-18 explain these terms and how the *vyāhṛtis* originated (v. 19).

14. The word *Bhuvarloka* is derived from *bhavana* by those who know *Nirukta* (Etymology). Hence the firmament is called the second Loka i.e. Bhuvarloka.

15. When Bhuvarloka had taken shape, the third word "*Bhavya*" was uttered by Brahmā and then the *Bhavya-loka* took shape.

16. The word *Bhavya* is used in the sense of what has not yet come about (i.e. the future). Hence this future world is remembered by the name *Diva* (Heaven).

17. Another third word "*Svaḥ*" was uttered (by Brahmā). Then the *Bhavyaloka* (future world) took shape. The word *Bhavya* is used in the sense of future time.

18. The Earth is remembered by the word *Bhūḥ*; the firmament is remembered as *Bhuvaḥ*; the heaven is remembered as *Bhavya*. This is the set of three worlds in a nutshell.

19. By the utterances in combination with the three worlds the three *Vyāhṛtis* (i.e. the mantras *Bhūḥ, Bhuvaḥ, Svaḥ*) originated. The root *Nath* is remembered in the sense of 'protection' by those who know the (meanings of) roots.

20. Since they are the Lord Protectors of the *Bhūta, Bhavya* and *Bhavat* worlds they are the *Nāthas* (Protectors) of the three worlds. They are termed as Indras by the Brāhmaṇas.

21. The Devendras who are the chiefs in the Manvantaras as well as those Devas who are their (subordinates) become partakers of shares in the *Yajñas*.

22. Yakṣas, Gandharvas, Rākṣasas, Piśācas, Uragas and Dānavas are all proclaimed as (the products of) the glory of the Devendras.

23. The Devendras are the elders (preceptors), protectors, kings and parents. Those excellent Devas protect all these subjects righteously.

24. Thus the characteristics of the Devendras have been briefly described. I shall now recount the seven sages who are stationed at present in the heaven.

25-28. They are: (1) Viśvāmitra of great penance, the intelligent son of Gādhi who was born of the family of Kuśika, (2) Jamadagni, the valorous son of Ūru (Aurva) the scion of the family of Bhṛgu, (3) Bhāradvāja of great penance, the son of Bṛhaspati, (4) Śaradvān the learned and the virtuous son of Utathya, belonging to the family of Gotama, (5) the fifth one Brahmakośa (otherwise known as) lord Atri, son of Svayaṁbhū (Brahmā,) (6) the sixth one, the son of Vasiṣṭha well known in the world as Vasumān, and (7) Vatsāra, son of Kaśyapa. All these seven are well honoured by good men. These seven sages, all of whom are Siddhas, exist in the present Manvantara.

29-31. Ikṣvāku, Nābhāga, Dhṛṣṭa, Śaryāti, the famous Nariṣyanta, Nābha, Uddiṣṭa, Karuṣa, Pṛṣadhra and Vasumān the tenth—these are the ten sons of Vaivasvata Manu glorified by me. The seventh Manvantara has been explained by me. O Brāhmaṇas, the second Pāda has been described by me in detail and in the proper order. What else shall I now explain?

SECTION 3 : ANUṢAṄGA PĀDA

CHAPTER FOUR

The Race of Prajāpati : Rebirth of Seven Sages

The Sages said :

1. On hearing the second section (in full) as narrated by the intelligent Sūta, Śāṁśapāyana thereafter asked him about (the subject matter of) the third *Pāda* (Section).

2. "The second *Pāda* has been narrated by you along with its sequel (Appendix); please recount the third *Pāda* in detail along with the (necessary) introduction" Being requested thus, Sūta began to speak with his inner soul highly delighted.

Sūta said :

3. O Brāhmaṇas, I shall recount the third pāda in detail along with (necessary) introduction. Even as I recount it, listen and understand it completely.

4. O Brāhmaṇas, listen in details and in proper order to the creative activity of the present Vaivasvata Manu of noble soul.

5-7. The (Manu) period is already calculated as being of seventyone sets of four Yugas. After bowing to Vivasvān (the Sun-god) I shall narrate the Vaivasvata creation beginning with Manu and ending with the future events. It comprises Deva-gaṇas, Sages, Dānavas, Pitṛs, Gandharvas, Rākṣasas, Bhūta-gaṇas, human beings, animals, birds and immobile beings.

8-9. The seven great sages who had passed away in the first Svāyaṁbhuva Manvantara and who were the creators and initiators then, are reborn in the Vaivasvata Manvantara after the lapse of the Cākṣuṣa Manvantara. It is due to the curse of Maheśvara that the noble souls, Dakṣa and the very powerful sages Bhṛgu and others manifested themselves (in this Manvantara).

10. The seven sages were born again as seven mental sons of Brahmā. They were adopted as sons by Svayaṁbhū (the self-born god Brahmā) himself.

11. The creative activity was initiated again as before and in the proper order, by those noble souls who manifested themselves and who created the series of subjects.

12. I shall mention the progeny of those people of pure knowledge and holy rites in brief as well as in detail (according to the context) and in the proper order.

13. This world consisting of mobile and immobile beings and embellished with planets and stars is filled with beings born of their families.

14. On hearing these words a doubt arose in the minds of the sages. Overwhelmed by the doubt, the sages of pure holy rites honoured Sūta and asked him for the sake of clarification of their doubts.

The sages said :

15. O excellent one, how were the seven sages born as seven mental sons at the outset ? How were they adopted as sons ? Please explain this to us.

Thereafter, the highly-splendid Sūta well versed in Purāṇas began the auspicious narration.

Sūta said :

16-17. How the seven great sages who had been great Siddhas in the Svāyaṁbhuva Manvantara, failed to attain the fruit of penance in the Vaivasvata Manvantara (I shall narrate.) Overwhelmed with the curse of Bhava (Śiva) they did not attain the (fruit of the) penance. Once they gathered together in the Jana Loka.

18-19. In the Jana Loka all the great sages spoke to one another: The blessed ones were talking to one another in the grand sacrifice of Varuṇa: "In the Cākṣuṣa Manvantara let us all be born as the sons of Pitāmaha. Then it will be conducive to welfare".

20. In the Svāyambhuva Manvantara they had been cursed by Bhava. In order to make (the curse) truthful (i.e. fulfilled), they were born again. From the Jana Loka they went to heaven.

21. We have heard that in the Yajña of the great lord, Brahmā assumed the form of Varuṇa. With a desire for progeny he had consigned the semen into the holy fire. It was then that the sages had their second birth.

22. Bhṛgu, Aṅgiras, Marīci, Pulastya, Pulaha, Kratu, Atri and Vasiṣṭha—these eight[1] were the sons of Brahmā.

23. In his grand elaborate Yajña all the Devas had come. All the *Aṅgas* (ancillaries) of the Yajña and *Vaṣaṭkāra* had assumed corporeal forms.

24. The Sāman mantras, thousands of Yajur mantras and the Ṛgveda embellished with Pada and Krama[2] (Pāṭhas) were present there in embodied form.

25. The Yajurveda enriched with (relevant) metres, brilliant with Oṁkāra as its mouth (face) was present here along with Sūktas, Brāhmaṇas and Mantras related to the *Arthas* (objects & purposes) of the Yajña.

26. The Sāma Veda so rich in (the variety of Vedic) metres and with all Mantra-Songs (which are) to be sung at the outset was present there along with Viśvāvasu and other Gandharvas.

27. The Brāhma Veda (Atharva Veda) was (present there) accompanied by terrible rites. (But) due to (the presence of the)

---

1. There are two discrepancies here. *Saptarṣis* means a set of seven sages but here *eight* sons of Brahmā are enumerated. Apart from this discrepancy in number the names of the *Saptarṣis* of this Manvantara as given in vv 25-28 of the last chapter are different from this list even though v. 28 of that chapter asserts that "these seven sages exist in the present Manvantara" (*ete saptarṣayaḥ siddhā vartante sāmprate'ntare*).

This previous list (3.25-28) agrees more with the one in VP.III.1.32 if the names therein are regarded as *gotras* of the sages.

2. *Krama* is a special method of reciting vedic texts. It is so called as the recitation proceeds from the first member, either word or letter to the second, then the second is repeated and connected with the third and so on.

Pratyaṅgirasas, it appeared to have a single head with two bodies.[1]

28. (The following details about the recitation of the Vedas) *Lakṣaṇas* (the characteristic topics), *Svaras* (notes), *Stobhas* (chanted interjections in a Sāman-song), *Nirukta* (etymologies), *Svarabhaktis* (insertion of vowel sound for ease in pronunciation), *Āśraya* (resting places or annexation), *Vaṣaṭkāra* (pronouncing '*Vaṣaṭ*'), *Nigraha* (suppression) and *Pragraha* (vowels not subject to Sandhi rules) (all these were physically present).

29-30. The brilliantly shining goddess Earth, the quarters, the intermediate quarters, the Lords of quarters, the celestial virgins, the wives of Devas, the mothers and Āyu—all these were present there in embodied form in front of the Lord (Brahmā) who was performing the Yajña assuming the form of Varuṇa.

31. On seeing the ladies, the semen virile of Svayaṁbhū fell on the ground. There is no doubt about this that it took place on account of the dispensation of the inevitable in the case of Brahmarṣis (Brahmanical sages).

32. Pitāmaha (god Brahmā) then took it up by means of Sruks and Sruvā (sacrificial spoons and ladles) and performed the *Homa* as if it were ghee, reciting the mantras duly.

33. Thereafter, the Prajāpati began the creation of living beings (or aggregate of elements). Due to the splendour that was beside, the fiery things were born; the Guṇas Sattva and Rajas were not pervaded by the Guṇa Tamas.

34. From the Saguṇa brilliance, Tamas stayed perpetually in the sky. All the living beings were born from the *Tamas* (darkness) and the *Tejas* (brilliance).

35. When the sons born of *Karman* were created, Brahmā took up his Semen Virile in the ghee-pot and performed the Homa.

36. When the Semen Virile was consigned to the holy fire, the great sages manifested themselves. They were embodied and very brilliant. All the seven (sages) had the attributes of new born infants.

37. When the Semen Virile was once poured into the fire,

---

1. The AV. consists of two sets of Mantras : the auspicious ones (*Atharvans*) and the terrible ones meant for the destruction of the enemies (*Aṅgiras*). Hence AV is said to have two bodies.

Kavi (i.e. Venus) came out of the flame. On seeing him coming out splitting up the flame, Hiraṇyagarbha (Brahmā) said: "You are Bhṛgu". Thereafter he is called Bhṛgu.[1]

38. Mahādeva saw him coming out like that and said to Brahmā: "I am desirous of a son and I am initiated. He is born to me, O lord. Hence may lord Bhṛgu be my son."

39. Mahādeva was permitted by god Brahmā who said: "So be it". Mahādeva adopted Bhṛgu as his son. All the descendants of Bhṛgu are called Vāruṇas. He became a holy lord (sage).

40. A second (ladleful of) Semen Virile fell on the burning coals. Aṅgiras was born of it with his limbs firmly united on fire (burning coals). Hence he is known as Aṅgiras.

41. On seeing his birth, the Fire-god spoke to Brahmā: "It was I who held your Semen Virile. Hence may this second son be mine."

42. The Fire-god was addressed by Brahmā: "Let it be so". Hence, we have heard that all the descendants of Aṅgiras are known as Āgneyas.

43. When the Semen Virile was consigned to the holy fire for six more times by Brahmā, the creator, the six Brahmās (sons of Brahmā) were born. So it is heard.

44. Marīci was the first among them, born from the rays (of sacrificial fire). Since the (second) son was born in the *Kratu* (sacrifice), he is called Kratu.

45. "I am the third" (Ahaṁ-Tṛtīya), saying thus the third son was born. So he is called *Atri*. The fourth son was born with sharp pointed hairs. Hence he is remembered as Pulastya.

46-47. The son born with long hairs is remembered as Pulaha. He who was born out of the Vasu (fire ?) was called Vasumān. He is called Vasiṣṭha by those who know the truth, by the expounders of Vedas. Thus these six great sages are the mental sons of Brahmā.

1. Cf. *Bṛhad-devatā* V. 97-101 for the story of the births of Bhṛgu, Aṅgiras and Atri. Etymologies of these names also are borrowed therefrom though grammarians offer different derivations.

48. They maintain the continunity of the worlds. These subjects are developed and nurtured by them. Hence Brahmā's sons are mentioned as Prajāpatis.

49-50. Others called Pitṛs were created by these great sages alone. The seven groups of sages are well known in the world, viz. Mārīcas,Bhārgavas, Āṅgirasas, Paulastyas, Paulahas, Vāsiṣṭhas and Ātreyas; these groups of Pitṛs are well-known in the world.

51. These three Gaṇas have been briefly mentioned before: They are *Apūrvas* (Rare), *Prakāśas* (Brilliant) and *Jyotiṣmantas* (Illuminated ones).

52. Their king is lord Yama and they have wiped off their sins by their (religious) observances. There are other Prajāpatis also. Listen to them attentively.

53-54. There are other Prajāpatis many in number, viz. Kardama, Kaśyapa, Śeṣa (?), Vikrānta, Suśruvas, Bahuputra, Kumāra, Vivasvān, Śuciśravas, Pracetas, Ariṣṭanemi, Bahula and many others.[1]

55. Kuśoccayas and Vālakhilyas had become great sages. They had the speed of the mind. They could go anywhere. They became Emperors.

56. The groups of sages called Vaikhānasas are honoured by Brāhmaṇas. They were born of the sacred ashes. They are engaged in penance and learning.

57. The handsome Aśvinas were born of his ears. The pure ones born of the eyes are known as *Akṣarajas*.

58. The elder Prajāpatis were born of his vessels. The sages were born of the hair pores in the skin and the sweat dirt.

59. From his tears and cry were born the terrible mouths Niryāsas (?), the junctions of fortnights, years, days and nights and the terrible light of Pitṛs.

60. Raudra they say is the blood. Lohita is remembered as gold. That should be known as Maitra also. The smoke is remembered as animals.

1. Different Purāṇas give different lists of Prajāpatis. For example, the lists in Mbh., Mt. P. or Garuḍa differ from our text (and Bd. P) and *inter se.*

61. The flames are Rudras and Ādityas. Divine human beings were born of the burning coal and the flame.

62. Brahmā born of Brahman is the primordial being in the world. Requesting (for the hand of) a virgin, the sages told him who bestowed everything:

63. "Brahmā, the eldest among Suras, is delighted with Devas. These lords will be giving birth to all the subjects.

64. All of them are Prajāpatis. All of them are sages. These rites will uphold these worlds with his grace.

65. They have developed couples increasing your splendour. Among Devas there are learned ones in Vedas. All the saintly kings are also such.

66. All of them are devoted to the Vedic Mantras. They have been born out of the attributes of Prajāpatis. The infinite Brahman is the Truth and the greatest penance.

67. O lord, all of us are your own children, the Brahman (Vedas), the Brāhmaṇas and all the worlds including the mobile and the immobile beings.

68. Beginning with Marīci and including all the sages, we Devas are thinking about and longing for children by your (blessings)".

69. (*Sūta said*) O highly blessed ones, Devas along with sages identifying (themselves) with the abodes and the time are born in this family during the Yajña.

70. In that very form, they may not establish these subjects. They may be stabilised from the beginning till the end of the Yugas.

71. Then the preceptor of the world (Brahmā), without any further thought, spoke—"O Devas, it was after deciding like this that the subjects had been created by me. There is no doubt about this. These sages have been born in your race".

72. Among them I shall recount in detail and in proper sequence the race of Bhṛgu, the ancient noble soul and the first Prajāpati.

73. Bhṛgu had two unequalled, excellent and auspicious wives of noble families. One was the daughter of Hiraṇyakaśipu, famous by the name 'Divyā' and the other was the fair-complexioned daughter of Puloman, named Paulomī.

74-75. Divyā bore to Bhṛgu the planet Śukra (Venus) who was the preceptor of Devas and Asuras, who was the son of Kavi, and was known as Kāvya, Śukra and Uśanas. He was the most excellent among the knowers of Vedas. Śukra's wife named Aṅgī was the mental daughter of the Soma-drinking Pitṛs and very famous. She gave birth to four sons.

76-77. He was endowed with Brahman's splendour and the most excellent among the knowers of Brahman. Śukra begot four sons of her, viz. Tvaṣṭṛ, Varūtrin, Śaṇḍa and Amarka. They resembled the sun and in their prowess they were equal to Brahmā.

78. Rañjana, Pṛthuraśmi and the scholarly Bṛhadgiras were the sons of Varūtrin. They were devoted to Brahman and became the priests of Suras.

79. They approached Manu with the motive of spoiling sacrificial rites. On seeing Dharma being violated, Indra spoke to Manu:

80. "I would rather have the sacrifice performed through you than through these". On hearing these words of Indra, they fled from that place.

81. When they absconded, Indra released (their) wife Cetanā. Then he followed her.

82-83. On seeing them come there again with the evil intention of killing Indra, he struck at them (while) they slept in the altar of the lord of Devas on the southern side. While they were being devoured by (dogs, jackals and wolves) their heads fell down simultaneously and became dates.

84. Thus, the sons of Varūtrin were killed by Indra formerly. Śukra begot (of his wife) Yajanī the daughter Devayānī.

85. The three-headed Viśvarūpa was the great son of Tvaṣṭṛ. Viśvakarman is remembered as the younger twin-brother of Viśvarūpa.

86. Twelve sons were born to Bhṛgu (and were known as) Bhṛgu (Gaṇa) Devas[1]. Lord Kāvya begot of Devī those sons.

---

1. Mt. P. gives a different list of these 12 Deva Yājñika Bhṛgus in its lists of Gotras and Pravaras.

87. They were—Bhuvana, Bhāvana, Anya, Anyāyata, Kratu, Śravas, Mūrdhan, Vyajaya, Vyaśruṣa, Prasava, Aja and the twelfth one Adhipati.

88. These twelve sons of Bhṛgu are remembered as twelve sacrificial Devas. Paulomī bore a lordly son having full self-control and engrossed in Brahman.

89. Since he was sickly in the eighth month of conception, he was forcibly taken out of the womb by dire means and so his name became Cyavana. He became conscious due to Pracetas. Through the anger of Cyavana (revived by) Pracetas, Cyavana alias Prācetasa burned the man-eaters through anger[1].

90. The son of Bhṛgu (i.e. Cyavana) begot of Sukanyā two sons honoured by saints, viz. Ātmavāna and Dadhīca.

91. The son Sārasvata was born to Sarasvatī and Dadhīca. The blessed lady Ruci, daughter of Nahuṣa, was the wife of Ātmavāna.

92. The sage Ūrva (Aurva in Bd. P. and Mbh.) of great renown was born of him after breaking through the thighs (of his mother)[2] Ṛcīka was the son of Aurva. He was brilliant (in complexion) like a blazing fire.

93-94. When the *carus*[3] (sacrificial offerings) pertaining to Rudra and Viṣṇu (charged with specific *mantras*) by Bhṛgu were interchanged, Jamadagni was born, as the *Caru* pertaining to Vaiṣṇava fire was (mistakenly) eaten (by his mother). Reṇukā bore to Jamadagni the son Rāma of unmeasured splendour. He was equal to Śakra (Indra) in valour and had the traits both of a Brāhmaṇa and a Kṣatriya.

95. Aurva had a hundred sons of whom Jamadagni was the eldest. Those descendants of Bhṛgu had thousands of sons due to mutual alliance.

---

1. The text *Prācetasāc cyavana-krodhād adhvānam puruṣādajaḥ* is defective. For this the corresponding text from Bd. P. II-3-1. is accepted.

2. Mbh. Ādi 177 informs that when Haihayas tried a genocide of the Bhṛgu clan, Bhṛgu women fled to hills. While running Cyavana's wife Āruṣi concealed her foetus in her thigh. When Haihaya officers arrested her to execute her, her foetus—a son—broke through his mother's thigh and blinded all Haihayas with his supreme brilliance. As this child broke through his mother's thigh (ūru), he was called Aurva (one born out of the thigh).

3. *ruci*—is a misprint for *caru*.

96. Among other sages outside (the original family) there are many other descendants of Bhṛgu. They are divided into seven *Gotras*, viz. Vatsa, Viśva, Aśviṣeṇa, Pāṇḍa, Pathya and Śaunaka. These seven clans are alternatively known as Bhārgavas.

97. Listen to the narration of the family of Aṅgiras, the intelligent son of Agni. It was in the family of Aṅgiras, the intelligent son of Agni, that Bhāradvājas along with Gautamas were born. The most important Devas belonging to the family of Aṅgiras are Tviṣimants (?) of great prowess.

98. Atharvan, Aṅgiras had three wives, viz. Surūpā the daughter of Mārīca, Svarāṭ the daughter of Kardama and Pathyā the daughter of Manu. I shall mention their progeny.

99. The heirs of Atharvan born of those wives were the uplifters of the family. They were born as a result of the great penance of that purified soul.

100-101. Bṛhaspati was born of Surūpā and Svarāṭ gave birth to Gautama. Pathyā gave birth of Avandhya, Vāmadeva, Utathya and Uśija. Dhisṇu was thes on of Pathyā. Saṁvarta was the mental son (of Atharvan). Vicitta, Āyasya and Śaradvān were the sons of Utathya.

102. Dīrghatamā was the son of Aśi. Bṛhaduttha was the son of Vāmadeva. Dhisṇu's son was Sudhanvan and his son was Ṛṣabha.

103. Rathakāras (Charioteers) are remembered as Devas. They are well-known as Ṛṣis (Ṛbhus ?). Bharadvāja of very great fame and well-known was born of Bṛhaspati.

104. The progeny of Saṁvarta, (mental) son of Aṅgiras, are considered as Devas. Listen to them. These Aṅgiras Devas are regarded as junior to Bṛhaspati.

105-108. Ten own sons of Aṅgiras were born of Surūpā. They were ten and their names are—Audārya, Āyu, Danu, Dakṣa, Darbha, Prāṇa, Haviṣmān, Haviṣṇu, Kratu and Satya. The following ten and five (i.e. fifteen) are to be known as belonging to the *Pakṣa* (i.e. *Gotra*) of Aṅgiras—Ayasya, Utathya, Vāmadeva, Uśija, Bhāradvājas, Śāṅkṛtikas, Gārgya, Kāṇva, Rathītara, Mudgalas, Viṣṇuvṛddhas, Haritas, Vāyus, Bhākṣas of Bhāradvāja family, Ārṣabhas and Kiṁbhayas. Many others (external) sages (belonging to the families outside) are remembered among other sages.

109. I shall now describe the race of Marīci consisting of excellent men as its scions. In his race was born the Universe consisting of mobile and immobile beings.

110. Contemplating on the waters (*Āpaḥ*) with a desire for progeny, Marīci desired the waters. The lord mentally conceived thus—"A son born of a praiseworthy woman, endowed with all good qualities and having good tastes is honoured".

111-112. All the waters were called. The lord dwelt in their company. The lord procreated an unequalled son named Ariṣṭanemi who became Prajāpati and who was of well-controlled mind. Vadhauveśa[1] (?) begot the son Mārīca, having the splendour of the Sun.

113. Contemplating on the speech of good men[2] he stayed under water for seven thousand years with a desire to beget sons. Hence (the son) became unequalled.

114. Kaśyapa was the knower of the sun (?) Hence he was on a par with Brahmā. In every Manvantara, he is born through a part of Brahmā.

115. The subjects[3] were angered by Dakṣa, it is said (?) for the sake of (his) daughters. Then he drank wine. The word '*Kaśya*' means wine.

116. *Haścekasas* (?)[4] should be known as Brahma's *Kaśya*. *Kaśya* is remembered by Brāhmaṇas as wine. Because he drank *Kaśya* (wine) he is called Kaśyapa.[5]

117. He used harsh words. On being cursed by Dakṣa, he became infuriated and thereby became *Kaśyapa*.

118. On being requested by Kaśyapa and urged by Brahmā Parameṣṭhin, Dakṣa gave his daughters to Kaśyapa. All of them were expounders of Brahman. All of them were the mothers of the worlds.

---

1. Bd. P. reads *nirata* : *so'psvatītapat* 'who performed penance in waters'.
2. Chaste goddess Vāk (Bd. P.).
3. Bd. P. (Ibid. v. 120) reads *Prabhuḥ* for *Prajāḥ* hereof. It means 'When the holy Lord got enraged at the over-bearing speech for his daughters'.
4. *Hāścekasa* is obscure. Bd. P. reads *hāsye kaśir hi vijñeyo* 'The word *Kaśi* should be understood in the sense of humour'.
5. A funny derivation. The sage Kaśyapa is so designated as he was a drunkard (*Kaśya*—wine) and whip-like (Kaśa—a whip) harsh in speech.

119. He who knows this holy creation of Ṛṣis through Varuṇa becomes long-lived and meritorious. He becomes Purified and attains excellent happiness. By listening to this and retaining this (in memory) he becomes free from all sins.

120. *Then all the sages spoke to Romaharṣaṇa*: "When the sixth Prajāsarga (creation of the subjects) of Cākṣuṣa Manu had been dissolved, the creation of Vaivasvata Manu began to function (How did it take place ?)."

Sūta said :

121. When the Vaivasvata Manvantara arrived, Dakṣa was commanded by the self-born lord himself—"Create the subjects". Dakṣa created mobile and the immobile living beings.

122. Then Dakṣa proceeded to create the four types of *Prajās* (subjects), viz. *Jarāyujas* (viviparous), *Aṇḍajas* (oviparous), *Udbhijjas* (plants that pierce the ground and grow), and *Svedajas* (those born of sweat).

123-125. He performed severe penance for ten thousand years. He became endowed with Yogic power and more particularly with supernatural powers like *Aṇimā* etc. As he possesses glorious power, he divided himself into human beings, serpents, Rākṣasas, Devas, Asuras and Gandharvas. All of them being endowed with divine bodies and wealth of beauty and splendour, they were lords equal to himself. He was desirous of creating other mental living beings of various kinds.

126. (He created) sages, Devas, Gandharvas, human beings, serpents, Rākṣasa's, Yakṣas, Bhūtas, Piśācas, birds, animals and deer.

127. When these mentally created beings did not flourish and multiply, he was rebuked by the intelligent lord Mahādeva.

128-129. He became then desirous of creating the different subjects by the process of sexual intercourse. He took to himself as wife the daughter of Vīraṇa, the Prajāpati. She was Asiknī who was endowed with great penance and who supported the worlds. The entire Universe consisting of the mobile and the immobile beings was sustained by her.

130-134. In this matter they quoted two verses about Dakṣa, the son of Pracetas. "When Dakṣa married Asiknī the great daughter of Vīraṇa, he created a million mobile wells along with those identifying with them. Creating them into rivers and mountains, the powerful Dakṣa pursued them. On seeing him the sages said, "He will establish the first and the second sets of creation of subjects of Dakṣa the Prajāpati." Thus after creating a million wells Dakṣa the Prācetasa married Asiknī, the daughter of Vīraṇa. Dakṣa the lord Prācetasa begot of Asiknī, daughter of Vīraṇa, a thousand sons of unmeasured splendour.

135. On seeing those subjects desirous of flourishing the extremely powerful celestial sage, Brahmā's son Nārada, fond of arguments, spoke evil words to them resulting in himself being cursed.

136. The Brāhmaṇa (Nārada) is sometimes called son of Kaśyapa. Due to his mean action the Brāhmaṇa sage was afraid of Dakṣa's curse.

137-140. Parameṣṭhin was born as Kaśyapa's son. Again due to the fear of curse of Dakṣa, he was born as his mental son. His second birth was as the mental son of Kaśyapa. He was formerly born as Nārada (son) of Parameṣṭhin. Formerly Dakṣa's sons famous as Haryaśvas were destroyed for the purpose of censure. They were undoubtedly annihilated. Lord Dakṣa became infuriated and attempted to destroy him (Nārada). Keeping the Brahmarṣis ahead, he (Dakṣa) was requested by Parameṣṭhin (not to kill Nārada).

141. Then Dakṣa stipulated the conditions with Parameṣṭhin: "Let Nārada be born of my daughter as your son".

142. Then Dakṣa gave his beloved daughter to Parameṣṭhin. Nārada was born thereof. The sage became calm and ceased to be afraid.

143. On hearing this those Brāhmaṇas became curious. They asked Sūta, the seer of truth, the foremost among the eloquent ones:

The sages enquired :

144. How were the sons of Prajāpati, the subjects born of Prācetasa destroyed by the noble-souled Nārada ?

145. On hearing these auspicious truthful words born of a desire to know, *he* (*Sūta*) *spoke* these sweet words endowed with all good qualities :

146. Haryaśvas, the sons of Dakṣa, desirous of procreating subjects, the extremely powerful ones came there and Nārada spoke to them:[1]

147. "Alas, all of you are childish. You do not know the entire surface of the world. What is within, what is above and what is below, you do not know. How will you create the subjects?

148. What is the extent of the Earth ? What are the things to be created ? Is it possible to create without knowing these ? Small or great defects are sure to be seen therein".

149. On hearing his words they went away to various quarters. On reaching the aerial zone, they were utterly non-plussed.

150. Wandering (here and there) intermingled with the (blowing) winds, they have not returned till this day. Thus those great sages are wandering after reaching the aerial zone.

151. When his sons were lost, Lord Dakṣa, the Prācetasa, begot again of Vīriṇī a thousand sons.

152-153. These sons (known as) Śabalāśvas (having horses of diverse colours), desirous of multiplying subjects were told the same words by Nārada. On hearing those words all those powerful young men spoke to one another—"The great sage has said well. Undoubtedly the track of our brothers should be followed.

154. After knowing the magnitude of the Earth we shall easily create the subjects". They too went the same way to all the quarters. Even to this day they have not returned like the rivers (not returning) after falling into the oceans.

155. Ever since then, if a younger brother goes in quest of a lost elder brother, he too gets lost. This is not to be done by one who knows.

156-158. When the Śabalāśvas were lost, lord Dakṣa became infuriated and cursed Nārada—"Be ruined, endure the

---

1. According to Mbh *Ādi*. 75.7-8, Nārada instructed Haryaśvas, the first batch of 1000 sons of Dakṣa, in Sāṅkhya Philosophy. Thereby all became recluses and frustrated Dakṣa's plan of populating the world. Here (vv. 147-48) Nārada advised them to know the magnitude of the earth, which they were going to populate.

pain of staying in a womb". When those noble-souled (sons) were lost, Dakṣa begot of Vīriṇī sixty daughters. Those daughters were accepted as wives by Lord Kaśyapa, Dharma, Lord Soma (the Moon god) and other great sages.

159. He who knows entirely this creation of Dakṣa precisely, becomes long-lived, famous, blessed and endowed with progeny.

CHAPTER FIVE

The Race of Dharma

The sages requested :

1. Please narrate in detail the birth and origin of all Devas, Dānavas and Daityas in the Vaivasvata Manvantara.

Sūta said :

2-3. I shall now recount the progeny of Dharma. (Listen and) understand. Dakṣa, the son of Pracetas, gave these ten daughters to Dharma as wives, viz. Arundhatī, Vasu, Yāmī, Laṁbā, Bhānu, Marutvatī, Saṁkalpā, Muhūrtā, Sādhyā and Viśvā.

4. Sādhyā bore to Dharma twelve sons called Sādhyas. The highly fortunate Sādhyas were born according to their wish and were partakers of shares in *Yajñas*. Those who are conversant with Devas (Devatā-lore) know them to be greater than other Devas.

5. It is reported that the Devas (called) Jayas were created out of the mouth of Brahmā through the desire for progeny. All of them are remembered as having Mantras as their bodies in the Manvantaras.

6-7. These names of those Jayas are famous : Darśa, Paurṇamāsa, Bṛhad Rathantara, Citti, Vicitti, Ākūti, Kūti, Vijñātṛ, Vijñāta, Manas and Yajña.

8-9. As a result of the curse of Brahmā, they were born

again in Svāyaṁbhuva Manvantara as Jitas; in Svārociṣa Manvantara they were born as Tuṣitas; and in the Auttama Manvantara they were born as Satyas. In the Tāmasa Manvantara, they were born as Haris and in the Raivata Manvantara they were born as Vaikuṇṭhas. In the Cākṣuṣa Manvantara the Sādhyas were born as Suras as per their will.

10. The blessed sons of Dharma, the twelve deathless ones (named) Sādhyas, had been formerly born in the Cākṣuṣa Manvantara.

11-12. The highly powerful Devas who had passed away in the Svārociṣa Manvantara assumed the name of Tuṣitas in the Cākṣuṣa Manvantara and spoke to one another. When the duration of Svārociṣā Manvantara remained but little, the Tuṣita Devas conferred with one another—"We shall enter the blessed Sādhyas and be born in the Manvantara. That will be conducive to our welfare".

13. After saying thus, all of them were born in the Cākṣuṣa Manvantara as the twelve sons of Dharma, son of Svayaṁbhū (god Brahmā).

14. Nara and Nārāyaṇa too were born there again. Vipaścit who was Indra and Satya who was Hari were in the Svārociṣa Manvantara the Tuṣita gods.

15-16. When Tuṣitas became Sādhyas, these names are mentioned—Manas, Anumantā, Prāṇa, Nara, the powerful Yāna, Citti, Haya, Naya, Haṁsa, Nārāyaṇa, Prabhava and Vibhu. They were born as the twelve Sādhyas.

17-18. In the Svāyaṁbhuva Manvantara at the outset, then in the Svārociṣa Manvantara these were the names of the Tuṣitas. (Listen and) understand them. They were—Prāṇa, Apāna, Udāna, Samāna, Vyāna, Cakṣus, Śrotra, Prāṇa(?), Sparśa, Buddhi and Manas.

19. Formerly only these names of Tuṣitas were remembered: Prāṇa, Apāna, Udāna, Samāna and Vyāna.

20. The Vasus were the sons of Vasu. They are remembered as the younger brothers of Sādhyas. These are glorified as the eight Vasus—Dhara, Dhruva, Soma, Āpa, Anala, Anila, Pratyūṣa and Prabhāsa.

21. Draviṇa and Hutahavyavaha were the sons of Dhara;

Dhruva's son was Bhava who in the name of Kāla became the impeller of the worlds.

22. Soma's sons were lord Varcā and Budha who is known as a planet. These two were born of Rohiṇī and are famous in the three worlds.

23. Dhāra, Ūrmi and Kalila—these three too were the sons of Candramas (Moon god). Āpa's sons were Vaitaṇḍya, Śama and Śānta.

24. Skanda and Sanatkumāra were born of the fourth part of Tejas (fire). Agni's son Kumāra was born in the Śara grove (a kind of reed). Śākha, Viśākha and Naigameya were his younger brothers.

25. Anila's (Wind god) wife was Śivā and her sons were Manojava and Avijñātagati. Anila had these two sons.

26. They know that the son of Pratyūṣa was sage Devala by name. Devala had two sons Kṣamāvān and Manīṣin.

27-28. Bṛhaspati's sister was an excellent woman, celibate and having Yogic Siddhis. Unattached (to the worldly affairs or things) she roamed the entire Universe. She who became the wife of Prabhāsa, the eighth among the Vasus, had a son Viśvakarmā who was the Prajāpati of all *Śilpis* (artisans and sculptors).

29. He is the maker of all arts and crafts. He is the carpenter of the Devas. He makes and causes others to make ornaments.

30. He makes the aerial chariots of all Devas. The human craftsmen depend upon (and emulate) his mechanical arts.

31-32. The ten renowned Viśvedevas were born of Viśvā. They were—Kratu, Dakṣa, Śravas, Satya, Kāla, Kāma, Dhuni, Kuruvān, Prabhavān and Rocamāna. [They] are remembered as the ten sons of Dharma. They were the auspicious sons born of Viśvā.

33. The Marutvants were the sons of Marutvatī. The Bhānu groups were remembered as the sons of Bhānu. The

Muhūrtas (auspicious hours) were born of Muhūrta[1]. Laṁbā gave birth to Ghoṣa.

34. The learned Saṁkalpa (conception) was born of Saṁkalpā. The Nāgavīthīs consisting of three paths were born of Jāmī (Yāmī).

35. All the objects on the Earth were born of Arundhatī. Thus the learned and eternal creation of Dharma has been narrated.

36. O men of holy rites, I shall mention the names of the *Muhūrta's* and *Tithis* along with their presiding lords.[1] Even as I recount, listen and understand.

37. (Incidentally I shall mention) the divisions of days and nights, the constellations in brief and all the Muhūrtas and stars that appear during days and nights.

38. More than six hundred Kalās are mentioned during days and nights. The manifestation of Ṛtus is based on the special movement of the Sun.

39. Those who know Vedas calculate *Tithis* as the basis of festivals. For the purpose of charitable gifts on behalf of Pitṛs, they utilise the different occasions (even if no apparent peculiarity is seen).

40-42. The divisions (*Muhūrtas* or *Bhāgas*) in the day are Raudra, Sārva, Maitra, Piṇḍya, Vāsava, Āpya, Vaiśvadeva, Brāhma—these *Muhūrtas* cover the period till mid-day. Prājāpatya, Aindra, Indra, Nirṛti, Vāruṇa and Āryamṇa and Bhāga: these Muhūrtas of the day are caused by the Sun. They are to be known in accordance with their magnitude by means of the gnomons.

43-45. Aja, Ahir-Budhnya, Pūṣā, Yamadevatā, Āgneya, Prājāpatya, Brāhma, Saumya, Āditya, Bārhaspatya, Vaiṣṇava, Sāvitra, Tvāṣṭra and Vāyavya—these are the fifteen Muhūrtas

1. This verse and vv. 36-45 present the names of the different Muhūrtas. *Muhūrta* shows 'time fit for performance of an auspicious act'. The names of Muhūrtas in Brāhmaṇas and Smṛtis are different. The names of the 15 Muhūrtas of the day and 15 Muhūrtas of the night agree with those in Bd. P. 2.3.39-46. But of these Mt.P. 253.8-9 mentions only 8 auspicious Muhūrtas for beginning a work. Purāṇas regard Muhūrtas as deities as every Muhūrta has a presiding deity.

occurring in a single night in order. The movements and rising of the moon are to be known from the *Nālikā* or the Pāda of its rise. These are the different periods of time remembered as Muhūrtas. Their presiding deities (are also mentioned).

46-48. Only three positions have been assigned for all the planets. They must be known in order as southern, northern and middle ones.

The place Jāradgava is the middle, the place Airāvata is the northern one and the place of Vaiśvānara has been indicated as the southern one factually.

The constellations Aśvinī[1], Kṛttikā and Yāmyā (i.e. Bharaṇī) are remembered as Nāgavīthī[2]*. The constellation Puṣya, Āśleṣā and Punarvasu are considered as Airāvatī Vīthī. These three Vīthīs are mentioned to be in the northern path.

49-50. The constellations Pūrvāphālgunī, Uttarāphālgunī and Maghā are remembered as Aryamī (Vīthī). The constellations Hasta, Citrā and Svātī are termed Govīthī). The constellations Jyeṣṭhā, Viśākhā and Anurādhā are remembered as Jāradgavī Vīthī. These three Vīthīs are mentioned to be in the middle path.

---

1. The enumeration of Nakṣatras from Aśvinī shows that this portion of the Purāṇa should be assigned to A.D. 300-400 as the Vedic list of Nakṣatras starts from Kṛttikā. *Vide* H.D. V.1 pp. 501-504 for a comparative table of the list of Nakṣatras in Vedic Saṁhitās, their deities, their modern names etc.

2. *Vīthis* are the divisions of planetary sphere comprising of three asterisms, e.g. Aśvinī, Bharaṇī, Kṛttikā constitute Nāgavīthī. Verse 48 states, *vīthīs* are three in number in the northern path but actually only two Nāga and Airāvatī are mentioned. The line regarding Gajavīthī seems to be omitted.

Verses 48-52 give the distribution of different Nakṣatras to different Vīthis. The sky is divided into three zones—the northern, the middle and the southern designated as Airāvatī, Jāradgavī and Vaiśvānarī respectively. Each of these have three (sub) Vīthis and to each (sub-Vīthi) three constellations are assigned (3+3+3=27 Nakṣatras).

*Here the line found in Bd. P. II.3-48a '*brāhmaṁ saumyaṁ tathārdrā ca gaja-vīthīti saṁjñitā* appears to be omitted. It continues the series of constellations after Kṛttikā and means : 'The constellations Rohiṇī, Mṛgaśiras and Ārdrā are termed Gajavīthī". Unless this line is included the words in 48.b

tisras tu vīthayo hyetā uttare mārga ucyate

would be meaningless as only two *Vīthīs* and *not* three are mentioned in the Vā. P.

51-52. The constellations Mūla, Pūrvāṣāḍhā and Uttarāṣāḍhā are termed Ajavīthī. The constellations Śravaṇa, Dhaniṣṭhā and Śatabhiṣak are the Gārgī Vīthī. The constellations Pūrvā Bhādrapadā, Uttarā Bhādrapadā and Revatī are glorified as Vaiśvānarī (Vīthī). These three Vīthīs are remembered by learned men to bein the southern path.

53. The twenty seven (constellations) daughters whom Dakṣa gave to Soma (Moon god) are glorified in Astronomy as Nakṣatras by name (i.e. Stars). They all bore children illuminated with unmeasured splendour.

54. From the daughters (of Dakṣa) who remained, Kaśyapa married fourteen[1] blessed ones. All of them are mothers of the worlds.

55. They were Aditi, Diti, Danu, Kālā, Ariṣṭā, Surasā, Surabhī, Vinatā, Tāmrā, Krodhavaśā, Irā, Kadru and Muni. O knowers of Dharma, listen and understand their progeny.

56. The twelve Vaikuṇṭha gods who were prominent in the Cāriṣṇava Manvantara that has passed, became Sādhyas, in the Cākṣuṣa Manvantara.

57-59. When the present Vaivasvata Manvantara had arrived, they were propitiated by Aditi. They gathered together and spoke to one another. "We shall enter this blessed Aditi alone, in the present Vaivasvata Manvantara by means of a moiety of our Yagic splendour and become her sons. That will be conducive to our welfare. Those who are born of Aditi will attain the status of Ādityas".

60. After saying this, all of them were born as the twelve Ādityas from Kaśyapa, the son of Marīci, in the Cākṣuṣa Manvantara.

61. Śatakratu (Indra) and Viṣṇu were born again as Nara and Nārāyaṇa in the present Vaivasvata Manvantara.

62. Death and birth are mentioned to happen even to those Devas. Just as the Sun rises and sets in this world, even so

---

1. Though the number of Kaśyapa's wives is stated to be fourteen, v. 55 gives the names of *thirteen* only.

there is manifestation and dissolution to Prajāpati (Brahmā), Viṣṇu and Bhava (Śiva) the noble soul.[1]

63. Since they are attached to the great Vedic tradition as well as worldly objects like sound and the eightfold superhuman powers like *Aṇimā* (minuteness) these Devas were born.

64-65. The attachment to sensual objects is declared as the cause of birth. Due to the curse of Brahmā, the Jayās were born in the Svāyaṁbhuva Manvantara as Jitas. In the Svārociṣa Manvantara, they were born as Tuṣitas and in the Auttama Manvantara they were born as Satyas. Devas were born as Haris in the Tāmasa Manvantara, Vaikuṇṭhas in the Cāriṣṇava Manvantara, Sādhyas in the Cākṣuṣa Manvantara and Ādityas in the present (i.e. Vaivasvata) Manvantara.

66-67. The follwing are remembered as the twelve Ādityas, the sons of Kaśyapa: Dhātā, Aryamā, Mitra, Varuṇa, Aṁśa, Bhaga, Indra, Vivasvān, Pūṣan, the tenth one Parjanya, Tvaṣṭṛ and Viṣṇu the last but not the least (i.e. really the great).

68-70. Purified by penance and blessed by Mahādeva the chaste Surabhī bore to Kaśyapa the eleven Rudras. They were Aṅgāraka, Sarpa, Nirṛti, Sadasaspati, Ajaikapāt, Ahirbudhnya, Ūrdhvaketu, Jvara, Bhuvaneśvara, Mṛtyu and Kapāla who was famous. With her great penance, Surabhī bore these elven Devas, the Rudras, the lords of the three worlds.

71. Then she gave birth to two daughters, viz. Rohiṇī having the lustre of Rudra and Gāndhārī the renowned.

72-74. Four daughters, very famous in the worlds were born of Rohiṇī, viz. Surūpā, Haṁsakīlā, Bhadrā and Kāmadughā. Kāmadughā and Surūpā gave birth to two sons. Haṁsakīlā gave birth to Nṛpa (king) and sages (?) and to Bhadrā were born the famous and blessed Gandharvas, the sons of Vājin (horse). The horses Uccaiśśravas were born then; they roamed about in the firmament with the speed of mind. They were of different colours, white, red, tawny, deer-coloured, green and gray and (also of the lustre of) Rudra. These horses were of Gandharva wombs. They were the vehicles of the Devas.

---

1. Verses 62-64 (in fact verses 56-65) stated that even gods like Brahmā, Viṣṇu and Śiva have their births and deaths due to their attachment to sensual objects. Non-attachment is the way to liberation. Cf. vv. 79-80 below.

75. Again to Surabhī was born (a bull) that was glorious, and had the good lustre like that of the moon. He had a garland on. He was lustrous with a (big) lump. He was born of the storehouse of nectar. With the permission of Surabhī he was given to Maheśvara as his banner.

76. Thus these sons of Kaśyapa, Rudras and Ādityas have been glorified. Sādhyas, Viśvedevas and Vasus are remembered as the sons of Dharma.

77. Ariṣṭanemi's wives had sixteen childern. The sons of the learned Bahuputra are remembered as Vidyuts. The excellent Ṛks honoured by Brahmarṣis are born of Pratyaṅgirasa.

78. The sons of Kṛśāśva, the celestial sage, are remembered as Devapraharaṇas. These are born again at the end of a thousand Yugas.

79-80. O Brāhmaṇas, all the thirty-three groups of Devas are *Chandajas* (born from Vedic chandas or mantras). These Devas too are said to have annihilation and birth. Just as the sun rises and sets in this world, so also these groups of Devas are born in every Yuga.

The sages enquired :

81-84. (How were) Sādhyas. Vasus, Viśvedevas, Rudras and Ādityas famous : by the nobility of their birth, greatness of the prowess or actions ? We wish to know the difference among Prajāpati, Viṣṇu and the noble-souled Bhava as to who excels whom among them ? Who originates from whom ? Who is established in whom ? Who is the eldest ? Who is the middle one ? who is the youngest among them ? Who is the most important among them ? Who is the greatest among them by means of actions, nobility of birth and prowess ? Please mention all these to us as you know these precisely.

Sūta replied :

85. In this context I shall describe the difference that is remembered among them. Listen to what I am going to say as to difference among Brahmā, Viṣṇu and Rudra.

86. The bodies of the Self-born Lord that are said to be born from time to time are proclaimed as Rājasa, Tāmasa and

Sāttvika.[1]

87. O excellent Brāhmaṇas, it is not possible to state the difference among these bodies, since they are dependent upon the increase of (a particular) Guṇa and the two-fold bondage due to *Anugraha* (blessing or favouring) and *Nigraha* (controlling).

88. O Brāhmaṇas, in accordance with my ability I shall recount *Pravṛtti* (activity), *Nivṛtti* (desistance from activity) and the increase of the Guṇas of the bodies. (Listen to it) and understand.

89. One among them, the Rājasa body creates all the subjects; the Sāttvika one staying in the ocean, blesses; and the Tāmasa one swallows the subjects and overthrows them at the proper time.

90. When god Brahmā manifests himself with the resurgence of Rajas guṇa, the Sāttvika body which is called Puruṣa vanishes.

91. With the excess of Tamas, when it assumes the form of Kāla (the destroyer), the Rājasa form designated as Brahmā disappears.

92. When with the dominance of Sattva, the lord becomes Puruṣa, the body named Kāla ceases to exist.

93. The form, name and activity of the Lord in favouring and controlling those prevailing in the three worlds disappear in due course.

94. When Brahmā manifests himself the difference is mentioned. When the lord is Brahmā, Puruṣa does not exist.

95-96. Just as the crystal jewel assumes various colours due to its purity, and as a result of the contact with other objects, the colours and sizes being in accordance with those objects, so also the self-born assumes shapes and sizes due to the

---

1. Verses 86-121: A philosophic synthesis of Brahmā, Viṣṇu and Śiva—'Three bodies of the single self-born lord' (v. 99) for the three activities of creation, protection and destruction (v. 104)—The Vedas, Dharma-śāstra, Sāṅkhya and Yoga hold unanimously that Reality or the Supreme Lord is one. Synthesization of the Trinity of gods (Brahmā, Viṣṇu and Śiva) as manifestation of the Supreme Lord (Brahman) is a favourite subject of Purāṇas.

Guṇas. In its singleness and separateness this is the example cited.

97-98. Just as the cloud, though single, remains (or seems) different in colour and form so also the self-born Lord though single one assumes different forms due to Guṇas and appears single, double or triple. The single entity has the three forms of Brahmā (the creator), annihilator and Puruṣa.

99. These three bodies are remembered as those of the single self-born Lord. The three bodies are Brāhma, Pauruṣa and Antakārī.

100. Herein what is (known as) His Rājasa body is verily the creator of subjects (i.e. the Universe). What is called the Tāmasa form is the annihilator of the subjects. The Sāttvika form called Pauruṣa is remembered as the bestower of blessings.

101-102. From the Rājasa part of Brahmā Marīci and Kaśyapa were born. From the Tāmasa form that causes dissolution was born Bhava. The Sāttvika or Pauruṣa form is called Viṣṇu. These three bodies of the self-born are thus remembered in the three worlds.

103. The supreme being, Kāla, assumes states for different functions (such as) creating the subjects in the capacity of Brahmā, supporting them in the status of Viṣṇu and devouring in the guise of Rudra, the subjects who had been blessed by the Vaiṣṇava form.

104. The Self-born one, Kāla, performs three activities through the three (bodies). It creates, supports and annihilates the subjects.

105. Thus the three bodies of the self-born God which are called Prājāpatya (belonging to Prajāpati or god Brahmā), Raudra (belonging to Rudra) and Vaiṣṇava (belonging to Viṣṇu) have been proclaimed.

106. Only one body is remembered in the Vedas, Dharma Śāstras and in the ancient (schools of) Sāṅkhya and Yoga by the intelligent sages who could see (both) analytically and synthetically, were conversant with nobility of pedigree and prowess and could visualize the Reality.

107. In the matter of unity and diversity people are of

different opinions. Advocates of different points of view say "This is great and this not so".

108. Some hold that Brahmā is the cause (of the Universe); some say that it is Prajāpati. Some say that Śiva is the greatest while others call Viṣṇu supreme. Out of ignorance and with the mind vitiated by passion, attachment etc. they think like this.

109. Considering the reality, time, place, cause and effects precisely, these deities are declared as working for diverse purposes.

110. He who censures one among them censures them all. He who praises one, praises all of them. They call him Brahmavādin (propounder of Brahman) who understands one Puruṣa.

111. The attitude of non-censure must always be adopted towards the deities by one who knows (the Reality). It is impossible to know Īśvara established in all *Aiśvarya* (prosperity, power and glory).

112-113. It is one supreme Soul. He becomes three and deludes the subjects. People seek difference among these three Beings, with diverse points of view, curiously testing their forms and saying, "This is the greatest; this is not (so)", out of deluded mind.

114-115. These deities permeate even Yātudhānas, Piśacas and human beings. The Self-born stays unified and separate deluding the subjects by means of the bodies solely consisting of the Guṇas. He who worships one among them, worships all the three.

116. These three deities remain non-different (factually). So where is separatness or unity? Where is their number? Whence do they come and go? Who is competent to know their unity or multiplicity?

117. Since in view of their being united with the Guṇas they create, sustain and devour the subjects in the three units of time, the supreme Being is said to be one.

118. Brāhmaṇas call that one lord, Rudra, Brahmā, Indra, guardians of the quarters, sages, Danus (Manus in Bd. P.) and Nārāyaṇa, in diverse ways.

119. The Prājāpatya body (i.e. that of Brahmā) and the Vaiṣṇava body (i.e. that of Viṣṇu) recur again and again in all the Manvantaras and Kalpas.

120. In splendour, fame, intellect, learning and strength they are born equal to Him. Know them also.

121. With the Rājasa part of Brahmā, Marīci and Kaśyapa were born. It is said that Rudra of the nature of Kāla was born with the Tāmasa part. With the Sāttvika part of Puruṣa Viṣṇu was then born in the Yajña.

122-124. The bodies born of parts of Brahmā occur in all the three units of time. Becoming Kāla, Rudra destroys the subjects again. When the end of the Kalpa approaches, the sun of seven rays becomes the Saṁvartaka Sun (the sun at the time of world dissolution) and burns the three worlds. With changes in name and form, Viṣṇu blesses i.e. sustains the subjects. In the different situations he is the cause of the origin of different things.

125. With the Pauruśa body of Bahmā which had a predominance of Sattva guṇa, the god was born here in the first Svāyaṁbhuva Manvantara as the mental son of Ākūti.[1]

126. Thereafter, when the Svārociṣa Manvantara arrived, he was born of Tuṣitā along with the previous Tuṣita groups of Devas and passed away along with them.

127. In the Auttama Manvantara also, he was known as Tuṣita. Born along with Vaśavartis (i.e. Devas of that name), Hari was again known as Vaśavartin.

128. He was born of Satyā, as Satya, along with the excellent gods Satyas. When the Tāmasa Manvantara arrived, Hari himself was born of Haryā along with the Haris.

129-132. In the Cāriṣṇava Manvantara, Lord Hari was again born of Vaikuṇṭha along with the Ābhūtarajasas. When the Cākṣuṣa Manvantara arrived that lord Vaikuṇṭha was born as Nārāyaṇa, Dharma and Sādhya along with the Sādhya group of gods. When the Vaivasvata Manvantara arrived, the lord Sādhya Nārāyaṇa, was born of Aditi and Kaśyapa, the son

1. Verses 125-132 state different incarnations of Viṣṇu in different Manvantaras, and his achievement as Trivikrama. But the unity of Brahmā, Vāmana and the great Ātman is emphasized.

of Marīci. Viṣṇu, of big steps, conquered all the worlds by means of three steps and handed them over to Indra and the Devas. Thus these seven bodies of the lord have appeared in the seven past Manvantaras. Thereby the subjects were protected.

133. Since, at the time of his birth, all the worlds were permeated by Vāmana (Lord in the form of a dwarf) he is remembered as Viṣṇu. The root √*viś* means 'to enter, to permeate'.

134. Thus the unity, separatness and the speciality of Brahmā and Vāmana, the great Ātman have been glorified.

135. The deities are born of the part of other deities. They are then born equal to them in brilliance, intellect, learning and strength, thanks to their blessings.

136. Know that whatever being exists endowed with special riches, glory and strength, is born of a part of Viṣṇu's brilliance.

137. Some men say that the lord alone is born partially. Others say that the deities are born of one anothers' part.

138. Thus arguing with one another they say after seeing them. For, there is no difference between *Manas* and *Cetas* Hence they are blessed. They become Kṣetrajñas.

139. Īśvara, though one, becomes manifold, due to the power of his lordship. For the same reason after becoming manifold he becomes one again.

140. From that (Lord) of good intentions and the diversity of brilliance are born the subjects consisting of mobile and the immobile beings in all the Manvantaras. When they are created once at the beginning of Sarga, they continue to live respectably (?)

141. Whenever any Kalpa comes to a close Rudra annihilates the subjects. Īśvaras are born by means of Yogic Māyā deluding others.

142. They are moving about due to their Aiśvarya and the non-Īśvaras (those devoid of Aiśvarya) are deluded. Hence there is nothing proper or improper in things where faults spread.

143. Those who spread scandal about living beings are wicked; those who are favourable to living beings are middling; those who slight and disregard living beings are competent. There are three Vedas for those who are eloquent.

144. (A line is missing from the the Text.) Because it is heard firmly, because it is heard before, bacause it is a rumour and because it is worldly, for these four reasons one does not get at the precise truth.

145. Formerly they meant and were used in another sense, and even after the lapse of time one does not accept the new sense out of spite.

146. He who is a solid among solids, he who becomes the attribute therein, he who is the creator of activities and minds and he who is great due to pedigree, are glorified by those who know the tradition, for these four reasons.

147. The incompetent and the infuriated know the deities only partially. They state these two verses in this connection in regard to Yogeśvara (Lord of Yogas).

148-149. The Yogeśvara makes replicas of himself and others in thousands by means of Yogic power. He moves about among them. He attains the (pleasures of) sensuous objects performing severe penance. Like the Sun withdrawing his brilliance and attributes (of heat etc.) he annihilates them all again.

CHAPTER SIX

Curse to Jaya Gods : Nṛsiṁha Incarnation
Race of Hiraṇyakaśipu : Birth of Marut-Gods

1. On hearing his words, the sages and ascetics of the Naimiṣa forest asked the most excellent one (i.e. Sūta) in due course.

The sages said:

2. How were the Devas, the extremely powerful Ādityas, the chief of whom were Indra and Viṣṇu, born in the seven

Manvantaras? O Romaharṣaṇa, please narrate all this in details to us.

3. On being urged and requested by the expounders of the Brahman (Vedas) the modest Sūta, the most excellent among eloquent ones spoke in accordance with the query of the great sages.

Sūta narrated :

4. All the Devas created from the mouth of Brahmā with a desire for progeny in the Manvantaras had their bodies constituted of Mantras.

5-8. The twelve Manus, the twelve sons of Brahmā were: Darśa, Paurṇamāsa, Bṛhad, Rathantara, Ākūta the first, Ākūti, Vitti, Suvitti, Ākūti (or Akūta the second?), Kūti, Adhīṣṭa, Adhīti, Vijñāti and Vijñata. These are the cumulative (names) of years. Seeing them Brahmā said, 'O Jayas, procreate the Devas. Perform the *Agnihotra* Yāga after marriage*'. After saying this, Brahmā vanished there itself.

9-12. But they did not act in accordance with the instruction of Parameṣṭhin (Brahmā). They found out defects even in those who abide by the mental, verbal and physical activities of a truthful nature; they saw the fruits of actions excessively reduced; they hated progeny and procreation. They were alert but free from the sense of my-ness (possession); they aspired for permanence; they were detached (from worldly objects); they saw defects (in worldly activities); they abandoned wealth, love and virtue; they adhered to knowledge pertaining to the supreme being and remained with their splendour withdrawn.

13. On realising the trend of their thought, Brahmā became angry. Brahmā spoke to those gods in despair.

14. "You have been created by me for the sake of further procreation and not otherwise. I have already told you to procreate and be victorious.

15-16. You have disregarded my words andh ave adhered to detachment. You hate your own birth. Hence you do not

*The text : *dārāgnihotrasaṁyage mithyāmārabhata* is obscure Bd. P. reads : *dārāgnihotrasaṁbandhaṁ vitatya yajateti ca* is better and hence adopted here.

appreciate (the necessity of) progeny. You have abandoned all rites in your ambition to achieve deathlessness (Immortality). Hence, having dishonoured (me) you will be born seven times."

17. On being urged by Brahmā thus, those Devas, the Jayas, began to propitiate him. "O great lord, forgive us for what has been done through ignorance".

18. When they bowed to him and implored, Brahmā said to them again: "Who deserves (i.e. is capable) to be independent in this world without being permitted by me ?

19. Everything is pervaded by me. As against my will how will living beings attain anything auspicious or inauspicious.

20. Whatever exists in the world or is endowed with *Sattva* (existence) or *Asattva* (non-existence) has been pervaded by me with intellect and soul. Who in the world dare to deceive me ?

21. Whatever has been conjectured, decided or considered by the living beings is entirely known to me.

22. The entire Universe consisting of the mobile and the immobile beings (created) has been established by me, thanks to the principle of hope and expectation. How can I approve of cutting it off ?

23. Since I have transformed myself for the sake of creation and not for any other purpose, who will be free from my will without beginning the performance of holy rites?"

24. After saying this to the group of Jaya Devas who accepted his punishment and who were dejected, Prajāpati spoke again to them (in consolation).

25. "Since, after open declaration to me, renunciation had been adopted by you formerly and since excessive effort, though fruitless, had been put in by you, O Devas, your future births will result in ultimate happiness.

26-27. O excellent Devas, your birth will be in accordance with your own will. In the six Manvantaras beginning with Svāyaṁbhuva and ending with Vaivasvata, O Suras, all of you will be moving ahead, deluded (by Avidyā)". After knowing them (i.e. their reaction) this ancient verse was recited by Brahmā.

28. "Those who perform holy actions such as the study of the three Vedas, maintenance of celibacy, procreation of progeny, performance of Śrāddhas, and Yajñas and practice of charity become free from sin (Rajas) and are always praised by others".

29. After reciting thus the verse he spoke to the Devas, Jayas again—"When the Vaivasvata Manvantara is over, you will come here near me.

30. Then you will attain eternal Siddhi along with me". After speaking thus to them, Brahmā vanished there itself.

31. When the lord had disappeared those Devas who were endowed with Yogic power and who possessed *Aṇimā* and other supernatural powers, continued practising Yoga fearlessly.

32. Thereafter, their bodies turned into twelve lakes. They came to be known by the name Jaya and they resembled the oceans.

33. Then, in that Svāyaṁbhuva Manvantara, those Suras (Gods) were born as the sons Ruci and Ajitā. They were twelve in number and were known as Ajitas.[1]

34. These mental sons known as the twelve Ajitas were Vidhi, Munaya (?), Kṣema, Nanda, Avyaya, Prāṇa, Apāna, Sudhāmā, Kratu, Śakti and Vyavasthita.

35. In Yajñas they are proclaimed as the partakers of the fruits of Yajñas along with the Suras in the Svāyaṁbhuva Manvantra. Again in the Svārociṣa Manvantara, they were born as the sons of Svārociṣa and Tuṣitā.

36-37. They were known by the names Tuṣitas[2] and Prāṇas. They were the Suras and partakers of Yajñas. Again theses Tuṣitas were born as the auspicious sons of Uttama and Satyā in the Uttama Manvantara. Then those Devas were remembered as Satyas in the Uttama Manvantara.

38-39. In the Dvāpara Yuga of the third Manvantara, they became the partakers of Yajñas. When the Tāmasa

1. Only 11 are enumerated.

2. The groups of gods are named after their mothers—a relic of matriarchcal society ?

Manvantara arrived, all those twelve Devas, the Satyas, were born as the sons of Tamas and Haryā ?[1] They were known by the name Haris and were partakers of Yajña.

40. When the Cāriṣṇava Manvantara arrived those Devas, the Haris, were born as the sons of Vaikuṇṭhā and Cariṣṇu. In the fifth Manvantara those Devas were known by the name Vaikuṇṭha[2].

41. In the Cākṣuṣa Manvantara, those Devas, the Vaikuṇṭhas were born as the twelve sons of Dharma and Sādhyā.

42-45. When the Cākṣuṣa Manvantara elapsed and the Vaivasvata Manvantara arrived at the beginning of the first Tretā Yuga (of that Manvantara), these Sādhyas were born as the twelve Ādityas, by means of their parts as the sons of Aditi and Kaśyapa, the son of Marīci. Thus those who were originally Jayas were born as Sādhyas in the Svāyaṁbhuva Manvantara as a result of the curse of (Brahmā). Again they were born in the Cākṣuṣa Manvantara and were born as Ādityas in the present Vaivasvata (Manvantara).

46. He who faithfully reads this story of the seven births of the Devas at the bidding of the lord, does not meet with any obstacle or sin.

47. Thus the seven births of Jayas with seven characteristics have been narrated by me.[2] What else do you wish to hear ?

The sages requested :

48. Narrate to us the origin and death in detail, of the Daityas, Dānavas, Gandharvas, Serpents, Rākṣasas, all the Bhūtas (goblins), Piśācas (ghosts), animals, birds and creepers.

49. Thus requested, *Sūta told these excellent sages*: "We have heard that Diti bore two sons to Kaśyapa.

50-51. Those two sons are remembered as the eldest of all the sons of Kaśyapa. The word *Kaśipu* means 'a mat'.

1. The same set of gods, viz. Jayas is born in the beginning of each Manvantara with different names such as 'Tuṣita' in Svārociṣa, 'Satya' in Uttama, Āditya in Vaivasvata. They derived their names from their mothers.
2. It is noteworthy that these gods also are named after their mother.

The seat of the chief *Ṛtvik* in a *Yajña* is a golden mat. Kaśyapa performed an Aśvamedha (horse-sacrifice). In the course of that sacrifice, during the performance of Atirātra sacrifice, on the day of *Sutya* (the day meant for extraction of Soma juice) the son of Kaśyapa came out of the womb of Diti and seated himself on the big seat of the *Ṛtvik* in the midst of the assembly (of the priests). As a result of this action, he is remembered as Hiraṇyakaśipu."[1]

The sages said :

52. O holy lord, mention in detail to us the name, origin and prowess of the noble-souled Daitya Hiraṇyakaśipu.

Sūta said :

53. Formerly the holy Aśvamedha of Kaśyapa was performed at Puṣkara. It was graced by (the presence of) deities and Gandharvas.

54. For the purpose of discourses etc. in accordance with the excellent injunctions (in sacred scriptures) there were five golden seats kept there.

55. Three of them were sanctified by means of Kuśa grass. The (fourth had a) bundle of Kuśa grass (over it) and (the fifth) a plank (over it). The four seats were intended for the chief Ṛtviks.

56. The fifth was an auspicious, divine, golden one intended for the *Hotṛ*. It was covered with divine cloth.

57. Diti who had been pregnant for ten thousand years was occupying the seat of *Patnī* (i.e. the wife of the sacificer, viz. Kaśyapa).

58-59. The boy in the womb came out of the belly of his mother and sat on the golden seat intended for the *Hotṛ*. Seated there he narrated the verses of the four Vedas and the fifth one, the Ākhyānas (Purāṇas) like Kāśyapa. On seeing him, the sages gave him that name.

60. Thanks to that act, he became renowned as Hiraṇyakaśipu. Hiraṇyākṣa was his younger brother. Siṁhikā was the

1. The author's fondness for popular etymologies (similar to that of Brāhmaṇa-writers) leads him to create such stories as in vv. 53-59.

younger sister. She was the lady who became the mother of Rāhu after marrying Vipracitti.

61. Hiraṇyakaśipu, the Daitya (son of Diti), performed severe penances for a hundred thousand years without taking any food and standing topsy-turvy.

62. Brahmā who was delighted (at his penance) gratified him with a boon (whereby he attained deathlessness from all living beings). O leading Brāhmaṇas, conquering Devas through his Yogic power he attained the lordship of all (*Lit.* the state of being all Devas).

63. (He requested further:) "May Dānavas and Asuras be equal to Devas and attain the greatness of Marut gods. May this boon be granted."

64. Thus requested Brahmā, granted him what he wished and after granting him the divine boons, he vanished there itself. Hiraṇyakaśipu, the son of Diti, has been glorified by the ancient people by means of verses.

65. "The Devas along with great sages made obeisance to that quarter which is resorted to by King Hiraṇyakaśipu."

66. O Brāhmaṇas, Hiraṇyakaśipu, the lord of Daityas, had such prowess. In ancient times, Viṣṇu, in the form of Man-Lion, became death unto him (i.e. killed him). He was torn by him by means of his claws. Hence the nails are remembered pure[1].

67-68. Hiraṇyākṣa had five valorous sons of great strength. Utkura, Śakuni, Kālanābha, the valorous Mahānābha and Bhūtasantāpana—these sons of Hiraṇyākṣa were invincible even to Devas.

69. Their sons and grandsons composed the group (of Daityas) named Bāḍeya. They were a hundred thousand in number and were killed in (the battle?) Tārakāmaya[2].

70. Hiraṇyakaśipu had four sons of great strength. Prahlāda was the eldest and the others were Anuhlāda, Saṁhrāda and Hrada. Understand the sons of Hrada.

---

1. Another reading—His nails were neither wet nor dry—Bd.P.
2. The battle fought after the abduction of Bṛhaspati's wife Tārā by Candra. In that battle Daityas sided with Candra.

71. Hrāda and Nisunda were the sons of Hrada. The valorous Sunda and Upasunda were the sons of Nisunda.

72. Brahmaghna, Mahāvīrya and Mūka became the successors of Hrada. Mārīca, son of Sunda, was born of Tāḍakā.

73. Tāḍakā was killed by the powerful Rāghava (Rāma). Mūka was killed by Savyasācī (i.e. Arjuna) in Kirāta (i.e. when Śiva assumed the form of a hunter to test Arjuna).

74. Their descendants purified themselves by means of great penance. They were the residents of Maṇivarta and reached the number of thirty million. Invinicible to Devas they were killed by Savyasācī (Arjuna).

75. Anuhlāda's sons were Vāyu and Śinīvālī. Their descendants running to a hundred thousand constituted the group of demons remembered as Hālāhala.

76. Vairocana, the son of Prahlāda, had five sons. Gaveṣṭhī, Kālanemi, Jaṁbha, Bāṣkala and Śaṁbhu (who was the youngest of them all) are remembered as the sons of Prāhlādi (i.e. Vairocana).

77-78. I shall mention their invincible sons in accordance with their importance. Śumbha, Niśumbha and Viṣvaksena—these were the sons of the powerful Gaveṣṭhin. Jaṁbha's sons were Śatadundubhi, Dakṣa and Khaṇḍa. Those three were Jaṁbha's sons.

79. Virodha, Manu, Vṛkṣāyu and Kuśalīmukha—these were the sons of Bāṣkala. Listen to the (enumeration of the) sons of Kālanemi.

80. Brahmajit, Kṣatrajit, Devāntaka and Narāntaka—these were the sons of Kālanemi. Listen to the progeny of Śaṁbhu.

81. Dhanuka, Asiloman, Nābala, Gomukha, Gavākṣa and Gomān—these are said to be the sons of Śaṁbhu.

82. Virocana's son Bali alone was very valorous. A hundred sons were born to Bali. All of them were kings.

83-84. Among them, four were very imporant. They were valorous and extremely powerful. The thousand-handed eldest son Bāṇa was wealthy and honoured (by all). The others were Kumbhanābha, Gardabhākṣa, Kuśi and others. Śakuni and Pūtanā were the two daughters of Bali. Bali's sons and grandsons numbered hundreds and thousands.

85. They constituted a group of demons famous by the name *Baligaṇa*. They were valorous and manly. Bāṇa whose mind was like that of Indra, had his capital city Lauhitya (Śoṇitapura in Assam).

86. Diti who lost her sons gratified Kaśyapa. Well-propitiated by her, the delighted Kaśyapa asked her to choose a boon freely. She chose the boon.[1]

87. The holy lord granted her the boon requested for. The son of Marīci, of fierce splendour, asked her, "What do you wish?"

88-89. She said to her gratified husband, Kaśyapa, the son of Marīci, with palms joined in reverence—"O holy lord, my sons have been killed by your sons born of Aditi. I wish for a son who will be endowed with penance of long duration and who will kill Śakra. I shall perform penance. It behoves you to impregnate me."

90. On hearing her words, Kaśyapa, the highly brilliant son of Marīci, replied to Diti who was extremely sad:

91. "May it be so. Welfare unto you. Be pure, O ascetic lady. You will bear a good son who will kill Śakra in battle.

92. If you (continue to) remain pure for full hundred years you will bear a son who will be the foremost in the three worlds".

93. After saying this, the holy lord of great brilliance had sexual intercourse with her. After embracing her, the holy sage went on his tour of the three worlds.

94. After the departure of her husband, that extremely delighted noble lady Diti went to the forest Kuśala and performed a very terrible penance.

95. While she was performing the penance, the thousand-eyed Indra, the most excellent among Suras, served her by means of his rich attributes.

---

1. Verses 86-134 describe the birth of Marut-gods from Diti and her final reconciliation with Indra. Indra's entry into Diti's womb and splitting of his prospective killer into 49 parts and the derivation of the name 'Marut' from Indra's threat '*mā rodīḥ*' (Don't cry) is a Purāṇic elaboration of a Vedic concept where the seven Maruts are said to be seven Prāṇas, Indra being the main Prāṇa controlling the Maruts (Śat. Br. 9.3.1.7). For similar elaboration cf. VP. I.21.32-41, Mt. P. Ch. 7. Bd. P. 2.3.5.45-81 is practically identical with our text.

96. He brought and gave her sacrificial fire and twigs, wood and Kuśa grass, fruits and roots. The thousand-eyed lord gave her whatever else she required.

97. By massaging her limbs and by assuaging her weariness, Śakra served her on all occasions. Thus propitiated, Diti spoke to Śakra :

98. "O excellent one among Suras, I am delighted with you; O dear son, only ten more years remain; welfare unto you; you will then see your brother.

99. On getting such a son I will fulfil my desire for conquest. With him, O son, I will conquer the three worlds."

100. After saying this to Śakra, and when the sun reached midday, the lady was over-powered by slumber. She crouched down keeping her head on her kness.

101. Seeing her impure inasmuch as her hair spread over her feet, Śakra laughed and rejoiced on getting that opportune moment.

102. Then Purandara (Indra) entered her open body. After entering and seeing the immense (unmeasurable) foetus of great power, Indra of great fame pierced the important enemy (?) with his thunderbolt.

103. On being split by the thunderbolt of hundred knots, the foetus cried in a high and terrible pitch, quaking again and again. Śakra then spoke to the foetus—"Do not cry (*Mā Rodiḥ*)[1]."

104. With his thunderbolt, Indra cut off the foetus into seven pieces and split each of the pieces into seven pieces again. Then Diti woke up.

105. "It should not be killed. It should not be killed", so shouted Diti. With due deference to the words of his mother, Indra jumped out of her belly. Armed with his thunderbolt, Śakra spoke to Diti with palms joined in reverence :

106. "O noble lady, you went to sleep in a defiled state since the hair were spread over your feet. On seizing that opportunity I have split the foetus that would have been the slayer of Śakra in battle. It behoves you to firgive me."

1. Cf. VP. I.21-39, Mt. P. 8.62 for similar etymology of 'Marut'.

107. When that foetus became fruitless, Diti became extremely distressed. Then she spoke to the thousand-eyed Indra these consoling words:

108. "O lord of Devas, O powerful son of a sage, it is not your fault, if the foetus had been rendered incapable as a result of my mistake.

109. There is no sin in killing an enemy. Hence, O (Indra) I do not curse you. I wish to do what is pleasing to you. Do a favour unto my foetus.

110. May my sons have seven abodes in heaven. Let my seven sons roam about these wind-regions (*Vātaskandhas*)[1] (Pathways of wind). May they be renowned as the seven Maruts, the seven sets of seven.

111. May the first *Skandha* (region) be on the Earth, the second in the Sun, the third in the Moon, aud the fourth should be known in the groups of luminaries.

112. May the fifth *Skandha* be among the planets, the sixth in the sphere of the Seven Sages and the seventh in Dhruva. That is the last region of the wind.

113. May my sons roam about among them on different occasions. May my sons walk through these Vātaskandhas.

114. The first *Skandha* extends from the Earth upto the clouds and it is called *Āvaha*. May the first set of my sons move therin.

115. The second *Vātaskandha* extends from the clouds upto the Sun. It is called *Pravaha*. Let the second set (of my sons) walk in the second *Vātaskandha*.

116. Above the solar region and extending upto the Moon is the *Vātaskandha* remembered as *Udvaha*. May the third set (of my sons) walk through the *Vātaskandha*.

117. Above the lunar region and extending upto the stars is the fourth *Vātaskandha* which is called *Suvaha*. O lord, may the fourth set of my sons walk therein.

---

1. This psuedo-scientific classification of higher space into seven strata (vide vv. 114-120) and the assignment of a Marut-god per stratum is found in other Purāṇas also.

118. Above the stellar region and extending up to the planets is the fifth *Skandha* which is called *Vivaha*. O dear boy, may the fifth set (of my sons) walk through the fifth *Skandha*.

119. Above the planets and extending up to the Seven Sages (Great Bear) is the sixth *Skandha* which is called *Parāhata* (*Anuvāha* in Bd. P.). May my sons who are in the sixth set walk therein.

120. Above the Seven Sages and extending up to Dhruva (Pole Star) is the seventh *Vātaskandha* which is called *Parivaha*. May my sons stay therein.

121. May my sons move about all these on different occasions. There let these be known by the name Maruts."

122. Then the mother and the son named them Maruts through the actions performed by them. They separately named the seven Maruts of each set.

123-125. The first set is said to consist of these: Sattvajyotis, Āditya, Satyajyotis, Tiryagjyotis, Sajyotis, Jyotiṣmān and another one. Listen and understand the second set. The second set consists of Ṛtajit, Satyajit, Suṣeṇa, Senajit, Satyamitra, Abhimitra and Harimitra. Listen and understand the third set.

126-128. The following constitute the other sets : Kṛta, Satya, Dhruva, Dhartā, Vidhartā, Vidhāraya, Dhvānta, Dhuni, Ugra, Bhīma, Abhiyu, Sākṣipa. This is known as Āhvayagaṇa*, Īdṛk, Anyādṛk, Yādṛk, Pratikṛt, Samiti, Saṁraṁbha, Īdṛk, Puruṣa, Anyādṛkṣa, Cetasa, Samita, Asamitadṛkṣa, Pratidṛkṣa and others.

129. These forty-nine are the different Maruts with their own separate names. They have been enumerated by Diti and Indra.

---

*There are some omissions and scribal confusion in the names and the sets of Marudgaṇas as given here. Bd. P. II. 3.5.96 and 97 state : The fifth set (of Marud-gaṇas) is as follows : (1) Īdṛk, (2) Anyādṛk, (3) Sarit, (4) Druma, (5) Vṛkṣaka, (6) Mita and (7) Samita.

The sixth class is as follows : (1) Īdṛk, (2) Puruṣa, (3) Nānyadṛk, (4) Samaccetana, (5) Sammita, (6) Samavṛtti, (7) Pratihartṛ.

Bd. P. does not give the names of the fourth and seventh groups of the Marudgaṇas.

A critical edition is essential for supplying the lacunae.

130. On hearing their names, Diti said to Indra, "O son, may my sons roam about in the *Vātaskandha*. May my sons walk in the company of Devas. Welfare unto you."

131. On hearing her words, the thousand-eyed Purandara joined his palms in reverence and said: "Mother, be it so.

132. Undoubtedly all this will happen as mentioned by you. These sons of noble souls (shall) become Devas and will be honoured by Devas. Similarly, your sons will become partakers of the fruits of Yajñas along with Devas."

133. Hence all those Maruts should be known as Devas (shining ones), younger brothers of Indra and *Amaras* (deathless ones). All of them, the sons of Diti were ascetics and gods.

134. After knowing this decisively, the mother and the son of ascetic nature went to heaven delightedly. Śakra too went to heaven.

135. He who reads or listens to the auspicious origin of Maruts shall become long-lived. He never meets with the fear of drought.

CHAPTER SEVEN

The Race of Kaśyapa : Danu's Progeny

Sūta said :

1. Henceforth, I shall recount the sons of Danu. Listen to and understand them. The sons of Danu, the great Asuras, have been famous in their race.

2. There were hundred demons of very fierce valour of whom Vipracitti was the chief. All of them had performed good penances and had been endowed with boons.

3. They were truthful, valorous, ruthless and expert in Māyā (illusive power). These Dānavas were very powerful, unfavourable to Brāhmaṇas and disinclined to perform Yajñas. I shall enumerate them all in accordance with their importance. (Listen to) and understand.

4-13. The chief of the sons of Danu were : Dvimūrdhā, Śaṅkuvarṇa, Śaṅku, Nirāmaya, Śaṅkukarṇa, Mahāviśva, Gaveṣṭhi, Dundubhi, Ajāmukha, prosperous Śila, Vāmanasa, Marīci, Rakṣaka, Mahāgārgya, Aṅgirāvṛta, Vikṣobhya, Suketu, Suvīrya, Suhṛda, Indrajit, Viśvajit, Suravimardana, Ekacakra, Subāhu, the powerful Tāraka, Vaiśvānara, Puloman, Pravīṇa, Mahāśiras, Svarbhānu, Vṛṣaparvan, the great Asura Muṇḍaka, Dhṛtarāṣṭra, Sūrya, Candra, Indra, Tāpina, Sūkṣma, Nicandra, Ūrṇanābha, Mahāgiri. Asiloman, Sukeśa, Sada, Balaka, Adaśa, Gaganamūrdhan, Kumbhanābha, Mahodara, Pramodāha, Kupatha, the valorous Hayagrīva, the Asura Virūpākṣa, the great Asura Supatha, Aja, Hiraṇmaya, Śatamāyu, Śambara, Śarabha and Śalabha. Sūrya (the Sun) and Candramas (the Moon) were the lords of Asuras formerly but now they are the lords of Suras. Thus the important scions of the family of Danu have been enumerated. Their sons and grandsons are unending and innumerable.

14. Those who are the sons (descendants) of Diti and Danu are (commonly known) as Asuras. Those mentioned just now are the sons and descendants of Danu. Svarbhānu is remembered as the son of Diti (i.e. a Daitya) and Anubhānu was the son of Danu.

15-16. Ekākṣa, Ṛṣabha, Ariṣṭa, Prabandha, Naraka, Indrabādhana, Keśī, Meru, Śamba, Dhenuka, Gaveṣṭhi, Gavākṣa and powerful Tālaketu—these were the sons of Danu but followed human rites and activities. So I remember.

17-20. The following sons of Vipracitti born of Siṁhikā became terrible, valorous in the clashes between Daityas and Dānavas. They are well known as Saiṁhikeyas. They are fourteen great Asuras, viz. Śatagāla, Balavān, Nyāsa, Śāmba, Anuloma, Śuci, Vātāpi, Sitāṁśuka, Hara, Kalpa, Kālanābha, Bhauma and Naraka and the eldest of all of them Rāhu who oppresses the Moon and the Sun. Thus these are the sons of Siṁhikā invincible even to Devas.

21. All of them were of terrible lineage, ruthless and haters of Brāhmaṇas. There are ten thousand other Asuras constituting the Saiṁhikeya group.

22. They were killed by the powerful son of Jamadagni of

the Bhṛgu Gotra. Prabhā was the daughter of Svarbhānu and Śacī was the daughter of Puloman.

23. Upadānavī was the daughter of Maya, Śarmiṣṭhā was the daughter of Vṛṣaparvan. Pulomā and Kālikā were the daughters of Vaiśvānara.

24. Nahuṣa was the son of Prabhā and Jayanta was the son of Śacī. Śarmiṣṭhā gave birth to Pūru and Upadānavī to Duṣyanta.

25-26. Pulomā and Kālikā, the two who were the daughters of Vaiśvānara became the wives of Mārīca. Sixty thousand leading Dānavas were the sons born of them. There were fourteen thousand other Asuras residents of Hiraṇyapura.

27. The Paulomas and Kālakeyas were Dānavas of great strength. They could not be killed by Devas, but were slain by Savyasācī (Arjuna).

28-29. All the sons born of Maya were heroic and valorous, viz. Māyāvī, Dundubhi, Vṛṣa, Mahiṣa, Bālika and Vajrakarṇa. A daughter Mandodarī was also born to him. Thus the creation of Daityas and Dānavas has been enumerated.

30. Five sons of great strength are remembered as born of Danāyuṣā, viz. Arūru, Bali, Jaṁbha, Virakṣa and Viṣa.

31. Arūru's son was a cruel great Asura named Dhundhu. It is reported that he was killed by Kuvalāśva at the instance of Uttaṅka.

32. The two sons of Bali were very valorous and unequalled in splendour. They were Kuṁbhila and Cakravarmā. (The latter) was Karṇa in his previous* birth.

33. Virakṣa had two sons Kālaka and Varaviṣa. Varaviṣa had four sons of cruel activities, viz. Śrāddhahā, Yajñahā, Brahmahā and Paśuhā.

34. The sons of Danāyuṣā have been enumerated. Now understand the sons of Vṛtra who were born of the terrible breath of Vṛtra while engaged in battle with Indra.

35. They were Rākṣasas of great strength and were the rulers mentally famous. They were a hundred thousand in number and are remembered as the followers of Mahendra.

---

*rather "in the future birth".

36. All were knowers of the Veda, gentle, righteous, subtle-formed. All were immanent in the subjects. All were very righteous.

37. Thus the creation of Daityas and Dānavas has been narrated. Pravāhī bore sons in the Yajña. They were excellent in singnig.

38-39. Sattvan, Sattvātmaka, Kalāpa, Vīryavān, Kṛtavīrya, Brahmacārin, the seventh one Supāṇḍu, Pana, Taraṇya and the tenth one Sucandra: These ten are to be known as Devas and Gandharvas. They have been enumerated.

CHAPTER EIGHT

Dynasties Descended From Kaśyapa[1]

Sūta said :

1-3. The holy Gandharvas and Apsaras-s are glorified as the children of Muni, viz. Citrasena, Ugrasena, Ūrṇāyu, Anagha, Dhṛtarāṣṭra, Puloman, Sūryavarcas, Yugapat, Tṛṇapat, Kāli, Diti, Citraratha, the thirteenth Bhramiśiras, the fourteenth Parjanya, the fifteenth Kali and the sixteenth Nārada—these divine Gandharvas are glorified as descendants of Muni.

4-8. There are their thirtyfour[2] younger sisters, the auspicious Apsaras-s, viz. Antarā, Dāravatyā, Priyamukhyā, Surottamā, Miśrakeśī Śacī, Parṇinī, Alambuṣā, Mārīcā, Mārīcī, Putrikā, Vidyud, Varṇā, Tilottamā, Adrikā, Lakṣaṇā, Devī, Rambhā, Manoramā, Suvarā, Subāhu, Pūrṇitā, Supratiṣṭhitā, Puṇḍarīkā, Sugandhā, Sudantā, Surasā, Hemasārā, Sutī, Suvṛttā, Kamalā, Subhujā, Haṁsapādā—these are the worldly[3] Apsaras-s.

1. This chapter enumerates the prominent members of clans of Gandharvas, Apsaras-s, birds, serpents, Yakṣas, Rākṣasas, Piśācas, Yātudhānas and other species possessing supernatural powers.

2. Even after splitting Vidyudvarṇā into Vidyut and Varṇā the number of these Apsaras-s is 32 and not 34 stated here. Bd. P. 2.3.7-5 states twentyfour as the number of Apsaras-s.

3. It is not understood why the sons of Muni are called '*Deva-Gandharvas*' (Divine Gandharvas) while their sisters, the Apsaras-s are called

These Gandharvas and Apsaras-s are glorified as descendants of Muni.

9. The daughters of Gandharvas had been (will be) narrated by me. Now listen to my enumeration of their names.

10. Suyaśā was the first among them. Gāndharvī comes next. Then are Vidyāvatī, Cārumukhī and Sumukhī of excellent face.

11. The sons of Suyaśā were very powerful and valorous. Yakṣas were the sons of Pracetas. Listen to their names.

12. Kaṁbala, Harikeśa, Kapila, Kāñcana and Meghamālī are said to constitute the group of Yakṣas.

13. Suyaśā's four daughters are remembered as Apsaras-s. Listen to and understand their names, as I recount them.

14. Loheyī was the eldest; Bharatā was the next. Then were Kṛśāṅgī and Viśālā who were unequalled in beauty.

15. From them other four groups of Yakṣas were procreated by the valorous and noble-souled Viśāla.

16. Loheya, Bharateya, the renowned Kṛśāṅgeya and Viśāleya were the groups of Yakṣas famous in the Purāṇa.

17. O excellent ones among the knowers of Loka and Aloka, (the worlds) have been occupied by these terrible Asuras of great strength and prowess.

18-19. The Gandharvas called Vāleyas were procreated by the noble-souled Vikrānta. They were the leaders of great Gandharvas. They possessed great prowess, and were richly endowed with valour and liberal-mindedness. I shall mention duly and in proper order the names of those highly mighty and valorous Gandharvas.

20. They were : Citrāṅgada, Citravarmā of great prowess, the highly fortunate Citraketu and the valorous Somadatta. There were three daughters also. Their names are being mentioned.

21. The first was Agnikā. Kaṁbalā was the next. Then was Vasumatī. All these had unequalled splendour.

'*Laukikyaḥ*' 'mundane, belonging to this world'. If the reading *ca laukikyaḥ* be emended as *cālaukikyaḥ*, 'not of this world, of the heavenly world' the equality between brothers (Gandharvas) and sisters (Apsaras-s) will be established.

22-23. Three other important groups of the chief Gandharvas were begotten of them by Kumāra. They were valorous and invincible in war. They were Āgneyas, Kāṁbaleyas and sons of Vasumatī. This world consisting of the mobile and the immobile is pervaded by these various groups.

24. They possessed learning and were procreated by the noble-souled Vikrānta. They were blessed and were richly endowed with beauty, learning and wealth.

25. Listen to the enumeration of the names of those noble-souled Gandharvas of distinctive prowess.

26. They were : Hiraṇyaroman, Kapila, Suloman, Māgadha, Candraketu, Gāṅga and the highly powerful Goda.

27. These were the first among the groups who were ascetics, valorous and pure on account of deep learning.

There were two daughters also of beautiful eyes.

28-29. They were Śivā and Sumanas. The groups Śaiveya, the valorous and Saumanasa as well were begotten of them by the noble-souled Viśravas. They practised learning. This world is pervaded by these three groups of Vidyādharas.

30. From these, many hundreds of groups of firmament-walkers were born in the world due to the activities of the Vidyādharas.

31. Horse-faced Kinnaras were procreated by the same noble-souled Vikrānta. They were called Aśvamukhas and Kinnaras. (Listen to and) understand the Kinnaras.

32-33. Samudra, Sena, Kālinda, Mahānetra, Mahābala, Suvarṇaghoṣa, Sugrīva, the valorous Mahāghoṣa and others are the leading ones of the noble-souled Kinnaras with the faces of horses. They are being glorified as extensive (in number) by scholars.

34. O Śāṁśapāyana, human-faced Kinnaras too were similarly procreated by the noble-souled Vikrānta.

35-36. Hariṣeṇa, Suṣeṇa, the valorous Vāriṣeṇa, Rudradatta, Indradatta, Candradruma, Mahādruma, Bindu and Bindusāra were the Kinnaras of the lunar race. Thus these excellent and auspicious Kinnaras have become famous in the world.

37. O excellent Brāhmaṇas, in this world there are hundreds of clans of these noble-souled Kinnaras, very efficient in dance and music.

38. They are Yakṣas calmed by Yakṣas (?) The beautiful daughter of Loheyā, named Suravindā was brilliant and honoured by the Siddhas.

39. (Defective Verse) The groups of Bhūtas (goblins) had been procreated by the terrible Upāyaketana. Listen to their names (?).

40. The groups of Bhūtas (goblins) should be known as those who haunt from within and without etc. (*āveśakas, niveśakas*). They are declared as being visible in the world.

41. Those that are the excellent ones among Bhūtas that move about in the sky are to be known as the leaders of these Bhūtas in the world. Undoubtedly they move about in the sky up to the tops of trees.

42. Almost all Devas and Gandharvas have been narrated by me. Those famous persons should be known as engaged in worshipping Devas.

43-45. Along with Gandharvas, Devas who are clever musicians and experts in dance and music stay in all the worlds. They worship Nārāyaṇa who is lotus-eyed, free from Rajas Guṇa and the foremost of gods, god Brahmā who is self-born and four-faced, great god Śaṅkara who is Īśāna and the lord of the Universe. (They worship) Rudras and Ādityas led by Indra, along with Vasus.

46-48. The blessed Variṣṭhā who is honoured by gods, gave birth to eight sons. Haṁsa was the eldest and the youngest was another. The middle ones were Hahā and Huhū. The fourth was Dhiṣaṇa. Then Vasiruci (was born). Tumburu was the sixth among them. Then Viśvāvasu. These Apsaras-s(celestial artiste) are considered as divine and of auspicious characteristics.

Ariṣṭā gave birth to eight (?) daughters, viz. Anavadyā, Anavaśā, Anvatā, Madanapriyā, Arūṣā, Subhagā and Bhāsī.

49-50. Manovatī and Sukeśā were the two daughters of Tumburu.

The following ten divine (celestial) Apsaras-s are called Pañcacūḍās. They are : Menakā, Sahajanyā, Parṇinī, Puñjikasthalā, Ghṛtasthalā, Ghṛtācī, Viśvācī, Pūrvacī, the one well-known as Pramlocā and Anumlocantī.

51. Urvaśī who was faultless (exquisitely beautiful) in every

limb and was born of the thighs of the beginningless and endless Nārāyaṇa is remembered as the eleventh.

52. Menakā was the daughter of Menā, delightedly engrossed in meditating upon Brahman. All of them are expounders of Brahman(Vedas) and great Yoginīs.

53. The groups of the holy Apsaras-s are fourteen. Among these fourteen *gaṇas* Āhūtas (is the first) and Śobhayantīs is the (fourteenth)[1].

54. (Āhūtas) are the mental daughters of Brahmā and Śobhayantīs are Manu's daughters. Vegavantīs are the daughters of Ariṣṭā and Agnisaṁbhavās are the daughters of Ūrja.[2]

55.[3] Āyuṣmantīs are shining groups born of the rays of the sun. The groups born of water i.e. produced from Amṛta (water, nectar) are remembered by the name Amṛtās.

56. The Vāyu-born groups are named Mudās, those born of the Earth are Bhavās, the groups Rucs are born of Vidyut (lightning) and the daughters of Mṛtyu are Bhairavās.

57. The group Śobhayantīs have the attributes of Kāma (Cupid). Thus the fourteen groups have been narrated. They have been created with exquisitely superb beauty by the groups of Suras including Indra and Upendra (Viṣṇu).

58. The divine lady Tilottamā is of auspicious features and extremely blessed. The celestial damsel Prabhāvatī richly endowed

1. Our text has given only the names of the first and the fourteenth group. Probably some lines missing in our text are found in Bd. P. 2.3.7.18-20a as follows :

"The meritorious groups(*gaṇas*)of Apsaras-s are well-known to be fourteen, viz. Āhṛtis (Āhūta in Va. P.), Śobhavatis, Vegavatis, Ūrjās, Yuvatis, Sruks Kurus, Barhis, Amṛtās, Mudās, Mṛgus, Ruks, Bhīrus and Śobhayantis". But the list in Vā. P. is incomplete and different.

2. The text needs emendation : 'The Ūrjās are born of the Fire-god' as Ūrjās are a *gaṇa* of Apsaras-s (vide Bd. P. 2.3.7..21).

3. Some lines appear to be missing. This translation is of the printed text of Vā. P. The missing lines are probably the same as Bd. P. 2.3.7.21b and 22. They mention the classes of divine damsels,viz. Yuvatis, Kurus, Sruks and Barhis who are respectively born from the Sun-god, the Moon-god, Yajña (Sacrifice) and Kuśavatī.

Bd. P. 2.3.7.23 corresponds to v. 55 above (of the Vā. P.)

with beauty and youth and renowned in the worlds, was born from the sacrificial fire-pit of Brahmā.

59. The celestial woman of great lustre, Vedavatī by name, was born from the bottom (surface) of the altar of the intelligent four-faced lord (Brahmā).

60. Similarly the daughter of Yama, the bright-eyed celestial woman Hemā had the lustre of excellent gold and possessed beauty and youth.

61. Thus there are many thousands of shining groups of Apsaras-s. They are the wives and mothers of Devas and Sages.

62. All the Apsaras-s are equally fragrant with the complexion of Campā (*Michelia Champacca*). During the course of their intercourse with their lovers, they are inebriated without imbibing wine. By their contact, their pleasure increases.

63. Vinatā had two sons Aruṇa and Garuḍa who had thirty-six sisters. They are remembered as their younger sisters.

64. Gāyatrī and other *chandas* (Vedic Metres), birds born of Garuḍa and also the Havyavāha groups present in the quarters (pertain to Vinatā?)

65. Kadrū[1] gave birth to a thousand serpents both mobile and immobile. They are hydra-headed noble souls, capable of traversing in the sky, since they are great in number. They have many names (but) learn the chief of them.

66-71. The most important of those serpents are Śeṣa, Vāsuki, Takṣaka, Karṇīra, Jaṁbha, Añjana, Vāmana, Airāvata, Mahāpadma, Kaṁbala, Aśvatara, Ailapatra, Śaṅkha, Karkoṭaka, Dhanañjaya, Mahākarṇa, Mahānīla, Dhṛtarāṣṭra, Balāhaka, Kumāra, Puṣpadanta, Sumukha, Durmukha, Śilīmukha, Dadhimukha, Kālīya, Śālipiṇḍaka, Bindupāda, Puṇḍarīka, the serpent Āpūraṇa, Kapila, Ambarīṣa, Dhṛtapāda, Kacchapa, Prahlāda, Padmacitra, Gandharva, Manasvika, Nahuṣa, Khararoman and Maṇi and many others like them. The sons of Kadrū have been enumerated by me. Understand those of Khaśā.

72. Khaśā gave birth to two sons who were well-known as

1. Verses 65-67 enumerate the names of most important of Kadrū's children, viz. serpents.

man-eaters. The eldest was in the latter number and the men in the east* (?)

73-76. At first, Khaśā gave birth to a very terrible son of the following description : He was excessively red in colour and devoid of ears. He had four arms, four feet, two heads and two-fold gait. He had hair all over the body. He had a huge body with a raised-up nose (like a snout) and a big belly. The head was big, the ears large and the hair like Muñja grass in accordance with his desire. The lips were like those of an elephant. The shanks were long. His fangs were like those of a horse. The chin was huge; the tongue red and the eyes had matted hair (?) The mouth was huge and the nose long. He was a Guhyaka (keeper of secrets (?)). The ears were variegated (?) in colour. He was extremely delighted and had a great face. Khaśā gave birth to such an extremely terrible son.

77-80. Khaśā gave birth to his younger brother, a second son. He had three heads, three feet and three hands. His eyes were black. The hair stood upright. The moustache was green in colour. His body was as firm as a rock. He had a huge body (short in stature). His arms were mighty and of great strength. His mouth was slit up to the ears. The eyebrows were suspended and the nose was stout. The lips were big. He had eight fangs and two tongues. He was pike-eared. His eyes were red and tawny-coloured. His complexion was tawny. He had matted hair. He had huge ears and broad chest. He was devoid of hips and the belly was slender. She gave birth to the younger brother who had claws and whose neck was red.

81. Immediately after the birth, they increased in size. Their bodies became mature and capable of sensual enjoyment. With their bodies thus grown up in size, they embellished their mother.

82. The elder one of the two who was ruthless, seized his mother. He said : "Mother, I am distressed with hunger. Come here as my prey."

83. The younger brother, however, forbade the elder one. He said frequently, "Save this Khaśā, our mother". Seizing him with both the arms, he released his mother.

---

*Obscure. But Bd. P. (2.3.7.38) : "The elder was born at dusk and the younger at dawn". *Śreṣṭham paścima-sandhyāyāṁ pūrvasyāṁ tu kanīyasam*/

84. At this time their father (sage Kaśyapa) appeared there. On seeing them hideous in form, he said, "Both of you stay here".

85. Those two strong ones, on seeing their father hurriedly (shrank in size) and began to lisp, clinging to the lap of their mother, by means of their Māyā.

86. Then the sage told his wife, "Tell us at the outset, how these two misbehaved.

87. A son adopts the traits of his maternal uncle and a daughter those of the paternal ancestors. A son adopts the same conduct of life as that of his mother.

88. Water certainly assumes the colour of that (bed of) earth on which it flows. Children become differnt due to the defects as well as the good qualities in the conduct of their mothers or through their faculty of discrimination.

89. Among (my wives), Aditi is interested in righteousness with her pious conduct and (inherent) strength[1]. She is endowed with piety, good conduct, enlightenment and strength.

90. Ariṣṭā is interested in music. Danu is remembered as fond of magic and illusiveness. The good lady Vinatā loves aerial movement.

91. Surabhi is embellished with the conduct of performance of penance. Kadrū is of a furious temperament. She is of unpleasant conduct due to anger.

92. The conduct of Danāyuṣā is characterised both by enmity and blessing. O blessed gentle lady, you are considered as of furious temperament by me.

93. The children adopt or change their character naturally or by observing other men. They are different in their activities, attempts, intellect, features, strength and patience. Changes occur due to the force of the objects conceived.

94. The forms of the whole Universe are naturally Rājasika, Sāttvika and Tāmasika. Your sons have taken after their uncle in their character and activities".

95. After saying thus to the incomparable Khaśā, he called the sons and made them fearless[2] by means of gentle words.

---

1. Kaśyapa describes the characteristics of his wives like Diti's fondness for fragrance etc. But the line is missing in the text. Hence the apparent duplication of adjectives.

2. *cakre somam abhītayaḥ* is obscure. Bd. P. 2.3.7.58 reads *cakre tābhyāṁ tu nāmanī* 'accorded names unto them'.

96. Then Khaśā told him what had been done by them to her. As the mother narrated their activities severally, the sage who saw the truth gave them names according to the meaning of the roots.

97. The root √ *yakṣ* means "to eat and to seize". Since he said '*Yakṣaye*' (I will eat), he will be a Yakṣa.

98. The root √ *rakṣ* means "to protect". Since he said "Save my mother Khaśā", your (second) son will be known by the name "Rākṣasa".

99. Then, on seeing them like that and searching (further) he was surprised*. The Prajāpati assigned to them blood and fat as their diet.

100. On seeing them hungry, the father granted them this boon: "Only at night can your hands feel the touch of anything.

101. You will move about and take your food during the night. By day, you will be enjoying sleep. You will be powerful during the night and will be sleeping during the day time.

102. Protect your mother. Let righteousness be practised." After saying thus to his sons, Kaśyapa vanished there itself.

103-105. When their father had gone, those two heroes, naturally terrible, began to behave (and do) what was exactly opposed (to their father's directions), eating anything they pleased and harassing living beings. They had great strength and energy. They were invincible and huge-bodied. They possessed the illusive *māyā* power. Sometimes they would be visible and immediately they would vanish. They assumed forms as they pleased. They were terrible and hideous naturally. Both of them became powerful by means of their diet in accordance with the forms (they assumed).

106-107. They used to roam about at night everywhere and for their food they were desirous of seizing Devas, Asuras, Sages, Gandharvas, Kinnaras, Piśācas, human beings, serpents, birds and animals. They were given the boons by Indra of not killing (not being killed?).

108-109, Once that Yakṣa (Rākṣasa) (the junior brother) was wandering alone at midnight, desirous of getting some food. Hearing a sound, he followed it. He met two Piśācas both of

*A reads: 'seeing them both hungry, he was surprised.'

whom were congenitally fierce. Their eyes were round and tawny and their hair stood upright. They were very terrible.

110-111. Their diet consisted of blood, flesh and fat. They were man-eaters of great strength. They were accompanied by their two daughters with a desire to do what pleased them. The two daughters could assume any form they pleased. Though they were splendid (in appearance), their behaviour was like that of (their father). They were wandering for the sake of food in the company of their daughters.

112-114. There they saw the highly powerful Rākṣasa who could assume any form as he pleased. As they met one another accidentally, they wanted to seize the other and save themselves. The father told the daughters, "Seize this young fellow alive-this fellow who is throbbing at every step and bring him here quickly". Then the two daughters approached him and seized him. Caught by both the hands, he was brought to the presence of their father by the daughters.

115. The two Piśācas asked that Rākṣasa who was caught hold of by the hands by them, "Who are you? Whose (son) are you?" He told them everything.

116. His antecedents were known. After knowing him as the foremost of Rākṣasas, Aja and Khaṇḍa, the two Piśācas who were delighted at his activity, gave him those two girls, their daughters.

117. (Defective Verse) By means of the Paiśāca form of matrimonial[1] alliance the Rākṣasa married the bright-toothed[2] (girls). Aja and Khaṇḍa then recounted their wealth.

118. Khaṇḍa said, "This is my daughter named Brahmadhanā. She is devoid of hair. She has Brāhmaṇas (along with their wealth) as her staple diet."

119. "This is my daughter beautiful in every limb. Her name is Jantudhanā. All the animals are her diet and wealth". (So said Aja.) Thus both of them narrated the wealth (of their daughters).

---

1. Out of the eight forms of marriage, Paiśaca is the lowest form wherein money is received by the father for the girl.

2. '*sudatyā buddha-vāhanaḥ*' in the text is obscure. Bd. P. 2.3.7.83 reads *rudantyāvudvavāha saḥ* 'He married them while they were crying'.

120. The daughter Jantudhanā had another name Sarvāṅgakeśī (having hair on every limb). The daughter who was called Brahmadhanā was devoid of hair and had no tip of the ears.

121. She gave birth to a boy Brahmadhana and a girl Dhanānā (?) Thus the two daughters of the Piśācas gave birth to two twins. Listen and understand even as I recount their progeny.

122-123. Heti, Praheti, Ugra, Pauruṣeya, Vadha, Visphūrji, Vāta, Āpa, Vyāghra and Sarpa—these were Rākṣasas, the ten sons of Yātudhāna. They were the followers of the Sun and they whirl along with him.

124. Laṅku was the son of Heti. Laṅku had two sons, Mālyavān and Sumālī. Now listen to the sons of Praheti. Praheti's son was the glorious and well-known Puloman.

125. Vadha's son was Nikuṁbha who was ruthless Brahmarākṣasa. Vāta's son was Virāga and Āpa's son was Jaṁbuka.

126. Vyāghra's son was Nirānanda who caused obstacles to all living beings. Thus all the cruel Rākṣasas have been enumerated.

127-128. Yātudhānas have been mentioned. Now understand the sons of Brahmadhāna. They were Yajña, Pitā, Dhuni, Kṣema, Brahmā, Pāpa, Yajñahā, Svākoṭaka, Kali and Sarpa. They were the ten sons of Brahmadhāna. The following are their sisters, terrible Brahmarākṣasīs.

129. They were—Raktakarṇā, Mahājihvā, Akṣayā and Upahāriṇī. Brahmarākṣasas were born of their families on the earth.

130. Generally they are found on the Śleṣmātaka (*Cardya Myxia*) trees. They live there. Thus Rākṣasas have been enumerated. Understand Yakṣas.

131-132. Yakṣa loved the Apsaras Kratusthalī otherwise known as Pañcasthūlā (stout in five limbs). Brooding over her and desirous of securing her, he wandered in the parks of Nandana, Vaibhrāja, Surabhi and Caitraratha. In the park of Nandana, he saw her seated along with Apsaras-s.

133. He did not know of any means of acquiring her despite his pondering, because he was defiled (ugly) in form and defiled and corrupt in his activities.

134. He thought, "All living beings are afraid and disgusted with me who am noxious and hurtful. So how shall I secure this lady of beautiful limbs?".

135. He thought of a plan and hastened to put it into action. The Guhyaka (Yakṣa) assumed the honoured form of a Gandharva. Then he seized Kratusthalī from the midst of (other) Apsaras-s.

136. Knowing him to be beautiful in form, she followed him with emotional attachment. Even as he was being observed by the group of Apsaras-s, he was embraced by her.

137. When he achieved his cause (i.e. desired object), a son of full-fledged sense-organs and height was born to him immediately. New-born though he was, he (as if) blazed in his glory.

138. He spoke to his father—"I am a king. I am Nābhi" The father replied, "Since you are born, there is no fear"

139. When the son emulated his mother in beauty and father in valour, Yakṣa was overjoyed and due to that exultation regained his original form.

140. Big Yakṣas and Rākṣasas regain their own form while dying, when asleep, angry or frightened and when extremely delighted.

141. Then that Guhyaka smilingly spoke to the Apsaras—"O lady of beautiful hips and excellent complexion, come to my house along with your son."

142. On seeing him who regained his form suddenly after saying this, all the Apsaras-s were furious, perplexed and frightened and they fled.

143. Kratusthalī followed the Apsaras-s who were fleeing. But the son consoled her with his words. He took her to the middle of Gandharvas and Apsaras-s and returned.

144. On seeing the birth of Yakṣa, the group of Apsaras-s spoke to Kratusthalī—"You are the mother of Yakṣas".

145. Then, accompanied with his son, Yakṣa went back to his abode named Nyagrodharohiṇaḥ (growing on the holy fig tree) where Guhyakas used to lie down. Hence the Nyagrodha tree is always a favourite place of residence to the Yakṣas.

146-148. The Yakṣa Rajatanābha was the grandfather of Guhyakas. He married Bhadrā, the excellent daughter of the

Daitya Anuhrāda. She gave birth to two sons—Maṇivara of good self-control, and Maṇibhadra who was equal to Śakra in exploit. The wives of these two brothers were sisters— two auspicious daughters of Kratusthalī. Their names were Puṇyajanī and Devajanī. Puṇyajanī bore the following (twentyfour) sons to Maṇibhadra.

149-152. (They were) Siddhārtha, Sūryateja, Sumanta, Nandana, Kanyaka, Yavika, Maṇidatta, Vasu, Sarvānubhūta, Śaṅkha, Piṅgākṣa, Bhīru, Mandaraśobhi, Padma, Candraprabha, Maghapūrṇa, Subhadra, Pradyota, Mahaujas, Dyutimān, Ketumān, Mitra, Mauli and Sudarśana. Thus there are twenty-four auspicious Puṇyajanas born to Maṇibhadra. All of them were characteristically meritorious. Their sons and grandsons were the auspicious Yakṣas and Puṇyajanas.

153-157. Devajananī (Devajanī) bore to Maṇivara the following sons—Pūrṇabhadra, Hemaratha, Maṇimān, Nandivardhana, Kustumburu, Piśaṅgābha, Sthūlakarṇa, Mahājaya, Śveta, Vipula, Puṣpavān, Bhayāvaha, Padmavarṇa, Sunetra, Yakṣa, Bāla, Baka, Kumuda, Kṣemaka, Vardhamāna, Dama, Padmanābha, Varāṅga, Suvīra, Vijaya, Kṛti, Pūrṇamāsa, Hiraṇyākṣa, Surūpa, and others. These sons of Maṇivara are remembered as Yakṣas and Guhyakas. Some are handsome and some are ugly. They are garlanded and very pleasing to see. They had hundreds and thousands of sons and grandsons.

158. There were other sons of Khaśā who became Rākṣasas who could assume forms as they pleased. Listen to and understand the important ones among them as they are being enumerated.

159-162. They were—Lālāvi, Kuthana, Bhīma, Sumālī, Madhu, Visphūrjita, Vidyujjihva, Mātaṅga, Dhūmrita, Candrārka, Sukara, Budhna, Kapiloman, Prahāsaka, Krīḍa, Paraśunābha, Cakrākṣa, Niśācara, Triśiras, Śatadaṁṣṭra, the Rākṣasa Tuṇḍakeśa, the Yakṣa Akaṁpana, Durmukha and Śilīmukha. These excellent Rākṣasas were valorous. In the form of groups, they move about in all the worlds. They have the ability to move on equal footing with the Devas.

163. She (Khaśā) had seven other daughters. Listen to them (their enumeration) in order, their progeny and the groups formed by them.

164. Ālambā, Utkacā, Kṛṣṇā, Nirṛtā, Kapilā, Śivā and the blessed Keśinī are the seven sisters remembered.

165. The following auspicious groups of Rākṣasas were born of them. They are the devourers of people, meat-eaters, killers and invincible in war.

166. The group called Ālambeya was cruel. Similarly the group Utkaceya was also cruel. The groups of excellent Rākṣasas were the Kārṣṇeyas and Śaiveyas.

167. The group of Rākṣasas called Nāirṛta comprised the progeny created by leading Gaṇeśvara who was the follower of Śiva.

168. These Yakṣas and Rākṣasas were procreated by the powerful (Gaṇeśvaras). They were valorous and endowed with heroism. These Devarākṣasas, the Nairṛtas had the renowned Virūpaka as their leader.

169. Many hundreds of these proud and noble-souled groups mostly follow Śaṅkara, the lord of the Universe.

170-173. The Kāpileyas, the Daityarākṣasas of great prowess, of huge body and of great strength and exploit were procreated by the noble-souled king of Daityas, Kuṁbha. The Yakṣa Kampana begot of Keśinī, very powerful Yakṣas and Rākṣasas. Keśinī's daughter Nīlā bore to Ālambeya Surasika many Rākṣasas of petty mentality. They are called Nailas. They were invincible and were terrible in their exploits.

174. Endowed with divine and worldly power, they move about on the entire earth. Since they are innumerable, the details of this creation cannot be recounted.

175. The same Nīlā had a daughter, the demoness Vikacā, naturally devoid of hair and possessing mediocre strength and exploit.

176. The same (Vikacā) bore terrible Asuras by the contact of the ugly Nairṛta. Listen to them in order.

177-178. They are Hārakas, Bhīṣakas, Krāmakas, Vainakas, Piśācas, Vāhakas and Prāśakas. All of them are hideous with their terrible fangs. They have huge ears and bellies. These are Bhūmi-rākṣasas (Earthly Demons). They possess manly exploit though slow-witted.

179. They assume multifarious forms and move about here and there unseen by others. Those whose strength and energy

are excellent and extraodinary are remembered as Khecaras ('Moving in the sky').

180. Those who appear to be very small, move in the sky to a small extent. This world is pervaded by these in hundreds and thousands.

181. The different countries all round are infested with these Bhūmirākṣasas and petty Rākṣasas of diverse forms and shapes.

182. In brief, it is said that there are eight Rākṣasa mothers. Therefore there are eight well-known clans (groups) of these (Rākṣasas).

183. Some constitute the Bhadraka group (Born of Bhadrakā). The cause of their origin is Yajña* (?). They are in hundreds and thousands and they move about in the human world.

184. There are many terrible Bhūtas having the same traits as their mother Pūtanā. They harass children in the human world like the evil planets, causing dejectedness.

185. The Skandagraha and other groups, the Āpakas, the Trāsaka and other groups—all these are to be known as Kaumāras ill-disposed towards children like evil planets.

186-187. There are hundreds of the groups of these evil (Rākṣasas) like the deceitful types of Skandagrahas and Bhūtas named Pūtanāṣ, lakhs and lakhs of them roaming about in the human world. They wander over the earth annoying the people.

188-190. There are Yakṣas called Puṇyajanas and others called Guhyakas. There are still others called Devajanas. All these are included in the group of Guhyakas. There are Rākṣasas called Āgastyas, Paulastyas and Viśvāmitras. The great king Kubera, the ruler of Alakā, is the king of all these Yakṣas and Rākṣasas including Paulastyas and Āgastyas.

191. Yakṣas drink blood, and swallow flesh and fat of men by merely looking at them. Rākṣasas do so by entering the body and Piśācas by crushing and harassing.

---

*Bd. P.V. 157 reads *ajña*—(born of) the ignorant ones.

192-194[1]. There are some beings of the following characteristics : They are endowed with all good qualities. They are equal to Devas in the matter of sphere of activities. They are brilliant and strong. They are masterly ones who can assume any form they please. Awe-struck, no one will dare to speak to them directly. They are valorous. They are bowed to by all the people. They are subtle and very powerful. They are pure and worthy of Yajñas. They are granters of boon. All these having the same characteristics as Devas are remembered as Asuras.[2] Gandharvas are inferior to Devas by three-fourths of their prowess.

195. All Guhyakas are inferior to Gandharvas by three-fourths. All Rākṣasas should be known as equal to Yakṣas in prowess. Piśācas are three times less powerful in their *Aiśvarya* (prosperity and glory) than Yakṣas.

196-197. Thus in wealth, beauty, longevity, strength, righteousness, affluence, mastery, intellect, penance, learning and exploits, the four Devayonis, beginning with Gandharvas and ending with Piśācas are (consecutively) three-fourths inferior to Devas and Asuras.

Sūta said :

198. Welfare unto you. Henceforth, hear about the progeny of the family of Krodhā. Krodhā gave birth to twelve daughters. They became the wives of Pulaha. Understand them by name.

199. They were—Mṛgī, Mṛgamandā, Haribhadrā, Irāvatī, Bhūtā, Kapiśā, Daṃṣṭrā, Niśā, Tiryā, Śvetā, Svarā and Surasā. They are well-known.

200. The sons of Mṛgī were the different types of deer, viz. *Hariṇas*, *Nyaṅkus*, *Rurus* and *Pṛṣatas* as well as such other animals as hares and *Śarabhas* (a fabulous eight-footed animal).

1. The Purāṇa-writer deserves credit for recording the greatness of Asuras and their equality with Devas.

2. Verses 192-197 describe the gradation (in descending order) of the divine and semi-divine beings as follows :

(i) Devas and Asuras
(ii) Gandharvas and Apsaras-s
(iii) Guhyakas (Yakṣas) and Rākṣasas
(iv) Piśacas.

201. The king of beasts (lion) was the son of Mṛgamandā as well as such other animals as *Gavayas* (blue cows), buffaloes, camels, boars, rhinoceros and *Gauramukhas* (a kind of black monkey with white face).

202 Hari's (Bhadrā's) sons were Haris (lions), bears, tigers, hyenas, different varieties of monkeys, Kinnaras and Kiṁpuruṣas and many other animals. Now understand the sons of Irāvatī.

203-205. Bhauvana (i.e. Viśvakarman) brought two egg-like skulls of Sūrya. Keeping them in his hands, he sang the Rathantara hymn. Suddenly an elephant arose out of the Sāman hymn.[1] Bhauvana presented that elephant to Irāvatī as her son. Being thus the son of Irāvatī, the elephant was called Airāvata. Since it was the vehicle of the king of Devas, it became the first king of elephants. It had the lustre of a pure cloud. The glorious elephant Airāvata has four tusks.

206. (Defective Verse) Only this elephant has the strength of being a vehicle, since it is born of water, has a single root, six teeth and the lustre of gold. It is of the Bhadra variety of elephants.

207. Airāvata had four sons, viz. Añjana, Supratīka, Vāmana and Padma. His mate was Abhramu.

208. Śvetā gave birth to four swift-footed sons who became the elephants of the quarters. They belonged to the varieties such as Bhadra, Mṛga, Manda and Saṁkīrṇa.

209-210. Añjana, though belonging to the Saṅkīrṇa variety is the vehicle of Yama. Supratīka who belongs to the Bhadra variety and is green in colour is the vehicle of the Lord of Waters (Varuṇa). Padma which belongs to the Manda variety and is of white colour is the vehicle of Ailavila (Kubera). (Vāmana) which was dark-coloured and belonged to the Mṛga variety was the vehicle of the Fire-god (Agni).

211.[2] (Defective) He has eight sons, viz. Padmottara

1. Verses 203-235 contain the Purāṇic "Elephant lore"; the geographical location of forests assigned to different types of elephants probably indicates that that type was found in that particular forest-area.

2. The text is very corrupt and is translated tentatively in the light of Bd. P. vv. 332-33a.

(Padma+Uttara?), two Gajas (Agata and Gajas ?), Varuṇa, Gaṇa, Upalepanameṣa (Upalepana and Meṣa ?).

212. In his race elephants possessing lofty stature, white nails and hair, yellowish colour are born. I shall recount Mataṅgaja and other (types) of elephants in due order.

213. The elephant Puṇḍarīka was grey-coloured and Rathānara had a flowery colour. Their sons were Supratiṣṭha and Pramardana.

214. (Defective Verse) Other types of elephants—spear-shaped, stout, with raised heads, having white (?) hair and nails, strong and energetic. They are called Ākulika elephants.

215. Puṣpadanta, Bṛhatsāman, Ṣaḍdanta, Dantapuṣpavān and Tāmravarṇa were his sons and companion tuskers.

216.[1] In his family are born elephants beautiful in appearance having protruding lips, dark-coloured, fierce and able to endure diverse kinds of ordeal (?)

217. Vāmadeva was as dark as collyrium. From Sāman was born Vāmana. His wife was Aṅgadā and the two sons were Nīlavān and Lakṣaṇa.

218. These elephants were fierce. Their necks and heads were beautiful. Their chests were broad and they were swift-footed. If they are bound by men, the elephants born become deformed.

219. There is no other elephant equal to Supratīka in beauty. He had three sons, viz. Prahārī, Saṁpātī and Pṛthu.

220. The animals with long palate and lips and with symmetrical portions of head and belly, of gentle birth (?) born in his family, become Mataṅgajas.

221. Añjanā was born to Añjanā and Añjanāvatī to Sāman. The mother of both of them is reputed to be the daughter(s) of Āyurajas.

222. In his family were born elephants with (distinctly divided) symmetrical heads, resembling the smooth clouds,

---

The verse enumerates the eight sons of that elephant the names of which are as follows: Padma, Uttama, Padmagulma, Agaja, Vātagaja, Gaja, Capala and Ariṣṭa.

1. *Pīḍāpatānanāḥ* in some editions is obscure and should be emended as *Pīḍāyatānanāḥ* 'with large and stout (big) faces (heads)', as in Bd. P. V. 338.

beautiful to look at, of well-built body having the lustre of lotuses and globular in shape. They are stout and have large, yellow faces.

223. From Candramas and Sāman were born Piṅgala and Kumudadyuti. Piṅgala's sons were Mahāpadma and Ūrmimālin.

224. Know that the elephants born of his family have equal and unrivalled tusks. They are fierce. Their strength is enormous. Their belly is large. They are fond of elephant fights.

225. In the course of wars between Devas and Asuras, Suras used them for the purpose of victory. When they achieved their object, those elephants were let off by them and they went to different directions as mentioned before.

226. Devas gave unto Lomapāda, the king of Aṅga and author of a Sūtra work, elephants born in these families and well-trained.

227-228. (The various names of elephants are to be etymologically derived as follows :)

Since it has two tusks it is called *Dvirada*; the word *Hastin* is derived from *hasta* (a trunk or hand); from the word *kara* (a trunk or hand) the word *Karin* is derived. *Vāraṇāt* (since it protects) it is called *Vāraṇa*. Since it has *dantas* (tusks) (prominently displayed) it is called *Dantin*. It is called *Gaja* because it trumpets (*garjanāt*). Since it roams about in the hedges (*Kuñja*) it is called *Kuñjara*. It is called *Nāga* because it is antagonistic to *Naga* (tree or mountain). Since it is born of Mataṅga it is called *Mātaṅga*. Since it drinks with two (i. e. trunk and mouth) it is called *Dvipa*. It is called *Sāmaja* because (the first elephant Airāvata) was born of a Sāman hymn.

229. The curvedness of their tongues and their muteness are due to Agni's curse. The fact that they are unaware of their strength and that the scrotum is concealed—these two are due to the curses of Svayaṃbhū and Suras.

230. Elephants of diverse inherent strengths are born of girls of Deva, Dānava, Gandharva, Piśāca, Uraga (Serpent) and Rākṣasa tribes through their union with the elephants of the quarters (*Diṅ-nāgas*).

231. The story of the origin, development and derivation of the names of elephants whose king is Vibhāvasu, should be known.

232. (Defective Verse) The forest in the east bound by the rivers Kauśikī and Gaṅgā and the sea belongs to Añjana and the family of elephants of which he is the founder (or of one tusk ?).

233. The forest of Supratīka is situated north of Vindhya, south of Gaṅgā and in between the land of Karuṣa and the source of Gaṅgā.

234. The fifth forest west of Utkala and extending upto the land of Vedi is remembered as the forest of Vāmana who is the sole Ātman (?)

235. The forest to the west of Lauhitya extending westwards upto the sea, is said to be the forest of Yama. It is near a mountain.

236-248. Bhūti gave birth to Bhūtas (goblins) who are the followers of lord Rudra. They were stout, lean, longish, dwarfish, short-statured and normal. The ears of some were hanging down. The lips of some were suspended. Some had tongues, breasts and bellies hanging down. Some had single form, some double form. The hips of some hung down. Some had stout calves of the leg. They stayed on the banks of rivers, lakes or seas. They were of all colours, black, white, blue, grey, red and pink. Some were smoke-coloured and some had variegated colours. Some were terrible like Rākṣasas and Kadrūs (?). Some had dishevelled hair like the Muñja grass. Some had hair standing up. Some wore serpents as the sacred thread. Some had eyes removed; some had hideous eyes. Some had small eyes. Some had only a single eye. Some had many heads. Some had no head. Some had a single head. Some had the head cut off. They were fierce and hideous. Some had no hair. Some had plenty of it. Some were blind. Some had matted hair. Some were yellow. Some were dwarfish. They resorted to the banks of rivers, lakes and oceans. Some had a single ear, some had large ears. Some were spike-eared, some had no ear. Some had fangs. Some had claws. Some had no teeth. Some had two tongues. Some had a single hand. Some had two hands. Some had three hands. Some had no hand. Some had a single foot. Some had two feet. Some three and some even more. Some were great Yogins. Some were highly dignified. Some were very strong. Some were *sutapakvas*[1] (*Sutapaskas*? 'of good penance'). They could go everywhere. They were unimpeded. They were the knowers of Brahman and could assume any form they wished. Some were terrible and ruthless. Some were pure, holy and auspicious. Some disputed and argued. Some had the Kuśa grass in their hands. Some had huge (long ?) tongues, long ears and large faces. Some ate with their hands, some with their mouths and some with their heads. Some wore skulls (round their necks). Some held bows. Some had iron clubs, swords or spears. Some had radiant faces and bright eyes; some wore garlands of variegated flowers and unguents. Some ate cooked food; some raw flesh. Some had many forms. Some had handsome appearance. Some roamed about at night or at dusk. Some were terrible. Some were gentle, roaming about during the day. Some were night prowlers, who were very terrible (or difficult) to look at; some were terrible night-wanderers.

249. All of them directed their minds towards lord Bhava (Śiva) as the greatest god. They had no wives or sons. All of them were celibate with sublimated sexuality.

250. These Bhūtas, the great *Ātmayogins*, numbered a hundred thousand. Thus all these noble-souled sons of Bhūti have been recounted.

251. Kapiśā, Kūṣmāṇḍī bore to Kūṣmāṇḍa twins of Piśācas who were tawny-coloured. Because they were brownish, they were called Piśacas.[2] All of them were flesh-eaters.

252. There are sixteen other twins. Their descendants are living now. I shall mention by names the man-eaters belonging to their family.

253-256. They are Chagala and Chagalī, Vakra and Vakramukhī, Sūcī and Sūcīmukha, Kuṁbhapātra and Kuṁbhī,

---

1. Bd. P. 2.3.7.367 reads *sumanaska* 'of very good minds'.

2. The Purāṇa distinguishes between *Bhūtas* and Piśācas. Bhūtas are noble-souled sons of Bhūti, celibate yogins and devotees of God Śiva. Piśācas are the progeny of Kūśmāṇḍī. The superstitions about Piśācas current at the time of this text are recorded in vv. 251-282.

Vajradaṁṣṭra and Dundubhi, Upacārā and Upacāra, Ulūkhala and Ulūkhalī, Anarka and Anarkā, Kukhaṇḍa and Kukhaṇḍikā, Pāṇipātra and Pāṇipātrī, Pāṁśu and Pāṁśumatī, Nituṇḍa and Nituṇḍī, Nipuṇā and Nipuṇa, Chalada and Uccheṣaṇā, Praskanda and Skandikā. The sixteen clans of Piśācas have been narrated.

257-259. These are the sixteen families born of Kūṣmāṇḍas : Ajāmukhas, Vakramukhas, Pūrins, Skandins, Vipādas, Aṅgārikas, Kumbhapātras, Prakundakas, Upacārolūkhalikas, Anarkas, Kukhaṇḍikas, Pāṇipātras, Naituṇḍas, Ūrṇāśas, Nipuṇas, and Sūcīmukhoccheṣaṇādas.

260. Those who are born as Sukalpas[1] (?) should be known as Piśācas. There are infinite number of sons and grandsons of hideous nature and ignoble activities. Hence, understand the characteristics of Piśācas.

261. Piśācas have hair on all their limbs. Their eyes are round. They have claws and fangs. Their limbs are crooked. They are man-eaters and their faces are turned down.

262. The Piśācas called Kūṣmāṇḍikas are devoid of hair on their heads or bodies. Skins and hides constitute their garments. They always eat gingelly seeds and flesh.

263. Some Piśācas have curved limbs, and feet. They walk in a zigzag manner. They should be known as Vakrapiśācas. They are of crooked gait. They can assume any form as they please.

264. Some Piśācas have protruding bellies. Their noses are like snouts. Their bodies are short. Their heads and arms are small. These are called Nituṇḍakas. Gingelly seeds form their diet. (They are fond of hearing pleasing things—*Priyaśrāvāḥ*?)[2]

265. Some Piśācas have dwarfish forms[3]. They are garrulous. They go about galloping. They are Ānarkamarka types of Piśācas. They are fond of staying on trees or taking food there.

266. Some Piśācas keep their hands lifted up (always).

---

1. Bd. P. *ibid* V. 384 reads *Sakulyas* 'belonging to the same family (?)'
2. This is obscure. Bd. P. V. 389 reads *Priyāsṛjaḥ* 'fond of (drinking) blood'.
3. Bd. P. V. 390 reads *Vānarākṛtayaḥ* 'having the form of monkeys'.

Their hair stands upright. Their abodes are high up on tall trees. They shed dust from their bodies. These Piśacas are called *Paṁśus*.

267. The Piśācas called *Upavīras* are very considerate about their veins*. Their bodies are dry. They have plenty of moustache. They wear bark garments. Cremation ground is their abode.

268. The Udūkhala (Ulūkhala) types of Piśācas have stable motionless eyes and long tongues with which they lick their lips. Their heads are as large as those of elephants and camels. They move about severally or jointly.

269. Those Piśācas are called Kuṁbhapātras, who take cooked food without seeing it (invisibly ?). They are small and yellow-complexioned with hairy bodies. They move about visibly and invisibly.

270. The Piśācas called Nipuṇas enter and infest those persons who go alone. Their mouths extend upto their ears. The eye-brows are long and the noses are thick.

271. (A line is missing from the text.) The Piśācas called *Bālādas* (devourers of children) are short-statured and they attack people with their hands and feet. Their eyes are turned towards the earth. They resort to lying-in-chambers.

272. Those Piśācas called *Piśitādas* (flesh eaters) drink blood from the battlefield. Their hands and feet are turned backwards. They are short and are as swift as wind.

273. The Piśācas called Skandins are naked and have no fixed abodes. They are globular in shape with long hair. There are other types of Piśācas eating leavings of food. Thus the sixteen types of Piśācas have been narrated.

274. On seeing these types of Piśācas deficient in intellect and in a dejected condition among his progeny, Brahmā sympathetically granted them the boons of vanishing and assuming forms as they pleased.

275-278. He permitted them to move about at the time of the two junctions (viz. dawn and dusk). (I shall mention) their abodes and way of maintaining themselves. Houses in

**dhamanī-matakāḥ*, but Bd. P. V. 392 reads *Bhramarī-sannibhāḥ* 'like black-bees'.

ruins, vacant or with very few people or completely dilapidated are their abodes. They live in those houses also where people do not follow rules of good conduct, which are not scrubbed and cleaned properly or not whitewashed or painted well. They live in the highways, sidelanes, kitchen gardens, quadrangles, portals, attics, paths of exit, sidewalks, pathways, rivers, holy centres, trees in the monasteries, trunk roads (these are assigned as their abodes). Piśacas occupy all these spots.

279-280. Unrighteous persons, those who violate the discipline of castes and stages of life and artisans and masons constitute the livelihood of these Piśācas as ordained by Suras. These Piśācas will be the presiding deities where holy rites are performed by means of money earned by unjustifiable means such as breach of trust and theft of nectar-like articles.

281-282. The oblations to Piśācas consist of honey (wine), flesh, cooked rice mixed with curds, powdered gingelly seeds, toddies and similar (intoxicating) beverages, incense, turmeric, Kṛśaras (i.e. balls of gingelly seeds in treacle), oil, rice mixed with jaggery, black cloths and flowers. At the junctions of Parvans, these things must be offered to Piśācas. Brahmā, the lord, ordained thus.

283. He made the trident-bearing Girīśa the lord of all Bhūtas and Piśācas.

The lady Daṁṣṭrā bore as sons tigers and lions.

284. Panthers, pythons and beasts of prey are also her sons.

Now listen to the progeny and procreation of Ṛṣā wholly. She had five daughters. Listen to their names :

285. Mīnā, Mātā, Vṛttā, Parivṛttā and Anuvṛttā are to be known (as her daughters). Listen to (the enumeration of) her children:

286. Sharks and crocodiles with a thousand teeth, the types of fish known as *Pāṭhīna*, *Timi* and *Rohita* and other groups are called Maina (born of Mīnā) groups. They are extensive.

287. The four types of *Grāhas* (crocodiles)—Anujyeṣṭhakas, Niṣkas, Śiśumāras etc. were born of Mātā.

288. Vṛttā gave birth to different types of tortoises and other aquatic animals as well as varieties of conches.

289. Anuvṛttā gave birth to different types of toads and frogs as well as different varieties of snails and Aṇeyas (black does) and Śaṁbūkas (shells and noxious insects).

290. Parivṛttā gave birth to different varieties of oyster-shells, cowrie-shells and conchs.

291. She produced the varieties of Kālakūṭa poison and leeches as well. Thus the race of Ṛṣā consisting of five branches has been enumerated.

292. The description of the first and early animals and insects is very extensive[1]. The varieties of sweat-born insects are a part of them.

293. O Brāhmaṇas, these insects are born of the bodies of *Svastipika*[2] (?). The producers are human beings. The insects known as *Uśanas* are born of dirt and sweat of men. So also the other insects and groups of ants moving about in rows.

294. There are varieties of insects born of conchs, pebbles which work like nails.[3] These and many others are the earthly groups of sweat-born creatures.

295. Similarly, these creatures are born out of water heated by the sun as well as of the rain water. Many of these insects are born of the bodies of other animals.

296-298. The following tiny creatures are born both of water and of sweat : Small shrimps (*mīnaka*), ants, (mosquito-like) biting or stinging creatures (*daṁśa*), *Tittira-putrikās* (tiny partridge-like creatures?). The Alakas (hair) are bluish or variegated in colour (*nīla-citrāḥ*) and very massive.

The insects called Nalada which are many-faced are born in water (stagnating) near the Kāśa grass. They are stated to be of three kinds—*Siṁhalas*, *Romalas* (Hairy) and *Picchalas* (Slimy). These and other groups of species are remembered as born of water as well as of sweat.

1. The line is corrupt. The corresponding line in Bd. P. V. 421 reads : *tiryāhetukam apyāhur bahulaṁ vaṁśa-vistaram*/ 'They say that there is an extensive line of living beings procreated by Tiryā'.

2. This obscure word is a misprint for '*Sveda-Klinna* 'born of bodies moisstened by sweat' (vide Bd. P. V. 422).

3. *Kīlakācārakāni* 'which work lik nails' in the text is rather obscure. Bd. P. V. 423 b reads *kīlakāvaraṇāni* 'Pebbles smaller than pins'.

299. Some creatures are born of ghee, black gram and green gram. Some are born of the fruits of Jaṁbū (Rose apple) Bilva, mango and arecanut.

300. Creatures are born of the dry hollows of trees and also of green gram, jack fruits and rice grains when kept (for a long time).

301. Creatures are born of other things also when kept for a long time. Germs and worms are born of horses and other (animals) and even from poison etc.

302. When cowdung is kept for a number of days, O Brāhmaṇas, creatures are produced from them. White ants and other creatures are born of (putrefying) wood.

303. Various kinds of blue flies are born of trees in due course. The creatures *Putrikās* (white ants ?) are born of drying and withering things.

304. Everywhere serpents are born seasonally from Śatikas (?). Scorpions and sweat-born creatures are produced from dry cow-dung.

305. O lord, many worms are born of the bodies of cows and buffaloes. Different types of fish etc. are born of eggs.

306. Different types of leeches are born of eggs such as *Caivīrikas* and *Gajas* and many other subtle creatures too.

307. Different types of flies etc. are born of eggs. These are laid generally on the leavings of food, water and sloughs.

308. Different types of mosquitoes and black bees are also born of eggs. The creatures known as nits (*Putrikās* and *Putra-bhāsakas*) are produced from grass.

309. The insects *Maṇicchedas* and *Vyālas* are said to be produced from foetus with no enveloping membrane (*potajas*). Varieties of *Śataveri* (?) are born of dry cow-dung.

310. Thus innumerable groups of sweat-born creatures have been enumerated by me in brief. It is to be remembered that these are born as a result of their actions in a previous birth.

311-312. There are other beings of Nairṛta nature (i.e. born of Nirṛti). They are remembered as *Upasargajas* (born of paroxysm due to possession by devils). Some beings are born of womb (*Yonijas*)and some are *Autpattikas* (born spontaneously). Generally all Devas are to be known as *Autpattikas*. Some

Devas are born of a womb (*Yonija*). Only some are born without cause.

313. The children of Saramā are the sons Tūlālāgha and Kola and a daughter Śivā. They are known as *Saramādi* group.

314. The Kadrukas (?) are *Śyāma* (dark-coloured), *Śabala* (of variegated colour), *Arjuna* (white), *Harita* (green-coloured), *Kṛṣṇa* (black), *Dhūmrāruṇa* (smoke-coloured and pink-coloured—Aruṇa), Tulālāgha (?).

315. Surasā gave birth to a hundred (serpents) with nectar in their heads (*Śiro' mṛtam*). The king of Sarpas (serpents) is Takṣaka and that of the snakes is Vāsuki. Thus this group belonging to the family of Krodhavaśā is mostly of Tāmasa quality.

316. Now understand the bosom creation of Pulaha from Tāmrā. Many well-known daughters were born of Tāmrā.

317. They are—Śyenī, Bhāsī, Krauñcī, Dhṛtarāṣṭrī and Śukī. Śyenī who was the wife of Aruṇa gave birth to two excellent birds of great strength and prowess, viz. Sampāti and Jaṭāyu.

318. Sampāti procreated one son and one daughter. Crows, vultures and *Aśvakarṇins* (a variety of vultures?) were the sons of Jaṭāyu.

319. The wives of Garutmān (Garuḍa) were Bhāsī, Krauñcī, Śukī, Dhṛtarāṣṭrī and Bhadrā. Their sons are being enumerated.

320-322. Śuki bore six well known sons to Garutmān, viz. the sweet-faced Triśira, Bala, Pṛṣṭha of great strength, Triśaṅkhanetra, Susukha of good form and Surasa the powerful. The sons and grandsons of these ruthless descendants of Garuḍa, the noble-souled serpent-eaters, numbering fourteen thousand. By procreation of sons and grandsons their family became extensive.

323-329. I shall mention in due order the lands where they spread themselves—the whole of Śālmalī Dvīpa, the mountain Devakūṭa, the leading mountains Maṇimān, Sahasra-śikhara, Parṇamāla, Sukeśa, Śataśṛṅga, Kauraja, Pañcaśikhara and Hemakūṭa—all these mountains were occupied by the noble-souled descendants of Garuḍa. They were brightened with ruby stones and (while flying) they produced gusts of violent winds.

Bhāsas (the bird vulture) Ulūkas (owls), crows and cocks were the sons of Bhāsī.

Peacocks, *Kalaviṅkas* (sparrows), doves and *Lāvas* and *Tittiris* also were born of Bhāsī. Krauñcī gave birth to *Vārdhiṇasa* birds (black birds with red legs, head and eyes). Śyenī gave birth to ospreys, *Sārasas* (a kind of crane) and cranes; she gave birth to other birds of prey also like these.

The beautiful lady Dhṛtarāṣṭrī gave birth to Haṁsas (swans) and Kalahaṁsas, *Cakravākas* and other types of (acquatic) birds too. These were the birds given birth to and their sons and grandsons were infinite.

330. Garuḍa's children have been enumerated. Listen to the progeny of Irā. Irā gave birth to three daughters with eyes like lotuses.

331. They were Latā, Vallī and Vīrudhā. They are the mothers of all types of plants, trees and creepers.

332. Latā gave birth to *Vanaspatis* i.e. the non-flowering plants growing on the banks of rivers etc. She herself gave birth to *Vṛkṣas* or trees with flowers and fruits.

333. *Vallī* gave birth to hedges, grasses and bamboo etc. of the same species. Vīrudhā gave birth to *Vīrudhās* i.e. creepers spreading all round. The description of the race is concluded here.

334. Thus the mobile and the immobile progeny of Kaśyapa have been enumerated. The whole Universe is filled with their sons and grandsons.

335. Thus a portion of the entire creation has been enumerated. The *Prajāsarga* of Mārīca (Kaśyapa) has been succinctly narrated. O Brāhmaṇas, it cannot be explained (in details) even in hundreds of years.

336. Aditi was of righteous, pious temperament. Diti is remembered as strong-minded. Surabhi was inclined towards the performance of penance. Danu was of a deceitful nature.

337. Kadrū was of ruthless mind. Krauñcī was disposed towards learning. Irā had the receptive capacity. Danāyu was interested in taking food.

338. Vinatā was capable of bearing burdens. Tāmrā was habituated to use nooses and strings. These are the natures and temperaments of the mothers of the worlds.

339. In piety, conduct, intellect, patience and strength they had the traits of qualities Sattva, Rājas and Tamas. Hence they were both righteous and unrighteous.

340. The bosom-born progeny of Kaśyapa were born with the traits of their mothers. (They were) Devas, Asuras, Gandharvas, Yakṣas, Rākṣasas, serpents, Piśācas, animals, deer, birds and creepers.

341. Since these were born of the daughters of Dakṣa who were human beings, hence human beings are the most excellent in all the Manvantaras.

342. Human beings are the aspirants of Dharma (Virtue) Artha (Wealth), Kāma (Love) and Mokṣa (Salvation). Therefore, Suras and Asuras are born as *Adhaḥ-srotas* (downward flow).

343. They are born again and again among human beings for the purpose of achieving their object. Thus the origin of the race of ascetics has been recounted.

344-346. The meritorious story of Suras, Asuras, Gandharvas, Apsaras-s, Yakṣas, Rākṣasas, Piśācas, Suparṇas, serpents, birds, pythons, peacocks, all medicinal herbs, worms, germs, insects, insignificant creatures born in water, animals and glorious Brāhmaṇas, is conducive to longevity and wealth. It is pleasing and beneficial. It is meritorious. It must be heard always and retained by one who is devoid of malice and jealousy.

347. He who regularly reads this story of the race (of ascetics) of noble souls in the assembly of Brāhmaṇas and physicians will attain children, abundant wealth and prosperity and the glorious goal after death.

CHAPTER NINE

The Race of Sages

Sūta said :

1-2. Thus when the entire mobile and immobile creations had been created and established by the noble-souled Kaśyapa, he the chief Prajāpati, crowned (the chiefs of them) as their Lords and began to assign them their respective domains in due order.[1]

3. He crowned Soma (the Moon) in the kingdom of the twice-born Brāhmaṇas, Kṣattriyas and Vaiśyas, creepers, constellations, planets, Yajñas and penance.

4. He made Bṛhaspati the lord of all the descendants of Aṅgiras. He crowned Śukra as the ruler over the realm of Bhṛgus.

5. He made Viṣṇu, the lord of Ādityas; Fire-god the lord of Vasus; Dakṣa the lord of Prajāpatis; and Vāsava (Indra) the lord of Maruts.

6. He made Prahlāda, the delighter of Diti, the king of Daityas : Nārāyaṇa the king of Sādhyas; and the Bull-bannered lord (Śiva) the king of Rudras.

7. He directed Vipracitti to be the king of Dānavas. He ordered Varuṇa to be the king of waters. He made Vaiśravaṇa (Kubera) the lord of Yakṣas, Rākṣasas and the wealth of (worldly) kings.

8. He coronated Yama, the son of Vivasvān (the Sun), in the kingdom of Pitṛs, and the trident-bearing Girīśa in the kingdom of all the Bhūtas and Piśācas.

9. He made Himavān the ruler of mountains; ocean, of the rivers; and Citraratha the ruler of Gandharvas.

10. He crowned Uccaiśśravas as the king of horses, tiger as the king of deer and cows, and bulls the lords of quadrupeds.

11. He made Garuḍa the most excellent among flying beings, the lord of all birds. He made Māruta the lord of scents and unembodied beings.

12. He made Vāyu, the most excellent among strong beings, the lord of sound, sky and strength. He made Śeṣa, the lord of all fanged (reptiles), and Vāsuki the lord of serpents.

13. He made Takṣaka, the lord of vipers, serpents and reptiles. He crowned Parjanya, one of the Ādityas, as the lord of oceans, rivers, clouds and rains.

14-15. He crowned Kāmadeva the king of all groups of Apsaras-s.

---

1. Verses 1-20 enumerate the heads of different categories of creation. Here one is reminded of the Vibhūtiyoga (BG.X).

He made Saṁvatsara (Year) the lord of *Ṛtus* (seasons), months and groups of seasons, fortnights (*Ārtavas*), *Vipakṣas* (the day of transition from one half of a lunar month to another), Muhūrtas, Parvans, Kāṣṭhās, Kalās and their magnitudes, the movements and the transits (of the Sun), of mathematical calculations and Yogas (astronomical divisions of time or combinations of Stars).

16. The Prajāpati crowned Sudhāman, the famous son of Rajas, as the king in the eastern quarter.

17. In the western quarter, he crowned the noble-souled Ketumān, the unerring son of Rajas, the king.

18. He made Vaivasvata Manu the lord of human beings. The entire earth consisting of seven continents along with the towns therein, is being ruled righteously by them in their respective areas.

19. They had been crowned formerly by Brahmā in the Svāyaṁbhuva Manvantara. Only those who become Manu are consecrated as kings.

20. In the Manvantaras that have passed, these kings (had ruled and) passed away. When the Manvantaras occur again, others will be crowned again. All the kings, past and future, are proclaimed as Lords of Manvantaras.

21. Pṛthu was crowned by these excellent men at the time of Rājasūya. The valorous king was made so in accordance with the injunctions of the Vedas.

22-23. The lord of Prajās, Kaśyapa, procreated these sons, for the purpose of the continuity of the progeny. Thereafter, desirous of his own lineage, he performed a severe penance. He contemplated—"May sons, the founders of the lineage, be born to me".

24. As Kaśyapa, the noble soul, contemplated, two powerful sons born of Brahmā's part were born to him.

25. They were Vatsara and Asita. Both of them were propounders of Brahman. Nidhruva and Raibhya of great fame were born of Vatsara.

26. The Raibhyas should be known as the (descendants) of Raibhya. Understand (those) of Nidhruva. Cyavana begot Sumedhas of Sukanyā.

27. Nidhruva's wife[1] was the mother of Kuṇḍapāyins. Brahmiṣṭha (Devala in Bd.P.) was born of Ekaparṇā and Asita.

28. On hearing (i.e. paying heed to) the words of Śāṇḍilya, Devala became excessively famous. Nidhruvas, Śāṇḍilyas and Raibhyas all these three formed the Kāśyapa Gotra later[2].

29. Vara (Vajrī i.e. Indra in Bd. P.) and other Devas are the progeny of Devala. These subjects function in Dvāpara Yuga that remains (i.e. occurs) after eleven cycles of the sets of four Yugas have passed.

30. Cariṣyanta (Nairiṣyanta in Bd. P.) was the son of Mānasa and his son was Dama. Mānasa who was well-known as Tṛṇabindu, was his heir and successor.

31. In the beginning of the third Tretā Yuga, he became the king. His daughter Iḍaviḍā was unrivalled in her beauty. The saintly king gave her to Pulastya.

32. The sage Viśravas was born of Iḍaviḍā. He had four wives who made the family of Pulastya flourish.

33. Bṛhaspati, the preceptor of the Devas, had a famous daughter named Devavarṇinī. He (Viśravas) married that girl.

34. He (Viśravas) married Puṣpotkaṭā and Vākā, the daughters of Mālyavān as well as Kaikasī, the daughter of Mālin. Listen to their progeny.

35. Devavarṇinī gave birth to his eldest son Vaiśravaṇa who had divine fate and saintly learning, (but) had the form of a Rākṣasa and the strength of an Asura.

36-37. He had three feet, a huge body, stout head, a large chin[3], eight fangs, green moustache, pike-like ears and red complexion. His arms were short and long (i.e. one short, one long). He was yellowish in colour (?) and very terrible to look at. He had the knowledge of the illusory world. He was enlightened with knowledge.

---

1. Sumedhaṣ as per Bd. P.

2. Bd. P. 2.3.8.33 reads *pakṣāḥ* for *paścāt* here. It means 'Nidhruvas, Śāṇḍilyas, Raibhyas are three branches of Kāśyapa Gotra'.

3. *Mahāvanum* in the text is a tautology. It should be *mahā-hanum* as in Bd. P. ibid V. 42.

38. On seeing such a son assuming a cosmic form, the father himself said—"This is *Kubera* (ugly-bodied one)".[1]

39. The word '*Ku*' is used to indicate contempt. The body is mentioned by the word *Bera*. Hence he is called *Kubera* because his body was deformed.

40. Since he was the child of Viśravas and he appeared like Viśravas, he will be known in the world by the name Vaiśravaṇa.

41. Kubera begot of Ṛddhi the famous (son) Nalakūbara. Kaikasī gave birth to four children Rāvaṇa, Kumbhakarṇa and Vibhīṣaṇa (the three sons and) a daughter Śūrpaṇakhā.

42-45. (Rāvaṇa) had pike-like ears and ten necks.[2] He was yellowish in colour with red hair. He had four feet and twenty arms. He was huge-bodied and very powerful. From his very birth, he resembled collyrium. He had fang-like teeth. His neck was red. He was like Rājasena (?) and was endowed with good features and strength. He was intellectually truthful. He had a firm body. He (was surrounded) by Rākṣasas. Naturally he was terribe and ruthless. He was called Rāvaṇa because he roared.

That king was Hiraṇyakaśipu in his previous birth. That Rākṣasa king ruled for thirteen cycles of four Yugas.

46-48. His span of life as reckoned by Brāhmaṇas, experts in calculation, extended to five crores and sixtyone lakhs of years. For sixty lakhs of years[3], this Rāvaṇa made Devas and Sages terribly sleepless (by means of his atrocities). In the twenty-fourth Tretāyuga, when his merit of penance declined, he met Rāma, the son of Daśaratha, (in battle) and was slain along with his followers.

---

1. Etymology of 'Kubera', the god of wealth.

2. The Purāṇa-writer entertained fantastic ideas about Rāvaṇa. Jaina Rāmāyaṇas give a sober and a more realistic picture of Rāvaṇa, e.g. Rāvaṇa was one-headed but due to the reflection of his face in the nine precious stones of his necklace, he was (poetically) called 'ten-headed'.

3. Rāvaṇa's harrasment is not thus delimited elsewhere. It should be a part of his span of life. Bd. P. 2.3.8.53 correctly reads *Ṣaṣṭiṁ caiva sahasrāṇi* 'sixty thousand years' as a part of Rāvaṇa's total life. For, a set of the four Yugas=4320000 years, thirteen such sets=56160000 years. Rāvaṇa is credited with this span.

49. Mahodara, Prahasta, Mahāpāṁśu and Khara were the sons of Puṣpotkaṭā and Kumbhīnasī was her daughter.

50. Triśiras, Dūṣaṇa, the Rākṣasa Vidyujjihva and the daughter Asalikā are remembered as the children of Vākā.

51. These are the ten Rākṣasa descendants of Pulastya. They were cruel in their activities. All of their followers were terrible and unassailable even by Devas.

52-55. All of them had secured boons. All of them were endowed with sons and grandsons.

Aiḍaviḍa (i.e. Kubera) whose left side was yellowish in colour and who was the descendant of Pulastya was the king of all these—all the Yakṣas, all the Rākṣasas belonging to the family of Pulastya, the cruel Brahmarākṣasas of the families of Agastya and Viśvāmitra, who were engaged in the study of the Vedas and who performed penance and holy rites.

Then, there were the other Rākṣasas called Yajñamukhas. Hence there are three groups of Rākṣasas: Yātudhānas, Brahmadhānas and Vārtas. These are *Divācaras* (moving about during the day). There are four groups of *Niśācaras* (those who wander in the night) who have been remembered (by wise sages).

56. Thus, there are seven classes of Rākṣasas (including the above three and the following four groups) : Paulastyas, Nairṛtas, Āgastyas and Kauśikas.

57-63. I shall describe the natural features of all these (Rākṣasas)[1] : They had round eyes. They were yellowish in colour. They had huge bodies and bellies. They had eight fangs; pikelike ears and hairs standing upright. They had their mouths extending (as if) upto the ears. Some had hair like the Muñja grass. Some had smoke-coloured upright hair. Some had stout heads shedding white lustre. Some were short-statured. Some had long arms. Some had copper-coloured faces. Some had long (dangling down) tongues and lips. Some had long eyebrows and stout noses. Some were blue-bodied with red necks and majestic eyes. They were terrific. They were excessively terrible-voiced and hideous. They went in groups. They were stout with promi-

1. Superstitions about Rākṣasas current at the time of Vā. P.

nent protruding noses. Their bodies were sturdy like rocks. They had terrible kinsmen and generally they were cruel, indulging in painful activities. They used to wear (ornaments like) ear-rings, bracelets and coronets. They wore crowns and turbans. They had diverse garments and ornaments. They wore garlands of variegated flowers. They applied fragrant scents and unguents. Some were flesh eaters and some ate cooked food. They are remembered as man-eaters. These attributes of Rākṣasas, common to many of them, have been enunciated by scholars. The full extent of their strength is not known because it is effected by Māyā.

64-65. The deer, all the fanged beasts of prey, Bhūtas, Piśācas, serpents, bees, elephants, monkeys, Kinnaras, Yamakiṁpuruṣas[1] (?) and all those mentioned by me as born of Krodhavaśā—all these were Pulaha's sons.

66. In that Vaivasvata Manvantara, Kratu is remembered as childless. He had neither a son nor a grandson. He remained with fully controlled splendour (semen) (i.e. He was celibate).

67. I shall now recount the lineage of Atri[2], the third Prajāpati. He had ten chaste and beautiful wives.

68-69. Bhadrāśva begot of Ghṛtācī the Apsaras, ten daughters. They were:Bhadrā, Śūdrā, Madrā, Śaladā, Maladā, Velā, Khalā, these seven and Gocapalā, Mānarasā and Ratnakūṭā.

70-71. The founder of the lineage of Atri was famous by the name of Prabhākara (the originator of lustre). He was their husband. He begot of Bhadrā, the famous son Soma (the Moon). When the Sun, struck by Rāhu, was falling down towards the earth from the sky, the whole world was enveloped in darkness and it was he (the sage Atri) who spread light everywhere whereby be got the name Prabhākara.

72. While the Sun was falling the words 'welfare unto you' were addressed to him. At these words of the Brāhmaṇa sage Atri (the Sun) did not fall on the earth from heaven.

73. Atri who was the performer of great penance founded excellent Gotras. Among Yajñas (the one called) *Atrighana* (?) is initiated by Suras.

1. Māyu-Kiṁpuriṣas in Bd. P.
2. The race of Atri is described in vv. 67-78.

74-76. He begot of them ten sons, all equal to him. They had no names. All the ten were purified by great penance. They were the sages famous by the name 'Svastyātreyas.' They were masters of Vedas. Among them, two were very famous, powerful and expounders of Brahman the eldest was Dattātreya and Durvāsas was his younger brother. The youngest daughter was Abalā who expounded Brahman. In this connection, the former (ancient) Paurāṇikas cite this verse.

77. Those who are conversant with Purāṇas say that Atri's son Dattātreya is embodied Viṣṇu. The noble-souled one is free from sins and tranquil in mind.

78. Four persons born in his spiritual lineage were famous on the earth. They were Śyāmas, Mudgalas, Balārakas and Gaviṣṭhiras. These are remembered as the groups of very powerful men.

79. From Kaśyapa Nārada, Parvata and Arundhatī were born. O excellent ones, (listen to and) understand (the sons)of Arundhatī.

80. Nārada gave Arundhatī (in marriage) to Vasiṣṭha.[1] Due to the curse of Dakṣa, the brilliant Nārada (was compelled to be) celibate.

81. Formerly when there was a great battle between Devas and Asuras, called Tārakāmaya, the whole world was oppressed by drought and Śakra was aggrieved along with Suras. The intelligent Vasiṣṭha sustained all the subjects by means of his penance.

82. Making use of the medicinal herbs, fruits and roots (the sage) sympathetically enlivened them.

83. (Defective Verse) O Brāhmaṇas, Vasiṣṭha begot Śakti of Arundhatī. Adṛśyantī (wife of Śakti) bore Parāśara to Śakti on the seashore (?)

84. Kālī bore Kṛṣṇadvaipāyana, the holy lord, to Parāśara. From Dvaipāyana, Śuka, endowed with good qualities, was born, at the Araṇi (the sacrificial twig with which fire is produced by attrition).

1. The lineage of Vasiṣṭha is described in vv. 80-90. A comparison of the race of sages as given in other Purāṇas e.g. *Matsya Purāṇa* shows many dissimilarities in the names of descendants though some names are common.

85-86. The following six children were born of Pīvarī to Śuka: five sons, viz. Bhūriśravas, Prabhu, Śaṁbhu, Kṛṣṇa and Gaura and a daughter Kīrtimatī by name. She was firm in her holy rites and a Yogic mother. She was the wife of Sāttvaguha and the mother of Brahmadatta.

87. There were eight groups (spiritual lineage) of Parāśaras of noble souls. They were Śvetas, Kṛṣṇas, Gauras, Śyāmas, Dhūmras, Samūlikas, Dārakas, the imbibers of hot (drinks?) (Ūṣmapas) and Nīlas.

88. Henceforth, understand the progeny of Indrapratima. Kuśīti, who was born of Kapiñjalī-Ghṛtācī to Vasiṣṭha is called Indrapratima.

89. Vasu was his son born of Pṛthu's daughter. Upamanyu was his son whose (descendants) were these Upamanyus.

90. Kuṇḍins who were famous as descendants of Mitrā-Varuṇa have one spiritual lineage. Others are well-known as Vasiṣṭhas. These are the eleven Gotras of Vasiṣṭhas.

91. Thus these eight renowned mental sons of Brahmā have been recounted. They were blessed brothers and their spiritual lineages have been established.

92. They sustain these three worlds consisting of groups of Devas and sages. Their sons and grandsons are hundreds and thousands. By them the entire Earth is pervaded as with the rays of the Sun.

CHAPTER TEN

The Procedure of Śrāddha[1]

1. After hearing this narrative of Sūta, the knower of Ātman, the Brāhmaṇas, subsequently asked him as follows :

---

1. *Śrāddha* is a form of ancestor worship. It is based on the belief in after-death survival of the deceased ancestors and their residence in a particular region called *Pitṛ-loka*. It is an important topic and forms an integral part of Hindu Dharmaśāstra. This belief is pre-Vedic as it dates back to the Indo-Iranian period (*vide* S.B.E. IV, p. 262). Ancestor-worship was regarded essential for the continuation of one's race and prosperity to

Śāṁśapāyana said :

2. How was Bhavānī who was formerly Satī, born for the second time ? She was Dākṣāyaṇī at first. How did she become Umā ?

3. The king of mountains begot her of Menā, the daughter of Pitṛs. Who were these Pitṛs whose mental daughter was Menā ?

4-5. (Who are the Pitṛs) whose grandson was Maināka and whose grand-daughters were Umā, Ekaparṇā, Ekapāṭalā and Gaṅgā, the most excellent one among rivers as well as the eldest of them all ? Even before this, all this has been already desired to be pointed out (by you). Please listen to all my requests.

6. Are there many Pitṛs ?[1] And then where do they stay ? Welfare unto you. I wish to hear the great procedure of Śrāddha.

7. Whose sons are they (*Pitṛs*) remembered to be ? How are they the Pitṛs ? How were the Pitṛs born and whose sons were they ? Of what nature are they ?

8. Are there other Pitṛs who are deities (i.e. worthy of worship) unto the Devas in heaven ? Thus I wish to hear the excellent creation of Pitṛs and how the Śrāddha performed by us (as per prescribed injunctions) propitiates Pitṛs.

9. What is regarded (in the Smṛtis) as the reason of their being not visible ? What types of Pitṛs stay in heaven and what types in hell ?

10-11. What Śrāddhas are to be offered (to Pitṛs) ? How do these Śrāddhas reach Pitṛs—the Śrāddhas that are offered uttering the names of father, father's father and great-grandfathter against the three rice-balls (*Piṇḍas*) ? How are they (Pitṛs), if stationed in hell, competent to grant benefits ?

12. Who are these called by the name Pitṛs ? Whom shall we worship again ? We have heard that even Devas in heaven worship Pitṛs.

---

one's family. The Gṛhya Sūtras and old Smṛtis like Manu and Yājñavalkya prescribe the procedure of Śrāddha which is generally followed in Purāṇas such as A.P. 163.2-42, G.P.I-210, K.P. II. 22.20-62, N.P. Ch. 28., Bd.P. 2.3-Chs. 9-20.

1. Verses 6-13 record all questions, doubts etc. about the performance of Śrāddha.

13. O extremely learned one, we wish to hear this in detail. It behoves you to explain the significance of this clearly.

14. On hearing the words of the sages, Sūta, the seer of reality, said in accordance with the questions and the desire in the minds of the sages.

Sūta said :

15. I shall describe to you (in detail) what I have heard (regarding Śrāddha), in accordance with my intellectual ability. In every Manvantara, Pitṛs are born as the sons of Devas.

16. In the past and the future Manvantaras, they are respectively the eldest and the youngest. I shall precisely recount the Pitṛs who have gone in the past Manvantaras along with Devas and who exist at present.

17. A *Śrāddha* of the human beings is what is offered with faith. Brahmā created Devas but they did not worship him. They forsook him and desirous of fruits for themselves created themselves* (?)

18. They were cursed by Brahmā—"O deluded ones! You will all become devoid of sense." They did not know anything. Then the whole world became deluded.

19. All of them bowed to god Brahmā and implored him. In order to bless the worlds, the lord spoke to them again.

20. "Perform expiatory rites for the transgression which has been committed. Ask your sons and therefrom you will attain knowledge."

21. Desirous of knowing (the procedure of) expiatory rites, Devas controlled themselves duly and asked their own sons mutually.

22. Those sons who were conversant with real Dharma and possessed self-control, explained to them the various modes of expiatory rites—verbal, mental and physical.

23. The heaven-dwellers who regained their senses became delighted and spoke to their sons—"You are our fathers (Pitṛs), since we are enlightened by you. What boon should be granted—virtue, knowledge or love?".

---

*Bd. P. 2.3.9.16 reads *ayajan* 'They worshipped themselves (instead of god Brahmā)'— a better reading than *asṛjan* of our text.

24. Then Brahmā spoke to them—"You are the speakers of truth. Hence what is spoken by you shall be so and not otherwise.

25. This is what is uttered by you—your own sons have been mentioned by you as your Pitṛs (fathers). They will be your Pitṛs. Let this boon be given to them."

26. On account of the words of Brahmā, Parameṣṭhin, the sons (Pitṛs) attained the status of fathers (of Devas) and Devas, the real fathers, the status of sons.

27. Hence it is declared (in Dharma-Śāstra) that the sons (of Devas) are Pitṛs and the status of Pitṛ-hood is proclaimed about them.

After declaring in this manner that the fathers are the sons and the sons as Pitṛs (fathers), god Brahmā addressed to them again for the development of their own selves.

28. "If anyone will perform any holy rite without worshipping Pitṛs in a Śrāddha, Rākṣasas and Dānavas will obtain the fruit (good results) thereof.

29. The Pitṛs propitiated and developed by means of Śrāddhas (develop) the imperishable Soma. Propitiated and developed by you all, they will always increase.

30. Soma (the Moon-god) strengthened and developed by means of Śrāddhas, will develop the people and the entire world, along with mountains and forests surrounded (=inhabited) by mobile and immobile beings.

31. Those men, who, desirous of nourishment, perform Śrāddhas are always granted development and progeny by Pitṛs.

32-33. Those (Pitṛs) to whom they (the performers of Śrāddha) offer three balls of rice (*Piṇḍas*) mentioning their names and Gotra up to great-grandfather, they (Pitṛs) who are present (everywhere), strengthen and develop their progeny by that offering of Śrāddha."

Such a behest has been declared formerly by the supreme god (*Parameṣṭhī*) Brahmā. It is by their grace that *Dāna* (charitable gift), *Adhyayana* (Vedic Study) and *Tapas* (Penance) fructify.

34. There is no doubt in this that Pitṛs grant you perfect knowledge.

In this manner Pitṛs are Devas and Devas are Pitṛs. Devas and Pitṛs are reciprocally Pitṛs.[1]

35. After hearing these words of Sūta possessing self-knowledge, the sages asked him again subsequently :

The Sages said :

36. How many are the groups of these Pitṛs ? At what time did those groups (come into existence)—Pitṛs who were the excellent ancestors of Devas and who developed and strengthened Soma?

Sūta said :

37. I shall recount to you the most excellent creation of Pitrs. This is the same question which had been formerly put to his father Bṛhaspati by Śaṁyu.

38. As Bṛhaspati, the great expert in all fields of knowledge, was seated, his son Śaṁyu endowed with humility, put this question.

39. "Who are these Pitṛs? What are their names? How were they born? How did they attain Pitṛ-hood?

40. What is the reason for which Pitṛs are worshipped at the outset in every Yajña? All the holy rites of noble souls begin with the performance of Śrāddhas.

41. To whom all these Śrāddhas are to be offered? What is the great benefit when they are offered? In which of the holy centres and sacred rivers does the Śrāddha performance yield ever-lasting benefit?

42. What are those holy centres in Which excellent Brāhmaṇas (ought to) perform Śrāddha to obtain all (desired) benefits? What is the (proper) time for Śrāddha? What is the procedure to be followed?

43. O holy sire, I wish that what has been enquired by me be explained in detail in the proper sequence."

---

1. Verses 20-34 explain the paradox why Pitṛs who were the sons of Devas became the fathers of their own fathers ? Manu III. 201, however, differs and states that Pitṛs sprang from Sages and from Pitṛs were born Devas (gods) and human beings.

44. On being asked thus clearly and specifically, the highly intelligent Bṛhaspati, the most excellent of those who understand (the implications of) questions, answered all the questions in the proper order.

Bṛhaspati said :

45. O dear one! I shall explain the solemn excellent question which you ask me with due propriety and proper humility.

46-47. At that time, there was neither the heaven nor the firmament, neither the earth nor the stars nor the quarters, neither the sun, nor the moon, nor the day, nor the night. O dear, the whole Universe was in complete darkness. Brahmā alone performed an austere penance difficult for others to perform.

48. Śaṁyu again spoke to his father who was the most excellent among the knowers of Brahman, who always performed holy ablutions in the form of rites and who was the most excellent of all knowers of perfect knowledge.

49. "What sort of a penance did Prajāpati, the lord of all living beings perform?"

Thus addressed, *Bṛhaspati* of excessive refulgence, *spoke* to him.

50. Of all types of penance, *Yukti* i.e. Yoga penance is the most excellent. Meditating on it, the lord then created all the worlds by means of that Yoga.

51. The past and future (items of) knowledge, the entire worlds and Vedas were created after practising Yoga by Brahmā, by means of his Yogic vision.

52. The worlds, the heaven are named '*Sāntānikas*' where the shining deities of the Devas well-known as 'Vairājas' stay.

53. Even at the outset then, the lord Brahmā, endowed with Yoga and penance, had created Devas after practising the eternal Yoga.

54. They are well known as *Ādidevas* (the primordial Devas). They have great splendour and energy. They are the bestowers of all desires. They are worthy of being worshipped by Devas, Dānavas and human beings.

55. There are seven groups of those Devas. They are worshipped by all the three worlds. Three of them are *Amūrtis* (devoid of forms) and four of them have splendid forms.

56. The three sets which have conceptual forms (*Bhāva mūrtis*) are stationed above. The four *Sūkṣmamūrtis* (having subtle forms) are stationed beneath them.

57. Thereafter, the (common) Devas are stationed and then the earth. This is the situation of the series of worlds. They (the groups of Devas) are stationed in this world. The clouds take their origin from them, rain-showers are due to them and, thanks to rain-showers, the worlds (and people) are created again.

58. Since they develop and strengthen the moon and the food-grains and make them flourish by means of Yogic power, they called them the Pitṛs of the world. They (Pitṛs) are the most excellent ones in the world.

59. They are as speedy as mind. *Svadhā* constitutes their diet. They have every requisite they desire. They are devoid of greed, delusion and fear. They are certainly devoid of sorrow.

60. After giving up Yoga, they have attained the worlds beautiful and pleasant to look at. They become divine, meritorious and sinless noble souls.

61. At the end of a thousand Yugas, they become expounders of Brahman. Regaining the Yogic power once again., they attain salvation in a bodiless state.

62. They forsake both the manifest and unmanifest (bodies) by means of their great Yogic power and perish (vanish) like a meteor or like the fading flash of lightning in the sky.

63. By abandoning all the bodies (and other adjuncts) by means of their great Yogic power, they attain the state of namelessness like rivers merging into the ocean.

64. Engaged everyday in holy rites and the worship of preceptors, Pitṛs develop their Yogic power and satisfyall (make them flourish).

65. Propitiated in Śrāddha, Pitṛs nourish Soma (the Moon) making use of their Yogic power whereby the three worlds sustain their lives.

66. Hence Śrāddhas must always be offered to Yogins[1] with (special efforts). Indeed, the mainstay of Pitṛs is Yoga and from (thanks to) Yoga the Moon functions.

67. One may feed thousands of Brāhmaṇas or as many as do come, but listen that one knower of Yogas, if delighted, deserves all (propitiating a Yogin is as fruitful as feeding thousands of Brāhmaṇas).

68. What is taken in by a thousand invited (ordinary Brāhmaṇas), or by a hundred *Snātakas* (Brāhmaṇas initiated into householder's life) or by one master of Yoga saves one from great fear.

69. One Yogin excels a thousand householders, a hundred *Vānaprasthas* (Forest-hermits) and a thousand *Brahmacārins* (celibate students).

70. Prajāpati has ordained : "(One may be) an atheist, an evil-doer, a person of mixed caste or a thief, (but) he cannot have redemption[2] (*Tāraṇam*) from anything else, except (by offering) a charitable gift unto those who have Yogic power.

71. His ancestors are delighted like the husbandmen by a good timely rain, even if his son or grandson feeds a (Yogic) meditator.

72. If meditating mendicants are not available, one should feed two Brahmacārins. When they too are not available, one should feed a householder not much engrossed in worldly affairs."

73. It is the injunction of Brahmā that a meditating Yogin is greater than one who (performs penance) for a hundred years standing on one leg and taking in nothing but air.

74-76. The Siddhas roam over the Earth in the guise of Brāhmaṇas. Hence one should approach the in-coming guest with palms joined in reverence. He should honour him with the vessel containing materials of worship. He shall offer him place of residence and food. The masters of Yoga assume diverse forms

---

1. Verses 66-64 emphasize the importance of feeding a Yogin at the time of Śrāddha. This is specifically re-iterated in a later chapter. It shows the deep regard for Yogins in ancient times.

Cf. VP. 15.23-24, Varāha P. 14.18-19.

2. *Kāraṇam* in the text is irrelevant and obscure. Hence *Tāraṇam*, the reading in Bd. P. ibid V. 71 is accepted.

and always roam over the ocean-girt earth. They are (no less than) Devas. They protect the people righteously. Hence every man should offer charitable gifts to a Brāhmaṇa guest. I shall recount those charitable gifts and the fruits thereof.

77-79. Housing the Yogins is far better than thousands of horse-sacrifices, hundreds of Rājasūya sacrifices and thousands of Puṇḍarīka sacrifices. The first of those seven groups of Pitṛs of unmeasured brilliance, has been recounted. This group exists always with the conception of Time[1] (?) Henceforth I shall narrate again all the groups of Pitṛs, their progeny, their situation and their *Bhāvanā* (conception) in the proper order.

CHAPTER ELEVEN[2]

The Birth of Skanda: Rules Prescribed for Śrāddha

Sūta said:

1. In heaven, there are seven excellent groups of highly intelligent Pitṛs. Four of them have forms and three are formless (*Amūrta*).[3] Understand as I shall recount their creative activity in the world.

2-4. (I shall describe) those who are proclaimed (in Smṛtis) as their daughters and daughters' sons. There are three excellent groups of those who assume Dhārmic bodies and forms. I shall briefly recount their names and creative activity. The disembodied groups of Pitṛs, the sons of Prajāpati, abide in the shining worlds named Virajas. O Brāhmaṇas, they belong to Virajas. Hence they are famous as excellent Vairājas. I have thus mentioned the first group of Vairājas.

1. 'Sanctifying the worlds'—Bd. P. V. 76.
2. This chapter is textually similar to Bd. P. 9.3.10. Reference are given to verses in that chapter.
3. For similar seven divisions of Pitṛs *vide* Pd. P. V.9.2-3, Bd. P. V-1.

5. Their fair-complexioned mental daughter Menā is the wife of the great mountain Himavān. From her the son Maināka was born.

6. The mountain Maināka, the holder of all medicinal herbs, the mine of all gems, the holy leader of mountains, was born of her. Krauñca was his son.

7. The king of mountains procreated three daughters of Menā, viz. Aparṇā, Ekaparṇā and the third Ekapāṭalā.

8. Two of them had support (They had their permanent abodes). But Aparṇā performed penance without an abode. Ekaparṇā had a Nyagrodha tree as her abode and Ekapāṭalā had Pāṭala (trumpet flower) tree as her abode. For a hundred thousand years, they performed such a penance as was difficult to be performed even by Devas and Dānavas.

9. A single leaf was the diet of Ekaparṇā and a single Pāṭala flower (trumpet flower) was the diet of Ekapāṭalā.

10. Both of them took their food once, (when) a thousand years had been completed. One of the daughters (viz. Aparṇā) remained without taking food. Their mother spoke to her thus.

11-12. Out of affection, the distressed mother forbade her with the words "*U*" "*Mā*" (O daughter! do not). Since she was addressed thus by her mother, the blessed gentle lady performing the difficult task (penance) became famous as "*Umā*". The auspicious lady got the name derived from her action.[1]

13. The world of (supported by ?) these three ladies will survive for ever. It will be proud of (*dṛptam*) their penance, while the earth lasts.

14. All the three, endowed with Yogic power, sustained their bodies by means of their penance. All those blessed gentle ladies possessed permanent youth.

15. All of them were expounders of Brahman. All of them were celibate. Umā was the greatest (eldest), the most excellent (girl) of the fairest complexion.

---

1. Kālidāsa refers to this in Kumārasaṁbhava I.26
umeti mātrā tapaso niṣiddhā |
paścād umākhyāṃ sumukhī jagāma ||

16. Endowed with great Yogic power, she attained Mahādeva (as her husband). Her adopted[1] son was Uśanas, the son of Bhṛgu.

17. Ekaparṇā was the wife of Asita. She was chaste and firm in her holy vows. She was given to that intelligent master of Yoga by Himavān. She gave birth to the mental son Devala who was engrossed in meditation on Brahman.

18. Ekapāṭalā, the third of these daughters, wooed Jaigīṣavya, the son of Śataśilāka, as her husband.

19. His sons Śaṅkha and Likhita,[2] are remembered as not born of the womb. Thus (these) are the blessed and auspicious daughters of Himavān.

20. Rudrāṇī was the best among them. She excelled others by her good attributes. Between Umā and Śaṅkara the mutual love (was ideal).

21. On realising that they were in close embrace, the slayer of Vṛtra (i.e. Indra) became apprehensive. (Fire-god) was sent near them by Indra who was afraid of the birth of a child from them engaged in sexual intercourse.

22. (He said to Agni) "O Fire-god, create an impediment in their sexual intercourse. You are present everywhere. So there cannot be any blame (on you in your going there)".

23. When he was told thus, Fire-god acted accordingly. Forsaking (i.e. aside from) the body of Umā, the semen virile was discharged on the ground (by Śiva).

24. O Śāṁśapāyana, then Fire-god was cursed by the infuriated goddess. With words choked with anger, she spoke to Fire-god thus:

25. "O Fire, since you have caused an impediment in sexual intercourse even before I had been satisfied, therefore you have committed an action which you should not have committed, you evil-minded one !

26. Since the lustrous semen virile of Rudra has not been retained (in my womb), you should hold the foetus yourself by way of punishment (for this act)".

1. The reading *danta-kāṇvośanā* is obscure. Bd. P. 2.3.10.18 reads *dattakaśco-śanas* etc. is clear and is supported by Purāṇas. Hence its acceptance here.

2. Smṛti works are attributed to them, though the antiquity of those works is doubtful.

27. Fire-god, who, due to the wrathful curse of Rudrāṇī, had to carry the foetus within himself, retained it for a number of years, O Brāhmaṇas.

28. Approaching (the river) Gaṅgā, he said—"O excellent river, may this be heard. Excessive distress is caused to me by the retention of the foetus.

29. O river, for my relief and welfare, please carry this foetus. Due to my gracious favour, your trouble will be less".

30. Saying "So be it", the highly delighted great river held the foetus (although) with a mind burning (as there was burning sensation within her).

31. Distressed by the great pain though she was, she retained the foetus for a long time.

32. The foetus was dropped into an auspicious crevasse of Himavān by her. There is an auspicious forest named Śaravaṇa where diverse trees were in bloom. It was there that she deposited the foetus that was blazing like fire.

33. It was there that the son of Rudra, Agni and Gaṅgā was born. He had rosy lustre. He was valorous and brilliant like hundreds of suns.

34. When that blessed son (Kumāra) of Jāhnavī (Gaṅgā) was born, the sky was covered (crowded) with aerial cars, as if by birds.

35. Celestial drums produced sweet sound in the sky. Siddhas and Cāraṇas moving about in the sky discharged showers of flowers.

36. The chief Gandharvas, Yakṣas, Vidyādharas and all the Siddhas and Kinnaras sang (laudatory songs) everywhere.

37. Thousands of great serpents and excellent birds approached with reverence the son of Śaṅkara born through Agni. Daityas, Dānavas and Rākṣasas were struck (down) by him by means of his prowess.

38. Even at the very outset, the son of Agni was observed by the wives of the Seven Sages (excepting Arundhatī) who had come there for their ablutions.

39. The lordly son of Rudra, resembling the rising sun, was surrounded by those ladies who were very affectionate (towards him), as though they were his real mothers.

40. Desirous of seeing all those ladies simultaneously, out of affection for them, the extremely lustrous son of Jāhnavī created six faces and he was very glorious.[1]

41. He was glorious and he resembled the midday sun. He had eyes like the petals of lotus. When he was born, the lustre of all the worlds was bedimmed.

42. The groups of Dānavas who could not brook Devas, had a purge (*Skandita*) when that great (deity) was born and (hence) that valorous (deity) became known as 'Skanda.'[2]

43. Because the ancient (deity), the slayer of Asuras, had been nourished (breast-fed and) nurtured by the Kṛttikās, he became famous as Kārttikeya.

44. While that enemy of Daityas was yawning, his (weapon) Śakti (spear) called Aparājitā (unvanquished) came out of his mouth, blazing with flames of fire.

45-46. For the purpose of Skanda's play, two birds named Prabhadrakas, a peacock and a cock, were created out of Garuḍa by Viṣṇu, the powerful god. A banner was given by Vāyu (Wind-god). A great Vīṇā (lute) of loud sound was presented by Sarasvatī. A goat was given by the self-born (deity) (i.e. Brahmā) and a ram was given by Śambhu.

47-48. O Brāhmaṇas, when the (mountain) Krauñca was felled down in his sport out of Māyā (his illusive power), when the rising leader of Asuras, Tāraka was also struck down, the lordly son of Agni, the valorous enemy of Daityas was crowned as commander-in-chief (of their army) by the blessed Devas including Indra and Upendra.

49-50. The commander-in-chief of the army of Devas is also called Naranāyaka (the leader of men), the harasser of the enemies of Devas, Skanda and the lord and master of all the worlds, by Pramathas, the different kinds of Devas

---

1. Mbh. *Anuśāsana* chs. 85 & 86 give a different version of Skanda's birth and the cause of his six faces.

2. According to Mbh. *Anu* 86.14. the child came to be known as Skanda due to the casting off of the semen of Śiva by Agni and Gaṅgā (*skannatvāt skandatām prāptaḥ*)

and the groups of Bhūtas, by the various mothers and the groups of Vināyakas.

[[1]Some lines are missing from the text.]

51. (While) Slipping from heaven and falling down, she saw the aerial chariots as small as a mote and in them she saw the fallen Pitṛs.

52. They were very subtle and unforsaken[2](?) (*a-parityaktān*). They were like sparks of fire imposed on sparks of fire. Falling down topsy-turvy, she appealed to them, "Save, ye".

53. She was consoled by them—"Do not be afraid". When thus urged, she became steady. Then she propitiated those Pitṛs with pitiable words.

54. Those Pitṛs spoke to the girl who fell down from her glory due to her transgression : "O lady of sparkling smiles, you are fallen from your prosperity due to your own fault. (Hence) you fall.

55. Deities (god) attain (experience) the fruits of their actions by means of the same bodies with which they perform those actions.

56. In the case of Devas, the actions fructify immediately. In the case of human beings, they fructify after death. Hence you will attain the status of the child of Amāvasu after death and will attain the fruit".

57. On being told thus (by her Pitṛs), she again propitiated Pitṛs. After meditating (for a while), they took pity on her and became pacified and pleased.

---

1. The missing lines are traceable to Bd. P. 2.3.10. vv. 53-b to 58. They are translated here to supply the lacuna: 53b-54. "It is heard that the Pitṛs named Barhiṣads are *somapas* (imbibers of Soma). The mental daughter of the Pitṛs was the river named Acchodā.

55. Those Pitṛs had never before been seen by her. She was born as their mental daughter. Hence she did not know her Pitṛs.

56-57. Transgressing those real Pitṛs, she chose Amāvasu as her father. He was traversing the sky accompanied by the Apsaras named Adrikā. He was seated in an aerial chariot in the firmament. But due to her transgression (of her real father), she was unable to move about in the sky.

58. After seeking another father (viz. Amāvasu) she slipped from her Yogic power and fell down."

After this comes verse 51 in our text.

2. But *aparivyaktān* 'not clearly visible or manifest' is a better reading in Bd. P. V. 59, as it describes their subtlety.

58-59. On foreseeing what is surely destined to happen, Devas, the Soma-imbibing Pitṛs spoke to the girl, "You will become the daughter of the noble-souled king Amāvasu who is born on the earth as a human being and thereafter attain these worlds of your own.

60. In the twenty-eighth Dvāpara Yuga you will be born of the womb of a fish; you will be the daughter of this very same king Amāvasu and (the celestial damsel) Adrikā.

61. You will give birth to the successor of the sage Parāśara. That Brāhmaṇical sage will divide the single Veda into four parts.

62-63. You alone will give birth to two sons who will heighten the glory of Mahābhiṣa (?) Śantanu—the sons Vicitravīrya, the knower of Dharma, and Citrāṅgada, the king endowed with the attributes of brilliance and strength. After giving birth to these sons, you will regain your own worlds.

64. Due to your transgression towards the Pitṛs, you will attain that despicable birth. You will become the daughter of the very same king and Adrikā.

65. After becoming (his) daughter, you will regain these worlds."

Thus addressed, she was born as Satyavatī, the daughter of a fisherman.

66. In the confluence of Gaṅgā and Yamunā, she was born of the fish Adrikā, She was born as the daughter of Amāvasu in Adrikā the fish.[1]

67. Indeed, she was the daughter of that king (being born of) the semen virile of the king.

The worlds named "Virajas" are in the firmament. There those groups (of Pitṛs) shine.

68. There the Pitṛs are the Agniṣvāttas of shining lustre. With a desire for (attaining) excellent fruits, groups of Dānavas, Yakṣas, Rākṣasas, Gandharvas, Kinnaras, Bhūtas, serpents and Piśācas worship them.

69. Thus, these sons of Pulaha, the Prajāpati, have been recounted. These groups are said to be three. They are auspicious and assumers of Dharma-form.

1. In the missing lines in the text supplemented from Bd. P. (vv. 55-58) and vv. 51-66, the Purāṇa writers have used the curse-motif to explain the unusual matrimonial life of Satyavatī.

70. Their mental daughter is (will be) famous by the name of Pīvarī. She was (will be) reputed to be a Yoginī, a Yogic wife and a Yogic mother.

71. In the (future) twenty-eighth Dvāparayuga (a sage) of great penance named Śuka will be born in the family of Parāśara.

72. O excellent Brāhmaṇas, he will be a glorious and great Yogin. Yoga (will spread) from him. He will be born of Vyāsa, from the Araṇī (a piece of wood used for the production of fire by attrition) like the smokeless fire.

73. In the (mental) daughter of the Pitṛs, he will beget these well-known Yogic preceptors, viz. Kṛṣṇa, Gaura, Prabhu, Śaṁbhu and Bhūriśruta.

74. He will beget a daughter Kīrtimatī who will be a Yoginī and a Yogic mother. She will become the queen of Aṇuha and the mother of Brahmadatta.

75-76. After begetting these children and attaining great Yogic power, he will become a great Yogin and ascetic. He will attain that goal from which there is no return. Like the rays of the sun, he will attain the status of no rebirth. The great sage will become omnipresent and liberated.

77. These three are the disembodied Pitṛs who assume Dharmic forms. There are four others. (Listen and) understand.

78. O excellent Brāhmaṇas! The Pitṛs whom I shall describe assume forms of great lustre. They are Kāvyas*, sons of Agni, Kavi (the wise one ?) born of Svadhā.

79. These are the Pitṛs shining in the worlds of Devas with their lustre amidst the luminaries. They are richly endowed with all desirable objects and the Brāhmaṇas revere them.

80. Their mental daughter was famous in heaven by

---

*The reading in our text is

utpannās te svadhāyās tu kanyā
hyagneḥ kaveḥ sutāḥ,

Here the nom. pl. *Kvayā* (*ḥ*) cannot be construed cogently as the Pitṛs are men (masculine). Bd. P. 2·3.10.85 reads *Kāvyāḥ* 'sons of Kavi' (a wise person or Śukra?) and appears plausible.

the name of Gau. Kumāra bestowed an army on her[1]. She became the beloved queen of Śukra.

81. There were thirty-one Pitṛs who heightened the glory of Bhṛgus. Their worlds were known as *Marīcigarbhas* (having rays within) which envelop the heavens.

82. Those sons of Aṅgiras, nourished along with Sādhyas, are remembered as the Pitṛs Upahūtas. They shine in heaven. Looking up to them, the Pitṛ Groups of Kṣatriyas, those who are desirous of benefits, revere them.

83. Their mental daughter is well known by the name of Yaśodā. She was the wife of Viśvamahān and the daughter-in-law of Viśvaśarmin.

84.[2] The gentle lady was the mother of the saintly king Khaṭvāṅga of noble soul, in whose Yajña Gāthā (a laudatory verse) was sung formerly by great sages.

85. After seeing the birth of fire (in the Yajña) of the noble-souled Śāṇḍilya, the deathless Devas conquering heaven with purity of mind observe the Yajamāna (under whose auspices the Yajña is performed) Dilīpa, the noble soul of truthful rites.

86. Ājyapas were the Pitṛs of Kardama, the Prajāpati, who was born of Pulaha. They were born of him again.

87. Moving about in the sky, they are stationed in these worlds that go about as they please. Groups of Vaiśyas who are desirous of benefits, revere these in Śrāddha.

88. Their mental daughter is famous by the name of Virajā. The chaste lady was the wife of Nahuṣa and the mother of Yayāti.

---

1. This is the translation of '*Dattasenā Kumāreṇa*.' The absurdity of the text is obvious. Bd. P. *ibid* V. 87 reads *Dattā Sanatkumāreṇa* 'She was given by Sanatkumara'. The reading in Bd. P. deserves adoption here as the next line reads "She became the beloved...of Śukra".

2. The combined verses can be constructed as follows:

That saintly lady was the mother of the noble-souled royal sage Khaṭvāṅga. On seeing the birth of the noble souled Śāṇḍilya from (sacrificial) fire at his sacrifice, the great sages sang the (following) laudatory verse (*Gātha*). :

"Those immortals who see the Yajamāna (the sponsor of the sacrifice) Dilīpa with full concentration (become) the conquerors of heaven—so much is noble-souled Dilīpa truthful in the observance of his vows".

89. Sukālas are the Pitṛs of Vasiṣṭha, the Prajāpati. They are the sons of Hiraṇyagarbha.

90. There are the worlds named Mānasas where these are stationed. Their mental daughter is Narmadā, the most excellent of rivers.

91. Flowing in the southern region, she sanctifies living beings. She was the wife of Purukutsa and the mother of Trasadasyu.

92. Manu became the lord of Manvantara by adopting these (Pitṛs). In the beginning of Manvantara, he initiates all types of Śrāddhas.

93. O excellent Brāhmaṇas, (I have recounted) all the Pitṛs in their proper order. Hence Śrāddha is to be offered with faith in accordance with one's Dharma.

94. A Śrāddha offered in silver vessels or those of silver alloy, after proferring Svadhā, propitiates Pitṛs.

95. By the propitiation of Soma, Agni and Vaivasvata (Manu) and by the performance of *Homa* in the sacrificial fire during the northern transit (of the sun), one shall attain the fruit of an *Aśvamedha* (a Horse Sacrifice).

96. Pitṛs delight him who propitiates Pitṛs with devotion. There is no doubt in this that Pitṛs bestow nourishment or progeny.

97. The rites of pitṛs are always far superior to the rites of deities. It is ordained that the propitiation of Pitṛs must be given priority over that of deities.

98. The subtle movement (or goal) of Yoga or the satiation of Pitṛs is not visible through the physical eye. Only by achieving special Siddhi by means of penance are they to be seen.

99. Thus Pitṛs, their worlds, their daughters, their grandsons, their Yajamānas and those who revere them have been recounted.

100. (Out of the seven classes of Pitṛs) four have forms and three are formless. Devas honour them and offer Śrāddhas to them devoutly and assiduously.[1]

---

1. The discussion about the seven classes of Pitṛs, their mental daughters and other particulars may be tabulated as below :

101-104. All the Devas including Indra concentrate their minds on them. They join their palms in reverence and devotedly worship them. Viśvedevas, Sikatas, Pṛśnijas, Śṛṅgins, Kṛṣṇas, Śvetas and Ajas worship them duly. Desirous of benefits, the subjects Vātaraśanas, Divākīrtyas, Lekhas, Maruts, Brahmā and other heaven-dwellers, Atri, Bhṛgu, Aṅgiras and all other sages, Yakṣas, Nāgas, Suparṇas, Kinnaras and Rākṣasas always worshipped Pitṛs.

105. These noble-souled (Pitṛs), if duly honoured and worshipped in Śrāddha, grant all desires hundred-fold and thousand-fold.

106. These grandfathers (Pitṛs) bestow Yogic Power (and prosperity) and liberation (from Saṁsāra) after one has abandoned the three worlds of normal existence involving old age and death.

107. Pitāmahas, the deities of subtle bodies, grant the means of salvation, *Aiśvarya* (prosperity), complete detachment and infiniteness.

108. Practised Yoga is *Aiśvarya*; and *Aiśvarya* is the excellent wealth. Without Yoga and *Aiśvarya* liberation (from Saṁsāra) is impossible (to be achieved).

Class of Pitṛs	*Names of their daughters and other particulars*
1. Vairājas	Menā, wife of Himavān, mother of Umā, Śiva's consort.
2. Barhiṣads	Acchodā, adopted king Amāvasu as father; cursed by Pitṛs; became Satyavatī, mother of Vyāsa and queen of Śantanu.
3. Agniśvattas	Pīvarī, married to Śuka, Vyāsa's son.
4. Kāvyas (sons of Agni and Svadhā)	Yogotpatti alias Ekaśṛṅgā married Śukra.
5. Upahūtas (sons of Aṅgiras)	Yaśodā, queen mother of king Khaṭvāṅga.
6. Ājyapas (sons of Pulaha)	Virajā, married to king Nahuṣa, mother of Yajāti.
7. Sukāla (sons of Vasiṣṭha	Narmadā (the river), wife of Purukutsa and mother of Trasad-dasyu.

Out of these groups (5), (6) and (7) are specially recommended for worship to Kṣattriyas, Vaiśyas and Śūdras. Manu III. 193-198 slightly differs in the assignment of Varnas to Pitrs.

109. It (Mokṣa) is as impossible as the movement of a wingless bird in the sky. *Mokṣa*-Dharma is the greatest of all Dharmas and eternal.

110. Pitāmahas (manes) grant thousands of aerial chariots attended by groups of Apsaras-s and richly equipped with all desirable things.

111. Intellect, nourishment, power of memory, brain, kingdom and health can be attained only through the grace of the noble-souled Pitṛs.

112. Pitāmahas grant crores of gems, pearls, *lapis lazuli*, garments and thousands of horses and elephants.

113. Pitāmahas always bestow on men chariots fitted with swans and peacocks, studded with pearls and *lapis lazuli* and decorated with tinkling bells and provided with perpetual flowers and fruits.

CHAPTER TWELVE

The Procedure of Śrāddha (*Continued*)

Bṛhaspati said :

1. It is said (in Dharma-Śāstra) that the vessels of (meant for) Pitṛs should be made of gold, silver or copper. A silver or silver-coated vessel is said to be befitting Pitṛs.[1]

2. Showing or gifting away of silver is proclaimed to be a suitable *Dāna* for Pitṛs and it is conducive to the attainment of infinite and everlasting heaven. Good sons enable Pitṛs to cross (hell) by means of this *Dāna* (religious gift).

3. O dear one, it was in silver vessel that Svadhā was formerly milked by Pitṛs seeking to get Svadhā. O dear one, if that is gifted, it yields everlasting benefit.

---

1. Cf. Viṣṇu Dh.S. 79.14-15. Yājñavalkya I. 236 specially recommends silver vessels. Cf also Mt. P. 17.19-22, Bd.P. 2.3.11-1.

4. The nearby presence, sight or gifting away of the hide of a black antelope is conducive to the destruction of Rākṣasas. It increases Brāhmaṇical splendour and enables Pitṛs to cross (hell).

5. Vessels made of gold, silver or copper, gingelly seeds, *Kutapa* (i.e. the eighth muhūrta of the day) or Kuśa grass, sesamum seeds, garments and *Tridaṇḍi Yoga* (i.e. the Yoga of mind, speech and body)—all these are holy objects.

6. In the holy rite of Śrāddha, the following ritual prescribed by god Brahmā is the most excellent and eternal. It is conducive to increase in fame, longevity, progeny, intellect and lineage.

7. In the south-east direction, especially at the intermediate point (corner) between them, (should be the place—altar in Bd. P.—for Śrāddha). It should be well-situated and square shaped with sides equal to an *Aratni* (the distance between the tip of the fist and the elbow).

8. I shall mention the proper spot for the holy rites of Pitṛs in accordance with the injunctions of the scriptures. It is conducive to the attainment of wealth, health and longevity. It enhances strength and brightness of complexion.

9. At the place (intended for Śrāddha), three pits (should be dug) and three sticks of Khadira wood should be placed. They (the sticks) should be an Aratni (distance between the tip of the fist and the elbow) in length and should be embellished with silver (bands). (The pits) should be a *Vitasti* (the span or the distance between thumb and little finger when they are extended on either side) in depth* and the four sides should be four *Aṅgulas* (fingers) each.

10. The sticks should not be hollow and they must be placed on the ground with their faces pointing to the south-east. (The performer of Śrāddha) should be pure and should wash them with holy waters or water rendered holy by the use of the ring of Darbha grass (called *Pavitra*) worn by the performer of Śrāddha.

**Kāryā* in the text but *gartāḥ* from Bd. P. 2.3.11.10 is better.

11. The purification (*Śodhana*) may be carried out with goat's milk or cow's milk and water. By means of this *Tarpaṇa* (holy water-offering) the satisfaction (of Pitṛs) will be permanent.

12. He will be prosperous here and hereafter. He will be (blessed with the fruits of) all holy rites. If a person always takes bath three times a day and worships Pitṛs with Mantras as per prescribed procedure, he gets the fruit of (performance) of a horse-sacrifice (*Aśvamedha*).

13. On the New Moon day, the Śrāddha materials should be placed in the pit in the ground four *Aṅgulas* square. These rituals are called *Triḥ-sapta-yajña* (Three-times seven Yajña). All the three worlds are sustained by them.

14. He will attain nourishment, prosperity, longevity and progeny. Various types of fortune will resort to him and he will gradually attain liberation (from Saṁsāra).

15. It removes sins. It sanctifies. It has the same fruit as a horse-sacrifice. I shall mention that *Mantra* composed by Brahmā. It is the *Amṛta* (immortal or nectarine) and it is honoured and worshipped by Brāhmaṇas and grants (the fruit of) Aśvamedha.

16. *The Mantra*: "Obeisance to all the deities, to Pitṛs, to the great Yogins, to Svadhā. Obeisance for ever to Svāhā.".[1]

17. At the beginning and the conclusion of the Śrāddha, this Mantra shall always be repeated three times. The devotee shall repeat this with purity of mind, when he offers the balls of rice also. Pitṛs arrive quickly and Rākṣasas flee.

18. Regularly repeated at the time of Śrāddha by expounders of Brahman, this Mantra enables Pitṛs to cross (hell) in the three worlds.

19. A person desirous of kingdom, should always repeat this Mantra with alertness. It increases virility, purity, wealth, sāttvic qualities, prosperity, longevity and strength.

20. I shall mention the Mantra *Saptārcis* that is auspicious and that bestows all desires. By repeating it regularly, Pitṛs are propitiated.

---

1. Hemādri regards this as Saptarcis Mantra : *vide Caturvarga Cintāmaṇi, Śrāddha* pp. 1079 and 1208. This mantra is accepted in Skanda P. VII. 1-206; 114-116., GP. (Ācāra) 218.6, A.

21. The Saptārcis[1] Mantra: "I always make obeisance to those who are engaged in meditation by means of the yogic vision, to the embodied and unembodied Pitṛs of brilliant splendour.

22. I bow to the Seven Sages and Pitṛs who fulfil all desires and who are the progenitors of Indra and other (Devas) and of Bhṛgu and Mārīca (Kaśyapa).

23-24. After bowing to all the Pitṛs who bestow welfare on Manu and other lords of Suras and on the sun and the moon, I bow down with palms joined in reverence to Pitāmahas, the progenitors of the constellations, the mobile (and the immobile beings) and of the heaven and the earth.

25. With palms joined in reverence I bow down to those who bestow fearlessness, to those who are revered by all the worlds and to the progenitors of the divine sages.

26. With palms joined in reverence, I bow down to Prajāpati, Kaśyapa, Soma, Varuṇa and to the lords of all Yoga.

27. Obeisance to the seven groups of Pitṛs in the seven worlds. Obeisance to the self-born Brahmā of Yogic vision."

28. Thus the Mantra honoured by the groups of Brahmarṣis along with the Seven Sages has been mentioned. It is highly holy and sanctified. It is conducive to prosperity and destructive of Rākṣasas.

29. The man who (performs Śrāddha) according to these injunctions attains three boons. Pitṛs grant food, longevity and childern (to the people) on the earth.

30. He who is endowed with great devotion, who has faith, who has controlled his senses and who always repeats this *Saptārcis Mantra* with purity, becomes the sole Emperor on the earth consisting of seven continents and oceans.

31. If any thing is cooked in the house, whether a dainty or ordinary eatable, it should never be eaten in that house without first offering it (to deities).

32. Henceforth, I shall describe in the proper order, the vessels intended for oblations to Pitṛs. Even as I mention listen

---

1. These seven verses 21-27 are called '*Saptārciṣ Mantra*'. Cf. Bd. P. 2.3.11 23-29. As against Hemādri our text calls this '*saptārcis*' Mantra.

to the respective benefits (in using oblations) in the different vessels.

CHAPTER THIRTEEN

The Procedure of Śrāddha Performance (*Continued*)

Bṛhaspati said :

1. It is cited (in scriptures that) a leaf of the Palāśa tree (*Butea frondosa*) is conducive to Brāhmaṇic splendour.[1] That kingdom is conceived (as the fruit, if leaves of) the Aśvattha tree (are used) : The lordship of all living beings is mentioned (in using the leaves of) Plakṣa (citron-leaved Indian fig tree) [i.e. the materials of oblations must be placed in cups made of these leaves or the wood as in the case of some of the following] .

2. Those who are desirous of prosperity, wisdom, intellect and power of memory (shall use the leaves of) the banyan tree. The vessel of the leaves of Kāśmarī (a large tree called Gambhārī also) is conducive to fame and destructive of Rākṣasas.

3. That which is offered in Madhuka (the tree *Bassia latifolia*) is considered excellent and conducive to good fortune. One who performs Śrāddha in the vessel of Phalgu (a kind of fig tree) attains all desires.

4. The performer attains supreme lustre, particularly all-round brilliance (if the sun-plant is used—Bd. P.). By using a Bilva vessel, riches, intellect and longevity are always attained.

5. If Śrāddha is performed in Bamboo vessels, Parjanya (cloud or the lord of rain) always showers in his fields, parks, lakes and all crops.

6. It is said (in *Śāstras* that) those who make Śrāddha

---

1. Verses 1-6 enumerate the different trees, the leaves (i.e. cups of the leaves) of which (if used for giving oblations to Pitṛs) confer different benefits. The Śrāddha Sūtra of Kātyāyana recommends the use of (cups of leaves of) sacrificial trees for *Arghya*.

offerings even for once in these excellent vessels, attain the fruit of all Yajñas.

7. He who always offers fragrant garlands to Pitṛs becomes endowed with riches and glory, and shines brilliantly like the sun.

8. He who offers incense, fragrant gum-resin and other things to Pitṛs, along with honey and ghee obtains the fruit of a horse-sacrifice.

9. One who offers shining fragrant *Dhūpa* (incense) to Pitṛs begets children of his wife (beneficial to him) here and hereafter. Hence he shall always offer it to Pitṛs.

10-11. He who always offers lamp to Pitṛs assiduously, obtains unequalled auspicious power of vision in the world. He becomes brilliant on the earth. He shines in Heaven with splendour, fame, refulgence and strength. He rejoices in the aerial chariot surrounded by Apsaras-s.

12. He should offer scents, flowers, incense and ghee. After propitiating at the outset, Pitṛs with fruits, roots and obeisance, with purity of mind and body, the devotee should later worship Brāhmaṇas with food and wealth.

13. Always at the time of Śrāddha, Pitāmahas (manes) assume aerial forms and on seeing Brāhmaṇas, they enter them. Hence I am saying this.[1]

14-15. Excellent Brāhmaṇas should be honoured with garments, foodstuffs, charitable gifts, food and beverages, (gifts of) cows, horses and villages. If Brāhmaṇas are honoured, Pitṛs become delighted. Hence, one should honour excellent Brāhmaṇas duly.

16. In the holy rite of Śrāddha, Brāhmaṇas should perform diligently the ritualistic scraping, digging and sprinkling of water (with Darbha) (*Ullekhana and Prokṣaṇa*) by means of the left and the right hands.

17. A learned man should keep ready for libation, Darbhas, balls of rice, foodstuffs, different kinds of flowers, scents, charitable gifts and ornaments.

---

1. Hence Brāhmaṇas are to be worshipped, fed and gifted at the time of Śrāddha. The belief that Pitṛs assume gaseous form and enter the bodies of the invited Brahmins is found in *Auśanasa Smṛti* V. 4-5. Cf. Manu III. 189.

18. After propitiating the persons present duly, the Brāhmaṇas shall perform the *Vaiśvadeva* rite and then perform the rites with *Abhyaṅga* (oil bath) with Darbha (leaves of the Kuśa grass) in accordance with the injunctions.

19. The excellent food-offering to Pitṛs should be made with reverse wearing of the sacred thread. After pronouncing (the names of Pitṛs) the thread must be offered to all of them in lieu of garments.

20. The rites of *Khaṇḍana*, *Poṣaṇa* and *Ullekhana* are to be performed only once in the case of Devas, and thrice in the case of Pitṛs.

21. Wearing a single *Pavitra* (a ringlike loop of Kuśa grass worn round a finger) in the hand and reciting the *Cailamantra*, the balls of rice are touched once for each of the Pitṛs. Then the benefit of showing (is attained) (?).

22. Always the balls of rice must be offered on the ground along with ghee and gingelly seeds. The devotee performing Pitṛ-Śrāddha, kneels on the ground with the left knee touching it.

23. He invokes the fathers, grandfathers and great-grandfathers and all ancestry of yore and properly sprinkles all round the balls of rice, by means of the holy water (*Pitṛtīrtha*) carefully from the right to the left (in anticlockwise manner).

24. Some men desire a separate Śrāddha for maternal grandfathers by means of food, water, flowers and foodstuffs of various kinds.

25. He should offer three *Piṇḍas* in the proper order (pressing them) with the thumb. They are conducive to the enhancement of nourishment. He should offer the Piṇḍas (by means of both hands placed) between the knees.

26. (In offering the *Piṇḍas*) the left hand should be placed over the right, repeating the Mantra[1] '*Namo vaḥ pitaraḥ śūkṣmaiḥ*[2] (?) always carefully in this manner.

1. The Text *dharme mantre ca paryayaḥ* is obscure and the sentence remains incomplete. Bd. P. 2.3.11.62 reads *dhārārtham mantram uccaran* 'should repeat the mantra (as follows for the sake of pouring water in the form of a thin current)'.

2. A reads *Suṣmai* and not *Sūkṣmaiḥ*.

The Mantra in A is recorded in Bloomfield's *Vedic Concordance*, p. 538 but no mantra with '*Sūkṣmaiḥ* is found. It is obviously a scribal error.

27. (Defective Verse) Carefully repeating the Mantra "*Nāmo vaḥ pitaraḥ saumyāḥ*" (Obeisance to ye, O gentle Pitṛs) he should offer the first Piṇḍa with both the hands and place it in the southern quarter.

28*. (Defective Verse) With both the hands, he draws the outline (?) of a mortar using the water from the water pot. He must be careful in the practice of piety.

29. He should offer a fresh thread of silk or jute or a cotton thread. Woven silk such as coloured cloth and Kauśeya should be avoided when offering thread to Pitṛs.

30. In the sacrifice, the thread taken even from a freshly woven cloth shall be avoided. These do not please Pitṛs. Those who give cannot flourish (?).

31. The collyrium obtained from the Trikūṭa mountain, they say, is always excellent. So also is the oil extracted from black gingelly seeds.

32. Sandal, Agaru (fragrant aloe wood), Tamāla, Uśira (fragrant root of the plant *Andropogon Muricatus*), lotus, fragrant incense, gum resin and (white) Turuṣka—all these are excellent articles (for use in Śrāddha).

33. White flowers are the most excellent. So also the red and blue lotuses. All other flowers can be used if they are fragrant.

34. The flowers China Rose, Bhāṇḍīra, Upakāma and Kuraṇḍaka should always be avoided in the Śrāddha rite.

35. Odourless flowers and flowers of obnoxious odour should be avoided at that time by one who seeks prosperity.

36. The Brāhmaṇas invited on that occasion should invariably face the north while sitting. The performer of the Śrāddha should duly face the south.

37. He should face them and offer the Darbhas and the

---

*Bd. P. 23.11-63-64 states that the first *Piṇḍa* is to be moved to the south with the mantra : *namo śoṣāya* and the other two *Piṇḍas* with the mantra *namo saumyāḥ*.

A comparison with the text in the Bd. P. 2.3-11.6 ff. shows that though the text in Vā. P. and Bd. P. is common, the lines are differently distributed in the verses of these texts.

Piṇḍas. He should worship his own grandfathers by means of this rite.

38-39. The following objects are said to be essential (in a Śrāddha): Green Piñjalīs (leaves of Kuśa grass) as smooth and soft as flowers, about a *Ratni* in size, softened and straightened by the holy water (Pitṛtīrtha), blue near the root and not defiled by pebbles etc. (should be used). So also Śyāmāka and Nīvāra kinds of rice.

40. This (story) has been narrated by the excellent Prajāpati.[1] His hairs fell down through the path of the sky on the earth.

41. Hence the Kāśa grasses are holy. They are always honoured in the Śrāddha rite. The *Piṇḍas* are to be offered on them by one who wishes prosperity.

42. Those who do so become free from sins and defects. Their children become nourished with splendour, fame and refulgence.

43. The devotee should sit facing the south and spread the Darbha grass once for the *Piṇḍas*. The tips of the Darbhas should be pointing to the south-east. The procedure shall be mentioned as follows :

44. A learned man should always perform Śrāddha with concentration of mind. He shall neither be dejected nor angry. His mind should not be distracted or diverted elsewhere.

45. (The following Mantra is to be repeated.) "I annihilate everything that has impurity in it. All Asuras and Dānavas have been killed by me. All Rākṣasas, Yakṣas, groups of Piśācas and all Yātudhānas (demons) have been killed by me."[2]

46. All Asuras avoid him who offers food to Pitṛs by repeating this Mantra. Rākṣasas avoid the place where this Mantra is recited.

---

1. There is some lacuna. Bd. P. 2.3.11.79-80 state that formerly Prajāpati assumed the form of a horse and his hair fell on the ground and became Kuśa grass.

2. Quoted in *Śrāddha Tattva*, p. 235. Verses of the same import and textual similarity are quoted by Aparārka but he adds the Vedic mantra *Apahatāḥ*' (Vāj. Saṁhitā II. 29) here.

47. A Brāhmaṇa should always perform Śrāddha according to this procedure. The manes (*Pitāmahas*) will grant whatever is desired in the mind (by him).

48. If Śrāddha is always performed assiduously, Pitṛs become delighted in mind and Rākṣasas become dejected.

49. Śūdras should always avoid the following in Śrāddha: *Kṣiracāśu*[1] (trees yielding white juice?), trees called Balvaja (*Eluesine Indica*, a species of coarse grass not liked by cattle) and other kinds of grasses such as Vāraṇa, Lava, Lava-varṣa.

50. They shall avoid applying collyrium, oil and unguents as well as wearing garlands. Their rites should be performed with Kāśas which grow again (when cut). All the benefits accrue (to them thereby).

51. Kāśa (grass) and the regrown Kāśa (grass) are (like) peacock's tail and its regrowth[2]. (So) Pitṛs are Devas and Devas are Pitṛs.

52-53. This is the Mantra intended for flowers, incense, scents etc. Pulling (the vessel of materials of worship) towards the south assiduously for the sake of Homa, he (performer of Śrāddha) should repeat the *mantra* "Svadhā unto Soma, the Pitṛmān (having Pitṛs). Obeisance to Aṅgiras". He should perform the Homa of non-heavenly or the worldly type for the purpose of the fructification of the holy rite.

54-55. Homa is to be performed after placing *Samit* (sacrificial twig) within. The devotee should keep the mind perfectly pure and keep the holy fire scrupulously pure, repeating the Mantra, "Svadhā unto Agni, the bearer of *Kavya*. Obeisance to Aṅgiras. Svadhā and obeisance unto Yama and Aṅgiras".

56-58. These are the Mantras in order intended for Homas. Homas shall be performed everyday from the southern direction to Agni and to Soma in the middle[3]. In between these two Homas, a Homa should be performed to Vivasvān (the Sun or his son Yama ?). *Upacāras* (ways of render-

1. *avi-kṣīram* 'milk of a variety of sheep called *Avi*' in Bd. P., *ibid* V. 87
2. *barhaṇa* 'a peacock' is rather inapplicable. Hence *barhi* (n) 'fire; kuśa grass' may be the probable reading.
3. *uttarataḥ* 'to the north' in Bd. P. *ibid* V. 95.

ing homage), repetition of Svadhā mantra, Ullekhana (ritualistic scrubbing), Homas, Japas, obeisance, particularly *Prokṣaṇa* (sprinkling), applying collyrium, oil bath and offering piṇḍas—(all these must be performed).

59. If they are performed with Mantras, they have the same benefit as a horse-sacrifice. All holy rites mentioned above shall be assiduously performed.

60. In the blazing fire plenty of ghee must be offered. Particularly Homa must be performed in a smokeless fire with curly leaping flames, for the fructification of the holy rite.

61. We have heard that if a *Yajamāna* performs Homa in a weakly burning smoking fire, he becomes blind and issueless.

62. If there is deficiency of fuel, if the flames are scattered all round and dried up or if the flames are defiled by smoke, the fire is not conducive to good results.

63. If the fire emits bad odour, if the flames are bluish or particularly black, or if the fire makes the ground crack, know that there is failure (in the holy rite).

64. The resplendent fire with a single globular flame, yellowish (golden) in colour, produced by the ghee, is conducive to the fructification of the rite. The flame shall be smooth and curling clockwise.

65. (That fire) is perpetually honoured and worshipped by both men and women. Thereby, the everlasting pitṛs become honoured and worshipped. They give everlasting benefits.

66. Mud-pots, vessels made of the leaves or wood of the Udumbara (*ficus glomerata*) tree, its fruits and *Samits*, all these are considered very holy in Śrāddha. They are very pure.

67-69. The different benefits of the various kinds of vessels that I have mentioned as regards the Śrāddha rite, O excellent Brāhmaṇas, are also true in regard to the holy rites of nativity. With regard to the *Samits* also, the same should be known. The devotee keeps the mind pure and says 'I am performing the rite in fire'. Then, after being permitted by excellent Brāhmaṇas, saying "Do", he should perform the Homa in the fire, accompanied by his wife and sons.

70. The following trees are equally sacrifice-worthy: Palāśa (Bd. P.), Plakṣa, Nyagrodha, Aśvattha, Vikaṅkata, Uduṁbara, Bilva and Candana.

71. The following trees are particularly recommended for the purpose of *Samits* (sacrificial twigs) : Sarala, Devadāru, Śāla and Khadira.

72. Rural thorny trees are also sacrifice-worthy. Some of them are honoured for the purpose of *Samits* in accordance with the words of Pitṛs.

73. Even as I recount, listen to the fruit of the holy rite to those who perform Homa with the *Samits* of the *Kalkaleya* (pomegranate) tree.

74-75. The Aloe wood is to be desired by all. It has the same benefit as that of a horse-sacrifice. The following trees should be avoided – Śleṣmātaka, Naktamāla, Kapittha, Śālmali, Nīpa, Vibhītaka and the creepers also. Similarly the trees on which birds reside must be avoided. Those trees which are considered unworthy of sacrifice should also be avoided.

76. In the course of the sacrificial rite, the word *Svadhā* is used at the end of the Mantra pertaining to Pitṛs and Svāhā is used in the case of Devas.

CHAPTER FOURTEEN

The Procedure Regarding Performance of Śrāddha: The Five Mahāyajñas

Sūta said :

1. Bṛhaspati declared (in reply) that as per (injunctions of) the Atharva Veda, Devas are Pitṛs but there are also other Pitṛs.

2. One should especially worship Pitṛs before Devas. (People) in the world do worship Pitṛs before Devas.

3. Dakṣa had a daughter famous in the world by the name of Viśvā. O knower of Dharma, she was given duly and righteously to Dharma. It is well-known that her sons are the noble-souled Viśvedevas.

4-5. They were very famous throughout the three worlds. They were revered by all the people in the world. On the beautiful peak of Himavān resorted to by Devas and Gandharvas, all those noble souls performed a very severe penance, performed by all the Apsaras-s and resorted to by all the Devas and Gandharvas.

6. The delighted Pitṛs spoke to them with a pure (frank) mind—"We are delighted. Request for a boon. What desire (of yours) shall we fulfil?"

7. When this was mentioned by Pitṛs, Brahmā, the creator of the three worlds, the lord of the subjects, spoke to the Viśvas (Viśvedevas).

Brahmā said:

8. "(Even) Mahādeva of great brilliance, has been scorched by them by means of the great penance. I am well-delighted by that penance. What desire of yours shall I fulfil?"

9. Thus urged by Brahmā, the creator of the world, all of them simultaneously spoke to Brahmā, the creator of the worlds.

10. "May we have a share in Śrāddha. This is the boon desired by us". Then Brahmā spoke to them who were worshipped in the heaven.

11-13. "What you desire will take place". Pitṛs said "So be it", and continued, "There is no doubt about it. Whatever is performed here shall be for you too along with us. In the Śrāddha intended by men for us, you will get the priority in being seated. We are telling you the truth. They will worship you at the outset by means of garlands, scents and food offerings.

14. Everything will be offered to you first and then to us. Our ritualistic farewell will occur first and the Devatās (i.e. you) will be ritualistically dismissed later.

15. The protection of Śrāddha and (according) of hospitality—these are the two ceremonial acts to be performed in the rite of Śrāddha offered to Pitṛs and Devatās and Bhūtas. If it is done duly according to injunctions, everything shall be all right."

16. After granting them the boon thus, lord Brahmā, the

benefactor of all living beings, went away happily along with the groups of Pitṛs.

17. Five great Yajñas have been prescribed in the Vedas. A Man shall always perform these five Mahāyajñas.

18. (Listen to) and understand where the performers (of those five Yajñas) go and where their abode is. They attain the abode of Brahman that is fearless, devoid of egotism, free from sorrow, strainless and free from pain. It yields all desires.

19. These five Yajñas are to be performed by a Śūdra also, but without reciting the Mantras. He who eats (enjoys) otherwise (without performing them), eats debts everyday.

20. He who cooks for himself is a sinful soul and he eats debts. Hence a sensible man shall perform the five great Yajñas.

21. Some wish that *Naivedya* (food-offering) should be assiduously offered even when Pitṛs are alive. Oblation should be offered along with libation of water. The water-pot also shall be offered.

22. The oblation should be made well announced. It shall be scattered by throwing it far above. Small oblations shall at first be offered on the horns of cows (?)

23. The *Piṇḍa* cannot be offered as *Naivedya* to Pitṛs. They should be duly fed by offering palatable foods and edibles. I am emphatically mentioning this as the procedure laid down in the Vedas.

24-26. These groups of Pitṛs are noble souls and lords of Devas. Some preceptors wish that Brāhmaṇas should be worshipped first everyday, and then the *Piṇḍa* should be offered. (But) Bṛhaspati* says to those who are experts in matters of Dharma (practice of rituals), that he (the performer of Śrāddha) should offer the Piṇḍa first and then feed

*These verses give two different views about the precedence of Brāhmaṇas to offering of Piṇḍas.

tad hi dharmārthakuśalān ityuvāca Bṛhaspatiḥ|

should better be emended as...*dharmārthakuśalo netyuvāca*.....as in Bd. P. 2.3.12.25 and would mean : "Bṛhaspati who is an expert in affairs of Dharma (ritualistic practice) has said that it (the precedence of Brāhmaṇa-worship to offering of Piṇḍa) should not be so".

Brāhmaṇas later. (For) Pitṛs are born of Yoga (Yogic Power) and are (themselves) Yogic souls and great ones. Pitṛs strengthen and develop Soma (the Moon).

27. Hence he (the performer of Śrāddha), remaining pure and devotedly attached to Yogins, should offer the Piṇḍas to Yogins. This shall be the *Havi* offering directly to Pitṛs.

28. If a single Yogin be in the seat of priority among thousands of Brāhmaṇas, he will enable the Yajamāna and the Brāhmaṇas partaking of the food, cross (the ocean of worldly existence) like a boat in water.

29. Where the wicked are accepted and honoured and where the good are disrespected, a terrible punishment meted out by the Devas befalls them immediately.

30. If a pious (Brāhmaṇa) who has come as a guest is left out and a foolish one is fed, the householder forgoes his prior holy rites and perishes (i.e. despite his merit in a previous birth he is faced with ruin).

31. He who seeks enjoyment (of worldly pleasures) should assiduously consign the Piṇḍa to the sacred fire.[1] He who seeks progeny shall give the middle Piṇḍa to his wife but after performing all the intervening rites and *mantras*.

32. He who wishes for excellent refulgence always offers it (the Piṇḍa) to cows. So also he who wishes for intellect, honour, fame and renown, offers it always to cows.

33. He who seeks long life gives it to crows. One desirous of comeliness offers (oblations) to the fowl.

34. Thus the benefit of offering Piṇḍas has been recounted. Or the devotee shall stand facing the south and pacify the sky (scatter the oblations in the sky)[2]. The abode of Pitṛs is the sky and their quarter is the south.

35. (Defective) Further, Brāhmaṇas mention one procedure of lifting up the Piṇḍa. After being permitted by Brāhmaṇas who say "Let it be taken up dry"

---

1. Verses 31-34 prescribe the disposal of Piṇḍas and the benefits accruing from it. Cf. Mbh. *Anuśāsana* 125.38-40, BM.P. 220.150-52 for similar views.

2. 'or scatter them in the water' if '*apsu*' (in Bd. P.) for '*Sthitau*' hereof be accepted.

36. The upper layer or the tip of flowers, fruits, edibles and cooked food shall be taken up and offered as oblation in the sacred fire.

37. After consigning the edibles, cooked food, beverage and the excellent fruits to the fire, he should face the south and offer the Piṇḍas.

38. He shall propitiate (them) with oily edibles, sweet scents and juices. With concentration and purity of mind, he should serve them standing (there) with palms joined in reverence. A man devoted to them and full of faith, obtains the desires.

39. The grandfathers (manes) bestow the (following) qualities on him : the state of not being mean and low (non-pettiness), gratefulness, chivalry, hospitality and the (ability for performance of) sacrifices and religious gifts.

40. Henceforth I shall recount the Saumya* (belonging to Soma) procedure after the Brāhmaṇas have taken food, in order. Listen to it, even as I recount it.

41-42. The devotee attached to Pitṛs should sprinkle the ground and scrub it at the outset. Then he should scatter (auspicious materials) in accordance with the injunctions. He shall request the excellent Brāhmaṇas to chant the Svadhā mantra and offer them plenty of Dakṣiṇās. He shall get the permission from them (as to what should be done with) the remnants of the food. With palms joined in reverence, he shall follow them after honouring them duly. He should then bid farewell.

---

*As there is no 'Lunar procedure' herein, this should be taken as vocative case, '*Saumya*' 'O gentle one', instead of the accusative as in the text.

CHAPTER FIFTEEN

Sacred Places[1] *for Śrāddha*

Bṛhaspati said :

1. Pitṛs worshipped even once become delighted. They are imperishable Yogic souls. They are noble souls of great power and free from sins and evils.

2-3. O gentle ones, I shall recount the holy lakes, rivers, sacred spots, places of pilgrimage, mountains and hermitages for performing Śrāddha, at which Pitṛs bless him (the performer) with fulfilment of desire for profuse riches (in this world), attainment of heaven after death and liberation from Saṁsāra in due course.

4-5. The mountain Amarakaṇṭaka[2] is the holiest and the most excellent in the three worlds. It is a sacred mountain resorted to by Siddhas and Cāraṇas. Formerly, holy lord Aṅgiras performed very severe penance (difficult for others to do) on it, for thousands of years, say, millions and crores of years.

6. As long as the earth holds (lasts), the god of death,

1. Due to their association with the founders of faith or with some great persons or events certain places have been regarded holy by all peoples of the world, e.g. Mecca by Muslims, Jerusalem by Christians, Bodha Gayā by Buddhists. These holy places have a deep psychological effect on religious-minded persons. Śrāddha is to be performed in one's own house. But as K.P. II. 22.17 states, holy places are the common property of all and not of a particular person. A list of such holy places is recommended in different Purāṇas like KP. II. 20-32-36, Mt. P. Ch. 22, Bd. P. 2.3.13. There is some divergence in the lists but there is a great deal of overlapping as a number of holy places like Prayāga, Vārāṇasī, Gayā, Puṣkara are deeply respected by all Hindus.

This age-old tradition of Tīrtha-yātrā claimed the fruit of certain sacrifices. The case of ablution in a sacred pond or river and its claim of equivalence with the performance of a sacrifice adversely affected the popularity of and tendency to perform sacrifices—an onerous job.

2. A mountain in Bilaspur District of Madhya Pradeṣh. *Viṣṇu Dh.S.* 85-6 highly glorifies the performance of Śrāddha on this mountain. Our text and Bd. P. 2.3.13.4-5 give the credit of its sanctity to the penance of Aṅgiras.

Asuras and Rākṣasas have no access there, nor is there any fear or misfortune there.

7. That excellent mountain shines with brilliance and renown, just as Saṁvartaka fire (Fire at the time of the annihilation of the world) blazes on the peak of mount Mālyavān.

8-9. The Kuśa (growing there) is famous as soft, sweet-smelling, pleasing to the eyes and golden-coloured. They are well known as 'calm and quiet' Darbhas. Drinking the waters* of Narmadā to the south of it, the holy lord Aṅgiras of great brilliance formerly performed Agnihotra after spreading those excellent Kuśas round the altar and he saw the steps leading to the heaven.

10. I shall recount the benefit attained by that intelligent man who offers *Piṇḍas* even once, on the Darbhas on the mountain Amarakaṇṭaka.

11. That Śrāddha becomes everlasting, increasing the pleasure of Pitṛs. On reaching that holy centre, they vanish for ever.

12. Even today the holy "*Jvālārasa*" is seen there everywhere. The river thereof (called Viśalyā—a branch of Narmadā) makes all living beings free from darts and thorns (sins and miseries).

13-14. To the south-east of that excellent mountain, there is a tank with a whirlpool in that part contiguous to the land of Kaliṅga. O excellent sages, there is that great holy centre Siddhakṣetra which increases the delight of Pitṛs. It is the greatest on the earth, approved of by both Devas and Daityas. Uśanas has sung a verse on it.

15. "Blessed are those men in the world who being devoted to Pitṛs propitiate them in Śrāddha after reaching Amarakaṇṭaka.

16. There is no doubt in this that they will attain Siddhi with very little penance. If they are worshipped even once on Amarakaṇṭaka, Pitṛs attain Heaven".

**piban-dakṣiṇa-narmadam*· but here 'drinking' is strange. Bd. P. 2.3.13.8. reads '*pari-dakṣiṇa-narmadam* 'to the south of Narmadā'.

17. On the beautiful Mahendra[1] mountain, there is a holy centre resorted to by Śakra. If one mounts it, Pitṛs are delighted. The Śrāddha (if performed) there, yields great fruit.

18. If one practises Yoga on its lower peak named Bilva (Vailāta in Bd.P.), one gets divine vision. He becomes invisible to all living beings and roams over the earth like a Deva.

19. If a man takes his holy ablution in the Saptagodāvara[2] and in the penance grove Gokarṇa[3], he attains the benefit of a horse-sacrifice.

20. A man becomes sanctified after taking his holy dip in Dhūtapāpa.[4] Rudra, Maheśvara, the lord of Devas, performed a penance there.

21. In the holy place Gokarṇa, a proof has been cited by Brāhmaṇas for (convincing?) the atheists. If a non-Brāhmaṇa recites the Gāyatrī mantra, he perishes.

22. Those who regularly ascend the peak, the abode of Devas and sages, resorted to by Siddhas and Cāraṇas, attain heaven.

23-24. Since the place is embellished with divine sandalwood and other trees and since the water mixed with the flavour of sandal flows continuously, a river named Tāmraparṇī[5] originates from them. It slowly winds its way to the southern

---

1. Although this name is applied to the mountain range from Orissa to Madura, here it is specially applied to the range of hills separating Mahānadi from Ganjam District. It is regarded as the resort of Paraśurāma.

—De 119, HD. IV. 177

2. Sapta-Godāvara : (1) The seven "mouths" (branches) of the Godavari falling into the sea; (2) Solañgipur, sixteen miles from Piṭhāpur in the Godavarī District.

—De. 178

3. Gokarṇa : A place sacred to Śiva on the western coast in Kumṭā Tehsil of North Kanara District.

—HD IV. 753

4. A tributary of Gaṅgā near Vārāṇasi.

5. The river rises in the Agastya-Kūṭa—mountain Malay. Flowing through the Pāndya country, it falls into the Gulf of Manar famous for pearl-fishery.

—De 203, HD. IV. 812

ocean like a young woman extremely distressed (while going to her husband's house for the first time?).

25. The waters of that river in confluence with the great ocean become conchs, pearls and pearl-like conchs.

26. People bringing its waters containing conchs and pearls, become free from mental agonies and physical ailments and go to the heavenly city of Amarāvatī.

27. According to Śruti (Veda), the charitable gift of sandal, conchs and pearls enables Pitṛs to cross (hell) even though they be perpetrators of sins.

28-29. So also is the case of Candratīrtha, (Kanyā) Kumārī, the perennial source of Kāverī, the holy centres of Śrīparvata[1], the mountain Vaikṛta, and the mountain Ośiraparvata where the trees Palāśa, Khadira, Bilva, Plakṣa, Aśvattha and Vikaṅkata are seen growing in one place. (The people taking ablutions and performing holy rites there attain heaven.)

30. O excellent Brāhmaṇas, this zone of holy centres is sacrifice-worthy and is conducive to great achievements. A person who casts his mortal coil here, quickly reaches the heavenly city of Amarāvatī.

31. Holy rites performed by oneself fructify in the subsequent birth. Rites of Pitṛs (though) performed with defects become as beneficial as duly performed rites.

32. The holy river Narmadā, the most excellent of all rivers, is the daughter of Pitṛs. Śrāddhas offered there, become everlasting (in yielding benefits).

33. In the holy forest of Māṭhara, resorted to by Siddhas and Cāraṇas, they do not vanish because they are attached to that great mountain.

34. There is a proof (test) for discrimination between the pious and the impious on the holy mountain of Vindhya. Sinners do not see the current (waterfall ?) Good men see the current.

35. The sins of some sinners are seen in its current. Us-

---

1. Śrīśailam in Kurnool District in Andhra Pradesh. It is one of the twelve Jyotirliṅgas.

ually the current is visible in the case of those of meritorious activities.

36. In Kauśalā there is the tank of Mātaṅga named Pāpaniṣūdinī (Remover of Sins). Even stray birds, flying as they please, go to heaven after bathing (casually) in that tank.

37-39. (Ablution) in the Kumārakośala Tīrtha on the mountain Pālapañjara[1] and on the banks of Pāṇḍu near the sea, in the Paṇḍāraka forest, performance of good actions in the Abhaya Prabhava which is pure and sinless, daily visit to Śrīvṛkṣa, Gṛdhrakūṭa, and Jaṁbūmārga and in the holy centre of Asita, the intelligent preceptor of Yoga—performance of Śrāddha (at these holy places)—gives everlasting benefits.

40. Śrāddha in Puṣkara[2] is ever-lasting. Penance there yields great fruits and the same is true of the holy centre Prabhāsa[3] on the great ocean.

41. In Devikā[4], there is a well named Vṛṣa resorted to by Siddhas. Its water always gushes up on hearing the sound of cows and bulls.

42. It is always resorted to by masters of Yogas who are beyond all sorts of sins. I shall mention the benefit resulting from the performance of Śrāddha therein.

43-44. The Śrāddha (there) yields all desires and is everlasting. It delights Pitṛs. There is a rock of Agni there called Jātavedaḥśilā. He who enters the fire there rejoices in

---

1. Pālamañjara in Bd.P.—near Śūrparaka or Sopārā near Bassein in Thana district of Mahārāshtra.

2. A sacred lake near Ajmer, Rājasthan. It is famous for the temple of god Brahmadeva.

3. Now known as Somanātha Pattaṇa in Saurashtra. Somanātha is a famous Jyotirliṅga which was attacked by Muslim rulers from the days of Mahmud Gaznavi to Aurangzeb. A new temple was built near the original spot by Ahalyabai Holkar in A.D. 1783 and it is still recognized as original Somanātha by all, though a new temple on the original spot in its original form is reconstructed after independence of India.

4. Variously identified as a tributary of Indus, Gandak, Śarayu by different scholars. Its identification with the Deeg or Degh in the Punjab is accepted by Pargiter and Kane (HD. IV. 746; De 55).

heaven. Once the fire is tranquil, he is reborn. Anything offered there gives everlasting benefits.

45. There is no doubt in this that the sacrifices performed at the holy centres called Daśāśvamedhika and Pañcāśvamedhika yield the benefits as indicated (in their names, viz. fruits of ten horse-sacrifices and of five horse-sacrifices).

46. The holy centre named Hayaśiras is famous as granter of boon immediately. Śrāddha performed there yields everlasting benefits. The devotee rejoices in heaven.

47. Śrāddha is said to be everlasting. So also are Japas, Homas and penances.

48. One should always propitiate the Pitṛs in the auspicious holy centre of Ajatuṅga. There the shadow of the heaven-dwellers is always seen on Parvan days. Whatever is given here becomes everlasting in the world. The Pāṇḍavas became free from ailment here.

49. It is always resorted to by masters of Yogas free from all sins. I shall mention the benefit of performance of Śrāddha there.

50. Pitṛs worshipped there always become delighted. He who keeps his sense-organs under control in this world shall rejoice after death in heaven.

51. The lake named Śiva is the most excellent. Vyāsa-saras and the divine lake Brahma-saras there are also holy.

52. The mountain Ujjanta[1] of the noble soul Vasiṣṭha is also holy. Centres called Kāpota, Puṣpasāhvaya, (and those named after the Vedas) Ṛg, Yajus, Sāman and (Atharva-) Śiras have been created by god Brahmā. After the creation of these the fifth Veda, viz. Purāṇas have been narrated by him.

53. After going there a Brāhmaṇa becomes free from sin like the eternal Fire-god Agni. Śrāddha, Japas, Homas and penances are of endless benefits.

1. In Aparanta as per HD. IV. 815. If identified with Ujjayanta, it is Mt. Girnar—De 211; but it is not associated with Vasiṣṭha but with Datta and Neminātha. Hence identification in HD probable.

54. In the great holy centre Puṇḍarīka, one attains the benefit (as sweet and fragrant) as lotus. One gets the fruit of a horse-sacrifice in the great holy centre of Brahma Tīrtha (by performing Śrāddha there).

55. In the confluence of the Sindhu river and the ocean and in Pañcanada, the benefit is everlasting. Kīrakātmā[1] (in Bd. P. Virajā) and Maṇḍavā on the mountain are sacred spots (?)

56. Śrāddha has to be performed in the holy centre Saptahrada and particularly in Mānasa.[2] On the mountains of Mahākūṭa, Vanda and Trikakuda also (Śrāddha should be performed).

57. In Mahāvedī (Mahānadī in Bd. P.) a great miracle is seen. It does not appear to one who has no faith (but) it does appear to a person who is firm in his religious vows.

58. The eternal rock of Agni himself is there. It is called Jātavedaḥśilā. Śrāddhas and holy rites in the fire performed there, have never-ending benefits.

59. Going there everyday in the evening, one who seeks never-ending benefits should always offer Śrāddha to Pitṛs there.

60. A man of purified mind or otherwise is known in the holy centre called *Svargyamārgaprada* (that which shows the path leading to heaven). It grants boons immediately. Casting off their mutual enmity in it, the Seven Sages went to heaven.

61. Even today signs of their extinct enmity are seen. Taking bath in that excellent Tīrtha, a man attains heaven.

62. There is a famous shrine there, resorted to by Nandin and Siddhas (or a Siddha named Nandin). The image of Nandīśvara is not visible to men of evil deeds.

63. Golden *Yūpas* (sacrificial posts) are seen there at sunrise. People circumambulating them vanish and go to

1. *Vairāṇi*, but *cīrāṇi* 'garments' in Bd. P. V. 2.3.61 is preferable for in the next verse *vairāṇi* 'enmity' is said to be 'visible even today. Visibility of abstract things is doubtful.

2. Lake Manas-sarovar situated in Kailāsa mountain in Tibet.

—De 123

heaven (or they—the golden posts—disappear and go to heaven when devotees complete their circumambulation ?).

64. The (land) all over Kurukṣetra[1] is especially an excellent holy place of Sanatkumāra, the noble-souled lord of the Yogic cult. It is glorified as yielding ever-lasting benefit if Pitṛs are offered gingelly seeds (there).

65. Śrāddha performed in the residence of Dharmarāja is conducive to brilliance and it is never-ending (in yielding benefit). Śrāddha offered on the New Moon day in accordance with injunctions and in the proper order also yields never-ending benefits.

66. Moreover, to those who are near about Kurukṣetra it is particularly efficacious. A dutiful son who worships Pitṛs there, becomes free from his indebtedness to them.

67-69. Śrāddha should be performed with the repetition of *Oṁkāra* by persons who wish for ever-lasting benefit, at the following places : Vinaśana,[2] on the Sarasvatī river, Plakṣaprasravaṇa[3], Vyāsatīrtha on the Sarasvatī and especially at Brahma Kṣetra, everywhere on the (banks of) Gaṅgā and on the excellent mountain Maināka and at the source of Yamunā. One gets absolved of sins (thereby). The proof for the same is the excessively hot and extremely cold water there.

70. (Yamunā) is Yama's sister and the daughter of Mārtaṇḍa (the Sun-god). It is holy. Śrāddha performed there is everlasting. It was so glorified by Pitṛs formerly.

71. One taking ablutions in the lake Brahmānuga becomes a Brāhmaṇa immediately. Śrāddha, Japas, Homas and penances performed there are everlasting.

72. Vasiṣṭha of great penance performed penance standing still like a stump. Even to-day trees are seen there studded with gems.

---

1. The famous sacred place in Haryana—the country round Thaneswar. Some of the holy places, e.g. Vyāsa-tīrtha or Dvaipāyana Hrada are in this area. Sarasvatī flowed through it.

2. The spot in the sandy desert in Sirhind district where Sarasvatī disappears. —De 37

3. The source of the river Sarasvatī in the hills of Sirmur in the Siwalik range of the Himalayas.

—De 180

73. There a weighing balance that indicates piety and impiety, is seen. People who get themselves weighed by Brāhmaṇas in it derive excellent fruits.

74-75. The daughter of Pitṛs, the great Yoginī, is famous by the name of Gandhakālī. It is she who will give birth to the great Yogin, the noble souled Vyāsa, who will divide the single Veda into four, who will be an intelligent great sage, the great scion of the family of Parāśara and who is a fourth part of Brahmā.

76. There is the lake Acchodaka[1] from which she originated as the river Acchodā. Again she (Gandhakālī) was born of the womb of a fish at the instance of Vāraṇa[2].

77. The place where she has a holy hermitage, is resorted to by meritorious persons. Śrāddha offered there once, is said to be everlasting. If Śrāddha is offered there even once, it causes the attainment of Yoga and *Samādhi* (Trance).

78. He who offers Śrāddha in Kuberatuṅga, Vyāmocca and Vyāsatīrtha is a holy Brāhmaṇa. The Śrāddha yields everlasting benefits.

79. In the north-eastern quarter there is Nandāvedī. It is resorted to by Siddhas for ever. It is not visible to non-self-possessed souls. (Those who perform Śrāddha there) do not return (i.e. they attain liberation from Saṁsāra).

80. In the holy centre Mahālaya,[3] the intelligent Mahādeva had imprinted his foot. It is a Siddhakṣetra resorted to (by Siddhas). People who go there do not return (i.e. attain Mokṣa).

81. (Partially defective) On (the peak called) Umātuṅga, in the shrine of the goddess (Umā) has performed penance standing on one foot for the period of a divine *yuga*, without taking any food[4]. And the water (also) stood (for that period?).

---

1. A lake at the foot of Mt. Candraprabha from which river Acchodā flows out. If identical with the Acchoda-sarovara in Bāṇa's *Kādambarī*, it is Acchāvat, six miles from Martaṇḍa in Kashmir.

2. For *Vāraṇena* Bd. P. *ibid* V. 78 reads *Kāraṇena* 'for some purpose' and it is a meaningful reading.

3. The same as Oṁkāranātha or Amareśvara in M.P. —De 117

4. Our text reads *nīhāra* 'snow' which is obscure. Bd. P. *ibid* reads *anāhāra* 'without taking food'. It is relevant to penance, hence accepted tentatively.

82-83. One becomes sanctified by visiting Umātuṅga, Bhṛgutuṅga, Brahmatuṅga, Mahālaya, Kādravatī, Śāṇḍilī and Vāmana's cave. Śrāddha performed there yields ever-lasting benefit. Japa, Homa and meditation—everything performed there becomes meritorious.

84. Those who observe *Brahmacarya* (celibacy), those who perform sacrifice and those who are devoted to their preceptors for a hundred years (enjoy good benefits). These and other similar benefits are attained immediately by taking a dip in those holy waters.

85. (The holy river) Kumāradhārā[1] there removes all sins (at its very sight). If one goes and settles there, one attains immediately what is attained when it is seen.

86. By regularly visiting Śailakīrtipura, one attains all cherished desires. Like Devas he remains invisible to all living beings and roams in the earth.

87. Śrāddhas should be offered everyday by one who seeks everlasting benefits at the great holy centre of Kāśyapa well known as Kālasarpi.

88. Śrāddha performed all round Śālagrāma[2] becomes ever-lasting. It is not directly visible to sinful persons.

89-90. The place is forbidden to the evil-minded and the good ones are allowed entry, since the pure divine king of serpents dwelling in the holy lake accepts the *Piṇḍa* of the good and not that of the bad. Even by the highly illuminated serpents, the food cannot be eaten (if offered by the bad).

91. In these two holy centres, Dharma is directly seen. In Devadāruvana[3] too the same proof can be seen.

92. The sins shaken off are visible to the meritorious soul. In Bhāgīrathī and Prayāga[4] (the Śrāddha performed) is said to be of ever-lasting benefit.

---

1. Near Vyasa's seat for dhyāna and Kāntipurī or ancient Kāthmāṇḍu in Nepal. —De 89

2. A place near the source of Gandak, the place where Sage Pulaha and Bharata performed penance.

3. Its site is on Gaṅgā near Kedar in Garhwal; Badarikāśrama is situated in this 'Vana'.

4. Modern Allahabad, U.P.

93. Śrāddha should be offered with efforts at Kālañjara,[1] Daśārṇa, Naimiṣa, Kurujāṅgala and the city of Vārāṇasī.

94. In that city, Yogeśvara is present for ever. Hence what is offered there is ever-lasting. Offering Śrāddhas in these holy places, one becomes sanctified. The Śrāddha yields ever-lasting benefits.

95. Penance, Homa, meditation, nay anything performed in Lauhitya,[2] Vaitaraṇī and Svarṇavedī, becomes meritorious.

96. Only once, is (Śrāddha) seen (performed) near the sea-shore by men of meritorious actions. So also in Gayā, Dharmapṛṣṭha and in Brahmā's lake.

97-98. The Śrāddha offered in Gayā and Gṛdhrakūṭa yields great benefit. Snow falls all round it upto a distance of five Yojanas (1 Yojana = 12 Kms.). The forest surrounding the hermitage of Bharata is remembered as the most meritorious. The foot-print of Mataṅga is seen there with the physical eye.

99. This spot is glorified as (conducive to) entire righteousness. It is an example for this world. Similarly the Pañcavana is very holy. It is resorted to by men of meritorious actions. The holy centre Pāṇḍuviśālā is also a ready example.

100. (Defective) The persons who perpetrate sins come to the surface (become exposed) by means of weighing balances, by its arcs[3] and by various scriptures when they get attached (visit) to that Tīrtha (?).

101. Highly efficacious is the Śrāddha offered at the silent (deep) great lake Pāvamaṇḍala in the (river) Kauśikī in the third quarter on the third *Tithi* (day).

---

1. The places mentioned are identified as follows:
   (i) Kālañjara—Kalinjar in Badausa sub-division of Banda district, Bundelkhand (M.P.).
   (ii) Daśārṇa—Eastern N. Malwa, including Bhopal in Madhya Pradesh. Its ancient capital was Vidiśā.
   (iii) Naimiṣa—Nimsar, 45 miles NW of Lucknow, Uttar Pradesh.
   (iv) Kurujāṅgala—a forest country situated in Sirhind, NW of Hastinapur. —De 110

2. The following are identified by De thus: Lauhitya (The Brahmaputra, Assam); Vaitaraṇī (the river Baitaraṇī in Orissa); Jaipur stands on this river.

3. It appears that sinners are supposed to be weighed in the balance.

102. After performing a very severe penance for many celestial Yugas, the intelligent deity Mahādeva set foot on Muṇḍapṛṣṭha.

103. Within a very short time, a righteous man discards his sin quickly like a serpent casting off its slough.

104-105. To the north of Muṇḍapṛṣṭha, there is a holy centre famous in the three worlds by the name Kanakanandī. It is well protected by day and night by terrible serpents of huge bodies and licking with their tongues, frightful to the sinners (but) very delightful to Siddhas. (Even) birds flying as they please take bath there and go to heaven.

106. Śrāddha offered there is said to yield everlasting benefit. An excellent man becomes free from his three-fold indebtedness by taking his bath there.

107. On the banks of that lake, there is a great shrine of the lord. After mounting up to it and performing Japas, one becomes a Siddha and thereafter goes to heaven.

108. After going to the northern Mānasa,[1] one attains excellent Siddhi. On going to the excellent city[2], a very wonderful thing is seen.

109. One should perform Śrāddha there according to one's capacity and physical strength. He should attain divine pleasures and the means to liberation (from *Saṁsāra*) for ever.

110-111. In the excellent Mānasa lake, a very wonderful thing is seen. The highly blessed goddess Gaṅgā of three-fold path, slipping dawn from heaven, shines in the sky. Falling off the lunar rays on to the earth, it appears like festoons in the sky with the brightness of the sun.

112. It is diving with golden splendour. It is like the gate to heaven thrown wide open. It is from this place that it flows again towards the eastern ocean in its final stage.

113. It sanctifies all living beings and particularly those who know righteousness. Candrabhāgā (Chenab) and

---

1. Can it be the Kara Kul of northern Pamirs as suggested by M. Ali (AGP P. 71)? The so-called Uttara Mānasa at Gayā is an ordinary pond.

2. No mention of any city is here in the context. Bd. P. *ibid* V. 117 reads *Saraśreṣṭhe* 'in that excellent lake'.

Sindhu both these are like Mānasa (in sanctity). The divine Sindhu, the most excellent of rivers flows towards the western ocean.

114-115. There is the mountain named Himavān. It is embellished with various kinds of minerals. It is said that it extends to eighty thousand Yojanas. It is crowded with Siddhas and Cāraṇas. It is served and resorted to by Siddhas and Cāraṇas. There is a Puṣkariṇī (lake) on it, well known by the name Suṣumnā.

116. One who is born there lives upto ten thousand years. Śrāddha offered there yields ever-lasting benefits, and great prosperity. The performer of Śrāddhas enables ten previous generations and ten succeeding ones to cross (hell).

117. Everything belonging to Himavān is holy. The Gaṅgā is sacred everywhere (throughout). The ocean-going rivers and all the oceans all round are holy.

118. A sensible man should perform Śrāddha in all these places and at similar ones. Even by taking bath, he becomes sanctified. By offering (Śrāddha* ?) he becomes so (all the more).

119-123. Śrāddha can be performed in the following places: On the high summits and ridges of mountains, crevasses, in the solitary sides, springs and fountains, on the sandy banks of rivers, on the auspicious anniversaries of the beginning of Yugas, on great oceans, in cowpens, in the confluence of two rivers, in the forests, well-cleaned and scrubbed ground, pleasing fragrant spots, in solitary houses, on the ground polished with cow-dung, etc. One should perform Śrāddha in these places in accordance with injunctions. Those who seek fulfilment of all desires shall perform Śrāddha in these places carefully. They should perform circumambulation in all the quarters. An intelligent man performing thus, shall attain the Siddhi of *Brahmatva* (Brahmahood).

124. The worship of Pitṛs becomes fruitful if anger etc.

---

*MS. Kha. In A reads *dattva dānam* 'giving a religious gift', for *dattvā dattvā* of our text. Bd. P. *ibid* V. 127 reads *hutvā dattvā* 'by offering oblations to fire and by religious gifts'.

is eschewed, the duties of the three castes are performed and the discipline of castes and stages of life is maintained.

125. Even a person who has committed sins becomes sanctified if he boldly and faithfully makes the pilgrimage to the holy centres and courageously controls his senses. What need be said in regard to a person of meritorious deeds ?

126. He is not reborn in an animal womb. He is not born again in an impious land. A Brāhmaṇa attains heaven and attains the means to salvation (Mokṣa).

127. These five do not attain the benefit of pilgrimage : those who have no faith, sinners, atheists, permanent doubters and those who always seek a cause (for everything).

128. Great *Siddhi* is achieved in the holy centre of *Guru* (the preceptor). He is the most excellent of all sacred objects and spots. Meditation is a still greater Tīrtha. It is the eternal Brahmatīrtha.[1]

129. Meditation is greater than observance of fasts. It makes all the sense organs shun (their objects). Those who are wedded to observance of fasts are reborn again and again along with their vital breaths.

130. One shall equalise Prāṇa and Apāna. One should restrain in mind objects and the sense organs and restrain the intellect in the mind. Then every sense-organ recedes.

131. Understand that undoubtedly *Pratyāhāra* (the withdrawal of all sense organs) is the sure means to salvation. Among the sense-organs, the mind is the most terrible. It makes the intellect and other organs function.

132. (The restlessness of the mind) is subdued by not taking food. Know that fasting is a penance. By restraining the intellect and the mind, the intellect is sublimated (the intellect becomes beautiful).

133. When all the sins are mitigated, when the sense organs are weakened (subdued) the pure soul attains bliss of liberation like fire without fuel.

---

1. The influence of Yoga is so profound on the Purāṇa writer that Yogic meditation is regarded superior to Tīrthayātrā (vv. 128-131). The importance of feeding a Yogin at the time of Śrāddhas has been already extolled in previous chapters.

134. A knower of Yogas separates the individual soul from all manifest and unmanifest causes and *Guṇas* by means of his Yogic power.

135. There is no place for him to go, whether manifest or unmanifest. He is neither *Asat* (non-existent) nor *Sat-Asat*. Nothing can be said of his existence.

CHAPTER SIXTEEN

The Śrāddha Ritual : Purificatory Rites

Bṛhaspati Said:

1. Henceforth, I shall recount the various types of *Dānas* (religious gifts) and the benefits thereof. I shall also mention the pure things to be used in the Śrāddha rite and those that should be avoided.

2. It should be performed on snow-capped precipice (?) or he should also bring snow from there (?). Hence *Agnihotra* is laid down (in the scriptures) as the greatest and holiest.

3. One shall avoid Śrāddha-performance during the night. On other occasions also, since Rāhu is seen, one should quickly perform Śrāddha as soon as Rāhu is seen[1] even by spending one's entire possession.

4. He who does not perform Śrāddha at the time of eclipse becomes distressed like the cow (stuck up) in mire. He who performs it, uplifts sinners like a boat in the ocean that saves those who are drowning.

5. During the sacrifice to Viśvedevas and Saumyas, the *Havis* can contain plenty of meat. But one should avoid the horn of the rhinoceros to mitigate the malice (of Pitṛs) (?)

6-8. Formerly while Tvaṣṭṛ was being prevented by the noble-souled Lord of Devas from drinking the Soma juice meant for Indra, the consort of Śacī, it (some part or drops of Soma)

1. Cf. Bd.P. 2.3.14. 3-4, KP. II. 16.8; Brahma P. 220-51-54 Eclipses are the proper times for *Kāmya* Śrāddhas.

fell on the ground. *Syāmākas* (a variety of rice) grew up that way (from drops of Soma). They are honoured for (the propitiation of) Pitṛs. The spray (of Soma juice) sticking to (and coming out of) his nostrils fell from them (and became *ikṣu*—sugarcane). Hence sugarcanes are phlegmatic, cool, pleasing and sweet.

One should perform all the Pitṛ-rites with Śyāmāka rice and sugarcane for the fulfillment of all desires.

He who performs Āgrayaṇa i.e. the first Soma libation at the Agniṣṭoma sacrifice (or of fruits after the rainy season) (with Śyāmāka and sugarcanes) attains the fulfilment of his desires quickly.[1]

9. Syāmāka (rice), Hastināman (?), Paṭola (fruit of *Trichosanthes Diaoeca*), fruits of Bṛhatī (Brinjals) and the crest of Agastya—all are very astringent.

10-11a.[2] Such other excellent and sweet things as Nāgara (?), Dīrghamūlaka (a kind of radish) should be offered (at Śrāddha). So also tender shoots of a bamboo, *surasa*, *sarjaka* (juicy parts of the Sāla tree) and Bhūstṛṇa (*andropogen schoenanthus*).

11b-14. I shall now mention those things that should always be avoided in Śrāddha. Garlic, carrots, onions, globular radish and *Karambha* (groats or flour mixed with curds) and other articles devoid of smell and with no taste should be avoided in Śrāddha.[3] The reason is also mentioned (as follows):

Formerly in the fight between Devas and Asuras, Bali was defeated by Suras. From his wounds drops of blood gushed out and from them these articles grew up. Hence they are avoided in the Śrāddha rite.

15. The exudations mentioned in the Vedas, the salts found in arid lands are to be avoided in the Śrāddha rites. Women in their monthly course shall not take part in Śrāddhas.

---

1. For the lists of kinds of corns to be used for Śrāddha food vide MKP. 29-9-11 (quoted by Hemādri), VP. III. 16.5-6, Viṣṇu Dhs. 80.1.

2. A comparison of our text with Bd. P. 2.3.14 shows that some lines are missing here while others are mixed up.

3. Cf. Bd.P. 23,14.22-27; *Smṛti Candrikā*—Śrāddha, pp. 415-416.

16. Foul-smelling water, water having froth and foams, water from puddles, water where cows are disinclined to drink and the water stored in vessels the previous night shall not be used in Śrāddha[1].

17. The milk of ewes, deer, camel, single-horned animals, buffalo and the Camarī deer should be avoided by a wise man.[2]

18. Henceforth I shall mention the places that should be avoided assiduously. I shall also mention, by whom Śrāddha should not be seen. I shall also recount what is pure and impure in a Śrāddha.

19. With great faith one should perform a Śrāddha by means of fruits, roots and foodstuffs available in forests. Thereby he attains desirable country, heaven and liberation (from Saṁsāra) as well as fame.

20. Places full of noise-pollution and teeming with insects and a place with foul smell shall be avoided for the performance of Śrāddha.[3]

21. A place within a distance of twelve Yojanas from all the rivers joining the sea (i.e. so far from their confluence with the sea), a door at the south-east as well as the land of Triśaṅku, should be avoided.

22. The land to the north of Mahānadī and to the south of Kaikaṭa is the land of Triśaṅku. It is forbidden for the rite of Śrāddha.[4]

23. The lands of Kāraṅkara (Karkal in south Kanara Dist.), Kaliṅga, the land to the north of Sindhu and those lands wherein the practice of the pious rites of different stages of life and castes are not in vogue, should be avoided scrupulously.

24. The naked and similar (apostates and non-Vedic sects) people should not see the Śrāddha rite.[5] This is the rule.

---

1. Mk. P. 29.15-17
2. Cf. Brahma P. 220.169; VP. III. 16.11; MK.P. 32.17-19.
3. Cf. Mk.P. 29.19.
4. It is not clear why places like Orissa, Telangana or regions north of Indus were declared unfit for Śrāddha-performance. Were they beyond the pale of Brahmanism when this section of the text came to be written? Cf. Bd.P. 2.3.14.31-33.
5. As explained below (vv. 26ff), those who do not have the protective covering of the Vedas. The term includes not only non-Vedic sects like

Such Śrāddhas as are seen by these, do not reach Pitṛs or Pitāmahas.

Śaṁyu said :

25. O holy lord, O leader of important Brāhmaṇas, please recount in detail and precisely to me who ask about the naked and similar people.

26. Thus requested, *Bṛhaspati of great brilliance said to him* : The *Trayi* (the three Vedas) is remembered as the protective covering unto all living beings.

27. Those who discard it out of delusion are the naked, O excellent Brāhmaṇa. If a man forsakes that protection, he becomes supportless and is ruined.

28. If a man discards Dharma and seeks liberation (*Mokṣa*) elsewhere, his labour therein is in vain. For he has not the correct perspective.

29-30. Formerly, all the Brāhmaṇas, Kṣatriyas, Vaiśyas and Śūdras were made heretics and placed in a deformed state by Asuras who were defeated in the battle between Devas and Asuras. This is not the creation of the self-born god Brahmā*. Nor are these :

31. Those who do not practise piety come under the category of "the naked and similar people" (Nagnādayaḥ). A Brāhmaṇa who keeps matted hair without any specific aim, who shaves off his hair for nothing and who goes about naked purposelessly is also called so.

32. He who observes holy rites in vain, he who performs Japas in vain is also called "'Naked etc." So also those who blow off their homes, the hunters and those who destroy property (are considered so).

Jains and Buddhists but includes apostate Brahmins, atheists, committer of gross sins (*mahā-pātakas*). Cf. Mbh. *Anuśāsana* 91-43-44, KP. II. 21-32, 23.4-25, Viṣṇu Dh. S. 89.3ff. The underlying idea is that the sacred food for Śrāddha would get polluted by the mere sight of these fallen people.

*The line : *Pāṣaṇḍa-vaikṛtasthāne naiṣā*
sṛṣṭiḥ svayambhuvaḥ/
is obscure. Bd. P. 2.3.14.39 reads
Pāṣaṇḍā vai kṛtās tāta, teṣāṁ sṛṣṭiḥ prajāyate

(The defeated Asuras), created heretics. Their progeny are *Vṛddha-Śrāvakas* (*Dvi-Śrāddhaka* is mis-spelling), *Nirgranthas* (nude Jainas), *Śākyas* (followers of Buddha) and *Puṣṭi-kalaṁ-kaṣas* (?)

33. They are denounced as men of evil ways finding fault with every action committed. The Śrāddha performed or witnessed by these, goes to men(and not to Pitṛs).

34. The Brāhmaṇa-slayer, the ungrateful, the atheists, the defilers of the preceptor's bed, robbers and wicked men are shunned at the very sight.

35. One shall avoid all those who commit sins and particularly those who indulge in slandering Devas and the divine sages.

36-40. Whatever is witnessed by these, goes over to Asuras and Yātudhānas.

Kṛtayuga is said to be the age of Brāhmaṇas. Tretāyuga is remembered as the age of Kṣatriyas. They say that Dvāparayuga is the age of Vaiśyas and Kaliyuga is remembered as the age of Śūdras.

Pitṛs said :

The Vedas are to be worshipped in Kṛtayuga. Similarly Suras are to be worshipped in Tretāyuga. Wars are always to be worshipped in Dvāpara and the heretics in Kaliyuga.

There is no doubt in this that these spoil a Śrāddha by their mere sight : the dishonoured, the unholy, fowl, domestic pig and dog. The Śrāddha materials touched by calves and the people having pollution and chronic ailments are defiled. Cooked food should never be seen by dirty or fallen persons. If they see, it cannot be used as Havya and Kavya (offerings to gods and Pitṛs).

41. The chief materials touched by them become desecrated. Solidified ghee shall be avoided at the very outset. Sprinkling with water mixed with clay is laid down (for the consecration of materials of Śrāddha).

42. Scattering of yellow mustard and black gingelly seeds should be done. The articles should be assiduously shown to the preceptor, the sun and the fire.

43-47. The following should be avoided in Śrāddha : that which is trodden upon by people while climbing on to their seats; that which is seen by the mobile beings that are defiled; dried up and stale things; partly eaten things, defiled objects; that which is licked at the tip; that which is defiled by gravel, pebbles and hair or worm-eaten; cooked rice and other foodstuffs in which salt has been added; gingelly seeds and barley ground and powdered like oilcake; and things shaken off from garments. There are certain people who profess to be very wise by showing their opposition to the Vedas. They are to be termed 'Ayajñapatis' (non-masters of sacrifice). They are as though the dusts of Śrāddha. Forbidden vegetables mixed with curds, as well as sour gruel or fomented liquids are avoided in a Śrāddha.

48. One should avoid (the egg-plant) and all distilled liquors. The salt extracted from the ocean (water) and from the (waters of the) Mānasa (lake) (is holy).

49-50. This is extremely holy. It is visible directly. It is put into the fire and then taken in the hands and carefully pressed. It is to be applied to the forehead. This is remembered as Brahmatīrtha. All the articles for Śrāddha should be sprinkled and offered in the sacrifice.[1]

51. Ariṣṭa (soap-berry), Tumula, Bilva, Iṅguda and Śvadana should be soaked in water and (water be) sprinkled (out of them).

52. All sorts of baskets (wicker-work) should be purified according to the conventional practice. Vessels made of tooth (ivory)-bone, wood and horns should be scrubbed and scraped.

53-54. All earthen pots should be burnt again (for purification). Gems, diamonds, corals, pearls and conchs are to be purified by (brushing with) the residues of powdered yellow mustard or gingelly seeds. The same can be used to purify sheep wool and all types of hair.

55. All kinds of sheep's wool can be purified with clay and water, (but) at the beginning and end of all purificatory processes washing with water is recommended.

56. Purification of cotton cloth is effected with sacred ashes. Flowers, fruits, pins and rods should be dipped in water.

57-58. Purification of the earth (ground) is by sweeping, sprinkling and smearing (with cowdung). Outside the village the ground (earth) is purified by the wind. Purification (cleansing) of bow and arrows is effected by (brushing) it with clay. Thus the excellent modes of purification have been mentioned.

1. Verses 50-58 describe the process of purifying different articles to be used in a Śrāddha.

Henceforth I shall mention further modes of purification. Listen to it even as I recount.

59. One should evacuate the bowels early in the morning at a distance of an arrow-shot from the house in the south-western direction and within the view of the house. He should cover the head (with a cloth). He shall not touch the head with the hands.[1]

60-61. (Before evacuating) the ground should be covered with dry grass, wooden sticks or leaves, bamboo chips or broken mud pots. He should take water in a pot and hold clay also in the hand in complete silence. He should sit facing the north during the day and the south during the night.

62. He should hold the water-pot with the right hand and wash the anus with the left hand applying clay three times.

63. He should scrub the left hand with clay ten times and then each of the two hands five times.

64. Washing the feet after applying clay, he should duly perform *Ācamana* (sipping of water). He should then pour water down three times with (invocation of) the sun, fire and water.

65. A sensible man should always keep a water-pot handy. Subsidiary actions and washing of the feet shall be done by means of this pot.

66. The performance of Ācamana and divine duties shall be done by means of a second (vessel). If such actions are performed with a defiled hand, one should observe fast for three nights.

67. In protracted cases of default, the rite of Kṛcchra is prescribed for expiation. After touching a dog or a Cāṇḍāla one should perform Taptakṛcchra rite.

68. If human bones are touched, fasting is the purification (for it). It is prescribed that if (the bones are) touched delibera-

1. After dealing with the purification of things or materials for Śrāddha, the author deals with the purification of the man performing the Śrāddha in vv. 59 to the end of the Chapter. The Purāṇa-writers (in fact the whole tribe of writers on Dharma-Śāstra in the mediaeval period) appear to have been so much obsessed with 'purity-psychosis' that they lost sight of the social necessity of assimilating foreigners or backward people in Hinduism and prohibited their own followers from going beyond the contracting geographical limits of Brahmanism (vide vv. 69-71).

tely, the fast is to be observed for three nights, and for one night, if touched unintentionally.

69-71. By going to unholy places, one acquires all sorts of sins. These unholy places are—Kāraskaras, Pulindas, Āndhras, Śabaras and others, the land of Bhūtilaya (if one drinks water there), the land of Yugandhara, up to the northen borderlands of Sindhu, the land of Divyantaraśata, sinful countries occupied by sinners and lands devoid of good men such as Brāhmaṇas who have mastered the Vedas.

72-73. Clarity of mind, fire, timely whitewashing—these things indicate purity. But one is always ignorant. If one makes default in the purificatory rites—except out of ignorance, undoubtedly the benefit goes to Piśācas and Yātudhānas.

74-75. One who has no faith in purificatory rites is born among Mlecchas. Those who do not perform Yajñas and sinners are born among the lower strata of animals. A man gets released from sins through purificatory rites and attains heaven. Devas indeed desire purity. This has been declared by Devas themselves.

76. Suras always forsake the hideous and the unclean. Men of auspicious rites perform three types of purificatory rites justifiably.

77-78. *Pitṛs* delighted with them for their pure rites, increase the Yogic power and bestow all cherished things available in the three worlds, on these people, viz. a man who reveres Brāhmaṇas, one who receives guests, an intelligent man who adheres to purity, one devotedly attached to parents, one who possesses self-control and one who is sympathetic, O Brāhmaṇas.

CHAPTER SEVENTEEN

The Test for Eligibity of a Brāhmaṇa (for Śrāddha Invitation)

The Sages said :

1. O intelligent Sūta, the *Śrāddhakalpa* has been recounted by you. The *Śrāddhakalpa* glorified by sages, has been heard by us.

2. Its extensive details have been particularly narrated. O extremely intelligent one, please mention the remaining topics too, according to the opinion of that sage.

Sūta said :

3. O blessed Brāhmaṇas, I shall recount the opinion of that sage in detail, in regard to *Śrāddha*. Listen to it from me.

4. The Śrāddha rite as well as the mode of its performance have been previously mentioned by me. I shall also mention what remains in the proper order as regards the Brāhmaṇas.

5. It is not that Brāhmaṇas should always be (subjected to) tests and investigation. But in regard to rites pertaining to gods and Pitṛs (employment of) tests has been laid down in the Śruti.[1]

6. One shall scrupulously avoid that person in whom defects are seen or who is shunned by good men or who, through contacts or staying together, is known to be wicked.

7-8. A sensible man should always test a Brāhmaṇa who is not known before, at the time of Śrāddha.[2]

---

1. Since the days of Gṛhya Sūtras, there was insistence on the antecedents, learning, character of the invitees (Brāhmaṇas) for rites pertaining to Devas and Pitṛs (Āśvalāyana G.S. IV.7.2, Baudhāyana G.S. II. 8.2-3, II 10.5-6). To these Smṛtis and Purāṇas added many more, but heredity, personality, Vedic learning, character remained the main considerations in the case of such invitees (cf. Mt.P. 16.8-10, NP.I, 28.6-10, KP. II. 21 and *Smṛti Candrikā*: *Śrāddha Kāṇḍa*—pp. 389-394). Self-control was the *sine-qua-non* of an invitee. Manu (II.118) declares, 'A Brāhmaṇa who knows only the *Gāyatrī Mantra* but is self-controlled, is preferable to a Brāhmaṇa who knows the three Vedas, but lacks in self-control.

2. Cf. Viṣṇu Dh.S. 82-1-2.

Indeed Siddhas roam over this earth in the guise of Brāhmaṇas. Hence one should approach the in-coming guests with palms joined in reverence. He should worship him offering water for washing the feet, oil for massage and food for eating.

9-10. Devas and the masters of Yoga roam about the ocean-girt earth in various guises, virtuously protecting the subjects. A man should worship and offer a Brāhmaṇa guest different types of food and vegetable dishes and fruits as well.[1]

11. It is heard that one attains the fruit of Agniṣṭoma (sacrifice) by offering milk (or water) to a guest.[2] By offering ghee he attains splendid vision as well as the fruit of a yajña of sixteen-day duration. By offering honey, he attains the fruit of *Atirātra* sacrifice.

12. A devout person who feeds Brāhmaṇas faithfully, offering them all desired objects, obtains the fruit thereof. He who offers all his possessions to all guests and Brāhmaṇas enjoys for ever the fruit of *Sarvamedha* sacrifice.

13. He who slights a guest after his coming at the time of Śrāddha or in a rite for Devas, is shunned by Devas in the manner a Hotṛ disregards another man's wealth.

14. For the purpose of blessing the worlds Devas, Pitṛs and Fire-god enter those Brāhmaṇas and take food.

15. If they are not worshipped, they burn; if they are worshipped, they grant all desires. Hence one should always worship guests by offering one's entire possession.

16. A forest-dweller, a householder, a person who visits the house, children, distressed persons and an ascetic—all there are to be known as *Atithis* (guests).

17. An *Abhyāgata* is the guest who begs for something. An *Atithi* will not beg. An *Atithi* is the most excellent because he

---

1. Verses 8-10 mean that an *atithi* (an uninvited guest)—a stranger—coming for food at the time of Śraddha is exempt from the qualifications on the specious ground that the stranger might be a *siddha* or a god in disguise.

2. Such cheap promises of getting the fruits of sacrifices like Agniṣṭoma or Atirātra by offering ordinary things like milk or ghee to Brāhmaṇas have adversely affected the Vedic institution of sacrifice. For the distinction between *Atithi* and *Abhyāgata* vide vv. 16-18 below.

has no *Tithi* (fixed date). This is said to be the etymological meaning of *Atithi.*

18. A real guest is neither terrible nor of a mixed caste, neither devoid of learning nor a very learned specialist, neither has he too many children nor is he servile. He is of good conduct.

19. A person who wishes (the fruit of) the performance of a Yajña should hospitably receive and give (food etc.) to a guest who has wandered a lot, is thirsty, tired and extremely hungry.

20-22a. By climbing on to Bhṛgutuṅga, by visiting (and taking holy dip in) the holy river Sarasvatī, the holy river-goddess Gaṅgā, Mahānadī, and other rivers originating from Himavān and those worshipped by sages, as well as lakes and holy centres, one becomes free from sins and is honoured in heaven.

22b-23. It is said that there is pollution due to death for ten nights particularly for a Brāhmaṇa. It is prescribed that a Kṣatriya has twelve days' pollution. A Vaiśya has pollution for half a month and a Śūdra becomes pure after a month.[1]

24-25. A woman in menses in all the castes becomes pure in three nights. It is laid down that by touching a woman in her menses, a woman lying-in-chamber, a dog, a Cāṇḍāla, a nudist like a Digambara Jaina and similar people and those who have borne a dead body, one gets polluted. He must take bath along with his clothes and smear clay twelve times on himself. Then he becomes pure.

26-27. The same purificatory rite should be followed in the case of sexual intercourse. Clay is to be applied nine times. After washing hands with clay (and water), a person shall perform the purificatory rite. After washing the hands with water and taking bath, a sensible man shall apply clay to the private parts twice.

28. This is the mode of purification to be observed by all the castes for ever. One should smear hands and feet three times and sprinkle them with water.

29. This is the purificatory rite for forest-dwellers

1. Verses 226-30 deal with personal purification

(*Vānaprasthas*). Henceforth I shall mention the procedure for village-dwellers (i.e. for householders). Clay is applied to the hands three times and three times to the feet.

30. Clay shall be applied fifteen times to the hands and other unclean parts. Clay shall be applied to the uncleaned parts and it shall be washed with water.

31. After tying a cloth round the neck or the head, if anyone walks on foot along the street, he shall wash the feet. Without washing the feet, even if he performs Ācamana, he shall be unclean.

32. After washing the feet and setting the waterpot down, he should perform Ācamana and then sprinkle it with water. The materials of Śrāddha etc. shall be sprinkled again.

33. Sprinkling is recommended on flowers etc., grass and *Havis*. Objects brought by others should be placed down and sprinkled with water.

34. In a Śrāddha and rites for Devas only, those articles that are sprinkled with water should be used. Whatever is brought to the altar should be brought at the northern end and taken away from the southern end.

35. If the procedure is altered in the rites pertaining to Devas or Pitṛs, it (the rite) becomes fruitless. With the right hand, one should touch the southern altar*.

36a It is auspicious to scatter ritualistically the offering to Devas and Pitṛs with both the hands.

36b. (*Ācamana* is the purificatory rite in the following cases:)

When one is agitated or enraged; after getting up from sleep; after urination and evacuation of bowels;

37-42. when one spits; after taking food; when feet are not washed; after conversing with a person excommunicated (by others); after working in unclean places (?); in all doubtful acts such as when the tuft of hair is untied and/or one is without the sacred thread; when the lips touch the teeth; when one

---

*The text reads: *dakṣiṇena tu hastena dakṣiṇām vedam ālikhet* out of which the last three words are confusing. Bd. P. 2.3.14.99 reads *dakṣiṇām vedim ālabhet* 'should touch the southern altar' which is more appropriate and hence accepted here.

sees Cāṇḍālas; after touching things clinging to the teeth with the tongue;snapping the fingers loudly; when seeing while bowing down etc. He who is in the midst of a sinful action, but out of delusion performs Ācamana is also unclean. He should then squat in a clean place and bow down facing the north or the east. After washing the hands and feet, he should perform Ācamana between the knees (keeping hands on laps ?). He should sip the still water thrice with concentration and purity of mind.

43. He should perform *Mārjana* (cleansing with water) twice and then *Abhyukṣaṇa* (sprinkling with water) once over the sense organs, head, hands and feet as well.

44-49. Anything not considered properly, shall be sprinkled with water. In this manner his Ācamana, Vedas (Vedic Study) Yajñas, penance, charitable gifts and vow of celibacy become fruitful. If an atheist performs holy rites without performing Ācamana out of delusion, all those rites shall undoubtedly be futile. All these following should be known pure—that which is pure in words, that which is cleaned, that which is undefiled and that which is not censured. The opposite of these is impure. A hungry Brāhmaṇa should never be told—"There is nothing". If anything is given to him after duly honouring him, it is called a sacrifice without erecting a sacrificial post. During Śrāddhas, an indigent but non-begging, solitary and shy Brāhmaṇa should always be fed with food neither over-cooked nor watery. He who offers food to the low castes only, is a wicked soul, a Brāhmaṇa-slayer.

50-51. Even if he takes a hundred births, he does not become free from that sin. A Brāhmaṇa who feeds the nobler and less dignified Brāhmaṇas in the same row, whether urged by others or not, incurs sin immediately. Even his merit resulting from digging wells and tanks becomes destroyed.

52-53. In a festival, an ascetic is the leader of all Brāhmaṇas.[1] An excellent Brāhmaṇa who reads all the Vedas with Itihāsa constituting their fifth (Veda), should be kept next

1. Verses 52-54 state the precedence to be given to Brāhmaṇas according to their learning, in the seating arrangement of Brāhmaṇas to be fed. It is noteworthy that a recluse or a Yogī gets the first place of honour.

to him by one who knows. A Brāhmaṇa who studies three Vedas comes next to him. One (a student) of two Vedas comes next to him.

54. Then a man of a single Veda and after him comes a person who studies the Nyāya System. For the purity of the row, I am mentioning them. Understand. I shall mention those who sanctify the row (?).

55-58. Those who are mentioned before, are mentioned in their order. The *Paṅktipāvanas*[1] (those who sanctify the row of diners) are the following:—Ṣaḍaṅgī (a person who has learnt all the six ancillary subjects of the Veda), Vinayī (the disciplined one), Yogin, *Sarvatantrasvatantra* (he who has mastered all systems of philosophy) and *Yāyāvara* (a wandering mendicant saint). All these five should be known as *Paṅktipāvanas*. He who has mastered completely one of the eighteen lores, he who fulfills his duty duly—all of them are also so. The *Triṇāciketas*[2] (a Brāhmaṇa who learns the three Vidyās of Naciketas), the *Traividya* (he who has mastered three Vidyas), the Brāhmaṇa who learns Dharmaśāstras, the Brāhmaṇa who has mastered the Bārhaspatya scripture—all these Brāhmaṇas are said to be those who sanctify the row.

59. If a Brāhmaṇa invited in a Śrāddha indulges in sexual intercourse with a woman, the Pitṛs lie down in his semen virile for the period of that month (?)

---

1. It was believed that persons of specially high character, merit, learning etc. purify excommunicated or degenerate members of the society by associating with them, by sitting in their row for dining or even by their beneficent look (v 91 below). The belief was probably current before the time of Dharma Sūtras: *vide* Āpartaṁba Dh. S.II. 7.17-22. Curiously enough, Gautama (15.28), Baudhāyana Dh.S. II. 8.2, Manu III. 185-186, Yājñavalkya Smṛti (I. 219) use the same words about these sanctifiers of diners (*Paṅktipāvanas*). We get a long list of such sanctifiers in Mbh. *Anuśāsana* 90.25-31, Mt.P. 16.7-23, KP. II.21-1-14. Bd.P. 2.3.15.28-32. Our text practically repeats the same lines.

2. *Trināciketa* is alternately explained as :

(i) A person who knows the *Naciketa* fire.

(ii) A person who has thrice kindled the *Naciketa* fire.

(iii) One who has studied the *Anuvāka* called *Virajas* (Tait. Br. III. 11.7-8) which describes the Nācikata fire and the story of Naciketas.

60. If the performer of a Śrāddha or he who takes food in a Śrāddha, indulges in sexual intercourse, undoubtedly the Pitṛs are stationed in his semen virile that month.

61-62. Hence a *Dāna* (religious gift) is to be made to the guest and a Brahmacārin (celibate person) is to be fed. The *Dāna* is to be made to one engrossed in meditation and having sympathetic feelings. In the Śrāddha rite, a righteous ascetic or a Vālakhilya (a mendicant who does not hoard anything) should be fed. A *Vānaprastha* (forest-dweller) and an *Upakurvāṇa* (Brahmacārin who completes his studies and pays his teacher and is about to be a householder) is propitiated by mere worship.

63. If a householder is fed, Viśvedevas are worshipped. By worshipping a Vānaprastha, sages are worshipped. By worshipping Vālakhilyas, Purandara (i.e. Indra) is worshipped.

64. In worshipping ascetics, Brahmā himself is worshipped. These Āśramas are holy. There are five Anāśramas through deceitfulness (?)

65. Four Āśramas (i. e. people in the four stages of life) are to be worshipped in the rites of Devas and Pitṛs. A Śrāddha should never be offered to those who are outside the four stages of life.

66. Even if he stays hungry, let him stay so outside the four stages of life. The non-ascetic and the salvationist—both of them are the defilers of the row.[1]

---

1. Verses 66-83 give a list of persons who are defilers of the row of diners (*Paṅkti-dūṣakas*). These lines are common to Smṛtis and other Purāṇas such as Manu III. 151-166, Yājñavalkya I. 222-224, Bṛhad Yama Smṛ. III. 34-38, Mbh. *Anuśāsana* 90.6-11, Mt.P. 16.14-17, BM.P. 220.127-135, NP. I. 30-4, KP. II. 21.27-46 to mention a few. Apart from the textual similarity, the lists are interesting from a sociological point of view. They indicate what class of persons, vocations, ways of life were disrespected by the elites of those times. Sects which insist on long fasts (e.g. Jainas), Sāṅkhyas (who were originally atheists), non-Brāhmaṇical mendicants like Bauddhas, Jainas, persons not following the vocations of their castes, are regarded as unworthy of being invited to a Śrāddha or receiving religious gifts (*dāna*).

67. Those who shave off their hair in vain, those who wear matted hair, those who wear all sorts of robes, those who are devoid of mercy, those who break all codes of good conduct and those who are indiscriminate in eating—are to be avoided.

68. In the matter of *Havya* and *Kavya*, one shall avoid Kārukas (a Śaiva sect) and men of no disciplined conduct of life, men ostracised from the Vedic Society, musicians and actors (who imitate deities).

69-70. A person who has social and other contacts with these, attains black complexion (taint). He who dines with Śūdras—all these are defilers of the row (of diners).

71. Killing (of animals etc.), destruction with force, agriculture, trading activities, animal husbandry, secret service to a person other than the preceptor—these should not be followed by a Brāhmaṇa.

72. Those who are real Brāhmaṇas, pursue knowledge and meditation. Even if they are born as Brāhmaṇas, those who have false conceptions are of evil conduct.

73. The preachers of wrong/heretic doctrines should be avoided. So also the arrogant, the scandal-monger, and people defiled by minor sins and great sins should be avoided.

74-75. Those who make use of Vedas as a means of employment out of greed and delusion or for profit are the sellers of Vedas. They are to be avoided in the Śrāddha rite.

Study of Vedas is not a profession. He who makes it a profession is a sinner. The partaker is deprived of the fruit of Vedic study. The donor is deprived of the fruit of charity.

76. A person hired to teach the Vedas and one who is taught by such a person—both of them do not deserve invitation to a Śrāddha as the sellers and buyers of the Vedas.

77. Those (Brāhmaṇas) who buy and sell for the purpose of livelihood are despicable ones. This is the profession of a Vaiśya but a sin unto Brāhmaṇas.

78. They say that he who depends for his livelihood upon the Vedas and he who depends upon those who know Vedas for livelihood do not deserve invitation to a Śrāddha. The husband of one's daughter also shall not be invited.

79. He who goes unto his wife in vain (i.e. an issueless person) and he who performs Yajña in vain—both of these do not deserve an (invitation to) a Śrāddha. A Brāhmaṇa (who is) an atheist also shall not be invited.

80. He who cooks food for himself only and he who does not offer anything to Devas and guests—both of them are fallen and they are Brahmarākṣasas. They do not deserve (invitation to) a Śrāddha.

81. Those whose wives eagerly await the nights and those who run after other men's wives, as well as those who are mad after wealth and love should not be invited to a Śrāddha.

82. Those who are opposed to the discipline and the duties of the four castes and stages of life, a thief and he who indiscriminately performs Yajña for everyone—all these are defilers of the row in the rite of Śrāddha.

83. Pitṛs do not partake of their share in the Śrāddha if the invited Brāhmaṇa eats like a boar, or eats off his palm or eats with his left hand.

84. The leavings of the Śrāddha food should not be given to women or a Śūdra unless he is an attendant. If anyone gives out of passion or delusion, it never reaches Pitṛs.

85. Hence in a Śrāddha rite, the leavings of food should never be given except curds and ghee and that too to a disciple and a son; not otherwise.

86. Only that which is not left over should be given, such as food particularly. Pitṛs are propitiated with flowers, roots and fruits too as with food.

87. The foodstuffs served are sanctified as long as they are warm. Pitṛs partake of the food as long as the invited Brāhmaṇas take their food, with control over their speech.

88. Charitable gifts, acceptance of gifts, Homa, taking food and oblations must be made with the thumb (touching them) lest they should go to Asuras.

89. All these rites and particularly the rite of gifting away, are thus performed. The rite of Ācamana is performed with the hands within the knees.

90. One should avoid persons with shaven heads, matted hair, and ochre-coloured robes, at the time of Śrāddha rite.

One should assiduously offer Śrāddha to those who wear tufts and to the *Tridaṇḍin* type of ascetics.

91. Those who are steadfast in their holy rites, those who seek knowledge and are engaged in meditations and the noble-souled devotees of Devas do sanctify (others) by their mere sight.

92. The whole of the three worlds is pervaded or ever by the masters of Yoga. Hence they (can) observe whatever there is in the universe.

93-94. The noble souls keep both the manifest and the un-manifest under their control. They control even that which is greater than all. Truth and falsehood have been perceived by them. *Sat*, *Asat* have been seen by them. All knowable things, absolution etc. are seen by the noble souls. Hence one who is devoted to them attains everything auspicious.

95. He who knows the *Ṛks* knows the Vedas. He who knows the Yajur Mantras knows Yajña. He who knows Sāman Mantras knows Brahman. He who knows Mānasa (? mind) knows everything.

CHAPTER EIGHTEEN

Benefit Derived from Charitable Gifts

Bṛhaspati said:

1. Henceforth I shall recount the various types of religious gifts and the benefits thereof.[1] A religious gift enables all living beings to cross (the ocean of worldly existence). It is the pleasing pathway unto heaven.

---

1. Though ancient works on Dharma Śāstra insist upon avoidance of lavishness in *Śrāddha*, later Purāṇas encourage profuse expenditure on Śrāddha, e.g. Pd. P. *Sṛṣṭi-Khaṇḍa* 9.179-181, Varāha P. 13.50-51, VP. III. 14.22-23. *Pitṛs* are reported to have two Gāthās expressing their desire to have a descendant who would bestow on Brāhmaṇas (for the benefit of Pitṛs) jewels, clothes, land, costly vehicles. This text encourages

2. That which is the most excellent in the world, that which is conducive to the attainment of heaven, nay, everything that is pleasing to oneself, must be offered to Pitṛs by one who seeks one's own eternal salvation.

3. A person who offers cooked rice, derives the benefit of attaining a divine golden chariot dazzling like the sun and filled with divine Apsaras-s.

4. He who gifts a cloth fresh from the loom at the time of the Śrāddha rite attains longevity, ample wealth, beauty and a son.

5. The knower of Dharmas who gives a sacred thread at the time of Śrāddha and offers water to all Brāhmaṇas attains the fruit of Brahmadāna (the gift of Vedic learning).

6. If anyone offers a good waterpot at the time of Śrāddhas to the Brāhmaṇas, a cow exuding honey and milk approaches the donor.

7. He who gives a circular waterpot at the time of Śrāddha obtains a milk-yielding divine cow that can be milked for whatever he wishes.

8. If anyone gives a complete bed-equipment decorated with garlands of flowers, it becomes a palace and follows him as he goes (to heaven).

9. By giving a house full of gems, furnished with bed, seats and food, at the time of Śrāddha to ascetics, one rejoices in heaven.

10-14. He obtains pearls, *lapis lazuli*, garments, varieties of precious stones, divine vehicles, hundred thousands and trillions in number and a divine aerial chariot that dazzles like a great blazing fire, that has the lustre of the moon and the sun and that is furnished with jewels according to one's desire. The aerial chariot has the speed of the mind and can go anywhere as per his pleasure. It is surrounded by Apsaras-s. He remains at the head of the aerial chariot eulogised by eveyone all round. The Gandharva-s and Apsaras-s sprinkle him with divine scents and showers of flowers. They sing and play on the instruments.

---

lavish gifts in Śrāddha. The reward promised is happiness in heaven. There is little rational co-relation between religious gift (dāna) and the reward obtained.

Youthful and prominent maidens accompanied by groups of Apsaras-s, wake him up in sweet pleasing voices.

15. By the gifts of a thousand horses, a hundred chariots and a thousand elephants, a man lives with a Yoginī.

16. He who offers water (and) lamp to Pitṛs and Yogins, attains the fruit of the gift of thousands of gold coins.

17. No other gift is more excellent than the gift of life. Hence, by all means protection to life should be given.

18. Non-violence is holier than all the Devas. It bestows everything. Learned men say that the gift of life is the noblest unto all living beings.

19. At the time of Śrāddha, one should give golden vessels having good characteristics. Sweet (divine) juices and beverages, good foodstuffs and good fortune approach him.

20. One shall give beautiful metallic vessel while feeding in Śrāddha. He will become a recipient of the objects of cherished desires and of beauty and wealth.

21. In the Śrāddha rite, one should give a silver or gold vessel. By giving it, the donor gets ample virtue (as reward).

22. He who makes a gift of a cow that has calved but once, along with a milking pot, at the time of a Śrāddha, obtains several cows and the nourishment of the cows.

23-26a. At the time of winter, one shall offer fire and plenty of wood. He who gives fuel to Brāhmaṇas at the onset of winter, becomes always victorious in battle. He shines with glory. One should honour Brāhmaṇas and offer fragrant garlands and sweet scents as well as vessels. Great rivers flowing with fragrant scents and all sorts of happiness approach the donor. So also youthful maidens of pleasing manners (approach him).

26b. Beautiful beds and seats, grounds and vehicles (are to be given).

27-28. He who gives the above-mentioned articles at a Śrāddha, attains the benefit of a horse-sacrifice. In ordinary Śrāddhas or at the time of Darśa Śrāddha, one should give to the Brāhmaṇas of good qualities, vessels full of ghee with very great respect. He shall attain good memory and fine intellect.

29. He obtains the benefit of many cows yielding potfuls

of milk. In this world, he rejoices with chariots and good horses.

30. By giving the thing wished for, at the time of Śrāddha, one gets the benefit of the sacrifice called Puṇḍarīka. By giving a beautiful residential place, one attains the fruit of Rājasūya sacrifice.

31-33. By giving a forest full of flowers and fruits, one obtains sweet smelling substances. By giving wells, parks, tanks, fields, cowsheds and houses, one rejoices in heaven as long as the moon and the stars stay. By giving beds and bedsheets embellished with jewels, one attains endless heavenly pleasure. Pitṛs are pleased with him. He is worshipped (honoured) by kings. He flourishes with wealth and grain.

34-35. Woollen and silk garments, excellent blankets, deer-skin, gold brocade, coloured cloth and wool—these should be given to Brāhmaṇas after duly feeding them. A person who has faith then gets the benefit of a hundred Vājapeya Yajñas.[1]

36. Many beautiful women, sons, servants and attendants, nay all living beings, become submissive to him in this world. He becomes free from all ailments.

37. He who gives silk, woven silk, cotton and velvet cloth, in Śrāddhas obtains the fulfilment of all his cherished desires.

38. He dispels all inglorious things and misfortunes immediately like the darkness at the time of sunrise. He shines on an aerial chariot like the moon among stars.

39. A garment is praised by all Devas; garment belongs to all the deities. In the absence af cloth, no holy rite—neither Yajñas nor (study of) Vedas nor penances, can be performed.

40. Hence clothes should be given at the time of Śrāddha particularly. He obtains all those things—Yajñas, the Vedas and the penances.

---

1. The promise of the fruit of sacrifices (which require a lot of trouble and expenditure) for *dāna* must have resulted as a disincentive for performance of sacrifice and these Brahmanical advocates of such cheap and easy ways of gaining sacrificial merits get the dubious credit of adversely affecting the Vedic institution of Sacrifice.

41. He who always gives them during Śrāddhas with faith and purity, obtains all his desires and all realms.

42-43. He obtains the fruit of a sacrifice richly equipped with all desirable things. He who gives different kinds of edibles, grains, flour mixed with curds, flour cakes, ghee and sugar, milk, milk puddings, Kṛśaras[1] and Madhuparka and pies fried in ghee, obtains the fruit of Agniṣṭoma.

44. Pitṛs are eager for curds and other milk products and different kinds of edibles and cooked rice during the rainy season and at the time when the constellation Maghā is ascendant.

45. One shall feed Brāhmaṇas with ghee. A little of ghee must be poured on the ground. By gifting elephants in Gayā, one can be free from all worries about Śrāddha.

46. By giving cooked rice, milk pudding, ghee, honey, fruits and roots as well as different types of food, one rejoices here and after death.

47. Beaten rice mixed with sugar and milk is always of everlasting benefit. If *Masūrā dāl* and Kṛśara (rice cooked with spices and pulses) are offered, Pitṛs will be pleased for a year.

48. Fried grain-powder, fried rice, pies, cooked horse-gram dishes—all mixed with curds—He who gives all these in Śrāddha obtains the treasure of Kubera.

49. He who assiduously gives fresh vegetables in Śrāddhas after duly honouring the guests, attains all enjoyments. He is revered when he goes to heaven.

50. The man who offers the most excellent foods and edibles, beverages, lambatives and juicy things, becomes the most excellent of all.

51. The flesh of the rhinoceros is the best *Havis* in the rites for Viśvedevas and Soma. But the best horn of the rhinoceros should be avoided to mitigate the malice (of deities) ?

52. The devotee, with palms joined in reverence, should offer the best seat to the guests while feeding. He shall then attain the excellent fruit of all the rites and Yajñas.

1. A dish consisting of sesamum and grain (mixture of rice peas with a few spices)—MW, p. 308.

53. Well-cooked food should be served hot and quick to the hungry. It should not be over-cooked. After honouring him assiduously vegetable dishes soaked in ghee should be offered devotedly.

54. The person who offers food attains an aerial chariot resembling the mid-day sun and fitted with swans for three crores of Kalpas (crores of maidens in Bd. P.).

55. There is nothing here greater than the gift of food and they are sustained by it without any doubt.

56. There is no gift nobler than the gift of life. The set of the three worlds lives by means of food. That is the fruit of offering cooked rice.

57. All the worlds are founded (dependent) on food. It is the fruit of the gift of the worlds. Food is Prajāpati himself. All these worlds are pervaded by it. Hence a gift on par with that of food has never been before nor will there be any ever in future.

58. A man devoted to Pitṛs immediately attains all the jewels, vehicles and women on the earth.

59. One should with palms joined in reverence, always offer shelter to the guests. They are the Devas awaiting in thousands, for the divine hospitality.

60. He who makes all gifts (mentioned before) shall be the sole emperor on the earth. He shall become happy even if he makes three, two or even one of those gifts.

61. Making gifts is the greatest virtue (*Dharma*). It is honourd and revered by good men. The Lordship of the three worlds is to be attained only through *Dāna*.

62. A king regains his kingdom; a poor man gets excellent wealth; a man about to die, attains longevity. Whatever a man devoted to Pitṛs desires in his mind, will be granted by his Pitṛs.

CHAPTER NINETEEN

The Benefit of Śrāddha Performance on Various Tithis

Bṛhaspati said :

1. Henceforth I shall describe the various types of *Śrāddha*[1] such as *Ajasra* or *Nitya* (daily, regular), *Naimittika* (occasional, conditional) and *Kāmya* (performed with some desired object in view) and the mode of worship (in them).

2. There are three sets of *Aṣṭakās*[2] (the 7th, 8th and 9th days of the dark half of a month) that bring about marriage, birth of a son and acquisition of wealth. The dark half of a month is the most excellent. The first *Aṣṭakā* is called Citrī.

3-4. The second *Aṣṭakā*, shall be Prājāpatyā (with Prajāpati as its deity) and the third one (is) Vaiśvadevikī. The first *Aṣṭakā* shall always be performed with flour cakes. The second should always be performed with meat. The third *Aṣṭakā* shall be performed with greens and vegetables. This is the injunction regarding the articles (for *Śrāddha*). The *Anvaṣṭakā* (the ninth day in the dark half of Pauṣa, Māgha and Phālguna) of the *Pitṛs* is also laid down permanently.

5. If there happens to be a fourth *Aṣṭakā*, a learned person should perform a special *Śrāddha* therein, even by spending his entire possession.

---

1. The '*Ajasra*' or '*Nitya*' Śrāddha must be performed everyday, e.g. *Pitṛ-yajña* in daily *Pañcamahāyajñas*. Śrāddha to be performed on an occasion which is uncertain (e.g. the birth of a son) is *Naimittika*. Śrāddha done with a desire for a fruit or reward (e.g. progeny) is *Kāmya*.

2. The word '*Aṣṭakā*' is formed from 'aṣṭan'. But according to Vārtika 9 on Pāṇini VII. 3.45, it means 'a rite with Pitṛs as deities'. *Āśvalāyana Gr. S.* II. 4-1 informs that the 8th day in the dark halves of seasons Hemanta and Śiśira are Aṣṭakās. As a season consists of two months there are (and should be) four *Aṣṭakās*. But most other Gṛhya Sūtras differ and regard the 8th day in the dark halves of Mārgaśirṣa, Pauṣa and Māgha as Aṣṭakā days. This Purāṇa does not follow Āśvalāyana. Though the above-mentioned Vārtika regards *Pitṛs* as the deities on these days, our Purāṇa regards the first Aṣṭakā as Citrī (Aindrī ? as in Bd.P.), the second has Prajāpati and the third has Viśvedevas as the deities and *Pitṛs* are conspicuous by their non-mention.

6. He (the performer of a *Śrāddha*) shall always be happy both here and hereafter. The worshippers shall attain progress and the non-believers, downfall.

7. Like cows approaching a water-trough, all these Pitṛs and gods approach the man (who performs a *Śrāddha*)—*Pitṛs* during the *Parvan* days and deities on different Tithis.

8. Let them not return without being worshipped during *Aṣṭakās*. The world (worldly life) will be in vain in regard to him (who does not worship). Even what is obtained by him, perishes.

9-10. Those who offer worship attain Devas. Those who do not offer are reborn as lower animals. A person who performs a *Śrāddha* on the Full Moon day obtains progeny, nourishment, memory, intellect, sons and prosperity.[1] He enjoys to the full. (The *Śrāddha* performed on) *Pratipad* (the first day of a fortnight) is conducive to the acquisition of wealth. What he has acquired does not perish.

11. He who performs a *Śrāddha* on the second day of the lunar fortnight, becomes the lord of bipeds. The third day (is to be selected for *Śrāddha*) by one who seeks excellent things, (for) *Tṛtiyā* (third day) is destructive of sins.

---

1. Verses 10-19 state the benefit accruing from performance of Śrāddha on different *Tithis* from the 1st to the 15th. *Āpastamba Dh. S.* II. 7.16-22, Mbh. *Anuśāsana* 87, Bd. P. 2.3.9-20, BM. P. 220.15-21, KP.II. 20.17.22 state the reward a man gets for performance of *Śrāddha* on these *Tithis*. But there is difference of opinion among these about the benefits. For example, see the comparative table of rewards of Śrāddha performance on various *Tithis*.

The Tithi	*Reward as per our Text*	*Reward as per K.P. II.* 20
1.	Acquisition of wealth	Auspicious sons
2.	Lordship over bipeds	Begets daughters
3.	Destroys sins	Gets animals
4.	Discovers weak points of his enemies	Gets small animals and things
5.	Attains prosperity and glory	Begets splendid sons
6.	Reverence from Brāhmaṇas	Blessed with lustre and good cultivation

The list need not be extended.

12. He who performs a *Śrāddha* on *Caturthī* (fourth day) finds the weak points of his enemies. A performer of a *Śrāddha* on the fifth day attains great prosperity and glory.

13-14. Brāhmaṇas revere him who performs a *Śrāddha* on the sixth day. The man who performs a *Śrāddha* on the seventh day regularly attains the fruit of *Mahāsatra* (great Soma sacrifice). He becomes the lord of Gaṇas (followers of Śiva). The man who performs a *Śrāddha* on the eighth day attains complete prosperity.

15. He who performs a *Śrāddha* on the ninth day, attains prosperity and a beloved wife. He who performs a *Śrāddha* on the tenth day, attains the glory of Brahman-hood.

16. He shall attain (mastery over) all the Vedas and the destruction of sins. The *Dāna* (religious gift) offered on the eleventh day yields prosperity for ever.

17. They say that he who performs a *Śrāddha* on the twelfth day acquires wealth, a kingdom and becomes victorious. He who performs a *Śrāddha* on the thirteenth day attains progeny, intellect, cattle, wisdom, freedom, excellent nourishment, long life and prosperity.

18. One shall offer a *Śrāddha* on the fourteenth day to those young men of the house who have met premature death and to those who have been killed by weapons.

19. With purity one should always offer a *Śrāddha* on the New Moon day to those children unfavourably born (e.g. a son after three daughters or a daughter after three sons) as well as to twin children.

20. One who regularly performs a *Śrāddha* attains all cherished desires and infinite heavenly pleasures. One shall always perform on the New Moon day the rituals and those great rites that involve extraction of Soma Juice (or that are conducive to the development of the Moon (?))

21. Thus developed, the Moon sustains the three worlds, being regularly eulogised by Siddhas, Cāraṇas and Gandharvas.

22. (The Moon) is eulogised by thousands of Apsaras-s dancing, singing and playing on instruments, by means of eulogies, flowers of great beauty and all the requisites for the fulfilment of desires.

23. Devas and Gandharvas and the groups of Siddhas eulogise that devotee of the *Pitṛs*, steady in his holy rites. They serve him by means of aerial chariots for sport.

24. The devotee of Pitṛs shall attain all cherished desires on the *Amāvāsyā* (New Moon) day, for *Pitṛs* are worshipped by him directly always.

25. The constellation Maghā has *Pitṛs* for its deities Hence a *Śrāddha* on that day yields everlasting benefit. The wise perform the rites for *Pitṛs* particularly on that day.

26. Hence the *Pitṛs* always desire Maghā. Those who are devoted to *Pitṛs* and deities attain the greatest goal.

CHAPTER TWENTY

Benefit of Śrāddha Performance under Different Constellations.[1]

Bṛhaspati said:

1. Listen to a detailed account of all those *Śrāddhas* which Yama mentioned to Śaśabindu. They are to be performed under different constellations severally.[2]

2. He who maintains the sacrificial fires for ever and performs a *Śrāddha* (when the Moon is) in conjuction with the Kṛttikā constellation, becomes free from worries and ailments along with his children.

3. A person desirous of children should perform a *Śrāddha* under Rohiṇī. By performing a *Śrāddha* under the Saumya (Mṛga-

1. This chapter is incorporated from Mbh. *Anuśāsana* 89.

2. Viṣṇu Dh.S. (78.8-15) mentions the rewards obtained by performing *śrāddha* under different constellations from Kṛttikā to Bharaṇī. Yājñavalkya I. 265-268, MK.P. 30.8-16, BM.P. 220.33-42, KP.II. 20.9-15, Bd.P. 2.3.18 deal with the same topic though there is some disagreement about the benefits promised.

The counting of Nakṣatras from Kṛttikā and not from Aśvinī shows that this chapter (and also the Mbh. chapter, the source of this chapter) was written some time before 500 A.D. when the Vedic counting of Nakṣatras was prevalent.

śiras) constellation one attains vigour and vitality. Generally the man of ruthless activities performs a *Śrāddha* under Ārdrā.

4-5. One performing a *Śrāddha* under the Punarvasu constellation becomes the possessor of fields and begets sons. He will be blessed with wealth and food-grains as well as sons and grandsons. A man who desires satisfaction and contentment should perform *Śrāddha* under Puṣya constellation. One shall attain heroic sons by worshipping *Pitṛs* under Āśleṣā.

6. He who performs a *Śrāddha* under Maghā becomes the most excellent among his kinsmen. A man worshipping *Pitṛs* in the (Pūrvā) Phalgunī constellation attains good fortune.

7. He who performs a *Śrāddha* under Uttarāphalgunī constellation becomes the leader (in his community) along with his children. He who performs *Tarpaṇa* to *Pitṛs* under the Hasta constellation becomes the chief of good men.

8. He who performs a *Śrāddha* in the Citrā constellation sees (has) handsome sons. He who performs a *Śrāddha* under the Svāti constellation becomes a scholar and attains profit.

9. A man wishing for sons shall perform a *Śrāddha* in the Viśākhā constellation. He who performs a *Śrāddha* in the Anurādhā constellation extends his realm.

10. He who performs a *Śrāddha* under the Jyeṣṭhā constellation attains lordship and excellence for ever. Those who desire health shall perform a *Śrāddha* under the Mūla constellation. Those who desire great fame should perform a *Śrāddha* under Pūrvāṣāḍhā.

11. A man performing a *Śrāddha* under the Uttarāṣāḍhā constellation shall be free from grief. By performing a *Śrāddha* under the Śravaṇa constellation, one shall attain the greatest goal in excellent worlds.

12. A man who performs a *Śrāddha* under the Dhaniṣṭhā constellation gains a kingdom and attains enormous wealth. By performing a *Śrāddha* under the Abhijit constellation, (he) obtains goats and sheep as fruit.

13. He who performs a *Śrāddha* in the Śatabhiṣak constellation attains success as a great physician. He who performs a *Śrāddha* in the Pūrvā-Bhādrapadā (Proṣṭhapada) constellation attains goats and sheep as the fruit.

14. He who performs a *Śrāddha* unfailingly under Uttarā Bhādrapadā shall obtain thousands of cows. He who performs a *Śrāddha* under the Revatī constellation gets much wealth. By performing a *Śrāddha* under the Aśvinī constellation one attains horses. He who performs a *Śrāddha* in the Bharaṇī constellation attains long life.

15. By performing a *Śrāddha* according to these injunctions Śaśabindu attained the entire earth. After attaining the entire earth he praised him (Yama).

CHAPTER TWENTYONE

Miscellaneous Topics : Qualifications of a Brāhmaṇa for Śrāddha-gifts : Merits of Performance of Śrāddha at Sacred Places

Śaṁyu said :

1. O foremost one among the eloquents, what is it that offered to the Pitṛs, delights them to a little extent ? What delights (them) for a long time ? What is it that is conducive to delight them infinitely ?[1]

---

1. The first topic discussed is about the vegetarian and non-vegetarian dishes liked by *Pitṛs* and therefore should be served to Brāhmaṇas while dining at a Śrāddha (vide vv. 3-9).

Āpastaṁba Dh.S. (600 B.C.) prescribes flesh-eating as obligatory at *Śrāddha* and enumerates the animals the flesh of which gratifies *Pitṛs* for a specific period e.g. the flesh of a *gavaya* (a cow-like animal) offered in *Śrāddha* gratifies the *Pītṛs* for a year (*saṁvatsaraṁ gavayena tṛptiḥ*). For other animals and the period of gratification etc., see Āpastamba Dh.S. II. 7.16-25; II.17.3. For refusal to accept non-vegetarian food at a *Śrāddha* one has to go to hell (*Viṣṇudharmottara* I. 140-49-50, also Manu V. 35; KP. II.17.40).

Manu III.267-272, Yājñavalkya I. 158-260, Mbh. *Anuśāsana* Ch. 88, Kātyāyana's *Śrāddha-Sūtra* (Kaṇḍikā 7-8), KP. II.40-42, Mt. P. 17.31-35, Bd.P. 2.3.19, VP. III.16.1-3 and such other Purāṇas specify the flesh of certain animals served at Śrāddha and the period of gratification of Pitṛs thereby. Hemādri opines that greater the period, greater is the gratification (*iha sarvatra prītyatiśayo vivakṣitaḥ*—Śrāddha p. 590).

Bṛhaspati said :

2. Listen to those sacrificial offerings which are to be made at the time of Śrāddha as the knowers of Śrāddha have understood. Listen also to the benefit of these in accordance with their strength.

3. Grandfathers are pleased for a month by a Śrāddha in which gingelly seeds, grains of rice, barley, black gram, water, fruits and roots are offered.

4. They are pleased for two months if fishes are offered; for three months if venison is offered; for four months if the meat of hare is offered; and for five months if the meat of birds is offered.

5. They are delighted for six months with the flesh of boars, for seven months with goats' flesh and for eight months with the flesh of a spotted doe.

6. The manes are delighted for nine months with the meat of the Ruru deer. They will have contentment lasting for ten months with the meat of *Gavaya* (a kind of ox).

7. They are propitiated for eleven months with the meat of a tortoise. Know that Śrāddha with (products of) cow's milk lasts for a year.

8. So also in the case of milk-pudding along with milk products, honey and ghee. The satisfaction with the meat of a *Vadhriṇasa* (a rhino-like animal ?) lasts for twelve years.

9. With the meat of *Khaḍga* (rhinoceros) during the rites of Pitṛs, the pleasure is everlasting. So also with the meat of a black goat and an alligator provides endless pleasure.

10. In this connection, those who know the ancient lores mention about the *gāthās* (traditional verses) sung by *Pitṛs*. I shall narrate them to you. Listen and understand precisely.

11-12. (*Pitṛs* sing) "Will a son be born in our own family who will give us on the *Trayodaśī* (thirteenth) day, cooked food, milk pudding, honey and ghee on the occasion of *Gajacchāyā Parvan* ?[1] Or give the same with the meat of a goat that is

In Southern India, though neither *Mitākṣarā* nor *Kalpataru* have prohibited flesh-diet at *Śrāddha*, strict vegetarianism is observed.

1. The conjunction that occurs when the Moon is in the Maghā constellation, the Sun is in Hasta and the *Tithi* is the 13th in the rainy season, it is called *Gajacchāyā* or *Kuñjaracchāyā*.

entirely red during the rainy season and under the constellation of Maghā ? It is better to wish for many sons. At least one of them will go to Gayā or marry a girl eight years old or discharge a blue ox[1] (free to wander)."

Śaṁyu asked :

13. O dear one, recount the benefit of the holy centres Gayā etc. to me who ask. Please mention the merit entirely that is derived by performing the rites of Pitṛs.

Bṛhaspati said :

14. O son, a Śrāddha performed in Gayā yields endless benefit. *Japas*, *Homas* and penances (performed there) are also beneficial endlessly. Hence on the anniversary day of the death of father, Śrāddha performed there is remembered as everlasting.

15. A son begot after marrying a girl of eight years sanctifies twentyone generations. Moreover, he sanctifies six generations in the family of his maternal uncle. This is remembered as the benefit (of such a marriage).

16. I shall recount the benefit derived from (discharging) a bull. Even as I recount listen and understand. The discharger of the bull sanctifies ten previous generations and ten succeeding generations.

17. At the time of letting free the bull whatever is sprinkled with water as it emerges from water on to the ground, is said to yield endless benefit.

18. There is no doubt in this that all those things touched by water tossed about by its tail etc., give endless satisfaction to Pitṛs.

---

1. This is called 'the rite of letting free a bull' (*Vṛṣotsarga-vidhi*). For the details vide *Viṣṇu Dh. S.* 86.1-20. *Viṣṇudharmottara* I.147. 1-19 repeat the same procedure. Though the words '*nīlam vṛṣam*' are translated as 'blue bull' the bull is not blue in colour. Though the adjective 'blue' (*Nīla*) is variously defined, Mt. P. 207.38 defines it as 'a bull having white legs, face & tail and the rest of the body as red' I could not trace the verse *lohito yastu varṇena* etc. in Bd. P. though Kane quotes it as ascribed to it (HD, IV p. 540, fn 1215).

For the benefit accruing from *Vṛṣotsarga* see the following vv. 16-20.

19. The ground dug up by the bull by means of its hoofs or horns, serves as canals of honey perpetually feeding Pitṛs.

20. The satisfaction derived by Pitṛs at the rite of letting free the bull is more than that when they hear that a tank, a thousand *Nalvas* square, has been dug (a *Nalva*=400 hands).

21. If anyone gives gingelly seeds mixed with honey and jaggery, it yields everlasting benefit.

Bṛhaspati said :

22. One should not test Brāhmaṇas always in order to give them anything. But testing is heard about (i.e. prescribed in śrutis) in regard to the rites of Devas (gods) and Pitṛs.[1]

23-27. One should invite these for the *Śrāddha* rite : Those who have studied all the Vedas and who have performed all rites; the Brāhmaṇas who are the sanctifiers of the row; important Brāhmaṇas who know the *Bhāṣyas* (Glosses on Aphorisms); those who regularly study Grammar; those who study Purāṇas and Dharmaśāstras; those who are conversant with the three-Naciketas-Vidyās; the worshippers of five fires; the *Trisuparṇas*, the knowers of the six ancillary subjects of the Vedas; a son of the Brāhma form of marriage; a master of Vedic Prosody (or chanter of the Vedas); a singer of the *Jyeṣṭha Sāman*; one who has taken baths in sacred waters (at holy places); those who have taken part in important Yajñas and taken the concluding (*Avabhṛtha*) ablutions; those who observe rites immediately; those who strictly adhere to their own duties; those who are not wrathful and those who are always calm and quiescent. And those who perpetually observe the ten meritorious deeds shall also be invited.

28. Whatever is offered to these, yields everlasting benefit. These are the sanctifiers of the row. Those Brāhmaṇas who observe Yogic rites and duties should be revered faithfully.

29. They are the foremost due to their adherence to the duties of their (specific) stages of life. In regard to the offering

---

1. Verses 22-31 state the qualifications of the Brahmins eligible for invitation to Śrāddha, though it has been already discussed in Ch. 17. Yogins are given the first preference as Yoga-dharma was regarded as the foremost among Dharmas.

of *Havyas* and *Kavyas*, they are the leaders. He who worships them worships the three deities Brahmā, Viṣṇu and Maheśvara.

30. One who worships these, worships all the worlds along with the Pitṛs. (*Yogadharma*) is the holiest of all holy things, the most auspicious of all auspicious things.

31. *Yogadharma* is mentioned as the first among all *Dharmas*.

I shall recount those who cannot be included in the row (i.e. cannot be invited) for a *Śrāddha*.[1] Listen and understand as I recount them :

32-36. A rogue, a drunkard, a patient of pulmonary consumption, a cattle breeder, an ugly person, a common servant of all in the village, a usurer, a professional musician, a merchant, an incendiary, an administerer of poison, a pimp, a seller of Soma juice, a person who undertakes sea voyage, one whose skin is defiled, a dealer in oil, a deceitful person, one who quarrels with his father, one who has a co-husband at home, a calumniated person, a thief, a person whose livelihood is arts and crafts, a tale-bearer, a person giving wrong information about holy days, one who is malicious to his friends, a group-beggar, an atheist, a discarder of the Vedas, a mad fellow, a eunuch, a knavish fellow, a destroyer of foetus, a defiler of the preceptor's bed, a follower of the physician's profession for livelihood, a messenger and an adulterer.

37. He who sells the Vedas, religious observances, holy rites and penances—all these are defilers of the row.

What is gifted to an atheist, ungrateful person or a censurer becomes lost.

38. What is given to a trader is not beneficial here or hereafter. The same is the case in regard to a person who misappropriates (deposits), who is knavish and who hates the Vedas.

39-42a. That which is given to a merchant or an artisan devoid of virtue becomes lost; a merchant despises (underrates)

1. Verses 31-42 give a list of persons unfit for invitation to a Śrāddha. Long lists of such unfit persons are given by Gautama Dh.S. XV. 16-19, Manu III. 150-166, Yājñavalkya I. 222-224, Mbh. *Anuśāsana* 90.6-11, Mt.P. 16.14-17, KP.II. 21.23-43.

the commodities while purchasing and praises (the same) while selling. Hence a merchant, the abode of untruth, does not deserve (invitation to) a Śrāddha. What is given to a widow's son (after remarriage) even if he be a Brāhmaṇa, is like what is oblated into ashes.

The following persons if invited to a Śrāddha destroy the merits of the donor: a one-eyed man (destroys) sixty (merits), a eumuch a hundred (merits), a sufferer from leprosy as long as he sees, a sufferer from sinful ailment a thousand (meritorious acts). A donor, by being childish, falls off from the benefit of *Dāna*.

42b-43. Brahmā has ordained that he who covers his head while taking food and one who eats food facing the south, he who takes food with shoes on and he who offers *Dāna* scornfully gives the entire share unto the leaders of Asuras.

44. Dogs and demons should not see the performance of a Śrāddha.[1] Hence it should be screened out all round, and gingelly seeds should be strewn around.

45. It is to ward off Rākṣasas that gingelly seeds are strewn and the screen is to prevent the dogs. Boars destroy the effect of a Śrāddha by having a look at it and a cock by fluttering its wings (or by the fall of its feathers within).

46. A woman in her monthly course destroys the Śrāddha by touching. If the performer of a Śrāddha becomes angry, he destroys the benefit derived. If anyone gets his friends to offer Śrāddha and Havis, they do not please Pitṛs or Devas. Nor does he attain heaven.

47. Grandfathers (manes) are delighted with what is given on the beautiful banks of the rivers and streams as well as of the lakes and in secluded places.

48. One shall not shed tears while performing a Śrāddha, nor should he take active part in irrelevant conversation. One should not munch or crunch anything while performing a Śrāddha. One should avoid mutual rivalry too.

1. Since the period of *Dharma Sūtras*, people believed that food for Śrāddha got polluted even by being looked by certain animals and certain categories of people. The list of such unworthies is given in vv. 44-46—an echo of Gautama Dh.S. 15.25-28, Manu III. 239-242, and Purāṇas like KP. II. 22.34-35, VP. III.16.12-14, Bd.P. 2.3.19, 43-44.

49. While performing a Śrāddha the sacred thread should be worn from right to left and the Darbhas should be held duly in the hands. One should perform a Śrāddha till one's death. Thus one delights Pitṛs.

50. At the outset, he should formally take permission of the preceptor or the invited Brāhmaṇas. He should then kindle a fire duly. The articles to be offered to Pitṛs should be placed on the ground over a winnowing basket or on a Kuśa mat.

51. During the bright half (of the month), the Śrāddha is to be performed in the forenoon by the skilful performer of a Śrāddha. During the dark half, it should be performed in the afternoon. In any case the *Rauhiṇa* period (the 4th *Muhūrta* of the day), should not be transgressed.

52. Thus the great and noble souls, the seers of time and place, the Pitṛs of great Yoga (yogic power) and great virility should be worshipped.

53. A person always devoted to Pitṛs attains the excellent Yoga. After eschewing both auspicious and inauspicious actions they attain salvation through meditation.

54. It is for the sake of (promotion of) sacrifices that after deluding the universe, it (Yoga) was eschewed and kept in the cavity (of the heart, i.e. kept secret) by the noble-souled Kaśyapa.

55. O excellent one among the knowers of Yoga, that nectarine (or immortal) Yoga, the eternal great Dharma was promulgated by Sanatkumāra.

56. It is a great esoteric secret of the Devas. It is the greatest resort of the sages. It can always (be attained) by the devotees of Pitṛs through filial devotion, piety and endeavour.

57. There is no doubt in this that one who is devoted to Pitṛs shall, with endeavour, attain everything of that Yoga in essence.

58. To whom are the Śrāddhas to be offered; which are the things that yield great benefits when given; what are the holy centres and sacred rivers wherein the Śrāddha offered bears everlasting benefits; by what means does one attain heaven—all these have been mentioned to you in brief.

Bṛhaspati said :

59. The man who after hearing this explanation of the procedure of Śrāddhas, becomes malicious, is an atheist enveloped in darkness. He will drown himself in the terrible hell.

60. He who has perfectly controlled his mind, finds all his great ailments terminated. He who is not mindful of the *Āśramas* (stages in life) stated in the Vedas attains the Kumbhīka hell. He attains the status of a thief and gets his tongue cut.

61. Those who censure Yoga become lumps of clay in the ocean[1] and decay as long as the earth exists. Hence, this is the Dharma (virtue) intended in the Śrāddha that it should be performed by a man with faith (in it).

62. Scandalisation of Yogins should be scrupulously avoided. By scandalising (them), a person becomes a worm and rolls there itself.

63. There is no doubt in this that he who censures Yoga, the cause of salvation unto those who meditate, goes to terrible hell. He who listens to it (the censure), also falls into the hell.

64. By denigrating masters of Yoga, a man certainly falls into the hell surrounded by darkness and terrible to behold.

65. There is no doubt about it that he who pays heed to the vilification of masters of Yoga of fully controlled selves, becomes submerged in the Kumbhīpāka hell for a long time.

66. One should eschew hatred for Yogins mentally, verbally and physically. He will reap the benefit of the same here itself as well as after death. There is no doubt about it.

67. A person who has mastered (all lores) does not get (realize) the Ātman. He wanders within the three worlds due to his own actions. A person who has mastered Ṛgveda, Yajurveda, Sāmaveda and all their ancillary subjects does not attain Brahman which is devoid of changes and aberrations (*avikāram*) and therefore, becomes distressed.

---

1. Verses 54-57, and vv. 61-71 show the blind faith of Purāṇic writers in Yogins. Since the times of Vasiṣṭha Dh.S. XI. 17, Yatis (recluses) and Yogins had a special place of honour among the invitees to a Śrāddha. But Purāṇa writers have prohibited denigration of Yogīs even orally.

68. (Defective verse)[1] He who has crossed the bounds of effects (of *Prakṛti*) goes beyond *Prakṛti*. Mastery of the three Vedas leads to the crossing (of the limits?) of three *guṇas* The (highest) principle is beyond the twentyfour Yogas (?). He is the master of all, who has passed beyond worldly existence. (?)

69.[2] (Defective verse) By means of his Yogic power, a knower of Yogas withdraws unto himself the dissolution of the Ātman, in the same manner as the entire creation of the principles by the Ātman. He alone becomes the master of all.

70. It is the knower of Yogas who knows the Vedas and attains the knowable. They call him the knower of the Vedas, and the master of Vedas.

71. After duly knowing the knowable and what should be known (one becomes the knower of Vedas). They call him the knower of the Vedas. All others are thinkers of the Vedas.

72. A person devoted to Pitṛs attains the (fruit of) Yajñas, Vedas, all cherished desires, different kinds of knowledge, longevity, progeny and riches.

73. He who invariably reads this *Śrāddhakalpa* during Śrāddha, in the end, gets all these (benefits) and the benefits of charitable gifts at the holy centres.

74. He shall be the sanctifier of the row (of diners). He shall be given priority in being fed among the Brāhmaṇas. Or he shall (be eligible to) teach all the Brāhmaṇas and attain all cherished desires.

---

1. The text is defective and requires slight modifications as per the same verse printed in the Bd. P. 2.3.19.64 which means: "One who has mastered all created things, the products of *Prakṛti* (the nature known as *Avidyā*), one who has mastered the good features in three Vedas, one who has mastered the three *guṇas* (Sattva etc.) and one who has mastered the twentyfour principles, is the person who has crossed the Saṁsāra to the other shore and is the master of academic studies".

2. The text is defective. The corresponding verse in the Bd. P.2.3.19.65 (with slightly different reading) means: "One who is devoted to Brahman duly and wholly, attains it. Similarly he comprehends the state where everything is merged into the soul".

The second line of the verse is different. It means, "A Brāhmaṇa who does not take to the Path of Yoga, cannot become the master of everything that comes under the perview of order, by knowledge."

75. He who always listens to this after subduing anger, being without malice and becoming free from greed and delusion, attains endless heavenly pleasure.

76. He attains the entire benefit of visiting holy centres, and making charitable gifts etc. This is the most excellent means to liberation. This is the greatest means of attaining heaven. He shall have the greatest contentment in this world too. Hence he should assiduously perform this.

77. He who reads these injunctions about (performance of) Śrāddha attentively and with purity of mind, in the assembly (of the learned) during *Parvan* days, becomes endowed with children. With great brilliance, he attains the same region as that of the heaven-dwellers.

78. Obeisance to that self-born deity by whom this Kalpa has been prescribed. I always bow down to the great masters of Yoga.

79. O dear one, these Pitṛs are the deities of Devas. Pitṛs are stationed in these seven abodes for ever. They are free from pain.

80. All these noble souls are the sons of Prajāpati. The first group is that of Yogins. That is eternal and is ever conducive to the increase in the Yogic Power (of Yogins).

81. The second group is that of Devas and the third is that of their enemies. The other groups are of the members of (four) other castes (*Varṇas*). Thus all have been recounted.

82-83. All Devas worship them. They are stationed in them (Pitṛs). The four *Āśramas* too successively worship them. The four castes also worship them in accordance with the injunctions. Similarly the mixed castes and the Mlecchas (alien outcastes) also worship them.

84. Pitṛs revere him who devotedly worships Pitṛs. Pitṛs in the form of grandfather grant nourishment, progeny and heavenly pleasure to him who desires nourishment or who desires progeny.

85. To a son, the rite for Pitṛs is preferable to the rite for Devas. Pitṛs are to be propitiated even before Devas.

86. The subtle movement of the Yogic power of Pitṛs is in-

comprehensible to the physical eye which is distant (not empowered by) penance.

87. To all of them a silver vessel or one accompanied with silver is ordained. It is said to be sanctifying and excellent (for the rites) of Devas along with (those of) Pitṛs.

88-89. The three Piṇḍas which the kinsmen offer invoking the names and Gotra, which they place on the ground strewn with Kuśa grass after wearing the sacred thread from right to left, delight the respective parents who are present everywhere. What constitutes the diet of the creature (i.e. the devotee who offers) is the diet of Pitṛs as well.

90. Just as in a cowpen the calf finds out its lost mother, so also the Mantra takes those articles where the *Jantu* (the man for whom the *piṇḍa* is intended) stays.

91. The name, Gotra and Mantra take the food offered to him. Even if they had taken a hundred births, the satisfaction follows them. (They are satiated by the Śrāddha offering.)

92. Thus this convention is established by Brahmā, the supreme god. This first creation of Pitṛs is for the worlds that seek everlasting bliss.

93-95. Thus these Pitṛs are Devas and Devas are Pitṛs. O sinless ones, all these (following) have been recounted by me—*Dauhitras*, (i.e. daughter's sons), Yajamānas, worlds, daughters, grandsons, sons, charitable gifts, along with the mode of purity, holy centres, fruit thereof, everlasting nature of the benefit, (the different types of) Brāhmaṇas and the rules governing Yāyāvaras (wandering ascetics). Everything has been mentioned in the manner that Brahmā prescribed formerly.

Bṛhaspati said :

96. This, Aṅgiras explained in an assembly while the sages sat listening when he had been asked to clear the doubts regarding Pitṛs.

97. It was formerly in the course of an extensive *Satra* (sacrifice) lasting for a thousand years wherein the lord of the house was the deity, Lord Brahmā.

98. It is heard that Brahmā presided over it for hundreds

of years. The following verses were also formerly sung by the sages, the expounders of Brahman (Veda).

99. "When Brahmā, the great Ātman, presided over the *Satra*, then Pitṛs were born for the benefit of the worlds seeking everlasting bliss, through Brahmā Parameṣṭhin."

Sūta said :

100. Bṛhaspati who had been asked by his intelligent son formerly, told thus. He recounted the family of Pitṛs. What he said has been mentioned (by me). Henceforth I shall recount (the race) of Varuṇa. Understand (it).

CHAPTER TWENTYTWO

The Race of Varuṇa : Birth of Aśvin Gods[1]

1. The sages to whom this (*Śrāddha Kalpa*) was narrated became very much delighted. Extremely eager to hear further, they asked him thereafter.

The Sages said :

2. Please narrate (to us) in proper sequence the condition of the races of the kings of unmeasured spledour as well as valour. We implore you.

3-4. Thus entreated, *Sūta Lomaharṣaṇa* an expert in the narration of tales and proficient in the art of speech, (observed) the desire of the sages to hear the story and *spoke these words*:

Hear and understand as I recount in the manner the sage recounted to me.

5. Even as I recount, listen, and understand the state and position of the dynasties of the kings of unmeasured splendour, in the proper order and their prowess.

1. This chapter corresponds to Bd.P. 2.3.59; only verse numbers from that chapter are quoted in notes.

6. Varuṇa's wife was the daughter of the ocean and was called "Śunodevī". She had two sons Kali and Vaidya and a daughter Surasundarī.

7. Kali had two very powerful sons (namely): Jaya and Vijaya. Vaidya too had two sons of great strength, viz. Ghṛṇi and Muni.

8. When the subjects became desirous of eating, they ate each other. Devouring each other, they perished.

9. Kali begot of Surā (a son). That son of his is remembered as Mada. Hiṁsā, the daughter of Tvaṣṭṛ, was the eldest wife of Kali. She was known as Nikṛti (too).

10. She bore four other man-eating sons to Kali, viz. Nāka, the famous Vighna, Sadrama and Vidhama.

11. Among them Vighna was devoid of head; Nāka had no body; Sadrama was single-handed; and Vidhama had a single foot.

12. Sadrama's wife was remembered as Pūtanā. She had Tāmasic qualities. Revatī was the wife of Vidhama. Their sons were in thousands.

13. Śakuni was the wife of Nāka and Ayomukhī was the wife of Vighna. Rākṣasas of huge heads roaming about at dawn and dusk (were born of them).

14. The sons of Revatī and Pūtanā are remembered by the name of Nairṛtas. All these Rākṣasas were evil demons known as Grahas. They particularly harassed children (by haunting them). With the permission of Brahmā, lord Skanda became their overlord.

15. Bṛhaspati's sister was a noble lady (named) Yogasiddhā. Observing celibacy and being detached, she roamed over the whole universe.

16. She became the wife of the eighth of the Vasus, viz. Prabhāsa. Viśvakarmā, the creator of arts and crafts was born as her son.

17. (He was known as) Tvaṣṭṛ. He created many forms. He was the grandson of Dharma. He was liberal-minded. He was the creator of thousands of arts and crafts. He was the Architect of Devas.

18. He made aerial chariots for all the Devas. Human beings

maintain their livelihood by following the craftsmanship of that noble soul.

19. Tvaṣṭṛ's wife was the famous daughter of Prahlāda and was the sister of Virocana and the mother of Triśiras.

20. Maya, the son of the intelligent preceptor of Devas in craftsmanship of all kinds, is remembered as Viśvakarmā also.

21. His younger sister, the daughter of Tvaṣṭṛ (originally) famous by the name of Sureṇu, became the wife of the Sun and was well known as Saṁjñā.

22. With the power of her penance, she bore the eldest son Manu to Vivasvān (the Sun-god). Then she gave birth to the twins Yama and Yamunā.

23-24. Assuming the form of a mare, the noble lady went to the land of Kurus. The blessed lady bore two sons to the Sun who had assumed the form of a horse. She gave birth to them through nostrils. They were the twin gods, the Aśvins, Nāsatya and Dasra. Both of them were the sons of Mārtaṇḍa (the Sun-god).

The Sages enquired :

25. Why is (the Sun) called Mārtaṇḍa by learned men? Why did she, in the form of a mare, give birth to them through the nostrils ? We wish to know this. Please explain this to us who ask you.

Sūta said :

26. For a long time, the egg did not break (did not get hatched). It was broken open by Tvaṣṭṛ. On seeing it, Kaśyapa became sad as he feared that the foetus was killed.

27. When the egg was broken into two parts, he looked into it and said to Tvaṣṭṛ, "This is certainly not an (ordinary)egg". (Then to the child he said) "O Sinless one, be Mārtaṇḍa".

28. The father affectionately said—"Indeed this (child) in the egg is not dead". On hearing his words, the relevancy of the name has been understood.

29. Since he was addressed by the father, "Be born of the dead (broken) egg", when the egg was broken, Vivasvān is cal-

led Mārtaṇḍa[1] by those who know the Purāṇas.

30. Henceforth I shall mention the progeny of Mārtaṇḍa Vivasvān. Formerly three children were born of his wife Saṁjñā to Savitṛ.

31. (Later) the younger Manu Sāvarṇi and Śanaiścara were born to (the shadow) Saṁjñā and the twin gods Aśvins to (the real) Saṁjñā. These seven are remembered as the children of Mārtaṇḍa.

32. Vivasvān of great fame, was born of Kaśyapa and a daughter of Dakṣa. The noble lady, the daughter of Tvaṣṭṛ became the wife of Vivasvān. Originally she was well known by the name Sureṇu and later came to be known as Saṁjñā.

33. The wife of lord Mārtaṇḍa of excessive splendour was a woman of great beauty in the prime of youth. She was dissatisfied with the dazzling form of her husband.

34. The dazzlingly brilliant person of Mārtaṇḍa, the son of Aditi, coming into contact with her body was not very pleasing to her.

35. Being unaware, Kaśyapa said out of affection, "Indeed this (child) in the egg is not dead". Hence he is called Mārtaṇḍa.

36. The brilliance of Vivasvān increased day by day whereby he, the son of Kaśyapa, scorched the three worlds.

37. Ravi (the Sun-god) begot of Saṁjñā three children, two sons of great prowess and the daughter Kālindī (Yamunā).

38. Manu was the eldest son of Vivasvān. He was a Prajāpati and known as Śrāddhadeva. Yama and Yamī were born as twins.

39. On seeing the whetted brilliance of Vivasvān and unable to endure it, Saṁjñā created her own shadow of the same complexion as hers.

40. That woman of earthly form, born of her shadow came to her humbly with palms joined in reverence and spoke to Saṁjñā:

---

1. The Vedic word is *Mārtāṇḍa* 'born of an (apparently) dead egg'. Mārtaṇḍa is a later Purāṇic form, though the derivation is the same.

41. "Tell me, what should be done by me ?" Saṁjñā spoke to her: "Welfare unto you. I will go back to my own father's house.

42. You must remain in my house without any hesitation. These two sons of mine and this daughter of splendid complexion (should be looked after).

43. This (arrangement) should not be mentioned to the lord, my husband".

Thus addressed, the earthly form of Saṁjñā spoke to Saṁjñā:

44. "O noble lady, until the hair is caught hold of, I will never speak your secret idea. O noble lady, go back to your own house".

45. After consoling Saṁjñā, she said, "So be it". She, the woman in a pitiable condition, went near Tvaṣṭṛ as though greatly ashamed.

46. On seeing her come back, the father became angry and spoke to Saṁjñā: "Go back to your husband. Do not hate Divākara (the Sun-god)."

47. Though urged thus by her father and compelled (to go) again and again, she lived in her father's house for a thousand years.

48. "Go to your husband's house". When insisted upon again and again thus, that uncensured (praise-worthy) lady concealed her real form and assumed the form of a mare. She went to the northern Kurus and began to graze grass.

49. Considering that she (the shadow of Saṁjñā) was the real Saṁjñā, the Sun begot of the shadow, the second Saṁjñā, two sons of the splendour of Āditya (the Sun).

50. The sons were Śrutaśravā, the knower of Dharma, and Śrutakarman. Both of those lordly ones were equal to Manu the eldest-born.

51. Śrutaśravas will become Sāvarṇi Manu. The planet Śanaiścara (Saturn) is to be known as Śrutakarman.

52-53. It is known that Sāvarṇi became Manu. The earthly form of Saṁjñā was affectionate only towards her (own) sons and not towards the earlier born ones. Manu bore it patiently, but Yama did not brook it.

54-55. On being insulted many times (by the step-mother) out of spite, Yama became distressed and threatened Saṁjñā with his leg. Out of anger or childishness or the force of the inevitable destiny, that lady, having the same complexion as his mother, cursed Yama out of anger.

56. "Since you are threatening the renowned wife of your father, this leg of yours will undoubtedly fall off."

57. With his mind deeply afflicted due to that curse, Yama of virtuous soul reported everything to his father, along with Manu (i.e. accompanied by him.)

58. "I am much distressed due to the fear of the curse (taking effect). I have been defeated (?) by the (statement) words of Saṁjñā. (This mistake is) due to my childishness or delusion. Sir, please protect me.

59. O lord of the worlds, foremost one among those who blaze, I have been cursed by mother. May your grace protect us from this great danger."

60. Thus implored, lord Vivasvān spoke to Yama: "O son, undoubtedly there will be a great reason behind this (incident).

61. That was why anger took possession of you who are the knower of virtue and the speaker of the truth. The words of your mother too cannot be falsified.

62. The worms will take away your flesh and go to the earth. Then you will regain your foot. O intelligent one, you will be happy again.

63. In this way, your mother's words will be true and effective. By removal of the curse, you will also be saved."

64. Āditya then spoke to Saṁjñā, "When the sons are all equal, why is more affection shown by you towards one ?"

65. Avoiding (the necessity of disclosing the secret) she did not say anything to Vivasvān. But by means of his Yogic power and concentration, the Sun found out the truth.

66. The infuriated Sun-god was about to curse her bringing about her destruction. She then confessed factually everything to Vivasvān.

67-68. On hearing it, Vivasvān was enraged and hastened to Tvaṣṭṛ. Tvaṣṭṛ honoured with due formalities the Sun-god who wanted to burn down everything. He pacified him slowly saying : "Your present form which is excessively dazzling, is not attractive.

69. It is because she could not endure it that Saṁjñā is wandering in the forests and meadows. You will see your wife of auspicious conduct today itself.

70. O lord of rays, by using your Yogic power, you will see your praiseworthy wife superbly endowed with youthful charm. Everything will be favourable if my condition is accepted.

71-74. O suppressor of enemies ! At the outset, I shall change your personal form into an excellent one". The form of Vivasvān, then, was sideways, upwards and below (i.e. the rays were diffused everywhere). Hence Divaspati (the Sun-god) was ashamed of that form. So the deity of great penance praised the wheel of Tvaṣṭṛ. Tvaṣṭṛ was then permitted to change the form. With the concurrence of the Sun-god (Mārtaṇḍa Vivasvān), Tvaṣṭṛ mounted him on the wheel and whetted his brilliance. Then the brilliance had pleasant refulgence due to reduction in dazzle.

75. The refulgence became very pleasing to behold. What was inauspicious before shone splendidly. Then (the Sun) made use of Yogic power and saw his wife in the form of a mare.

76. She had been invisible to all living beings due to her brilliance and observance of rites. In the form of a horse, Mārtaṇḍa approached her and declared his love.

77. In the physical activity of sexual intercourse, she suspected him to be someone other than her lord. She therefore discharged the semen virile of Vivasvān through her nostrils.

78. From that semen were born the twin gods Aśvins, the excellent physicians, Nāsatya and Dasra. They are remembered as Aśvins.

79. They are the sons of Mārtaṇḍa, the eighth Prajāpati. Bhāskara (the Sun-god) showed his beautiful form to her.

80. On seeing him the wife was satisfied and fascinated. Yama was much afflicted in the mind due to that curse.

81-83. He pleased (all) by means of his Dharma. Then he became known as Dharmarāja. By means of his auspicious activity, he became extremely refulgent and attained the lordship of Pitṛs and guardianship of the quarters. Sāvarṇi Manu of great fame shall become the Manu in the Sāvarṇika Manvantara. Even today the holy lord performs penance on the beautiful ridge of the Meru mountain.

84. Their brother Śanaiścara attained the status of a planet. With the (chopped off) brilliance (of the Sun) Tvaṣṭṛ made Viṣṇu's discus.[1] It was unobstructed (irresistible) in battles to check Dānavas.

85. Their younger sister Yamunā of great fame, became the excellent river Yamunā, the purifier of all the worlds.[2]

86. I shall now narrate the details of Vaivasvata Manu who was the eldest among them. He had great splendour and his creation is current (and he presides over the present Manvantara).

87. He who listens to or reads the origin of Devas, the seven powerful sons of Vivasvān, shall be released, if he attains misfortune. He shall attain great glory.

CHAPTER TWENTYTHREE

Creative Activity of Manu: The Story of Sudyumna.

Sūta said:

1. When the Cākṣuṣa Manvantara had elapsed, when the Devas (pertaining to that epoch) too had gone, the kingdom of the earth was assigned to the great Vaivasvata (Manu).[3]

---

1. The creation of Viṣṇu's discus Sudarśana from the pruned part of the Sun-god is mentioned in VP. III. 2.11.

2. This story of the Sun-god, his wife Saṁjñā and Chāyā, his children from them, pruning of the Sun-god's excessive lustre, his approach to his wife Saṁjña (who was in a mare's form) and birth of Aśvin gods—these are traditional accounts found in Mbh. *Ādi* 76, *Anuśāsana* 150, VP. III. 2 and other Purāṇas.

3. Description of dynasties of kings is an integral part of a Purāṇa of five characteristics. Vaivasvata Manu, being the progenitor of these dynasties, is described in all Purāṇas.

This chapter corresponds to Bd.P. 2.3-60, hence only verse nos. from Bd.P. are given.

2. O Brāhmaṇas, I shall recount in the proper order the race of that noble-souled current Manu, the son of Vivasvān. (Listen to) and understand what is being narrated.

3. (I shall narrate the story) now taking up the present creation of Vaivasvata Manu. The first born Manu had nine sons equal to him.

4. These nine are remembered as the sons of Manu: Ikṣvāku, Nahuṣa, Dhṛṣṭa, Śaryāti, Nariṣyanta, tha tall (*Prāṁśu*) Nābhāga, Ariṣṭa, Karūṣa and Pṛṣadhra.

5. Know that formerly Manu, on being urged by Brahmā, began to create willingly, but he was unsuccessful.

6. Then Prajāpati, desirous of sons, performed a great *Iṣṭi* (Yajña). Manu offered the oblation (*Āhuti*) in the share of Mitra and Varuṇa.

7. It is heard, that Iḍā[1] was born thereof. She wore heavenly garments and was bedecked in celestial ornaments. Her body too was divine.

8-10. It is remembered that Manu, the bearer of the staff of justice, addressed her as 'Ilā' and said, "Welfare unto you, I shall follow you". Ilā replied to the Prajāpati who was desirous of sons, in the following words sanctioned by Dharma. "O foremost of the eloquent ones, I am born in the share of Mitra and Varuṇa. I will (first) approach them. May not Dharma violated by us kill us". After speaking thus, the noble lady went near them (Mitra and Varuṇa).

11. After going near them, the beautiful lady spoke these words with palms joined in reverence: "O Devas, I am born in your share. What should I do?

12-14. I have been requested by Manu, thus, 'Follow me' ". When the chaste lady Iḍā spoke thus, both of them, Mitra and Varuṇa spoke these words: "O fair-complexioned lady of beautiful hips, O knower of Dharma, we are delighted by your humility, self-control and truthfulness. O blessed lady, you will become renowned as our daughter".

---

1. In RV. it was used in the sense of 'refreshing draught' Later on it came to mean 'a cow', and 'a goddess of speech'. In Śat. Br. Iḍā is Manu's daughter. But in our text she is the daughter of ('born of the share of') Mitra and Varuṇa.

15-16. The son of Manu, the righteous-souled promoter of Manu's race is the beloved of the universe. He who is revered in the three worlds is famous as Sudyumna. He has attained the form of a lady.[1] That noble lady returned to her father after securing the boon.

17. After getting an opportune moment, she was invited for love making (sexual intercourse) by Budha (the planet Mercury). From Budha, the son of Soma, Purūravas, the son of Ilā was born.

18. After giving birth to the son born of Budha, she became Sudyumna again. Sudyumna had three sons, all extremely virtuous.

19. They were Utkala, Gaya and Vinatāśva. The land of Utkala went over to Utkala. The western region went over to Vinatāśva. In the quarter of the Wind-god (north-west) was Gayā, the city of Gaya, the saintly king.

20. (Defective verse) When Manu was abandoned (created) the Sun (Divākara) created the subjects and divided the whole region of the earth into ten.

21. Ikṣvāku had ten other sons. In view of his being a lady (as well), Sudyumna had no share.

22-23. At the instance of Vasiṣṭha, the establishment of the noble-souled Sudyumna, the virtuous king of great lustre, was (took place) in Pratiṣṭhāna. After getting the kingdom, he, of great renown, gave it to Purūravas. The characteristics of women and men among human beings, O blessed ones, (will be duly manifest). Sudyumna, the son of Manu, attained the status of a woman again.

24. On hearing this the sages asked thereafter: "How did Sudyumna, the son of Manu, attain womanhood?"

Sūta said :

25. The beloved goddess (Umā) spoke these words to her lover (Śiva) for the sake of his love: "O Lord, the man who enters my personal hermitage will certainly become a woman. She will be auspicious and on a par with the celestial damsels."

---

1. This strange story of Vaivasvata Manu's bi-sexual child is found in Mbh. Ādi 75, Anuśāsana 147, Bh.P. IX. 1.

26. All the living beings there, Piśācas, and the animals became women and played with Rudra like heavenly ladies.

27-28. That king who had gone a-hunting entered Umā's forest. He attained womanhood along with the Piśācas, Bhūtas and Rudras. Hence that king attained womanhood. By the grace of Mahādeva, he shall attain the lordship of the Gaṇas.

CHAPTER TWENTYFOUR

A Dissertation on Music: The Definition of Mūrcchanā[1]

Sūta said :

1-3. (Listen to and) understand the details of Manu's sons. Pṛṣadhra tortured the cow of his preceptor and ate it. Due to the curse of the noble-souled Cyavana, he attained the status of a Śūdra.

Karūṣa's son Kārūṣa was a Kṣatriya invincible in war. He became as valorous as the group of a thousand Kṣatriyas. Bhalandana, son of Nābhagariṣṭa[2](?) was a scholar.

4. Bhalandana had a very powerful son named Prāṁśu. Prāṁśu had a son who became well known as Prajāni.

5. Prajāni had a valorous son named Khanitra. His son was the glorious Kṣupa of great fame.

6. Kṣupa's son was Viṁśa who had no one equal to him. Viṁśa's son was Viviṁśa, the righteous performer of religious rites.

7. Viviṁśa's son was the virtuous-souled and valorous Khaninetra. In the beginning of Tretāyuga, his son Karandhama was born.

8. Karandhama's son was the vigorous Āvikṣit. By means of his good qualities, Āvikṣit surpassed his father.

---

1. The term '*Mūrcchanā*' means the changing of key or modulation of voice (and sounds) in the Science of Music. For more explanation see Footnote No 3, p. 662.

2. A. reads: Nābhāga was the son of Ariṣṭa. Bhalandana was a scholar.

9. (His son) named Marutta was a virtuous-souled king equal to an emperor. He was taken to heaven by (sage) Saṁvarta along with his friends and kinsmen.

10. In this connection a great dispute arose between Saṁvarta and Bṛhaspati. On seeing the magnificence of the Yajña, Bṛahspati became angry with him.

11. When the Yajña was brought to a successful conclusion by Saṁvarta, he (Bṛhaspati) became more furious. He was intent on the destruction of the worlds but he was propitiated by the deities (gods).

12. Emperor Marutta obtained Nariṣyanta (as son). Nariṣyanta's successor was the king Dama, wielding the staff of justice and punishment.

13. The valorous king Rāṣṭravardhana was his son. His son was Sudhṛtin and Sudhṛtin's son was Nara.

14. Kevala was his son and Bandhumān was the son of Kevala. The virtuous-souled king Vegavān was Bandhumān's son.

15. Budha was Vegavān's son and Tṛṇabindu was the son of Budha. He became king at the beginning of the third Tretā-yuga.

16. His daughter was Draviḍā (Iḍaviḍā in Bd. P.) who became the mother of Viśravas. He had a son also named Viśāla. He was an extremely virtuous king.

17. The city of Viśālā (Vaiśāli)[1] was built by king Viśāla. Viśāla's son was the king Hemacandra of great strength.

18. After Hemacandra (his son) Sucandra became very famous. Sucandra's son was the well known king Dhūmrāśva.

19. Dhūmrāśva's son Sṛñjaya became a great scholar. Sṛñjaya's son was the glorious and valorous Sahadeva.

20. Kṛśāśva was Sahadeva's son. He was extremely righteous. The valorous Somadatta of great brilliance was Kṛśāśva's son.

21. Janamejaya was the son of the saintly king Somadatta. Janamejaya's son named Pramati was very famous.

22. By the grace of Tṛṇabindu, all the kings ruling over Viśālā were long-lived, noble-souled, valorous and very righteous.

---

1. Besāḍ in the district of Muzaffarpur. The name is now officially changed as 'Vaiśāli', though local people still call it Besāḍ.

23. Śaryāti begot twins, a son and a daughter. The son became well known as Ānarta and the daughter was Sukanyā who became the wife of Cyavana.

24. Ānarta's successor was the heroic (king) named Reva. His kingdom was Ānarta[1] and the capital city was Kuśasthalī.

25. Reva's son was Raivata. He was very virtuous and was also known as Kakudin. He was the eldest of a hundred brothers. He became the king and ruled over Kuśasthalī.

26-27. He went to lord Brahmā's presence accompanied by his daughter and heard the musical performance of the lord of Devas for the duration of a Muhūrta which was equivalent to many *yugas* according to the calculation of human beings.[2] He returned to his own city in his own prime of youth, but the city had been occupied by Yādavas. It had been renamed by them as Dvārāvatī, a beautiful city with many gates.

28-30. It was then protected by Vasudeva and other leading Bhojas, Vṛṣṇis and Andhakas. On hearing the story (of the occupation of Dvārakā by Yādavas) with all the facts, Raivata, the suppressor of enemies, gave his daughter of good rites named Revatī, to Balarāma in marriage and went to a peak of mount Meru and became engrossed in penance.

Virtuous-souled Rāma (Balarāma) sported with Revatī.

On hearing the story, the sages enquired thereafter.

The Sages asked :

31. O son of Sūta, O holy lord, how is it that even after the lapse of a long period of many Yugas, Revatī did not become old ? How did her hair not turn grey ?

32. After going to the mountain Meru how did Śaryāti's son have progeny of his own ? How did they survive till now on the earth ? We wish to hear precisely.

33. How many are the groups of gods ? How are the Gandharvas ? How was that music on hearing which Raivata considered a long period as only a Muhūrta ?

---

1. Ānartta, old name of Gujarat (including Saurāshtra) and Kuśasthalī is modern Dwārkā.

2. Accidentally Einstein is anticipated by the imaginative Purāṇa-writer.

Sūta explained :

34. To a person who goes to the world of god Brahmā, there is neither hunger nor thirst. He has neither old age nor fear of death. No ailment affects him.

35. O excellent sages, as to the question put to me on *Gāndharva* (science of music), I shall explain it precisely, O good sages of holy rites.

36. The *Svara Maṇḍala*[1] (the whole group pertaining to musical notes) is comprised by seven *Svaras* (notes), three *Grāmas*[2] (basic scales), twentyone *Mūrcchanās*[3] (the modes of

---

1. It suggests the ascent and descent of seven notes, known as *Svara-saptaka*. See v. 37.

2. *Grāma* : *Grāma* means the group of seven notes. The three *Grāmas* mentioned in Purāṇas are (1) Ṣaḍja-grāma, (ii) Madhyama-grāma and (iii) Gāndhāra-grāma. These three were the basic scales—the *Sā*-scale, the *Ma*-scale and the *Ga*-scale. These had the notes *Sā*, *Ma* and *Ga* as the starting points. Thus the order of notes in these scales will be as follows :

(i) The *Sā*-scale : *Sā, Ri, Ga, Ma, Pa, Dha, Ni*

(ii) The *Ma*-scale : *Ma, Pa, Dha, Ni, Sā, Ri, Ga*

(iii) The *Ga*-scale : *Ga, Ma, Pa, Dha, Ni, Sā, Ri*

Out of these Ga-scale fell into disuse later. Dattila, an ancient writer on Music, states that it is not found in this world while later scholars say that it went to Heaven. They say that due to the extremely high and low notes it disappeared. But for the reasons given by later writers like Śargadeva, it seems that it was not perfect in its aspect of consonance. And consonance is vitally essential for the melodic music of India. Bharata, in his *Nāṭya-śāstra* describes the *Sa*-scale and *Ma*-scale on the basis of the fourth (*Sa-Ma Saṁvāda*) and the consonance of the fifth (*Sa-Pa Saṁvāda*). In the *Sa-scale* the consonance of the fifth was more prominent (*Sa-Pa, Ri-Dha* and *Ga-ni*) while that of the fourth in the *Ma*-scale (*Sa-Ma* and *Ri-Pa*).

The number of *Śrutis* (the microtones) in the Saptaka fixed by Bharata is 22. The *Śruti* intervals were distributed in the notes as follows :

Sa-Scale : 4*Sa*, 3*Ri*, 2*Ga*, 4*Ma*, 4*Pa*, 3*Dha*, 2*Ni*=22

Ma-Scale : 4*Ma*, 3*Pa*, 4*Dha*, 2*Nī*, 4*Sa*. 3*Ri*, 2*Ga*=22

The *Sa-Ma* consonance has the interval of 9 *Śrutis* and the *Sa-Pa* consonance that of 13 *Śrutis*.

3. *Mūrcchanā* :

Mūrcchanā was the gradual ascent and descent of the seven notes of the basic scale. The word is derived from the root √*mūrcch*—'to increase', 'to pervade'. As *Mūrcchanās* started from each note of the scale, there were seven *Mūrcchanās* of each scale. Thus the *Mūrcchanās* of three *Grāmas* numbered twentyone.

gradual ascent and descent of the seven notes of the basic scale) and fortynine *Tālas*[1] (*Tānās*).

37. The following are the names of the *svaras* : *Ṣaḍja* (*Sā*), *Ṛṣabha* (*Ri*), *Gandhāra* (*Ga*), *Madhyama* (*Ma*), *Pañcama* (*Pa*), *Dhaivata* (*Dha*), and *Niṣāda* (*Ni*). These are the seven *svaras* (notes).

(The Text dealing with Music is corrupt and obscure. An

For example, the *Sā*-scale *Mūrcchanās* would be :

(1) *Sā Ri Ga Ma Pa Dha Ni*......

(2) *Ni Sā Ri Ga Ma Pa Dha*......

(3) Dha Ni Sā Ri Ga Ma Pa......etc.

The *Sāman*-scale was descending having the notes *Ma Ga Ri Sā Dha Ni Pa* as per *Nāradīya Śikṣā* (I. 5, 1 and 2). Due to the influence of the *Sāman*-scale, there was the descending order followed in the case of starting notes of the *Mūrcchanās*. *Mūrcchanās* served as the basis of different types of songs. They also brought in the notes of the low (*Mandra*), high (*Tāra*) registers (*Sthāna*). If the first *Mūrcchanā* of the *Ma*-scale is rendered taking *Ma* as the Ṣaḍja and the remaining notes accordingly, then it would be indicated as :

4*Sa*, 3*Ri*, 4*Ga*, 4*Ma*, 2*Pa*, 3*Dha*, 2*Ni*=22 *Śrutis*

This gives the Gāndhāra of 4 *Śrutis* called *Antara Ga*, Its consonant note would be *Nī* of 4 *Śrutis* called *Kākali Ni*. These two were called the *Sādhāraṇa* notes. Their use was restricted. Their employment was allowed when the songs had two *Śruti Ga* and two *Śruti Ni* notes in small measure. The *Mūrcchamās* with these two *Sādhāraṇa* notes were called *Sādhāraṇīkṛta Mūrcchanās*.

1. *Tāla* or *Tāna* :

Tāna is the *Mūrcchanā* in which one or two specific notes are dropped. When one specific *Svara* (Note) is dropped, it is called *Ṣāḍava Tāna* (a Tāna consisting of six notes) and when two specific notes are dropped, it is called *Auḍuva Tāna* (a Tāna consisting of five notes). According to Purāṇas, there are twenty *Tānas* of *Madhyama-grāma*, fourteen of *Ṣaḍja-grāma* and fifteen of *Gāndhāra-grāma*. Thus the number of *Tānas* of the three *grāmas* is given as forty-nine.

According to Bharata (*Nāṭyaśāstra*) when the single note *Sa*, *Ri*, *Pa*, or *Ni* is dropped from the *Mūrcchanās* of the *Madhyama Grāma*, twentyone *Ṣāḍava Tānas* would be effected (7x3=21).

By dropping *Sa Pa Ga Ni* or *Ri Dha* from the Mūrcchanās of the *Sa*-scale twenty-one *Auḍuva Tānas* would be effected (7x3=21). When *Ri Dha* or *Ga Ni* are dropped from the *Mūrcchanās* of the *Ma*-scale, there would take place fourteen *Auḍuva Tānas* (7x2=14). Thus the total number of the *Tānaṣ* of the two *Grāmaṣ* is eighty-four according to Bharata. These are given as *Śuddha Tānas* by later Ācāryas.

attempt is made to emend it with similar verses on Music in Bd. P. and other Purāṇas.)

38-39. The *Mūrcchanās* of the *Ma-scale* (*Madhyama-grāmikā*) are known as Saubīrī (Sauvīrā in Bd. P.) of the Madhyama-grāma, Hariṇāsyā, Kalopabalopetā (also known as Kalopanatā) the fourth Śuddha-madhyamā, Śārṅgī, Pāvanī and Dṛṣṭākā in the serial order. *Mūrcchanās* of Madhyama-grāma are explained. Now understand (the Mūrcchanās of) the *Sa-scale* (*Ṣaḍja-grāma*).

40. Uttara-mandrā, Rajanī, Uttarāyatā, Śuddha-ṣaḍjā should also be known as the seventh.[1]

41a. Know the *Mūrcchanās* of the *Ga-scale* (*Gandhāra-grāmikā*) as they are being described by me.[2]

41b-48. (The names of the *Tānas* are as follows :) .

The first of the series is Āgniṣṭomika, the second is Vājapeyika; the third is called Pauṇḍraka; the fourth is Aśvamedhika; the fifth is Rājasūya; the sixth is Cakrasuvarṇaka; the seventh is Gosava by name; Mahāvṛṣṭika is the eighth; Brahmadāna is the ninth; the next is Prājāpatya; the later should be known as) Nāga-pakṣāśraya, Gotara, Hayakrānta, Mṛga-krānta; the charming Viṣṇukrānta, the most excellent Sūryakrānta, Mattakokila-Vādin, Sāvitra, Ardhaśāvitra, Sarvatobhadra, Suvarṇa, Sutandra, Viṣṇu, Vaiṣṇuvara, Sāgara, Vijaya which is charming to all beings. We know Haṁsa and Jyeṣṭha as dear to Tuṁburu (or 'Tumburupriya' be taken as a separate name), the pleasing Adhātrya.

These are followed by Gandharvas, desired by Alaṁbuṣā and dear to Nārada. It is mentioned by Bhīmasena that they are liked by citizens. (Bd. P. takes '*Nāgara-priya*' as the name of a Tāna.)

49-50a. (The Tāna) called Karopanīta—Vinatā, Śrīḥ, Bhārgava-Priya.

---

1. The text omitted the names Abhirudgatā, Matsarikṛtā and Aśvakrāntā.

2. Strangely enough neither our text nor Bd. P. gives the *Mūrcchanās* of the *Ga-scale*.

N. P. II.50.35b-36a records them as follows :

Nāḍi, Viśālā, Sumukhī, Citrā, Citravatī, Mukhā and Balā. Without any introduction the text proceeds to enumerate the *Tānas* from 41b.

The Purāṇic concept of a *Tāna* is different from that of today.

The *Ma-scale* (*Madhyama-grāma*) consists of twenty (*Tānas*) while fourteen (*Tānas*) constitute the *Sa-scale* (*Ṣaḍja-grāma*). They desire (opine) that there are fifteen (*Tānas*) belonging to the *Ga-scale* (*Gāndhāra-grāma*).

(*The deities associated with Mūrcchanās*)

50b. The *Mūrcchanā* Gāndhārī accompanied with Sauvīrā is hence sung by god Brahmā.

51. And god Brahmā is the presiding deity here of the *Uttarādi-svara*.

Hariṇāsyā is originated in the region of Hari. Mūrcchanā Hariṇāsyā has Indra as its presiding deity.

52. The *Mūrcchanā Karopanīta-vitatā* was sung by Maruts in *Svara-Maṇḍala*. That is *Kalopanītā*. Hence its presiding deity is Māruta.

53. The *Mūrcchanā Śuddha-madhyamā* originated in the Manu (ru?) deśa.

Śuddha Madhyamā is the note here and the presiding deity is Gandharva.

54. Since it moves along with the deer for the guidance of Siddhas, it is, hence, called *Mārgī*. The Lord of animals (the Lion) is its deity.

55. As the *Mūrcchanā* is associated with hermitages and also with the various (human) voices of citizens, it is called *Rajanī* due to its association with *rajas* (dust/atmosphere).

56. The *Tāla* (beating time) is known as having *Ṣaḍja* as its deity. Hence *Uttara-tāla* is known first as well extended.

Hence it is Uttara-mandrā whose diety is Dhruva.

57. Since it is after Apāna (?), Uttarāyaṇa having *Dha* (Dhaivata) as the starting point, is the Mūrcchanā the deities of which are Pitṛs (manes), the deities (worshipped in) Śrāddhas.

58. The great sages worship the Fire-god with the *Śuddha-Ṣaḍja* (pure *Sa-*) note; it should be known as *Śuddha-Ṣaḍjika.*

59. It starts from the *Pañcama* note causing delight to the good people.

The Mūrcchanā belonging to Yakṣīs (female Yakṣas) is called Yākṣikā Mūrcchanā.

60. (Defective) That Mūrcchanā which serpents of poisonous eyes do not approach and the serpent-deities become as it

were drawn by Brahmā, is called the Mūrcchanā of serpents (*Ahi-mūrcchanā*) and here the deity is Varuṇa.

61. The Mūrcchanā with which Kinnaras (sing) in imitation of birds, is the excellent (*Uttamā*) *Mūrcchanā*. Its deity is the Lord of Birds (Garuḍa).

62. By the sound of Gandhāra Rāga, the earth (or cow?) is held in support. Hence it is called Viśuddha-Gāndhārī (of pure *Ga*). And Gandharva is its presiding deity.

63. The Mūrcchanā Uttara-Gāndharī is so called as it was created after Gāndhāra. Its (presiding) deities are Vasus.

64. The Ṣaḍja Mūrcchanā first approached god Brahmā (Pitāmaha). Hence its greatness. Its deity is the Fire-god.

65. The Mūrcchanā called Mandaṣaṣṭhā is divine and extensive. The names of its qualities cannot be described. Its deity is Pañcama (the note *Pa*).

66. All the seven Notes (*Svaras*) and the *Mūrcchanās* are recounted completely. *Mūrcchanās* with Sādhāraṇa Svaras[1] (e.g. Antara Gāndhāra, Kākalī Niṣāda) are many. Only six of them are known.

CHAPTER TWENTYFIVE

The Science of Music: The Embellishments

1. After knowing the views of earlier teachers, I shall explain in due order, the thirty embellishments of music. Listen to them while I am expounding.

2. The *Alaṅkāras* (embellishments of music) are to be explained along with their *Varṇas* (movements of notes such as 'steady', 'ascending' and others) as their specific basis and also along with their associated configuration (*Saṁsthāna*), always in regard to dramatic performance[2] etc.

1. The *Sādhāraṇa Svaras* are :
(i) *Antara Gāndhāra* i.e. modern *Śuddha Gāndhāra*
(ii) *Kākalī Niṣāda* i.e. modern *Tīvra Niṣāda*

2. *Vide* Bharata's *Nāṭyaśāstra* Volume. IV, pp. 79-92 (Baroda Edition)

3. The fulfilment of embellishment is achieved by the implications of sentences and connotations of the word-combinations.

The words of a song are said to be either preceding or following the embellishment.

4. One should understand that there are three place of utterance. They are the chest, the throat and the head. The best procedure (of production of notes) begins in these three places.

5. In the original stage (*Prakṛtau*), there are four varṇas (tone-patterns) with fourfold movement. The alternative movement is eightfold;[1] and gods know it as sixteenfold.

6. [*The designations of Varṇas:*]

The first Varṇa is *Sthāyin*; the second is *Pra-sañcārin*, the third is *Avarohaṇa* (=*Avarohin*) and the fourth Varṇa is known by the experts in the knowledge of Varṇas to be, *Ārohaṇa* (=*Ārohin*).[2]

7. There is one (Varṇa viz. *Sthāyin*) which has steady employment. *Sañcara* is a mixed movement. One should indicate the descent of Varṇas (i.e. *Svaras*) as *Avarohaṇa*.

8a. And the experts in the knowledge of Varṇas know (that Varṇa) as the *Ārohaṇa* Varṇa by the ascent of notes.

8b. Now understand the embellishments of these specific Varṇas.[3]

9. There are four embellishments, viz. *Sthāpanī*,

---

1. These are mentioned in the Purāṇas, only later writers do not refer to them.

2. The exigencies of the metre have led to the change in the order of *Varṇas*. The order should have been :
   (i) *Sthāyin* (i.e. *Sā Sā Sā*)
   (ii) *Ārohin* (e.g. *Sā Ri Ga* etc.)
   (iii) *Avarohin* (e.g. *Ni Dha Pa* etc.)
   (iv) *Sañcarin* (e.g. *Sā Ri Sā Ri Ga Ri Sā* etc.).

3. Although I have referred to the section on *Alaṅkāras* in *Saṅgīta Ratnākara* (I.VI) only a few Alaṅkāras like *Śyena* (p. 133 of S.R.) shed some light. Though S.R. is much later than Vā.P or Bd.P., I consulted it as S.R. preserved some of the Purāṇic traditions.

Kramareṇina, *Pramāda* and *Apramāda*. I shall (henceforth) explain the characteristics of these.[1]

10. (Names of Alaṅkaras still continue as follows:) *Visvara*, *Aṣṭakala*[2] which has an interval of one place (from its original place?). *Āvarta* and *Kramotpatti*—these two should be effected according to their proportion.

11a. One should know the other one to be *Kumāra* and *Vistara*.[3]

11b. And this indeed is the *Apāṅga* (Alaṅkāra) and *Kutāreka* (?) possesses one more kalā (time-measure).

12. *Śyena* is originated as having one interval and situated in the midst of Mātrās of a Kalā. In it there abides the increase in the order of the note different from it (e.g. *Sā—Pa, Ri—Dha, Ga—Ni*).

13. The descent of the *Śyena Alaṅkāra* is called *Uttara*. The *Alaṅkāra* called *Bindu* is originated due to the measure of Kalās.

14a. One Kalā (measure of time) should be employed of the Varṇas. Then it would be *Sthāpita* (Sthāyin?) (established).

14b. *Durghaṭita* is that which has the note even in the reverse order.

15a. *Ekāntara* (*Ekottara-svara*) has the highest note from *Ṣaḍja*.

15b. *Ākṣepāskandana* should be effected as having high amplitude like the (harsh) crowing of the crow.

16a. The two *Santāras* belong to the *Sañcārin Varṇa* either as the cause or the effect.

16b. *Ākṣipta* belongs to the category of the descending (*Avarohin*) *Varṇa*.

17. The *Alaṅkara* called *Preṅkholita* has the twelfth place of Kalā having one interval. Thus it is endowed with *Svaras* (Notes).

18a. *Puṣkala* is said to be due to the transfer of the notes.

---

1. Some verses after this must have been lost as neither our text nor Bd.P. explains these anywhere.

2. *Uṣṭrakala* in the text being obscure, is emended as per Bd. P.

3. The text is obscure both here and in the Bd. P.

18b. *Prakṣipta* is due to Kalā——(?)

19a. It is called *Hrāsita* (*Bhāṣita* in Bd. P.) in which there is the use of two Kalās as before.

19b. *Visvarārūḍhā* (*Visarārūḍhā*) has got eight notes in ascendance.

20a. That[1] which is a descent from high or low register.

20b. These are placed verily with one interval and have the same note at the end.

21ab. The *Alaṅkāra* called *Makṣipracchedana* is declared to have a group of four Kalās. Thus, these are the thirty *Alaṅkāras* explained.

21c-22. Due to the employment of *Varṇa* and *Sthāna* having the measures of Kāla and Mātrā are the configuration, proportion, modification and characteristics. This should be known as the purpose of embellishments (of music)[2].

23. Just as in the case of beautification (of one's person) it is extremely censured if it is used at the wrong place, similarly unfavourable (discordant) embellishment of the *Varṇas* also (is censurable) as it is produced by oneself.

24. Just as with the use of various ornaments, a woman gets herself beautified, so are the (musical) embellishments to a Varṇa, (but) if discordantly used, it is bitterly denounced.

25. The ear-ring is not seen (worn) on the feet; nor a girdle round the neck. So also the embellishment (in music) if used in the wrong place, is reproached.

26. When the embellishment is effected, it should indicate the Rāga (melody) ; just as the path intended to be undertaken is characterised.

27a. The characteristics, its opposites are indicated (with business ?) by scribes (*Varṇika*?)

27b. I shall describe realistically (as it is)————? (Obscure).

28a. (Obscure) Twenty-three and eighty is the inversion (of their order ?)

---

1. If the reading from Bd.P. is referred to the name of this Alaṅkāra is *Vāpa*. But I am not sure of the correctness of the reading in the Bd.P.
2. *Vide Saṅgīta-ratnākara* I. 6.64 which enumerates *Rakṭilābha* etc.

28b. (Obscure) Even the *Ṣaḍja* becomes a deficient note (in the middle?)

29a. Similarly these result in the confusion between the Grāmas of *Ṣaḍja* and *Madhyama.*

29b. Obscure.

30. Obscure*.

31a. (Obscure) A part of the note *Ma-Madhyama*—is the deviation before Ṛṣabha?

31b. (Obscure) Their division is a guide (*mārgasaṃsthita*) to songs ?

32a. (Obscure) [*Svasāra* and *Svarāntara* have been indicated by me.]

32b. The reverse would take place in the case of the order of seven notes.

33a. The four *Mandraka gītas* (songs) are sung with Gāndhāra as the key note.

33bc. In *Mandraka* gītas, we know the notes *Pañcama* (*Pa*), *Madhyama* (*Ma*), *Dhaivata* (*Dha*), *Niṣāda* (Ni), *Ṣaḍja* (*Sā*), *Ṛṣabha* (*Ri*) as the remaining notes.

34a. One should know two Aparāntika songs.—(The rest is obscure).

34b. (Obscure but with Bd.P. text) In the Aparāntika songs, *Gāndhāra* (*Ga*) is employed in the original and modified form by flute players (*Vaiṇava*). [Bd.P : *Gāndhāra* is employed in the original and modified forms.]

35a. The *Pada* has got three forms (?). The *Kaiśika* [*Ki*] song has seven forms.

35b. The key-note procedure is declared with the entire use of *Gāndhāra.*

35c. This is also the order intended for its *Madhyama* as the key note.

36. The songs which have been mentioned with particular emphasis on the form should be effected with seven notes and the *Kaiśiki* [*-ka*] of the sevenfold form.

---

*(A tentative translation:) The embellishment of Svaras is remembered as the experience (?) of all following. The external music(?) is known to have five deities.

37a. This is called the indication of the component parts (of songs?)

(*The Topic of Tāla*)

There are two even measures.

37b. (Obscure)———the *mātrā* is not advanced (*abhipratiṣṭhitā*)?

38. In Uttara songs in the original form, the *Mātrā* is thus deleted (the rest of the verse obscure).

39. With one foot (*Pada*) in the Mātrā and with one foot deficient————— when there is the *Upahanana* (deficiency, error?) of numbers in it, it is called *Yāna*.

40. The second break in the foot is well established with *Graha* (the starting point of the song) and in the Aparāntika (songs). The first, the eighth, the third and second are established with *Graha* (?)

41. (Obscure) With half of the equivalent of a Pāda and in the one-fifth portion of the Pāda, the *Pāda-bhāga* (one fourth of the Pāda) also along with the one and a quarter (of a pāda) (?) is established in the original form)

42. In the *Uttara* and *Mandraka* songs in their original form, the Kalā exists as explained of the Dakṣiṇa Mārga (way of the Tāla—procedure).[1]

43[2]. Obscure (both here and in Bd.P.)

44. When there is the use of one and the use of two, O best of Brāhmaṇas, and when there is the combination of many *Patākā*[3] etc. are declared.

45a. There are three *Vṛttis*[4]—*Citrā*, *Vṛtti* and *Dakṣiṇā* (the text is obscure and hence emended).

1. Some lines are perhaps missing (*vide* Bd.P. 2.3-62.40-41).
There were three *Mārgas* (ways of the Tāla-procedure) viz. *Citrā*, *Vārtikā* and *Dakṣiṇā* having the Kalā of two *mātrās*, four *mātrās* and eight *mātrās* respectively. The forms *Ekakala*, *Dvikala* and *Catuṣkala* were associated with Mārgas.

2. (Tentative translation): The two feet and their *Āharaṇa*(?) beyond this are not laid down.

3. *Patākā* was one of eight *mātrās*, which was indicated by moving the hand upwards. These *mātrās* were to be employed in the *mārgas* as specifically directed.

4. The *Vṛttis* are the styles of rendering songs. They were three in number viz. *Citrā*, *Vṛtti* and *Dakṣiṇā*. They were associated with the three

45b The *Samavāyas* (combinations of?) are eight; similarly the Mūrcchanā is Sauvīrā.

45c. Obscure.

(Last foot of 45c.) Thus the *Svara-maṇḍala* of seven *Svaras* (notes) (is explained).

CHAPTER TWENTYSIX[1]

The Ikṣvāku Dynasty

Sūta said :

1. When Raivata, otherwise known as Kakudmin, went to that world (of Brahmā) the entire Kuśasthalī was over-run and destroyed by Puṇyajanas and Rākṣasas.

2. The hundred brothers of that noble-souled virtuous king, on being harassed by the Rākṣasas, fled away in great terror.

3. Fleeing in terror, those Kṣatriyas established their families in different places.[2] O excellent Brāhmaṇas, these families were very great.

4-5. As they were virtuous, they were famous in all the quarters as "*Prayatas*"[3] (the pure ones). The family of Dhṛṣṭa, the Kṣatriyas named Dhārṣṭakas, became quite invincible in war. Thus there were three thousand groups of noble-

---

Mārgas : *Citra, Vārtika* and *Dakṣiṇa*, the three *Layas* (Tempi) and *Grahas* etc.

In *Citra* the music of stringed instrument was prominent and song (vocal) subservient. In *Dakṣiṇa*, the song was prominent and instrumental music subservient and in *Vṛtti* both were employed with equal prominence.

1. This chapter corresponds to Bd. P. 2-3-63. The references are to the verses in this chapter.

2. Though the chapter is mainly concerned with the Ikṣvāku dynasty, vv. 3-7 mention a dynasty of the pre-Yayāti period, before *circa* 3000 B.C. (*The Vedic Age*, p. 276, BVB's *The History and Culture of the Indian People* Vol. 1.)

3. Śāryāta in Bd. P. *ibid* v. 5

souled Kṣatriyas. Nabhaga's successor Nābhāga was very powerful.

6. Aṁbarīṣa was the son of Nābhāga. His son was Virūpa. Virūpa's son was Pṛṣadaśva and his son was Rathītara.

7. These (Rathītaras), though born as Kṣatriyas, were known as Aṅgiras-s. The prominent members (descendants) of Rathītara were Brāhmaṇas with Kṣatriya-like (heroic) prowess.[1]

8. Formerly when Manu sneezed, Ikṣāvaku was born.[2] Ikṣvāku had hundred sons. All of them were liberal-minded (distributing enormous wealth as Dakṣiṇā).

9. The eldest son was Vikukṣi. His younger brothers, Nemi and Daṇḍa (two were famous). He had five hundred sons, the chief of them being Śakuni.

10. They were the kings and protectors of the land of Uttarāpatha (northern region). Forty-eight of them ruled in the southern region.

11. Twenty of them were very important. They protected the whole of the southern region.

Ikṣvāku ordered Vikukṣi on the occasion of Aṣṭakā.[3]

12. The king said : O powerful one, kill deer and bring the meat worthy of the Śrāddha. Undoubtedly the *Aṣṭakā Śrāddha* has to be performed today.

13. Vikukṣi who went a-hunting at the instance of the intelligent (king) killed thousands of deer. Though very powerful, he became very tired. He then (killed and) ate a hare.

14. When Vikukṣi returned with the meat along with the army, the king urged Vasiṣṭha, "May the meat be sprinkled with the holy water".

---

1. This indicates the fluidity of the caste-system in ancient India.

2. From v. 8, the Purāṇa describes the Ikṣvāku dynasty. His three sons—Vikukṣi, Nemi and Daṇḍa—founded separate dynasties at Ayodhyā (U.P.), Videha (Bihar) and Daṇḍaka (North Deccan) respectively. Nemi is mentioned as 'Nimi' in Buddhist Jātakas.

3. The Śrāddha performed on the 7th, 8th and 9th days after the Full Moon in the three months of Pauṣa, Māgha and Phālguna.

15. Thus urged by the king, Vasiṣṭha said "So be it" and came there for the due performance (of the *Śrāddha*). On seeing the meat desecrated, he became angry and spoke to the King:

16. "O king of great lustre, the meat has been desecrated by your son (behaving like a) Śūdra. The meat offered by you cannot be eaten, as he had eaten a hare.

17. O excellent king, O sinless one, a hare has been eaten by the wicked one before (the *Śrāddha*) at the forest. Hence this meat has been defiled and made unworthy of the Pitṛs."

18-19. The infuriated Ikṣvāku then spoke thus to Vikukṣi: "Commanded by me for the purpose of the rites of Pitṛs, you went for hunting the deer. In the forest you mercilessly ate the flesh of a hare before the Śrāddha. Hence I banish you. Go away along with your fate (as a result of your own action)." Thus at the instance of Vasiṣṭha the son was abandoned by Ikṣvāku.

20-23. When Ikṣvāku passed away, the hare-eater attained this earth. He was a very virtuous-souled king of Ayodhyā. Urged and guided by Vasiṣṭha, he ruled over the kingdom. Thereafter, being full of that sin, the king, ruling over the kingdom declined in power as time elapsed.[1] After understanding (the import of) this story, no one shall eat (meat) outside the injunction. Learned men explain the etymology of *Māṁsa* (Meat) thus—'In the other world that will eat me, *Māṁ Sa* (*Bhakṣayitā*) the flesh of which I eat here now'.[2]

24-25. Śaśāda's successor was Kakutstha, the powerful. Formerly he had sat on the hump of Indra who had assumed the form of a bull, in the course of the war named Āḍībaka.[3]

Hence he is remembered as Kakutstha[4] (The occupier of the hump).

Anenas was the son of Kakutstha. Pṛthu was the son of Anenas.

---

1. or went to an inferior world (hell) after death.
2. Quoted from Manu V. 55.
3. *Āḍī-baka*—The deadly combat fought by Vasiṣṭha and Viśvāmitra after assuming the forms of *Āḍi* and *Baka* (two acquatic birds). Devas and Asuras fought with each other forming an alliance with Vasiṣṭha and Viśvāmitra.
4. Kālidāsa, however, explains the epithet *Kakutstha* as 'one who

26. Vṛṣadaśva was Pṛthu's son. From him was born the powerful Andhra. Yavanāśva was Andhra's son. Śrāvasta was his son.

27. Śrāvasta was the king by whom Śrāvastī[1] was built. Śrāvasta's successor was Bṛhadaśva of great fame.

28. It is heard that Kuvalāśva was the son of Bṛhadaśva. By killing Dhundhu that king became known as Dhundhumāra.

The Sages said :

29. O highly intelligent one, we wish to hear how Dhundhu was slain, whereby Kuvalāśva attained the title of Dhundhumāra.

Sūta said :

30-32. Bṛhadaśva had twentyone thousand sons. All of them were experts in Vidyās. They were powerful and invincible. All of them were righteous. All of them were performers of Yajñas with profuse Dakṣiṇā. Bṛhadaśva, the king, crowned Kuvalāśva who was very powerful, heroic, excellent and virtuous, in that kingdom. After transferring the royal position and glory to his son, the king went to the forest.

33. Uttaṅka, the Brāhmaṇa sage, prevented the great heroic king Bṛhadaśva who was excellent and virtuous and who was proceeding to the forest (for penance).

Uttaṅka said :

34. "O King, protection must be offered by you. It behoves you to do it. I am unable to perform penance undisturbed.

---

occupies a prominent place among kings' in *Raghuvaṁśa* VI. 71 as follows:

Ikṣvāku-vaṁśyaḥ kakudaṁ nṛpāṇām
Kakutstha ityāhita-lakṣaṇo'bhūt /

Mallinātha, the commentator, correctly mentions the Purāṇic episode (*vide* his comm. on *ibid.*).

1. Modern Sahet-Mahet on the Rāpti (ancient Airāvatī or Acirāvatī) in the Gonda District in U.P.

35. In the wild desert region near my hermitage, there is a vast sea full of sand, O king.[1]

36. There is a huge-bodied, extremely powerful being lying beneath the ground covered with sand. He cannot be killed even by Devas.

37. He is the son of Manu. His name is Dhundhu. He is cruel and terrible. He is performing a severe penance for the last hundred years for the destruction of the worlds.

38. He breathes out (once) at the end of a year. But when he exhales the whole earth along with forests quakes and shakes.

39. A great column of dust is raised by the air exhaled by him. It covers up the path of the sun and the earth-quake continues for a week.

40. It is accompanied by very terrible flames of fire, sparks and smoke. O King, I am not therefore able to stay in my own hermitage.

41. O brawny-armed king, restrain him with a desire for the welfare of the worlds. The great deity Viṣṇu will further develop your prowess by means of his own splendour.

42. The worlds will be happy and relieved today when the Asura is killed. O King, you are hence competent to kill him.

43-44. O Sinless one, a boon has been granted to me (that you would help me by killing him) formerly by Viṣṇu. Hence Dhundhu of great virility cannot be slain by anyone of less splendour even in hundreds of years. His virility is so great that it cannot be brooked even by the Devas."

45. Thus requested by the noble-souled Uttaṅka, that saintly king entrusted his son Kuvalāśva with the job of restraining Dhundhu.

1. Verses 35-40 describe a sandy region with occasional earthquakes and something like volcanic eruptions. Scholars differ about its identification. B.C. Law conjectures that this volcanic pit near the western sea was submerged with sea-water and the volcanic action ceased by the efforts of Kuvalāśva (*Tribes in Ancient India*, p. 126). Pargiter regards this as a shallow sand-filled sea in Rajasthan which prevented Aryan expansion (*AIHT* pp. 260-61).

46. The King said, "I have already laid aside my weapons. Here is my son. O Excellent Brāhmaṇa, he will undoubtedly become the slayer of Dhundhu."

47. After ordering his son who was ready to slay Dhundhu, the king of praise-worthy holy observances retired to the mountains for performing penance.

48. The righteous-souled king Kuvalāśva, obeying the behest of his father, went ahead to Dhundhu's haunt, accompanied by his twentyone thousand sons and Uttaṅka, in order to restrain Dhundhu.

49. Due to the imploring entreaty of Uttaṅka, and with a desire for the welfare of the worlds, lord Viṣṇu entered him with his own brilliance.

50. When that invincible (king) started, a loud voice arose in heaven—"This king shall be the slayer of Dhundhu (Dhundhumāra) with effect from today."

51-52. The Devas honoured him with divine flowers. It was a wonderful thing. That tiger-like man (the king) of great prowess went to that vast sea of sand accompanied by his sons and dug it up without any waste (of time). That saintly king had already been developed (empowered) extra-ordinarily by the splendour of Nārāyaṇa.

53-54. He became still more powerful by staying under the control of Uttaṅka. Dhundhu was found out by his sons who were digging. He had been lying hidden beneath the sand on the western side. He seemed to be furiously covering the worlds by means of the fire coming out of his mouth.

55. O excellent one among the imbibers of Soma, by means of his Yogic power, he exuded water like the great ocean at the time of Moon-rise. It was a vast sheet of water with currents and waves.

56. His sons excepting three were burnt by the Rākṣasa. Then the king of great strength destroyed all the attendants and kinsmen of Dhundhu.

57. The king who was a Yogin, drank up his behemence in the form of water-flood (let loose by him) by means of his Yogic power and extinguished the fire by means of water.

58. Then he overpowered the huge-bodied aquatic

demon by means of his strength. The king, having successfully accomplished his task, showed him to Uttaṅka.

59-60. To the noble-souled king, Uttaṅka granted the boons of everlasting wealth, invincibility (in battles) by his enemies, perpetual interest in Dharma and everlasting residence in heaven. To the sons who were killed by the demon, he granted everlasting worlds in heaven.

61. Dṛḍhāśva was the eldest of his three sons who survived. Bhadrāśva and Kapilāśva were the younger ones.

62. Dṛḍhāśva was known as Dhaundhumāri (son of Dhundhumāra). Haryaśva was his son. His son was Nikuṁbha who was always engaged in Kṣātra Dharma (military Profession).

63. Saṁhatāśva was the son of Nikuṁbha. He is reputed as an expert in warfare. Kṛśāśva and Akṣayāśva were the sons of Saṁhatāśva.

64. His wife was Haimavatī who was like the river Dṛśadvatī to the minds of the good. She was famous in the three worlds. Her son was Prasenajit.

65. Yuvanāśva was his son. He was very brilliant and famous in the three worlds as highly virtuous. The chaste lady Gaurī was his wife.

66. She was cursed by her husband and turned into the river Bāhudā.[1] Her son Gaurika became an emperor.

67. Māndhātā, the son of Yuvanāśva, became a king conquering the three worlds. In this connection, Brāhmaṇas well versed in Purāṇas, cite these two verses.

68. "The entire region from the place where the Sun rises up to (the place) where he sets, the whole of it, is called the territory of Māndhātā, son of Yuvanāśva".

69. People who know the (details of) different races also quote this verse. "Those who know Purāṇas call the son of Yuvanāśva, noble-souled, a performer of sacrifices and (a king) of unmeasured splendour. Māndhātā is the embodied form of Viṣṇu."

---

1. Modern Dhumela or Burha-Rapti, a feeder of the Rapti in Oudh (U.P.). Sage Likhita had his amputated arm rejoined by a bath in this river. Hence she is *Bāhu-dā* 'Granter of arms'—De 16

70. His wife Caitrarathī was Śaśabindu's daughter. She was known by the name of Bindumatī also. She was a chaste lady and had no equal in beauty all over the earth.

71. She was the eldest sister of ten thousand brothers. She was devotedly attached to her husband. Māndhātā begot three sons of her.

72. They were Purukutsa, Aṁbarīṣa and Mucukunda. Ambarīṣa's successor was another Yuvanāśva.

73. Harita was Yuvanāśva's son. Descendants of Harita are remembered by the name Śūris. They were the (adopted) sons of Aṅgiras (spiritual lineage). They were Brāhmaṇas endowed with martial qualities.

74. Purukutsa's successor was Trasaddasyu of great fame. He was born of Narmadā. His son was Saṁbhūta.

75. Saṁbhūta's son was the valorous Anaraṇya. He was killed by Rāvaṇa formerly while he was conquering the three worlds.

76. Trasadaśva was the son of Anaraṇya. His son was Haryaśva. From Haryaśva Dṛṣadvatī gave birth to king Vasumata.

77. His son was the virtuous king Tridhanvā by name. The scholarly king Trayyāruṇa was the son of Tridhanvan.

78-79. He had a powerful son named Satyavrata. Vidarbha's wife was abducted by him after killing (i.e. defeating) the heaven-dwellers, when all the sacred mantras of marriage ceremony had been chanted and the ceremonies concluded. Viṣṇuvṛddha was his son whence his descendants are remembered as Viṣṇuvṛddhas. They were also the (adopted) sons of Aṅgiras endowed with martial qualities.

80. That (sin) was committed by him out of lust, or (pride) due to his strength, or to the powerful force exerted by the inevitable destiny, though he was intelligent.

81. His father Trayyāruṇa banished him as he was sinful. Being infuriated with him, he repeated many times, "Be degraded (and gone)".

82. He spoke to his father again and again, "I am alone. Where shall I go?" The father ordered him: "Live among the Cāṇḍālas.

83. O defiler of the family, I don't seek to be a father with such a son as you." On being repulsed thus by the words of the king, he went out of the city.

84. Vasiṣṭha, the holy lord and sage, did not give him asylum. The bold and intelligent Satyavrata, discarded by his father, lived near the hutments of Cāṇḍālas. The father too went to the forest.

85. On account of that unrighteous deed, Indra did not bring showers to that land for full twelve years.

86. Viśvāmitra of great penance left his wife in that land and performed a severe penance in the marshy land near the sea.

87. His wife tied her own bosom-born middle son (with a rope) round his neck and offered him for sale in exchange for a hundred cows for maintaining (the remaining ones).

88-89. On seeing the son of the sage tied round the neck, the excellent man of good rites, the virtuous-souled Satyavrata of great intellect, got him released by being sold. He nurtured him in order to propitiate Viśvāmitra and gain his sympathy.

90. The boy came to be known as Gālava because he had been tied round the neck (*Gala*). That descendant of Kuśika, a great sage of severe penance had been redeemed by that powerful (King).

91. On account of his (?) sacred vow, devotion, mercy and solemn declaration, the king who adhered to the rules of discipline, sustained Viśvāmitra's wife also.

92. After killing deer, boars, buffaloes and other forest animals, he cooked that flesh near the hermitage of Viśvāmitra.

93-94. At the behest of the father, he adopted a secret vow (*Upāṁśu Vrata*) and for that purpose took initiation extending to twelve years. As the king (Satyavrata's father) had gone to the forest, the sage Vasiṣṭha, in the capacity of the king's priest, protected Ayodhyā, the kingdom and the harem.

95. Out of childishness, or due to the force of the inevitable destiny, Satyavrata nursed a great grudge against Vasiṣṭha.

96. While he was crying on being exiled by his father and banished from the kingdom, the sage Vasiṣṭha had not restrain-

97. The Mantras chanted during the celebration of a marriage are concluded at the seventh step (of the *Saptapadī* rite) but Satyavrata abducted her (the bride of Vidarbha) at the seventh step.

98. 'Vasiṣṭha the knower of Dharmas does not wish to repeat the Mantras.' So Vasiṣṭha was inwardly angry with Satyavrata*(?)

99. It was because of being fully mindful of his position as preceptor that Vasiṣṭha did so then. Nor did Satyavrata understand the secret vow of (the sage).

100-102. (Defective verses) When the father of lofty mind passed away, Indra did not shower for twelve years. Thereby all the people on the earth became weak. All these years the son was having *Dīkṣā* (i.e. performing holy rites in accordance with his fathers' injunction). Vasiṣṭha thought that the people would be saved if he was crowned again. So he restrained Satyavrata from keeping out of the kingdom further.

103-106. The powerful (younger king) performed the holy rites for twelve years. When there was no meat available, the son of the king saw the cow of the noble-souled Vasiṣṭha, Kāmadughā (i.e. the yielder of desired objects). Out of spite, due to delusion and exhaustion and because he was hungry, the foremost among powerful persons who had adopted the practice of Dasyus (robbers and Cāṇḍālas), killed the cow. He himself ate the meat and fed the sons of Viśvāmitra also. On hearing it Vasiṣṭha abandoned him then. The holy lord Vasiṣṭha spoke also thus to the son of the king (i.e. Satyavrata):

107. "O base one among men, had it not been for the fact that you have already three Śaṅkus (sins), O cruel one, I would have let this iron Śaṅku (rod) fall on you.

108. Your transgression (commission of sins) is of three forms: One because of the dissatisfaction of your father, the other due to the slaughter of the preceptor's cow and (finally) due to the partaking of unsanctified (flesh)."

---

*The line needs emendation as in Bd. P. v. 97:
iti satyavrato roṣaṁ vasiṣṭhe manasā 'karot /
'So Satyavrata entertained anger about Vasiṣṭha in his mind'.

109. Thus (observing out) the three sins, the sage of great penance called him, "Triśaṅku" by which name he is remembered.

110. After returning (from his penance), Viśvāmitra was delighted (on hearing that Satyavrata) had looked after his wife (in his absence). He granted boons to Triśaṅku.

111-112. When he was asked to choose a boon as he pleased, the son of the king (Satyavrata) requested him to be his preceptor. When the danger of the drought lasting for twelve years was averted, the sage (Viśvāmitra) crowned him in the hereditary kingdom and presided over his sacrifice. Even as Devas and Vasiṣṭha were watching, the holy lord Kauśika (Viśvāmitra) made him ascend to heaven along with his physical body.

113. To Vasiṣṭha who was watching, it was very surprising. In this connection, people well-versed in the Purāṇas cite these two verses:

114-115. By the favour of Viśvāmitra, Triśaṅku shines in heaven with great brilliance in the company of Devas. It is the result of the blessing of that intelligent one. A beautiful woman bedecked by the moon in the season Hemanta proceeds slowly. She is embellished by the three Bhāvas and adorned by the heavenly body—a planet (called) Triśaṅku.

116. Satyaratā hailing from the Kekaya family was his wife. She gave birth to a son, Hariścandra, the sinless.

117. That king Hariścrndra was well known as Traiśaṅkava (son of Triśaṅku). He was renowned as an emperor and a performer of Rājasūya sacrifice.

118. Hariścandra's son was Rohita, the powerful. Harita was Rohita's son. Cañcu is called Hārīta (son of Harita).

119. Vijaya and Sudeva were the sons of Cañcu. Since he was the conqueror of all Kṣatriyas, he is remembered as Vijaya.

120. Ruruka was his son. He was a king, a great expert in matters pertaining to religion and wealth. Hṛtaka (or Dhṛtaka) was the son of Ruruka and Bāhu was born of him.

121. The king (viz. Bāhu) who was addicted to vice was

defeated by Haihayas, Tālajaṅghas, Śakas, Yavanas, Kāṁbojas, Pāradas and Pahlavas.

122. Even in that righteous Satyayuga that king was not very virtuous. Sagara was born as the son of Bāhu. He was born with a body containing poison in the hermitage of Bhṛgu. He was saved by Turva (Aurva).

123. After obtaining the missile pertaining to Fire-god from Bhārgava, the king Sagara went over the whole of the earth and killed Tālajaṅghas along with Haihayas.

124. The unerring king repudiated the Dharma (code of conduct, rites etc.) of Śakas and Pahlavas. He who was conversant with Dharma cast out the Dharma of (his opponents) Kṣatriyas and Pāradas (i.e. excommunicated them).

The Sages enquired :

125-126. How was the king Sagara (*Sa-gara*) born with poison (inside)? Why did the infuriated unerring king repudiate the traditional holy rites of those powerful Kṣatriyas such as the Śakas and others?

Sūta said :

It is reported that the kingdom of the vicious king Bāhu was taken over by Haihayas and Tālajaṅghas who came along with Śakas ?

127. These five clans, viz. Yavanas, Pāradas, Kāṁbojas, Pahlavas, (and Śakas) attacked him.

128. His kingdom was plundered and taken by these powerful leading Kṣatriyas. King Bāhu whose realm was seized, renounced the world. Accompanied by his wife the righteous-souled king entered the forest and performed penance.

129. After some time the king once went to fetch water. Due to advancing years and weakness he died midway.

130. His wife Yādavī who was pregnant then, followed him. Poison had been administered to her by her co-wife with a desire to kill the foetus.

131. She prepared the funeral pyre of her husband, got him placed and lit it and was (about) to enter into the fire, when Aurva, descendant of Bhṛgu made her desist from it out of sympathy.

132. In his (Aurva's) hermitage, she delivered the foetus (child) along with the (administered) poison. Thus she gave birth to her son, the mighty-armed virtuous Sagara.

133. Aurva performed the post-natal holy rites for that noble soul. After teaching him Vedas and Śāstras he instructed him in the use of miraculous weapons and missiles.

134. Then he learnt the use of the miraculous missile of Fire-god from the son of Jamadagni (in fact Aurva)—a missile which could not be endured even by Asuras. Naturally strong and with the added strength of those missiles the infuriated king killed Haihayas like Rudra destroying *Paśus* (Individuals).

135. Then the king attempted to exterminate completely Śakas, Yavanas, Kāmbojas, Pāradas and Pahlavas.

136. Being harassed and victimised by the heroic and noble-souled Sagara, all of them desirous of protection sought shelter and protection from Vasiṣṭha.

137. Having stipulated some conditions, Vasiṣṭha agreed. Promising them protection from fear (of extermination by Sagara), the great sage restrained Sagara.

138. Remembering his own vow and on hearing the words of his preceptor, Sagara put an end to their traditional rites of worship and made them change their dress and apparel.[1]

139. He got half of the heads of Śakas shaved and released them. He got the heads of Yavanas and Kāmbojas completely shaven.

140. Pāradas were compelled to keep their hair dishevelled and Pahlavas were made to grow their beards. They were debarred from Vedic study and the use of *Vaṣaṭkāra* by that noble-souled king.

141-142. Śakas, Yavanas, Kāṁbojas, Pahlavas, Pāradas, Kelisparśas, Māhiṣikas, Dārvas, Colas and Khasas—all these were clans of Kṣatriyas. Their traditional religious rites were prohibited by the noble-souled Sagara at the instance of Vasiṣṭha.

---

1. Verses 139-140 describe the ways of hair-dressing etc. of these tribes and attribute to Sagara the credit of imposing these non-kṣatriya ways on them.

143. Conducting his conquests righteously, the king conquered the earth and took initiation for the performance of a horse-sacrifice. He let loose the horse.

144. As it was being taken round, it was stolen near the shore of the south-eastern sea and made to enter beneath the earth.

145-146. The king made all his sons to dig the whole area. Then ultimately, in the great ocean, they met with the primordial Being, Lord Viṣṇu, Lord Hari, Kṛṣṇa, the Lord of subjects, Lord Haṁsa, Lord Nārāyaṇa, in the form of Kapila.

147. They came within the range of the vision of that brilliant being. Then all those sons (of Sagara) were burnt and four of them survived.

148. They were Barhiketu, Suketu, Dharmarata and the heroic Pañcavana. All these continued the lineage of the lord (Sagara).

149. Lord Hari, Nārāyaṇa granted him boons such as the everlasting nature of his race, the benefit of a hundred horse-sacrifices, the all-pervading *Samudra* (ocean) as the son and perpetual residence in heaven.

150. Taking the horse with him, the ocean, the lord of rivers, came there and bowed to him. On account of that action he earned the title of "Sāgara" (born of Sagara).

151. After regaining the horse from the ocean the king performed horse-sacrifices again and again making up the total of one hundred.

152. We have heard (it reported) that there were sixty thousand sons. Those sixty thousand sons were burnt. Those noble-souled sixty thousand sons entered (merged in) the divine brilliance of Nārāyaṇa.

The Sages enquired :

153. By what means did the sixty thousand sons of Sagara become powerful and valorous? Please narrate.

Sūta replied :

154. Sagara had two wives. By means of penance they had burnt all their sins. The elder of them named Keśinī was the daughter of Vidarbha.

155. The younger wife was very virtuous. She was the daughter of Ariṣṭanemi. In beauty she was unrivalled on the earth.

156. Propitiated by meàns of penance, the holy lord Aurva granted them these boons—"One of them will give birth to a son who will establish the lineage and who will be coveted. The other will give birth to sixty thousand sons."

157. On hearing the words of the sage in the king's assembly, Keśinī, the elder one, chose the boon of a single son who will be the cause of the perpetuation of the race.

158. Sumati, the sister of Suparṇa, accepted the boon of sixty thousand sons from the noble-souled sage, in accordance with her wish.

159. After some time the elder wife gave birth to the eldest son (subsequently) famous as Asamañja (Asamañjasa), the son of Sagara, the scion of the family of Kakutstha.

160. Sumati, the famous lady, gave birth to a gourd-like foetus. From the gourd-like foetus all the sixty thousand sons came out.

161. The king caused (pieces of) the foetus to be deposited in (sixty thousand) jars of ghee and engaged as many nurses to look after them individually.

162. Then, In the course of nine months, they grew well and came out of them (jars) hale and hearty; those blessed sons heightened the pleasure of Sagara.

163-164. After a long time those sixty thousand sons (of Sagara) attained youth. Of those who (later) (closely) followed the horse (of Aśvamedha) the eldest son of Sagara was a tiger among men. The powerful one was famous as Asamañja, otherwise known as Barhiketu.

165. Since he was engaged in activities against the interest of the citizens, he was banished by his father at the very outset. The son of Asamañja was the powerful Aṁśumān.

166. His son was a virtuous soul. He was well-known by the name of Dilīpa. From Dilīpa was born Bhagīratha, a hero of great splendour.

167. Gaṅgā, the most excellent of rivers, rendered beautiful with aerial chariots, was (brought here in this world) by him. She was given the status of a daughter by the (king), the

performer of the sacrifice (*ijānena*), from the sea[1] (?) In this connection, people well-versed in Purāṇas cite this verse.

168. "Bhagīratha brought down Gaṅgā by means of his active endeavour. Hence Gaṅgā is called Bhāgīrathī by those who are the foremost ones among those conversant with genealogies (of kings)."

169. Bhagīratha's son was Śruta by name. His successor was Nābhāga. He was always engaged in religious activities.

170. Aṁbarīṣa was his son. Sindhudvīpa succeeded him. It is well-known that the knowers of the Purāṇa of genealogies sing thus:

171. "Protected by the arms of Aṁbarīṣa, son of Nābhāga, the earth became completely free from three types of *Tāpa* (distress)".

172. Ayutāyu, the powerful, was the son of Sindhudvīpa. Ṛtuparṇa of great fame was the successor of Ayutāyu.

173. He was the knower of the divine *Akṣahṛdaya Mantra* (the Mantra with which people become sure winners at the game of dice). He was a powerful king and a friend to Nala.

There are two Nalas of stead ast holy rites, very famous in the Purāṇas.

174. One of them was the son of Vīrasena and the other a leading member of the Ikṣvāku race. Ṛtuparṇa's son was Sarvakāma who was lord of the people.

175. King Sudāsa was his son. He was *Haṁsamukha* (one with the face of a swan)[2]. Sudāsa's son was the king Saudāsa.

176. He was well-known by the names of Kalmāṣapāda and Mitrasaha. Vasiṣṭha, of great brilliance, begot of Kalmāṣapāda's wife the son Aśmaka, for the purpose of making the line of Ikṣvāku flourish (and perpetuate).

177. Urakāma was the son of Aśmaka and his son was Mūlaka. As regards King Mūlaka, they cite the following (verse).

---

1. The text: *ijānona samudrādvai* is obscure and gives an awkward meaning, especially of *samudrāt*. Bd. P. v.167: *ihānītā sureśād vai* etc. 'was brought here (in this world) and was assigned the daughterly status from the lord of Suras.'

2. *Indra-sakho* 'a friend of Indra' in Bd. P. v. 175 is better.

178. "That lordly king, frightened of Rāma (i.e. Paraśurāma) always stayed surrounded by women. Seeking protection, he abandoned his (manly) apparel and had the coat of mail (in the form) of women."

179. The righteous king Śataratha is remembered as the son of Mūlaka. From Śataratha was born the powerful king Aiḍiviḍa.

180. The son of Aiḍiviḍa was the glorious and valorous Kṛtaśarmā. He had a daughter also and his son was Viśvamahat (Viśvasaha in Bd.P.)

181. Dilīpa was his son. He became well known as Khaṭvāṅga. Having attained a span of life extending to a Muhūrta, he returned to this world from *svarga* (celestial world). By means of his intelligence and truthfulness the three worlds were mastered by him.

182. Dīrghabāhu was his son and Raghu was born of him. Aja was the son of Raghu. From him (Aja) was born that powerful king Daśaratha, the cause of delight for the race of Ikṣvāku.

183. The heroic Rāma, the knower of Dharmas, well-known in the worlds, Bharata, Lakṣmaṇa and Śatrughna of great strength were the sons of Daśaratha.

184. After killing Lavaṇa, the son of Madhu, Śatrughna entered his Madhuvana and founded the city of Mathurā there.

185. Subāhu and Śūrasena, his sons, born of the princess of Videha, protected the city of Mathurā, accompanied by (their father) Śatrughna.

186. Aṅgada and Candraketu were the sons of Lakṣmaṇa. Their territories at the border of mountain Himālaya were very prosperous and flourishing.

187. Aṅgadīyā, the capital city of Aṅgada, was in the land Kārapatha.[1] Candravaktrā, the city of the mighty Candraketu, was very auspicious.

188. Takṣa and Puṣkara were the heroic sons of Bharata.

1. Modern Kārābāgh or Bāghān on the west bank of the Indus, at the foot of salt range called Niti hill in the Bannu district (cf. *Raghuvaṁśa*. XV-90).

—De 92

The cities of those two noble-souled ones were in the Siddha land of Gāndhāra.

189. The beautiful city of Takṣa, viz. Takṣaśilā[1] is renowned in all the quarters. Puṣkarāvatī,[2] the city of the heroic Puṣkara, is also well-known.

190. The people who know the Purāṇas sing this Gāthā (laudatory verse): "All the principles are fettered to (concentrated in) intelligent Rāma due to his greatness."

191. Rāma was a dark-complexioned, youthful, red-eyed, bright-faced hero with arms extending upto the knees. With a smiling face and leonine shoulders, that mighty-armed (one) uttered only measured words.

192-193. Rāma reigned for ten thousand years. The sound of the chanting of Ṛk, Sāman and Yajur Mantras and the twanging of his bow string were always heard.

"May it be given. May it be enjoyed". These utterances were continuously heard in the realm. While staying in Janasthāna[3] he carried out the work of Devas.

194. Proceeding in search of Sītā, that renowned leader of men killed the (demon) of the family of Pulastya, who had committed sins before.

195. Rāma, son of Daśaratha, was brilliant with his own splendour. He possessed Sāttvic qualities. He was richly endowed with good attributes. He surpassed even the Sun and the blazing fire in brilliance.

196. Thus the mighty-armed scion of the family of Ikṣvāku killed Rāvaṇa along with all of his followers and then went back to Heaven.

197. Śrīrāma's son was called Kuśa, He had another son Lava of great prowess. Understand (the names of) their realms.

---

1 Taxila, in the district of Rawalpindi in W. Panjab, (now) Pakistan.

2. According to VR. VII. 101.10-15 it was founded by Bharata. Probably the same as 'Poukelaotes' mentioned by Greeks as being sacked by Alexander the great. De (p. 163) identifies it with Charsaddah, eighteen miles north of Peshawar, on the Landi near its junction with the Kabul river.

3. Modern Nasik or Pañcavaṭi in Mahārāshtra.

198. The realm of Kuśa was Kośalā. The capital city was Kuśasthalī.[1] This beautiful city was founded by him on the ridges of the Vindhya mountains.

199. Uttara-Kośala was the kingdom of the noble-souled Lava. (His capital) Śrāvastī was renowned in the worlds. Understand the descendants of Kuśa.

200. Kuśa's son was the pious-souled Atithi who loved to receive guests hospitably. Atithi's son who was more well-known than his father was a king named Niṣadha.

201. Nala was the son of Niṣadha and Nabha was Nala's son. Puṇḍarīka was born of Nabha and Kṣemadhanvan was his son.

202. The valorous king Devānīka was Kṣemadhanvā's son. Devānīka's son was lord Ahīnagu by name.

203. Ahīnagu's successor was Pāriyātra of great fame. His son was Dala and from him was born the king Bala.

204. Bala's son was a pious-souled (king) Auṅka[2] by name. His son was Vajranābha whose son was Śaṅkhaṇa.

205. Śaṅkhaṇa's son Dhyuṣitāśva was a renowned scholar. King Viśvasaha was the son of Dhyuṣitāśva.

206. Hiraṇyanābha belonged to Kośala. His son was Vasiṣṭha. He was remembered as the disciple of the grandson of Jaimini in all auspicious rites.

207. He had studied five hundred Vedic Saṁhitās.[3] The Yoga philosophy was learned from him by the intelligent Yājñavalkya.

208. Puṣya, his son, was a great scholar. His son was Dhruvasandhi. Sudarśana was his son and Agnivarṇa was born of Sudarśana.

209. Agnivarṇa's son was Śīghra and Manu (Maru in Bd. P.) is remembered as the son of Śīghraka. Manu adopted

---

1. De (p. 111) identifies it with Ujjain but our text locates it on the ridges of the Vindhya mountain.

2. 'Ulūka' as per Bd. P.v. 205. Pargiter, in the list of kings of Ayodhya, calls him 'Uktha' (*AIHT*, p. 149).

3. Bd.P. v. 207 states that Pauṣyañji was his teacher in Sāma Veda. Pauṣyañji, a disciple of Sukarman, taught 500 branches of the Sāma Veda.

Yogic practice and stayed in the village Kalāpagrāma.[1] In the nineteenth Yuga, he would be the lord who originated and made the Kṣatriya race flourish.

210. Manu's son was Prasuśruta. His son was Susandhi. Susandhi's son was Amarṣa, otherwise known by the name Sahasvān.

211. Sahasvān's son was the king known by the name Viśrutavān. Viśrutavān's son was the king Bṛhadbala.

212. These are the mostly remembered kings, the successors of Ikṣvāku. The most important members of the race have been enumerated here.

213-214. One who reads well this creation of Vivasvān, the son of Aditi, becomes endowed with progeny. He attains identity with Vaivasvata Manu, lord Śrāddha-Deva who bestows prosperity on the subjects. He becomes free from sins and Rājasic qualities. He becomes long-lived and does not swerve from the righteous path.

CHAPTER TWENTYSEVEN

The Nimi Dynasty[2]

Sūta said:

1-3. Now (listen to and) understand the race of Nimi[3], the younger brother of Vikukṣi. It was he who founded a city well known as Jayanta near the hermitage of Gautama. It (the city) was comparable to the city of Devas. In his race a very intelligent son named Nemi was born to Ikṣvāku of great

1. Probably a fictitious place. It is regarded to have been situated somewhere near Badrinath in the Himalayas. It was a pleasure haunt of Urvaśī and Purūravas according to our text. Maru (Manu) and Devāpi, the last kings of the Solar and Lunar races are practising Yoga, waiting to re-establish their kingdoms at Ayodhya and Hastinapur after the incarnation of Kalki.

2. This chapter corresponds to Bd. P. 2.3.64., so from Bd. P. only verse numbers are mentioned.

3. Nimi is a respectable king in Brahmanical, Bauddha and Jaina traditions. As a popular etymology, 'Videha' (mod. Tirhut) is traced to his being bodiless due to Vasiṣṭha's curse (see v. 4-5 below).

brilliance. He was extremely pious-souled and revered by all living beings. He was born in the course of a Yajña, the procreator (*Janaka*) being an excellent sage.

4-5. By the curse of Vasiṣṭha, he became *Videha* (devoid of body). His son named Mithi was procreated in the course of three Parvans. This king of great fame was born of *Araṇi* (a piece of wood from which fire is kindled for sacrificial purpose) while it was being churned. He was well known by the name of Mithi. Since his birth was of this type, he became (known as) Janaka.

6. Mithi was a king of great prowess whereby the capital city became (known as) Mithilā[1] and the king was Janaka. Janaka's son was Udāvasu.

7. From Udāvasu was born the extremely pious-souled Nandivardhana. From Nandivardhana was born the heroic and pious Suketu.

8. From Suketu was born the pious-souled Devarāta of great strength. It is heard that the pious-souled Bṛhaduccha was Devarāta's son.

9. Bṛhaduccha's son was the valorous Mahāvīrya. Dhṛtimān was the son of Mahāvīrya and his son was Sudhṛti.

10. The pious-souled Dhṛṣṭaketu, the oppressor of enemies, was the son of Sudhṛti. Dhṛṣṭaketu's son was well known by the name of Haryaśva.

11. Maru was Haryaśva's son. Pratitvaka[2] was Maru's son. The pious-souled king Kīrtiratha was the son of Pratitvaka.

12. The son of Kīrtiratha was well known as Devamīḍha. and Vibudha was the son of Devamīḍha and Vibudha's son was Dhṛti.

13. Mahādhṛti's son was Kīrtirāja, a king of great valour. Kīrtirāja's son was a scholar well known as Mahāromā.

---

1. Also called Janakapur, capital of Videha in the district of Darbhanga (Bihar). It was famous for its Brahmanical University (upto 14th cent. A.D.). Now a new Sanskrit University has been founded there some years back.

2. Pratimbaka in Bd.P. v. 11. Pargiter records 'Pratindhaka' as his name (*AIHT*, p. 147).

14. From Mahāromā was born the famous Svarṇaromā. Svarṇaromā's son was the king Hrasvaromā.

15. It is heard that the son of Hrasvaromā was the scholar Sīradhvaja. While this king was ploughing, Sītā, of great fame, was born. She became the chaste queen of Rāma. She was devoted to her husband and a virtuous wife.

Śāṁśapāyana enquired:

16. How was Sītā of great fame born while (the field) was being ploughed. Why did the king plough the field wherein she was born ?

Sūta replied :

17. While the Agnikṣetra (the field where sacrifice was to be performed) was being ploughed in accordance with the injunction in the course of the horse-sacrifice of the noble soul she was born out of it.

18. From Sīradhvaja was born the Maithila (king of Mithilā) named Bhānumān. His brother was Kuśadhvaja, the lord and king of Kāśī.

19. Bhānumān's son was the valorous Pradyumna. His son was Muni and from him Ūrjavaha is remembered (as born).

20. From Ūrjavaha was born Sutadvāja. Śakuni was his son. Śakuni's son was Svāgata.[1] Suvarcas is remembered as his son.

21. Śruta was his successor. Suśruta was his son. Jaya was Suśruta's son. Vijaya was the son of Jaya.

22. Vijaya's son was Ṛta and Sunaya was the son of Ṛta. From Sunaya was born Vītahavya, and Vītahavya's son was Dhṛti.

23. Dhṛti's son was Bahulāśva and Bahulāśva's son was Kṛti.[2] It is with him that the race of Janaka is terminated. Thus the Maithilas (kings of Mithilā) are enumerated. Understand the race of Soma also.

---

1. The list in *AIHT*, p. 144 shows that our text and Bd.P. jumped twelve generations downwards and declared Svāgata as the son of Śakuni.

2. Kṛtakṣaṇa in *AIHT*, p. 149.

CHAPTER TWENTYEIGHT

The Nativity of Soma and Saumya (Budha)

Sūta said:

1. O Brāhamaṇas, the progenitor of the Moon-god was Atri, the holy sage. He surpassed all the worlds by means of his brilliance. He was a holy lord.

2-3. He always performed only holy rites physically, mentally and verbally. We have heard that formerly, for a period of three thousand years, he performed a penance that was indeed very difficult to be performed in the worlds, wherein with his arms upraised he stood firm (unmoved) like (a piece of) wood, a wall or a piece of rock.

4. The highly intelligent Brāhmaṇa had sublimated his sexual urge. He stood without even winking his eyes. His body attained the status of Soma.

5. The sage of sanctified soul in the state of Soma rose up (to the sky). The Soma juice exuded from his eyes illuminating all the quarters.

6. On being ordered by Vidhi (Brahmā), the ten Devīs (i.e. the quarters) gathered together there and received it in their womb collectively, but could not do so (for long).

7-8. When those goddesses (ladies) were unable to hold the foetus in their wombs, the foetus endowed with lustre, illuminated the worlds like the Moon (now) blessing everyone; it emerged from the quarters (womb of the ladies) and fell on the ground (assuming the form of) the Moon along with them (the goddesses).

9. On seeing Soma falling, Brahmā, the grandfather of the worlds, placed him in a chariot, with a desire for the welfare of the worlds.

10. O Brāhmaṇas, indeed he (the Moon) was a Deva (god) himself, a seeker of righteousness and truthful to the promise. We have heard that (the chariot) was (fitted with) yoked to a thousand white horses.

11. When that great soul, the son of Atri, had fallen, Devas and the seven famous mental sons of Brahmā eulogised (him).

12. There itself, the sons of Aṅgiras and Bhṛgu eulogised by means of Ṛks, Yajur mantras and many Atharva Āṅgirasa mantras.

13. The brilliance of the shining Moon who was being eulogised, developed further and it purified all the three worlds.

14. In that prominent chariot, he circumambulated the earth extending upto the ocean twenty-one times.

15. His splendour that reached the earth became medicinal herbs. They sparkle by means of his brilliance.

16. O excellent Brāhamaṇs ! He sustains subjects of four types and the universe with them (herbs). Lord Soma is indeed the nourisher of the universe.

17. Having acquired splendour through the penance (of Atri), the eulogy (of Devas and sages) and his own religious activities, the blessed one (Soma) performed penance for ten times ten *Padma* years. (one *Padma* = a thousand billion).

18. Soma who is famous by his own Karmans will be the pervader of those (ten) gold-complexioned goddesses (viz. quarters) who sustain the whole world.

19. Thereafter, Brahmā the foremost among the knowers of Brahman, entrusted him with the kingdom of seeds, herbs, Brāhmaṇas and waters.

20. Being naturally the foremost among those who shine brilliantly and, thereafter, being crowned over a big kingdom, (Soma) of great splendour became the king of kings and purified the worlds and developed them.

21. Dakṣa, the son of Pracetas, gave twenty-seven Dākṣāyaṇīs (daughters of Dakṣa) of great holy rites to Indu (the Moon). They (people) know them as Nakṣatras (constellations).

22. Having attained that great kingdom, Soma the lord of possessors of Soma (i.e. Brāhmaṇas) performed the Rājasūya sacrifice, wherein the Dakṣiṇā amounted to hundred thousands.

23-24. In that sacrifice, Hiraṇyagarbha was the Udgātṛ (the presiding priest who recites mantras); Brahmā occupied the seat of Brahmā and lord Nārāyaṇa Hari was the Sadasya (member of the witnessing assembly). He was surrounded by Sanatkumāra and other leading original Brahmarṣis. O Brāhmaṇas, we have heard that Soma gave the three worlds as

Dakṣiṇā (sacrificial fee) to those important Brāhmaṇa sages who were the members of the Assembly.

25. Nine Devīs, viz. Sinī, Kuhū[1], Vapus, Puṣṭi, Prabhā, Vasu, Kīrti, Dhṛti and Lakṣmī served him.

26. After finishing his concluding ablutions (of the sacrifice), he became free from worries. He had been revered by all Devas and sages. That supreme emperor of emperors shone over the ten quarters.

27. After having attained such a rare glory praised even by the sages, O Brāhmaṇas, his mind became confounded. His humility was suppressed by his immodesty and impertinence.

28. Slighting all the sons of Aṅgiras, all of a sudden, he abducted Tārā of great fame, the wife of Bṛhaspati.

29. Though implored by Devas and celestial sages, he did not give up Tārā to Aṅgiras (Bṛhaspati).

30. O Brāhmaṇas, Uśanas, one of the Aṅgiras (?) took his side. Indeed, he had been the highly brilliant disciple of Bṛhaspati's father.

31. Thanks to that affection, lord Rudra took up his bow Ajagava and sided Bṛhaspati.

32. The great miraculous weapon was discharged by that noble soul aiming at the chief Brāhmaṇa sage and Devas whereby their fame was destroyed.

33. There ensued a great battle directly (between Devas and Asuras). It was called Tārakāmaya[2] (concerning Tārā ?). It caused great destruction of Devas, Dānavas and all the worlds.

34. Only three Devas survived. They are remembered by the name Tuṣitas. They sought shelter in Brahmā, the primordial lord, the grandfather of the worlds.

35. Then Pitāmaha (Brahmā) himself prevented Uśanas and Rudra, the eldest (deity) Śaṅkara, (from fighting) and handed over Tārā to Aṅgiras (Bṛhaspati).

---

1. Sinī and Kuhū are deities presiding over (i) the day preceding the new moon day on which the moon rises with scarcely visible crescent and (ii) the new moon day when the moon is invisible, respectively.

2. Out of the twelve wars between Devas and Asuras this was the fifth one.

36. On seeing that Tārā, the lady with a moon-like face, was pregnant, the Brāhmaṇa Bṛhaspati said: "Don't you cast off the foetus ?

37. In (your) body belonging to me another foetus shall by no means be held in the womb." Still she did not cast off the child '*Dasyu-hantama*' (the slayer of robbers).

38. Like the fire that blazes after catching the Īṣikā grass, the son surpassed the beautiful bodies of Devas at the very instant he was born.

39. Their suspicion having been aroused, Suras spoke to Tārā : "Tell us the truth, whose son is he, Soma's or Bṛhaspati's ?"

40. When she, out of bashfulness, did not tell Devas, 'yes' or 'no', the boy Dasyuhantama was about to curse her.

41. Preventing him, Brahmā said to Tārā, "(We have) suspicion that it is Candra's (Moon's), O Tārā; therefore, speak the truth. Whose son is this ?"

42. With palms joined in reverence, she said this to lord Brahmā, the granter of boons, that the noble-souled boy Dasyuhantama was Soma's.

43. Thereafter, sniffing at the head of his son, Lord Soma, the Prajāpati, named his intelligent son as Budha.

44. (Defective verse) While rising up to go towards the east*, Budha begot a son of the princess (Ilā).

45. Purūravas, his son of great brilliance, was born of Ilā. In Urvaśī, six sons of great prowess were born (to Purūravas).

46. Then, being violently attacked by pulmonary consumption Soma became exhausted and helpless. Overwhelmed by consumption, the Moon's disc became pale and weak. He, therefore, sought refuge in his own father Atri.

47. Atri, of great fame, quelled his sin (disease). He was cured of the pulmonary consumption and so he shone with brilliance all round.

48. O excellent Brāhmaṇas, thus the origin of Soma has been recounted by me. Listen to and understand his race that is being recounted to you, O excellent Brāhmaṇas.

---

*The reading Bd. P. v. 2.3.66-44: *Pratighasram...budhaḥ*, 'Buddha rises in the east everyday.'

49. It is conducive to wealth, health and longevity. It is holy and destructive of sins. Only by listening to the origin of Soma, one is relieved of all sins.

CHAPTER TWENTYNINE

The Lunar Race[1] : *The Amāvasu Dynasty*

Sūta said :

1. Buddha was Soma's son and his son was Purūravas. He was very brilliant and munificent in charitable gifts. He performed *Yajñas* with vast amounts distributed as *Dakṣiṇā*.

2. He was an expounder of Brahman (Vedas), destroyer of foes and invincible in battle. He regularly performed Agnihotra and granted gifts of lands to sacrificial priests.

3. He was truthful in speech and intelligently engaged in holy rites. Handsome in features, he indulged in sexual intercourse in great privacy. He was an extraordinarily dutiful son, and in beauty of form was unequalled in all the worlds.

4. Eschewing her pride in personal prestige, the renowned Urvaśī wedded that righteous, truthful (king), conversant with Dharmas and expounder of Brahman (Veda)

5-8. The vigorous king stayed with her (in all for sixty-four years) spending ten, eight, seven, six, seven, eight, ten and eight years in the beautiful Caitraratha park, on the banks of Gaṅgā, in the excellent forest Nandana, in the extensive Alakā, at the foot of the Gandhamādana mountain, on the peak of the excellent mountain Meru, in the northern Kurus, and in the village Kalāpagrāma respectively. With great

1. The present chapter which corresponds to Bd.P. 2.3.66, opens with the episode of Purūravas, the founder of the Lunar race and Urvaśī, the celestial nymph. This episode gives the background of the famous "Dialogue" sūkta in the RV. This romantic story inspired Kālidāsa to write his immortal play *Vikramorvaśīya*.

joy, the king accompanied by Urvaśī sported about in their main forests and parks (usually) frequented by Suras (gods).

The Sages asked :

9. Urvaśī was a Gandharva lady. Forsaking Devas, how did she attain the king, a mere human being ? O (sage) of extensive learning, please explain it to us.

Sūta replied :

10. She was overwhelmed by the curse of Brahmā and therefore had to approach a human being. The beautiful lady (became the wife of) Aila Purūravas under certain stipulated conditions.

11. In order to redeem herself from the evil effects of the curse, she stipulated that she should not see him naked except at the time of sexual intercourse or when swayed with passionate love.

12. (She said further) "O King, two rams will always be kept near our bed.[1] My sole diet will be ghee which I shall take only once a day.

13. If these conditions are fulfilled, O king, as long as you strictly adhere to these stipulations, I shall stay with you. This is our mutual agreement".

14. The king scrupulously adhered to her conditions. Thus that beautiful lady stayed with Purūravas.

15. Deluded by her curse, Urvaśī became a human lady and stayed with him devotedly for sixty-four years. The Gandharvas became worried due to this.

---

1. Urvaśī, as her name indicates, seems to have hailed from the ancient central Asian town Ur. It appears that fashionable ladies from Ur had a fascination for rams in the fourth millennium B.C. In his excavation at Ur, Sir Leonard Wooley discovered in a queen's tomb of 3300 B.C. a pair of rams, "beautifully and intricately made. Their bodies were covered with fleece of shell.... their heads and legs were of gold" (quoted on p. 8 in A. J. Karandikar's introduction to his Marathi book *Background of the Mahābhārata —Mahābhāratācī Pārśvabhūmi*, Poona, 1980. This fascination for rams may be the cause of the inclusion and importance attached to this term in the marriage-contract between Purūravas and Urvaśī.

Gandharvas said :

16. O blessed ones, ponder over the means whereby that excellent lady, the ornament of heaven, Urvaśī, may again come back to Devas.

17-19. Then the foremost of the eloquent ones (Gandharvas), named *Viśvāvasu spoke thus*:

"O sinless ones, I consider that some conditions must have been stipulated by her there. I shall tell you the means whereby she will forsake the king due to the breach of agreement. I shall immediately engage myself to achieve your task". After saying thus, that (Viśvāvasu) of great fame went to the city of Pratiṣṭhāna.

20. He came there at night and took away one of the two rams. The lady of sweet smiles had been no less than a mother unto the two rams.

21. On realising that the Gandharva had come, the renowned lady (Urvaśī) lying on the bed told the king, "My son is being taken away".

22. Thus requested, the king thought, "The queen will see me naked and there will be a breach of the agreement."

23. Then the Gandharvas took away the second ram as well. When the second ram was taken away, the queen spoke to Aila:

24. "O Lord, O king, my sons are taken away as though they are the sons of a helpless woman". Thus taunted the king got up and rushed out (though he was) naked.

25-26. The king rushed out seeking the sheep taken away by the Gandharvas, whereupon a great Māyā (i lusion) was produced by them. The great palace became illuminated suddenly and she saw the naked king. On seeing the king naked, the Apsarā lady (Urvaśī) who could assume any form she wished, vanished (from there).

27. On realising that she had vanished, the Gandharvas abandoned the rams there and disappeared themselves.

28. On seeing the abandoned rams, the king, the lord, took them with him and returned. Unable to see her there, the king became extremely dejected and lamented.

29-30. Seeking her here and there, the king roamed over

the earth. The powerful king saw her at Kurukṣetra. She was taking her bath in the deep waters of Puṣkariṇī (lotus pond) in the holy centre of Plakṣatīrtha. She appeared very splendid, sporting there in the company of five Apsarās.

31-32. The lady of splendid evebrows saw the king not very far. Urvaśī then spoke to her friends : "Here is that excellent man with whom I lived." She pointed out the king to them. Then those ladies, the Apsarās (with five braids of hair) appeared in front (of him).

33. On seeing her (Urvaśī) the king was delighted. He began to lament in diverse ways. "O cruel lady, come (unto me). Stay willingly, stand by your words."

34-35. These and similar subtle words they exchanged. Urvaśī then spoke to Aila : "O lord, I have been rendered pregnant by you. Undoubtedly your son will be born within a year." The king stayed for a night with her.

36. The king went back to his city with great delight. When a year elapsed, the king of great fame came to Urvaśī again.

37. After staying with her for a night, the lofty-minded king became overwhelmed by passionate love. In a pitiable tone he spoke: "Be mine for ever".

38. Urvaśī then said to Aila: "The Gandharvas will grant you (that) boon. O great king, choose that boon and tell them this yourself:

39. 'I choose the boon of *Sālokya* (having the same world) with the noble-souled Gandharvas' ". The king accepted the suggestion saying "So be it", and requested the Gandharvas for the boon. The Gandharvas replied, "So be it".

40. After filling the *Sthāli* (mud-pot) with fire, the Gandharvas spoke to him: "O king, performing the sacrifice with this, you will attain that world."[1]

41. He took the fire and went back to his city along with the prince. He placed the fire in the *Araṇi* and went to his abode along with his son.

---

1. As vv. 40-45 show, this Purāṇa attributes to Purūravas, the institution (or encouragement) of the performance of Yajña out of the fire created from *Araṇi* (of Aśvattha wood) by attrition. Bd.P. 2.3.66.19 gives the credit of introducing three fires (Dakṣiṇāgni etc.) to Purūravas.

42. He returned and saw the fire. He found an Aśvattha (holy fig tree) there. On seeing the Aśvattha near it, he was surprised.

43. In order to inform the Gandharvas about it, he went to heaven with the fire. On hearing everything they asked him to make use of *Araṇi*.

44. They said: "Make an *Araṇi* out of the Aśvattha, churn it and kindle the fire, in accordance with the injunctions. O king, performing the sacrifice with it, you will attain the same region as ours. The king churned and prepared three fires and performed the sacrifice.

45. After performing different kinds of *Yajñas*, he attained *Sālokya* with the Gandharvas. It was in the Tretā Yuga that this great (hero) lived. Originally there was only a single fire. Aila made (introduced) three fires.

46-47. O excellent Brāhmaṇas, the king Aila had such a prowess. He ruled over his kingdom in Prayāga, the holiest of lands embellished by the great sages, on the northern banks of Yamunā, in the city of Pratiṣṭhāna.

48-49. (He had) six sons having the brilliance comparable to that of Indra and well-known in the regions of Gandharvas. They were Āyu, Dhīmān, Amāvasu,[1] Viśvāyu, Śatāyu and Gatāyu—all born of Urvaśī. Amāvasu's son was king Bhīma, the conqueror of the whole universe.

50. Śrīmān, the successor of Bhīma, was a king with golden lustre (otherwise known as Kāñcanaprabha). The scholarly and powerful Suhotra was the son of Kāñcana (i.e. Kāñcanaprabha).

51-55. Jahnu was the son of Suhotra, born of Keśikā's womb.

While his elaborate sacrificial rite was going on, Gaṅgā turned her course and flooded that territory on account of the vision of the inevitable future (events). Seeing the sacrificial enclosure flooded all round by Gaṅgā, the son of Suhotra, the granter of boons, became infuriated. Flashing red eyes he spoke to Gaṅgā: "O Gaṅgā, have the recompense of this outrage

---

1. Amāvasu was the founder of Kānyakubja kingdom—Pargiter, *AITH*, p. 144.

immediately. I shall make all your efforts in vain. I shall drink up your waters." On seeing the waters of Gaṅgā drunk up the saintly king, Suras and sages brought out the blessed river as his daughter (and known as Jāhnavī). Jahnu married Kāverī, the grand-daughter of Yauvanāśva.

56-57. It was a result of the curse of Yuvanāśva that Gaṅgā was produced by him. Kāverī, the most excellent of all rivers, became the praise-worthy wife of Jahnu. Jahnu begot a beloved righteous son named Suhotra, of Kāverī. Suhotra's son was Ajaka.

58. Ajaka's successor was Balākāśva of great fame. Gaya, Śīla and Kuśa are remembered as sons born to him.

59. Kuśa had four sons brilliant due to their Vedic knowledge. They were Kuśāśva, Kuśanābha, Amūrtārayaśas and Vasu.

60. The excellent king Kuśastamba desirous of a son, performed a penance. When a thousand years were completed he saw Śatakratu (Indra).

61-62. On seeing him who performed severe penance, the thousand-eyed Purandara decided to become his son, as he was competent to do so. The enemy of Pāka (i.e. Indra) became his son and took the name Gādhi. He was called Kauśika also, being a member of the family of Kuśa.

63. Kuśastaṁba's wife was Paurukutsā and Gādhi was born of her. Lord Gādhi gave his eldest daughter, the splendid and blessed Satyavatī, to Ṛcīka who was a descendant of Bhṛgu (Kāvya?).

64-67. Her husband, himself a descendant of Bhṛgu and the delighter of the Bhṛgu family, prepared *Caru* (consecrated cooked rice) for the sake (of the birth) of a son to himself as well as to Gādhi. The courageous sage Ṛcīka, the descendant of Bhṛgu, called (his wife Satyavatī and said): "O splendid lady, this *Caru* should be taken by you and this by your mother. A brilliant leader of Kṣatriyas will be born to her. He cannot be conquered by Kṣatriyas in battle. He will be the destroyer of prominent Kṣatriyas. This *Caru* will give you, O splendid lady, an excellent Brāhmaṇa as a son. He will be courageous and quiescent, possessing penance as his wealth (i.e. he will become a great sage)."

68. After saying this to his wife, Ṛcīka, the scion of the family of Bhṛgu, ever engaged in penance, entered the forest.

69. In the course of his pilgrimage, king Gādhi came to Ṛcīka's hermitage in order to see his daughter. He was accompanied by his wife also.

70. Satyavatī brought the two types of *Carus* given by the sage to her mother. Delightedly but without excitement, she told her what her husband had mentioned to her (about them).

71. As fate would have it, the mother gave the *Caru* intended for her to her daughter. Out of ignorance, she took in the *Caru* intended for her daughter.[1]

72. Then Satyavatī conceived in her womb a foetus that was splendid but competent to destroy Kṣatriyas. With her illuminated body, she became terrible to view.

73. On seeing it and pondering over it by means of Yogic power, Ṛcīka, the excellent Brāhmaṇa, spoke to his fair-complexioned wife:

74. "O gentle lady, due to the interchange of the *Carus*, an extremely terrible son of cruel deeds will be born as your son and your mother will be successful (in getting a good son).

75. Your mother will give birth to such a saintly son. The entire Brahman (Vedic knowledge) has been instilled into it by me.

76. Thus warned by her husband, the blessed lady Satyavatī propitiated her husband: "May my son never be like this. Let another be a base Brāhmaṇa". Thus requested, the sage said :

77. "O gentle lady, this has never been thought of nor desired by me or by you. The son may be one of terrible activities due to the fault of his father or mother".

78. Thus addressed, Satyavatī spoke again these words: "O sage, if you wish, you can create many worlds. What then a mere son?

---

1. This explains why Paraśurāma, though a Brāhmaṇa, was of a militant nature and Viśvāmitra, though Kṣatriya by birth, attained Brāhmaṇa-hood.

79. O holy lord, O master, it behoves you to grant me a son who will be quiescent and straightforward. O Lord, say 'Let such a son be born'.

80. O excellent Brāhmaṇa, nothing other than this can be done to me". Thereafter, by means of the power of his penance, he made her delighted.

81. "O fair-complexioned lady, it makes no difference as far as I am concerned whether it is the son or the grandson. O gentle lady, everything shall be in accordance with the words spoken by you."

82. Therefore Satyavatī gave birth to a son, the scion of the family of Bhṛgu. He was Jamadagni, the quiescent and self-controlled. He was interested in penance.

83. Formerly when there was an interchange of Raudra and Vaiṣṇava *Carus* in the Yajña of Bhṛgu, he ate (*Jamanāt*) the Vaiṣṇava fire and so he came to be known as '*Jamadagni*'.

84. Having obtained Viśvāmitra as his successor, Gādhi the delighter of Kuśikas (members of the family of Kuśika) attained the status equal to that of Brāhmaṇa sages. He was selected to be such by Brahmā.

85-86a. The meritorious Satyavatī, engaged in truthful rites, became the great river well known as Kauśikī. Kauśikī the most excellent and distinguished river began to flow thus.

86b-88. There was a king in the race of Ikṣvāku. His name was Suveṇu. His daughter was a blessed lady named Reṇukā otherwise known as Kāmalī. Ṛcīka's son, Jamadagni, endowed with the power of penance and fortitude begot of Kāmalī alias Reṇukā, the terrible son Rāma who was the most excellent of those who had mastered all lores and the science of archery as well. He became the destroyer of Kṣatriyas and shone like the blazing fire.

89. In this manner, the lofty-minded Jamadagni, the foremost among those who know Brahman, was born of Satyavatī, thanks to the semen virile of Aurva Ṛcīka. The middle son was Śunaḥśepha and the youngest was Śunaḥpuccha.

90. The pious-souled Viśvāmitra is remembered by the name Viśvaratha also. By the favour of Bhṛgu, he was born of Kauśika, as the perpetuator of the race of Kauśika.

91-93. Śunaḥśepha is remembered as the eldest of all the sons of Viśvāmitra.[1] He became a sage. In the Yajña of Hariścandra, he was intended (appointed) as the sacrificial animal. He was given over (to Viśvāmitra) by Devas. Hence he became Devarāta. Śunaḥśepha is remembered as the eldest son of Viśvāmitra. Madhucchanda, Naya, Kṛta, Deva, Dhruva, Aṣṭaka, Kacchapa and Pūraṇa were the other sons of Viśvāmitra. The Gotras (spiritual lines) of those noble-souled Kauśikas are innumerable.[2]

94-97. These following are remembered as Kauśikas: Pārthivas, Devarātas, Yājñavalkyas, Samarṣaṇas, Udumbaras, Udumlānas, Tārakas, Yamamuñcatas, Lohiṇyas, Reṇavas, Kārīṣus, Babhrus, Pāṇins, Dhyāna-Japyas, Śālāvatyas, Hiraṇyākṣas, Syankṛtas, Gālavas, Devalas, Yāmadūtas, Śālaṅkāyanas, Bāṣkalas, and many other descendants of the intelligent Viśvāmitra. They entered into matrimonial alliance with the families of other sages.

98. Some other families of the Brahmarṣi Kauśika, the holy descendant of Purūravas are: Sośrumas and Saindhavāyanas.

99. Aṣṭaka, born of Dṛṣadvatī, was also Viśvāmitra's son. Aṣṭaka's sons (and descendants) constituting the Jahnu family have already been recounted by me.

The Sages enquired:

100. What are the characteristics of Dharma, penance and learning whereby Brāhmaṇa-hood was attained by Viśvāmitra and other kings?

101. What are the various names under which the Kṣatriyas who had attained Brāhmaṇa-hood (are known?). We wish to know the special features of the penance and charitable gifts (whereby they had attained the same).

---

1. This confirms the story in the *Aitareya Brāhmaṇa*, though Śunaḥśepa's release from bonds by his prayer of Varuṇa is not mentioned here. Viśvāmitra adopted him as a son.

2. The list of Gotras of Kauśika clan given in vv. 91-97 is incomplete (*vide Mt. P. A Study*, pp. 406-409).

102. Thus requested, *he (Sūta) spoke these meaningful words:*

Even if a man is desirous of acquiring Dharma and his mind is engaged in Yajña, he does not attain the fruit of holy rites if he gathers the requisites thereof by means of illegally acquired wealth.

103-106. A sinful soul, a base man, may give charitable gifts to Brāhmaṇas after proclaiming his intention to perform righteous deeds to the people out of hypocrisy. An uncontrolled man overwhelmed by passion and delusion may perform severe Japas and in the end may give charitable gifts for the purpose of sanctifying himslf. But these charitable gifts offered by him do not yield fruits. The charitable gifts of a wicked-souled man indulging in violence, do not stay (i.e. do not yield fruits) even if he engaged himself in holy rites. Similarly the *Dānas* offered by one who has amassed wealth by painful violent deeds also do not fructify.

107-108. Riches acquired by just (proper) means must be gifted to pious, deserving persons. If one performs *Yajñas* and makes charitable gifts without harbouring any specific desire in his mind, he attains the fruits of that *Dāna*. His *Dāna* results in happiness. One attains enjoyment through *Dāna* and goes to heaven through truthfulness.

109. By means of well-performed penance one pervades the worlds and stays. After fixing himself firm in the worlds that brilliant person enjoys everlasting (bliss).

110. *Yajña* is more beneficial than *Dāna* Penance is more beneficial than *Yajña*. Renunciation is more beneficial than penance, and *Jñāna* (perfect wisdom) is remembered as better than that.

111-114. It is reported that the twice-born castes who were born as Kṣatriyas attained Brāhmaṇa-hood by penance,[1] e.g. Viśvāmitra, King Māndhātā, Sankṛti, Kapi, Kapi's son Purukutsa, Satya, Anṛhavān, Pṛthu, Ārṣṭiṣeṇa, Ajamīḍha, Bhāgānya(?)[2], Anya, Kakṣīva, Śijaya, and many other heroic ones, Rathītara, Runda, Viṣṇuvṛddha and other kings. These are remembered as sages with Kṣātra qualities who attained

1. This is an evidence of social mobility in ancient India.
2. *Bhargavyoma* in Bd. P.

sagehood due to penance. All these saintly kings attained great Siddhis.

Henceforth I shall recount the race of Āyu, the noble soul.

CHAPTER THIRTY[1]

The Origin of Dhanvantari[2]; Vārāṇasī Cursed; Raji's Exploits

Sūta said :

1-2. O Brāhmaṇas, five noble-souled sons of great strength were born of Prabhā as the sons of Svarbhānu. Nahuṣa was the first among them. The next one is remembered as Putradharmā[3]. Dharmavṛddha's (Kṣatravṛddha's?) son was Sutahotra (Sunahotra?) of great fame.

3. Sutahotra's successors were three extremely righteous ones, viz. Kāśa, Śala and lord Gṛtsamada.

4-5. Śunaka was the son of Gṛtsamada and his son was Śaunaka. In his race Brāhmaṇas, Vaiśyas and Śūdras were born as a result of their diverse Karmans. O Brāhmaṇa, Śala's son was Ārṣṭiṣeṇa and Caranta was his son.

6. The Śaunakas and the Ārṣṭiṣeṇas were Brāhmaṇas endowed with qualities characteristic of Kṣatriyas. Kāśa's sons were Kāśaya, Rāṣṭa and Dīrghatapas.

7. Dharma was the son of Dīrghatapas. The scholarly Dhanvantari was his son. He was of great brilliance due to his

1. This Chapter corresponds to Ch. 2.3.67 in Bd. P. The references are to verses of the chapter in Bd. P.

2. As stated at the end of the last chapter, this chapter describes the race of Āyu who ruled at Kāśī. Dhanvantari, the famous physician-king, the founder of the systematic science of Āyurveda was born in Āyu's lineage. Hence the title specifically refers to him in preference to his forebears.

3. Kṣatravṛddha in Bd. P. A line is missing here. Bd. P. supplies the names of the remaining three sons, viz. Raṁbha, Raji and Anenas (Bd.P. *Op. Cit.* v. 2).

penance. He was born to that intelligent king, when he had become old.

Then the sages asked Sūta in the following words.

The Sages asked:

8. How was Dhanvantari, a god, born among human beings?

We wish to know this. Please explain this matter which is pleasing to us.

Sūta said :

9. O Brāhmaṇas, may the origin of Dhanvantari be heard. He was born formerly when the ocean was being churned for the sake of nectar.

10. He was born prior to everyone.[1] He was enveloped in a halo of glory all round. On seeing him with perfectly shaped limbs, (gods) stood surprised and said, "You are Aja (the unborn)". Hence he is remembered as Aja.

11. Aja spoke to Viṣṇu: "O lord, most excellent of gods, I am your son. Please assign me my share (in *Yajña*)."

12-14. Thus addressed, the lord looked at him and said: "The share in *Yajña* has already been allotted by Suras who are worthy of Yajñas. The *Homa* in accordance with the Vedic mantras has already been laid down by the great sages. It is never possible to arrange for another Homa similar to it. O god, you are a later born son· (of mine). O lord, your name alone is a mantra[2] You will become famous in your next birth.

15. Even while in the womb, you will have the Siddhi (spiritual powers) of *Aṇimā* (minuteness) etc. O lord, with that very physical body, you will attain Deva-hood. Brāhmaṇas will perform *Yajñas* for you by means of *Carus*, *mantras*, ghee and scents as offerings.

---

1. *kalaśāt pūrvam* 'before the emergence of the pot of nectar' a better reading in Bd.P. v. 11.

2. *tava mantro na vai prabho* 'no mantra is assignable to you' (Bd.P. v. 15).

16. You will propound the Āyurveda system of medicine. This is bound to happen surely. It has been already ordained by the lotus-born deity (Brahmā).

17. In the second Dvāpara Yuga, you will undoubtedly be born." Then after granting him the boon, Viṣṇu vanished from there.

18. At the advent of the second Dvāpara Yuga, the king of Kāśī Dīrghatapas belonging to the family of Sunahotra, performed a penance with desire for a son.

19. The king propitiated Deva Aja (i.e. Dhanvantari) for the sake of a son. The delighted Dhanvantari offered the king the choice of a boon. The King requested:

20. "O lord, if you are satisfied, be pleased to be born as my righteous son." After agreeing to it saying "So be it", he vanished there itself.

21. God Dhanvantari was born in his house. The great king, king of Kāśī became the destroyer of all ailments.

22. Sage Bharadvāja created the science of Āyurveda along with its therapeutics.[1] The king divided it into eight parts and taught them to his disciples.

23. Dhanvantari's son was famous by the name Ketumān. Ketumān's son was the powerful king Bhīmaratha. He was famous by the name Divodāsa[2] and he was the king of Vārāṇasī.

24. In the meanwhile, the city of Vārāṇasī had become desolate and a Rākṣasa named Kṣemaka occupied it.

---

1. Though our text does not mention it, Bd.P. 2.3.67. 23-24 informs us that Dhanvantari learnt *Āyurveda* (the science of medicine) along with its therapeutics from Bharadvāja. Dhanvantari divided it into eight sections and taught them to different disciples.

2. He is regarded as the contemporary of Daśaratha of the Ikṣvāku dynasty of Ayodhyā. It was during his reign that god Śiva occupied it by first making it desolate through crafty machination of one of his chief Gaṇas (aptly called demon) Kṣemaka. To get a flourishing capital city vacated for one's honey-moon in the manner described later (vv. 36-53) is not creditable to a great god ie. Śiva.

25. Formerly that city had been cursed by the noble-souled Nikuṁbha, 'The city (of Vārāṇasī) will be desolate for a thousand years'. He had repeated the curse many times.

26. As soon as the city was cursed, Divodāsa the king, founded a beautiful city on the banks of Gomatī, near the extremities of his realm.

The Sages said :

27. Why did Nikuṁbha curse Vārāṇasī in the days of yore ? Nikuṁbha was a righteous soul. Why did he curse the holy centre of Siddhas ?

Sūta said :

28. After gaining the city, King Divodāsa, the saintly king of great splendour lived in that flourishing city.

29. In the meantime, Maheśvara who had married (Umā) stayed near the Devas* and desired to do what was pleasing to the goddess.

30. His attendants and the saints assuming various forms continued to delight the great godddess by means of their diverse forms mentioned before.

31. Mahādeva used to be delighted with them, but Menā was not at all pleased. Everyday she began to abhor the lord and goddess.

32. (She said to Umā) "Your husband Maheśvara is carrying on ill-mannered activities in (my) presence. O sinless girl, he is by all means very indigent. Without wearying himself out, he sports and dallies".

33. On being thus taunted by her mother, she did not brook it as was but natural to women. After smiling (at the words of her mother) the goddess, the granter of boons, went near Hara (Śiva).

34. With a dejected face the goddess spoke to Mahādeva: "O my lord, I will not stay here. Take me to your abode".

35. Thus requested, the great god, Maheśvara of great splendour, surveyed all the worlds. O excellent Brāhmaṇas, he

---

*A. reads *Śvaśurāntike* 'near (at the residence of) his father-in-law'.

liked Vārāṇasī, the holy centre of the Siddhas on the earth, as his residence.

36. On knowing that that city was occupied by Divodāsa, he called Kṣemaka, the chief of Gaṇas who was by his side and spoke to him :

37. "O lord of the Gaṇas, Go to Vārāṇasī and make it desolate. You must employ soft and subtle means. That king is extremely valorous".

38-39. Nikuṁbha then went to the city of Vārāṇasī and revealed himself to a barber named Maṅkaṇa in his dream and said, "O sinless one, I shall bring welfare unto you. Assign a place for me. Make an image of my form and place it at the outskirt of the city."

40. O Brāhmaṇas, the barber did everything in accordance with what he was told in dream. After getting the permission of the king, he did everything duly at the gate of the city.

41-42. Everyday splendid worship was offered with scents, incense, garlands etc. Food was offered. The whole thing was wonderful. Thus the lord of Gaṇas was worshipped there everyday.

43. He used to grant thousands of boons to the people of the city, such as sons, gold, longevity and similar desires.

44. The senior queen-consort of the king was well-known by the name Suyaśā. That chaste lady was urged by the king and she came (to that deity) with a desire to have a son.

45. She performed (his) worship on a grand scale and requested him for sons. She frequented (the shrine) again and again for (the boon of getting) a son.

46. There was a reason behind Nikuṁbha's not granting sons. If the king were to be infuriated something could be done.

47-50. After the lapse of a long period, the king became furious. (He thought) 'This spirit at the main gate delightedly bestows hundreds of boons on the town-people but does not do anything (for me). In my city he is worshipped by my people. He has been worshipped by my queen there for that specific reason. Though he eats much, he does not grant me a son. He is ungrateful. Hence he does not deserve further worship at all by me. So, I shall destroy the abode of the chief of Gaṇas. He was evil-minded (indeed).'

51. Having determined thus that wicked, sinful and evil-minded king destroyed that sacred place of the chief of Gaṇas.

52-53. On seeing the shrine shattered, the lord (of Gaṇas) approached the king (and said), "O king, since, without any offence on my part, my shrine has been destroyed by you, the city will be void and desolate all of a sudden". Then, due to that curse Vārāṇasī became desolate.

54. Nikuṁbha brought Mahādeva to that desolate cursed city. Mahādeva rebuilt that desolate city by means of (the powers of) his great soul.

55. The city was befitting the *Vibhūti* (prosperity and glory) of the goddess and the lord. The goddess sported there, even as lord Maheśvara too sported there.

56. But the goddess did not derive (permanent) pleasure due to her surprise at the (peculiar) house. For the sake of playing with the goddess, lord Īśāna spoke these words.

57-58. "I shall not abandon my abode. My abode is *Avimukta*[1] (unabandoned)". He laughed and spoke again to her: "My abode is *Avimvkta*. O Goddess, I shall not go away (from here). You may go. I shall sport here". Hence indeed it is *Avimukta* since it was said so by the lord himself.

59. This is the story of how the city of Vārāṇasī was cursed and then glorified as '*Avimukta*'. In it lives the lord revered by all Devas in the three Yugas. The pious-souled Maheśvara is accompained by the goddess also.

60. He vanished during the Kali age. That city of the great soul is reoccupied by the people when the lord vanishes.

61-63. Thus Vārāṇasī was cursed and was re-inhabited. King Divodāsa killed king Bhadraśreṇya's one hundred sons who were noted for their mastery in archery and occupied (his capital). The kingdom of Bhadraśreṇya was usurped by that powerful king. But the son of Bhadraśreṇya named Durdama was let off by Divodāsa, out of mercy, thinking that he was only a boy.

64-65. Heroic Pratardana was born of Divodāsa and Dṛṣa-

1. This explains why Vārāṇasī is called 'Avimukta'.

dvatī. The son (of Bhadraśreṇya) desirous of wreaking revenge recaptured it (kingdom). Pratardana had two sons, Vatsa and Garga, who became well-known.

66. Vatsa's son was Alarka and his son was Sannati. These two old verses are sung about the saintly king Alarka.

67-69. "Alarka ruled as excellent king of Kāśī for sixtysix thousand years. He was endowed with handsome features and he maintained his youth (all along). He attained his great longevity by the grace of Lopāmudrā." At the end of the period of curse, he killed the Rākṣasa Kṣemaka and rebuilt the beautiful city of Vārāṇasī.

70. Sannati's successor was the righteous king named Sunītha. Sunītha's successor was the pious Suketu.

71. It is heard that Suketu's son was Dharmaketu. Heroic Satyaketu was the successor of Dharmaketu.

72. Satyaketu's son was the king named Vibhu. Suvibhu was the son of Vibhu and Sukumāra was his son.

73. Sukumāra's son was Dhṛṣṭaketu. He was very virtuous. Dhṛṣṭaketu's successor was the king Veṇuhotra.

74. Veṇuhotra's son was Gārgya. He was very famous. Vātsya was the son of the intelligent Vatsa.

75. The sons of these two were very virtuous Brāhmaṇas and Kṣatriyas. They were strong, valorous and famous for their leonine exploits.

76. Thus these kings of Kāśī have been enumerated. Now listen and understand the (descendants) of Raji. Raji had a hundred sons. Two of them were very powerful and well-known on the earth as the group of kings "Rājeya". Those Kṣatriyas caused terror to Indra too.

77. When a terrible war broke out between Devas and Asuras[1], both of them spoke to Pitāmaha (god Brahmā).

78. "O lord of all the worlds, O great lord, who will be victorious in the battle between us. Please tell us. We all wish to hear."

Brahmā said :

79. There is no doubt in this that they on whose behalf

1. This is the twelfth (and the last) war between Devas and Asuras as far as Purāṇic records are concerned.

lord Raji takes up arms in the battle and fights, will conquer the three worlds.

80. Where there is Raji, there will be Lakṣmī (fortune, wealth). Where there is Lakṣmī, there is fortitude. *Dharma* abides where there is fortitude and where there is *Dharma*, there is victory."

81. On hearing about the victorious (-ness of) Raji, Devas and Dānavas approached the excellent king. They eulogised him as they wished for success.

82. With a delighted heart, all Devas and Dānavas requested the king: "Please take up your excellent bow for enabling us to be victorious."

Raji replied :

83. I will defeat you all in the battle, as well as Devas led by Śakra. I shall become the righteous-souled Indra and then shall I fight in the battle.

Dānavas said :

84. Our Indra is Prahlāda. We shall be victorious on his behalf. O king, please stand by this agreement urged by our Lord.

85. Even as he was about to say, "So be it" he was urged by Devas also. He was invited by Devas saying, "After conquering you will become Indra."

86-88. He killed all the Dānavas in front of Indra (who was armed with thunderbolt). He was endowed with self-control and the greatest prosperity. Lord Raji killed all Dānavas and redeemed the lost glory of Devas. Accompanied by Devas, Śatakratu (Indra) spoke to Raji, "I am Raji's son", and continued as follows, "O king, there is no doubt in this that you are Indra of all Devas. O destroyer of enemies, O, Indra, I shall become renowned as your son".

89. On hearing the words of Śakra, he was deceived by him by means of his Māyā. The delighted king said, "So be it".

90. When that king who was on par with Devas attained heaven, Raji's sons took away all the legacies from Indra.

91. Those hundred sons forcibly occupied most of the region of *Svarga* (heaven), the abode of the consort of Śacī.

92. When a long period elapsed, the powerful Indra whose kingdom was seized and whose share in sacrifices was confiscated spoke to Bṛhaspati:

93. "O Brāhmaṇa sage, please allot Puroḍāśa (sacrificial oblation) unto me at least of the size of the fruit of Badarī (the jujube tree) whereby I can sustain myself with my splendour developed further.

94. O Brāhmaṇa, be pleased with me. My kingdom has been seized by the sons of Raji. My food has been taken away. I have been rendered devoid of prowess, emaciated, confounded by the sons of Raji."

Bṛhaspati said :

95. O Śakra, if only I had been urged by you earlier in this matter, this would not have happened. O sinless one, there is nothing that should not be done for the sake of pleasing you.

96. O Devendra, O highly splendoured one, I shall endeavour for your welfare so that you will regain your share in the Yajña as well as your kingdom ere long.

97. O Śakra, I shall go (now). Let not your mind be dejected.

Thereafter, he performed such great rites as increased Indra's splendour.

98. The highly intelligent (Bṛhaspati) created delusion in the intellects of those (sons of Raji). They became devoid of Dharma and mad with passion.

99. They became haters of Brāhmaṇas. Hence they became deprived of their virility and exploit. So (Indra) regained the glory of Suras and his former excellent position (of Indra-hood).

100. He killed all the sons of Raji who were overwhelmed with lust and anger. He who listens to this story of Raji or the holy rehabilitation of Śatakratu will never meet with evil.

CHAPTER THIRTYONE[1]

The Story of Yayāti[2]

The Sages said :

1. How was his daughter given to the king by Maruta,[3] the great soul ? Of what prowess were the daughters of Maruta born with great souls[4] (?)

Sūta said:

2. Endowed with great splendour yet desirous of food, the king performed the sacrifice *Marut-Soma* to Prajeśvara every month, for sixty years.

3. Thereby the Marut-gods were pleased by the Marut-Soma sacrifice of that king, and granted him never-ending food with requisites for the fulfilment of all desires.

4. His food, cooked once, never got exhausted during that day and night even though given to crores (of people) right from sunrise.

5. Mitrajyoti was born of the daughter of the intelligent Maruta. From him were born (sons) of great strength, knowers of Dharma and seers of salvation.

---

1. This chapter corresponds to Bd.P. 2.3.68. For comparison or reference only the verse number is quoted.

2. This immortal story with a profound moral is repeated in many Purāṇas. The story is originally given in details in *Mbh Ādi*. Chs. 84 and 85. The immortal verse uttered by Yayāti :

na jātu kāmaḥ kāmānām upabhogena śāmyati |
haviṣā kṛṣṇa-vartmeva bhūya evā'bhivardhate ||

has been quoted in Purāṇas. It has been the main theme of an epoch-making Marathi novel *Yayāti* by V.S. Khandekar, which secured the much coveted Bhāratīya Jñānapīṭha Prize.

3. Verses 1-11 speak of Maruta and Mitrajyoti and his descendants. But they are unrelated to the main story of this chapter.

4. The reading *jātā marutakanyakāḥ* in the text translated above is contradictory and obscure. If emended : *jātā maruta-kanyayā* (as in Bd. P. 2.3.68.1) meaning '(of what heroic ability were the noble-souled persons) *born of the daughter of Maruta*', it gives cogentness. The references to the Bd.P. are to the above-mentioned chapter. Only verse number is quoted in these notes.

6. After renouncing domestic rites (the duties of householders), they resorted to detachment. Maintaining the duties of recluses (*sannyāsins*), they attained absorption in Brahman.

7. Anapāya was born of him. His son was Dharmapradattavān. Thereafter was born Kṣatradharma and from him Pratipakṣa (Pretīpaka in Bd. P.) of great penance.

8. Pratipakṣa's son named Sañjaya was well-known. Jaya was the son of Sañjaya and Vijaya was born of him.

9. Vijaya's son was Jaya (the second) and his son is remembered as Haryandvata and Haryandvata's son was the valorous king Sahadeva.

10. Sahadeva's son was virtuous-souled. He was well-known as Adīna. Adīna's son was Jayatsena and his son was Saṅkṛti.

11. Saṅkṛti's son was the pious-souled Kṛtadharmā of great fame. These were fully endowed with Kṣātra qualities*. Now understand (the descendants) of Nahuṣa.

12. Nahuṣa's successors were six. They had the brilliance comparable to that of Indra. These sons of great prowess were born of Virajā, the daughter of the Pitṛs.

13. They were Yati, Yayāti, Saṁyāti, Āyāti and the twins Viyati, Kṛti, (Bd. P.) who were the fifth-born (?) Yati was the eldest of them and Yayāti was the younger brother.

14. Yati attained Gā (Gau), the daughter of Kakutstha as wife. Saṁyāti became a sage. Attaining absolution, he became one with Brahman.

15. Among the (other) five, Yayāti became a king. He attained Devayānī, the daughter of Uśanas, as his wife.

16. He married the Asura lady Śarmiṣṭhā, the daughter of Vṛṣaparvan. Devayānī gave birth to Yadu and Turvasu.

17. Śarmiṣṭhā, the daughter of Vṛṣaparvan, gave birth to very powerful sons comparable to divine sons, viz. Druhyu, Anu and Pūru.

18. The delighted Rudra gave him a divine golden chariot that shone brilliantly and that could never get stuck up (impeded). He gave him two great inexhaustible quivers also.

---

*were the descendants of Kṣatradharma ?'

19. That chariot was fitted with horses as fast as the mind. It was in this chariot that he drove at the time of his marriage. With the same important chariot he conquered the earth.

20. Yayāti was invincible in battle to Devas, Dānavas and human beings. That chariot belonged to all the Paurava kings.

21. It remained with them upto the time of Kaurava Janamejaya born of a good land(?) The chariot got lost through the curse of the son of Garga, the intelligent sage, when Parīkṣit's son became a king.

22. The unwise king Janamejaya (the first) who was evil-minded and was known as *Loha-gandhin*[1] (having the odour of iron) killed the (young) son of Gārgya.

23. The saintly king with iron odour began to run here and there. He was abandoned by the citizens and the people of the land. Nowhere did he derive happiness.

24. He was extremely miserable. He did not get peace anywhere. Excessively dejected, he sought refuge in the sage who was the cause of his curse.[2]

25. The sage of liberal mind was famous by the name Indrota. This Indrota, the excellent Brāhmaṇa, a descendant of Śunaka, made the king perform an Aśvamedha for the sake of purification.

26. After reaching his abode, the iron-ore odour was quelled.[3] That divine chariot left him and reached Vasu, the king of Cedi.

---

1. Emend as in Bd.P. v. 22, as syntactically the text here is obscure. The text : *Lohagandham narādhipam* is emended as *Lohagandhī narādhipaḥ*, as in Bd.P.

2. The text is confusing. The king did not take resort to Gārgya who cursed him (see v. 22 above) but Indrota Śaunaka (see the next verse). The reading in Bd. P. 68.24: *sa prāyācchaunakam ṛṣim*—'he resorted to the sage Śaunaka' is relevant and deserves adoption.

3. Bd. P. v. 26 reads *avabhṛtha* for *avasatha* hereof and means, 'The king died when he reached the Avabhṛtha stage of the sacrifice'. The Bd. P. reading is preferable for if the curse of iron odour was removed and the king was rehabilitated, the divine chariot should have continued with him.

27. Then it was obtained by Śakra who was delighted. From him, Bṛhadratha got it. Killing Jarāsandha afterwards, Bhīma, the scion of Kaurava family, gave that excellent chariot to Vāsudeva with pleasure.

28. Attaining old age, the saintly king Yayāti, the son of Nahuṣa, spoke these words to his eldest and most excellent son Yadu:

29. "O dear one, old age, wrinkles and greying hairs have come over (surrounded) me due to the curse of Uśanas, Kāvya (i.e. Śukra). Nor am I fully satiated with youthful age.

30. O Yadu, accept all my sins along with my old age. Take my old age". Yadu replied to him:

31. "I have promised to give alms to Brāhmaṇas but have not given. That can be achieved only by exertion. (So) I will not take up your old age.

32. There are many defects and ailments in old age affecting (the abilility to) drink and eat. Hence, O king, I am not enthusiastic enough to accept your old age.

33-34. In the prime of youth, I do not wish to become a pitiable figure with white moustache and beard, shattered (in every limb) by old age, (skin) with many a wrinkle, with the body bent down, faced with a miserable state, the very form indicating weakness, and incompetent to perform any action. I would be overwhelmed (attacked) by great frightful effects. I do not desire that old age.

35. O King, O knower of virtues, you do have many sons even more beloved than I am. May they take it up. Please request some other son".

36. On getting this rebuff from Yadu, (Yayāti) the foremost among the most eloquent ones, became infuriated. Censuring his eldest son, he said thus:

37-39. "What other Āśrama do you have? What other holy rite do you have for which you disregard me and say thus? O evil-minded one, O new instructor!" After saying this the angry king cursed Yadu: "Since you, though born of my bosom, do not pass on your (youthful) age unto me, O fool, your progeny shall not get the kingdom." (Then he said to Turvasu) "O Turvasu, accept my sin along with my old age".

Turvasu said :

40. O father, I do not like old age that destroys the (worldly) pleasures of love. There are many defects in old age affecting (the ability to) drink and eat. Hence, O king, I am not enthusiatic enough to accept your old age.

Yayāti said :

41. You, though born of my bosom, do not exchange your (youthful) age with me; O Turvasu, your progeny will meet with utter ruin.

42-43. O deluded one, you will be a king among people of mixed religious rites and practices*, born of anti-caste marriages and other mixed castes, who are meat-eaters and others. There is no doubt that you will be a ruler of the brutish Mlecchas, barbarians and outcastes who are after outraging the modesty of their preceptors' wives and who (are destined to be) born as loweranimals.

Sūta said:

44. After cursing his own son Turvasu thus, Yayāti spoke these words to his son Druhyu born of Śarmiṣṭhā:

45. "O Druhyu, you accept my old age that destroys your complexion and beauty. Give unto me in exchange your youth for a period of one thousand years.

46. When the thousand years are completed, I shall return your youth and take back again my sin along with the old age."

Druhyu said :

47. An old man does not enjoy (a ride on) elephants, chariots and horses, nor can he enjoy a woman. He has no one to be in contact. Hence I do not like the old age.

Yayāti said :

48. Since you, though born out of my own bosom, do not

**asaṁkīrṇā ca dharmeṇa* is obscure as '*asaṁkīrṇa*' is a compliment and not a part of a curse. Bd. P.v. 43 reads : '*saṅkīrṇeṣu ca dharmeṇa*'. 'of mixed or impure religious practices' is better. Hence accepted here.

give unto me your (youthful) age, O Druhya, the pleasures that you love and seek will not be realised by you anywhere.

49. You will be perpetually staying in a place where people move about in canoes and rafts. You will always be there as a non-king though born of a royal family.[1]

50. (He said to Anu) O Anu, you accept my sin along with my old age. Thus I can move about for a thousand years with your youth.

Anu said :

51. (Defective verse)[2] An old man gives (the gift of age) to a child. (If I give up my youth) I shall become impure with your old age. An old man does not perform Homas at the proper time. I do not like that (type of) old age.

Yayāti said :

52-53. Since you, though born out of my own bosom do not give unto me your (youthful) age, all those defects of old age mentioned by you will visit (afflict) you. Your children will die on attaining youthful age. You will have to devote to the scattering of fire like this (after cremating your children).

54-56. (He then spoke to Pūru) O Pūru, you accept my sin along with the old age. O dear one, old age, wrinkles and greyish hairs have overwhelmed me as a result of the curse of Kāvya Uśanas (Śukra). I am not satiated with the pleasures of youth. I shall enjoy the worldly pleasures with your youth. When a period of thousand years is completed I shall return you your youthful age. I shall also take back my own sin along with the old age.

Sūta said :

57. Thus requested, the son immediately replied to his father, "O father, I shall do as you wish.

---

1. *arājabhrājavaṁśas tvam* in the text is obscure. Bd.P. v. 51 reads : *arājā rājavaṁśas tvam* which is better and is accepted here.

2. *jīrṇaḥ śiśuvaram datte* is obscure though translated above. For this Bd. P. 52 reads:

jīrṇaḥ śisur ivāśaktaḥ—'An old man is weak like a child'.

58. O king, I shall accept your sin along with your old age. Take from me my youthful age. Enjoy the pleasures as you wish.

59. I shall become disguised by your old age, assuming your form and age. Giving up my youthful age, I shall carry out what would be suitable (to the age assumed)".

Yayāti said:

60. O Pūru, I am pleased with you. Welfare unto you. Delightedly I grant this unto you. All the subjects in your kingdom shall flourish and enjoy all pleasures (or your progeny will realise their desires, be affluent and rule over a kingdom).

Sūta said :

61. Permitted by Pūru and by the grace of Bhārgava, king Yayāti transferred his old age to Pūru.

62. By means of the youthful age, Yayāti, the son of Nahuṣa, became highly delighted and enjoyed all worldly pleasures.

63. In accordance with his desire and enthusiasm, in a way conducive to happiness and at the proper time, the leading king enjoyed the pleasures without prejudice to virtuousness (Dharma) and it was what he alone deserved.

64. He propitiated Devas by means of *Yajñas*; *Pitṛs* by means of *Śrāddhas*; the poor people by favourable presents; and the excellent Brāhmaṇas by whatever they desired.

65. He delighted guests with foods and drinks; Vaiśyas by affording due protection; and Śūdras by (prevention of their harassment) showing kindness. He checked robbers by restraining and killing them.

66. Duly delighting the subjects by means of virtuous actions, Yayāti ruled the realm like another Indra.

67. The king of leonine exploits and youthful age indulged in worldly pleasures. Without prejudice to Dharma, he enjoyed excellent pleasures.

68-69. In the parks of Vaibhrāja and Nandana, he sported with (the celestial damsel) Viśvācī. He scrutinised all sexual pleasures to find out the hidden defect[1]. When the king saw that the desire to enjoy was increasing the more he enjoyed it, he approached Pūru and took back his own old age.

70. After enjoying the pleasures and desires, the king was both contented and dejected. The king then remembered the stipulated time-limit of one thousand years.

71. Counting (even the small units of time such as) *Kalās* and *Kāṣṭhās,* he considered that the time limit was complete and so he spoke to his son Pūru:

72. "O son, O suppressor of enemies, with your youthful age, all worldly pleasures have been enjoyed by me in accordance with my zeal befitting the time and in a way conducive to happiness.

73. O Pūru, I am delighted. Welfare upto you, you take back your own youthful age. Accept the realm too. You alone have been my beloved son who carried out what is pleasing to me".

74. King Yayāti, the son of Nahuṣa, took back his old age and Pūru regained his own youthful age.

75. When the king evinced his desire to crown his youngest son Pūru, people of all castes with Brāhmaṇas as the chief of them, spoke these words.[2]

76. "O lord, why do you set aside (the claim of) your eldest son, the excellent Yadu, the grandson of Śukra, the son of Devayānī, and bestow the kingdom on Pūru?

77. Yadu is your eldest son. Turvasu was born next to him. Śarmiṣṭhā's eldest son is Druhyu, then comes Anu and then only Pūru.

78. How can the younger son deserve the kingdom superseding (the claims of) the elder ones? Hence we urge you to abide by the (traditional) Dharma."

---

1. Bd. P.v. 69 reads : *atad-doṣa-nidarśanāt* 'because he failed to notice the defects (of passionate indulgence)'. This is a better reading as it states why he went with Viśvācī.

2. Verses 75-86 show that subjects did not allow injustice even if committed by the king. Some sort of public sanction seems to be necessary for appointing a new king.

Yayāti said:

79. O people of all castes with Brāhmaṇas as leaders! Let all of you listen to my speech why I do not intend to give the kingdom to the elder ones.

80. Only that son who carries out the words (orders) of his father and mother is considered praiseworthy. My behest was not obeyed by the eldest son Yadu.

81. That son who is antagonistic to his father is not honoured or approved by good men. He is the real son who does his duties to his parents.

82. I have been slighted by Yadu and also by Turvasu. Much discourtesy was shown by Druhyu and Anu too.

83. I have been specially honoured by Pūru who had carried out my behest. Though he is the youngest, he shall be my successor. It was he who accepted my old age. It was he who fulfilled all my desires. Everything has been done by Pūru who carried out his duties as a son.

84. This boon has been granted by Śukra, Kāvya, Uśanās, himself—'O highly intelligent one, that son who is favourable to you shall be the king to succeed you.'

85. Permitted by you all, may Pūru be crowned as the ruler of the kingdom. The son who is endowed with all qualities and who is always loyal to his parents deserves all welfare. He is to be the lord (the king), though he may be the youngest.

86. "Pūru who is your favourite son and who has done what is pleasing to you, deserves this kingdom. Due to the boon granted by Śukra, nothing more can be said (against this decision)."

87-89. Thus addressed by the delighted citizens and the people of the realm, the son of Nahuṣa crowned his own son Pūru in his own realm. He established Turvasu in the south-eastern territories. The king established the eldest excellent Yadu in the south-western territories. Druhyu and Anu were established in the west and the north. After conquering the earth consisting of the seven continents and the oceans, the son of Nahuṣa, king Yayāti, divided it into five regions and gave them to his five sons.

90. The whole of this earth consisting of the seven conti-

nents and (many) towns is being ruled over by them, the knowers of Dharma, righteously and in close adherence to their own respective lands.

91. Thus handing over the earth to his sons and transferring his royal glory to them, king Yayāti, the son of Nahuṣa, became delighted.

92. Leaving aside his bow and arrows, entrusting his kinsmen with all duties and responsibilities and his sons with the kingdom, the king became glad.

93. In this connection the following *Gāthās* (verses)[1] have been sung by the great king Yayāti, who after desiring pleasures, withdrew from them all like a tortoise that withdraws all its limbs (within itself).

94. "Never can lust subside by enjoyment of pleasures. Just as the fire gets ablaze all the more by ghee-oblations, so also desires get increased by indulgence.

95. All the grains and barley seeds, all the gold, all the cattle and all the women in the world are not sufficient for even one (person). He who realises this, does not become deluded.

96. When one maintains the purifying (auspicious) attitude to all living beings in thought, speech and action, one attains (realizes) Brahman.

97. When one is not afraid of others, when others are not afraid of him, when one neither desires nor hates (anything), one attains Brahman.

98. Happiness comes to one who eschews *Tṛṣṇā* (covetousness), which cannot be got rid of by evil-minded ones, which does not subside even when one grows old and which is a foul disease full of fatal faults.

99. When one grows old, the hairs grow old; the teeth decay along with old age; but the hope for longevity and acquisition of wealth never grow old.

100. The happiness arising from enjoyment of lust or by attaining the great pleasure in heaven does not deserve even a sixteenth part of the happiness resulting from the destruction of covetousness".

1. Verses 94-100 are the immortal verses quoted in various works and they constitute the moral of this episode.

101. After saying this, the saintly king went to the forest along with his wife. He performed a great penance on Bhṛgu-tuṅga[1] and performed hundreds of holy rites. Earning great fame, he attained Svarga.

102. His races are five thus. They are holy and revered by Devas and sages. The whole earth is pervaded by them as if with the rays of the sun.

103. An excellent Brāhmaṇa who reads this entire narrative of Yayāti or listens to it, shall become wealthy, long-lived and renowned. He will be blessed with children.

CHAPTER THIRTYTWO

The Birth of Kārtavīrya[2]

Sūta said :

1. I shall recount the race of the eldest (son of Yayāti) Yadu, of excellent splendour. Listen and understand, even as I recount it in detail and in the proper order.

2. Yadu had five sons, all comparable to the sons of Devas. Sahasrajit was the eldest. (The others were) Kroṣṭu, Nīla, Jita and Laghu.

3. Sahasrajit's son was the glorious king named Śatajit. Śatajit had three sons who were well known as very virtuous.

4. They were Haihaya, Haya and the king Veṇuhaya. It is heard that Haihaya's successor was Dharmatattva.

5. Dharmatattva's son was Kīrti and his son was Saṁjñeya. Saṁjñeya's successor was the king named Mahiṣmān.

6. Mahiṣmān's son was the valorous Bhadraśreṇya who was the king of Vārāṇasī and has already been mentioned.

1. A mountain in Nepal on the eastern bank of Gandak. Here was the hermitage of Bhṛgu. (De 34).

2. This chapter describes the Haihaya line of Yadu in which the greatest ruler of the Narmadā valley, Kārtavīrya Arjuna, was born. This chapter is captioned after that illustrious king. This chapter corresponds to Bd. P. 2.3.69 & verse-numbers in the notes refer to that chapter.

7. Bhadraśreṇya's successor was the king named Durmada and Durmada's successor was an intelligent (king) well known by the name Kanaka.

8-9. Kanaka's successor (sons) were four and they were famous in the worlds—Kṛtavīrya, Kārtavīrya, Kṛtavarmā and Kṛta the fourth. Kṛtavīrya's son was Arjuna. Born with a thousand arms, he was a king who ruled over the seven continents.

10. He performed a very severe penance for ten thousand years. Kārtvīrya thus propitiated Datta, born of Atri.

11-13. Datta granted him four excellently glorious boons. At the outset, (Arjuna) chose the boon of (being endowed with) a thousand arms. The second was (the ability of) the prevention (of the world) given up in evil by good people.[1] (The third was the competence) to protect the earth righteously after conquering it in the same (righteous) way.

The fourth was victory in numerous battles after killing thousands of enemies but meeting death in a battle (fighting) with a superior warrior.

14. The entire earth consisting of seven continents and many towns and surrounded by seven oceans, was conquered by him in a manner befitting a Kṣatriya.[2]

15. When he started fighting in a battle, banners and chariots befitting it and a thousand arms used to appear by means of the Māyā of that intelligent one.

16. It is heard that without any difficulties ten thousand Yajñas had been performed by that intelligent king in all the seven continents.

17-18. All the Yajñas performed by that mighty-armed king were profoundly splendid. All of them were provided with golden altars with golden sacrificial posts. All of them were graced by the presence of blessed Devas seated in aerial

1. Bd. P. 2.3.69. reads : ability to prevent one from evil the moment he plans it.

2. Verses 14-37 describe the exploits, munificence, righteousness and glory of Kārtavīrya. The *Gāthās* sung by Nārada about him (vv. 20-22) record in a nutshell Arjuna's achievements. Generally these Gāthās are quotations from ancient traditional verses.

chariots; all of them were always rendered splendid and attractive by Gandharvas and Apsaras-s (celestial damsels).

19. After observing the conduct and the grandeur of that saintly king, Nārada and Gandharvas sang the following verse(s) of glory of that king.

20. "Certainly no man can emulate (none can attain) the goal or status of Kārtavīrya by means of Yajñas, Dānas, penances, exploits and learning.

21. In all the seven continents he is seen moving about with his sword drawn and the excellent bows and arrows kept ready as well as seated in his chariot. Though he is the king, he behaves as though he is the follower.*

22. While he was protecting the subjects righteously, none of his subjects lost his wealth, no one was grief-stricken and no one had any confusion, thanks to the prowess of that great king".

23. That king became the sole monarch and emperor of the seven continents for eightyfive thousand years.

24. (In his realm) he himself was the protector of cattle and the fields. As a Yogin, Arjuna became *Parjanya* (Lord of clouds and rains) and showered in plenty.

25. With his thousand arms rendered tough by frequent contact with the bowstring, he shone like the Sun with his thousands of autumnal rays.

26. Having conquered the royal assembly of (the serpent king) Karkoṭaka in Māhiṣmatī with a thousand elephants, he established his capital there.

27. (Defective) The lotus-eyed king used to check the forceful (speedy) waves of the sea during the rainy season (when the sea is stormy). In a happy mood, he sportingly spewed out water and made an (artificial) rainy season.

28. Shaken and tossed about by him during his (water-sports), Narmadā, wearing garlands with golden fillets approached the king in an apprehensive mannar, with eyebrows like waves producing the gentle (murmuring) sound.

---

*Bd.P. *ibid* v 21 reads *yogāt* (by means of his Yogic Power) for *'nyo'gāt* in our Text.

29. Formerly, following its (Narmadā's) course, that (king) had plunged into the great ocean and flooded the forest near the shore creating artificial rainy season.

30. When the great ocean was agitated by his thousand arms, the great Asuras in the nether-worlds used to become stunned and motionless.

31. Giant fishes and great serpents concealed under great billows were crushed and scattered in the flood of foam, the eddies and whirlpools which were unbearably furious.

32. Agitating it by means of his thousand arms, the king made the ocean resemble the milky sea churned by Devas and Asuras.

33. (Defective verse) On seeing the terrible, prominent king, the (aquatic beings) were afraid that the ocean was once again being churned by the Mandara mountain for the sake of *Amṛta* (nectar) and at once felt uprooted (*utpāṭita* in *A*).

34. Great serpents bent down their heads and stood motionless like the stumps of the plantain trees standing still in the evening hours, when the wind does not blow.

35. (Defective verse) Proudly he went to Laṅkā. With his bow and five hundred arrows he overpowered Rāvaṇa along with his army. He defeated and brought him to Māhiṣmatī and imprisoned him there.

36. (Sage) Pulastya himself went to Arjuna and propitiated him. The king released Paulastya (Rāvaṇa) at the request of Pulastya.

37. The sound produced by the twang of the bowstrings by his thousand arms was like the thunder at the time of the close of the Yugas, when the trees* of the clouds of dissolution seem to burst.

38. Sad indeed that his thousand powerful arms were cut off by Bhārgava (Paraśurāma) in battle, as though they were golden palm trees.

39. Once upon a time, the thirsty Sun-god begged alms of him. The Lord of the people bestowed on the Sun-god the seven continents as alms.

**Vṛkṣa* in the text needs emendation as *Vṛnda* as in Bd. P.v. 38. It means 'a collection, a mass' (of clouds).

40. With a desire to consume (everything), the Sun-god blazed at the tips of his arrows and burnt cities, cowherd colonies, villages and all the towns.

41. Thanks to the prowess of that chief of men (Arjuna), the (Sun-god) of great fame burnt the mountains and forests of Kārtavīrya.

42. The Sun-god in the company of Haihaya (Kārtavīrya) burnt everything including continents along with forests. He burnt the empty hermitage of Varuṇa's son completely.

43. Varuṇa had obtained this glorious and excellent son formerly. He was famous by the name of sage Vasiṣṭha otherwise known as Āpava.

44-45. Out of anger the powerful Āpava cursed Arjuna then,[1] "O Haihaya, since you have not spared this forest of mine another man will set aside even this difficult task achieved by you. He will be Kuntī's son named Arjuna.[2] He will not be a king.

46-47. O Arjuna, the extremely powerful Rāma, the foremost among those who strike with weapons, will cut off and shatter your thousand arms. The powerful. Brāhmaṇa and Sage of great strength will kill you." Then, as a result of the curse of that intelligent (sage), Rāma became the cause of his death.

48. Such a boon had been chosen by the king himself formerly (from Datta). He had a hundred sons, five of whom were great warriors. .

49-50. They were Śūrasena, Vṛṣṭyādya, Vṛṣa and Jayadhvaja. All of them were well-trained in the use of miraculous weapons. They were heroic, strong, pious-souled and re-

---

1. The curse motif and that of boon were very popular with Purāṇa-writers to explain an unlikely or miraculous event. Here both are used to explain Kārtavīrya's death at the hands of Paraśurāma. Kārtavīrya is stated to have sought such a boon from Datta (*supra* v. 13) and received a curse from Āpava Vasiṣṭha (vv. 46-47) for destroying (i.e. helping the Sun-god to destroy) his hermitage.

2. Āpava's curse was of a twofold nature. Kārtavīrya Arjuna will meet physical death at the hands of Paraśurāma and he will be superseded in reputation by another Arjuna (Kuntī's son) for a similar act (viz. burning of Khāṇḍava forest).

nowned. They ruled over Avantī. King Jayadhvaja's son was the valorous Tālajaṅgha.

51-52. He had a hundred sons who constituted the clan of Tālajaṅghas. Five families among those noble-souled Haihayas are very famous, viz. the numerous Vīrahotras (Vītihotra in Bd.P.), Bhojas and Āvartis, Tuṇḍikeras and the valorous Tālajaṅghas.

53. Vīrahotra's son was king Ananta. Durjaya was his son. His son was Amitradarśana.

54. That king had the boon of never losing his wealth. The great king protected the subjects by means of his prowess.

55-56. An intelligent person who recounts the story of the birth of Kārtavīrya, shall regain lost wealth. He will not lose wealth (further). He will be rich. His Dharma will flourish and he will be honoured in heaven like Tvaṣṭṛ or like a man of charitable inclination.

CHAPTER THIRTYTHREE

The Dynasty of Jyāmagha and Vṛṣṇi

The Sages said :

1. Why was the world (hermitage) of the noble-souled Āpava burnt by Kārtavīrya forcibly?[1] Please explain it to us who ask.

2. We have heard that the saintly king was a protector of his subjects. Being a guardian, therefore, why did he destroy that hermitage?

Sūta said :

3. Āditya (the Sun-god) desirous of satisfaction (of hunger) approached Kārtavīrya in the guise of a Brāhmaṇa (and said), "Please give me food. Undoubtedly I am Āditya."

1. Verses 1-13 explain in details again why the hermitage of Āpava Vasiṣṭha was burnt by Kārtavīrya. As these verses deal with the curse of Āpava, they should have formed a part of the last chapter after v. 39. Vv. 1-13 hereof are unrelated to the present chapter (Race of Kroṣṭu)

The King said :

4. O Lord Sun, please tell me with what you will be satisfied. What type of food I should give to you; I shall serve it.

The Sun said :

5. O most excellent one among donors, give unto me all the immobile beings as my food. I shall be satisfied only thereby O king, and not by anything else.

The King said :

6. O the most excellent one among those who blaze, no fiery splendour of human beings can burn down all immobile beings. I bow unto you.

Āditya replied :

7. I am delighted. I shall give you an inexhaustible quiver of arrows that are conducive to all happiness* and that never fail. When discharged they will burn because they are charged with my brilliance.

8. When it is commanded, it will dry up the clouds and the oceans. When it is dry, I will reduce it to ashes and shall be delighted thereby, O king!

9-11. Then Āditya gave Arjuna those arrows. Securing them, (Arjuna) burnt all the great immobile beings, hermitages, villages, cowherd colonies, cities, penance groves, beautiful forests and parks etc. and then circumambulated the Sun-god. The earth burnt down by the splendour of the Sun, became tree-less and grass-less.

12-13. In the meantime the great sage (Āpava) who had been residing under water for ten thousand years, completed his holy observance. Then the ascetic of great splendour emerged out (from water). The great sage then saw his hermitage burnt down by Arjuna. Out of anger he cursed the saintly king as already recounted by me to you.

Sūta said :

14. Listen to the race of the saintly king Kroṣṭu consi-

***sarvato-mukhān* 'capable of facing i.e. going in all direction' in Bd.P. 2.3.70.7 is a better reading than *sarvatosukhān* hereof.

sting of excellent men. In his family was born Vṛṣṇi, the founder of the dynasty of Vṛṣṇis.

15. Kroṣṭu had only one son Vṛjinīvān of great fame. (The people) liked the son of Vṛjinīvān, Svāhi, the foremost among those possessing Svāhā (i.e. performers of Yajñas wherein 'Svāhā' is repeated).

16. King Raśādu, the foremost among donors was the son of Svāhi. (The people) liked Ghṛtamprasūta, the eldest and the best son of Raśādu.

17. He performed many types of great Yajñas with adequate Dakṣiṇās. His son Citraratha was also endowed with (the inclination) to perform diverse holy rites.

18. Thus the heroic Citraratha performed many Yajñas giving vast wealth as Dakṣiṇā. His successor was Śaśabindu, who followed (the footsteps) of saintly kings.

19. He was an emperor of great prowess. He was very powerful and he had many children. In this connection, this genealogical verse has been cited by those who know ancient traditions.

20. "Śaśabindu had ten thousand sons. They were all very intelligent. They possessed vast wealth and great splendour. They were worthy (of their father).

21-22. Six of them were very important; they were known as '*Pṛthuṣaṭkas*' (six men who had the word *Pṛthu* i.e. great added on to their name). They were—Pṛthuśravas, Pṛthuyaśas, Pṛthuñjaya, Pṛthukīrti and Pṛthundātā. All the sons of Śaśabindu were kings. All the Purāṇas praise Antara who was the son of Pṛthuśravas. He was the same Antara as was the son of Yajña formerly."

23. After getting the earth (i.e. having become king) the same pious-souled excellent, righteous (king) performed a hundred horse-sacrifices.

24. His son was Marutta[1] who followed (the footsteps of) saintly kings. Heroic Kambalabarhis is remembered as Marutta's son.

---

1. Our text has dropped two generations between Antara (Akṣara in Bd.P.) and Marutta—*vide* Bd.P. 2.3.70.23-25.

25-26. Scholarly Rukmakavaca was the son of Kaṁbalabarhis. This Rukmakavaca had formerly attained excellent glory by killing (many) warriors wearing coats of mail and armed with bows, with his sharp arrows. He attained great fame as a performer of horse-sacrifices and gave profuse wealth (as Dakṣiṇā) to Brāhmaṇas.

27. From king Rukmakavaca were born five very strong sons of great prowess who killed heroic enemies without turning away (from the battlefield).

28. They were Rukmeṣu, Pṛthurukma, Jyāmagha, Parigha and Hari. The father established Hari and Parigha in (the land called) Videha.

29. Brahmeṣu[1] (? Rukmeṣu) became king and Pṛthurukma became his dependent. Banished from the kingdom by them, Jyāmagha[2] lived in a hermitage.

30. He was quiescent (by temperament). He lived in the terrible forest but he was actuated by a Brāhmaṇa. Taking up his bow he went to the middle of the land, seated in his chariot and waving his flag.

31. He (wandered) along in the marshy place on the banks of Narmadā. After passing through Mekala mountains and the mountain Ṛkṣavān, he entered Śuktimanyā (?)

32. Jyāmagha's wife was Śaibyā who was very strong. Though the king had no son, he did not take a second wife.

33. He became victorious in a battle and won a girl therein. The king then came to his wife and said, "Here is your daughter-in-law".

34. On being addressed thus she said, "This daughter-in law of yours is loveable. She will be the wife of your son who will be born (who is yet to be born)."

35. By performing a severe penance, the beautiful chaste lady Śaibyā gave birth to his son Vidarbha in her old age.

36. Vidarbha begot of that daughter-in-law two scholarly

1. *Brahmeṣu* is a mistake for *Rukmeṣu*. In *AIHT* p. 146 Parāvṛt is named as the successor of Rukmakavaca.

2. Jyāmagha's dynasty was famous but he is personally noted as a henpecked husband in Purāṇas, *vide* vv. 32-34, also Bd.P. 2.3.70. 33-36.

princes, Krathu and Kauśika who were heroic and experts in battles.

37. The very virtuous (king Vidarbha) later begot a third son Lomapāda. Vastu was the son of Lomapāda and his son was Āhṛti.

38. Cidi was the son of Kauśika. The Caidya kings are remembered as his descendents. Kunti was the son of Krathu who was Vidarbha's son.

39. Dhṛṣṭa was born as the son of Kunti. He was very proud and valorous. Dhṛṣṭa's son was the pious-souled Nirvṛti, the slayer of brave enemies.

40. His son was Daśārha who was very strong and valiant. Daśārha's son was Vyoman and his son is called Jīmūta.

41. Jīmūta's son was Vikṛti and his son was Bhīmaratha. Bhīmaratha's son was Rathavara.

42. He was a donor interested in Dharma (holy rite) perpetually. He was well-behaved and invariably truthful. His son was Navaratha. Daśaratha came after him.

43. His son was Ekādaśaratha. Śakuni was his son. From him was born the archer Karambhaka. Devarāta came thereafter.

44. King Devakṣatra of great fame was the son of Devarāta. Devana, the delighter of Kṣatriyas, was born as the son of Devakṣatra.

45-46. Madhu was born of Devana. His son was Medhārtha-saṁbhava. Madhu had other sons as well, viz. Manu of great brilliance, Manuvaśa, Nandana of great splendour and Mahāpuruvaśa. Purudvān, the most excellent man, was the son of Puruvaśa.

47. Purūdvaha was born of Bhadravatī as the son of Purūdvān. Aikṣākī was the wife (of Purudvān). Sattva was born of her. From Sattva was born Sāttvata who was endowed with Sattvaguṇa. He increased the fame (of the race).

48. After perfectly understanding this creation (race) of the noble-souled Jyāmagha, one obtains childern and attains *Sāyujya* (identity) with the intelligent king Soma.

CHAPTER THIRTYFOUR

The Race of Vṛṣṇi[1]

Sūta said :

1-2. Sāttvata's wife Kauśalyā gave birth to handsome sons, viz. Bhajin, Bhajamāna, Divya, Devāvṛdha the king, Andhaka, Mahābhoja, Vṛṣṇi and Yadunandana. They established four races. Listen to them in detail.

3. Bhajamāna begot of Śṛñjayī two sons, Bāhya and (the next) Bāhyaka. Bāhyaka married Śṛñjaya's two daughters

4. His wives, the two sisters, gave birth to many sons[2], viz. Nimi,, Paṇava, Vṛṣṇi and Parapurañjaya.

5-6. (Defective verse) Bhajamāna begot of Śṛñjayī other sons also, viz. Ayutāyutajit, Sāhasrajit, Śatajit and Vāmaka. Out of those who were born of Bhajamāna, king Devāvṛdha performed a severe penance.

7. He had this thought in his mind, 'May a son endowed with all good qualities be born to me'. After concentrating on this in Yoga, he touched the waters of the river Parṇāśā.[3]

8. On being touched by him, the river, the most excellent of all rivers, desired for the welfare of the king.

9-10. Anxiously engrossed in thought, the river decided thus : "I do not find any woman in whom a son like this, endowed with all good qualities, will be born to the king Devāvṛdha. Hence I shall myself become his wife (*Sahavratā*—a woman who performs holy rites in one's company)." She assumed hands[4] (i.e. human form) in accordance with her intention.

11. Taking the form of a girl, Sāvitrī (the river)repeated the

---

1. This chapter corresponds to Bd.P. 2.3.71. Hence only verse-numbers of this chapter are mentioned for comparison.

2. The list of sons in Bd.P. (vv. 3-6) differs. It gives the names of the sons as follows : Nimloci, Kiṃkaṇa, Dhṛṣṭi, Parapurañjaya.

3. The river Banas in Rajasthan—a tributary to Chambal. De 146.

The Purāṇa writers had a romantic concept of showing rivers falling in love with Kings and Sages and sometimes marrying them in human form such as Gāṅgā with Śantanu, Narmadā with Kārtavirya Arjuna. Kosı, Bahudā and other rivers had similar affairs.

4. *Hasta* translated here is obscure. Bd. P. 2.3.71.11 reads *hṛtstha* for *hasta* hereof. It means (in Bd. P.) II '(her emotional attachment) welled up in her heart'.

great words (?) She thought of the king. The king desired her (as his wife).

12-13. The liberal-minded (king) rendered her pregnant. She conceived a brilliant (son). In the ninth month, the most excellent of rivers gave birth to a son endowed with all good qualities as desired by Devāvṛdha. About this race, the Brāhmaṇas who know the Purāṇas, sing this Gāthā (glorificatory verse).

14-15. People of noble souls glorifying the good qualities of Devāvṛdha say—"He is seen at close quarters exactly as he is heard from a distance. Babhru is the most excellent among men. Devāvṛdha was equal to Devas. Seventy thousand and sixtyfive men of the line of Babhru and Devāvṛdha attained immortality (liberation from *Saṁsāra*).

16. That highly fortunate, most valiant hero among Sāttvatas, was a performer of sacrifices, the chief of the most prominent ones among the donors of liberal gifts, a brave warrior, a patron of Brāhmaṇas, truthful in speech, scholarly and (most) famous (in the world)."

17. (Defective verse) Sumahābhojayas and Imārtikābalas were born in his race[1] (?) Gāndhārī and Mādrī were the two wives of Vṛṣṇi.

18-19. Gāndhārī gave birth to Sumitra and Mitranandana. Mādrī gave birth to the sons Yudhājit, Devamīḍhusa and Anamitra. The two (last mentioned) were excellent men. Nighna was Anamitra's son. Nighna had two sons.

20. They were the blessed Prasena and Śakrajit. Sūrya[2] (the Sun-god) was an intimate bosom friend of Śakrajit.[3]

---

1. *tasyānvaye sumahābhojayemārtikābalāḥ* in the text is obscure. Bd. P. 2.3.71.18 reads :

tasyānvayaḥ sumahān bhojā ye bhuvi viśrutāḥ ||

'His race is very great. The kings of his line are well known on the earth as Bhojas'.

2. *Pūrva* in the text is wrong. *Sūrya* (as in A and Bd. P.) is accepted here as the following verses also confirm it.

3. Compare the Story of the Syamantaka gem in Bh.P. X. Chs. 56 and 57; Bd. P. 2.3.71.22-99.

21. Once, at the close of a night, the king who was driving in his chariot, got down near the bank (of a river) in order to perform the worship of the Sun with water libation.

22. While he was worshipping, Vivasvān, the Sun-god, the lord with his brilliant halo, stood before him but his form was not clearly visible.

23-24. Then the king addressed the Sun-god who was standing in front of him: "O lord of the luminaries, I see you in front of me also in the same form with brilliant halo as I see you in the sky. What special significance is there in your coming to me as a friend?"

25. On hearing this, the lord took off the excellent jewel Syamantaka from his neck and tied it round the king's neck.

26. The king then saw the Sun-god in his actual (physical) form. He gazed at the form for the duration of a Muhūrta.

27. When the Sun-god was about to start (on his journey) again, king Śakrajit requested him, "It behoves you to present me this excellent jewel of fiery splendour wherewith you traverse the worlds".

28. The Sun-god thereupon gave him the Syamantaka jewel. Wearing it the king re-entered the city.

29. The people flocked round him, saying, "Oh! here comes the Sun-god". The people in the king's assembly, the city and the harem all were surprised.

30. Out of affection, the king Śakrajit handed over the excellent divine jewel Syamantaka to his brother Prasenajit.

31. The clouds shower at the proper season in the land where the jewel Syamantaka is present. There is no fear of any epidemic or sickness.

32. Govinda (Kṛṣṇa) desired to have the jewel Syamantaka from Prasena. But he did not get it. Though he was powerful, he did not take it by force.

33. Once, bedecked with that jewel Prasena went a-hunting. For the sake of Syamantaka he met a terrible death from a lion.

34. Jāmbavān, the king of bears, killed that lion. Taking that jewel with him he entered his den.

35. The elders of Vṛṣṇis and Andhakas thought it to be the

work of Kṛṣṇa. Considering him covetous of the jewel, they all suspected him alone (as the perpetrator of the crime).

36. Unable to endure the false accusation, the lord, the powerful slayer of foes, roamed about in the forest (to trace Prasena).

37-40. He went over all the places where Prasena was hunting. With the help of trustworthy men, he followed the footsteps of Prasena and searched the great mountain Ṛkṣavān and the excellent mountain Vindhya. He became completely exhausted due to the search. The noble-minded (lord) then saw Prasena (lying) killed along with his horse. He did not get the jewel there. The lion was seen lying dead not far from the dead body of Prasena. Apparently the lion had been killed by a bear as indicated by the footprints. The scion of the family of Yadu (i.e. Kṛṣṇa) traced by means of footprints of the bear and found out the cave of the bear.

41. He heard the voice of a young woman deep inside the great cave. O Brāhmaṇas, the nurse had been playing with the infant son of Jāmbavān along with the jewel. The words "*Mā rodiḥ*" (Do not cry) were uttered by her.

The Nurse said:

42. The lion killed Prasena. The lion was killed by Jāṁbavān. O tender child, do not cry. This Syamantaka is for you.

43. (The words were clearly audible.) As soon as everything was made clear by those words, he entered the cave. He had already seen Prasena (lying dead) torn to pieces very near that cave.

44. Quickly entering the cave of the bear, the liberal-minded lord saw Jāṁbavān, the king of bears.

45. Vāsudeva fought with Jāṁbavān in his cave. For twentyone days Govinda had a hand to hand fight (with him).

46. When Kṛṣṇa entered the cave, the attendants of Vāsudeva returned to Dvārāvatī and reported (to others) that Kṛṣṇa (also) was killed.

47. After defeating the powerful Jāmbavān, Vāsudeva won the hand of his daughter Jāṁbavatī with the permission of the king of bears.

48. Overwhelmed by the splendour of the lord, Jāṁbavān gave the jewel as well as his daughter Jāṁbavatī to Viṣvaksena (Kṛṣṇa).

49. It was to clear himself that the lord took the Syamantaka jewel. Consoling the king of bears, he came out of the cave.

50. After redeeming the jewel thus and clearing himself of the scandal by his own efforts, the lord handed over the jewel to Satrājit in the presence of the Sāttvatas.

51. Madhusūdana (Kṛṣṇa) thereafter duly married the girl Jāṁbavatī. Janārdana got himself acquitted of the false accusation.

52. He who knows this story of the false accusation of Kṛṣṇa and the subsequent acquittal will never be accused fraudulently.

53. A hundred sons were born to Śatrajit from his ten wives who were sisters. Among them three were famous. Bhaṅgakāra was the eldest. The others were the heroic Vratapati, and Apasvānta the beloved (Supriya).

54. Bhaṅgakāra's wife named Dvārāvatī had good children. She gave birth to three daughters endowed with beauty and good qualities.

55. Satyabhāmā was the most excellent of all ladies. She was steadfast in performing holy rites and severe penances. The father gave her to Kṛṣṇa.

56-57. The jewel that Kṛṣṇa (redeemed and) gave to Satrājit was worn by Babhru (?) Akrūra who was desirous of wealth, coveted the jewel Syamantaka, requested for Satyabhāmā of excellent (unblamed) beauty through Śatadhanvā of the Bhoja family.

58. Therefore the mighty Śatadhanvā killed Bhadrakāra (? Bhaṅgakāra) at night. He stole the jewel and handed it over to Akrūra.

59. Akrūra, a prominent person, took that gem and entered into an agreement (with Śatadhanvā). "This should not be made known to anyone else by you.

60. Should you be attacked by Kṛṣṇa, we shall help you. Undoubtedly the whole of Dvārakā will be under my control."

61. When her father was killed, the grief-stricken Satyabhāmā of great fame got into a chariot and went to Varaṇāvata.

62. Telling her husband about the (criminal) act of Śatadhanvan of Bhoja family, the distressed (lady) Satyabhāmā stood near him and shed tears.

63. After offering (obsequies such as) the water libations to the Pāṇḍavas who were (supposed to have been) burnt (in Varaṇāvata), Hari (Kṛṣṇa) employed Sātyaki to be on a par with his brothers (in performance of remaining rites).

64. Hastening back to Dvārakā, the glorious slayer of Madhu spoke these words to his elder brother Balarāma (*Halin*—one armed with ploughshare).

65. "Prasena was killed by the lion, Satrājit was killed by Śatadhanvan (all for the sake of the jewel, Syamantaka). I seek that Syamantaka (as the legal owner). O Lord, strike him.

66. Hence get into the chariot quickly. After killing the mighty Bhoja, O mighty-armed one, the Syamantaka will be ours."

67. Then a tumultuous fight ensued between Bhoja and Kṛṣṇa. Śatadhanvā (i.e. Bhoja) could not see Akrūra anywhere round.

68. Both Bhoja and Janārdana were on horseback (while fighting). Akrūra did not wholeheartedly help him although he was competent and he could have done so.*

69-72. Hence (Bhoja) became frightened and thought of running away. Bhoja's mare was a divine one named Vijñātahṛdayā (that which understood the heart or mental feeling of the rider). She had a speed of a hundred Yojanas. It was seated on this mare that he fought with Kṛṣṇa. On his speedy mare Bhoja went a hundred Yojanas away. On seeing the quick motion of the chariot, Kṛṣṇa harassed Śatadhanvan. Then the mare became extremely exhausted. O Brāhmaṇas, the vital airs

---

*The line : *śakto'pi sādhyād vārdhakyān nākrūro' bhyupapadyata* is obscure. Bd. P.V. 70 reads :

śakto'pi śāṭhyād hārdikyo nā'krūro'bhyupapadyata /

'Though he was competent to do so, Akrūra, the Hārdikya, did not do so through perfidy'.

of the mare rose up into the sky (i.e. it died). Then Kṛṣṇa spoke to Rāma.

73. "O mighty-armed one, stay here. The defects of the horses (mares) have been observed by me. I shall go on foot and bring away the excellent jewel Syamantaka".

74. Going on foot alone, Acyuta, the knower of great miraculous weapons, killed Śatadhanvan, the king of Mithilā.

75. He could not see the Syamantaka (on his person) even after killing the mighty Bhoja. When Kṛṣṇa returned, the bearer of ploughshare (i.e. Rāma) asked him, "Give me the jewel".

76. "I don't have it", said Kṛṣṇa. Then the infuriated Rāma repeatedly cried "Fie upon you", and spoke to Janārdana.

77. "I tolerate it (and excuse you) as you are my brother. Welfare unto you. I am going. I have nothing to do with Dvārakā nor with you nor with the Vṛṣṇis."

78. Then Rāma, the suppressor of enemies, entered Mithilā. With all desirable presents, the king of Mithilā himself welcomed and honored him.

79. In the meantime Babhru (Akrūra), the foremost among the intelligent ones, performed unimpededly different kinds of Yajñas.

80. The son of Gādhi, the king of great fame, adopted a coat of mail in the form of *Dīkṣā* (initiation for sacrifices) for self-protection, in order to preserve the Syamantaka jewel.

81. In the performance of these Yajñas (which continued) for a period of sixty years, he utilised (donated) vast wealth, excellent jewels and different kinds of materials.

82. These Yajñas of that noble-souled (King) became famous by the name "Akrūra Yajña". Much food and wealth was given as Dakṣiṇā. All of them fulfilled the cherished desires of all.

83. Thereafter lordly king Duryodhana went to Mithilā and underwent divine training in mace fighting under Balabhadra.

84. O Brāhmaṇas, after a great deal of persuasion and pleading (Balabhadra) was brought back to Dvārakā by the leading persons among Vṛṣṇis and Andhakas along with the noble-souled Kṛṣṇa.

85. After killing Śatrughna along with Bandhumān in battle Akrūra, the powerful leader of men, went away along with Andhakas.

86-87. These two excellent men, Śatrughna and Bandhumān, were the sons of Bhaṅgakāra, the leader of Andhakas. They were born of Narā, the daughter of Śvaphalka. They were very mighty and famous. Kṛṣṇa was not pleased at the killing of Bhaṅgakāra.

88. As he was apprehensive of a split amongst his kinsmen, he (Kṛṣṇa) ignored him (Akrūra). After the departure of Akrūra, Indra did not shower rain there.

89. The whole land was oppressed by drought and was about to perish. Then Kukuras and Andhakas pacified and consoled Akrūra.

90. When (Akrūra), the lord (the most prominent) of charitably disposed persons, returned to Dvārāvatī, Indra showered everywhere, even within the ocean.

91. In order to please Vāsudeva Akrūra, the glorious leader of Yadus, gave him his virgin sister of approved good conduct.

92. After knowing by means of his Yogic power that the Syamantaka jewel was with Babhru, Kṛṣṇa Janārdana said to Akrūra in the open assembly.

93. "O honourable Lord, please hand over to me the jewel which has come into your possession. Please do nothing ignoble unto me.

94. The anger raging in my heart for the last sixty years has become great and deep-rooted. A long time has elapsed by now."

95. Then at the instance of Kṛṣṇa, Babhru, the highly intelligent one, handed over the jewel without any demur in the assembly of all the Sāttvatas.

96. The suppressor of enemies (Kṛṣṇa) obtained the jewel from Babhru in a straightforward manner. With a delighted mind, he gave it back to Babhru again.

97. The son of Gāndinī (i.e. Akrūra) obtained Syamantaka, the excellent jewel handed over by Kṛṣṇa. Wearing it (round his neck) he shone like the Sun.

98. He who knows this story of the false accusation and the subsequent excellent clearance of the Lord will by no means become a victim of false accusation.

99-100. From the youngest son Animitra (? Anamitra) of Vṛṣṇi Śini was born. His son was Satyaka who was truthful in speech and endowed with truthful temperament. The son of Satyaka (Sātyaki) was Yuyudhāna and his son was Bhūti.

101. Yugandhara was Bhūti's son. Thus the descendants of Bhūti, the Bhautyas have been recounted. Pṛśni had two sons, Śvaphalka and Citraka.

102. Wherever the pious-souled great king Śvaphalka stayed, no sickness or fear of drought oppressed the people.

103. O excellent Brāhmaṇas, once Indra did not shower rain in the realm of the lord, king of Kāśī, for three years.

104. He made the highly honoured Śvaphalka stay there. Due to the presence of Śvaphalka, Indra showered rain there.

105. Śvaphalka married the daughter of the king of Kāśī. She was a praise-worthy (uncensured) lady named Gāndinī. Everyday she gifted a cow to a Brāhmaṇa.[1]

106-108. It is said that she remained in the womb of her mother for many hundreds of years. She did not come out. The father said to her even as she was in the womb, "Be born quickly. Welfare unto you. Wherefore do you stay there?" Remaining in the womb itself the girl said, "I shall be born if a cow is given everyday. O Father, do you desire it?" The father said, "So be it" and fulfilled her desire.

109. Akrūra is remembered as her son. He was munificent, a performer of Yajñas, learned, heroic and fond of guests. Śvaphalka himself was very liberal in giving Dakṣiṇā.

110-111. Śvaphalka had other sons also—Upamaṅgu, Maṅgu, Mṛdura, Arimejaya, Girirakṣa, Yakṣa, Śatrughna, Arimardana, Dharmabhṛt, Śṛṣṭacaya, Vargamoca, Āvāha and Prativāha. He had a beautiful daughter Vasudevā also.

112. Akrūra begot of Ugrasenī two sons who delighted the family. They were Deva and Anupadeva. They were equal to Devas.

1. A popular etymology of the name 'Gāndini'.

113-114. Citraka's sons were : Pṛthu, Vipṛthu, Aśvagrīva, Aśvabāhu, Supārśvaka, Gaveṣaṇa, Ariṣṭanemi, Aśva, Suvarmā, Varmabhṛt, Carmabhṛt, Abhūmi and Bahubhūmi. Śraviṣṭhā and Śravaṇā were the two (daughters).

115. The daughter of (the king of) Kāśī bore four sons to Satyaka, viz. Kakuda, Bhajamāna, Śamīka and Balabharhis.

116. Vṛṣṭi was Kakuda's son. Vṛṣṭi's son was Kapotaromā and his son was Revata.

117. His son was a scholar and a friend of Tumburu. He is famous by the name Candanodakadundubhi.[1]

118-119. His son was Abhijit and his son was Punarvasu. The excellent man (King) had performed a horse-sacrifice for the sake of a son. In the course of that sacrifice, while the rites of Atirātra were being performed, he was born in the middle of the assembly. Therefore Punarvasu became a scholar, donor and righteous performer of Yajñas.

120. He had twin children—Āhuka[2] and Āhukī both of whom were foremost among intelligent ones. They say that Āhuka was invincible, thanks to his (mighty) arms and arrows.

121-123. About Āhuka the following verses are cited : "He had ten thousand war-chariots fully equipped with quivers, martial requisites, banners and flagstaffs, rumbling like clouds. No one (in his family) was a speaker of untruth, non-performer of Yajñas or non-giver of thousands (as Dakṣiṇā). No one was unclean or unrighteous. No one was unlearned or emaciate." We have heard that Dhṛti was the son of Āhuka.

124-126. (Partially defective) With his white-liveried retinue, the king who was like Āhuka, marched towards the eastern direction displaying (accompanied by) one million and eighty youthful horses (cavalry). He surpassed Bhoja's twenty-one thousand elephants the ropes of which (elephants) were made of gold and silver (wires?). An equal number of thousands (of elephants) of Bhoja (were posted) in the north. (The bells of these elephants) made a tinkling sound.

---

1. *AIHT*, p. 150 records 'Nandanodaka-dundubhi' as his name. His other name 'Andhaka' is not recorded there.

2. According to the genealogy on p. 105 of *AIHT*, Āhuka is the son of Punarvasu.

127. Āhuka gave his sister Āhukī to Āhukāndha. A daughter and two sons were born to Ahukāndha*.

128. The sons were Devaka and Ugrasena. Both of them were brilliant as if born of divine womb. Heroic sons comparable to Devas were born to Devaka.

129. They were Devānāṁdeva, Sudeva and Devarañjita. Their sisters were seven whom he gave to Vasudeva.

130-131. They (the sisters) were Vṛkadevā, Upadevā, Devarakṣitā, Śrīdevā, Śāntidevā, Mahādevā and Devakī who was the seventh. She was very beautiful to look at. Ugrasena had nine sons, the eldest of whom was Kaṁsa.

132. The others were Nyagrodha, Sunāma, Kadvaśaṅku, Bhūmaya, Sutanu, Rāṣṭrapāla, Yuddhatuṣṭa and Supuṣṭımān.

133. Their sisters were five: Karmavatī, Dharmavatī, Śatāṅku, Rāṣṭrapālā and the comely lady Kahvā.

134. Ugrasena, who was born of Kukura family and had a large number of children, was famous.

A man remembering this race of Kukuras of unmeasured splendour shall make his own race vast and be endowed with children.

135. Bhajamāna's sons were Rathimukhya, Vidūratha Rājyādhideva, Śūra and Vidura.

136-138. The sons of Śūra were more powerful. They were Vāta, Nivāta, Śoṇita, Śvetavāhana, Śamī, Gadavarmā, Nidāta, Śakra and Śakrajit. Śamī's son was Pratikṣipta and his son was Svayaṁbhoja. Hṛdika was born of Svayaṁbhoja. Hṛdika's ten sons were all of terrible exploits.

139-140. Kṛtavarmā was the eldest and Śatadhanvā was the middle one. The other sons were Devārha (Devabāhu in Bd. P.), Vanārha, Bhiṣak, Dvaitaratha, Sudānta, Dhiyānta, Nakavān and Kanakodbhava. A scholarly son Kamalabarhiṣa was born to Devārha.

---

*This seems to be a wrong statement. Āhuka gave his sister (to the prince of Avantı). Āhuka married princess of Kāśi. From her he had two sons Devaka and Ugrasena. Bd. P. 2.3.71.128 clearly states :

āhukāt kāśya-duhitur dvau putrau sambabhūvatuḥ

Vide *AIHT*, p. 105.

141. His sons were Asamaujas and the famous Susamaujas. Kṛṣṇa gave Sudaṁṣṭra and Surūpa[1] (as sons in adoption) to Asamaujas to whom no son was born (*ajātaputrāya*). Thus Andhakas have been recounted.

142. There is no doubt in this that he who daily glorifies this race of Andhakas, gains an extensive race for himself.

143. Śūra begot Devamānuṣi of Asmakī. Śūra begot of Māṣī (Māriṣī in Bd. P.) (the son) Devamīḍhuṣa.

144. Ten men (i.e. sons) were born of Bhāṣī (Māriṣī in Bd. P.), the daughter of Bhoja, and Śūra. The mighty-armed Vasudeva was the eldest. He was originally known as Ānakadundubhi.

145-146. As soon as he was born, *Dundubhi* (divine drum) sounded in heaven. A loud sound of ānakas (military drums) rose up in heaven. A heavy shower of flowers fell in the house of Śūra. In the entire human world there was no one equal to him in handsome features.[2]

147-149. The fame of Vasudeva who was foremost of men, was as brilliant as that of the moon. The other sons were Devabhāga, Devaśravas, Anādṛṣṭi, Kaḍa, Nandana, Bhṛñjina, Śyāma, Śamīka, and Gaṇḍūṣa. Four daughters, all excellent ladies, were also born, viz. Pṛthā, Śrutavedā, Śrutakīrti and Śrutaśravā. There was another (daughter) Rājādhidevī. All these five became mothers of heroic sons.

150-151. Kunti of Bhoja family adopted Pṛthā as his daughter. Pāṇḍu married her. Śūra had given her in adoption to the aged Kuntibhoja as he had no child. Hence Pṛthā became known as Kuntī and daughter of Kuntibhoja. Pāṇḍu the chief of Kurus, a great hero, took her as wife from him.

152. Pṛthā gave birth to three sons who were brilliant like fire. They were heroes with none to match them in the whole world. They were equal to Indra in exploit.

1. Sucandra and Vasurūpa according to Bd.P. v. 143.

2. Vasudeva's unparalleded handsomeness is recorded in Jaina works also. According to Jaina records Vasudeva was banished by his father, as complaints were lodged to him by citizens of Mathura about the seductive effect of his beauty on their women. A Prakrit work called *Vasudeva-Hiṇḍi* (*circa* A.D. 600) makes Vasudeva a hero whose wanderings were a marriage campaign. The work, however, is a Prakrit version of Guṇāḍhya's Paiśāci *Bṛhat-Kathā*, though here the hero is Vasudeva instead of Naravāhanadatta.

153. Pṛthā gave birth to Yudhiṣṭhira from Dharma, to Bhīma (Vṛkodara) from Māruta and to Arjuna (Dhanañjaya) from Indra.

154. It is well-known that Nakula and Sahadeva were born of Mādravatī. Both of them were endowed with handsome features and inherent strength and good qualities.

155. The powerful and heroic lord of Karūṣa named Dantavaktra was born of Śrutadevā as the son of Vṛddhaśarman.

156-158. Santardana was born of Śrutakīrti, the wife of the prince of Kekaya. Cekitāna and Bṛhatkṣatra were the other two mighty (sons). Brothers Vinda and Anuvinda who were very powerful, were born of the king of Avanti (?) as sons of Rājādhidevī.

The king of Cedi[1], Śiśupāla, was born of Śrutaravā as the son of the saintly king Damaghoṣa. His manliness is well known. He was formerly the ten-necked (Rāvaṇa), the slayer of enemies.

159-161. Yaduśravā and Rujakanya were his younger brothers. Vasudeva had thirteen excellent ladies as wives. Of them Pauravī, Rohiṇī, Madirā, Aparā, Bhadrā, Vaiśākhī and Devakī the seventh (were the chief queens). Two lady attendants Sugandhi and Vanarāji and two others (also were married to him). Rohiṇī and Pauravī were the daughters of Vālmīka.[2]

162-163. The blessed lady, the eldest wife of Ānakadundubhi, Rohiṇī gave birth to eight children. The eldest son was Rāma. The others were Sāraṇa, Niśava, Durdama, Damana, Śubhra, Piṇḍāraka and Kuśītaka. She had a daughter named Citrā.

164-165. His grandsons born to Rāma were famous as Niśīta and Utsuka. Rāma had other sons as well: Pārśvī, Pārśvanandī, Śiśu, Satyadhṛti, Mandabāhya, Rāmāṇa, Girika, Gira, Śuklagulma, Gulma and Daridrāntaka.

166-171. Sāraṇa had five daughters who were born prior to these. They were Arciṣmatī, Sunandā, Surasā, Suvacā and Śatabalā. The following are remembered as the sons and grandsons of Rohiṇī : Bhadrāśva, Bhadragupti, Bhadra-

1. Bundelkhaṇḍa and the adjacent territory from former Central Provinces (now the whole of Cedi is included in new Madhya Pradesh).

2. 'Younger sisters of Bāhlīka' as per Bd. P.V.163.

vighna, Bhadrabāhu, Bhadraratha, Bhadrakalpa, Supārśvaka, Kīrtimān, Rohitāśva, Bhadraja, Durmada and Abhibhūta.

The sons and daughters of Madirā were : Nanda, Upananda, Mitra, Kukṣimitra, Acala, Sthita (?), Puṣṭi and Sudeva (sons) and Citrā and Upacitrā (daughters).

Upabiṁba, Biṁba, Sattvadanta and Mahaujas, these four were the powerful and famous sons of Bhadrā.

172-173. Śauri (i.e. Vasudeva) begot the excellent son Kauśika of Vaiśākhī. He begot six sons of Devakī. They were: Suṣeṇa, Kīrtimān, Tadaya (Udarṣī in Bd. P.), Bhadrasena, Yajudāya the fifth, and Bhadravit the sixth. Kaṁsa killed all of them.

174. Under these circumstances Viṣṇu, the lord of the worlds, lord of the subjects, was born as the long-lived Kṛṣṇa.

175. After him was born Subhadrā who used to speak pleasantly. She was otherwise known as Kṛṣṇā. This girl of the family of Vṛṣṇis named Subhadrā became famous as Kṛṣṇā.

176. The heroic Abhimanyu was born of Subhadrā and Pārtha (Arjuna). Listen and understand the names of the other heroic sons born of Vasudeva and his seven highly fortunate wives.

177-178. The heroic son Bhayāsakha was born of Sahadevā. Śārṅgadevā gave birth to Tambu. Śauri (thus) begot a son who made the family flourish. Four more sons of his, viz. Upasaṅga, Vasu, Deva and Rakṣita were killed by Kaṃsa. Thus he had ten sons. Kaṁsa killed all of them.

179. Upadevā gave birth to all these blessed sons : Vijaya, Rocana and Vardhamāna. (Bd. P adds : Devala.)

180. Vṛkadevī gave birth to noble-souled Svagāhava. (This lady was known by these names as well) Āgāhī, Svasā, Śiśirāyiṇī and Surūpā.

181. Devakī of beautiful nose gave birth to Bhū (Śrīkṛṣṇa ?) as her seventh son. (Afterwards) she gave birth to the blessed Gaveṣaṇa, who could fight in battle in wonderfully diverse ways.

182. Śauri (Vasudeva) begot of Śaibyā the immutable (economical ?) son (Kauśika alias Śrāddhadeva) who formerly

implanted a forest[1], O Brāhmaṇas.

183. Sugandhi and Vanarājī (the servant-maids mentioned before) were also the wives of Śauri. Puṇḍra and Kapila were Vasudeva's sons born of Sugandhi (Bd.P.v.186). Of them Puṇḍra became a king and Kapila went to the forest.

184. Of the other lady (Vanarājī) Vasudeva had another powerful son who was a foremost wielder of bow. He was a king called Niṣāda.

185. Mahābhāga was the famous son of Devarāta. They call the son born of Devaśravas as one honoured by scholars.

186. Nivarta begot of Aśmakī the sons Anādṛṣṭi of great fame, Śrāddhadeva of great strength and Śakraśatrughna.

187. (Defective verse)[2] Śrādhadeva was well known as the founder of Niṣadha (Niṣāda) (?) kingdom. Ekalavya of great prowess was nurtured and brought up by Niṣādas (hunting tribes).

188. With pleasure Kṛṣṇa gave his sons Cārudeṣṇa and Sāmba who had all praiseworthy characteristics and who had learned the use of miraculous weapons, to Gaṇḍūṣa who was childless.

189. Tantija and Tantimāla were Kanaka's own sons. Vasudeva of great exploit gave them to Vastāvani who had no child. Sauti gave his heroic sons Śauri and Kauśika to him.

190. (Other members of this family were) Tapas, Krodhanu, Virajas, Śyāma and Sṛñjima. Śyāma was childless and he went to the forest. He contemptuously treated his status as a member of the Bhoja clan. He secured the status of a Rājarṣi (a royal sage).

191. He who reads this story of Kṛṣṇa's birth after regularly observing rites, and also narrates it to Brāhmaṇas shall attain great happiness.

192. Lord Nārāyaṇa of great splendour, lord of Devas, the lord of subjects (Prajāpati) was formerly born among men out of sportfulness.

---

1. Reading in A adopted.

2. Bd. P.v. 190 gives a better reading and means: 'Ekalavya, the highly lucky son was born to Śrāddhadeva. He was brought up by Niṣādas (a forest tribe) and so he was well known as Naiṣādi.'

193. The lotus-eyed lord was born of Devakī and Vasudeva, thanks to their penance. It should be known that he had divine form with four arms. He was endowed with glory.

194. Even after becoming the son of Aditi (Devakī), the delighter (or scion) of the Yādava clan (Kṛṣṇa) is well-known as god Viṣṇu, the younger brother of Indra.

195. Though Nārāyaṇa took birth, he is still *Avyaya* (the unchanging). The Lord Nārāyaṇa is still eternal even after becoming Hari.

196. It was he who created the primordial being Prajāpati formerly. Even after becoming the son of Aditi (Devakī) the delighter (or scion) of the Yādava clan (Kṛṣṇa) is well known as god Viṣṇu, the younger brother of Indra.

197. It was he who blessed Aditi with his grace and was born as her son for the purpose of slaying Daityas, Dānavas and Rākṣasas, the enemies of Suras.

198. The family of the intelligent Vasudeva, born of the race of Yayāti, became certainly meritorious and holy because Lord Nārāyaṇa resorted to it.

199. While Janārdana was being born, the oceans trembled, the mountains shook and the sacrificial fires blazed.

200. While Janārdana was born, the winds blew auspiciously. All dust subsided. All the luminaries shone more brilliantly.

201. The asterism on the day when Janārdana was born was Abhijit by name. The night was called Jayantī (the 8th of the dark half of Śrāvaṇa with the constellation Rohiṇī rising at midnight). And the Muhūrta (the specific period at the time of his birth) was Vijaya by name.

202. The unmanifest, eternal Lord Hari, Nārāyaṇa, Kṛṣṇa fascinated the people with his eyes as he was born.

203. The lord of Devas (Indra) showered flowers from the firmament. Eulogising Madhusūdana (Kṛṣṇa) with auspicious words thousands of great sages and Gandharvas offered prayer unto him.

204. Vasudeva saw lord Adhokṣaja (whose form is beyond the ken of the physical sense-organs) born at night as his son endowed with the characteristic curl of hair called *Śrivatsa* and accompanied by various divine signs in heaven.

Vasudeva thereafter requested: "O lord, withdraw your form.

205. I say this, O dear one, as I am very much afraid of Kaṁsa. My sons, your elder brothers, were very wonderful in appearance but were killed by him".

206. On hearing the words of Vasudeva, the lord withdrew his form. Permitted by him (the lord), the father took him to the abode of Nandagopa. Abiding by the suggestion of Ugrasena,[1] he gave (the child) to Yaśodā then.

207. Yaśodā and Devakī had been pregnant simultaneously. Yaśodā was the wife of Nandagopa, the Lord of (herd of) cows.

208. Yaśodā had given birth to a daughter in the same night as Kṛṣṇa was born as the lord of the race of Vṛṣṇi.

209. Protecting the son born to him, Vasudeva of great fame, handed him over to Yaśodā and took the daughter with him.

210. Handing him over to Nandagopa, (Vasudeva) spoke, "Save me. This (adopted) son of your shall be the bestower of all happiness to Yādavas. This is that (long expected) child of Devakī. He shall put an end to all our pain and misery."

211. Ānakadundubhi took that girl to the son of Ugrasena (i.e. Kaṁsa) and informed him: "This is the girl of auspicious characteristics".

212. Kaṁsa had not known (till then) that a child had been born to his sister. The wicked-minded one became delighted and spared that girl.

213. The foolish one muttered within himself: "If it is a girl she is already slain !" That daughter grew up well respected in the abode of Vṛṣṇis.

214-215: (Defective) Just as gods bring up gods[2], they protected her like a son. They said that a daughter had been

---

1. '*ugrasena-mate*' in the text is confusing. Bd. P.v. 212 reads "gopa (who was staying) in the house of Ugrasena".

2. The text '*Putravat paripālyanto devā devān yathā* /' translated above is irrelevant to the context. It gives cogent sense if emended as in Bd. P. 2.3-72, 220, as follows :

putravat pālayāmāse devī devīṁ mudā tadā

'Then the goddess (Devakī) gladly brought up the goddess (Ekādaśā) like (her own) son.'

duly born: "(Goddess) Ekādaśā is born for the protection of Keśava. With delighted minds all the Yādavas will worship her. Kṛṣṇa, the lord of Devas, of divine physical form is well protected by her."

The Sages said:

216. Why did Kaṁsa, the king of the Bhoja family, kill the sons of Vasudeva even when they were (mere) infants? It behoves you to explain this to us.

Sūta said:

217-218. Listen why the foolish Kaṁsa killed the infant sons of Ānakadundubhi (Vasudeva) immediately after their birth. (I shall explain) how, out of fear, the mighty-armed Kṛṣṇa was taken elsewhere immediately after birth and how Govinda, (though) the supreme person was brought up among the cows.

219. It is reported that Kaṁsa, then the crown prince, acted as a charioteer of the self-possessed Vasudeva along with Devakī (in their marriage).

220. Then there arose in the sky a divine voice of some incomprehensible person. It was distinctly loud and clear and was witnessed by all people. Thereby Kaṁsa remained panicky perpetually (throughout his life).

221. "O Kaṁsa, the seventh (?) child of this lady whom you drive in your chariot out of affection, will be the cause of your death."

222. On hearing that (aerial) voice, the foolish Kaṁsa became distressed. Unsheathing his sword, he evinced his desire to kill her.

223. The mighty-armed and valorous Vasudeva spoke to Kaṁsa, the son of Ugrasena, out of friendliness and affection.

224-228, "It does not behove any Kṣatriya to kill a woman at any time. O scion of the family of Yadus, I have seen a way out in this matter. O King, I shall hand over to you the seventh child that will be born of her. You may do whatever you deem fit then. Even now, O liberal one in giving Dakṣiṇā, you can do as you wish[1]. I shall (even) promise that I will give you all her childern. O excellent man, this promise will never be falsified". Thus implored and propitiated Kaṁsa (agreed to the proposal of) seizing all the children. Vasudeva rejoiced in having got back his wife (alive). So Kaṁsa, the foolish man of sinful deeds, went on killing the sons (one after the other).

The Sages said:

229. Who is this Vasudeva who begot Viṣṇu ? Who is this Devakī, the lady of fame, who gave birth to Viṣṇu? Who is this Nandagopa and who is this famous lady Yaśodā who brought him up?

Sūta said :

230. All the men (of the Yadu race) were the incarnations of Kaśyapa and all the women of Aditi[2]. The mighty-armed lord (thus) fulfilled the desires of Devakī.

231. The lord entered a human body and moved about on the earth. By means of his Yogic Māyā the Yogic-souled lord infatuated all living beings.

232. When Dharma declined, Viṣṇu himself incarnated in the race of Vṛṣṇis in order to reestablish Dharma and to annihilate Asuras.

233-234. He married the girl Rukmiṇī, Satyā the daughter of Nagnajit, Satyabhāmā the daughter of Satrājit, Jāmbavatī, Rohiṇī, Śaibyā, Sudevī, Mādrī, Suśīlā, Kālindī, Mitravindā, Lakṣmaṇā, Jālavāsinī and others.

235. Thus he had sixteen thousand wives. After consulting Devas, Śakra had sent down to the earth the most

---

1. The words *tvam tvidānīm* in the text are absurd as they would mean free permission to Kaṁsa to kill Devakī. They need emendation as *natvidānīm*, as in Bd.P. ibid v. 233. It means "Do not behave now in the way you wish". Vasudeva wanted to save Devaki's life and hence requested Kaṁsa not to kill her.

2. This is a strange statement. Bd. P. v. 238 states that Vasudeva and Devaki were Kaśyapa and Aditi in their former life. Our text does not answer who was Nandagopa and Yaśodā but Bd.P.v. 239 informs that Nanda was a Vasu called Droṇa and Yaśodā, his wife Dharā. Bh. P. X.8.48.51 confirm it.

excellent ones among the celestial damsels of whom it is said there are fourteen groups.

236. In order to become the wives of Vāsudeva, they, were born in royal palaces. These were the blessed ladies famous as Viṣvaksena's wives.

237-240. Pradyumna, Cārudeṣṇa, Sudeṣṇa, Śarabha, Cāru, Cārubhadra, Bhadracāru, and Cāruvindhya were the sons of Rukmiṇī. She had a daughter Cārumatī.

Sānu, Bhānu, Akṣa, Rohita, Mantraya, Jarāndhaka, Tāmravakṣas, Bhaumari and Jarandhama were the sons of the Garuḍa-bannered lord (Kṛṣṇa) and Satyabhāmā. They had four sisters, viz. Bhānu, Bhaumarikā, Tāmraparṇī and Jarandhamā.

Now listen to the children of Jāṁbavatī.

241. Bhadra, Bhadragupta, Bhadravindra and the famous Saptabāhu were the sons; Bhadrāvatī and the famous Sambodhanī were the daughters. These should be known as Jāmbavatī's children.

242. Saṅgrāmajit, Śatajit, and Sahasrajit are glorified as the sons of Sudevī and Viṣvaksena (i.e. Kṛṣṇa).

243. Vṛka, Vṛkāśva, Vṛkajit, Mitrabāhu and Sunītha were the sons. Vṛjinī and Suraṅganā[1] were the daughters. These are the children of the daughter of Nagnajit (i.e. Satyā).

244. Thus know that he had thousands of sons. (Some say) that Vāsudeva had hundred thousands of sons.

245. Ten thousand and eight of them (or eighty thousand of them) were heroic and experts in battle. The family of Janārdana has been recounted to you factually.

246. Bṛhatī (known also as) Nartakonneyī was united (in wedlock) with Sunaya. She was the daughter of Bṛhaduktha the noble-souled scion of the family of Śuni (Śauneya).

247. Her sons were three in number. They were well known as shining splendidly in war, viz. Aṅgada, Kumuda and Śveta. She had a daughter too named Švetā.

248. Avagāha[2], Citra and the heroic Citravara (were

1. The reading *varāṅganā* in Bd.P. v. 252 implies that excellently beautiful Vṛjinī was the only daughter of Satyā.

2. Bd. P.v. 257 reads *Avagāhasya* and implies Citra, Śura and Citravara as his sons.

famous members of the Vṛṣṇi race). Citravaras son was Citrasena and his daughter was Citravatī.

249. Tumba and Tumbabāṇa were the two sons of Janastamba. Vajrāra and Kṣipra are remembered to be the sons of Upāṅga.

250. Bhūrīndrasena and Bhūri were the two sons of Gaveṣa. Yudhiṣṭhira's daughter Sutanu was well-known.

251. The famous son of Aśva named Vajra was born of her. Vajra's son was Pratibāhu and Sucāru was his son.

252. Kāśmā (Princess of Kāśī—Bd.P.) gave birth to the son Supārśva and Sāmbā to Tarasvin. The sons of the noble-souled Yādavas were three crores.

253. Six million of them were extremely valorous and very strong. All these men of great prowess were born of the parts of Devas.

254. They were born in the family of Yādavas in order to exterminate the Asuras of great penance who had been born among human beings in this world and were harassing them. These Asuras had been killed in the battles between Devas and Asuras.

255. There were eleven distinct families of the noble-souled Yādavas. But in the family of Viṣṇu (i.e. Kṛṣṇa) all of them merged as though into one family.

256. Viṣṇu was their authority and the leader for them. All of them, all human beings*, obeyed his behests and abided by his directions.

257. Thus the progeny of Vṛṣṇis has been glorified succinctly and in details. The glorification of these bestows fame and fulfilment of cherished desires.

*The text is a bit obscure. If '*sarva-mānuṣāḥ*' in the 2nd line is emended as '*sura-mānuṣāḥ*' (as in Bd. P.v. 262) it means 'suras and human beings are bound by those who abide by his (Kṛṣṇa's) behests'.

CHAPTER THIRTYFIVE[1]

Wars between Suras and Asuras: Bhṛgu curses Viṣṇu: The Eulogy of Śaṁbhu by Śukra

1-3. Understand the Devas who had assumed human nature and born as they are being glorified.

Saṁkarṣaṇa, Vāsudeva, Pradyumna, Sāmba and Aniruddha—these five are glorified as the race[2] (of Vṛṣṇis).

The Seven Sages, Kubera, the Yakṣa Maṇivara, Śalaki, Bādara, the scholarly Dhanvantari, Nandin Mahādeva (?), Śālaṅkāyana, Jiṣṇu (Viṣṇu in Bd. P.), the primordial god along with these divine beings (are being narrated).

The Sages said :

4. Why did Viṣṇu incarnate? How many incarnations are remembred? How many are the future manifestations of the great soul?

5. Why is he born in Brāhmaṇa and Kṣatriya families at the closing periods of the Yugas? Why does he incarnate again and again among human beings? Please explain it to us who (being curious to know) enquire of you.

6. We wish to hear completely and in detail all the activities of the intelligent Kṛṣṇa, the slayer of enemies in different bodies (incarnations).

7. O Sūta, O holy lord, it behoves you to narrate in the proper order his various activities, the different manifestations as well as his nature to us.

8. How did that lord Viṣṇu (well-renowned) among Suras as the slayer of their enemies, adopt the state of being the son of Vasudeva, in his family?

9. O Sūta, what (special) meritorious act was performed by the deathless Devas who invariably perform meritorious deeds, as a result of which (the lord) left the region of Devas and came over to the world of mortals?

---

1. This chapter corresponds to Bd. P. 2.3.72; the references are to the verse numbers of that chapter.

2. The list shows the influence of Pañcarātra school in that period.

10. Why did the leader of Devas and human beings, Hari, the source of origin of the worlds Bhūḥ and Bhuvaḥ, install his divine soul in a human womb?

11. It is he who makes the mental cycles of human beings revolve and function. He is the foremost among the wielders of discus. Why did he decide to be born among human beings?

12. It is he who affords protection to all the worlds and the whole universe. Why did that lord Viṣṇu descend to the earth and emulate (an ordinary) cowherd?

13. He is the Ātman of all living beings. He has created and sustained all the great Bhūtas (elements). He is the *Śrīgarbha* (having glory and splendour, Śrī, within him). How was he retained in the womb by a woman of the earth?

14. It was he who measured the three worlds in three paces at the request of Devas. It was by him that the three paths of the worlds consisting of the three *Vargas* (i.e. Dharma, Kāma and Artha?) were laid down.

15. At the time of dissolution of the universe he assumed the form consisting of waters and drank up the whole universe. He made the whole world a vast sheet of water through the visible and invisible paths.

16. In the Purāṇas he is (eulogised as) *Purāṇātmā* (the ancient soul). He assumed the physical form of a Boar. He is the most excellent of Suras who redeemed the earth and gave it over to Suras.

17. Hiraṇyakaśipu, a demon of yore, who possessed great prowess, had been killed by him assuming a leonine body divided into two (as half man, half lion).

18. Formerly, the omnipresent lord became the Aurva fire (also called) the Saṁvartaka fire (fire of dissolution), and stationed himself in the nether worlds within the ocean. He drank *Havis* (sacrificial offerings) in the form of water.

19. It is he whom they (the sages) call in every Yuga as the lord with a thousand feet, thousand rays, the lord having thousands (of forms), and thousand heads.

20. When the whole world was a vast sheet of water, the abode of god Brahmā (Pitāmaha) came out of his navel even as fire comes out of Araṇi. It (the abode) was a Paṅkaja (a lotus,

but literally 'one born of mud') but it was not born of any *Paṅka* (mud).

21. It was by him that Daityas were killed in the Tārakāmaya battle[1] after adopting a body consisting of all (the spirits of) Devas and holding all weapons.

22. The haughty Kālanemi was defeated and struck down by him (the lord) seated on the back of Garuḍa.

Resorting to his eternal Yogic power and enveloping (everything) in dense darkness, he reclines (on his serpent couch) on the northern part of the ocean of milk, the ocean that yielded nectar. He (wards off) the great darkness (of ignorance).

23. (Defective verse) Thanks to the intensity of her penance, formerly Aditi ratained him in her womb like Araṇi (holding fire within it). When Indra was surrounded by the hosts of Daityas, it was he who saved him by contemptuously warding them off from the womb?

24. When the Wind-god[2] (?) deprived (Daityas) of their hold (from all positions) in the world and made Daityas remain sub-merged in waters, the primordial Lord made Devas the resident of heaven and made Indra (Puruhūta) the Lord of Devas.

25-26. It was the same Ādideva[3] who laid down the process of preparing the Āhavanīya fire by means of Gārhapatya and Anvāhārya rites. He created the altar, the Kuśa grass, the *prokṣaṇīya śruvā* (the sacrificial ladle with which the offering is taken or holy water sprinkled) and the materials for *Avabhṛtha* (the final ablution). He laid down the rules of selecting the three persons[4] (?) entitled to offer Havya in a sacrifice.

27. He made Suras the partakers of Havyas and Pitṛs the partakers of Kavyas. In order to enjoy (him-

1. The battle that ensued after the abduction of Tārā by Soma.

2. Purāṇas do not attribute this feat to the Wind-god. Bd. P. 2-3.72.23 reads *padāni yo* for *yadā'nilo* hereof. Bd. P. reading means 'He made the regions of world as the abodes of the people'.

3. Verses 25-29 give to Viṣṇu the credit of founding the institution of sacrifice.

4. The reading *'atha trīn iha yaścakre* (translated here as 'selecting three persons') is wrong. Bd. P. 2.3.72.26 reads *atharṣīn ścaiva yaścakre* 'then he created sages' (for participation in sacrifices).

self) by the sacrificial procedure, he himself became Yajña, in the sacrificial rite.

28-29. By dint of his supreme power, he created and made resplendent the requisite material for sacrifices such as *Yūpas* (sacrificial posts), *Samits* (holy twigs), *Sruvā* (sacred ladles), Soma (the creeper or its juice called soma), *Pavitra* (the special holy ring of Kuśa grass), *Paridhi* (the holy twigs of Palāśa etc. laid round the sacrificial fire), the sacrificial fires, *sadasyas* (members of the sacrificial assembly), *Yajamāna* (the performers of sacrifices) and excellent sacrifices like horse sacrifice and others.

30-31. After creating the three worlds in order in accordance with the Yugas, he made all the following things: (Measures of Time such as) *Kṣaṇas* (moments), *Nimeṣas, Kāṣṭhās, Kalās,* and all the three periods of time (past, present, and future), periods of time such as *Muhūrtas* (periods of 48 minutes each), *Tithis* (days of the lunar fortnight), months, days, years, seasons, various specific *yogas* of time, the three kinds of *Pramāṇas* (means of valid knowledge) etc.

32-34. He created the span of life, *Kṣetras* (?fields), increase, characteristics, beauty of form, intellect, wealth, heroism, the ability to comprehend the sacred lore, the three castes, the three *Vidyās* (Lores), the three fires, the three periods of time, the three rites, the three Māyās* and the three Guṇas (Sattva, Rajas and Tamas). It was by his infinite power (of creation) that he created the worlds, gods. All the Bhūtas and Gaṇas were created by him who is the *Ātman* (soul) of them all (living beings and Bhūta Gaṇas).

35. He sports in the sense-organs of men by means of his Yogic power. He is the lord of diverse things. He is present everywhere. He is the leader of arrivals and departures (*Gata* and *Āgata*) i.e. all sorts of movements.

36. He is the goal unto those endowed with piety and virtue and is inaccessible to those of sinful deeds. He is the source of origin of the system of four castes and protector of the same.

*Probably *Mātrās* 'units of time' as in Bd. P. 2.3.72.32.

37-38. He is the knower of the four Vidyās, viz. *Ānvīkṣikī*, *Trayī*, *Vārtā* and *Daṇḍanīti*, and the supporter of the four *Āśramas* (stages of life). He is the space between quarters, the sky, the earth, the waters, the fire, the wind, the quarters, the two luminaries, the sun and the moon. He is the lord of the Yugas and the night wanderers (Rākṣasa?). In the Vedas he is spoken of as the great lord and as the great penance.

39. It is he who is greater than penance; they call him the supreme one, the possessor of the great soul. He is the lord, first among the Ādityas (sons of Aditi). He is the lord, the destroyer of the Daityas.

40. At the close of the Yugas, he is the annihilator. He is the slayer of the destroyers of the worlds. He is the bridge (or the boundary) of all the boundaries of the worlds. He is the purest among all those of pure rites.

41. He is the *Vedya* (one who should be known) for the Vedic scholars; he is the lord of all powerful persons. He is the Soma to all living beings; he is the Agni (Fire-god) for those of fiery splendour.

42. He is the mind of men; he is the penance of the ascetics; he is the modesty of those satisfied with good policy and he is the splendour of the refulgent.

43-44. He is the *Vigraha* (body) of all embodied beings. He is the goal of those who achieve their goal[1].

Vāyu is born of Ākaśa (Ether). Hutāśana (Fire) has Vāyu as its vital essence. Devas have their vital essence in fire and Madhusūdana (Kṛṣṇa) is the vital essence of Agni.

Rasa (the lymphatic juice) becomes blood; flesh is developed out of blood.[2]

45-47. From flesh fat is produced and bone is developed from fat. Pith and marrow are developed from bone and semen virile is generated from marrow; foetus is developed from semen through the assimilative activity of *Rasa*—bodily fluid (or through the activity rooted in sexual pleasure). At

1. Or : He is the velocity of those which are in motion.

2. Verses 44b-57 deal with embryology with special emphasis on Viṣṇu's power.

first it is in fluid state. This is called the *Saumya Rāśi*. It is called the second Rāśi when it is heated by the warmth (temperature) in the womb. Semen should be known as of the nature of Soma (Moon) and menstrual blood as of the nature of fire.

48. These two secretions (evolutes) follow *Rasa* (lymphatic juice). In semen (the mixture of semen and menstrual blood) there are Soma (Moon) and fire. Semen comes under the category of *Kapha* (phlegmatic humour) and menstrual blood comes under the category of *Pitta* (bilious humour).

49. The receptacle of *Kapha* is heart. *Pitta* is held in navel. Heart in the centre of body is the place of mind.

50. Lord Hutāśana (Fire) is stationed in the umbilical cavity. Mind should be known as Prajāpati (Brahmā) and *Kapha* is considered as Soma (Moon).

51. *Pitta* is considered as fire. Hence the universe consists of Agni and Soma. The foetus thus originating stays there like a patch of cloud.

52. Vāyu enters and becomes united with the great soul. It is divided into five within the body and develops (the foetus).

53. The five divisions are *Prāṇa*, *Apāna*, *Samāna*, *Udāna* and *Vyāna*. Among them *Prāṇa* moves round and develops the great soul.

54. *Apāna* is situated in the lower half of the body. *Udāna* circulates in the upper half of the body. *Vyāna* is called so because it pervades the whole body. *Samāna* is present in all the joints.

55. Thereafter, the five elements, viz. Earth, Wind, Ether, Water and Fire the fifth one, are attained by the foetus. Then it becomes perceivable by the sense-organs.

56. All the sense-organs enter into that (foetus) and perform their respective functions. They call it then the earthly (physical) body and the wind is called *Prāṇātman* (having the characteristic form of Prāṇa, the vital air).

57. The pores of the body have Ether as the source of their origin. It is from the element water that the liquid form-

ation (and exudation) in the body take place. The fiery element enters the eyes in the form of moonlight (?) The groups of objects function due to his prowess.

The Sages enquired:

58. How did Viṣṇu, the Puruṣa who creates all these and all the worlds, attain human state in the mortal world?

59. O intelligent one, this is our doubt. Our wonder is excessive. He is the ultimate goal of those who attain their goal (*Mokṣa*). How did he come to assume the human body?

60. We wish to hear about the very wonderful exploits of Viṣṇu in the proper order. Viṣṇu is described to be so by the Vedas and Devas.

61. O highly intelligent one, please tell us the story of the wonderful nativity of Viṣṇu. May the wonderful and pleasing narrative be recounted.

62. The manifestations of the noble soul of reputed strength and prowess are wonderful. The inherent power of Viṣṇu who has become miraculous on account of his wonderful deeds be please narrated.

Sūta said :

63. I shall glorify the manifestation of the noble soul, how that lord of great penance was born among human beings.

64. His incarnations in the human world as a result of Bhṛgu's curse were seventyseven in number*. He incarnates at the closing periods of the Yugas for realising the purpose of Devas.

65-66. Listen and understand (the details of) the divine personality of Viṣṇu, as I recount it. When the *Yuga-Dharma* (practice of *Dharma*—virtue—peculiar to a Yuga) gets reversed and declined and the time becomes slack and inactive, the Lord incarnates in order to stabilise righteousness (Dharma) in human beings. (These incarnations are) due to the curse of

---

*The text *sapta-sapta-tapaḥ proktā* is not supported in the subsequent narrative. Bd. P. 2.3.72.63 reads *bhṛgu-strī-vadha-doṣeṇa* 'due to his (Viṣṇu's) fault of killing (sage) Bhṛgu's wife'. As the episode is given in the following verse the reading deserves adoption.

Bhṛgu brought about by (the mutual struggle between) Devas and Asuras.

The Sages enquired:

67. How can he incarnate as a result of the mutual struggle between Devas and Asuras? We wish to know this, How did the mutual clash between Devas and Asuras take place?

Sūta replied:

68. Listen and understand even as I narrate it, the clash between Devas and Asuras in the manner it has taken place.

Formerly, Hiraṇyakaśipu, a Daitya, ruled over the three worlds.[1]

69. Thereafter the suzerainty over the three worlds was hereditarily established by Bali. There was great friendship between Devas and Asuras.

70. For ten Yugas all the inhabitants of the universe mixed together without any interruption. Both Devas and Asuras abided by the directions of those two (Daityas).

71. (Later on) a terrible, violent dispute arose between Devas and Asuras. It caused horrible devastation to both of them.

72. Many battles were fought between them for their respective share in the patrimony.[2] It is remembered that in this Varāha Kalpa twelve battles ending with the participation of Ṣaṇḍāmārka (took place).

73. Listen to them even as I am recounting them succinctly by their names. The first war is called Nārasiṁha (that caused by the Man-Lion). The second was Vāmana the act of the Dwarf (incarnation of Viṣṇu.)

74. The third war is Vārāha (that of the Boar incarnation); the fourth was at the time of the churning of the ocean for nectar. The fifth was the terrible war of Tārakāmaya (on the abduction of Tātā by Candra).

1. Verses 68-70 show that Asuras and Suras were cousin-clans who lived amicably under Asura Kings also. See vv. 88-92.

2. Verses 72-87 describe the twelve wars between Devas and Asuras, which made Viṣṇu to incarnate to help Devas. The list of Viṣṇu's incarnations is different (*vide Introduction*—Vaiṣṇavism).

75. The sixth war was Āḍibaka and the seventh war was remembered as Traipura (that of the burning of the three cities). The eighth war was Andhakāra and the ninth one was Dhvaja (Flag).

76. The tenth war should be known as Vārta (Vārtra ?) (pertaining to Vṛtra); the next one is Halāhala. The twelfth war among them is remembered as the terrible Kolāhala.

77. Hiraṇyakaśipu, a Daitya, was killed by Narasiṁha. Bali was bound by Vāmana when the three worlds were overtaken (were measured by Vāmana's steps).

78. Hiraṇyākṣa who was of very great strength and prowess and who had never been defeated in wars, was killed in a duel (by Viṣṇu in his incarnation as the Boar), when the clash with Devas ensued.

79. It was then that the Earth was lifted up on his curved fang by the (divine) Boar.

At the time of the churning of the ocean for nectar Prahlāda was defeated in battle by Indra.

80. Virocana, the son of Prahlāda, always attempted to kill Indra. In the Tārakāmaya war he was killed by Indra by means of his exploits.

81. Jaṁbha who had acquired the boon of *avadhyatā* (the state of not being killed or immunity from death) along with special miraculous weapons was killed in the sixth war by Viṣṇu who entered the body of Śakra.

82. When Devas were unable to protect the city of three gods* (?) all Dānavas along with (the demon) Tripura were killed by the three-eyed god Śiva.

83-84. In the eighth war, Asuras, Rākṣasas who were Andhakārakas (causing blindness, invisible ?) were defeated

---

**Tri-daivatam* is obscure as the city called Tripura belonged to Asuras. Bd.P. 2.3.72.81 b reads

aśaknuvatsu deveṣu param soḍhum adaivatam /

'When Devas became unable to endure (the greatness of) Asuras. If '*para*' in this line be emended as '*puram*', *adaivatam puram* would means 'the city of demons' and that would suit the context better. Scribes many times forget to indicate the signs of the vowels *-i-*, *-u-*, *-e-*.

by Devas and human beings in alliance with the Pitṛs. All these well protected Dānavas were wholly exterminated by Mahendra helped by Viṣṇu.

85-86. The mighty-armed Vipracitti began to fight with Mahendra hiding himself by means of his Māyā. Indra aimed at his banner and cut him down.

In the war called Kolāhala, Raji was surrounded by all Devas. He killed all Daityas and Dānavas who formed an alliance: By means of the nectar (generated) from Yajña[1] Ṣaṇḍa and Amārka were defeated by Devas.

87. These twelve battles took place between Devas and Asuras resulting in exhausting both Devas and Asuras. They brought about misfortune to the people also.

88. Hiraṇyakaśipu shone as the ruler and king of the three worlds for one hundred and seven million two hundred and eighty thousand years.

89. By succession Bali became the king and he ruled for one hundred and three million and sixty thousand years.

90.[2] Prahlāda ruled in the company of Asuras for as many years as the period of Bali's administration.

91. These three were very famous as the Indras of Asuras. They were very mighty. All these worlds were under Daityas for a period of ten Yugas.

92. Then the entire kingdom was free from enemies for a period of ten Yugas. Then the three worlds began to be protected by Mahendra without any change.

93-94. When the kingdom of the three worlds (inherited) by Prahlāda was taken away by the lapse of time, when the kingdom of the three worlds came to Indra (the chastiser of Pāka) by rotation, Yājña forsook Asuras and went over to Devas.

When Yajña went over to Devas, those Asuras spoke to Kāvya (Śukra), their preceptor:

95. "Even as we are looking on, Yajña went over to

---

1. Production of nectar from Yajña is not known. Bd. P. 2.3.72.87 reads *yajñasyā'vabhṛthe* 'at the time of the valedictory—*avabhṛtha*—bath'.

2. This verse should have been 89 as Prahlāda succeeded his father Hiraṇyakaśipu.

Devas, forsaking our kingdom. We cannot stay here. We shall, therefore, enter Rasātala (nether worlds) today."

96. Thus addressed, he became depressed. In consoling words, he spoke to them: "O Asuras, do not be afraid. I shall sustain you by means of my spiritual brilliance.

97. Rainfall, medicinal herbs and the two things, the Earth and Wealth—all these are retained by me. Only a fourth of it is with Suras. I shall hand over to you everything that I hold".

98-99. On seeing Asuras sustained by the intelligent Kāvya, Devas consulted among themselves. They were dispirited and desired to be victorious then. They said: "This Kāvya, spoils everything we do, by his strength. Well, we shall go there quickly lest he should strengthen them further. Killing them forcibly, we shall compel those who are left off to flee to Pātāla."

100. With great fury Devas rushed at Dānavas and killed them. Being harassed by them, Dānavas hastened to Kāvya (for protection).

101. Kāvya saw that the sons of Diti were attacked by Devas and that they were in great distress because they were wounded in battle by various weapons[1].

102. On seeing Devas also standing there he reflected over the fate.[2] Remembering the previous incidents, he spoke to them (Asuras):

103. "All the three worlds were conquered by Vāmana by means of three paces. Bali was bound. Jaṁbha was killed. Virocana was slain.

104. In twelve great and terrible battles they were killed by Suras. By various means most of the important persons have been killed.

105. Only a few of you have been spared in these latest battles. I shall now employ a great strategy. Please wait for a short while.

---

1. Bd. P. v. 103 reads : *samarakṣata saṁstrastān* 'protected the frightened (sons of Diti)'

2. *Daivam* in Bd. P.

106. I shall go to Mahādeva for acquiring Mantras for the sake of your victory. Bṛhaspati is performing Homa and worshipping Agni by means of Mantras.

107. Hence I shall go unto the lord Nīlalohita (Śiva) for the sake of Mantras. I shall bless you all after my return.

108. All of you perform penance in the forest clad in bark garments. Devas will not kill you until I return.

109. After obtaining the Mantras that will never go against us, from Lord Maheśvara, we shall fight Devas again. You will surely gain victory."

110-112. After deliberating thus Asuras spoke to Devas :

"We have set aside our dispute with you. All of you can occupy the worlds. We shall be clad in bark garments and we shall perform penance in the forest". On hearing these words of Prahlāda, Suras believed that he was speaking the truth. Then Devas returned without fighting. They rejoiced. When Daityas laid aside their weapons, Devas went back to their respective places from where they had come.

113. Then Kāvya said to them: "Wait for some time performing penance without enthusiasm, waiting for an opportunity to achieve the object in view. All Devas including Vāsava are in my father's hermitage."*

114. After instructing Asuras thus, Kāvya approached Mahādeva. After bowing to the lord, the cause of origin of the universe, he said:

115. "O lord, I wish to secure such Mantras as are not in the possession of Bṛhaspati. I want them to be the bestowers of fearlessness on Asuras. I wish to defeat Devas".

116. Thus requested, the lord said : "O Brāhmaṇa ! do you wish for the Mantras ? Perform then the holy rites indicated by me, with purity of mind and observing celibacy.

117. For full thousand years you must stay in a topsy turvy position inhaling the smoke from the holy sacrificial fire-pit. Welfare unto you. If you perform (a sacred rite) like this, you will obtain the Mantra from me."

---

*This is a strange statement. Bd. P. reads relevantly : *sampratīkṣata dānavāḥ* : "O Dānavas, stay waiting (in my father's hermitage)."

118-119. Thus advised by the lord of Devas, Śukra of great penance, touched the feet of the lord and said: "Yes, my lord, I shall perform the holy rites and observe all the other things as instructed." Then he was engaged by the lord inhaling the smoke from the holy fire-pit.

120-121. When Śukra had gone to Maheśvara and was staying there observing celibacy for the acquisition of the Mantras with the welfare of Asuras in view, Devas understood that the kingdom was set aside by Asuras as a measure of strategy. Finding that loophole, the infuriated Devas attacked them. They had sharp weapons in their hands and Bṛhaspati led them all.

122. On seeing Devas armed with weapons again Asuras became frightened and fled suddenly.

123-125. "We have laid down our weapons and conceded victory unto them. Our preceptor is observing holy rites. Devas have abrogated the terms of agreement. They are desirous of slaying us, (their) enemies. Welfare unto you all, we are now without a preceptor (to guide us). We had been credulous. We remained quiet performing penances. We are clad in bark and coarse garments. We have no holy rite. We have nothing to grasp and hold on to. By no means are we able to conquer Devas in war. In this nasty situation* it is better that we seek refuge in the mother of Kāvya.

126. We shall wait here till the return of the preceptor. We shall tell him everything. When Kāvya returns we shall fight with Suras."

127-131. Saying this to one another, they sought shelter with the mother of Kāvya. They had been frightened but the boon of fearlessness was offered unto them as they sought shelter. (The mother of Kāvya said :) "O Dānavas, do not be afraid, do not be afraid. Cast off all fear. You need not be afraid as long as you are with me." On seeing Asuras frightened, Devas pursued them earnestly without caring for strength or weakness. On seeing the frightened Asuras being harassed by Devas, the gentle lady (the mother of Kāvya) became infuriated and said to them : "I shall cause *Anindratva* (the state of

*Bd. P. : *ayuddhena* 'without being involved in fighting.'

Indralessness i.e. destruction of Indra)". She made Indra immediately benumbed and stunned and she went on with her other activities.

132. On seeing Indra in that helpless condition after being rendered motionless like the sacrificial post, Devas became afraid and fled from there.

133. When the groups of Suras had gone, Viṣṇu said to Indra: "O lord of Suras, welfare unto you. Enter me. I shall take you away."

134. Thus advised Purandara (Indra) entered Viṣṇu. On seeing him saved by Viṣṇu, the infuriated lady spoke these words:

135. "O Maghavan, here itself I will burn you down along with Viṣṇu even as all the living beings observe. May the power of my penance be witnessed."

136. The lords Indra and Viṣṇu, on being oppressed by her, conversed (under their breath). Viṣṇu asked Indra—"How can both of us get free jointly ?".

137. Indra replied : "O lord, kill her before she burns us both. Especially I have been attacked. Hence, kill her. Do not delay."

138. Then on seeing her (thus intending to kill them) Viṣṇu got ready (even) to kill that woman. Caught in adverse circumstances, the lord hurriedly remembered his discus.

139. While she was hastening to kill them, the discus (Sudarśana), the destroyer of the enemies of Suras, hastened still more. On realising the ruthless attempt of the woman (the mother of Kāvya) Viṣṇu became furious. Taking up that weapon the husband of Mā (i.e. Lakṣmī) cut off her head.

140. On seeing that terrible slaughter of a woman (his wife) the holy lord Bhṛgu became furious. Then Viṣṇu was censured and cursed by Bhṛgu for the murder of his wife.

141. "Since (according to Dharma) a woman should not be killed and that you have killed one even though you are conversant with what is Dharma, you will have to take birth among human beings seven times".

142. Thereafter, as a result of that curse he incarnates again and again in the world (of mortals) for the welfare of all, whenever virtue (Dharma) declines.

143. After speaking those words of curse to Viṣṇu, he (i.e. Bhṛgu) took up the head (of the lady) himself and joined it to her body. Taking up water he said:

144. "O truthful lady, I am hereby resuscitating you who had been killed by Viṣṇu. If all virtues and holy rites have been understood and practised by me, come to life. If I speak the truth, come to life, thanks to that truth".

145. Thus addressed with the emphasis on truth, the gentle lady regained her life. Then he sprinkled her with cool water and uttered, "Get up".

146. On seeing her getting up as if from sleep, all living beings loudly applauded "Well done ! Well done !" Such an applause of invisible (incorporeal) voices arose from all the quarters.

147. Even as all living beings were observing, the lady was resuscitated to life by Bhṛgu. That was really miraculous.

148. On seeing his wife resuscitated to life by Bhṛgu without the least agitation Śakra was not at all happy, because he was afraid of Kāvya (all the more).

149. Indra had no sleep at all (after the incident). The intelligent chastiser of Pāka (i.e. Indra) called his daughter Jayantī and spoke to her.

150. "O daughter, this Kāvya is performing a terrible penance for the sake of my destruction (lit. Indra-less-ness). I have been rendered much dispirited by that (Brāhmaṇa) of great fortitude.

151. Go and honour him with auspicious (services) removing his fatigue and by rendering alertly and deligently service pleasing to his mind".

152-154. The gentle lady Jayantī, the daughter of Indra, of auspicious conduct, saw Kāvya engaged in meditation. Although he was weak, he was quiet and self-possessed, endowed with fortitude, as her father had already mentioned to her. She rendered every service to Kāvya in accordance with the behest of her father. In sweet and pleasing words she eulogised him. Frequently she massaged his body and served him in various other pleasant ways. Thus she stayed there for many years.

155. When the terrible rite of inhaling the smoke lasting

for a thousand years was completed, the delighted Bhava asked him to choose a boon freely.

156-160. He said thus : "O Brāhmaṇa, such an observance (of a vow) as this has been performed by you alone and not by anyone (so far). Hence you will excel all Devas in penance, intellect, learning, strength and brilliance. O son of Bhṛgu, whatever I possess by way of the esoteric secret of Yajñas, Upaniṣads etc. along with their ancillaries and esoteric secrets (*Rahasya*) will be known to you alone, from the beginning to the end and not to anyone else. Thereby you will become an excellent Brāhmaṇa surpassing all". Thus granting the boons one after the other, to the son of Bhṛgu, he granted him invincibility, lordship of wealth and immunity from death. On attaining these boons, Kāvya became exhilarated. Hairs on his body stood on their end due to excessive pleasure.

161. Due to his excessive joy, the following hymn to the lord Maheśvara manifested itself. Prostrating (before the Lord), he eulogised Nīlalohita (Lord Śiva):

The Hymn to Śambhu[1] (Lord Śiva)

162. "Obeisance to *Śitikaṇṭha* (Blue-throated god) to *Surūpa* (of good form), to *Suvarcas* (of good brilliance), to *Ririhāṇa* (one who exhibits the mystic *mudrā* of frequently licking with the tongue), to *Lopa* (the destroyer), to *Vatsara* (the presiding deity of the year), to the *Jagatpati* (the lord of the universe).

163. To *Kapardin* (having matted hair), to *Ūrdhvaroman* (having hair standing up erect), to *Haya* (the horse), to *Karaṇa* (the instrument), to *Saṁskṛta* (the consecrated), to *Sutīrtha* (the holy centre), to *Deva-deva* (Lord of Devas), to *Raṁhas* (velocity personified).

164. To *Uṣṇiṣin* (one with a turban or turban-wearer), to *Suvaktra* (one with a charming face), to *Sahasrākṣa* (god with a thousand eyes), to *Mīḍhvan* (bountiful), to *Vasureta* (distributer

---

1. Praising deity by giving him/her various attributes is found common in the Mbh. and Purāṇas. This hymn of Śiva is strongly influenced by Rudrādhyāya from *Tait. Saṁhitā IV*. 5 as most of the epithets of Rudra mentioned therein are incorporated here.

(?) of wealth), to *Rudra* (terrific roarer), to the performer of penance, to *Cīravāsas* (wearer of bark garments).

165-166. To *Hrasva* (the short), to *Muktakeśa* (one with untied tresses of hair), to *Senānī* (the commander-in-chief of the army of gods), to *Kavi* (the poet), to *Rājavṛddha* (the old ruler), to *Takṣakakrīḍana* (one who plays with Takṣaka), to *Giriśa* (Lord of mountains), to *Arkanetra* (god with the sun as the eye), to the ascetic, to *Jāmbava**, to *Suvṛtta* (one of good antecedents), to *Suhasta* (one with good hands), to *Dhanvin* (one wielding a bow), to *Bhārgava* (a good archer).

167. To *Sahasrabāhu* (one with a thousand i.e. infinite arms), to *Sahasrāmalacakṣus* (one with a thousand clean eyes), to *Sahasrakukṣi* (one with a thousand bellies), to *Sahasracaraṇa* (one with a thousand feet).

168. To *Sahasraśiras* (one with a thousand heads), to *Bahurūpa* (multi-formed), to *Viśvarūpa* (immanent in the universe), to *Śveta* (the white one), to *Puruṣa* (primordial man).

169. To *Niṣaṅgin* (one with a quiver), to *Kavacin* (one wearing a coat of mail), to *Sūkṣma* (the subtle one), to *Kṣapaṇa* (the destroyer), to *Tāmra* (the copper-coloured), to *Śiva* (the benevolent one).

170. To *Babhru* (the tawny-coloured), to *Piśaṅga* (reddish brown), to *Piṅgala* (yellowsih brown), to *Aruṇa* (the pink coloured), to *Mahādeva* (the great god), to *Śarva* (the destroyer), to *Viśvarūpaśiva** (the auspicious omnipresent god).

171. To *Hiraṇya* (the golden one), to *Śiṣṭa* (the self-controlled one), to *Śreṣṭha* (the excellent one), to *Madhyama* (the middling), to *Pinākin* (wielding the bow Pināka), to *Iṣumān* (possessing arrows), to *Citra* (the miraculous one or one of variegated colours), to *Rohita* (reddish-tinged).

172. To *Dundubhya* (worthy of being honoured with the sound of war-drums), to *Ekapāda* (single-footed), to *Arha* (the deserving), to *Buddhi* (the intellect), to *Mṛgavyādha* (one who has assumed the form of a hunter of deer in Dakṣa's sacrifice), to *Sarpa* (the serpent), to *Sthāṇu* (motionless like a tree-trunk in meditation), to *Bhīṣaṇa* (the terrible).

---

*Bd. P. reads : Ājyapā (imbiber of ghee-offering).

173. To *Bahurūpa* (the multiformed), to *Ugra* (the fierce), to *Trinetra* (the three-eyed), to *Īśvara* (the supreme ruler), to *Kapila* (tawny-coloured or identical with Kapila), to *Ekavīra* (the single hero), to *Mṛtyu* (the death), to *Tryaṁbaka* (the three-eyed).

174. To *Vāstoṣpati* (the protective deity presiding over the foundation of a house), to *Vināka* (one beyond heaven), to *Śaṅkara* (the benefactor), to *Śiva* (the auspicious one), to *Āraṇya* (the forest-dweller), to *Gṛhastha* (the householder), to the *Brahmacārin* (the religious student observing celibacy).

175. To the *Sāṅkhya* (one accessible through the *Sāṅkhya* system of philosophy), to *Yoga* (one realizable through the Yoga system), to *Dhyānin* (the meditating one), to *Dikṣita* (the initiated), to *Antarhita* (unmanifest, hidden), to *Śarva* (destroyer of the world), to *Mānya* (the honourable), to *Mālin* (one wearing garland).

176. To *Buddha* (the enlightened one), to *Śuddha* (the pure), to *Mukta* (the liberated one), to *Kevala* (the sole one without a second), to *Rodhas* (staying on the mountain slope), to *Cekitāna* (the sentient), to *Brahmiṣṭha* (merged in Brahman), to *Maharṣi* (the great sage).

177. To *Catuṣpāda* (one having four feet), to *Medhya* (one worthy of sacrifice), to *Dharmin* (the virtuous), to wearer of an armour (*Varmin* as in Bd.P. v. 178), to *Śighraga* (one going fast), to Ś*ikhaṇḍin* (one with tuft of hair), to *Kapāla* (one holding the human skull), to *Daṁṣṭrin* (one with curved fangs), to *Viśvamedhas* (of universal intellect).

178. To *Apratighāta* (the unimpeded), to *Dīpta* (the illuminated), to *Bhāskara* (the creator of lustre), to *Sumedhas* (of excellent intellect), to *Krūra* (the cruel one), to *Vikṛta* (the deformed), to *Bībhatsa* (the hideous), to *Śiva* (auspicious).

179. To *Saumya* (the gentle one), to *Puṇya* (the meritorious) to *Dhārmika* (the righteous), to Ś*ubha* (the auspicious), to *Avadhya* (one who cannot be killed), to *Mṛtāṅga* (one whose body is dead?), to *Nitya* (the eternal one), to Ś*āśvata* (the perpetual one).

180. To *Sādya* (one with a beginning), to Ś*arabha* (the eight-footed fabulous animal), to Ś*ūlin* (the trident-bearing god), to *Tricakṣus* (the three-eyed god), to *Somapa* (the imbiber of Soma

juice), to *Ājyapa* (the imbiber of ghee), to *Dhūmapa* (the inhaler of smoke), to *Ūṣmapa* (drinker of hot stuff).

181. To *Śuci* (the pure and clean), to *Rerihāṇa* (one repeatedly licking), to *Sadyojāta* (born in a trice), to *Mṛtyu* (death), to *Piśitāśa* (the meat-eater), to *Kharva* (the dwarfish), to *Megha* (the cloud), to *Vaidyuta* (the lightning).

182. To *Vyāśrita* (having no dependent), to *Śraviṣṭha* (the most famous), to *Bhārata* (one engaged in brilliant light), to *Antarikṣa* (the firmament), to *Kṣama* (the competent), to *Sahamāna* (the enduring), to *Satya* (the truthful), to *Tapana* (the blazing one).

183. To *Tripuraghna* (the destroyer of the three cities), to *Dipta* (the illuminated), to the *Cakra* (the discus), to *Romaśa* (the hairy one), to *Tigmāyudha* (having sharp weapons), to *Medhya* (the cleanest), to Siddha, to Pulasti.

184. To *Rocamāna* (one who is appealing), to *Khaṇḍa*, to *Sphita* (the flourishing), to *Ṛṣabha* (the bull, the chief one), to *Bhogin* (the enjoyer), to *Yuñjamāna* (the united one), to *Śānta* (the quiescent one), to *Ūrdhvaretas* (of sublimated sexuality).

185. To *Aghaghna* (the destroyer of sins), to *Makhaghna* (destroyer of Dakṣa's sacrifice), to *Mṛtyu* (god of death), to *Yajñiya* (one belonging to sacrifice), to *Kṛśānu* (fire), to *Pracetā*, to *Vahni* (the fire, bearer of offerings), to *Kiśala* (?)

186. To *Sikatya* (belonging to sand?), to *Prasanna* (the delighted), to *Vareṇya* (the most excellent), to *Cakṣus* (the eye), to *Kṣipragu* (having a fast bull), to *Pramedhya* (the excessively pure), to *Piva* (the corpulent one?)

187. To *Rakṣoghna* (the destroyer of Rākṣasas), to *Paśughna* (destroyer of animals), to *Vighna* (the obstacle), to *Śayana* (the lying one), to *Vibhrānta* (the revolving one), to *Mahānta*. (having great end), to *Anti* (the nearest one), to *Durgama* (difficult to attain).

188. To *Dakṣa* (the dexterous), to *jaghanya* (the last one), to the lord of the worlds, to *Anāmaya* (the non-ailing), to *Ūrdhva* (the topmost one), to *Saṁhatya Adhiṣṭhita* (to one estabilished in masses).

189. To *Hiraṇyabāhu* (of golden arms), to *Satya* (the truthful), to *Śamana* (the tranquiliser),. to *Asikalpa* (one like a

sword), to *Māgha* (the month Māgha), to *Ririṇya* (?), to *Ekacakṣus* (the one-eyed).

190. To *Śreṣṭha* (the excellent one), to *Vāmadeva*, to *Īśāna* (supreme ruler), to *Dhīmān* (the intelligent one), to *Mahākalpa*, to *Dipta* (the illuminated), to *Rodana* (the crying), to *Hāsa* (the laughing).

191. To *Vṛtadhanvan* (*Dṛḍhadhanvan*—having firm bow), to *Kavacin* (one wearing a coat of mail), to *Rathin* (having a chariot), to *Varūthin* (having a host of army), to *Bhṛgunātha* (the lord of Bhṛgu), to Śukra, to *Vahniriṣṭa* (?), to *Dhīmān* (the intelligent).

192. To *Agha* (the sin), to *Aghaśaṁsa* (the despiser of sin), to *Vipriya* (having no beloved), to *Priya* (the beloved). O *Digvāsas* (having the quarters as garments), obeisance be to you, the wearer of elephant hide and destroyer of Bhaga.

193. Obeisance to the lord of *Paśus* (individual souls), to the lord of living beings. Obeisance to *Praṇava*, the Ṛk, the Yajus and the Sāman, to *Svadhā* and *Sudhā* (nectar).

194. Obeisance to you of the form of *Vaṣaṭkāra*. Obeisance to you, O *Antātman* (soul of all ends). Obeisance to you, the creator, the sustainer, and the annihilator, to the *Hotṛ* and the destroyer.

195. Obeisance to you, of the form of Kāla, past, present and future. Obeisance to Vasu, Sādhya, Rudra, Āditya and Aśvin.

196. Obeisance to you, the Viśva (Viśvedevas), to Maruts, the Ātman of Devas. You are Agni, Soma, Ṛtvik, *Ijyā* (sacrifice), the sacrificial animal, the Mantra and the medicine.

197. You are *Dakṣiṇā*, *Avabhṛtha* (sacred ablution of concluding rites), and the *Yajña* itself. You are *Tapas* (penance), *Satya* (truth), *Tyāga* (renunciation) and *Śama* (self-control).

198. Obeisance to you, the embodiment of nonviolence and non-covetousness. You are of good demeanour, the surpassing one. Obeisance to you, the *Yogātman* (of Yogic Soul), the soul of all living beings.

199. Obeisance to you, of the form of all worlds, the earth, the firmament, the heaven, Mahar, Jana, Tapas and Satya (Lokas).

200. Obeisance to you, the unmanifest, the great, the element, the sense organs, the Tanmātras, the end of the *Mahat*. Obeisance to you, of the form of the Reality.

201. Obeisance to you, the eternal one, the Arthaliṅga (of meaningful index?), the subtle one, the sentient, the pure, the omnipresent, the permanent soul.

202. Obeisance to you in the three worlds beginning with Bhūḥ and ending with Svaḥ (i.e. Bhūḥ, Bhuvaḥ and Svaḥ) and in the four worlds beginning with Satya and ending with Mahaḥ (i.e. Satya, Tapas, Jana and Mahaḥ).

203. O lord, you are friend and sympathiser of Brāhmaṇas. In this prayer of obeisance both correct and incorrect things[1] have been uttered by me. It behoves you to forgive everything thinking like "He is my devotee".

CHAPTER THIRTYSIX

Glorification of Viṣṇu's Greatness

Sūta said :

1-2. After propitiating Īśāna, Nīlalohita, the lord of Devas, Śukra spoke words of prayer bowing to him with palms joined in reverence uttering *Brahman* (Vedic Mantras). Śiva who was delighted, touched the body of Kāvya with his hand, accorded him a full vision of His own form and vanished there itself.

3. When the lord of the Devas[2] had vanished, he spoke the following words to Jayantī who was standing near him, with palms joined in reverence.

---

1. The reading *'sadasat'* needs emendation as *'yadasat'* as in Bd.P. 2.3.72, 195 as there is no point in begging pardon for saying correct things.

2. The obscure reading *deveśānucare* is probably a scribal error and should be emended as *deve sānucare* 'God (Śiva) along with his retinue'. Bd. P. 2.3.73.3 supports the emendation suggested.

4. "O beautiful lady, whose (daughter) are you? When I was distressed, you too were distressed. Who are you? What for did you take care of me when I was performing the great penance ?

5. O lady of beautiful hips, O fair-complexioned one, I am delighted with your steady devotion, humility, self-control and affection.

6. O beautiful damsel, what do you wish? What is your cherished desire which should be fully gratified? Even if it be very difficult to be fulfilled, I shall get it realised (for you)".

7. On being asked thus, Jayantī said : "O sage merged in Brahman, it behoves you to know it by means of the power of your penance. In fact, you already know precisely what I have desired to achieve".

8. On being told thus, the sage saw everything by means of his divine vision and said: "O beautiful maiden, you are the daughter of Mahendra. You have come here to render service to me.

9. O woman of beautiful lips, O lustrous woman, you desire to live in contact with me for ten years without being seen by any other living being.

10. O beautiful lady with (brilliant) complexion of the Lord of Devas and of fire* ! O lady of beautiful eyes, you choose (the fulfilment of your) desire from me, O lady of sweet voice.

11. Let it be, O fascinating woman, we shall go home". Thereafter the holy lord returned to his abode, accompanied by Jayantī.

12. He stayed along with her for ten years. Being envelop-ed with Māyā (illusive power), he was invisible to all living beings.

13. On seeing (learning) that Kāvya had returned after realising his desires, all Daityas delightedly came to his house desirous of seeing him.

---

*For '*devendrānalavarṇābhe*' hereof, Bd. P. v. 10 reads '*devīndranīlavarṇābhe*' 'O goddess with the shining lustre of blue sapphires' which is worth consideration.

14. Having gone there, they could not see their preceptor who was concealed by Jayantī. Thinking that it was part of his clever strategy*, they returned to their respective homes.

15-16. On knowing that Kāvya was held in restraint by Jayantī for ten years in her desire to do what was beneficial to her father, Bṛhaspati knew that to be an opportunity offered by Daityas. He assumed the form of Kāvya, the preceptor of Daityas, and spoke to Asuras.

17. Looking at the Asuras who had assembled, Bṛhaspati said : "Welcome to my disciples for whom I perform sacrifices. For your welfare, I have come back to this place.

18. I shall teach you all. That (great) Vidyā has been acquired by me". With a delighted mind, then they approached him for the sake of attaining the Vidyā.

19-20. After the period of ten years was over, Śukra's ambition was completely realised. (His delusion vanished) and his intellect was awakened at the same time. At the end of the period of agreement, Devayānī, his daughter was born (of Jayantī). Then Śukra decided to look after his disciples.

21. Śukra said: "O gentle lady, let us go to see your disciples, O lady of sweet smiles and of tremulous eyes, O chaste lady, O lady of large eyes of three colours".

22. The lady replied : "O sage of great holy rites, please resort to your disciples. It is the sacred Dharma, O Brāhmaṇa. I shall not make you swerve from it."

Sūta said :

23. Then he went to Asuras and saw that they had been deceived by the intelligent preceptor of Devas by assuming the form of Kāvya. He spoke to Asuras :

24. "O dear ones, know me to be the (real) Kāvya. This is the son of Aṅgiras. O Dānavas, in spite of my power, you have been deceived".

---

* *dākṣiṇya*. But *lakṣaṇam* (the sign of his non-return), in Bd. P. ibid. v. 14.

25. On hearing him speak thus, Daityas were confused. They looked at both of them smiling pleasantly.*

26. They stood there utterly confused. They were unable to understand anything. When they were (seen) confused like this, Kāvya spoke to them again :

27. "I am your preceptor Kāvya. This is the praceptor of Devas, the son of Aṅgiras. All of you follow me. Leave off this Bṛhaspati".

28. On being addressed thus, all the Asuras stood gazing at them. They could not see any difference between them.

29-30. Unperturbed by anything, Bṛhaspati told them: "O Daityas, this is Aṅgiras. I am Kāvya, your preceptor. This is Bṛhaspati in my guise. O Asuras, he deludes you all by assuming my form". On hearing his words, they consulted one another and spoke these words:

31. "This holy lord and sage has been imparting instructions to us continuously for the last ten years. This Brāhmaṇa is desirous of coming in between".

32. Then all those Dānavas bowed to and paid respects to him (Bṛhaspati in the guise of Kāvya). Deluded by a long practice they accepted only his words.

33. All the infuriated Asuras spoke to him (the real Kāvya) (staring at him) with reddened eyes: "This is our preceptor and benefactor. You may go. You are not our preceptor.

34. Whether he is Bhārgava (son of Bhṛgu) or Āṅgirasa (son of Aṅgiras) let him be our preceptor. We shall abide by his guidance. Do not tarry (here any longer). That will be in your interest."

35-37. After saying this, all the Asuras resorted to Bṛhaspati (as their teacher). When the Asuras did not accept his suggestion for their great benefit, Bhārgava became angry at their arrogance. He told them again : "O Dānavas, although I had apprised (and instructed) you, you are not resorting to me. Hence, you will become deficient in sense and will attain defeat after defeat". After saying this to them, Kāvya went away the way he had come.

*The word *sitāsita* is obscure. Bd. P. v. 25 read *sthirāsīnau* which means 'sitting firmly'.

38. On realising that the Asuras had been cursed by Kāvya. Bṛhaspati got his object fulfilled. With great delight, he re-assumed his own real form. To his great contentment, he realised that the Asuras had fallen and doomed and he vanished from the scene.

39. When he had disappeared, the dismayed Dānavas spoke to one another: "Oh fie upon us! In this matter we have been deceived.

40. We have erred in our duties. So the fate is against and we have been struck by it. We have been used (by him i.e. Bṛhaspati) in his own interest and burnt by means of his Māyā".

41-42. Then the Asuras became extremely frightened of the Devas and fled from that place. Keeping Prahlāda at the head, they approached Kāvya again. On approaching him, they stood there with heads bent down. On seeing his disciples (lit. ones for whose benefit he performed Yajñas) Kāvya said to them:

43. "In spite of being cautioned by me at the proper time, you did not honour and respect me. So, on account of that arrogance, you met with a defeat".

44. Then Prahlāda entreated him: "O Bhārgava, (please) give up (forget) your wounded sense of honour. O Bhārgava, do not forsake us, your own disciples, particularly attached to you with devotion and prayerfulness.

45-46. When asked by you, we had been deluded by the preceptor of Devas. Knowing this by means of your long-ranged vision, it behoves you to save us. O son of Bhṛgu, if you are not going to favour us, we are (no better than) cursed by you. So we shall enter *Rasātala* (the nether worlds) to-day."

Sūta said :

47. On being thus implored, eulogised and informed Kāvya realised the truth. Out of mercy and sympathy, he controlled his anger.

48. He spoke these words : "Do not be afraid. Do not go to Rasātala. Even though I was alert this incident befell you because it was inevitable.

49. Destiny which is very powerful cannot be altered. The sense that you have lost, you will regain now.

50. Brahmā too had mentioned that the period adverse to you had arrived. It was due to my favour that you had enjoyed the great pleasures of the three worlds (so long).

51. For full ten Yugas you have reigned over Devas. Brahmā has ordained your rulership only for that length of period.

52. In the Sāvarṇika Manvantara you will again have suzerainty. Your grandson Bali will become the lord of all the worlds.

53. It has been mentioned by Brahmā himself to me that when later on the worlds will be seized from him, his power of penance will not be of any avail.

54. Since his activities will be devoid of undue attachment, Brahmā will be pleased with him and (the kingdom) will be bestowed on him in the Sāvarṇika Manvantara.

55. The lord has told me, 'The kingdom of Devas will come to Bali'. Hence he bides his time remaining invisible to all living beings.

56. You have been granted immortality by the delighted self-born deity. Hence, without exhibiting undue curiosity and agitation you have to bear with the change.

57. Before the (proper) time, it is not possible for me to save you. O lord, I have been forbidden by Brahmā who knows the future.

58. These two are my disciples. They are equal to me.* and Bṛhaspati. They will sustain you all when attacked by Devas."

59. When the Daityas, the chief of whom was Prahlāda, were given this advice by Kāvya of indefatigable energy and activity, they went away along with those two (disciples i.e. Ṣaṇḍa and Amārka).

60. On hearing about the inevitability of future events

*Probably Ṣaṇḍa and Amārka are mentioned here as will be clear by later verses 63 etc.

from Śukra, Dānavas took the words of Kāvya to mean victory for them (at least) for once.

61-62. They equipped themselves with various weapons and the coats of mail and challenged Devas for fighting. On seeing Asuras advanced for battle, Devas got ready with all equipments and fought them in return. The battle between Devas and Asuras continued for a hundred years. Asuras defeated Devas. The beaten and distressed Devas spoke thus among themselves.

63-65. Devas said : "We do not know the (extent of the) power of Ṣaṇḍa and Amārka on Asuras. Hence, what is conducive to our welfare must be done by preparing for a Yajña. After knowing about and capturing those two, we will defeat Asuras".

Devas then invited both Ṣaṇḍa and Amārka and said, "We shall invite you for the Yajña. O Brāhmaṇas, forsake Asuras. After defeating them we will make you receive a share".

66. In this manner, Ṣaṇḍa and Amārka thereafter forsook Asuras. Devas were victorious and Dānavas suffered disastrous defeat.

67-69. After defeating Asuras, Devas approached Ṣaṇḍa and Amārka. Asuras who had already been overwhelmed by the curse of Kāvya had no support now. Harassed by Devas, they entered Rasātala. Thus Dānavas were crippled and rendered inactive by Śakra.

Thereafter, whenever the cult of Yajñas and other holy rites was slack, Lord Viṣṇu incarnated again and again as a result of Bhṛgu's curse*, in order to stabilise Dharma and destroy Adharma.

70. Lord Brahmā pronounced that all those Asuras who did not follow the directions of Prahlāda would be killed by human beings.

71. Hence Nārāyaṇa was born of Dharma in the Cākṣuṣa

*Viṣṇu's incarnations were due to Bhṛgu's curse. Verses 71ff. give the list of those incarnations but they are different from our usual list (*vide* Intro., Vaiṣṇavism).

Manvantara. In the Vaivasvata Manvantara, he popularised Yajña in Caitya[1] (sacrificial shed).

72-73. At the time of the manifestation of the other (i.e. Pṛthu) Brahmā himself was the priest. In the fourth Yuga, when Asuras[2] were in distress, he was born within the ocean for the purpose of killing Hiraṇyakaśipu[3].

The second (incarnation was that of the terrible Narasiṁha, keeping Suras at the head.

74. The third incarnation, that of Vāmana, took place in the seventh Tretāyuga when all the three worlds had been overrun by Daityas and were ruled over by Bali.

75-76. Withdrawing all the limbs within himself (Assuming the form of a Dwarf) the son of Aditi approached the son of Virocana, Bali, the king of Daityas, who was performing a Yajña. Bṛhaspati too accompanied him. Assuming the form of a Brāhmaṇa on an auspicious occasion, he requested Bali: "O king, you are the lord of the three worlds. Everything is in you. It behoves you to grant me (the space covered by) three paces".

77. "I will give", promised the king Bali, the son of Virocana. On knowing that he was a Vāmana (dwarf), he was delighted much.

78. But, O excellent Brāhmaṇas, that lord Vāmana measured the entire Universe, the Earth, the Heaven and the Sky by means of three paces.

79. That Bhūtātman (the immanent soul of all living beings) of great fame excelled even the sun by means of his brilliance. He illuminated all the quarters and the intermediate directions with his refulgence.

80. The mighty-armed Janārdana brightened up all the worlds and shone. Seizing the royal glory of Asuras from all the three worlds, he forced them to retreat to the bottom of the nether-world along with their sons and grandsons.

---

1. 'Vainya' i.e. King Pṛthu in Bd. P. v. 72. It is a better reading as this and other sources give the credit of Yajña to Pṛthu in this Manvantara.

2. *Suras* (in Bd. P. v. 74) is the correct reading.

3. It implies Varāha incarnation, but Varāha killed Hiraṇyākṣa and Nṛsiṁha incarnation was for killing Hiraṇyakaśipu.

81. Namuci, Śaṁbara and Prahlāda (were among them). The cruel Dānavas were killed. Those who were rudely shaken were forced to flee in various directions.

82. Mādhava, the immanent soul of all living beings showed, the Brāhmaṇas there a great miracle, viz. all the great elements with their special features and the entire Time.

83. They saw the entire Universe and themselves in his cosmic body. There was nothing in the worlds which was not pervaded by the noble-souled lord.

84. Seeing that form of Upendra (i.e. Vāmana) Devas, Dānavas and human beings were fascinated. All of them were enchanted by Viṣṇu's refulgence.

85. Bali was bound with great nooses along with his kinsmen, friends and followers. The entire race of Virocana was consigned to Pātāla.

86. After handing back the entire riches and glory of Devas to the noble-souled Indra, the mighty-armed Janārdana manifested himself before the human world.

87. These three incarnations of the lord were divine and auspicious. Listen and understand the seven incarnations as human beings as a result of the curse.

88. In the tenth Tretāyuga when Dharma had been ruined he had his fourth incarnation as Dattātreya with Mārkaṇḍeya as his preceptor.

89. His fifth incarnation was in the fifteenth Tretāyuga as Māndhātṛ, the Emperor. Tathya (Utathya?) was his preceptor.

90. The sixth incarnation was that as the son of Jamadagni in the nineteenth Tretāyuga. He annihilated all the Kṣatriyas. He had Viśvāmitra as his preceptor (Purohita).

91. In the twentyfourth Tretāyuga, he took his seventh incarnation as Rāma, the son of Daśaratha. In his sacrifice Vasiṣṭha was his priest. It was for the purpose of killing Rāvaṇa.

92. In the twentyeighth Dvāpara Yuga, Viṣṇu took his eighth incarnation as Vedavyāsa born of Parāśara. He had Jātukarṇa as the preceptor.

93. Viṣṇu who had been born earlier as the son of Aditi and Kaśyapa took his ninth incarnation as the son of Devakī and Vasudeva with the Brāhmaṇa Gārgya as his preceptor.

94-95. The lord is *Aprameya* (one whocannot be measured). He is *Niyojya** (freely ordered about and employed bydevotees). He moves about as he pleases. He has full self-control. He sports about in the world like a boy playing with toys. This mighty-armed Madhusūdana cannot be measured. There is nothing greater than the cosmic form of the Lord.

96-97. In the twentyeighth Dvāpara Yuga, when a slight portion of the end of Dvāpara remained and when Dharma had been destroyed, Lord Viṣṇu was born in the family of Vṛṣṇis in order to establish Dharma and destroy Asuras. By means of his Yogic Māyā, the Yogic soul fascinated all living beings.

98. Entering human womb, he moved about on the Earth fully concealed (from the view of ordinary mortals) for the sake of the sport among the human beings. He was accompanied by Sāndīpani as his preceptor.

99-100. In that incarnation, the powerful lord slew the following Daityas who had taken human bodies : Kaṁsa, Śālva, Dvivida the great Asura, Ariṣṭa, Vṛṣabha, Keśin the horse, Kuvalayāpīḍa the elephant, the chief of wrestlers, the officer in-charge of the abode (of Kaṁsa) (Cāṇūra) and the demoness Pūtanā.

101. The thousand arms of Bāṇa of wonderful exploits were cut off by him. The Asura Naraka and the powerful (Kāla-) Yavana were killed by him in battle.

102. All the precious gems and jewels of kings were confiscated by him through his splendid refulgence. All the kings of evil conduct in Rasātala were killed by him.

103-104. These incarnations of the noble-souled lord were for the sake of the benefit of the worlds.

In this Kaliyuga, towards its close, when the period of junction will begin, the powerful Kalki will be born under the name Viṣṇuyaśas, as the son of Parāśara. He will be accompanied by Yājñavalkya as his preceptor. This is his tenth and future incarnation.

---

*Better *a-niyojya* 'uncontrollable; one who cannot be ordered' as in Bd.P. It fits here with an *Avagraha* (S)— *aprameyo' niyojyaśca.*

105-109. He will be leading all the armies consisting of elephants, horses and chariots. He will be surrounded by hundreds and thousands of Brāhmaṇas armed with weapons. He will be killing those who are not very religious and those who hate religion, viz. the northerners, those of the middle lands, those who live to the west of the Vindhya mountain, the southerners (such as) Draviḍas along with Siṁhalese, Gāndhāras, Pāradas, Pahlavas, Yavanas, Śakas, Tuṣāras, Barbaras, Pulindas, Daradas,Khaśas, Laṁpākas, Andhakas, Rudras and Kiratas. The powerful lord will destroy Mlecchas making his discus whirl. He will be invisible to all living beings and move about on the Earth.

110. Viṣṇu will be born as a human being with a part of the intelligent god. In the previous birth he would have been born as the powerful Pramiti.

111. In bodily splendour he was (will be) like the moon and will be born when the Kaliyuga is complete. Thus the ten incarnations of the lord have been recounted.

112. The lord takes incarnations in the different periods with a part of his powerful splendour in the three worlds for different purposes and ends in view. He is born in different wombs in accordance with the function he has to perform.

113. When the twentyfifth Kalpa has started and twenty-five years have elapsed, he will be killing all living being and men.

114. By means of his ruthless activities he will make the Earth left with only the seeds. He would have (then) massacred all Vṛṣalas and almost all impious persons.

115-120. Then Kalki will have achieved his object along with his army. The subjects then would be destroyed by their own actions. But they will become Siddhas again by themselves.

Urged by the inevitable destiny, they will become unreasonable, infuriated and deluded, causing mutual destruction. Along with his followers, he will undertake eternal rest in the middle of Gaṅgā and Yamunā. When Kalki passes away the kings will die along with their ordinary soldiers. People will be without anyone to restrain them.[1] When the arrangement for security ceases to be, they will kill one another in battle. The will lose confidence in one another. They will be fretting and fuming and will be extremely distressed. Having no belonging left, they will leave off their cities and villages together. All the Vedic Dharmas will be defunct. All the rites of castes and stages of life will be extinct. People will be short in stature and short-lived. They will be residing in forests.

121-125. They will be resorting to rivers and mountains. Leaves, roots and fruits will constitute their diet. They will be wearing leaves and barks of trees or hides. There will be a highly indiscriminate fusion of castes. In the last junction of the Kali age they will be short-lived and highly distressed. Their means of sustenance will be destroyed. They will be overwhelmed with many adversities. They will undergo sufferings. The people will be completely extinct along with the Kali age. When the Kali age lapses and the Kṛta Yuga starts again, all objects will regain their original forms naturally and not otherwise. Thus I have recounted the activities of Devas and Asuras. In the context of the narration of Yadu race the great fame of Viṣṇu has been recounted. I shall now recount the race of Turvasu, Pūru and Druhyu.

CHAPTER THIRTYSEVEN[2]

Royal Dynasties
(Conclusion of the Anuṣaṅga Section)

Sūta said :

1. Vahni was the son of Turvasu. Gobhānu was the son of Vahni[3]. The unconquered heroic Trisānu was Gobhānu's son.

---

1. These verses (to the end of the chapter) describe a gloomy picture of the society at the end of Kali Yuga. All Purāṇas are unanimous in depicting the terrible state of the public as Kali advances.

2. This chapter correspond to Bd.P. 2.3.74. Reference are to verse numbers.

3. Genealogy of Turvasu as recorded in *AITH*, p. 149 shows Garbha as the predecessor of Gobhānu.

2. Karandhama was the son of Trisānu and his son was Marutta. Another Marutta mentioned before was the son of Avikṣit. He was also a king.

3. Marutta was childless. I have heard that he too was a king. All the (people) made Duṣkṛta[1] a descendant of Pūru, his son.

4. Thus, due to the curse of Yayāti in connection with the transference of his old age the line of Turvasu merged with that of Pūru.

5. The successor of Duṣkṛta was the king named Śarūtha. After Śarūtha came Janāpīḍa and he had four sons.

6. They were Pāṇḍya, Kerala, Cola and Kulya with their kingdoms named after them, viz. Pāṇḍya, Kerala, Cola and Kulya.

7. Druhyu had two heroic sons well known as Babhru and Setu. Aruddha was the son of Setu and Ripu was the son of Babhru.

8. This strong (king) Ripu was killed in war with very great difficulty by Yauvanāśva. Their great war lasted continuously for fourteen months.

9. Aruddha's successor was the king named Gāndhāra after whom the great lan d of Gāndhāra took its name.[2]

10. The horses bred in Gāndhāra land are the most excellent horses. Gāndhāra's son was Dharma and Ghṛta (Dhṛta) was his son.

11. Durdama was born to Ghṛta (Dhṛta) and his son was Praçetas. A hundred sons were born to Pracetas. All of them were kings.

12. All of them were the rulers of the Mleccha territory in the northern direction (region). Anu had three noble-souled sons. All of them were highly righteous.

13. They were Sabhānara, Pakṣa and Parapakṣa. The son of Sabhānara was the scholarly king Kālānala.

14. Kālānala's son was the pious-souled Sṛñjaya who was righteous. The heroic king Purañjaya was the son of Sṛñjaya.

---

1. Duṣyanta in Bd. P.v. 3.
2. This shows that Druhyu's descendants ruled over a part of Afghanistan.

15. Janamejaya of great strength and vitality was the son of the saintly king Purañjaya.

16. This king was equal to Indra. His fame was established (even) in heaven. Mahāmanas was the son of Mahāśāla. He was very pious.

17. He was the lord of the seven continents. He was an emperor of great fame. Mahāmanas procreated two famous sons.

18. They were Uśīnara the knower of Dharma and Titikṣu the righteous. Uśīnara had five wives. They were born of the races of saintly kings.

19. They were Mṛgā (Nṛgā in Bd. P.), Kṛmī, Navā, Darvā and Dṛṣadvatī the fifth. Uśīnara had five sons from them. They made his race flourish. They were virtuous and grew old with the performance of great penance.

20. Mṛga (Nṛga in Bd. P.) was the son of Mṛgā (Nṛgā), Nava was the son of Navā. Kṛmi was the son of Kṛmī and Suvrata, the virtuous, was the son of Darvā.

21-22. O Brāhmaṇas, the son of Dṛṣadvatī was (popularly called) Auśīnara Śivi. The city of Śivi was famous as Śivapura[1] and that of Mṛga was the Yaudheya city. Navarāṣṭram belonged to Nava and the city Kṛmilā to Kṛmi. That of Suvrata was Vṛṣṭā (Ambaṣṭha). Now listen and understand Śivi's sons.

23. The four sons of Śivi called Śivis were very popular among the people. They were Vṛṣadarbha, Suvīra, Kekaya and Madraka.

24. Their territories were very flourishing. They were Vṛṣadarbhas, Sūcīdarbhas, Kekayas and Madrakas. Now listen to the progeny of Titikṣu.

---

1. These places are located as follows :
   (I) Śivapura—The country of Siaposh. It includes Kafiristan (DE. 211).
   (II) Yaudheya—The country between the Hydaspes and the Indus (DE 215)
   (III) Navarāṣṭra—Nausari in Baroach Dist. of Gujarat (DE 139).
   (IV) Kṛmilā—untraced.

25. The mighty-armed son of Titikṣu named Uśadratha was the well-known king in the eastern quarter. His son was Hema.

26-32. Sutapā was born to Hema and Bali was the son of Sutapas* (Bd. P.). The noble-minded Bali who was a great Yogin was bound (by Vāmana). He took birth in the human womb, being desirous of children, as the family was nearing extinction due to absence of issues. He begot sons who established the discriplines of four castes on this earth. He procreated the sons Aṅga, Vaṅga, Sulha, Puṇḍra and Kaliṅga. These are called Bāleya Kṣatras (the Kṣatriyas born of Bali). That lord had Brāhmaṇa sons also called Bāleya Brāhmaṇas. They established the line (of Bali). Many boons were granted to the intelligent Bali by the delighted Brahmā. The boons granted were *Mahāyogitva* (the state of being a great Yogin), longevity of life lasting for a Kalpa, invincibility in war, great inclination towards righteousness and piety, the vision of the three worlds, importance among his descendants, unrivalled state in strength as the ability to see the true principles of Dharma. "You will establish the (discipline of) four castes"—on being thus told by the lord, king Bali attained great peace (of mind).

33-34. After a long period the scholarly Bali went back to his own abode. The territories of the sons were Aṅgas, Vaṅgas, Sulhakas (Suhma), Puṇḍras and Kaliṅgas. They were very flourishing territories.

Listen to and understand their race. These sons were his Kṣetrajas (born of his wife) through the contact of a sage. They were born of (sage) Dīrghatamas of great virility in Sudeṣṇā (the wife of Bali).

The Sages said :

35. O holy lord, how were these five Kṣetraja sons of Bali procreated by the sage Dīrghatamas ? Please narrate this to us who ask.

**Sutayaśā* in the text is obscure. Hence the form *Sutapas* is accepted.

Sūta said :

36. Formerly there was an intelligent and renowned sage named Aśija. The wife of this noble-souled sage was named Mamatā.

37. Bṛhaspati who was the younger brother of Aśija, whose splendour was great and who was the preceptor of the heaven-dwellers (gods) coveted Mamatā.

38-40. Not desirous of having sexual intercourse with him, Mamatā spoke thus to Bṛhaspati : "I am pregnant due to my contact with your elder brother. This is the eighth (month). O Bṛhaspati, this great child in the womb cries much. The son of Aśija that he is, he has learned the Vedas with their six ancillaries and he repeats the Vedic Mantras.

Your semen virile too is never-failing. It does not behove you to have sexual intercourse with me. O holy lord, when the period (of gestation) lapses (you may do) as you deem fit".

41. Though emphatically told thus by her, the noble-souled Bṛhaspati of excessive refulgence did not restrain himself, as he was overwhelmed by passion.

42. The virtuous-souled Bṛhaspati did have his sexual intercourse with her. Even as he was discharging the semen virile; the child in the womb spoke thus :

43. "No *Snātaka* (a Brāhmaṇa who just had his sacred ablution after completing his Vedic study) shall deposit his (semen virile) here. There is no space here for two. You too are one with never-failing semen virile. I have come here first."

44. Bṛhaspati, the sage of divine attributes, became infuriated on being told thus. He cursed the son of Aśija, his brother, who was yet in the womb:

45. "You have spoken thus to me on an occasion coveted by all living beings. Since you have spoken thus out of delusion, you will enter a long period of darkness".

46-47. Due to that curse, the sage thereafter came to be called Dīrghatamas.

Āśija (son of Aśija—Dīrghatamas) too was highly renowned by virtue of his power (of penance) like Bṛhaspati. He too stayed in the hermitage of his brother observing celibacy. He heard of *Godharma* (the law of cattle—behaving like a bull or cow) from the bull, the son of Surabhi (Kāmadhenu).

48. Aśija's brother, his uncle, had built a house for him. While he was staying there, a bull came there casually.

49. Surrounded by cows he grazed the Darbha grass that had been brought for the *Darśa*[1] rituals. Dīrghatamas caught hold of the quivering bull by its horns.

50. Caught by him, the bull could not move even a step. Then the bull spoke to him : "O foremost one among the strong persons, leave me off.

51. O dear one, a strong one like you has not been met with by me anywhere, even though I had been bearing the three-eyed lord (everywhere), as a result of which I have come down to the earth.

52. O most excellent one among strong persons, leave me off. I am pleased with you. Choose a boon". On being told thus, the sage told the bull: "Where will you go alive, away from me?

53. Hence I will not release you, the quadruped that eats others' wealth". Then that bull replied to Dīrghatamas:

54. "O dear one, to us nothing is sinful. There is no theft. We do not distinguish between what should be eaten or what should not be eaten or what should be drunk or should not be drunk.

55. We do not know what should be done or what should not be done, what should be approached or what should not be approached. O Brāhmaṇa, we are not sinners. This is remembered as the Dharma of cows and bulls".[2]

56. On hearing the name of cows mentioned, he became confused and released him. Thanks to his devotion to the cows as ordained by the Vedas, he propitiated the bull.

---

1. The sacrificial rite to be performed on the New Moon Day.

2. This practice of open and unconcealed sexual intercourse is mentioned in the M.Bh. (MW 365A) and seems to have been followed by Dīrghatamas. The Buddha mentions this Dharma in derision.

57. When the bull went away, fully propitiated, he began to deliberate on the Dharma of cows devoutly. He was fully engrossed in it and devoted to it pondering mentally over it again and again.

58. As ill luck would have it, he became foolish and silly-minded and molested the wife of his younger brother Autathya, even though she struggled and wept.

59. Considering it to be his arrogance, Śaradvān did not brook it. Using force and following Godharma (the practice of cattle), he had approached his daughter-in-law (the wife of younger brother).

60. On seeing this trespass, Śaradvān reflected. The noble-souled (Śaradvān) knew what was destined to happen. So he did not confer death on him (Dīrghatamas).

61. With eyes turned red due to anger, he shouted to Dīrghatamas: "You do not distinguish between whom to approach and whom not to. Following *Godharma* you have solicited your daughter-in-law.

62. You are a man of despicable conduct. I am casting you off. Go away along with your evil action. In spite of being blind, old and dependent on others for maintenance you have committed a deplorable, sinful action. Therefore, you are forsaken. I am convinced that you are a person of evil conduct".

Sūta said:

63. Thereafter he thought of a ruthless action. After rebuking Dīrghatamas many times, he caught hold of him by his arms, put him in a sealed casket and hurled it into the waters of Gaṅgā.

64. For seven days the sealed casket was wafted by the current. King Bali, the knower of the principles of Dharma, who was in the company of his wife, saw the sinking casket borne towards him by the current.

65. Bali, the righteous-souled son of Virocana, saved him and took him to his harem where he propitiated him with different kinds of food and drinks, and looked after him.

66. The delighted sage asked Bali to choose a boon according to his desire. The leading Dānava chose the boon for (blessing him with) a son.

67. Bali said: "O blessed one, O bestower of honour, it behoves you to procreate in my wife sons endowed with virtue and wealth, so that my line will be perpetuated".[1]

68. On being requested thus by him, the sage said to the king, "So be it". The king thereupon sent his wife named Sudeṣṇā unto him (the sage).

69. On seeing him blind and old, the queen did not go unto the sage. She bedecked her servant-maid in ornaments and left her with him.

70-73. The righteous-souled sage of good self-control begot of that Śūdra woman two sons of great prowess, Kakṣīva and Cakṣus. They studied the Vedas duly and became masters and expounders of Vedas, great enlightened Siddhas and excellent ones with direct vision of Dharma. On seeing them, Kakṣīva and Cakṣus, the king, Bali, the son of Virocana, asked the sage, "Are these my sons?" The sage said, "O excellent Asura, no, that is not the case. They are mine. Due to your deception, these god-like children are born of Śūdra womb.

74. Considering me blind and old, Sudeṣṇā, your queen, sent the Śūdra servant-maid unto me and disrespected me".

75. Bali, thereupon propitiated the excellent sage again. The lord rebuked his wife Sudeṣṇā.

76-78. He bedecked her in ornaments and gave her unto the sage. The sage Dīrghatamas spoke thus to the queen : "O splendid lady, if, without showing aversion, you lick from head to foot my naked body smeared well with curds mixed with salt, you will obtain those sons mentally desired by you". The queen, thereupon, carried out all his instructions.

79. When she reached the anus, her aversion was so great that she avoided it. Thereupon that sage said to her : "O auspicous lady, since you avoided the anus, the eldest son you will give birth to will be without anus".

---

1. This Purāṇa has mixed up two different Balis—Bali or Mahābali, the rival of Indra, who donated three feet of land to Vāmana, was not childless. Bāṇa, Uṣā's father, was his son. This Bali is another East Indian King who being childless requested thus to Dīrghatamas.

80. Then the queen replied to the sage Dīrghatamas, "O blessed one, it does not behove you to give me a son like that".

81-82. The sage said: "O gentle lady, this is your own fault. It will not be otherwise. O queen of good rites, I shall bestow a son unto you. Even without anus, he will perform all bodily functions". Touching her belly, the sage Dīrghatamas continued—

83-84. "O lady of sweet smiles, since you have licked up the curds from my body, your womb is filled like the ocean on the Full Moon Day. Five splendid sons comparable to the sons of Devas will be born to you. They will be refulgent, valiant and righteous and performer of sacrifices."

85. Then Aṅga, the eldest son of Sudeṣṇā, was born. The other sons born to her thereafter were Vaṅga, Kaliṅga, Puṇḍra and Brahma (Suhma in Bd. P. v. 87).

86. These five were the sons born of Bali's wife. They perpetuated his line. Thus, they were given as sons to Bali formerly by Dīrghatamas.

87-88. For certain reasons, his (Bali's) progeny had been prevented by Brahmā, saying, "Let there not be any offspring of this noble-souled (king) by his own wives"* That was why he begot children of human wombs. Then the delighted bull, the son of Kāmadhenu, spoke these words to Dīrghatamas:

89. "Since you have done this after pondering over *Godharma*, I am pleased with you. I shall release you (from the curse).

90. Hence, look, I shall remove your long period of darkness and gloom, as well as the curse of Bṛhaspati along with the other sins that may be lingering, sticking to your body.

91. After sniffing at you, I shall remove your fear of death and old age." As soon as he was sniffed at, the darkness was destroyed and he began to see.

92. He regained his eye-sight. He became a young man

***apatyāmạtyadāreṣu* is a misprint for *apatyāmātmadāreṣu*
Cf. Bd. P. v. 89 : *apatyamasya dāreṣu sveṣu mā'bhūt mahātmanaḥ!*

blessed with long life. Thus that Dīrghatamas was transformed by the bull and he became Gautama.

93. Thereafter Kakṣīvān went to Giripraja (Girivraja—Bd. P.) along with his father. He performed extensive penance for the sake of his father as conceived (originally).

94. After a long period, he became purified through his penance. After shaking off his defects, the lord (sage) attained Brāhmaṇahood along with his younger brother.

95. Then spoke his father: "O Lord, now I am (really) one blessed with a son. By having a famous and good son (like you), I have achieved my objective (and am happy and contented) in life."

96. With his soul united in Yogic practice, he attained Brahman-hood and extinction of (worldly bondage). After obtaining Brāhmaṇa-hood Kakṣīvān procreated a thousand sons.

97-99. Those dark-skinned Gautamas (descendants of Gautama) are remembered as the sons of Kakṣīvān. Thus the association of Dīrghatamas and Bali, the son of Virocana, has been narrated. So also the progeny of both. After the coronation of his five sinless sons, the contented Bali resorted to Yogic practice. The lord of Yogic soul bides his time roaming (on the earth) while remaining invisible to all living beings.

100. Dadhivāhana, the son of the saintly king Aṅga, became king. Due to the blunder of Sudeṣṇā, this king was Anapāna (devoid of anus).

101. King Diviratha is remembered as the son of Anapāna. The scholarly son of Diviratha was king Dharmaratha.

102. It was this selfsame glorious Dharmaratha by whom Soma (Soma juice) was drunk in the course of a Yajña along with the noble-souled Śakra on the mountain Viṣṇupada.

103. Listen, (the son) of Dharmaratha was king Citraratha. From Citraratha was born king Daśaratha. He was famous as Lomapāda and his daughter was Śāntā.[1]

1. Some words missing here in the text are supplied here.
The missing lines after v. 103 are given in A (p. 374). They are translated as follows:—

104. The elephant of Śakra was born as his elephant Caṇḍika. By means of Mantras (?) he brought the excellent vehicle to the earth.

105. Haryaṅga's successor was the king Bhadraratha. Bhadraratha's son was Bṛhatkarmā, the lord of subjects.

106. Bṛhadratha was his son and Bṛhanmanā was born of him. Bṛhanmanā procreated the son Rājendra.

107. He was otherwise known as Jayadratha and from him was born king Dṛdharatha. The son of Dṛdharatha was Janamejaya, the conqueror of the universe.

108. His successor, the king of Aṅgas, was Karṇa. Karṇa's son was Śūrasena and Dvija is remembered as his son.

The Sages said :

109. How was Karṇa known as the son of a charioteer and how did he become a member of the family of kings of Aṅgas? This we wish to hear. Indeed you are very efficient (in narration).

Sūta replied :

110. King Bṛhanmanā was born as the son of Bṛhadbhānu (earlier he was mentioned as Bṛhadratha). He had two wives. Both of them were the daughters of Caidya.

111. They were Yaśodevī and Satyā. The race is bifurcated on account of these two wives. Jayadratha otherwise known as Rājendra was born of Yaśodevī.

---

104. That noble-minded heroic son of Daśaratha, Caturaṅga, the promotor of his family, was born through the grace of Ṛṣyaśṛṅga.

105. It is reported that Pṛthulāśva was Caturaṅga's son. The son of Pṛthulāśva was (?) of Campā. The (capital) city of Campā was beautiful. It became the beautiful Mālinī (real name of Campā).

106-107. The city of Campāvatī (alias) Campā was inhabited by people of four Varṇas (castes). They lived in Campāvatī for sixty thousand years. By Brāhmaṇas, Kṣattriyas, Vaiśyas, by all, their own duty (Dharma) was followed. All were devoted to Viṣṇu by performing penance and following the duties of their (respective) caste.

Haryaṅga became his son by the grace of Pūrṇabhadra.

—Vā.P. (Anandashram, Pune, p. 374)

112. (Defective verse) Satyā gave birth to the famous Vijaya who was of mixed Brāhmaṇa-Kṣatriya caste (?) Vijaya's son was Dhṛti and his son was Dhṛtavrata.

113. Dhṛtavrata's son was Satyakarmā of great fame. Satyakarmā's son was Adhiratha, the charioteer.

114. He adopted and looked after Karṇa. Hence Karṇa was known as the son of a charioteer. Thus everything that had been asked about Karṇa has been mentioned to you.

115. Thus all the kings in the family of Aṅga have been recounted by me. Now listen to the progeny of Pūru in detail and in the proper order.

Sūta said :

116. The mighty-armed son of Pūru, Janamejaya became a king. His son was Aviddha who conquered the eastern region.

117. From Aviddha was born as son the great hero Manasyu. King Jayada was the son of Manasyu.

118. His successor was the king named Dhundhu. Bahugavī was the son of Dhundhu. Sañjāti was his son.

119. Sañjāti's son was Raudrāśva. Understand his sons. Raudrāśva begot ten sons of the celestial damsel Ghṛtācī.

120-123. They were Rajeyu, Kṛteyu, Vakṣeyu, Sthaṇḍileyu, Ghṛteyu, Jaleyu, Sthaleyu the seventh, Dharmeyu, Sannateyu and the tenth son Vaneyu. He had ten daughters also, viz. Rudrā, Śūdrā, Madrā, Śubhā, Jāmalajā, Talā, Khalā (these seven and then), the daughter who is remembered as Gopajalā, then, Tāmrarasā and Ratnakūṭī. The husband of all of them was Prabhākara by name. He belonged to the Ātreya line (Gotra).

Anādṛṣṭa was a saintly king. Riveyu was his son.

124. Riveyu's wife named Jvalanā was the daughter of Takṣaka. That saintly king begot of that gentle lady a son named Ranti.

125-126. Ranti, the king, begot splendid sons of his wife Sarasvatī. They were Trasu, Pratiratha and Dhruva, who was exceedingly righteous. His daughter Gaurī is famous as the splendid mother of Māndhātā. Dhurya was Pratiratha's son and his son was Kaṇṭha.

127. (Defective verse) His son was Medhātithi from whom the Brāhmaṇas Kāṇṭhāyanas originated. Itinā (?) was the daughter of Anuyama (?). She gave birth to sons.

128-129. Trasu obtained his favourite son Malina who was an expounder of Brahman. Thereafter he obtained Upadātā and the (following) four sons of Itinā (?) : Suṣmanta, Duṣyanta, Pravīra and Anagha. The son born to Duṣyanta was an excellent king and he became an emperor.

130. That son Bharata was born of Śakuntalā. It is from him that (the land) took its name Bhārata. A disembodied (celestial) voice spoke to king Duṣyanta.

131-132. "O Duṣyanta, the mother is but a leathern pouch (or bellows). The son belongs to the father. He is identical with him by whom he is begotten. Śakuntalā tells the truth. Maintain your son. O lord of men, he who discharges the semen virile redeems the son from the abode of Yama. You are the progenitor of this child in the womb. Do not dishonour Śakuntalā".

133. Bharata begot of his three wives nine sons. "These are not befitting me". Saying this, the king did not approve of them. (He disowned them).

134. Then those infuriated mothers slew their sons. Thus the births of those sons to the king were futile.

135. Then the powerful son Bharadvāja, the son of Bṛhaspati, was brought over there by the Maruts in the course of the sacrifices and handed over to him.

136. In this connection, they cite this story of the intelligent Bharadvāja, his birth and the transfer unto Bharata by the Maruts.

137. When his wife was in the advanced state of pregnancy, it is said that Aśija died. Looking at his brother's wife, Bṛhaspati said : "O auspicious lady, embellish your body with ornaments and give me (the pleasure of) sexual intercourse with you."

138. On being told thus, she said to him, "O holy lord, I am pregnant now. The foetus has reached the advanced state of maturity. The child repeats the Vedic Mantras.

139. You too are one whose semen virile never goes in

vain. This activity (of sexual intercourse with you) is despicable". On being told thus, Bṛhaspati said smilingly:

140. "You need not at all instruct me in good behaviour". With great delight, he forcibly indulged in sexual intercourse with her.

141. "O father (uncle) Bṛhaspati", said the foetus to Bṛhaspati who was in a state of exhilaration, "I am already embedded here, having come here before.

142. You are one whose semen virile never goes in vain. There is no space here for two (children)." On being told thus by the child in the womb, the infuriated Bṛhaspati said again:

143. "Since you prevent me at such a time as this, desired by all living beings, you will enter a long period of darkness".

144. The (vaginal) passage of his mother was covered with his feet by the child. The semen virile of Bṛhaspati, being obstructed in between them became an infant.

145. On seeing the son instantaneously born Mamatā said, "O Bṛhaspati, I am going to my house. Bhara (Nurture), Dvāja (that which is born of two)."

146. When she went away after saying this, he (too) forsook the son instantaneously." "*Bharasva* (Nurture). *Bāḍham* (very well)". Since this was said, he came to be known as 'Bharadvāja'.

147. On seeing the infant abandoned by both the mother and the father, the Maruts took away the child Bharadvāja out of mercy.

148-149. At that time Bharata had performed various Yajñas and other *Kāmya* and *Naimittika* (sacrifices) with the desire for obtaining a son. In spite of those Yajñas, the lord did not obtain any son. Thereafter he performed the *Marut-Soma* Yajña for the sake of a son.

150. Being propitiated by that Marut-Soma sacrifice, the Maruts (gave) him Bharadvāja, the intelligent son of Bṛhaspati.

151. On obtaining that son Bharadvāja, Bharata said: "O lord, with you as my son, I am satisfied, since all my previous children had been killed".

152. The births of his (i.e. Bharata's) previous sons had

been in vain (*vitatha*). So Bharadvāja was known by the name Vitatha.

153. Hence the Divine child Bharadvāja turned into a Kṣatriya from Brāhmaṇa-hood. He is remembered by the names *Dvimukhyāyana* (having two important abodes) and *Dvipitṛka* (having two fathers).

154. After the birth (succession) of Vitatha, Bharata went to heaven (passed away). Vitatha's successor was Bhuvamanyu.

155. Four sons comparable to the Mahābhūtas (great elements) were born to Bhuvamanyu. They were Bṛhatkṣatra, Mahāvīrya, Nara and the powerful Gāgra.

156. The son of Nara was Saṁkṛti. His sons were very powerful. Guruvīrya and Trideva are remembered as the sons of Saṁkṛti. There were none greater than they.

157. The successors of Gāgra were born of Śinibaddha. Therefore the Gāgryas (descendants of Gāgra) are remembered as Brāhmaṇas with the traits of Kṣatriyas.

158. Bhīma was the son of Mahāvīrya. From him was born Ubhakṣaya. His wife Viśālā gave birth to three sons.

159. She gave birth to Trayyāruṇi, Puṣkarin and the third son Kapi. Kapi's descendants were excellent Kṣatriyas and those of the other two are said to be great sages.

160. The descendants of Gāgra, Saṁkṛti and Mahāvīrya were Brāhmaṇas endowed with Kṣatriya traits too. They merged with the line of Aṅgiras. Now the line of Bṛhatkṣatra will be recounted.

161. Bṛhatkṣatra's successor was a pious one named Suhotra. Suhotra's successor was one named Hastin. Formerly this city named Hastināpura was built by him.

162. Hastin's successor were three, viz. Ajamīḍha, Dvimīḍha and Purumīḍha. They were all extremely devout and pious.[1]

163-164. Ajamīḍha's sons were splendid. They perpetuated the auspicious line. They were very pious. They were

1. The following additional verse numbered 167 in A, is translated as follows :

"The queens of Ajamīḍha were auspicious and perpetuators of the Kuru race. They were (by name) Nilini, Keśini and the beautiful Dhūmini'.

born to the great king in his old age after a great penance, thanks to the grace of Bharadvāja. Listen to their extension. Kaṇṭha was born to Ajamīḍha and Keśinī.

165. Medhātithi was his son and from him were born the Brāhmaṇas called Kaṇṭhāyanas. King Bṛhadvasu was born to Ajamīḍha and (his second wife) Dhūminī.

166. Bṛhadvasu's son was Bṛhadviṣṇu who was very strong. His son was Bṛhatkarmā whose son was Bṛhadratha.

167. His son was Viśvajit, whose son was Senajit. The four sons of Senajit were well known in the world.

168. They were Rucirāśva, Kāvya, Rāma of steady bow and Vatsa, the king of Avantī from whom the *Parivatsara* (era started).

169. Rucirāśva's successor was Pṛthuṣeṇa of great fame. Pāra was the son of Pṛthuṣeṇa and Nīpa was born of Pāra.

170. We have heard that a hundred sons were horn to Nīpa. They are called 'Nīpas'. All of them were kings.

171. The most glorious king among them who raised the fame of the race and stabilised the race was Samara with his capital in Kāṁpilya. He was fond of war.

172. Samara had three sons endowed with all good qualities. They were Para, Pāra and Sattvadaśva. Pāra's son Vṛṣu shone well.

173. A son named Sukṛti endowed with all good qualities was born to Vṛṣu, thanks to his meritorious activities. Vibhrāja was his son.

174. Vibhrāja's successor was the king named Aṇuha who was very famous. He was the husband of Ṛcī and so the son-in-law of Śuka.

175. Aṇuha's successor was Brahmadatta of great penance. Yogasūnu was his son and his son Viṣvaksena became a king.

176. Vibhrāja's sons became kings, thanks to their meritorious activities. Viṣvaksena's son was Udaksena.

177. His successor was Bhallāṭa by whom the king was killed formerly. Bhallāṭa's successor was king Janamejaya. On his behalf, all the Nīpas were destroyed by Ugrāyudha.

The Sages asked :

178. Whose son was Ugrāyudha ? In which family was he born and glorified ? What for were all the Nīpas destroyed by him ?

Sūta said :

179-180. The scholarly Yavīnara was the son and successor of Dvimīḍha. Dhṛtimān was his son. His son was Satyadhṛti. Satyadhṛti's son was the valorous Dṛḍhanemi. The king named Suvarmā was Dṛḍhanemi's son.

181. The valorous Sārvabhauma (lord of the entire earth) was Suvarmā's son. He shone as the sole lord of the earth and he became famous as Sārvabhauma.

182. In his great family was born (a king named) Mahatpauravanandana. King Rukmaratha is remembered as the son of Mahatpaurava.

183. Rukmaratha's son was the king named Supārśva. Supārśva's son named Sumati was very virtuous.

184. The son of Sumati was lord Sannatimān, the righteous-souled king. His son was named Sanati and Kṛta was his son.

185. He was a disciple of the noble-souled Hiraṇyanābhi of the Kauthuma branch (of Sāmavedic study). Twentyfour Sāman-Saṁhitās were expounded by him.

186. The sons of Kṛta, the singers of Sāman hymns, are remembered by the name 'Prācyas' (Easterners). The heroic Ugrāyudha was one of the sons of Kṛta. He was the scion of the family of Pūru.

187. The mighty-armed lord of Pañcālas named Nīla, who was the grandfather of Pṛṣata, was killed by him (Ugrāyudha) (and thereby) he exhibited his valour.

188. Ugrāyudha's son (successor) was a very famous king named Kṣema. Suvīra was born of Kṣema. Suvīra's son was Nṛpañjaya. Vīraratha was born of Nṛpañjaya. Thus these are remembered as Pauravas (descendants of Pūru).

189. King Nīla was born of Nīlinī (the third wife) of Ajamīḍha. Suśānti was born of Nīla, thanks to his severe penance.

190. Purujānu was the son of Suśānti. Riksa was born of Purujānu. The following were the sons and successors of Rikṣa.

191. They were : Mudgala, Sṛñjaya, the king Bṛhadiṣu, Vikrānta who was younger to him and Kaṁpilya, the fifth.

192-193. For the sustenance and the upkeep of all the five, the father spoke to them thus : "Know that there are five flourishing territories for all the five of you." Since the five were sufficient, all the territories were together well known as Pañcālas.* Maudgalyas, the descendants of Mudgala, were Brāhmaṇas endowed with Kṣatriya traits.

194. These were known as Kaṇṭhamudgalas and they merged into the Āṅgirasa Gotra. Mudgala's eldest son was very famous. He was engrossed in the meditation of Brahman.

195. From him Indrasenā conceived Badhyaśva. We have heard that Menakā bore to Badhyaśva twins.

196-197. They were Divodāsa the saintly king and Ahalyā of great fame. Ahalyā bore Śatānanda the excellent sage to Śāradvata. His son was Satyadhṛti of great fame. He was a master of the science of archery.

198. On seeing an Apsaras (celestial damsel) in front, the semen virile of Satyadhṛti was emitted in the bush of Śara-grass and twins were born.

199-200. Śantanu who had come that way ahunting took them out of mercy (Kṛpā). The boy is remembered as Kṛpa and the girl Kṛpī. She was also known as Gautamī. Thus the race of Gautama, known as Śāradvatas and Ṛtathyas, has been recounted.

Henceforth I shall recount the progeny of Divodāsa.

201. Divodāsa's successor was king Mitrayu who was engrossed in meditation on Brahman. Maitreya was born of him. It is rememberd that these too got merged (in other families).

202. These too got merged into the family (of Bhṛgu). They were (Brāhmaṇas) endowed with Kṣatriya traits. They were known as Bhārgavas. King Cyavana was born (in that family). The scholarly Pratiratha was born of him.

**Pañca* (five) + *alam* (sufficient)

203. The intelligent Sudāsa was born of Cyavana. Sahadeva was born as the son of Sudāsa. Somaka was his son.

204-205. When the race was about to be extinct, Ajamīḍha was born again. That was Somaka. Somaka's son was Jantu. When he was killed, hundred other sons were born to the noble-souled lord Ajamīḍha in his birth as Somaka. The youngest of them, Pṛṣata was Drupada's father.

206-209. His son was Dhṛṣṭadyumna and Dhṛṣṭaketu was his son. Dhūminī, the queen of Ajamīḍha, was desirous of a son. In her rebirth she performed a very difficult penance for a hundred years. She performed Homas in the fire. She kept awake. She ate but little and that too only the holy food. She performed great holy rites. Day and night she stayed on the Kuśa mattress alone. By these rigorous activities, she became smoke-coloured. The powerful Ajamīḍha begot of her Ṛkṣa, a smoke-coloured son, who was elder brother of Sita (one of white colour). Saṁvaraṇa was born of Ṛkṣa. Kuru was born of Saṁvaraṇa.

210. After treading on (conquering) Prayāga, he built Kurukṣetra. The excessive-splendoured king ploughed it for many years.

211. While it was being ploughed, Śakra shone there and granted this boon : Your (Kurukṣetra) shall be beautiful, holy and resorted to by meritorious persons.

212-213. Persons born in his family were excellent kings famous as Kurus. Kuru's beloved sons were Sudhanvan, Jahnu, Parīkṣita the great king, Putraka and Arimardana. It is remembered that the intelligent Suhotra was the successor of Sudhanvan.

214-215. Cyavana was his son. The king was an expert in religious affairs. Kṛta was the son of Cyavana. He performed great penance and many Yajñas. The king procreated his famous son Vidyoparicara who claimed friendship of Indra. He was a great hero who could traverse the sky and was known as Vasu too.

216-217. Girikā bore seven sons to Vidyoparicara—Bṛhadratha, a great warrior, who became famous as the king of Magadha, Pratyagṛha, Kuśa, one whom they call Maṇivāhana Māthailya, Lalittha and Matsyakāla the seventh.

218. Bṛhadratha's successor was famous by the name of Kuśāgra. Kuśāgra's son was a powerful king named Ṛṣabha.

219. Ṛṣabha's successor was a virtuous king named Puṣpavān. King Satyahita is remembered as his valorous successor.

220-221. His son was Sudhanvan. From him the valorous Ūrja was born. Ūrja's son was Nabhasa and from him was born that powerful king Jarāsandha. He was born in two pieces and he was joined by Jarā. Jarāsandha was mighty-armed because he was joined by Jarā.

222. This Jarāsandha of great strength was the conqueror of all Kṣatriya kings. Jarāsandha's son was the valorous Sahadeva.

223. Sahadeva's son was the glorious Somādhi of very great penance. Śrutaśruva was the son of Somādhi and is glorified as Māgadha.

Sūta said :

224. Janamejaya was the successor of Parīkṣita. Śrutasena's successor was named Bhīmasena. (lines missing).

225. Jahnu begot a son named Suratha who became a king. Suratha's successor was the heroic king Vidūratha.

226. It is well known that Vidūratha's son too was Sārvabhauma. Jayatsena was born of Sārvabhauma and Ārādhi was his son.

227. Mahāsattva was born of Ārādhi and Ayutāyu came thereafter. Akrodhana was the son of Ayutāyu. It is remembered that Devātithi was born of him.

228. It was Ṛkṣa who became the successor of Devātithi. Bhīmasena was born of Ṛkṣa and Dilīpa was his son.

229. Pratīpa was the son of Dilīpa. It is remembered that three sons were born to him. Those three were Devāpi, Śantanu and Bāhlīka.

230. King Saptabāhlīśvara should be known as (the son) of Bāhlīka. Somadatta too, of great fame, was the son of Bāhlīka.

231. Bhūri, Bhūriśravas and Śala were born of Somadatta. With a desire to accumulate virtue Devāpi (renounced everything and) went to the forest.

232. Sage Devāpi became the preceptor of Devas. To this noble-souled sage, two sons Cyavana and Iṣṭaka were born.

233. Śantanu became king. He was a scholar and a great physician (*Mahābhiṣa*). About this Mahābhiṣa they cite this verse.

234. "Whomsoever does the king touch, be he very old due to the efflux of time, becomes a youth again. Therefore they know him as *Śaṁtanu* (*Śam*—happiness, *Tanu*—body)."

235. Therefore the quality of his being *Śaṁtanu* was well known among the subjects. That righteous king Śaṁtanu married Jāhnavī (Gaṅgā).

236. The lord begot a son of her, named Devavrata (who later became) Bhīṣma. That Bhīṣma became famous as the grandfather of the Pāṇḍavas.

237-238.* After some time Śaṁtanu begot his most favourite son Vicitravīrya who as king did much for the welfare of the subjects. Kṛṣṇadvaipāyana begot of Vicitravīrya's wife (*kṣetra*), Dhṛtarāṣṭra, Pāṇḍu and Vidura. Gāndhārī bore to Dhṛtarāṣṭra a hundred sons.

239. Duryodhana was the eldest among them. He became the lord of all Kṣatriyas. Mādrī and the queen Pṛthā became the wives of Pāṇḍu.

240-241. Sons bestowed by gods were born of them on behalf of Pāṇḍu. Yudhiṣṭhira was born, thanks to the grace of Dharma; Vṛkodara was born of Vāyu; Dhanañjaya whose valour was equal to that of Śakra was born of Indra. Sahadeva and Nakula were born to Mādrī, thanks to the grace of Aśvins.

242. Five sons were born to Draupadī from the (five) Pāṇḍavas. Draupadī bore Śrutividdha, the eldest of them, to Yudhiṣṭhira.

243. Hiḍaṁbā bore her son Ghaṭotkaca to Bhīmasena. Kāśyā too bore her son Sarvavṛka to Bhīmasena.

244. Vijayā, the princess of Madra land, bore Suhotra to Sahadeva. Niramitra was born to Karematī of Vaidya (?) as the son of Nakula.

245. The heroic Abhimanyu was born of Subhadrā as the son of Pārtha. Parīkṣit was born of Uttarā, the princess of Virāṭa, as the son of Abhimanyu.

246. King Janamejaya was the successor of Parīkṣit. He established Vājasaneyika Brāhmaṇas.

247-248. The infuriated Vaiśaṁpāyana (said to him), "O evil-minded one, your directions (rule) will not remain long here in this world without an enemy (without being protested against). As long as I am alive in this world, this (act of yours) cannot be praised." Thereupon, Janamejaya was faced with difficulties all round.

249. He worshipped lord Prajāpati by offering *Havis* in the Paurṇamāsa Yajña. He saw that the different materials were offered in the sacrifice of the lord. Still he was in difficulties?

250. Janamejaya, the son of Parīkṣit, the descendant of Pūru, then performed Aśvamedha twice. Thereafter, he made those Vājasaneyaka Brāhmaṇas function. Janamejaya was crippled (defeated) three times.

251. Crippled at the hands of Aśvakomukhyas, crippled at the hands of the residents of Aṅgas, and crippled at the hands of the people of Madhyadeśa (Middle Lands), Janamejaya became *Trikharvī* (crippled three times). He was distressed. Being cursed along with those Brāhmaṇas, he suffered ruin.

252. Śatānīka of truthful exploit and strength was his son. After him (Janamejaya), the Brāhmaṇas crowned his son Śatānīka.

253-255. The powerful Aśvamedhadatta was the son of Śatānīka. Adhisāmakṛṣna was born as the son of Aśvamedhadatta. He conquered the cities of his enemies. He is the present ruler, of righteous soul and great fame. It is under his rule that you have been able to perform this *Dīrghasatra* (sacrifice of long duration) for three years. It is very difficult to be performed. O excellent Brāhmaṇas, (besides) there is another Satra lasting for two years, which is being performed in Kurukṣetra on the banks of the river Dṛṣadvatī.

The Sages said :

256. O highly intelligent Sūta, we wish to hear the future events of the subjects along with the kings. The past kings have been already mentioned by you.

257-259. We wish to hear all these—the activities that will be undertaken by them, and their names, the kings who will be born, their time calculated in years, the extent of the Yugas, their good points and their defects, their happiness and misery and those of the subjects, their religious activities and their passionate pursuits as well as their monetary dealings. Enumerate all these to us who ask you.

On being requested thus, Sūta the most excellent among the intelligent ones, mentioned everything in the manner it would occur and as he had seen and heard.

Sūta said :

260-261. Even as I recount listen and understand the future events,[1] the Kaliyuga and the Manvantaras in the manner they had been described to me by Vyāsa of wonderful activities. Henceforth, I shall mention the kings who will be born in future.

262-265. I shall mention the descendants of Aila, Ikṣvāku, Sudyumna and other kings in whom this splendid territory of the Ikṣvākus will be vested. I shall mention all other kings also besides these who will be born in future, viz. Kṣatriyas, Paraśavas, Śūdras and Brāhmaṇas, Andhas (Āndhras), Śakas, Pulindas, Tūlikas, Yavanas, Kaivartas, Ābhiras, Śabaras, and all other Mleccha (outcaste) tribes.

I shall mention those kings by names and the duration in years of their rule.

266. This present king Adhisāmakṛṣṇa is a king belonging to the Pūru dynasty. I shall mention all the future kings in his family.

267. Nirvaktra will be the son of Adhisāmakṛṣṇa. When his city Hastināpura is swept away by Gaṅgā he will abandon it and live happily at Kausāmbī.

---

1. Verses 260-310 describe the 'future' dynasties of kings. The dynasties mentioned here are (1) Bṛhadratha, (2) Pradyota, (3) Śiśunāka (Śiśunāga), (4) Nanda, (5) Maurya, (6) Kāṇva and (7) Āndhra. Guptas (if the reading be correct) are merely mentioned and Mleccha and other rulers are also referred to.

268. His son will be Uṣṇa. Citraratha will be born of Uṣṇa. Śucidratha will be born of Citraratha, and Vṛtimān will be born of Śucidratha.

269. Suṣeṇa of great fame and prowess will be born thereafter. To Suṣeṇa will be born the king named Sutīrtha.

270. Ruca will be born of Sutīrtha. Then Tricakṣa will be born. Tricakṣa's successor will be Sukhībala.

271. Sukhībala's son will be the king Paripluta. King Sunaya will be born as the son of Paripluta.

272. King Medhāvī will be the son of Sunaya and Medhāvin's son will be Daṇḍapāṇi.

273. Daṇḍapāṇi's son will be Niramitra and Kṣemaka will be the son of Niramitra. These twentyfive kings (?) will be born in the race of Pūru.

274-275. In this connection the following verse describing the subsequent race has been cited by Brāhmaṇas who know ancient lore. "This race which has produced Brāhmaṇas and Kṣatriyas, and which is honoured by Devas and sages, will be extinct in the Kali age after coming to Kṣemaka". Thus the race of Pūru has been enumerated precisely.

276. (The race) of the intelligent son of Pāṇḍu, the noble-souled Arjuna (has been narrated).

Henceforth I shall mention the race of the Ikṣvākus of great souls.

277-278. Bṛhadratha's successor was the heroic king Bṛhatkṣaya. His son was Kṣaya. Vatsavyūha was the son of Kṣaya. After Vatsavyūha, Prativyūha became king. His son is Divākara and this king is ruling over the city of Ayodhyā now.

279. Divākara's son will be the renowned Sahadeva. Bṛhadaśva will become the successor of Sahadeva.

280. Bhānuratha will be his son. His son will be Pratītāśva. Supratīta will become the son of Pratītāśva.

281-282. Sahadeva will be his son and his son will be Sunakṣatra. Kinnara, the oppressor of his enemies, will become the son of Sunakṣatra. Antarikṣa, the son of Kinnara, will be a great (king).

283-284. Suparṇa will be born of Antarīkṣa and Amitrajit

will be born of Suparṇa. His son will be Bharadvāja. Dharmin will be his son. A son named Kṛtañjaya will be born to Dharmin. Vrata will be the son of Kṛtañjaya and his son will be Raṇañjaya. To Raṇañjaya will be born the heroic king Sañjaya. Śākya will be born as the son of Sañjaya. From Śākya will be born Śuddhodana.

285. In the family of Śākya, Rāhula will be born to Śuddhodana (?) Then Prasenajit will be born. Kṣudraka will be born then.

286. Kṣulika will be the son of Kṣudraka. From Kṣulika will be born Suratha. Sumitra, the son of Suratha, will be the last king.

287. All these mentioned are the future Ikṣvāku kings in the Kali age. They will be born in the race of Bṛhadbala in the Kali age. All of them will be heroic, learned and truthful. They will be the conquerors of the sense-organs.

288. In this connection the following verse describing the subsequent race is cited by those who know the future. "This race of the Ikṣvākus will end with Sumitra. After coming to the king Sumitra, it will become extinct in the Kali age." Thus the Kṣetra (domain ?) originating from Manu and descending from Aila has been described.

289. Henceforth I shall mention the kings of Magadha, the descendants of Bṛhadratha, i.e. the kings of the race of Jarāsandha and the family of Sahadeva.

290. I shall mention the past, present and future kings in accordance with their importance. Even as I recount, listen and understand.

291. In the Mahābhārata war Sahadeva fell. His son Somādhi, the saintly king, ruled over Girivraja.

292. He ruled over the kingdom for fiftyeight years. His son Śrutaśravas ruled for sixtyfour years. Ayutāyu ruled for twentysix years. Niramitra enjoyed the earth for a hundred years and passed over to heaven.

293. Sukṛtta ruled over the earth for fiftysix years. Bṛhatkarman ruled the kingdom for twentythree years.

294. Senajit enjoys the kingdom (now). (His son) Śrutañjaya will be king for forty years.

295. Mahābala, the mighty-armed and endowed with great intellect and exploit, will become king and rule over the earth for thirtyfive years.

296. Śuci will remain in the kingdom for fiftyeight years. Kṣema will be the king for full twentyeight years.

297. Bhuvata the powerful will maintain the kingdom for sixtyfour years. Then Dharmanetra will be the king for full five years.

298. Nṛpati (?) will then enjoy the kingdom for fifty-eight years. Suvrata's rule will be for thirtyeight years.

299. Dṛḍhasena will be the king for forty, ten and eight (i.e. fiftyeight) years. Then Sumati will be in possession of the kingdom for thirtythree years.

300. Sucala will enjoy the kingdom for twentytwo years. Thereafter, Sunetra will enjoy the kingdom for forty years.

301. Satyajit will enjoy the earth for eightythree years. After attaining the kingdom Vīrajit will enjoy it for thirtyfive years.

302. Ariñjaya will be in possesssion of the earth for fifty years. These thirtytwo kings will be the future rulers in the line of Bṛhadratha.

303-304. Altogether they will rule for full thousand years. When the descendants of Bṛhadratha cease to rule and when the Vītahotras occupy the throne, even as all the Kṣatriyas stand gazing Pradyóta* Munika will kill his master and crown his own son as the king.

305. That king of the future will be devoid of statesman-ship or just policies. All the vassals will bow down before him. That excellent man will be king for twentythree years.

306. Thereafter the king named Pālaka will rule for twentyfour years. Then king Viśākhayūpa will rule for fifty years.

307. The rule of Ajaka will be for thirtyone years. His son Vartivardhana will rule for twenty years.

308. Thus the five future sons (and successors) of Pradyota will rule for one hundred and thirtyeight years.

---

*As per Bd. P. v. 123, Pradyota is the prince enthroned and Munika was his father.

Destroying their fame entirely, Śiśunāka (Śiśunāga) will become king (at Vārāṇasī).*

309-310. His son will attain Girivraja in Vārāṇasī. The suzerainty of Śiśunāka (Śiśunāga) will be for forty years. His son Śakavarṇa will rule for thirtysix years. Then for twenty years Kṣemavarmā will be the king.

311. Ajātaśatru will be the king for twentyfive years. Thereafter Kṣatraujas will rule the kingdom for forty years.

312. King Bimbisāra will rule for twentyeight years. King Darśaka will rule for twentyfive years.

313. The next king will be Udāyī who will rule for thirty-three years. In the fourth year of his rule, he will build his capital city named Kusumapura (Mod. Patnā) on the southern bank of Gaṅgā.

314 The king Nandivardhana will live for fortytwo years. The king Mahānandin will be the king for fortythree years.

315. Thus the kings of the Śiśunāka (Śiśunāga) dynasty will be ten in number. They altogether will rule for three hundred andsixtytwo years.

316. All the members of the Śaiśunāka (Śaiśunāga) family will be the contemporaries of the following kings who will be kinsmen to Kṣatriyas.

317-319. Those are twentyfour Ikṣvāku kings, twentyfive Pāñcālas, twentyfour Kālakas, twentyfour Haihayas, thirtytwo Kaliṅgas, twentyfive Śakas, twentysix Kurus, twentyeight Maithilas, twentythree Śūrasenas and twenty Vītihotras. All these kings will rule simultaneously.

320. Mahāpadma will be born of a Śūdra wife of Mahā-nandin. He will be a king over all Kṣatriyas.

321. Thereafter all the future kings will be born of Śūdra wombs. Mahāpadma will be the sole ruler with a single royal umbrella.

322. He will rule over the earth for twentyeight years.

******Vārāṇasyām* the 1st word from the next verse (no. 309) be better connected with Śiśunāga's becoming a king at Vārāṇasi to avoid confusion in v. 309.

Due to the power of the inevitable future, he will uproot all the Kṣatriyas.

323. His sons will be thousands. For eight years twelve of them will rule as kings. In succession to Mahāpadma they will become kings in order.

324. Kauṭilya will exterminate all of them by means of the twice eight of them (sixteen). After enjoying the kingdom of the earth[1] for a hundred years, the moon in the form of Nanda will set and fall down.

325. Kauṭilya will instal Candragupta as king. King Candragupta will be ruling for twentyfour years.

326. Bhadrasāra (?), the next king, will be king for twentyfive years. King Aśoka will rule over the men for twenty-six years.

327. His son Kunāla will rule for eight years. Kunāla's son Bandhupālita will enjoy the kingdom for eight years.

328. Bandhupālita's successor Indrapālita will rule for ten years (?) King Devavarmā will be king for seven years.

329. King Śatadhara, his son, will rule for eight years. King Bṛhadaśva will be the ruler for seven years.

330. These are the nine kings who will enjoy the earth. The earth will be in their possession for full one hundred and thirty seven years.[2]

331. The general Puṣpamitra will drive out Bṛhadratha and will rule over the kingdom continuously for sixty years.

332. The sons of Puṣpamitra will be kings for eight years. The eldest of all of them will be the king for seven years.

333. Thereafter Vasumitra, his son, will be king for ten years. Then Dhruka (?), his son, will rule for two years.

---

1. Instead of *bhuktvā mahīṁ* hereof, Pargiter's suggestion (*Dynasties of the Kali Age*, p. 26) '*bhuktā mahī*' 'the earth that was enjoyed (for 100 years)' is a better reading.

2. Reading *tebhyaḥ śuṅgān gamiṣyati* 'from them the earth will go to Śuṅgas.'

334. After him the Pulindakas will rule for three years. King Ghoṣasuta too will rule for three years.

335. Thereafter* Vikramamitra will be king for many years. King Bhāgavata will rule for thirtytwo years.

336. His son Kṣemabhūmi will rule for ten years. Ten Tuṅga (? Śuṅga) kings will enjoy the earth.

337. (Defective verse) They will enjoy the earth for full hundred and twelve years and it perhaps will go to Sudeva who will not be a (born) king but an indulgent fellow ever since his childhood. He will then become a king.

338. There will be another king Devabhūmi among the Śṛṅgas (? Śuṅgas). He will be a Kāṇṭhāyana (Kāṇvāyana—'Belonging to Kaṇva gotra') and will rule for nine years.

339. Bhūtimitra, his son, will be king for twentyfour years. After him king Nārāyaṇa will rule for twelve years.

340. His son Suśarmā will rule for ten years. These four kings of lofty activities will be Kāṇṭhāyana (Kāṇvāyana) Brāhmaṇas.

341. They will make the vassals bow down to them. They will rule for fortyfive years. After the change of their rule, Andhras will come in.

342. Driving out Kāṇṭhāyanas (Kāṇvāyanas), over-powering Suśarman and making the remaining forces of the Śṛṅgas (? Śuṅgas) dwindle down, Sindhuka of the Andhra race will gain possession of the earth.

343. King Sindhuka will rule for twentythree years. After him Bhāta (Kṛṣṇa) will rule for ten and eight years (?)

344. His son, Śrīsātakarṇi will be very great. Sātakarṇi will rule for fifty and six years.

345. Āpādabaddha, his son, will rule (first) for ten years, (then) for twentyfour years and (then) for six years.

346. Nemikṛṣṇa will rule for twentyfive years. Then for full one year Hāla will be the king.

---

*Bd. P. v. 154 reads *sapta* for *tato* hereof. But Bd. P. reading fixed the period of the king's reign.

347. Five (or) seven kings (of this race) will be very powerful. Putrikaṣeṇa will rule for twentyfive years.

348. Sātakarṇi will be king for one year. Śivasvāmī will rule for twentyeight years.

349. King Gautamīputra will rule for twentyone years among men. Thereafter Yajñaśrī of the Sātakarṇi family will be the king for nineteen years.

350. After him, king Vijaya will rule for only six years. Daṇḍaśrī Sātakarṇi, his son, will for three years.

351. Pulovā (Pulumāyi) will rule for seven years. There will be other kings as well. Altogether there will be thirty Āndhra kings who will enjoy the earth.

352. The rule of the Āndhras will cover a period of four hundred, five and six (four hundred and eleven) years. There will be five families of the Āndhras and all of them will be (are) equal (in power).

353-355. There will be ten and seven Ābhīra kings, seven Gardabhins (Gardabhillas), ten Śakas, eight Yavanas, fourteen Maunas, as kings. Āndhras will enjoy the earth for two hundred and one hundred years. Śakas will enjoy the earth for three hundred and eighty years.

356. Yavanas will enjoy the earth for eighty years. It is remembered (prophesied) that Tuṣāras will be in possession of the earth for five hundred years.

357. Thirteen Maruṇḍa families will rule for four hundred and fifty years along with (other) Śūdras. There will be other Mleccha tribes as well.

358. Eleven of those Mlecchas will enjoy (the earth) for three hundred years. Then the Śūdra tribes (Kilakila) Kolikilas (?) will rule for an equal period (?)

359. Vindhyaśakti will take over the administration from Kolikilas. Having supervised over the administration for ninetysix years, he will pass away.

360. Listen to and understand the future Śūdra clans called Diśakas (?) Svarapurañjaya will be the son of Śeṣa, the king of serpents (Vaidiśaka—residents of Vidiśā?).

361-362. That king, born of the race of serpents, will be a king who will enjoy. The following kings: Sadācandra who will be a part of the moon, Nakhavān the second, Dhanadharma the next one, Viṁśaja the fourth and Bhūtinanda thereafter, will be kings in the foreign land (or at Vidiṣā?)

363. At the close of the rule of Nandana of the Aṅgas, Madhunandi will become the king. His younger brother will be Nandiyaśas by name.

364-365. There will be three kings in his family: Dohitra, Śiśuka and Pravīra. Śiśuka will rule over Purikā. The powerful Pravīra will be the son of Vindhyaśakti, He will rule over the city Kāñcanaka (along with the others) for sixty years.

366. They will perform Vājapeya Yajñas with the offerings of excellent Dakṣiṇās. His four sons will become great rulers of men.

367. When the family of Vindhyakas becomes extinct, three kings of Bāhlīkas will enjoy the kingdom for thirty years. Supratīka and Nabhīra (will be the prominent kings).

368. The king named Śakyamā will be the ruler of Māhiṣīs. Puṣpamitras and Paṭṭamitras will rule for thirteen years.

369. Seven excellent kings will rule over Mekalā (Amarkaṇṭaka). The kings in Komalā (Comilla, Bengal) will be very strong and powerful.

370. Nine kings of great intellect and well known as Meghas will become the kings of the Niṣadha (Marwar, De 140) land. They will rule till the end of the Manvantara.

371. Those strong and powerful kings will be born in the race of Nala. Viśvasphāni, the powerful, will become the ruler of Magadhas.

372. After exterminating all the other kings he will make Kaivartas, Pañcakas, Pulindas and Brāhmaṇas as well as the other castes (rule over the kingdom).

373. He will establish kings in different lands, thanks to his excessive splendour. Viśvasphāni will be very powerful and strong in war like Viṣṇu.

374. It is said that in external appearance, Viśvasphāni will be like a eunuch. He will destroy the existing Kṣatriyas and make other Kṣatriya clans.

375. After propitiating Devas, Pitṛs and Brāhmaṇas many times that strong king will reach the banks of Jāhnavī (Gaṅgā) and cast off his body.

376. After forsaking his body, he will go to Śakra's region. Thereafter, the nine Nāka (Nāga) kings will enjoy the city of Campāvatī.

377. The seven Nāgas will enjoy the beautiful city of Mathurā.

Kings born of the family of Guptas[1] will enjoy all the territories near Gaṅgā such as Prayāga, Sāketa and Magadha.

378. The descendants of Maṇidhānya will enjoy the territories of Niṣadha, Yaduka, Śaiśīta and Kālatopaka.

379. Devarakṣitas (?) will enjoy the territories of Kośalas, Āndhras, Pauṇḍras and Tāmraliptas along with the oceans as well as the beautiful city of Campā.

380. Guha will protect Kaliṅgas, Mahiṣas, Mahendranilaya and other territories.

381. (The king) named Kanaka will enjoy Strīrāṣṭra (the women's territory, Kāmarūpa) and Bhakṣyakas. All these kings will be contemporaries.

382. Thereafter,[2] the untruthful and unrighteous Yavanas of great fury and of little grace will rule here spreading their religion, spending vast riches and giving vent to their lust.

383. Those kings will not be duly crowned. They will have all the defects of the (Kali) Age. They will commit evil actions.

384. During the remaining period of the Kali Age, the kings will enjoy the Earth, not even hesitating to kill women and children and to destroy one another.

385. The races of those kings will gain continuous ascendancy (at some time or in some places) or flourish and perish in succession in due course.

386. They will be devoid of piety, true love and real wealth. All the common people coming into close contact with them, too will follow the customs and habits of Mleccha (aliens and outcastes).

387. They will be acting contrary to accepted traditions.

---

1. Bd. P. v. 195 reads *Sapta* for *Gupta* hereof.

2. Verses 382-405 depict a gruesome picture of the advanced Kali Yuga. The description (including identical verses) are found in other Purāṇas as well. R.C. Hazra in *PRHRC* states that such was the actual condition of the people from 200 B.C. to 200 A.D.—the period in which these Purāṇas came to be composed.

They will destroy their subjects. The kings will be greedy and devoted to mendacious behaviour.

388-389. When their turn is over, women will outnumber men in that Age. People will become more and more deficient in learning and strength. Their span of life will grow less and less. When their decline reaches the limit the ruling kings overwhelmed by Kāla will be ruined.

390. Struck down by Kalki, all the Mlecchas will be destroyed. All the heretics and the unrighteous will be doomed.

391-393. The very name king will disappear when the Kali Age comes to the period of junction. Only very few people will survive and they will be helpless and destitute without any belonging, as Dharma would have been destroyed by that time. There will be none to console them. They will have no where-withals. They will be afflicted by diseases and sorrows. They will be overwhelmed and ruined by drought and mutual slaughter. They will have none to support them. Being distressed (and due to fear) they will forsake their avocations and professions. Deserting their own villages and towns they will resort to forest.

394-395. When the kings are destroyed, the subjects will leave off their homesteads. All the feelings of friendliness and affection will be lost. In acute distress, even the closest of friends will become bereft of affection. The discipline of castes and stages of life will become distrubed. Terrible mixture and mingling of the castes will result. People will take shelter on mountains and riverbanks.

396-397. They will resort to rivers, marshy foreshores of the seas and mountains. They will gather together in the territories of Aṅgas, Vaṅgas, Kaliṅgas, Kāśmīras, Kāśī, Kośalas, the mountain ravines of Ṛṣika and other places. Men will seek shelter on the ridges of Himavān and the coasts of the briny sea.

398. The Āryas will flock to the forests with the Mleccha tribes. Men will sustain themselves with the meat of deer, fishes, birds and beasts of prey as well as with sugar-cane plants, honey, greens, fruit and roots.

399. Like the sages (of yore) they will wear different kinds

of leaves and barks of trees as well as hides of deer which they themselves will make.

400. Desirous of growing foodstuffs (grains) through seeds, they will dig the earth deep with wooden pikes. They will strenuously rear goats and sheep, donkeys and camels.

401. The men then will resort to the banks of rivers for the sake of water. By means of their activities they will harass one another as well as the rulers of the land.

402. They will consider it honourable to be issueless. They will not observe rules of cleanliness and good behaviour. Then the men will be engrossed in evil actions and behave in this manner.

403. The subjects will follow the worst of religious observances. No one will live beyond their twentythird year.

404-405. They will be weak. They will be debilitated and fatigued due to sensuality. They will be overcome by (premature) old age. Their diet will consist of leaves, roots and fruits. Bark garments and deer skins will constitute their clothings. In search of livelihood they will be roaming over the earth. Towards the end of Kaliyuga, the people will come to such a plight.

406. When the Kali Age, the duration of which is a thousand divine years, comes to a close, the subjects will be annihilated along with the Kaliyuga. When it expires along with the period of junction, the Kṛta Age will come in.

407. When the moon, the sun, Tiṣya and Jupiter come together in a single sign of zodiac, the Kṛta Age will set in.

408. Thus the past, present and the future races have been enumerated in due order.

409-412. From the time of the coronation of Mahādeva* (Mahāpadma?) to the birth of Parīkṣit the duration was a thousand and fifty years. The period between Mahāpadma and the future kings ending with Āndhras whom I have narrated, has been calculated as eight hundred and thirtysix years by the learned sages, the knowers of Purāṇas.

**Mahānanda* in Bd. P. v. 227.

(Defective verse) The Seven Sages then said that a hundred years elapsed when Pratīpa was king (?) You should calculate twentyseven hundreds again (?)

413. The stellar mansions are altogether twentyseven. The Seven Sages stay in each of these, for hundred years in succession. This is remembered as the Yuga of the Seven Sages. The years are calculated according to those of the Devas.

414. (Defective verse) The hundred years of the Seven Sages are equal to sixty divine years and seven (divine) days.

415. (?) The Seven Sages are seen in the east at first and then in the north of the zone of the constellations. Thereafter they are seen parallel to those constellations seen in the middle of the firmament.

416. It should be known that the Seven Sages are united with it (the zone of the constellations) in the sky for a hundred years. This is the evidence of the union of the Sages and the constellations.

417. In my opinion the Seven Sages were stationed in the Maghā (tenth) constellation at the time of Parīkṣit. At the time of Andhras they will be in the twentyfourth constellation (i.e. Śatabhiṣak).*

418. At that time the subjects will be afflicted very much. They will be doomed through their mendacious nature in the affairs of virtue, wealth and love.

419. When the Vedic and Smārta (pertaining to the Smṛtis) rituals (Dharma) become lax and the rigorous discipline of the castes and the stages of life becomes very loose, the deluded subjects will be weak in their soul-power and undergo a mixing and mingling of the castes.

---

*The corresponding Bd. P. v. 230a reads :

saptarṣayas tadā prāptāḥ pitrye pārīkṣite śatam |

If the reading is accepted, the verse means : During the period of Parikṣit the Saptarṣis were in the Pitrya (Maghā) constellation for a hundred years. Hence the period of the dynasty of Āndhras will be two thousand and seven hundred years ? The words in our text need correction.

420. Śūdras will become merged with the twice-born castes. Brāhmaṇas will begin to officiate as priests in the Yajñas of the Śūdras. Śūdras will begin to compose Mantras.

421-423. Desirous of securing means of livelihood, Brāhmaṇas will approach them reverentially. Declining gradually and bit by bit, all the subjects will be destroyed and when the Yuga expires, they will be completely destroyed.

Kali Yuga had started on the very day when Kṛṣṇa passed away. Understand the duration of Kali Age. Kaliyuga is said to be of the three hundred and sixty thousand years according to human calculation.

424. According to divine calculation it is one thousand years. The Sandhyāṁśa (the period of junction) is also mentioned. (That period is extra.) When it has expired completely Kṛta Age comes in.

425. The races of Aila and Ikṣvāku are said to become extinct with Sumitra.

426-427. Those who know about the Lunar race know that the Kṣatriya race of Aila will become extinct with Kṣemaka. The sons and descendants of the Sun of the past, present and future have been glorified. They were and will be the heighteners of their fame. In that race there were Brāhmaṇas, Kṣatriyas, Vaiśyas and Śūdras.

428-429. Many noble-souled kings are born and have passed away in every Yuga. Their names are legion. When the members of every family are calculated, many names are repeated. Hence they have not been mentioned by me. The race of Nimi comes to an end in the Vaivasvata Manvantara itself.

430. I will recount how the Kṣatriya race originates in this Yuga. Even as I recount listen and understand.

431-432. Devāpi will be born in the Kalāpa village. He will be a king of Pūru's family and considered (greater) than Ikṣvāku. He will be endowed with great Yogic power.*

---

*The corresponding verse of Bd. P. (v. 250) states : Devāpi belonging to the family of Pūru and Maru who belongs to Ikṣvāku family—these two are endowed with great Yogic Power. They stayed in the village called Kalāpa."

Suvarcas, the son of Soma, will be born in the family of Ikṣvāku. In the twentyfourth cycle of four Yugas, they will be the founders of the Kṣatriya race and traditions.

433. In the twentieth Yuga (? cycle of four Yugas ?) there will not be any founder of the Lunar race. Devāpi being unrivalled, will be the first king in the family of Aila.

434. In the four Yugas these two will be the founders of Kṣatriya race. Everywhere this should be known as the characteristic feature, for the sake of progeny (the perpetuation of the line).

435-436. When Kali Yuga declines and Kṛta Yuga sets in and again in the first Tretāyuga they will be the activisors of the Kṣatriya lines along with the Seven Sages. In the Dvāpara period, Kṣatriyas do not stay along with the sages.

437-438. When Kṛtayuga and Tretāyuga decline, the Seven Sages and the kings will take birth for the sake of seed of the Brāhmaṇa and Kṣatriya races. For the sake of progeny, they (the Seven Sages) abide by the kings in all the Manvantaras in every Yuga.

439. The annihilation of Kṣatriyas leads to their contact with Brāhmaṇas again (?) In all the seven Manvantaras all the progeny have been heard of (?)

440-442. In view of their long life the Seven Sages know the series of Yugas, the origin, activities and the decline of those active persons belonging to Brāhmaṇa and Kṣatriya races. The birth of the Brāhmaṇas in the families of Aila and Ikṣvāku is in this manner (?) Born in the Tretā Age and extinct in the Kali Age, they will follow the Age till the end of the Manvantara.

443. When all the Kṣatriyas were eliminated by Rāma, the son of Jamadagni, the Kṣatriyas of the two families were born again. I shall recount them. Listen and understand.

444. The families of Aila and Ikṣvāku spread once again. A series of other kings of the Kṣatriya race became rulers.

445. A hundred families undergoing coronation became famous among each of the races of Aila and Ikṣvāku.

446. The extent of Bhojas is up to twice of that (i.e. two hundred). Thus there were three hundred Kṣatriya

families. They were divided into four according to the four quarters.

447-449. Listen and understand even as I recount the past and the present kings among them. Prativindhyas were a hundred; Nāgas were a hundred; Hayas were a hundred; Dhṛtarāṣṭras were a hundred and one; Janamejayas were eighty; Brahmadattas were a hundred; Śīrins and Vīrins were a hundred (each); then Pulomans were a hundred; Śvetas, Kāśas, Kuśas etc. were a hundred; the other Śaśabindus who passed away were a thousand.

450. All of them performed horse-sacrifices with lakhs and lakhs in Dakṣiṇā. Thus hundreds and thousands of saintly kings have passed away.

451-452. Know that the descendants in this world of the present Vaivasvata Manu cannot be mentioned in detail and in full even in hundreds of years.

453. In the Vaivasvata Manvantara already twentyeight cycles of four Yugas have passed along with their saintly kings. Listen and understand those who yet remain.

454-458. Forty excellent kings will be born in the future. Then the Vaivasvata Manvantara will come to a close. Incidentally I have mentioned everything in detail and in brief. Many are repeated. As they are too many they could not be mentioned in full. The twentyfive families of Yayāti's sons were highly beneficent to the people. They have been glorified. They even now sustain the worlds.

He who listens to and remembers these attains rare things of the world. They attain longevity, fame, wealth, sons, heaven and infiniteness. O Brāhmaṇas, thus the third section has been recounted by me. What more shall I say?

SECTION 4 : UPASAṀHĀRA PĀDA

CHAPTER THIRTYEIGHT

The Manvantaras & Dissolution of the Universe

1. After hearing the third section completed (narrated in full) by the intelligent Suta, the excellent sages asked him about the fourth Section.

The Sages said :

2. The third section called *Anuṣaṅga Pāda* has been completely narrated out of affection by you. Now narrate to us in details the fourth *Pāda* called *Saṁhāra* (annihilation or conclusion).

3-4. Please recount all the Manvantaras, the ones that had elapsed along with the others (the future ones), the Seven Sages who exist now in the current Manvantara and the details of the creation and expansion of the noble-souled Manu. Narrate everything in detail and in the proper order.

Sūta said :

5. O excellent sages I shall narrate everything to you precisely; the fourth and the concluding section, along with the (description of) annihilation.

6. O Brāhmaṇas, listen to the creative activity of the current noble-souled Vaivasvata Manu in detail as well as in proper order.

7. Even as I recount, listen and understand the gist of the (past) Manvantaras along with the seven future ones as well as the dissolution of the worlds.

8. All these (past) seven Manvantaras have already been recounted by me. Now listen to the brief description of the future Manvantaras from me.

9. I shall speak about the current Vaivasvata Manu and the future Sāvarṇa Manu briefly. Listen and understand.

10-12. The future Seven Great Sages are remembered as follows : Kuśika's descendant Gālava, Jamadagni's son Bhārgava (Paraśurāma), Dvaipāyana of Vasiṣṭha lineage, Kṛpa the descendant of Śaradvān, Dīptimān of Atri's lineage, Ṛṣyaśṛṅga of Kaśyapa's lineage, Droṇa's son Aśvatthāmā of great fame and belonging to Bhāradvāja Gotra—these noble-souled ones are the future Seven Great Sages.

13. There will be three groups of Devas, viz. Sutapas, Amitābhas and Sukhas (? Mukhyas). Each of these groups consists of twenty Devas.

14-15. I shall enumerate them. Listen and understand attentively. Rita, Tapas, Śukra, Dyuti, Jyotis, Prabhākara, Prabhāsa, Bhāsakṛt, Dharma, Tejas, Raśmi, Ṛtu, Virāṭ, Arciṣmān, Dyotana, Bhānu, Yaśas, Kīrti, Budha and Dhṛti—these twenty Devas constituting the group Sutapas, are glorified by their names.

16-17. Prabhu, Vibhu, Vibhāsa, Jetā, Hantā, Arihā, Ritu, Sumati, Pramati, Dīpti, Samākhyāta, Mahas, Mahān, Deha, Muni, Naya, Jyeṣṭha, Sama, Satya and Viśruta—these are the twenty Devas mentioned as Amitābhas.

18-19. Dama, Dātā, Vida, Soma, Vitta, Vaidya, Yama, Nidhi, Homa, Havya, Huta, Dāna, Deya, Dātā, Tapas, Sāma, Dhruva, Sthāna, Vidhāna and Niyama—these twenty are mentioned as constituting the Mukhya (Sukha) group of Devas in the first Sāvarṇa Manvantara.

20. All these are the sons of the noble-souled Kaśyapa, the son of Marīci who exists now. They will be born in the Sāvarṇa Manvantara.

21-22. He who was formerly Bali, the son of Virocana, will become their Indra. Nine sons will be born to Sāvarṇa Manu, viz. Vīravān, Avarīyān, Nirmoha, Satyavāk, Kṛti, Cariṣṇurājya, Viṣṇu, Vāca and Sumati.

23-24. I shall mention nine more in the other Sāvarṇa Manvantaras. Other Sāvarṇa Manus will be born as Brahmā's (future) sons. They are seen as Merusāvarṇis by those endowed with divine vision. They are the grandsons of Dakṣa, the sons of his beloved daughter.

25. They are endowed with great penance and great splendour. They live on the ridges of Meru. They are procreated by Brahmā and other (Devas) as well as by the intelligent Dakṣa.

26. They were born in the previous Cākṣuṣa Manvantara. These noble persons had been in the Maharloka. After returning from there they will resort to Meru.

The Sages said :

27. How were the sons procreated by Dakṣa in his own daughter? How were they created by Bhava, Dharma and Brahmā the noble souls?

Sūta said :

28. After bowing to Pracetas, henceforth, I shall mention the future Manus who are the Sāvarṇa Manus, their origin as well as their prowess.

29. When a short period of Cākṣuṣa Manvantara remained and the Vaivasvata Manvantara had begun, those who will be the Manus in the future Manvantara were born.

30. Of those Manus who are the daughter's sons of Prācetasa Dakṣa, the five named Sāvarṇas and four are born from great sages.

31. One Sāvarṇa is the son of Saṁjñā born of Vivasvān (the Sun-god). The eldest son of Saṁjñā is Lord Manu, son of the Sun-god (Vivasvān)

32. Their auspicious manifestation was (took place) at the advent of the Vaivasvata Manvantara. The fourteen Manus are glorified as the enhancer of fame.

33. These Manus are described in the Vedas, Śrutis* and Purāṇas as very powerful Prajāpatis. All of them were the lords of all living beings.

34. The entire Earth consisting of the seven continents and mountains is to be protected by these kings for a full thousand Yugas.

35. Their details will be mentioned along with their progeny

*Smṛtis in Bd. P. v. 30.

and penance. These creations of Svāyaṁbhuva and others should be known as fourteen.

36. They hold office as the presiding Authorities in the Manvantaras only once each. After the tenure of their office they resort to Maharloka.

37. (Defective verse) Among them eight have already ceased to operate; (excepting) six more Manus are the others who will come in the future. At present it is Lord Vaivasvata Manu who rules.

38. I shall mention those who remain, those who are the future Brāhmaṇas (Manus), along with Devas, Dānavas and sages as well as their (other) creation of the subjects.

39. The details of the creation of these Manus are to be known through the creative activity of Vaivasvata Manu, since they are neither inferior nor superior to those of Vaivasvata Manu.

40. I am not recounting their details for fear of repetition and due to their multiplicity in both the past and the future Manvantaras.

41. I shall mention them, the creative activities in the different families only partially. The remaining things should be known through their details and in order.

42. Dakṣa had a pious daughter who was well known as Suvratā. Although she was the youngest of the daughters, she was the most excellent and the most pious. Once the father took her with him and approached Brahmā.

43. He was in the Vairāja region seated along with Dharma and Bhava. Brahmā spoke to Dakṣa in the presence of Dharma and Bhava.

44. "O Dakṣa, this, your daughter Suvratā will give birth to four sons who will become the auspicious Manus and stabilise the discipline of four castes."

45. On hearing the words of Brahmā, the three—Dakṣa, Dharma and Bhava approached that girl mentally along with Brahmā.

46. The girl immediately gave birth to four sons who were similar to and befitting those four divine personages as they were of truthful meditation.

47. Those sons were born fully endowed with physical bodies, born in a trice but capable of all enjoyment, and competent to perform all activities. They were endowed with glory.

48. On seeing them, those deities who had realised Brahman began to claim "This is my son, This is my son". They began to tug at them furiously.

49. Since they mentally created sons through meditation, they said to one another : "Let us select that boy as our respective son who is similar to us physically.

50. If a boy is similar to one in features, prowess and name as well as complexion, one shall take him as one's gentle son.

51. A son emulates the features of his father invariably. Hence the son is born taking after the father and the mother."

52-53. After coming to terms like this, they took those boys who were similar in complexion (*Savarṇa*) to them. Since the boys were similar in complexion to god Brahmā and others, they are called Sāvarṇa. Since they were meditated upon and were accepted respectfully, they are remembered as Manus.

54. When the Cākṣuṣa Manvantara expired and the Vaivasvata Manvantara set in, a son named Raucya was born to Ruci, the Prajāpati.

55. He who was born of Bhūti became known by the name Bhautya. In the Vaivasvata Manvantara two sons were born to Vivasvān.

56. One is well known as Vaivasvata Manu and the other as Sāvarṇa. The learned Lord Vaivasvata Manu was the eldest son of Saṁjñā.

57-58. The other Vaivasvata Manu was the son of Sāvarṇa (i.e. Chāyā, the shadow of Saṁjñā). The four Sāvarṇa Manus born of the great sages will be equipping themselves with (the power of) penance. They will achieve all their tasks in their respective future Manvantaras.

59. (Defective verse) The sons of the first Merusāvarṇi Manu who was the son of Dakṣa were the three groups, Marīcigarbhas, Suśarmans and Pāras. All these noble-souled ones were born in the Vaivasvata Manvantara.

60. They are the sons of Rohita, the Prajāpati, the son of Dakṣa. In future each of these groups will consist of twelve Devas.

61. (Defective) Aiśvarya-Saṅgrāha, Rāha, Bāhuvaśa (and the remaining) should be known as twelve Pāra gods. Understand the later ones.

62-63. Vājiya, Vājijit, Prabhūti, Kakudī (?), Dadhikrāva, Ayapakva, Praṇīta, Vijaya, Madhu, Tejasmān and two Nathavas—these twelve constitute the Marīcis. I shall recount the Suśarmans mentioning the names. Listen to (them) and understand.

64-65. Varṇa, Aṅga, Viśva, Muraṇya, Vrajana, Amita, Dravaketu, Jambhostha, Ajasra, Śakraka, Sunemi and Dyutapas—these twelve constitute Suśarmans. Their future Indra will be known by the name Adbhuta.

66-69. The seven sages in the Rohita Manvantara were—Skanda of fiery nature and resembling Soma and otherwise known as Kārtikeya, Medhātithi of Pulastya lineage, Vasu of Kaśyapa Gotra, Jyotiṣmān of Bhṛgu family, Dyutimān of Aṅgiras lineage, Vasita of Vasiṣṭha Gotra, Havyavāhana of Atri's Gotra and Sutapas of Paulava family.

The following nine are glorified as the sons of the first Sāvarṇi—Dhṛtiketu, Dīptiketu, Śāpa, Hasta, Niramaya, Pṛthuśravas, Anīka, Bhūridyumna, and Bṛhadratha.

70-71. In the tenth revolution (i.e. cycle of four Yugas?) the second Sāvarṇi, the son of Dharma, will be the Manu. In his Manvantara, there will be two groups of Devas, viz. Sukhāmanas and Viruddhas. All of them will be Tviṣivants ('highly effulgent') a hundred in number and mutually equal(?)—alike.

72. They are said to be controlling the breath in (other ?) persons by the sages. They will be the Devas at the time of the Manu, son of Dharma.

73-74. Their Indra will be the great scholar Śānti. The Seven Great Sages will be the glorious Haviṣmān of the Pulaha family, Sukīrti of Bhṛgu race, Āpomūrti of Atri lineage, Āpava (?) of Vasiṣṭha family, Pratipa of Pulastya family, Nābhāga of Kaśyapa family and Abhimanyu of Aṅgiras family.

75-77. The ten sons of Manu will be—Sukṣetra, Uttamaujas, Bhūriṣeṇa, Vīryavān, Śatānīka, Nirāmitra, Vṛṣasena, Jayadratha, Bhūridyumna and Suvarcas. In the eleventh revolution (cycle of four Yugas) when the third Sāvarṇi will be the Manu, the following three groups of noble-souled Devas will be famous : Nirmāṇaratis, Kāmajas (Kāmagas in Bd.P.) and Manojavas.

78-80. Each of these groups consists of thirty units. The thirty days in a month mentioned by the poets constitute the Devas Nirmāṇaratis. The nights (known as ?) Vihaṅgamas (constitute the Kāmaja Devas). The Muhūrtas constitute the Devas Manojavas. These are the three groups of Devas mentioned. These future Manus are remembered as the sons of Brahmā.

81. Their Indra, the king of Suras, will be called Vṛṣa. Listen and understand their Seven Sages who are being glorified.

82-86. They are—Haviṣmān of Kaśyapa family, Vapuṣmān of Bhṛgu's race, Vāruṇi of Atri lineage, Bhaga of Vasiṣṭha's family, Puṣṭi who should be known as hailing from Aṅgiras family, Niścara of Pulastya race and Agnitejas of Pulaha family. They are also the Devas in the eleventh Manvantara. The following are the sons of Prājāpatya (son of Prajāpati) Sāvarṇa Manu—Sarvavega, Sudharmā, Devānīka, Purovaha, Kṣemadharmā, Gṛheṣu, Ādarśa and Pauṇḍraka.

In the twelfth revolution (Manvantara) Ṛtusāvarṇi, the son of Rudra, will be the Manu. He will be the fourth Sāvarṇi. Listen to the Devas in that Manvantara. The future Devas are said to consist of five groups.

87. The Devas will be—Haritas, Rohitas, Sumanas, Sukarmans and Supāras. These are remembered as the five groups of Devas.

88-89. They are the mental sons of Brahmā. Each of these groups consists of ten Devas. The following ten constitute the Harita group of Devas : Aruntija, Hari (? Havi), Vidvān (whose followers are) in thousands, Parvatānucara, Āpas, Aṁśu (prob. Apāṁśu as in Bd.P.), Manojava, Urja, Svāhā, Svadhā and Tārā.

90-91. The following ten constitute the Rohita group:

Tapas, Jāni, Bhṛti, Vācā, Bandhu, Rajas, Rāja, Svarṇapāda, Vyuṣṭi and Vidhi. Know these to be the Sumanas: the thirty-three Devas who have been glorified (before), viz. Uṣita and others.

92-93. Understand the Sukarmans. They are—Suparvā, Vṛṣabha, Pṛṣṭa, Kṛpi, Dyumna, Vipaścita, Vikrama, Karma, Nibhṛta and Kānta. These Devas are Sukarmans. Now understand their sons (i.e. Supāras ?)

94-95. They are : Varyodita, Jiṣṭa, Varcasvī, Dyutimān, Havi, Śubha, Havikṛta, Prāpti, Vyāpṛtha and Daśama (?) These are the mentally created ones the Supāras, the Devas mentioned (before). Ṛtadhāmā of great fame should be known as their Indra.

96-99. The Seven Sages are—Kṛti the son of Vasiṣṭha, Sutapas of Atri's family, Tapomūrti of the Aṅgiras race, Tapasvin of Kaśyapa Gotra, Tapośyāna of Pulastya family, Taporati of Pulaha Gotra and the seventh of them should be known as Tapomati of Bhṛgu family. These are the Siddhas, the Seven Sages in the Sāvarṇika Manvantara. The following are the sons of the twelfth (?) Manu : Devavān, Upadeva, Devaśreṣṭha, Vidūratha, Mitravān, Mitrabindu, Mitrasena, Amitrahā, Mitrabāhu, and Suvargas.

100. In the thirteenth revolution (Manvantara), the Raucya Manvantara, three groups of Devas are mentioned by the self-born deity (Brahmā).

101. All those noble souls are Brahmā's mental sons. They are Sutrāmans, Sudharmans and Sukarmans.

102-103. They are said to be the future Somapāyins (Imbibers of Soma juice), the groups of Devas. Along with the performers of Yajñas, the deities are thirtythree in number. They include the Ājya, Pṛṣadājya and Grahajyeṣṭha groups of Devas. Listen to and understand that the thirtythree Devas are separate ones.

104-105. The Sutrāmans are the present Prayājyas and Ājyapas. The Anuyājyas and those who partake Pṛṣadājya are Sukarmans. The Upayājyas are Sudharmans. Thus the Devas have been recounted. Divaspati of great prowess will be their Indra.

106-109. The sons of Ruci should be known as the grandsons of Pulaha. The Seven Sages in the thirteenth Manvantara will be—Dhṛtimān of Aṅgiras family, Pathyavān of Pulastya race, Tattvadarśin of Pulaha family, Nirutsaka of Bhṛgu Gotra, Niṣprakaṁpa of Atri's family, Nirmoha of Kaśyapa Gotra and Svarūpa of Vasiṣṭha lineage. The following are the sons of Raucya Manu in the thirteenth Manvantara : Citrasena, Vicitra, Tapas, Dharmadhṛta, Bhava, Anekabaddha, Kṣatrabaddha, Surasa, Nirbhaya and Pṛtha.

110. In the fourteenth Bhautya Manvantara, the future groups of Devas are five.

111. The five groups of Devas are—Cākṣuṣas, Kaniṣṭhas, Pavitras, Bhājaras and Vācāvṛddhas.

112-113. Know that the seven different parts are those named Cākṣuṣas. They understand Bṛhada and other Sāmans as the Kaniṣṭhas. The seven worlds are Paritras (Pavitras ?) The Bhājiras (Bhājaras) are the seven Sindhus (oceans, rivers). Know the sages to be Vācāvṛddhas belonging to Svāyaṁbhuva Manu (?) All the Indras of the Manvantaras should be known as having equal characteristics (and powers).

114. Those Indras excel all the mobile and the immobile living beings in the three worlds by means of their splendour, penance, intellect, strength, learning and exploits.

115. The Indras (or Devas) are Bhūtāpavādins, Hṛṣṭas, Medhyasthas, Bhūtavādins, Bhūtānuvādins. The three Vedas are competent in respect to *Pravādins* (arguers ?)

116. Agnidhra, Kāśyapa, Paulastya, Māgadha, Bhārgava, Agnibāhu, Śuci, Āṅgirasa, Ojasvin, and Subala are the sons of Bhautya Manu.

117. All these four Sāvarṇa Manus are the sons of Brahmā. One Sāvarṇa Manu is called the son of Vivasvān.

118. Raucya and Bhautya, these two Manus belong to Pulaha and Bhṛgu families. While Bhautya rules over, the Kalpa becomes complete.

Sūta said :

119. When all things are dissolved completely, when all the Manvantaras come to a close and many Yugas pass on, it is called *Saṁhāra* (Annihilation).

120-122. Then, at the end of the Manvantara, the seven Devas of the Bhṛgu family, the powerful sovereign rulers, who had enjoyed the three worlds for seventyone cycles of four Yugas by remaining within them, and who used to perform Yajñas along with the Pitṛs, Manus and the Seven Sages will then abandon the three worlds and go to Maharloka along with their devotees and those who perform Yajñas. When they proceed upwards, and when the Manvantara expires, all the three worlds will be rendered without any support.

123. O Brāhmaṇas ! Thereafter, the abodes presided over by deities become vacant and fall down along with constellations, stars and planets getting hurled and destroyed.

124-125. Thereafter, when the lords of the three worlds including the eight Indras pass away, the fourteen groups of Devas beginning with (A)jita and others and ending with Cākṣuṣas—the Devas who were very mighty and full of splendour in all the Manvantaras—will go to Maharloka where they will become identical with those Devas who stay there till the end of the Kalpa.

126-127. It is reported that when the time of *Saṁhāra* (lit. heaping and collision—*Saṅkalana*) comes those fourteen groups of Devas will forsake Maharloka and go to Janaloka with (i.e. preserving) their physical bodies and accompanied by their followers.

128-129. Thus when the Devas have gone from Maharloka to Janaloka, when *Bhūtādi* (Cosmic Ego—*Ahaṁkāra*) and other (prime causes of the universe) remain and (even) immobiles have come to an end, when the abodes of the worlds beginning with Bhūḥ and ending with Mahaḥ have become void, when the Devas have gone upward and become united with the Kalpavāsins (those who stay till the end of the Kalpa),

130. after withdrawing (annihilating) those Devas, Sages, Pitṛs and Dānavas, god Brahmā with his powerful vision sees that it is the end of the Yuga and puts an end to his creation.

131. The knowers of day and night of god Brahmā understand that the day of Brahmā consists of a thousand cycles of four Yugas and similarly the night too consists of a thousand cycles of four Yugas.

132. This *Pratisañcara* (Dissolution & Reabsorption) of all

living beings is of three types, viz. *Naimittika* (periodical), *Prākṛtika* (pertaining to Prakṛti) and *Ātyantika* (the ultimate one).

133. The *Naimittika* dissolution is the burning (of the Universe) at the end of the Kalpa and complete withdrawal (of all beings) by god Brahmā. The destruction of Karaṇas (instruments or means and causes) of living beings during *Pratisarga* (absorption) into Prakṛti is called Prākṛta type of dissolution.

134. The dissolution due to dawning of spiritual knowledge is said to be the ultimate one (*Ātyantika*) as it renders the seeds (causes) of Saṁsāra, impossible.

135. After dissolving all the Devas residing in the three worlds at the end of his day and when he feels the urge to sleep (?), Lord Brahmā destroys all the subjects and dissolves all the creation.

136. Then at the end of a thousand cycles of *Caturyugas*, when the period of annihilation of Yuga arrives, Prajāpati (Lord of subjects, viz. Brahmā) begins to make the subjects abide in him (i.e. absorb in himself).

137-138. Then a drought sets in lasting for a hundred years. Those living beings on the surface of the Earth, (still left) being deficient in strength become dissolved and are merged into the Earth. The Sun then rises up with seven rays constituting his chariot.

139. Lord Sun of unbearable rays begins to suck up water through his rays. Those seven rays will be green in colour and of dazzling lustre.

140. Spreading over the forest ('the sky'—Bd.P.) gradually they get transformed again. The wood over the earth, wealth and refulgence begin to blaze with water (?)

141. Hence it is water that is said to be the cause of the blazing of the Sun. With drought the Sun does not blaze. With drought the Sun has no halo (?)

142. With drought the rays of the Sun do not pick up things (from the ground). The Sun blazes with water. Hence, sucking up water, the Sun blazes in the sky.

143. His seven rays suck up water from the great ocean. With that as his diet, the single Sun proliferates into seven Suns.

144. Then those seven rays assuming the forms of seven Suns, burn the four quarters and the four worlds like fires.

145. The fiery rays reach the top and bottom (of the worlds). Seven Suns and the blazing fires of dissolution shine fiercely.

146. Ignited and illuminated by means of the water, thousands of rays envelop the sky and scorch the Earth.

147. Being burnt by their blazing heat, the Earth inclusive of the oceans and the mountains becomes bereft of moisture and viscidity.

148. The nether regions, the upper regions and the sides are restrained by the illuminated rays of the Sun of various colours and spreading everywhere.

149. The scorching rays of the Sun and the leaping flames of the fires mingling with one another appear to be a single unit with a single flame.

150. That fire becomes a mass of fiery zone creating the destruction of all the worlds. With its brilliance it scorches all the four worlds.

151. All the mobile and the immobile beings get dissolved. The Earth, devoid of trees and even grass, appears like the back of a tortoise shell.

152. The entire universe destroyed and affected by misfortune appears like a frying pan. The whole of the sky, filled with the burning rays, blazes fiercely.

153. All the living beings in the nether worlds and in the great ocean become dissolved and one with the Earth.

154. The continents, mountains, sub-continents, the great oceans—all these will be reduced to ashes by that cosmic fire, the soul of everything.

155. The excessively kindled fire sucks up water from everywhere, the oceans, the rivers and the nether worlds. Spreading over the Earth it blazes up.

156. Then the big Saṁvartaka fire (the fire of dissolution) transcends the mountains and destroys all the worlds. It becomes a terribly kindled fire.

157. It then pierces through the Earth and dries up Rasātala. After burning up Pātālas it burns down the world of serpents.

158. After burning the Earth from below, it burns the firmament above spreading through thousands, lakhs and trillions of Yojanas.

159. Many flames leap out from that Saṁvartaka fire. Glowing fiercely the Saṁvartaka fire consumes Gandharvas, Piśācas, the great serpents and Rākṣasas. Everything is reduced to a huge globular mass (of ashes).

160. The deadly fire thus burns all the four worlds, viz. Bhūrloka, Bhuvarloka, Svarloka and Maharloka in a terrible manner.

161. When all the worlds are enveloped with fire on all sides and above, the entire universe is slowly permeated with brilliance and shines like a (red hot) ball of iron.

162. Thereafter the terrible Saṁvartaka clouds begin to rise in the sky. They assume the shapes of the herds of huge elephants and are embellished with lightning streaks.

163. Some are dark-coloured like the blue lotus. Some are like the white lilies, some resemble *lapis lazuli* and others are like emerald and sapphire.

164. Others are (white) like the conch shell and the *kunda* flowers. Some are (black) like the natural collyrium. Some clouds are smoke-coloured and some clouds are yellow.

165. Some clouds have the (grey) colour of a donkey, some resemble the red lac, others have the lustre of the red arsenic and there are dove-coloured clouds.

166. Some glow-worm-coloured clouds rise up in the sky; some are as vast as the expansive cities and the Earth and some are as huge as herds of elephants.

167. Some clouds are like mountains and some are like rocky regions. Some resemble large basins and some huge shoals of fish.

168. Terrific in appearance and multi-formed, all those clouds thundering terribly, fill the entire firmament at that time (of dissolution).

169. Then the terrific fresh clouds identifying themselves with the Suns, organise themselves in seven groups and extinguish the fire.

170. The clouds then shower energetically and quell the entire inauspicous and terrible fire.

171. The universe is filled with waters of the heavy downpour. The brilliance of the burning fire is overcome by the waters and the fire enters (i.e. merges) into water.

172. When in the course of a hundred years the whole fire is quelled, the clouds that arise from the fire inundate the entire universe with huge quantities of showers.

173. Urged by the self-born deity (Brahmā), they fill the universe with their showers. Others assail the sea-shore with large quantities of water. The entire Earth with its continents and mountains is covered with water.

174. O Brāhmaṇas, the entire quantity of water showered by the clouds enters the ocean. There it is sucked up by the rays of the Sun.

175. The water sucked up by the rays of the Sun clings to the clouds. It falls again on to the Earth whereby the oceans are filled up.

176. Then the oceans overflow their shores all round. Mountains crumble down and the Earth sinks into the water.

177. Whirling up suddenly, a violent wind of terrible nature envelops all those clouds in the sky.

178. In that *Ekārṇava* (a single vast sheet of water) all the mobile and the immobile beings get dissolved. When a thousand cycles of four Yugas pass away, it is called a complete Kalpa.

179. Learned men call this vast sheet of water whereby the entire world is enveloped, *Ekārṇava*. All separate entities are lost sight of. Neither the surface of the Earth, nor the atmosphere, neither the wind nor the firmament is visible distinctly.

180. Objects of *Pārthiva* (Earthly) nature, waters of the ocean and all *Haima* (i.e. of the elements of fire, Gold standing for Tejas) objects form one unit termed *Salila* (water).

181. When only water is seen flowing hither and thither it is called *Salila*. When it stands covering the whole Earth, that (mass of) water is called *Arṇava* (an ocean).

182-183. The word *Bhā* indicates *Vyāpti* (pervasion) and *Dipti* (splendour). Since water shines and pervades all the ashes (of the universe) it is called *Ambaḥ*. The root √*Ar* means multiplicity and quickness. In that *Ekārṇava* waters are not quick. Hence they are called "Narās".

184. At the end of that period of a thousand sets of four Yugas, one day of Brahmā passes off. During the whole of that period the entire universe becomes sub-merged in the *Ekārṇava*. All the activities of Prajāpati (Brahmā) cease (to exist).

185-186. When in that *Ekārṇava* the mobile and the immobile beings become annihilated, Brahmā assumes this form—with thousand eyes, thousand feet, thousand heads, beautiful mind, thousand legs, thousand eyes and faces, thousand speeches (tongues), thousand arms and the lustre of the Sun. He is called the first Prajāpati and the Puruṣa in the path of Trayī (three Vedas).

187. He has brilliant complexion like the Sun. He is the protector of the worlds. He is single and the first *Turāṣāṭ* (forestaller of the enemies). He becomes Hiraṇyagarbha, the great Puruṣa. He goes beyond the darkness (of ignorance).

188. At the end of the period of a thousand cycles of four Yugas when everything around is flooded with water, the lord becomes desirous of sleep and creates a dark night without light.

189. When Brahmā lies down with the four types of creation withdrawn in the *Aṇḍa* (Cosmic Egg), the Seven Great Sages see that noble-souled Kāla (god of Time or Death).

190. At that time they move about in Janaloka. By means of penance they have gained (divine) vision. They are the noble souls—Bhṛgu and others. Their characteristics have already been recounted by me.

191. With their divine vision only they see the seven worlds—Satya and others. They visualize Brahmā during the great nights of Brahmā.

192. The Seven Sages see him at the time of his sleep. He is cited to be the first Parameṣṭhin, because he stays beyond all Kalpas.

193. In the beginning of every Kalpa, he becomes the creator of all living beings again and again. After withdrawing all creations within himself Prajāpati (creates them again).

194. The excessively brilliant one, the creator of everything takes (withdraws) everything into himself and thereafter stays within the single vast sheet of water for the whole of that night.

195. Then, when the night passes off, Prajāpati wakes up. He is induced (in his mind) with the desire for creation once again.

196-198. At the time of the *Naimittika* (periodic) dissolution (by Brahmā), when Prajāpati grows calm, in the course of withdrawal effected all the living beings get separated from their bodies. All the Bhūtas become burnt by the rays of the Sun; even gods, sages and the excellent Manus (are affected by it in that water of flood.). In that collision all the living beings beginning with Gandharvas and ending with Piśācas who have not been scorched in the beginning of the Kalpa resort to Janaloka.

199. The living beings of the lower strata of animals and those that have fallen into hell—all those become burnt up and get absolved from sins. As long as the universe is submerged in water, they abide in Janaloka.

200. When the night of Brahmā whose source of origin is the Unmanifest, dawns again all those living beings are born again.

201. The sages, Manus, Devas and all the four kinds of living beings (are alike in this respect). Those Siddhas too die and are born.

202. Just as the Sun is rising and setting in this world (it happens regularly), so also the living beings are seen to have birth and destruction.

203-205. The rebirth after the dissolution of all living beings is called Saṁsāra (worldly existence). Just as all living beings (e.g. trees) germinate after the rains fall, so also the subjects and the immobile and other beings are born in every Kalpa. Just as in successive seasons the different forms of the characteristics of the seasons appear in the same succession as before, so also at the time of (every) creation the mobile and the immobile beings (appear in the same manner as they were) before Brahmā's nights and the dissolutions.

206. All the living beings come out and re-enter the creator of subjects, Brahmā, the great lord, Prajāpati of great Yogic power.

207. The great Deva who is both manifest and unmanifest

becomes the creator of all living heings again and again in the beginnings of the Kalpas. The entire universe is his.

208. It is he by whom the waters are created at first, the waters that reach the surface of the earth along the path taken before.

209. Just as mortal beings revolve through those (*Yonis* or births) due to their auspicious and inauspicious activities, so they move upwards and downwards due to the (pull of) the Sun, as transfer from one body to another is inevitable.

210. [1]So also Devas, Manus, Prajeśas and other Siddhas who have attained heaven naturally assume the forms of righteous living beings on being subjected to the inevitable future.

211. Henceforth, I shall recount the period of dissolution of all living beings (*Ābhūtasaṁplava*). O Brāhamaṇas, the Manvantaras have already been explained by me along with Prajñānisarga[2] (creation through intellect.) and the fourteen Manus.

212. All the Manvantaras consist of a thousand cycles of four Yugas. When two thousand cycles of four Yugas are completed it is said that a Kalpa is finished entirely.

213. This should be known as one day of Brahmā. Understand its calculation. The time taken to utter a short syllable or to wink once is called Nimeṣa. It is equal to a Mātrā.

214. Fifteen such Nimeṣas of human beings constitute one Kāṣṭhā. One Lava is equal to five Kṣaṇas and twenty Kāṣṭhās constitute three Lavas

215. According to another calculation seven and a half measures (*Prasthas*) of water constitute a Lava.[3] Thirty Lavas should be known as a Kalā and thirty Kalās, one Muhūrta.

216. Thirty such Muhūrtas make one day and one night or nine hundred Kalās make one day and one night.[4]

---

1. Obscure. So is the corresponding text in Bd. P.3.41.207.
2. *Prajānisarga* 'creation of subjects' in Bd.P.v.209.
3. Perhaps it indicates that the time taken by so much of water to drip through the hole in the mechanical device used to calculate time, is one *Lava*.
4. The reading here of *vyadhikāni śatāni ṣaṭ* should be emended as *tryadhikāni* etc. meaning 'six (hundred) increased by three hundred'.

217. The movement of the Moon and the Sun should be known by counting these: Fifteen Nimeṣas make one Kāṣṭhā. Thirty Kāṣṭhās make one Kalā.

218. Thirty Kalās make one Muhūrta. Some say that Kalā is a tenth part of a Muhūrta. Forty Kalās are termed (by others) one Muhūrta.

219-220. Muhūrtas and Lavas are determined (thus) by those who know the measure. (Instead of the above) through water also time is measured. Thirteen Palas of water make a Prastha according to the calculation current in Magadha. Four Prasthas of water make one Nālika Ghaṭa (a jar with a tube fitted in).

221. The bottom plate of the device is four Aṅgulas square. There are four holes in it, each of the size of a golden *māṣa* (the pulse, black gram). Two Nālika Ghaṭas of water flow through those holes in the period of a Muhūrta. It is the same both in the day and in the night.

222-223. Thanks to the special movement of the Sun, the maximum number of Kalās is six hundred and five in all the Ṛtus always. This is to be known as one human day. The Stellar day contains ten more. A human year is calculated through Sāvana months.

224. It is decided in the scripture that a human year is one day and one night for the Devas. Through this day, the months, Ayanas and years should be calculated.

225. Knowledge of this is arrived at by this method. The terms given are only indicative. Since Kalā constitutes the basic unit time is mentioned as Kāla.

226. One day of Brahmā is constituted by ten million two hundred and ninety thousand divine years.

227. On hearing this, the sages were very much surprised. They asked Sūta thereafter to make their knowledge clearer numerically.

The Sages said:

228. We wish to hear the magnitude of the period of dissolution on the basis of human calculation, briefly, consisting of small words and syllables.

229. On hearing their words, lord Vāyu endowed with divine attributes, and celestial vision and engaged in the welfare of the worlds spoke in brief.

230. "The day and the night of Brahmā have already been mentioned. I shall now mention their duration based on worldly calculation.

231-233a. According to human calculation, four hundred and thirtytwo crores eight millions nine hundred and eighty thousand (4328980000) human years constitute the period of dissolution.

233b-236. Then seven Suns rise up. All the four types of creations become merged in the great elements of the worlds. The universe is flooded with water. All the mobile and the immobile beings are destroyed. After completing the annihilation Prajāpati becomes quiescent. When everything is burnt, light vanishes and everything is surrounded by nocturnal darkness. The entire vast sheet of water is then presided over by Īśvara. The duration of the period of *Ekārṇava* is the same as that of the day of the lord. The period of night is as long as everything is submerged in water. When that recedes, it is remembered as day.

237. The night and day of Brahmā succeed each other. This successive period of night and day of the lord is what is called *Ābhūtasaṁplava*.

238. It is called *Ābhūtasaṁplava* because whatever living beings there be whether mobile or immobile in the entire range of three worlds upto the elements (*bhūtas*) become merged.

239. (Another explanation) Prajāpati is called *Bhūta* because he exists at the very outset before all the subjects and creations. Everything floats and merges in *Bhūta*. Therefore the the final dissolution is called *Ābhūtasaṁplava*.

240. The word *Ābhūtasaṁplava* is also used in the sense of permanency and deathlessness (?) The past, present and future subjects are calculated up to *Aparārdha** (infinite number) by means of divine number.

241. The maximum longevity (of Brahmā) is mentioned as twice Parārdha. This much is the period of stay of Aja (the

*Probably the reading is 'ā-parārdha' upto Parārdha—vide v. 241.

unborn) Prajāpati. At the end of the stay of Brahmā, Parameṣṭhin, there is the *Pratisarga* (secondary creation).

242. Just as the flame of a lamp is blown out by the gust of wind, so also Brahmā becomes quiescent as a result of the Pratisarga.

243. (Defective) The principles beginning with *Mahat* become withdrawn in the great Īśvara; Mahat merges into the Unmanifest and all the three Guṇas attain equilibrium.

244-245. Thus *Ābhūtasaṁplava* has been recounted by me briefly. This withdrawal by complete merging in water is a periodic (*Naimittika*) reabsorption in relation to Brahmā. What more shall I tell you?

He who always retains this in memory, he who listens to this frequently, shall attain great Siddhi as a result of glorification and listening attentively."

CHAPTER THIRTYNINE

Worlds from Maharloka to Śiva's City[1]

Vāyu said :

1-6. Those Brāhmaṇas of acute discernment, who are of extra-ordinary good behaviour, who subsist on the residue of what is consigned to sacred fire in *Homa*, and who maintain special piety, become the residents of *Maharloka* along with Devas.

The fourteen Manus, the increasers of fame who had been glorified before, and who belong to the past, present and the future, are born here again and again along with sages, Devas, Gandharvas and Rākṣasas and take up their duties in the Manvantaras.

---

1. This chapter corresponds to Bd. P. 3.4.2. Only verse numbers from it are mentioned for reference. The chapter is an epitome of *Bhuvana Kośa*.

Devas, Seven Sages, Manus and Pitṛs pass away gradually and resort to Maharloka along with the righteous Brāhmaṇas, Kṣatriyas and Vaiśyas. They are accompanied by those who perform truthful actions, who are faithful and devoid of arrogance and who regularly maintain Vedic and Smārta rites and who maintain the rigorous discipline of Varṇas and Āśramas. Afterwards when the period of a Manvantara expires, they cease to operate in their offices (and go to Maharloka).

The Sages said :

7-8. O Powerful Mātariśvan (Wind-god), of what nature is that world which has been called Maharloka by you? In every world many (meritorious souls) will be presiding. Hence, O Lord, recount to us with pleasure, how many are those worlds and how they are burnt (if at all). You alone know this precisely.

9. On being requested thus by those disciplined-souled sages, Vāyu, the knower of reality, spoke these sweet and truthful words.

Vāyu said:

10. There are only fourteen abodes called *Lokas*[1] (worlds) described by great sages and (meritorious men) stay therein.

11-12. They call seven of them *Kṛtas* and the other seven *Akṛtas*. The seven worlds, enumerated as Bhūḥ etc. are the *Kṛtas*. The seven *Akṛtas* are the Prākṛta ones (created by

1. Verses 10-48 describe the seven *Lokas* (worlds), viz. (1) Bhūr, (2) Bhuvar, (3) Svar, (4) Mahar, (5) Jana, (6) Tapas and (7) Satya. The location of 1-4 is (1) the Earth, (2) the space between the Earth and the Sun, (3) the space between the Sun and Dhruva (the Polar Star), (4) the space between Dhruva and Jana-Loka.

Verses 24-27 explain the significance of Lokas [5-7]

(5) Jana—Birth-place of subjects of Svāyambhuva Manu and such other people. (6) Tapas—Region of the performers of penance like Ṛbhu, Sanatkumāra. (7) Satya is *Sattā-mātra* (pure existence), the region of god Brahmā.

God Brahmā created these worlds by uttering seven *Vyāhṛtis*, viz. Bhūr, Bhuvaḥ, Svaḥ etc.

Prakṛti). The Kṛtas are the abodes created along with their *Sthānins* (persons identifying themselves with them).

13. The Earth, the firmament, the heaven and what is remembered as *Mahaḥ*—these four abodes are remembered as *Ārṇavakas*.

14. These abodes are having decline and increase. Those not endowed so will be mentioned (later). Those that are *Naimittikas* (periodical ones) last till the final dissolution.

15. *Jana*, *Tapa* and *Satya*—these three abodes are exclusive ones. They last till the (final) *Prasaṁyama* (dissolution).

16. I shall mention the *Vyakta* (manifest) ones. They are the seven abodes. *Bhūrloka* is the first among them. The second one is remembered as *Bhuvaḥ*.

17. The third one should be known as *Svaḥ*; the fourth is remembeted as *Mahaḥ*. *Jana* is the fifth world and *Tapaḥ* is considered as the sixth.

18. *Satya* is the seventh world. Beyond that there is darkness. When (Brahmā) said "*Bhūḥ*" *Bhūrloka* originated.

19. Second time when he said "*Bhuvaḥ*", firmament originated. For the third time when he said "*Svaḥ*", heaven appeared.

20-21. By means of these three *Vyāhāras* (utterances) Brahmā created the worlds. Hence *Bhūḥ* is remembered as *Pārthiva Loka* (Earth) and firmament is remembered as *Bhuvaḥ*. *Svarloka* is heaven. This is the conclusion in the Purāṇas. Agni (Fire-god) is the lord of *Bhūtas*. Hence he is remembered as *Bhūtapati*.

22. Vāyu is the lord of *Bhuvaḥ*. Hence he is *Bhuvaspati*. The Sun is the lord of *Bhavya* i.e. *Svaḥ*, hence is *Divaspati*.

23. When he uttered "*Mahaḥ*", *Maharloka* originated. The residence of the Devas who retire from their offices is there.

24. *Jana* is the fifth Loka. Janas (people) are born there. It is called Janaloka because the subjects of Svāyaṁbhuva Manu and others were born there.

25. Those subjects of Svāyaṁbhuva Manu and others, who have already been glorified, set out for *Tapoloka* when all the worlds are consumed by the fire at the end of the Kalpa.

26. That world is called *Tapoloka* because Ṛbhu, Sanatkumāra and other holy personages of souls purified by *Tapas* (penance) and of sublimated sexuality stay in that world.

27. The word *Satya* refers to Brahmā. It refers to pure existence as well. Hence Brahmā's world is Satya. It is the shining seventh world.

28. All the Devas are the residents of *Svarloka* along with Gandharvas, Apsaras-s, Yakṣas, Guhyakas and Rākṣasas. All Bhūtas, Piśācas and Nāgas are residents of the Earth along with men.

29-30. Although Maruts, Mātariśvans (Wind-gods), Rudras, (some) Devas and the Aśvins have no fixed abode and they roam about in the atmosphere, they have their main residence in *Bhuvarloka.* The heaven-dwelling Ādityas, Ṛbhus, Viśvedevas, Sādhyas, Pitṛs, and the sages of Aṅgiras Gotra resort to *Bhuvarloka* also.

31. All these Devas move about in aerial chariots and reside in the constellations and planets also. Thus all the (worlds) born of the utterances (*Bhūḥ, Bhuvaḥ, Svaḥ*) of Brahmā have been recounted in order.

32. *Bhūrloka* is the first of these worlds and the last one is *Maharloka.* They are created by the Tanmātras. They are mutually pure i.e. they are separated from one another.

33. Those who have gone away after resorting to the Earth, viz. Śukra and others ending with Cākṣusa (Manu?) reside in Maharloka till the end of the Kalpa.

34-37. The seven Suns burn with their rays those worlds beginning with *Bhūrloka* and ending with *Maharloka.* All the following : Marīci, Kaśyapa, Dakṣa, Svāyaṁbhuva, Aṅgiras, Bhṛgu, Pulastya, Pulaha, Kratu and others, are the Prajāpatis and they live there with them. They are devoid of possessions and free from the feelings of my-ness. They are of sublimated sexuality. Ṛbhu, Sanatkumāra and others are ascetics of great detachment. These worlds are the causes of the rebirth of all the fourteen Manvantaras including those of the Sāvarṇas.

38. Practising Yoga, penance and truthfulness and meditating on the soul, they return to the sixth Loka (i.e. *Tapoloka*) then at the end of the day (of Brahmā i.e. during dissolution).

39. *Satya* is the seventh Loka. It is the region from which there is no return. It is unobstructed (i.e. eternal). It is god Brahmā's Loka.

40. In (velocity?) of rotation and in magnitude *Bhūrloka* is the meeting place (i.e. in the middle?). The firmament, the space between the Earth and the Sun is remembered as *Bhuvaḥ* (-Loka).

41. This space between the Sun and Dhruva (the Pole Star) is *Svarloka* (Heaven). It is called *Diva* also. The space between Dhruva and Janaloka is called *Maharloka*.

42. The seven worlds have been recounted well. Now I shall recount the Siddhis of those worlds. All the living beings in *Bhūrloka* are the imbibers of juice and eaters of cooked food-grains.

43-44. All the residents of *Bhuvarloka* and Svarga are the imbibers of Soma and *Ājya* (ghee-oblations). Those who stay in the fourth Loka, *Maharloka*, should be known to possess the mental Siddhis of five characteristics. Everything that they desire mentally is immediately realised.

45. These Devas are of the past, present and future. They mutually worship by means of Yajñas.

46. The middle ones worship the earlier ones (by sacrifice) and the present ones worship the middle ones. When the groups of Devas pass off, the contact and relations cease (to exist).

47. It should be known that they still retain their series of mental Siddhis even though they cease to hold positions of authority. Their series of Siddhis is pure and should be known as mental.

48. O Brāhmaṇas, the four worlds situated lower than *Janaloka* have been briefly recounted by me to you. I shall recount them again.

Vāyu said:

49-50. Marīci, Kaśyapa, Dakṣa, Vasiṣṭha, Aṅgiras, Bhṛgu, Pulastya, Pulaha, Kratu and others are born at the outset as the mental sons of Brahmā. After establishing their subjects, they resort to *Janaloka*.[1]

51-52. When the worlds beginning with *Bhūḥ* and ending with *Mahar* are pervaded by the flames of Saṁvartaka fire at the end of the Kalpa, when the black fires blaze and burn, Yāma and other groups of Devas residing in *Maharloka* resort to *Janaloka*. All those stationed there are of very subtle bodies.

53-54. The (newcomers) assume the same features and excellence as they (the residents of *Janaloka*) and move about in *Janaloka* as long as the universe is submerged in water.

55. When the night of Brahmā whose source of origin is the Unmanifest, dawns into day, they are reborn in the same order as before.

56. On the death of their predecessors all those aspirants beginning with Svāyaṁbhuva (Manu) and ending with Marīci are reborn.

57-58. Thereafter the Yāma groups of Devas are reborn in the (chronological) order, the eldest first and the younger afterwards. In the family of Devas are remembered seven *Saṁbhūtis* (Manifestations). These *Saṁbhūtis* are born with the Kalpa —*Kalpajāḥ*. Four of these manifestations have passed away, while the three others (still) survive.

59-61. Undergoing transmigration again and again upto ten times in order those Devas observe the evanescence of all created beings. Thanks to the force of the inevitable future and as a result of that power of their own meritorious deeds, they attain mental equilibrium. They desist from all activities and leave off *Janaloka* with a calm mind. They then attain the *Vairāja Loka*.

62-63. Practising Yoga perpetually, performing penance and preaching dharma for a long time, they are born in the families of meritorious persons. Whether they attain Devahood, sage-hood or human form, they do fulfil the duties of those respective positions.

---

1. In vv. 49-69, we are told that at the end of the world, when Maharloka suffers from the Saṁvartaka fire, gods etc. resort to Janaloka. Time being endless, the process of the same gods, sages etc. taking re-incarnations in the same state, continues *ad infinitum* (except for the Jīvas who attain Mokṣa).

64. Thus these groups of Devas resort to the *Vairāja Loka* after ten repetitions of births. There they stay for ten Kalpas.

65-66. As each of the Kalpas is completed in the *Vairājaka* (Kalpa) (Loka?), they move on to Brahmaloka in their due order of priority. In the world of Brahmā, when a Kalpa of *Vairājaka* (pertaining to Brahmā) passes away, they again get assigned a position lasting for a Kalpa in *Vairāja* (loka).

67. Thus in the order mentioned before they frequently go to Vairāja as a result of their penance up to ten times and return to Brahmaloka.

68. Thus thousands of Devayugas have passed. They attained death along with the sages in Brahmaloka.

Sūta said:

69. It is impossible to recount them in detail and in the proper sequence because time is beginningless and it is impossible to count everything completely. Still you need not have any doubt. Everything has been mentioned by me precisely.

70. On hearing that statement the sages were over-whelmed with doubts. They then spoke to Sūta who was conversant with the Purāṇas, whose intellect was great and who was Vyāsa's disciple.

The Sages said:

71. Please mention precisely what constitutes the diet of these people in *Vairāja Loka*, what the extent of their exploit is, what their support is and how long they stay there.

72. On hearing the statement uttered by the Sages, Sūta who was well-versed in the Purāṇas and who knew the reality of the world, spoke thus with humility.

Sūta said:

73. Those people who become the purest of the pure (by means of meritorious actions) attain that world (*Vairāja*) and stay there for ten *Ābhutasaṁplavas* (periods of final dissolution).

74. All of them have only subtle bodies. They are learned. Their forms and features are like those of clouds. Since they abide in a permanent world there is no Bhūta (the elements) in them.

75-77. When a change is imminent (i.e. when they are about to leave), Sanatkumāra and other Siddhas of Yogic rites and practice mention (reveal) their time of (periodic) change. The inclination to abandon the abode occurs simultaneously. Then all of them, of pure intellect, say to the Vairājas and to one another: "O blessed ones, now we shall enter into Praṇava and stay in Brahmaloka. It is conducive to our welfare to proceed to Brahmaloka".

78-79. After saying thus, all of them striving to attain Brahman practise Yogic rites and stay there uniting the *Ātman* with *Paramātman*. Like the flames of a lamp that has ceased to burn (for want of oil), they become extinct and become merged in Brahman wherefrom a return is rarely achieved. (There is no return.)

80. After attaining that world full of meditation, they attain the bliss of Brahman and the state of immortality.

81. Brahmaloka is mentioned to be six times higher up beyond the Vairāja worlds. And god Brahmā is the *Purohita* (one who has been put in charge beforehand).

82. All of them are *Praṇava*-souled (i.e. have concentrated their souls in the mystic syllable *Om*). They are endowed with enlightenment, purity and penance. After deriving the bliss of Brahman, they enjoy the state of deathless-ness.

83. They are not affected by mutually clashing opposites (like happiness and sorrow etc.). They are devoid of the three *Bhāvas* (states of existence, i.e. birth, growth and decay). They possess majestic lustre. They are in every respect equal to Brahmā except in the matter of over-lordship.[1]

84. They are endowed with majestic lustre, victory, *Aiśvarya* (divine faculties of omnipotence etc.), *Sthiti* (continuous existence), *Vairāgya* (non-attachment), *Darśana* (vision) on par with Brahmā.

85. Those learned men of holy rites and activities and in an enlightened state at the end of penance, attain the goal that transmutes them. When the *Pratisañcara* (re-absorption) in

1. Cf. *Brahma Sūtra* IV.4.17-21 which state that the Liberated Soul has all the powers of Brahmā except that of creation of the world.

Prakṛti is imminent they see it in a moment and get dissolved in the Unmanifest along with Brahmā and Devas.

86. Thus Devas and Sages partake of, i.e. worship the *Sattra* (the sacrificial session in the form of) Brahman. The *Sattra* (i.e. Brahman) is eternal (*sanātana*), immortal, resplendent, ever-existent, imperishable and immutable.

87. They are of sublimated sexuality. They traverse a path of no return. The purity they have attained by means of the practice of holy rites is supplemented by the knowledge of Vedāntas.

88. There they engage themselves in the practice of Yogic union (with the Supreme Brahman). They worship the highest goal. They abandon their physical body which is the cause of all sins and proceed ahead to (the state of) immortality.

89-90. They are devoid of passion. They have conquered anger. They are rid of delusion. They speak the truth invariably. They are quiescent. They are of dedicated souls endowed with mercy and sympathy. They have conquered the sense organs. They are devoid of attachment. They are pure. They are remembered as ones who have attained *Sāyujya* (identity) with Brahman. They are the heroic souls who have burnt all their sins by means of acts of penance uncontaminated by desires. Theirs are those worlds from which there is no falling off. It is remembered that the pleasure therein is immeasurable.

91. This is the immortal region of Brahman. It is superbly resplendent in the most exalted firmament. After attaining it along with Brahmā, Devas cease to be worried and sorrowful (i.e. attain Liberation—Mokṣa).

The Sages said :

92. O excellent one, whence is this Parārdha (Infinite, Infinity) ? What is this called *Para* (the greatest) ? We wish to know this. Please speak.

Sūta said :

93-95. Listen from me the definition of *Parārdha*[1] and

1. Verses 93-104 give the technical terms for numbers and the digits up to *Parārdha*.

Para. One, ten, hundred and thousand are the (main) numbers known (well) to you. Ten times thousand make *Ayuta*. One hundred thousand is called *Niyuta* by learned men. Similarly *Arbuda* and *Koṭi* can be calculated. Hundred *Niyutas* make a *Koṭi* (crore). Thonsand *Niyutas* make one *Arbuda* (one hundred million). *Arbuda* is ten *Koṭis*. They consider hundred *Koṭis* as *Abja*.

96. Learned men call a thousand crores a *Kharva* and ten times a *Kharva* make a *Nikharva*.

97-98. A huudred thousand *Koṭis* make (what is called) *Śanku*. People who know numbers (and calculation) say that a thousand times thousand *Koṭis* multiplied by ten make a *Samudra* (i.e. *Jaladhi*). Ten thousand times a thousand *Koṭis* is called *Madhya*. A hundred thousand times a thousand *Koṭis* is termed *Anta* (*Antya*).

99. A thousand crores multiplied by a crore is called *Parārdha*. Learned men call twice a *Parārdha*, a *Para* (great).

100-102. The number hundred they say is *Paridṛḍha* (*Parivṛdha* in Bd.P.). A thousand is *Paripadmaka*. Thereafter the other numbers (each number is multiplied by ten to get the next number) are *Ayuta*, *Niyuta*, *Prayuta*, *Arbuda*, *Nirbuda*, *Kharbuda*, *Kharva*, *Nikharva*, *Śaṅku*, *Padma*, *Samudra*, (*Antya*), *Madhyama*, *Parārdha* and *Para*. In calculation these are the eighteen digits.

103-104. These are the terms given by sages. A *Parārdha* (? years) from the beginning of creation constitutes a Kalpa (?) of Brahmā (only a day). A period extending as much also remains, at the end of which there is *Pratisarga*. Thus *Para* and *Parārdha* have been (calculated) explained by me.

105-107. As Brahmā's prowess is the greatest, his longevity the highest, (his power of) penance, strength, piety (or Dharma), learning, fortitude, knowledge, realization of Brahman and faculties such as omnipotence (*aiśvarya*) etc. are of the highest magnitude, there is no living being who is greater than Brahmā. He is established in the highest position, so he is the greatest of all objects.

The greatest Brahmā has been reckoned (calculated and explained) by me (as *Para*). Half of *Para* is *Parārdha*.

108. The countable yet ever uncountable is the trinity·

The countable is observed through numbers. All numbers up to Parārdha can be expressed.

109. When the mass is seen there is no specific number. It is the characteristic of countlessness. If we say as many as sand particles it means infinite. These are the five characteristics (?).

110. That can be calculated by Īśvaras of divine vision because of their purity. Since he is established in perfect knowledge, Brahmā sees everything.

111. On hearing this, all the sages residing in Naimiṣa forest had their eyes bedimmed with tears (of joy). Their (voice) was choked up due to delight.

112-113. Those expounders of Brahman asked Mātariśvan (the Wind-god) : "O holy lord, we wish to hear precisely how far is Brahmaloka in so many Yojanas. What is the magnitude of Yojana and Krośa?"

114. On hearing their words, Mātariśvan (Vāyu) of humble speech spoke as follows in sweet words, in the proper order and in the same manner as was seen (by him).

Vāyu said:

115. I shall recount this to you. Listen to what I intend to say. The *Vyakta Bhāga* (that which is manifest) is grosser than *Avyakta*.

116. There are ten parts of *Mahat*. The gross part is called *Bhūtādi* (*Ahaṁkāra* or the Cosmic Ego). The magnitude of *Paramāṇu* (an atom) is little more than the tenth part of *Bhūtādi* (?)

117. A *Paramāṇu* is very subtle. It cannot he seen by the (naked) eye. It can be imagined; what cannot be (ultimately) split in the world should be known as *Paramāṇu*.

118. When the Sun's rays enter through the window, the subtlest dust particle that is seen is called *Paramāṇu* It is the first among the units of magnitude. It is called *Paramāṇu*.

119. When there is an aggregate of eight *Paramāṇus* it is called *Trasareṇu* or *Padmarajas* (pollen-dust of a lotus).

120. When eight *Trasareṇus* join together that is remembered as one *Ratharenu* (chariot dust). When eight *Ratharenus* are combined they form what is remembered by learned men as one *Bālāgra* (tip of the hair).

121. Eight *Bālāgras* form a *Likṣā* (the egg of a louse). Eight *Likṣās* form *Yūkā* (a louse). Eight *Yūkās* form what is called *Yava* (a grain of barley) and eight *Yavas* form one *Aṅgula* (the distance between the joints in a finger).

122. Twelve *Aṅgula*-joints make a *Vitasti* and twentyone *Aṅgula*-joints make a *Ratni* (a cubit—the distance between the elbow and the closed fist).

123. Twentyfour *Aṅgulas* form one *Hasta* (the distance between the elbow and the tip of the middle finger). Two *Ratnis* or fortytwo *Aṅgulas* should be known as a *Kiṣku.*

124. Learned men say that ninetysix *Aṅgulas* form one *Dhanus* (a bow). This *Dhanus* is a unit used in measuring *Gavyūti* (Explanation in verse 126).

125. *Dhanus, Daṇḍa, Yuga* and *Nāli*—all these contain equal number of Aṅgulas. Persons who know calculation say that three hundred Dhanus units make a *Nalva.*

126. It is taught that two thousand *Dhanus* units make one *Gavyūti.* Eight thousand *Dhanus* units make one *Yojana.*

127. The measurement of the distance of a *Yojana* is based on this unit of *Dhanus.* It should be known that a thousand of these *Dhanus* make the distance of a *Śakra-Kroṣa* (or a *Krośa*).

128. Calculation in *Yojanas* is made by those who are experts in the knowledge of numbers. Listen to the distance of Brahmaloka, in so many *Yojanas.*[1]

129. Divākara (Sun) is a hundred thousand Yojanas above the surface of the Earth. *Niśākara* (Moon) is a thousand Yojanas above the disc of the Sun.

130. The entire stellar zone shines a full hundred thousand Yojanas above the Moon.

---

1. Verses 128ff. give the distances from the earth to other planets and their locations. Though other Purāṇas endorse this information, it is imaginary. It shows the limits of the knowledge of Astronomy in those times.

The same remark applies to the distances to Mahar Loka and other mythical worlds.

131. The Meru mountain is a hundred thousand Yojanas high. The distance between planets above the stellar zone is twice this (height) and they are one above the other.

132. *Budha* (Mercury) moves about beneath all stars and planets. *Śukra* (Venus) moves about above it. Above it is the planet *Lohita* (Mars).

133-135. Above it is *Bṛhaspati* (Jupiter) and above that is *Śanaiścara* (Saturn). A hundred thousand Yojanas above Saturn shines the entire zone of the Seven Sages (Great Bear). A hundred thousand Yojanas above the Seven Sages shines Dhruva (Pole star), son of Uttānapāda. He is the main pivot of all stars in the heaven. He has the compact divine stellar aerial chariot.

136-137. The height of the three worlds has been recounted by me in Yojanas. In the course of the Manvantaras, worldly Yajñas are performed for Devas by the people of different castes and stages of life. These Yajñas alone are conducive to the sustenance and stability of Devas.

138. The set of the three worlds has been explained. Understand what is beyond this. Above *Dhruvaloka* is *Maharloka* wherein those people staying till the end of the Kalpa reside. It is ten million Yojanas from *Dhruva*—that is the conclusion (of wise men).

139. *Janaloka* is twenty million Yojanas from *Maharloka*. In it stay those *Sādhakas* (aspirants) —Dakṣa and others, the sons of Brahmā. They live till the end of the Kalpa.

140. It is remembered that *Tapoloka* is forty million Yojanas above *Janaloka*. It is here that the Vairāja groups of Devas stay. They are exempt from the effects of burning of all living beings in the destruction of the universe.

141. Sixty million Yojanas from *Tapoloka* is *Satyaloka*. It is called *Brahmaloka* of those who are devoid of death and desire and so who never return to the *Saṁsāra* therefrom.

142. It is remembered (proclaimed) that the space above *Brahmaloka* upto the (upper crust of the) Cosmic Egg is a crore and fifty *niyuta* (a fifteen million) Yojanas.

143-144. The lower part extends to fortysix million five hundred thousand Yojanas. This lower half consists of movement (of stars, planets, etc.). In the upper half the movement ceases. Dhruvaloka and its top has been explained as has been heard by me mentioning the distance in Yojanas.

145. Now I shall mention the allotment of abodes to those living beings who deserve falling into hells due to their cruel actions.

146-149. The following are the hells[1] : *Raurava*, *Rodha*, *Sūkara*, *Tāla*, *Taptakumbha*, *Mahājvāla*, *Śabala*, *Vimocana*, *Kṛmi*, *Kṛmibhakṣa*, *Lālābhakṣa*, *Viśaṁsana*, *Adhaḥśiras*, *Pūyavaha*, *Rudhirāndha*, *Vaitaraṇa*, *Kṛṣṇa*, *Asipatravana*, *Agnijvāla*, *Mahāghora*, *Saṁdaṁśa*, *Śvabhojana*, *Tamas*, *Kṛṣṇasūtra*, *Loha*, *Asija*, *Apratiṣṭha*, *Vīcyaśva* and others.

150. All these dark and gloomy hells are under the jurisdiction of Yama. Men of evil deeds fall into these severally.

151. All these hells *Raurava* etc. are reported to be beneath the Earth. A perjuror, a person taking up a side by making false statements and untruths falls into the hell *Raurava* of ruthless grasp.

152. A slayer of a cow, a destroyer of a foetus and one who commits arson in the city fall into the hell *Rodha*. A slayer of a Brāhmaṇa, a drink-addict and a stealer of gold fall into the hell *Sūkara*.

153. A slayer of a Kṣatriya, of a Vaiśya in miserable circumstances or of a Brāhmaṇa as well as a defiler of the preceptor's bed falls into the hell *Tāla*.

154. He who indulges in sexual intercourse with his sister and the soldier of a king (i.e. murderer of a king) fall into the hell *Taptakumbha*. A trader in (stolen) horses and protector of one who is kept in legal bondage fall into the hell *Taptaloha*.

155. He who sells his chaste wife, he who forsakes a devotee and he who indulges in sexual intercourse with his daughter or daughter-in-law falls into the hell *Mahājvāla*.

156-157. He who sells the Vedas, he who blasphemes the Vedas, those who abuse or disrespect elders or hit them with wounding words and one who carnally approaches forbidden

1. Veases 146-184 deal with the hells, the tortures therein and the sins that lead to these hells. The total number of hells is twentyeight.

women—all these fall into the hell named *Śabala*. A thief or a trespasser falls into the hell *Vimoha*.

158. He who dismantles or spoils public roads falls into the hell *Kīṭaloha*. Those who hate Devas and Brāhmaṇas, those who do not worship preceptors and those who contaminate precious gems fall into the hell *Kṛmibhakṣya*.

159. He who eats food keeping his wife, friends and daughter (starving) falls into the foul-smelling hell *Lālābhakṣa*.

160. A manufacturer of arrows, a potter, a person who takes away gold coins, a professional physician, one who sets fire to a garden—all these fall in (the hell called) *Viśaṁsana*.

161. He who accepts monetary gifts from evil men, he who officiates as a priest in the Yajña on behalf of an ineligible man and the man who maintains himself by stellar calculation fall into the hell *Adhomukha*.

162. He who sells milk, wine, flesh, lac, scents, juices, gingelly seeds and similar things falls into the terrible hell *Pūyavaha*.

163. He who captures, fetters or ensnares fowls, cats, boars, birds, deer, rams and sheep will also fall into the same hell.

164-166. Learned men say that these (following) sinners fall into the hell *Rudhirāndha*: a Brāhmaṇa who rears goats, sheep and buffaloes, handles wheels and banners or makes a livelihood with the sale of dyes and colours (or by staging plays etc.); a dealer in birds; he who performs Yajñas on behalf of all and sundry in the village; he who burns other men's houses; he who poisons others; he who makes a living by pimping and pandering; he who sells Soma juice; a drunkard; a flesh-eater; wilful slayer of animals; a slayer of buffaloes and deer; he who creates (imaginary) festivals; a tailor by profession; and one who is treacherous to one's friends.

167. There is no doubt in this that those who feed the people sitting in the same row with different sorts of food-stuffs (and thus are partial), fall into the terrible hell *Viḍbhuja*.

168. He who invariably utters falsehood, he who is voluble in scolding others, he who is inauspicious—these sinners fall into the terrible hell named *Mūtrākirṇa*.

169-170. Men who kill those who offer libations of honey, fall into *Vaitaraṇī*. Insane persons, persons of dejected mind, those who are devoid of purity of conduct, persons of furious temperament, persons who make others miserable, persons given to deceitful ways, fall into the hell *Asipatravana*. Persons killing *Urabhras* (rams) or hunting deer, are cut, mutilated, dragged and pulled in a terrible manner in that hell.

171. Those who eat and drink (forbidden stuffs) in a hermitage fall into the hell *Agnijvāla*. They are eaten by steel-beaked crows of dark and diverse colours.

172. Persons with the vow of holy rites and celibacy, breaking those vows by discharging semen even in dreams, fall into the hell *Sandaṁśa*.

173. Those who are taught or ordered about by their sons invariably fall into the hell *Śvabhojana*.

174. Those who perform actions contrary to the rules of castes and stages of life on being urged by anger or elation, go to hell (*Niraya*).

175. The hot-centred great hell *Raurava* is white (?) from outside and terrible. The extremely terrible *Tapaḥ* is beneath it. It is cool-centred.

176. Listen and understand these being described in serial order. Beneath the Earth only seven hells are mentioned.

177. They are the outcome of *Adharma* (sin). They are *Andhatāmisraka* and others. *Raurava* is the first among them. Then there is *Mahāraurava*.

178. Beneath this is the other hell which is both cold and scorching. This third hell is *Kālasūtra* which is remembered as *Mahāhavividhi** also.

179. The fourth hell is *Apratiṣṭha*, and *Avici* is remembered as the fifth. The next one is *Lohapṛṣṭha* and *Avidheya* is the seventh.

180. The first hell is called *Raurava* because it is very terrible. Although it contains water, it is remembered as one that scorches. Beneath it is the hell *Tapaḥ* that is terrible, cold and very low.

**mahāhir-vividhaḥ* (Bd. P.v. 181) having great serpents of various kinds.

181. Biting serpents are said to be in the terrible *Kālasūtra*. Nothing can stay in the hell *Apratiṣṭha*. There is a terrible whirling in it.

182. *Avīci* is said to be very terrible because the sinners are crushed by means of mechanical contrivances. The hell *Loha* (*Pṛṣṭha*) is still more terrible, because all Karmans are exhausted in it (by experiencing the fruit thereof).

183. (Defective verse) Though the beings in the hell are without bodies, the harassment, afflictions and sufferings that they undergo in the *Avidheya* hell are irremediable.

184. All these hells are as terrible as mountains and devoid of light above. In all these the misery due to sin is very intense.

185-186. These two worlds on the top are devoid of any light whatsoever. Although they are like the other worlds, the sufferings in these two worlds by means of fiery piles (?) are the worst. They take up bodies capable of experiencing these sufferings as a result of their previous actions. Intensity of suffering is common to all these worlds.

187-188. The sufferings of the beings doomed to hell are innumerable. They undergo misery. When the sins have been exhausted, they are born again in the womb of lower animals or as Devas. Devas are stationed above and Nārakas (beings doomed to hell) are stationed below.

189. Caused by *Dharmas* or *Adharmas* they develop befitting bodies for the purpose of experiencing the fruits thereof.

190. Devas see the hellish beings standing topsy turvy below them. The hellish beings too see all the Devas standing topsy turvy.

191. There is no distinction in Lokāloka as to the top or bottom because these worlds have no tip or root. They are held in position naturally.

192. This situation, this *Saṁjñā* (? name) is natural to Lokāloka (?).

The Brāhmaṇas who were performing the Satra then spoke to Vāyu.

The Sages said :

193-194. Mention completely the number of living beings

residing in Lokāloka and moving about in the world of existence.

On hearing the words of the sages, Māruta spoke these words.

Vāyu said :

195-196. O excellent ones among men, all the creatures can by no means be entirely enumerated.[1] They are beginningless and endless. They are jumbled and mixed with one another. Only a general inference can be made to fix their number. The number cannot be positively asserted. They are mentioned to be numerous. Even with a divine vision they cannot be known. How can I with limited knowledge and ordinary vision fix their limit ?

197. Actually no question is asked on what cannot be conceived or known. Understand what has been named and numbered by Brahmā.

198. The earthly worms born of *Saṁseka* (sprinkling or watering) etc. form about a thousandth part of the number of immobile beings.

199. This has been decisively arrived at that all the aquatic creatures together come to about a thousandth part of the creatures born of *Saṁseka*.

200. All the worldly birds should be known as forming a thousandth part of the number of aquatic living beings.

201. All the animals, the quadrupeds, should be known as constituting a thousandth part of the number of birds.

202. The bipeds (men) in this world should be known as constituting a thousandth part of all the quadrupeds.

203. Righteous men should be known to constitute a thousandth part of the entire number of bipeds.

204. Of the righteous men only a thousandth part goes to heaven. Of those righteous men who go to heaven only a thousandth part qualify themselves for absolution (*Mokṣa*).

205. Persons staying in the abodes of torture are equal to those who go to heaven. Those wicked souls who fall into the dark *Raurava* after death are harassed by both chill and heat.

1. Verses 195-208 give the Purāṇic notions about the number of Jīvas in each species.

206. They suffer bitter pain. The bodies of those who reach the abodes of torture become benumbed. *Raurava* should be known as hot. Blazing splendour and hot liquids flow there.

207. The *Tapa* hell is in solid form and always chill. Good and righteous people going to heaven are very rare.

208. This fixation of number is made by the self-born lord Īśvara himself. Human calculation recedes. Only the calculation of Brahmā decides (properly).

The Sages said :

209-210. Mahaḥ, Jana, Tapaḥ, Satya, Bhūta, Bhavya and Bhava—all these worlds have been recounted by you. Please mention precisely what their difference is and what the distance between them is.

On hearing these words of the sages of sublimated sexuality, Vāyu, who has seen the real truth mentioned these facts to them.

Vāyu said:

211. Learned men see that manifest through inference; the Yogins see it directly by means of Yogic power and those who habitually perform holy rites observe it through *Pratyāhāra* (withdrawal of physical senses), meditation and penance.

212-214. The enlightened Ṛbhu, Sanatkumāra and others who possess pure intellect, the Virajas (those who are free from Rajoguṇa) free from sorrow, those excellent saintly men like Brahmā himself who are never fading (always) full of delight, Yogins adhering to Brahman, and the sages Vālakhilya and others—all these have observed the residence of the eternal lord from close quarters. That residence cannot be conceived or argued about. It makes good men contented. I too have observed it by remaining close at hand.

215-216. Since Īśvara is so subtle as the atom, he can only be conceived by learned men. The following ten everlasting attributes are always present in Śaṅkara—*Jñāna* (perfect knowledge), *Vairāgya* (detachment), *Aiśvarya* (overlordship or possession of mystic powers), *Tapas* (penance), *Satyam* (truthfulness), *Kṣamā* (forgiveness), *Dhṛti* (fortitude), *Draṣṭṛtva* (supervision), *Ātmasaṁbandha* (contact with the soul) and *Adhiṣṭhānatva* (the state of being the support of all).

217. He is *Vibhu* (all-powerful and omnipresent). The fire of Yogic power of the Yogins is kindled by his blessings. Assuming physical bodies, he helps the world of human beings.

218. The abode of that eternal lord is imperishable, fixed and untarnished by worldly chaos. It is the eighth (one beyond the seven Lokas). It is conceived by Māyā and the greatest of all.

219. The eightfold Prakṛti and its creations are created by him through Māyā. Lord Maheśvara is *Māyin* (Master or possessor of Māyā). The withdrawal (annihilation) of Devas is done there (in his abode).

220. Listen to and understand even as I recount in detail and in the proper order. The distance between Bhūrloka and Brahmaloka is one hundred and thirtyone million five hundred thousand Yojanas.

221. The space of Brahmāṇḍa above Brahmaloka is fifteen million Yojanas.

222-223. This is the highest point that can be reached. Beyond that no one can go. The eternal, uncountable, subtle Prakṛtis supported by mutual Guṇas exist there. Their attribute is to create the *Kṣetrajña* termed Brahmā who makes them function and is present there.

224-226. It is in them that all these exist: the possessor of Prakṛti, the subtle, supporting, the eternal one, the unproduced, great abode, the great atom, the great one lying down, the undying, the unimaginable, unembodied, the mental form, the manifestation, the disappearance, the maintenance and the blessing. Vidhi (Brahmā) cannot be compared to anyone else. The great Īśvara is like Paramāṇu. With his brilliance he makes this illuminated. He is beyond the darkness.

227. The golden egg that was evolved at the outset as *Aupasargika* (a relevant adjunct) was very huge and wholly circular. It was evolved out of Īśvara.

228. The germination of seed is from Īśvara. Kṣetrajña (individual soul) is considered as the seed. They speak of Prakṛti as the *Yoni* (the source of the origin) and that is of the nature of Nārāyaṇa.

229. The creator of all the worlds, the noble-souled omnipresent lord in contact with Prakṛti creates Brahmaloka and Brahmāṇḍa through his body, for the purpose of the creation and maintenance of the worlds.

230. Beyond Brahmaloka and beneath the upper crust of the Cosmic Egg—in between these two is the *Pura* (city), his divine abode *Manomaya* (consisting of the mind).[1]

231. That is the abode of the embodied Īśvara of unmeasured splendour. The city named Śiva is there and it is the refuge of those who are afraid of rebirth.

232. O excellent Brāhmaṇas, it is full one hundred thousand Yojanas in extent. Within, it is as extensive as the sphere of the Earth.

233-34. It is surrounded by a massive gold rampart of solar splendour. It has brilliance of the mid-day Sun outshining the lustre of all others. It has four golden portals embellished with strings of pearls. The enclosures are well-constructed with bright golden adjuncts.

235. That divine city (shines well) with the sounds of bells reverberating in the sky. Neither the fear of death, nor distress nor the exhaustion of old age finds a place there.

236. No other city deserves to be compared to this city. It extends to a hundred thousand Yojanas to the ten quarters.

237. That city is pervaded by the brilliance of the bull-bannered lord and so it stands (firm). The creation of that golden city is by means of mental conception.

238-240. The city shines much with scattered diamond dust. In the gardens and parks therein, there are divine lotuses which have the lustre of the autumnal Moon, which resemble the rising Sun, which are half white and half red and which are made of gold. With their stalks having the lustre of Marakata (emerald) gem they are of the size of the wheels of chariots. In fragrance, beauty and tenderness they are unequalled.

241-242. Some lotuses resemble the wings of a bee; some are golden. Some are half black and half red. Their inner

1. Verses 230-300 give a poetic description of the city of Śiva and the description of the residents therein.

surfaces are very tender. The lotuses covering up the whole place seem to be so many umbrellas.

There are seven great rivers there. Understand their names.

243. The following are the beautiful rivers in that excellent city : Varā, Vareṇyā, Varadā, Varārhā, Varavarṇinī, Varamā and Varabhadrā.

244. The excellent rivers contain water shining like split jewels. It is mixed with the petals of red and blue lotuses. Foams and whirlpools add to their beauty.

245. Neither Brahmarṣis nor Devas, nor Asuras nor Pitṛs nor others knew that city of the inconceivable lord.

246. Only those noble-souled ones who perform meditation without agitation and who have conquered their sense-organs by means of good yogic power, see that city of the bull-bannered one.

247-248. There is a splendid golden palace in the middle of that excellent city of unequalled splendour. It is divine and it resembles the great Meru mountain. It is enveloped in gracious glory. It has a thousand 'feet' (columns). It is embellished all round with incomparable gems and jewels.

249-254. Its splendour all round is increased by means of invaluable and incomparable gems. It is embellished in some sections with crystals, in some sections with lunar stones, in other sections with lapis lazuli, in some sections with shining gems resembling the Moon, in some with brilliant gems as beautiful as the rising Sun, in others with golden jewels refulgent like fire, in some sections with jewels shining with silver lustre, in other sections with blue sapphire gems and in some sections with firmly fixed diamonds. It was heightened in splendour by means of brilliant windows and ventilators of various sizes. It is decorated with festoons and flags shining like the rays of the Moon. Sounds of golden bells reverberate in it. Joy and revelry are ever present there. Its refulgence is heightened by the residences of Kinnaras, which have the shape and lustre of the evening clouds. Just as the mountain-lord Meru shines with its golden peaks, so also the palace shines with shining water currents all round abounding in golden flowers.

The whole city shines with golden flags and banners. Similarly the lordly palace shines with its terraces and landing spots.

255-257. In this abode of the three-eyed lord there is a statue of Vasanta (Spring). The goddesses Lakṣmī, Śrī, Kīrti, Śobhā and Sarasvatī are present there in physical bodies (created through Māyā). These eternal goddesses endowed with beauty and fragrance are innumerable and of mutually dependent (complementary) qualities. They are the ornaments of all precious stones and source of the origin of loveliness and dalliance. The highly blessed goddesses divided themselves into a hundred crores and diligently wait upon the Lord with Umā.

258. They have thousands of other maid-servants behind them, beautiful and endowed with splendour and glory. They all have eyes like the petals of lotuses.

259. They rejoice along with the Gaṇas as huge as mountains and as brilliant as fire; they exhibit their extremely attractive amorous gestures and sportive activities.

260-264. Some are hunch-backed; some are dwarfish; some have beautiful bodies; some are horse-faced; a few are slender like the red variety of sugarcane; some are hideous and terrible with flat faces; some have loosely hanging bellies; a few have short arms. Some have no eyes, some are small-footed; a few have the faces of the lord of beasts; others have faces and bellies like those of elephants; others are elephant-faced; a few are lion-faced and tiger-faced; some have red eyes; some beauties have huge breasts and charming eyes; there are beautiful ladies with curly locks of hair and comely eyes; others can assume any form they wish. There are women with different dresses and features. They are worthy of the abode of the lord; they move about everywhere within the palace. Lord Maheśvara of ten arms sports therein.

265-266. He lives with Nandin and the noble-souled Gaṇas of universal forms as well as Rudra-gaṇas of equal exploits and liberal-mindedness. They resemble sons of fire. They have hideous faces with curved fangs as huge as the sacrificial posts. He is being respected and diligently worshipped by those people moving about in aerial chariots.

267-268. He wears the garland of flowers of every season on his chest and inhales their fragrance. He is of a dark complexion like the blue lotus. His eyes are large, wide and copper-coloured. His hanging lips are a bit hideous. His sharp curved fangs appear to add to his beauty. His eyes are turned upwards. It is impossible to see him straight in the face. He is beautifully clad in bark garments.

269-270. He stands with his right arm (hand) clasping the left arm (hand) and keeping both of them clinging to his side—the hand that has destroyed the enemies of Devas and has never exhausted by fatigue in battles. In his left hand shines the weapon Paṭṭiśa (a spear with a sharp edge). There also shines much his wonderful bow of ten colours, the twanging sound of which is very terrible. There is no other bow to equal its strength.

271. Again there is his Trident which has the refulgence of lightening. It never fails in destroying enemies. It has the most excessive splendour and it blazes brilliantly.

272. The sword of the noble-souled lord of Devas is the most excellent of all shining objects. Similarly does the cool-rayed Moon shine with its brilliant splendour and gorgeous body like the flame of fire in the sacrificial altar.

273. In front of the lord is the great golden Kamaṇḍalu (water pot). It is full of water and it shines splendidly.

274-275. The first (or the head) female doorkeeper (portress) of the goddess, named Vijayā stands there shining splendidly after making obeisance to the lord. She is a blessed lady with four arms. She is very popular. She wears whitish garments. A sword hangs from her (waist). There is a great pearl necklace covering her chest. She shines like another goddess Śrī. She is unequalled and great.

276. There are other ladies behind her. They are accompanied by groups of celestial ladies. With their newly wed and beloved husbands they worship Śaṅkara.

277. Groups of Gandharvas endowed with all characteristic features and accompanied by all musical instruments, sing songs of prayer before the lord of Devas.

278. The Lord of bulls, of broad chest and great height, shines there. He has the lustre of the autumnal cloud. He rejoices much in his (lord's) house.

279. Then there is Skanda, his son, of unmeasured prowess.

He wears red garments. He is glorious and his eyes resemble the petals of an excellent lotus. He stays there with his followers.

280-281. He has four followers (attendants), viz. Śākha, Viśākha, Naigameya and Aṣṭavān (?) They are devoid of vicious indulgence. They are not cruel. They are engaged in protecting the subjects. The deity having peacock for his vehicle (i.e. Skanda) shines in their company. He has great prowess. There, the lord having faces all round (i.e. six-faced) sports with big serpents as his toys.

282-283. Those kings who make gifts of gold to leading scholars, those householder Brāhmaṇas who live at home expounding Brahman, those who perform their Vedic study and penance in secret and those who maintain themselves by gleaning (grains)—all these become the honoured councillors of the lord of Devas.

284. Many Manvantaras expire and new Manvantaras come (yet the assembly of the lord stays as it was before). May the excellent and wonderful feats of Bhava, the lord of Devas, be heard.

285. Tigers are his followers. They have great speed and the lustre of gold. They are created by the lord himself and they move about as they please.

286. They are like Death unto god of Death. They subdue the arrogance of Yama. Who will (adequately) mention the innumerable superhuman faculties and excellences (of the Lord)?

287. Henceforth, I shall recount again the excellent and wonderful activities of Bhava, pursued sympathetically for the sake of blessing the living beings. Listen and understand.

288-292. (Defective verse) There are a thousand living (beings) created through Māyā and fettered to eight pillars in that abode of the three-eyed lord. They have the excellent features of the lords of the quarters by having these attributes:

1. They are as huge as the Mandara mountain and shine like it.
2. In strength and prowess they are unequalled.
3. They have the colour of pearl necklace, Kunda flower and the Moon.

4. They roar like the rumbling cloud (illuminated by) lightning.
5. They wear crystalline jewels on their heads.
6. They have cloud-like dark garments (covering their bodies).
7. They are marked with Śrīvatsa mark in Vajra (adamant).
8. Their fingers (toes) with their claws resemble the Trident and hence they are termed Śūlapāṇin (armed with trident).

To the excellent shining columns of that important palace they are severally tied by means of fiery fetters. Thus they live there very happily.

Appreciating these words of Vāyu, the surprised sages, the saints residing in the Naimiṣa forest said:

293. "O omnipresent lord, O holy lord, the vital air of all living beings, who are those great beings in the forms of lions? Where are they born? Of what forms are they?

294. What is their guilt for which those lions have been severally bound by means of Vaiśvānara (fiery) fetters by the lord of all living beings?"

295. On hearing their words Vāyu spoke thus: "Those thousand lions are the embodied forms of the Furies of the lord and created by the noble-souled Īśvara after removing them from his own body. They are given the physical forms of lions.

296-297. After granting the boon of freedom from fear to all living beings, they had been fettered formerly by means of the fiery bonds. When (dispute arose with Dakṣa) regarding his share in the Yajña, that Yajña of Dakṣa was completely destroyed sportfully by a single lion that had been released from bondage at the behest of Īśvara after knowing that the wrath of the goddess has been incurred (by him).

298. At that time the great goddess Mahākālī came out of Mahādevī (goddess Umā), the eternal witness of all rites, along with the Bhūtas (goblins) as her followers.

299. That fury is the holy lord Vīrabhadra who permanently resides in Rudra's abode. He is of incomprehensible form. He is the wiper (remover) of the anger of the goddess.

300. Thus the palace, the incomparable residence of the

lord of Suras, the highest secret of all, has been recounted by me to you.

301-303. Henceforth I shall describe the other residents and objects of that city which is the most excellent of all beautiful cities. It is situated in the atmospheric regions. There are many other palaces decorated wonderfully with various kinds of gems. There are many flags there heightening their beauty. The palaces are richly endowed with things fulfilling all desires. They are beautified splendidly by parks and gardens. Some are made of silver and some of gold. Some are like the evening clouds (red) and some resemble the Kailāsa mountain (white). All are lofty.

304. In those excellent palaces, the followers of Bhava who perform good rites, rejoice enjoying various means of pleasures liked by them such as sweet melody etc.

305. Different kinds of auspicious mythological stories are recounted along with the chanting sounds of Vedas. The sounds of songs and musical instruments are heard all round; chantings of prayers (echo everywhere).

306. These sounds are incomparable. All of them mingled together (are very pleasing). These and similar things occur on the tops of those palaces.

307. The palaces are auspicious and built of gold. Each of them has a thousand columns. It is embellished all round with excellent and incomparable gems and jewels.

308. They are beautified with crystals like the Moon, with brilliant lapis lazuli stones and pieces of gold resembling the rising Sun and having the lustre of fire."

309. On hearing this, the ascetics residing in the Naimiṣa forest expressed loudly (their wonder). Their doubts being aroused, they spoke these words to the Wind-god.

The Sages said :

310. Who are those noble-souled followers of Bhava there ? Indeed they are the most worthy of being blessed. Well do they rejoice in that excellent city.

Having heard the words of the sages, *Vāyu spoke* :

311-314. O sages ! May this be heard.[1] Only the following have attained *Sālokya* (residence in the same region—that of Śiva) with Rudra, the eternal and never changing region. They alone attain identity of forms and excellent features with Bhava. They are the people who are devoted to the lord of Devas. They are of bashful temperament (ashamed to do sinful things). They are powerful but not covetous. They are vigorous but have perfect self-control. They observe the middle course in taking food and other activities. They have conquered their sense organs and they revel in their own souls (meditating on souls). They are far above the influence of *Dvandvas* (mutually opposed pairs like pleasure-pain). They are gentle and extremely enthusiastic. They are devoid of jealousy and enmity. They love all living beings. They are quiescent, unagitated and they do not exert themselves (in worldly pursuits.) Their conscience is pure. They are pure in mind, speech and activity. With single-minded attention they seek refuge in Maheśvara.

315-318. Those who live in Śiva's palace are all universal-formed with fire-like faces. They have *kaparda* (matted hair). Their throats are blue in colour, the neck white and the fangs very sharp. They are three-eyed with the crescent Moon forming their coronet. Matted hair is worn by them. All of them are heroic. They have ten arms and have the fragrance of lotus. All of them resemble the midday Sun in brilliance and wear yellow garments; all of them are armed with Pināka bows. They ride white bulls. They are endowed with glory; they wear ear-rings; they are embellished with pearl necklaces; in brilliance they are superior to Devas; they are omniscient and observers of everything.

319. They divide themselves into various forms and enjoy various sports and pleasures, rare for others. They are devoid of death and old age.

320. They can go anywhere they please. They are great Siddhas themselves and they are further enlightened by other Siddhas. Thus the attendants of the eleven Rudras of great souls are crores and crores.

---

1. A Purāṇic way of describing the *Salokatā*, *Samīpatā* and *Sarūpatā* types of liberation.

321. With them, Maheśvara, the noble-souled lord of Devas, the beloved lover of Pārvatī, rejoices there fully sympathetic with his devotees.

322. I do not find any difference between those Rudras and the noble-souled Bhava. I am speaking the truth unto you.

323-324. The lordly Mātariśvā (Wind-god) thus concluded the holy story. All the sages resplendent like the Sun, considered that they attained great blessing on hearing the extremely meritorious story of the three-eyed Lord. They were delighted much. Honouring him suitably they spoke thus to Vāyu of great strength.

The Sages said :

325-326. O highly exalted and fortunate Wind-God ! The excellent holy *Aupasargika* eighth abode of Īśvara and its magnitude has been recounted precisely to us by you. It is redolent with the excellent fragrance of the great Ātman.

327. The grandeur of Mahādeva is difficult to be understood even by Suras. Due to the greatness belonging to himself, the lord of unmeasured splendour has thousand Gaṇas.

328-329. Non-delusion is effected by him in his devotees in order to bless them. In the abode of the lord of Devas, the *Vibhūti* (excellence, grandeur) that assumes a cosmic form shines very well. It is unequalled and is served (attended) by Brahmalakṣmī (the glory of Brahma or Brahman) itself. It appears like the Moon that pervades the sky with the moonlight.

330. You have also mentioned everything regarding the noble-souled Rudras who are equal to Mahādeva. All these stories came out of your mouth like nectar.

331. Without drinking it devoutly, of what use are our excellent holy rites ? There is nothing (?) which is not known by us. O Prāṇa (life-breath), O excellent one among Devas, it behoves you to answer our question precisely.

Sūta said :

332. That lord (Wind-god) spoke: What else shall I explain again ? O sages of excellent rites, what should be recounted by me ? I shall tell it.

The Sages said :

333-335. Please precisely recount to us what, at the time of *Ābhūtasaṁplava*, will be the state of the Ādityas who stand by as attendants (near the lord), the lions who had been the outcome of the lord's furious outburst, the Vaiśvānara groups of Bhūtas (goblins), the tigers and other followers about whom you have mentioned along with the groups of lions and tigers. What will be their state as well as the state of those who have attained Siddhi at the time of the terrible dissolution, when all living beings are destroyed?

(On hearing it) *Mātariśvā* (*the Wind-god*) *said* :

336-338. This is the greatest and (secret) reality.[1] I shall recount it. Please listen. Those who have gone there before, the sons of Brahmā, viz. Sanaka, Sananda and Sanātana, Voḍhu, Kapila, Āsuri of great fame, Sage Pañcaśikha and others have known the existence of Īśvara, the unmanifest source of origin (and attained salvation).

339-341. Thereafter, when much time elapses, at the close of the Kalpas, when even the great *Bhūtas* (Elements) are destroyed and utter annihilation takes place, many crores of Rudragaṇas delightedly (meditate on) Maheśvara, closely adhere to eight types of truth (?), desist from enjoying melody and other objects of pleasure, enter all the living beings through their brilliance accompanied by perfect knowledge and attain the unagitated *Vaihāyasapada* (the abode of firmament) in order to bless the living beings sympathetically.

342. The noble-souled ones attain to Maheśvara of the subtle nature of Paramāṇu (Atom) there. They cross the river of births and deaths of great eddies and whirlpools of terrific nature.

343. Then they see Śarva and the great Brahman. They are accompanied by those seven goddesses who have been glorified (before).

1. Here is a description of what happens to the residents of Śiva's city after *Ābhutasaṁplava*. They enter Lord Śiva who is a subtle *Paramāṇu*. The concept of Śiva as an atom shows Vaiśeṣika influence. Historical Śāṅkhya teachers like Kapila, Āsuri, Pañcaśikha are elevated to the exalted position of sages like Sanatkumāra, Sanaka.

344-345. Lord Śaṅkara draws within him the thousand lions, the Ādityas, the Vaiśvānara groups of *Bhūtas*, the tigers and his own followers (the *Rudragaṇas*). Thereafter he draws these seven Lokas that rush (towards him) and the five Mahābhūtas (the great elements).

346-347. Accompanied by Viṣṇu, he makes (the worlds) united (sustained) and annihilates. He is Rudra who is of the nature of Sāman and Yajur (Vedas). He is warped and woofed both within and without, decisively. O Brāhmaṇas, he is the only lord and leader. He is beginningless. He is the annihilator.

348-349. Then all those sages (of Naimiṣa forest) refulgent like the Sun consecrated the sacred fire in their own hermitage. They thereafter devoted themselves to the worship of Maheśvara by means of the purity of their inner soul mentally, verbally and physically.

350. They were merciful towards all living beings and engaged themselves in observing fasts and holy rites. All their doubts were cleared and the unequalled divine Yoga was attained by them.

351. After attaining these by means of the mind endowed with perfect knowledge and their greatest devotion, the *Sālokya* form of salvation was attained by them. It is the eternal and unchanging region.

352-355. He who regularly reads this hymn of prayer narrated by Vāyu, whether a Brāhmaṇa, a Kṣatriya or a Vaiśya but observing his duties, attains *Sālokya* with Rudra. He will be endowed with devotion and be free from ailments. A Śūdra who is not addicted to wine, who is a devotee of Bhava and who has conquered his sense organs, remains till the time of dissolution without obstacles and attains the leadership of Gaṇas or the abode coveted by all. If he is a wine addict, he rejoices with those groups of Bhūtas who are drunkards. Being worshipped on the earth he will be the granter of boons to men. Thus the Wind-god the excellent lord spoke these words.

CHAPTER FORTY[1]

Dissolution of the Universe

Sūta said:

1. I shall now recount the process of dissolution (*Pratyāhāra*) at the end of *Para* (one full day and night) of the self-born god Brahmā, when the period of existence of the Lord comes to a close.

2. During the process of *Pratyāhāra*, Īśvara swallows the unmanifest ones[2] entirely and clearly (*vyaktam*) in exactly the same manner as he does the subtle ones.

3-4. [3]This activity of re-absorption of creations begins even as the Kalpas have not fully expired. This terribly critical period sets in at the closing period of the tenure of the office of the Manu named Druma (?) towards the end of Kaliyuga then. The entire creation merges in the *apratyakṣa* (the invisible i.e. the unmanifest). It is called annihilation.

5-7. When that period of 'great washing off' begins to function,[4] when the withdrawal of the creation is imminent, elements gross and subtle (*Bhūtas* and *Tanmātras*) are destroyed. All evolutes beginning with *Mahat* and ending with *Viśeṣa* be-

---

1. This chapter corresponds to Bd.P.III.4.3 Only verse numbers are referred.

2. The word *avyaktān* in the line: *avyaktān grasate vyaktam* creates confusion. If emended as '*avyaktam*' as in Bd.P.v.2 the verse means 'during the process of *Pratyāhāra*, the *Anyakta* (the Unmanifest one) swallows the *Vyakta* (the Manifest one, the whole universe) entirely in the same way as Īśvara created the manifest universe which is very subtle.'

3. For *Paraṁ tad anukalpānām apūrṇe* Bd.P.3 reads *Parānta-dvyaṇukādyānāṁ sampūrṇe*: It means '(when the extremely dreadful destruction) of everything beginning with molecules of two atoms and ending with *para* (greatest thing) is imminent it is called *Saṁhāra*.

4. Verses 5-33 state the process of involution of *Tattvas*. Thus at the end of a Kalpa, the element *Pṛthvī* is swallowed by water; *Prithvī* loses its special quality, viz. smell and merges in water. The process of 'Swallowing' a lower element by the higher element may be summarised as follows:

The element Pṛthvī merges in——→Water——→Fire——→Wind——→ Ether————→Bhūtādi(Buddhi)————→Mahat————→Guṇa-Sāmya (equilibrium of Guṇas—Sattva, Rajas and Tamas) or Prakṛti.

come annihilated. All this happens naturally. At the outset the vast sheet of waters absorbs the quality of smell of the (element) earth. The earth devoid of smell becomes dissolved. When thus the quality of smell of the earth is dissolved, the earth assumes the form of water.

8-9. The waters of great velocity and loud report spread throughout the entire universe and stay by awaiting destruction (?). The special attribute of the waters (*Rasa*—taste) becomes merged in *Jyotis* (fiery element). At the destruction of the subtle element *Rasa*, the waters too get dissolved.

10. When *Rasa* is absorbed by *Tejas* (fiery element), the waters become merged in it. When the waters are thus absorbed, only *Tejas* is seen all round.

11. The fire element, pervading everywhere, absorbs the waters. The entire universe is gradually filled up with flames of fire.

12. When this (entire universe) is filled with flames, the flames spread on all sides, above and below. Vāyu (the wind element) swallows up *Rūpa* (colour or form), the luminous quality of *Jyotis* (the fire element). The entire fire element merges in the cosmic air, like the flame of lamp in the great wind.

13. When the Rūpa *Tanmātra* (the essential quality) is dissolved, *Vibhāvasu* (the element of Fire) becomes bereft of *Rūpa* (colour). *Tejas* then subsides. The great *Tejas* is then blown off by Vāyu.

14. When the entire universe thus becomes bereft of light, the element of *Tejas* having merged in Vāyu, the element of Vāyu resorts to the source of its origin.

15. It shakes everything above, below and the sides in all the ten quarters. Then *Ākāśa* (Ether) absorbs the quality of Vāyu, viz. *Sparśa* (Touch).

16. The element of Vāyu subsides and the open firmament alone remains, *sans* colour, *sans* taste, *sans* touch and *sans* smell. It has no physical body as well.

17. The great circular hole, the Ākāśa, characterised by its quality of sound, shines filling everything with its sounds.

18. The *Śabda*-characterised Ākāśa envelops everything and

remains (steady). Then *Bhūtādi* (the Cosmic Ego) absorbs the the quality of sound belonging to it.

19. Then the Bhūtas and the sense-organs get merged simultaneously in *Bhūtadi*. *Bhūtādi* is of the form of Cosmic Ego. It is said to be of the quality of Tamas.

20. The principle *Mahat* characterised by *Buddhi* (the cosmic intellect) absorbs *Bhūtadi*. The *Mahat* principle is to be known to be of the form of *Saṁkalpa* (conception) and *Adhyavasāya* (determination, will).

21. Philosophers who ponder over reality call it by the synonyms *Buddhi* (Intellect), *Manas* (Mind), *Liṅga* (the Symbol), *Mahat* (Great) and *Akṣara* (the Imperishable).

22. When all the Bhūtas become dissolved, the Guṇas remain in equilibrium, the entire universe becomes dark and gloomy; the groups of causes of the worlds remain merged in Ātman.

23-24. The creation becomes re-absorbed in Prakṛti; neither the beginning nor the end of anything is perceived; nothing is seen; no name or form remains; even those endowed with perfect knowledge do not become aware of anything; no going in or coming out is observed.

25-27. Such a situation is inferred and conceived mentally and the following account is given. All objects become established in that existent-cum-non-existent (*sad-asad-ātmika*) eternal great cause. This automotive activity cannot be pointed out through any specific cause. The dissolution of the Seven Prakṛtis occurs in this manner. At the time of the reabsorption of creation, they enter into one another. That by which the globular Egg is enveloped becomes dissolved.

28. The seven continents, the seven oceans, the seven worlds and the seven mountains are enveloped by the covering of water. This *Udakāvaraṇa* (water-covering) becomes merged in *Jyotis* (Fire).

29. (Defective verse) The *Taijasa* (fiery) *Āvaraṇa* (covering) is absorbed by the Wind element. The cover of the wind element is absorbed by the element Ether.

30. *Bhūtādi* (the Cosmic Ego) absorbs the Ethereal *Āvaraṇa*. *Mahat* characterised by cosmic intelligence (*Buddhi*) absorbs *Bhūtādi*.

31. The Unmanifest absorbs the principle of *Mahat.* Thereafter the Guṇas attain equilibrium. This annihilation and extension of creation is pursued through the unmanifest Prakṛti stationed in Brahman.

32. It creates and absorbs the *Vikāras* (created objects) for the sake of creation and annihilation. The Siddhas who are endowed with perfect knowledge have all instruments in the activity of annihilation (?)

33. Attaining a quick motion in these abodes due to their self-control, these *Kṣetrajñas* become bereft of *Karaṇas* (sense organs and organs of activity).

34. They call the *Avyakta* (the Unmanifest) by the term *kṣetra* and Brahmā (or Brahman) is called *Kṣetrajña.* Their union is beginningless but is caused by *Sādharmya* (similarity of characteristics) and *Vaidharmya* (dissimilarity of characteristics).

35. O Brāhmaṇas, it is thus that one should know with regard to all *Sargas* (creations) and *Kṣetrajñas.* By the knowledge of the *Kṣetras* separately and severally, a *Brahmavid* (man with the knowledge of Brahman) should be known.

36. The state of being the object of knowledge (*Viṣayatva*) and of not being so (*Aviṣayatva*) are proclaimed (as the characteristics) of *Kṣetra* and *Kṣetrajña.* Brahmā should be known as *Aviṣaya* (not object of knowledge, the knower) and *Kṣetra* is called *Viṣaya* (object of knowledge)*.

37. *Kṣetra* is presided over by *Kṣetrajña* and so is said to be for his sake. Since the bodies are many, the *Śarīrin* (the embodied soul) is remembered as many.

38. These souls are stationed without any arrangement (*avyūhāt*) and are unmixed (*a-saṅkarāt*) like luminaries. Since there is the perception of happiness and sorrow severally in the

---

*The text in Vā.P. condradicts the 1st line of the verse. It runs thus : *Brahmā tu viṣayo jñeyo'viṣayaḥ kṣetram ucyate* 'Brahma should be known as Viṣaya (object of knowledge) and Kṣetra is called Aviṣaya (non-object, knower).

Bd. P. v. 302 gives correct reading : *Brahmā tvaviṣayo jñeyo viṣayaḥ kṣetram ucyate.* If *tu viṣaya* be emended as *tv-aviṣaya* (*tvaviṣaya*) and the avagraha after *viṣayo* is dropped, the Vā.P. text will not be a contradiction.

different bodies, the multiplicity of Puruṣas should be known by one who is wise.

39. When the withdrawal of those different beings sets in, that is brought about naturally after the lapse of a great deal of period.

40. At that time the passion for sustenance of the worlds of the self-born god Brahmā recedes, along with all the residents of Brahmā's heaven.

41. Then the attachment for the sustenance of those residing (in meditation) in Ātman recedes and they begin to see defects therein of their contemporaries.

42-43. Then their (sense of) detachment is aroused and it dispels their *Ātma-vāda* (egotism). *Bhojya* (object of enjoyment) and *Bhoktṛtva* (the state of being the enjoyer)—through this they comprehend Saṁsāra. They have been *Kṣetrajñas* due to their vision of their separateness. Then the residents of Brahmaloka (see the multiplicity of individuals but) they are beyond the cause of Prakṛti.

44. Now they dwell in the Ātman alone. They are quiescent and endowed with (true) vision. All of them are pure, free from blemish and in conscious or unconscious stage.

45. It is proclaimed that they attain complete absolution there itself and they do not return to Saṁsāra since they are devoid of Guṇas (state of *nirguṇatva*) and the sense of identity with the body (*nirātmatva*).

46-47. Thus the process of dissolution by the Self-born Brahmā through Prakṛti has been recounted. In this *Prasaṁyama* (final curbing and restraint) the *Karaṇas* (organs of activity) of all living beings differ. Thus is the curbing of the *Tattvas* (Principles) along with that of the *Karaṇas*. This *Tattvaprasaṁyama* is remembered as capable of repetition.

Sūta said :

48-50. Dharma and Adharma, penance, perfect knowledge, the auspicious, the inauspicious, truth, falsehood, superiority, inferiority, happiness, sorrow, likes, dislikes—all these are mere attributes of one who has gone* (i.e. who has attained salvation).

**Prapañcastham* in Bd. P. v. 26 'current in the worldly existence' is logically a better reading.

Whatever is meritorious and sinful, auspicious and inauspicious is regarded as the nature of Guṇas of the (spiritually) wise who are devoid of (attachment to) sense organs—all merits and demerits are stabilised in Prakṛti. It is the Prakṛti which is the source of origin. (Merit and demerit) are deposited in the nature of embodied beings.

51. The merits and demerits of living beings that have been stabilised in Prakṛti, are declared to lie unmanifested. The same merits and demerits (in different situations) join this body or the next.

52. Dharma and Adharma (virtue and sin) are merely two qualities of creatures. They flourish in the form of the body along with the organs of sense (*Karaṇa*) of creatures.

53. The sentient Guṇas (i.e. Sattva etc.) presided over by Kṣetrajña get dissolved during the primary creation and secondary creation in the world. The creatures come into contact or get separated from their *Karaṇas* (organs of activity) and they move about (i.e. undergo worldly existence and suffering).

54. The *Vṛttis* (proclivities, causes of activities) are threefold according as they are of the nature of Sattva, Rajas or Tamas. They function on being presided over (and activised) by Puruṣa.

55. The (attribute) Sattva of the divine nature is conducive to attain the upper part (heaven) and Tamas is of the nature of (falling off) to the lower part (hell). The activiser of the two, in the middle is Rajas which moves about repeatedly in this world.

56-57. In all the worlds, within all the living beings these three types of emotional activities are the original causes of the nature of Guṇas. One who knows need not entertain much doubt about this. Urged by (?) Avidyā,[1] activities are pursued by men and they derive meritorious, sinful or non-committal goals through these three.

1. Verses 56-72 discuss the nature of Avidyā, three bondages created by it, the defects such as *Rāga* (Attachment), *Dveṣa* (Hatred) resulting from it and leading to hell (67-69) and birth in lower species (70-72).

58. All living creatures do not understand the reality due to their being overwhelmed by Tamas. But not realising the Tattva (Reality), they are fettered in three ways.

59. He is bound by three types of bondages:

(i) *Prākṛta Bandha* (bondage of Prakṛti)

(ii) *Vaikārika Bandha* (bondage of its evolutes)

(iii) Bondage called *Dakṣiṇa* (a technical term in the Sāṇkhya System for the third bondage).

And being bound thus; the creature turns round and round here (in Saṁsārā).

60-61. These are the three types of bondage due to ignorance. The following are the usual defects (due to them)—Seeing permanence in what is transcient; perception of happiness in what actually is the cause of misery; feeling of possessiveness in what does not belong to one; and decisive knowledge of purity in what is impure. Those who have these mental defects have the defects of knowledge through misapprehension.

62. The cessation of attachment (*Rāga*) and hatred (*Dveṣa*) is called knowledge. Ignorance is the root-cause of Tamas. Rajas has two-fold Karman (the auspicious and inauspicious) as its result. The resumption of the physical body once again is the result of Karmas. Thus great misery begins to function.

63. The various sins committed by ears, eyes, skin, tongue and nose are the causes of the rebirth and misery.

64. A man with a craving is said to be a *Bāla* (an immature or ignorant person). As a result of actions committed by himself, the individual soul goes round and round there only (in the Saṁsāra) like the bull yoked to the oil-pressing machine.

65. Hence it is taught that gross ignorance is the cause of all miseries. Realising that it is the sole enemy one shall endeavour to acquire knowledge.

66. One renounces (*tyajate**) everything by perfect knowledge. As a result of renunciation the intellect becomes detached; one becomes pure as a result of detachment; the pure one becomes liberated by means of Sattva Guṇa.

67. Henceforth I shall explain *Rāga* (passion and attachment) that overwhelms living beings. Due to this attachment,

---

*Reading in A. '*vijayati*' in our text is rather confusing.

all living beings become indulgent in worldly pleasures in spite of themselves.

68. Attachment is undesirable and calamitous inasmuch as it yields pleasure, sufferings and dejection. Suffering is due to the misery that befalls (when the desired object is not acquired) and the recollection of (previously experienced) happiness.

69. It is the attachment to worldly pleasures that is declared as the cause of births. In all the physical worlds beginning with Brahmā and ending with the immobile beings, this attachment alone is the cause of birth and that is the result of ignorance. Hence one shall avoid ignorance.

70-71. If one does not accept the words of sages as authority nor has regard for good manners as practised by virtuous and respectable men; if one is opposed to the discipline of (four) castes and stages in life; and if a man is antagonistic to wise men and scriptural injunctions—that is the cause of rebirth in lower species.

72. There are various kinds of tortures in remaining (or taking birth) among the six kinds of lower animals. There is complete obstruction in the matter of cause and object of knowledge (?).

73. The entire non-attainment of *Aiśvarya* (glory and prosperity) is in the nature of *Pratighāta* (obstacle) (to the desires). Thus the four types of Tāmasa proclivities of the living beings etc. have been recounted.

74-75. The mind can be considered mainly Sāttvic if the Sāttvic traits are evinced. *Tattvas* can be comprehended only after viewing them in accordance with reality. And the knowledge of the multiplicity (? difference) of Sattva Guṇa and Kṣetrajñas is the perfect knowledge. It is said that Yoga originates from perfect knowledge.

76. Bondage is for one who is fettered to it (the worldy existence) and liberation is for one who is released therefrom. When the worldly existence recedes, the liberated soul is released even from the Liṅga Śarīra (the subtle frame or body consisting of Prāṇas, subtle sense organs etc.).

77. Devoid of any *Saṁbandha* (contact) and in a state of being unconscious (of the external world), he abides in his own

self. Even while remaining within his own self, he is touched (contaminated) by diversity and multiplicity.

78. Thus the characteristic features of perfect knowledge and liberation have been succinctly explained. That liberation is declared by those who see truth.

79-80. The first one is the separation from worldly impressions, thanks to perfect knowledge. The second one is due to destruction of passion (passionate attachment) whereby the liberated soul attains *Kaivalya*, because even the *Liṅga Śarīra* (the subtle inner body) is absent. Through *Kaivalya* he becomes *Nirañjana* (unsullied). By not being sullied, he becomes *Śuddha* (pure). In this state of liberation there is no guide or leader. The third type of cause of liberation is by the destruction of *Tṛṣṇā* (thirst) (for enjoyment).

81-82. The liberated souls do not experience misery caused by the obstacle to the worldly objects of desired melody etc. These eight things caused by Prakṛti adhere to the *Kṣetrajñas*. They are called *Guṇas* and *Mātras* (the three *Guṇas* and the five *Tanmātras*).

Henceforth I shall explain detachment, arising from the sight of faults.

83. One should practice non-hatred and absence of attachment to the five *Viṣayas* (objects of sensual enjoyment) of both divine and human nature, after seeing the defects therein.

84. One should avoid heart-burn, pleasure and dejectedness. By having recourse to non-attachment the embodied soul becomes free from *Mamatva* (the feeling of my-ness i.e. possessiveness).

85. He should decide in his mind (intellect) that (the worldly existence) is non-eternal, inauspicious and conducive to misery. Then with Sāttvic traits he should perform pure activities.

86-87. When the attachment to worldly objects of pleasure becomes firm, he becomes able to see defects and blemishes entirely.

At the time of the journey[1] (i.e. at the time of death) the heat in the body becomes virulent due to conditioning causes

1. Verses 87-92 describe the process of death.

e.g. *Doṣas* (disorderly state of the humours in the body produced by causes dependent on particular circumstances).

88. Due to the chilliness, the virulently excited Vāyu (life breath) pierces the centres of Prāṇas (vital airs), cuts off vulnerable parts of the body and rises up.

89. It is the breath stationed in the abodes of vital airs of all living beings. By contraction, Jñāna (consciousness and knowledge) becomes covered up and the activities are enshrouded.

90. The Jīva (the individual soul) being bereaved of the supporting body, is induced by its own actions committed before. It then dislodges the Prāṇas from the eight limbs.

91. (In the end) abandoning the body, it ceases to have breathing activity. Being abandoned by the vital airs thus, the person is called "Dead".

92. This is something like this. When someone holds the glow-worm in his hand and goes about here and there he too is visible in its light. He who kills it, though a carrier (of the glow-worm) ceases to be a carrier (leader).

93-94. The third, viz. the elimination of thirst or covetousness is spoken as the characteristic of liberation. It is the (result of) observation of defects in five objects of sensual pleasure such as sound and others. Absence of hatred, absence of intense attachment, avoidance of pleasure and agony (about objects of pleasure)—these are the dissolutions of the eight Prakṛtis (primary essences which evolved the whole Universe).

95. All the eight Prakṛtis mentioned before should be known in order, beginning with *Avyakta* (the Unmanifest) and ending with *Bhūtas* (Elements). These are called the dissolution of the Prakṛtis.

96. Those who follow the rigorous discipline of the four castes and stages of life and those who do not go contrary to the injunctions of the scriptures are called *Śiṣṭas* (the eminent and the distinguished). The practice and adherence of the discipline of Varṇas and Āśramas is conducive to the attainment of the abodes of the Devas (i.e. Heaven).

97. The eight groups of Devas (and their abodes) are those

beginning with Brahmā and ending with Piśācas. The Siddhis conducive to *Aiśvarya* (supernatural powers), *Aṇimā* (minuteness) etc. are the causes eight in number.

98-102. Those who stay in those abodes do not experience the misery due to the obstacle to the achievement of such desired objects as sweet melody etc. These are the eight Prākṛta forms in order. They come into contact with the *Kṣetrajñas*. They are of the nature of the three Guṇas and five *Tanmātras*. People do not see with their eyes the clouds distinct from the water therein in the course of the rainy season. (Similarly ordinary people do not see the individual soul. They can only infer.)

The Siddhas, however see it like this by means of their divine vision. The soul takes all kinds of bodies such as those of Brāhmaṇas and those of Cāṇḍālas*.

Thus he moves about in a certain order up and down as well as in the sides (as a result of his own Karmans). He is called by these various names, all synonymic, viz. *Jīva* (individual soul), *Prāṇa* (vital air), *Liṅga* (the symbol), *Kāraṇa* (cause). In both manifest and unmanifest (worlds) he is an authority.

103. After realising categories ending with *Avyakta* (the Unmanifest) and what is presided over by the *Kṣetrajña*, he becomes pure and becomes liberated through knowledge.

104-106. When the truth is realized, the principle that was obscure comes out. But in different bodies that have completely ceased to exist, the *Kāraṇa* (the individual soul) differs from the *Avyakta* and the *Jñānin*. One who is completely liberated from the body in the form of Guṇas as well as Prāṇa etc. does not take up another body, just as sprout never comes out when seed is burnt.

107. Due to knowledge he becomes enlightened and pure of the four *Daśās* (conditions). He follows the Prakṛti. They say that Prakṛti is the reality, while *Vikāras* (its evolutes) are unreal.

---

*The reading *śvāviti śvānapānaśca* is obscure. Bd. P. v. 78 reads *khādataś cānnapānāni* 'Siddhas see...even as they take food, drinks, enter different yonis.'

108. Its *Sad-bhāva* (apparent? existence) should be known as *Anṛta* (unreal). *Sadbhāva* (State of being existent) is called *Satya* (Reality). *Satya* (Brahman) is without name and form.[1] They called *Kṣetrajña*[2] as possessing name and form.

109. Because he knows (thoroughly) the *Kṣetra* (the field i.e. the body) he is called *Kṣetrajña*. *Kṣetrajña* is auspicious because of the perception of *Kṣetra*.

110. *Kṣetrajña* is remembered. Hence it is mentioned as *Kṣetra* by those who know it. *Kṣetra* is seen to be without intelligence but *Kṣetrajña* is always endowed with intelligence.

111. Those who know *Kṣetra* call it so because of its *Kṣayaṇa* (destruction), *Karaṇa* (being created), *Kṣatatrāṇa* (protection from wound), *Bhojyatva* (state of being what is eaten or enjoyed) and *Viṣayatva* (state of being the object).

112. All categories beginning with *Mahat*, ending with *Viśeṣa* possess variety of forms and they are characterised as *Vikāra* (an evolute, change). Hence they are peculiar (*Vilakṣaṇa*). Hence verily *Akṣara* (imperishable) approaches the *Kṣara* (perishable)[3].

113. That evolute (*Vikāra*) is called *Kṣara* as it wastes away and perishes.[4]

114. Happiness, misery, delusion are called *Bhojya* (that which is to be experienced). It is *Viṣaya* (object of enjoyment) as it is insentient. That which has the opposite quality[5] is remembered as *Vibhu*.

115. It is called *Akṣara* (imperishable) for the following reasons : It does not waste away (*na kṣiyate*). It does not perish (*na kṣarati*). Evolutes spread from it. It is not diminished.

---

1. The compound: *anāmarūpa-kṣetrajña-nāmarūpa* is split in Bd. P. as *anāmarūpam* and *Kṣetrajña*.

2. Verses 108-130. A desultory discussion of *Kṣetrajña*. It incidentally explains the terms *sadbhāva, kṣetra, karaṇa, akṣara, urpuṣa* and others.

3. *Sākṣarakṣaram eva ca* in the text is obscure. Hence the reading in Bd P. v.90, *so'kṣaraḥ kṣaram eti ca*/ is accepted.

4. A adds as v. 114 (ch.102 in A, p.417) here. It is untraced in our Text. 'That which protects man from Saṁsāra and hells and also from 'misery is called Kṣetra.'

5. *tad hi dharmavibhuḥ smṛtaḥ* in the text is obscure. Hence *tad vidharmā vibhuḥ smṛtaḥ* in corresponding Bd. P. v.93 is accepted.

116. Since it lies in *Pur* (*puri anuśete*) it is called Puruṣa. The term Puruṣa is derived also as follows: Since it is *Purapratyayika*—that is the *Pratyayi* (the knower) of the *Pura* (Body), it is called so.

117-118. He is other than what can be called existent, non-existent, bound, liberated, mobile, stable. As he is devoid of any cause, he cannot be specified (by any of these terms).[1]

119. Since he is very pure, he cannot be indicated specifically. Since he is full of bliss, it is of equal vision. Since he is the cause (*Kārin*) of *Ātmapratyaya* (the knowledge of Ātman), no causal expression applies to it[2] (?) It can be imagined or inferred. Those who perceive thus are not deluded.

120. When he sees the knower who is quiescent in regard to all objects, who is of the nature of Vision, and who is the only one to be pointed out among the visible and invisible objects, his emancipation (uplift) takes place.

121-122. After having realised this great Being, the perfect knower attains quiescence (calmness). He, the perfect knower, does not see the separateness in the effect, cause, the physical objects of intellect etc., that is in contact or severed, and him who is dead or alive.[3]

123. The causal Ātman controls that Ātman (the individual soul) by means of his own self. He abides in the Prakṛti, in its cause and in his own Ātman.

124-125. He exists. He does not exist. He is he or he is another. He is here or he is hereafter. He has oneness or separateness. He is Kṣetrajña or Puruṣa. He possesses Ātman or he is devoid of Ātman. He is sentient or non-sentient. He is a doer or non-doer. He is the enjoyer or he is only the enjoyed.

126. On realizing the unsullied Kṣetrajña, there is no further return to Saṁsāra. It is called *Avācya* (inexpressibe) because it cannot be described by means of logic or by arguments it cannot be grasped.

127. It is (called) *Apratarkya* (that which cannot be argued about) because it cannot be conceived. After attaining that

1. Bd.P. v. 96 reads: *jñātājñānavivarjitaḥ* 'He is a knower, devoid of ignorance'. A better reading.

2. Bd. P. v. 98 reads *anyūnaṁ vāpyahetukam* 'not deficient and not caused—spontaneous'.

3. Some lines in the text mixed up.

principle along with the mind, he (the soul) does not become attached (to other objects).

128-130. When the Kṣetrajña is free from Guṇas, when it is pure, quiescent, unsullied, exhausted, devoid of both happiness and misery, when it is checked and attains calmness and when it becomes *Nirātmaka* (devoid of ego?), there is neither *Vācyatva* (state of being expressed) nor *Avācyatva* (the state of not being expressed) (?) These two, annihilation and creation are manifest and unmanifest. Puruṣa creates and swallows (the entire world). Everything functions again with the *Kṣetrajña* presiding over.

131. At its end, it consciously resorts to the *Adhiṣṭhāna* (substratum). Their mutual contact is known as being brought about by *Sādharmya* and *Vaidharmya* (similarity and dissimilarity). The *Saṁyoga* (contact) of the great Puruṣa is beginningless.*

132. As long as creation and subsidiary creation last Prakṛti keeps Puruṣa restrained and stays: At the outset it functions unintelligently but in favour of it. Its function is for the sake of Puruṣa.

133. This creation and dissolution are effected by Pradhāna as well as by Īśvara. But it is beginningless and endless. Prakṛti approaches the Universe even while terrifying it with the feeling of identification.

134. Thus the third creation of Prakṛti characterised by *Hetu* (cause) has been recounted. One who strictly adheres to it becomes liberated as mentioned by poets (seers).

135. Thus three types of dissolution have been recounted to you in detail as well as in proper order. What shall I explain further?

---

*After slightly correcting obvious mistakes, with the help of Bd. P. 109.

CHAPTER FORTYONE*

Recreation of the Cosmic Egg

The Sages said :

1-4. O Sūta, a great narrative has been recounted by Your Holiness.[1] You have narrated the wonderful deeds of all subjects along with Manus, of Devas along with sages, of Pitṛs, Gandharvas, Bhūtas (goblins), Piśācas (ghosts), serpents, Rākṣasas, Daityas, Dānavas, Yakṣas and birds. Their *Vidhi*-supported decision of their Dharmas and their excellent and fine births have been narrated in wonderful stories. Being narrated to us in your sweet voice (or in charmingly polished words), O son of Sūta, it rendered pleasure to our ears and minds for ever till the end of the creation of living beings.

5. After having thus propitiated and honoured Sūta, all the great sages, the performers of the *Satra* (sacrifice) asked him about the process of creative function.[2]

6-7. "O highly intelligent Sūta, how does creation reappear? To us who ask you, please narrate how the creation begins again, when the bonds have dissolved, when all the Guṇas have attained the state of equilibrium, when everything is enveloped in darkness, when the groups of *Vikāras* (created beings) have become inactive and stationed in the unmanifest Ātman and when all the Kṣetrajñas have attained *Sāyujya* (identity) with Brahman."

8. On being thus requested, Sūta Lomaharṣaṇa again began to narrate the process of creation.

---

*This chapter corresponds to Bd.P. 3.4.4. References are to verse nunbers therein.

1. The speech of sages shows that this must be the last chapter. They have duly honoured Sūta. They performed *Avabhṛtha* bath and went to heaven (42). The review of the contents, *Phalaśruti* and the genealogy of teachers who handed down the text of this Purāṇa—all these confirm the above conclusion.

2. Dissolution of the Universe and its recreation form an important characteristic (*Lakṣaṇa*) of a Purāṇa. As the topic of recreation of the Brahmāṇḍa was not properly dealt in previous chapters, it is taken here to fulfil the *Pañcalakṣaṇa* criterion.

9. "I shall recount to you how the creation functions (again). The order of the creation should be known (to occur) as (it took place) before.

10. I shall mention what is seen and what can be inferred. I shall mention cogent arguments. From it (the principle of creative function), all words recede without reaching it along with the mind (i.e. the mind cannot conceive it, the words cannot express it).

11. Just as the unmanifest is invisible and incomprehensible, (the objects of creation too) are invisible and incomprehensible. When the *Vikāras* (evolutes) become dissolved they are seen nowhere. The Guṇas attain equilibrium and the created things recede.

12. Pradhāna stands on a similar footing with Puruṣas. The Dharmas and the Adharmas of living beings too merge in *Avyakta* (the Unmanifest).

13. Their Dharma of the nature of Sattva gets settled in the Guṇa of Sattva, while Adharma of the nature of Tamas (darkness) abides in the Guṇa Tamas.

14. These two Guṇas are devoid of distinction when the Guṇas are in the state of equilibrium. In all the functions of Pradhāna the activities will be backed by the intellect.

15. The Kṣetrajña will preside over those Guṇas without the (intermediary) intellect. Thus the *Pura* (physical body) will be attained through *Abhimāna* (the act of identification).

16. When it becomes necessary to function both[1] the Kṣetra and Kṣetrajña begin to interact mutually; they become united together in the relationship of *Bhojya* (that which has to be enjoyed) and *Bhoktṛ* (the enjoyer).

17. The only refuge for them is the Avyakta. Stabilised in the state of equilibrium, the group of Guṇas become presided over by the Kṣetrajña (at the time of the beginning of creation) and then their equilibrium is upset.

18. Then both Kṣetra and Kṣetrajña reach the state of

---

1. After describing the state of *Guṇa-Sāmya* (Equilibrium of all Guṇas), vv. 16ff. describe how that state gets disturbed and how the evolution (creation) of the Universe takes plaee. The influence of Sāṅkhyas is obvious in the description of evolution and involution of the Universe.

Vyakta (manifestation). Sattva (Guṇa) presided over by Ksetrajña will produce *Vikāra* (evolutes).

19. The twentyfour principles of the nature of Guṇas beginning with *Mahat* and ending with *Viśeṣa* (which are called Vikāras) attain the Kṣetrajña, Pradhāna and Puruṣa.

20. Then in the Brahmāṇḍa (the Cosmic Egg) Īśvara will be born (manifest) first. He will be the lord of all living beings, of the entire knowable universe. He is Śiva.

21. He is the overlord of all liberated souls. He is the great Brahmā of the nature of Brahman. He is the primordial lord and it is said that his manifestation is for the sake of blessing Pradhāna.

22. Kṣetra and Kṣetrajña are self-born and beginningless. They are remembered as subtle. Their union is beginningless. They are aware of all Kṣetras.

23. They are joined together without the intermediation of intellect (*Abuddhipūrvakam*) like *Maśaka* (mosquito) and *Udumbara* tree. They are stationed beginninglessly and inconceivably like water and fish.

24. The creation functions again as it had functioned before. The *Ajña* (non-knowing) Prakṛti transforms itself into the universe functioning through its Guṇas, viz. Rajas, Sattva and Tamas.

25. At the time of the functioning (of Prakṛti) the Kṣetrajña human beings are overwhelmed by Rajas Guṇa and attain the (benefit of) the principles of Mahat, Ahaṁkāra etc. ending with Viśeṣa and the sense organs. Then the Guṇas reach their end (?)

26. God Brahmā is of truthful conception. While he was meditating on the *Sat*, the Guṇas Rajas, Sattva and Tamas though mutually dissimilar became manifest as caused by the *Sat* (the existent).

27. Kṣetrajñas (knowers of the Kṣetra or body) are ever produced both at the beginning and at the end. *Abhimānins* (*Ātmans* who identify themselves) become born with instruments of actions readily achieved.

28. All beings are produced from the *Avyakta* (Unmanifest) at the outset itself, who had been Sādhakas (spiritual aspirants) or non-Sādhakas (?)

29. All of them undergoing the process of worldly existence along with their *Sthānas* (abodes) and *Prakaraṇas* (contexts?), attain their effects and are born again and again.

30. Dharma and Adharma are solely of the nature of quality. They begin (give rise to) each other through boons and blessings.

31. All are equal for the purpose of creation. It is at the beginning of creation that they undergo transformation. The Guṇas rush to him and hence it is liked by him.

32-33. The Kṣetrajñas attain again and again only those qualities which they had in the previous creation. Being created again and again they attain only them. Qualities of violent or non-violent temperament, softness or cruelty, virtuousness or sinful nature, truthfulness or falsehood—had already been conceived by them (in the former creation); they attain them again and hence they appeal to them.

34. It is through Guṇas that the multiplicity and diversity in the great Bhūtas (elements), in the sense-objects and in physical forms as well as the separation of living beings take place.

35. Thus I have recounted briefly to you the subsequent creation. Now I shall briefly recount the birth (manifestation) of Brahmā.[1]

36. From that *Avyakta* (unmanifest) cause which is eternal one and of the nature of *Sat* and *Asat* (existence and non-existence) Maheśvara (the great Lord) is born through Pradhāna and Puruṣa.

37. With the appellation 'Brahmā', he becomes the evolver. He creates the worlds once again of the nature of (i.e. characterised by) *Abhimāna* (referring all objects to the self) and Guṇas (Sattva etc.).

38. Ahaṁkāra (Cosmic Ego) is born of Mahat (the cosmic intellect) and Bhūtas are born of it (Ahaṁkāra).

---

1. Sūta narrates the recreation of the Universe by bringing in Purāṇic deities like Maheśvara and Brahmā and synthesizing the Sāṅkhya and Purāṇic accounts.

Bhūtas and *Indriyas* (sense organs) are born simultaneously from the Ātman. The different living beings are born from Bhūtas (elements).

It is thus that the creation begins to function.

39. The ramifications of these are extensive. I have recounted to you in accordance with my intellect and in the manner I have heard it, formerly. Know them in the same manner."

40. The sages living in the Naimiṣa forest heard the story of the origin, maintenance and destruction of the worlds and then finished the holy ablution of *Avabhṛtha* in the *Satra*. They became pure and attained the meritorious world.[1]

41. In the same manner, you worship duly Devatās (deities) etc., take the valedictory bath (*Avabhṛtha*) after the sacrifice and become pure. At the end of life be contented (that you have done your duty), abandon bodies, attain the meritorious world and proceed (to enjoy) as you please.

42. All the residents of the Naimiṣa forest, the performers of the *Satra* went to heaven after taking the ablution, *Avabhṛtha* on the conclusion of the sacrifice.

43. O excellent Brāhmaṇa, in the same manner you will also go to heaven at the end of your life after performing the various kinds of sacrifices and taking the *Avabhṛtha* bath in the end.

44-45. The Wind-god himself who is engaged in the welfare of the worlds, has narrated this popular *Purāṇa* consisting of the four Pādas[2] (sections), viz. *Prakriyā* is the first section, where the story is taken up (the other sections are) *Anuṣaṅga*, *Upodghāta* and *Upasaṁhāra*.

46-47. He narrated it to the sages after going to their *Satra* in the Naimiṣa forest. It is due to his favour, O excellent sages, that the story of the origin and dissolution of the living

1. Conclusion of the *Satra* (sacrificial session) and the completion of the narration of the Purāṇa synchronised. The author exhorts the later audience of the Purāṇa to perform sacrifices and go to heaven just as the sages in Naimiṣāraṇya did formerly.

2. A brief review of the main *Pādas* (Sections) of the Purāṇa.

beings has been learnt without any doubt. After clearly understanding this creation of the Pradhāna effected by Īśvara, an intelligent man will not be deluded.

48-49. The scholarly Brāhmaṇa who listens to or narrates or teaches this ancient *Itihāsa* rejoices in the worlds of Mahendra for eternal years.[1] After attaining *Sāyujya* with Brahman along with Brahmā he becomes liberated.

50. Eulogising those Prajāpatis, the famous noble-souled lords of earth,[2] he attains the status of Brahman.[3]

---

1. Verses 48-57 contain the *Phala-Śruti* of listening to or narrating this Purāṇa.

2. MS. Kha used by A. (Anandaśrama edition) contains the following additional verses:

(1) The learned scholar who narrates (makes other hear) this (Purāṇa) attains the high goal. He is endowed with wealth, food-grains, happiness and prosperity. There is no doubt about this.

(2) A Brāhmaṇa will attain knowledge (or learning) and union with Brahman. A Kṣatriya attains victory (in battles) and excellent position in the region of gods.

(3) A Vaiśya will get (ample) riches, food-grains and money. A Śūdra being blessed with progeny (sons and grandsons) gets happiness.

(4) He who learns or hears a verse, or a part of a verse of this Purāṇa goes to Viṣṇu's city (Vaikuṇṭha) after death and never experiences grief—*A. edition* p. 421.

3. A. records the following additional verses from the same (Kha) MS. after the words *Brahmabhūyāya gacchati*: They are translated from p 421 of A edition as follows:

(1) He by whom the sacred Bhārata (Purāṇa) as narrated by Vāyu is heard (once or) frequently, attains heaven by the grace (of the Wind-god).

(2) He who devoutly reads this Vāyu Purāṇa will be blest with a long life. The goddess of wealth will be stable (stay permanently) in his house.

(3) After writing down the Purāṇa or getting it written and after worshipping it (the MS of the Vāyu Purāṇa) duly, there is no fear of fire, thieves or fear from the (unfavourable) planets, diseases etc.

(4) All those (evil influences, fear and such other) troubles get destroyed till the moon and stars exist (to the end of the world). Being absolved of all sins, he will go to Viṣṇu's city (Vaikuṇṭha).

(5-6) There is not the least danger from cholera. He will get happinesss everywhere. He will be blest with longevity, health, prosperity, wealth, sons and grandsons for ever. No question (doubt) need be raised about this.

51. This Purāṇa narrated by Kṛṣṇa Dvaipāyana, the expounder of Brahman (Vedas), is conducive to wealth, fame, longevity and great merit. It is on a par with the Vedas.

52. He who extols the fame of the lords of Manvantaras, of the Devas and sages endowed with enormous wealth and splendour, is released from all sins. He shall attain great merit.

53. A scholar who always narrates this on every festive occasions, shakes off his sins, conquers heaven and becomes capable of being merged in Brahman.

54. If one at the time of Śrāddha recites a section of this (Purāṇa) to Brāhmaṇas, it ultimately passes on to Pitṛs bestowing everything desired and everlasting benefit.

55. The word Purāṇa is derived thus: *purā ananti iti purāṇam*, i.e. that which has been established in ancient times. He who knows this derivation becomes liberated from all sins.

56-57. Those men of the three higher castes who listen to this Purāṇa and turn their attention to virtuous activities, rejoice in heaven for as many crores of years as there are hair-pores in the skin. After attaining *Sāyujya* (absorption) with Brahman they rejoice along with Devas.

58. Brahmā handed over to Mātariśvan[1] (Wind-god) this sacred text of the ancient Purāṇa which dispels all sins, which is holy and meritorious and which is conducive to fame.

59. From him it was acquired by Uśanas, and Bṛhaspati secured it from him. Thereafter, Bṛhaspati narrated it to Savitṛ.

60. Savitṛ recounted it to Mṛtyu and Mṛtyu handed it over to Indra. Indra narrated it to Vasiṣṭha and he taught it to Sārasvata.

A Kṣatriya who studies this has inexhaustible fruit (benefits).

(7) In this world, he get excellent reputation. He becomes victorious (in battles). He gets the happiness of begetting sons and having grandsons. After death, he will dwell in *Svarga* (Heaven).

(8) If a non-Śūdra (Śūdra, if the *Avagraha* [S] in *adhīyate'śūdraḥ* be a misprint) teaches it or narrates it repeatedly, the goddess of Wealth stays permanently in his house. This is true (definitely), true and not otherwise.

1. Verses 58-66 give the genealogy of teachers who handed down the Purāṇa up to Sūta, the present narrator.

61. Sārasvata handed it over to Tridhāman; Tridhāman gave it to Śaradvān. Śaradvān taught Triviṣṭa and he gave it to Antarikṣa.

62. Antarikṣa gave it to Varṣin and he gave it to Trayyāruṇa. Trayyāruṇa taught it to Dhanañjaya and he gave it to Kṛtañjaya.

63. Tṛṇañjaya got it from Kṛtañjaya and he gave it to Bharadvāja. Bharadvāja gave it to Gautama and he handed it over to Niryantara.

64. Niryantara narrated it to Vājaśravas. He handed it over to Somaśuṣma, who gave it to Tṛṇabindu.

65. Tṛṇabindu narrated it to Dakṣa and Dakṣa taught Śakti. Even as he was in the womb, Parāśara heard this from Śakti.

66. O excellent Brāhmaṇas, Jātukarṇa learnt this from Parāśara. From him holy lord Dvaipāyana got it. From Dvaipāyana this was secured by me.

Śāṁśapāyana said:

67. Thus the words uttered by Brahmā, the first preceptor, were mentioned by me to my son Amitabuddhi (of unmeasured intellect); it is narrated orally by (a line of preceptors) of whom Brahmā was the first.

68-70. Preceptors should be earnestly bowed down to by learned men. This story is conducive to wealth, fame and longevity. It is meritorious and achieves all objects (of desire). It destroys sins. This must always be regularly listened to by Brāhmaṇas. This sacred story should not be mentioned to an impure person, a sinner, nor to a disciple who has not put in at least a year's disciplined student life. Nor should it be mentioned to one who never pays heed, nor to one who is not a scholar, nor to one who has no son, nor to one who is inimical.

71-73. With great mental purity, I bow down to Brahmā,[1] the first Maheśvara whose source of origin, they say, is *Avyakta*

1. This salutation to Mahādeva who is identified with the Primordial Puruṣa shows that it is a Śaiva Purāṇa. The *Maṅgalācaraṇa* of this Purāṇa pays obeisance to Lord Śiva.

(the Unmanifest), whose body is the Manifest. Kāla that has gone in, whose mouth is Vahni (fire), whose eyes are the Sun and the Moon, whose ears are the quarters, whose nose, they say, is Vāyu, whose words are Vedas, whose body is the firmament, whose feet are the earth, whose hair pores are the stars, whose limbs are similarly constituted, all the Vidyās are the tail, who is the lord of Devas, who creates people, who is firmly stationed in all the worlds, who is the foremost of all and who is Maheśvara, the granter of boons.

CHAPTER FORTYTWO

Dissipation of Vyāsa's Doubts[1]

The Sages Śaunaka and others said:

1-2. O Sūta, O blessed one, eighteen Purāṇas have been entirely narrated along with the connected anecdotes in the manner of *Upakrama* (beginning) and *Upasaṁhāra* (conclusion), by you, the holy one, who have understood all the sacred texts by the favour of Vyāsa.

3-11. You have clearly narrated *Matsya Purāṇa*[2] containing fourteen thousand verses; the *Bhaviṣya Purāṇa* containing an equal number of verses with five hundred more; the beautiful

---

1. This chapter is a later addition as it is found only in one MS(Ka) used by A. The very fact that it comes after *Phalaśruti* and formal completion of the Purāṇa shows its supplementary nature.

2. Verses 3-11 give a list of 18 Mahāpurāṇas along with the total number of verses in each. Here only the *Vāyu Purāṇa* is narrated. But the credit of narrating eighteen Purāṇas is given to Sūta. This being a mere Appendix, various topics are included herein. These verses give the traditional number of verses in each Purāṇa without verifying them, unless we presume that that much number of verses was found at the time of this Purāṇa writer. Thus *Kūrma Purāṇa* is credited with 17000 verses but actually we find therein only 6000 verses; the *Bhāgavata Purāṇa* is credited to have 18000 verses but actually it has less than 15000 verses.

Mārkaṇḍeya containing nine thousand verses; the *Brahmavaivarta* containing eighteen thousand verses; the *Brahmāṇḍa* containing twelve thousand and one hundred verses; the divine *Bhāgavata* containing eighteen thousand verses; the *Brahma Purāṇa* (the Purāṇa called Brahma of ten thousand verses); the Purāṇa named *Vāmana* containing ten thousand verses; the *Ādipurāṇa* containing ten thousand and six hundred verses; the *Anila* (*Vāyu*) *Purāṇa* containing twentythree thousand verses (?); the *Nāradīya* containing twentythree thousand verses; the *Vainateya* (*Garuḍa*) containing nineteen thousand verses; the extensive *Padmapurāṇa* containing fiftyfive thousand verses; the beautiful *Kūrma* containing seventeen thousand verses; the wonderful *Śaukara* (*Varāha*) *Purāṇa* containing twentyfour thousand verses and the extensive *Skanda Purāṇa* containing eightyone thousand verses. Thus eighteen big Purāṇas have been narrated. In these Purāṇas many holy rites (Dharmas) have been explained by you.

12-15. The holy rites and duties (Dharma) of those with and without attachment, those of ascetics, the religious students, householders, forest-hermits, women and Śūdras have been particularly explained by you. Similarly the rites and duties of Brāhmaṇas, Kṣatriyas, Vaiśyas and the mixed castes have been recounted. You have described the big rivers Gaṅgā and others. Many kinds of Yajñas, holy rites and penances have been explained in those Purāṇas. Many kinds of religious gifts, all kinds of *Yamas* (restraints and holy observances), the duties of Yoga, Sāṁkhya and Bhāgavata (pertaining to the holy devotee of the lord) have been explained in them. The paths of devotion, knowledge, and detachment have been explained. The procedures for the *Upāsanā* (special forms of worship) with water and wind (i.e. such as Prāṇāyāma where the breath is controlled) by those whose minds have been purified by holy rites, have been mentioned.

Though our text reiterates 18 as the number of Mahā Purāṇas actually a list of 16 Purāṇas is given. The *Ādipurāṇa* hereof is either Viṣṇu or Agni or Liṅga but that number of verses approximates to those of Liṅga Purāṇa. The number of verses attributed per Purāṇa differs in different Purāṇas. But that is a minor point as these Purāṇa writers had no opportunity or inclination to verify the actual number of verses in each Purāṇa.

16. The systems (of philosophy and devotion), the Brāhma (pertaining to Brahma), Śaiva (that of Śiva), Vaiṣṇava (that of Viṣṇu), Saura (that of the Sun), Śākta (that of Śakti, the goddess), Ārhata[1] (that of Arhat, Jina), the six systems of philosophy and the materialistic philosophy—all these and many other things have been explained in the Purāṇas.

17. It is not known whether there is or not anything beyond this that is excellent and worth knowing.

18. Could it be that Vyāsa or you, holy sir, are hiding anything? Please clear our doubts in this respect, since you are a complete Paurāṇika (knower of Purāṇas).

Sūta said :

19. O Śaunaka, listen. I shall explain this intricate problem. This is a great secret of divine nature. It should not be mentioned (to anyone and everyone), so say (the sages).

20. After writing the story of the Purāṇas wherein all the meanings of the Vedic passages have been included, Vyāsa, son of Parāśara, thought thus in his mind.[2]

21. "The duties of the different castes and stages of life have been clearly explained by me. Different paths leading to salvation without infringing the Vedic injunctions have been mentioned by me.

22. In my decisions (incorporated) in the (*Brahma sūtra*), the (alleged) distinction between Jīva (individual soul), Īśvara and Brahman has been completely refuted. Brahman the supreme soul has been explained on the basis of Vedic passages, cogent arguments and deliberations.

1. Mention of Jainism and non-mention of Buddhism shows that Buddhism had either disappeared from India at that time or the inclusion of the Buddha as an incarnation of Viṣṇu was probably regarded a sufficient ground not to mention it as a separate system of philosophy. I believe in the first alternative (disappearance of Buddhism on a large scale).

2. Cf. Bh. P. I.4.26-31 and the subsequent two chapters 5 & 6. That episode in the Bh. P. is the basis of this episode of Vyāsa's dejection. The mention of *Brahma Sūtras* shows that at the time of this Purāṇa the authors of the Mahābhārata, the Purāṇas and the *Brahma sūtra* were believed to be one single individual called Kṛṣṇa Dvaipāyana Vyāsa.

23. The supreme Brahman is imperishable. It is the supreme soul, and the greatest region. It is for its realization that the religious students, forest-hermits and ascetics perform holy rites.

24-25. Highly intelligent persons perform *Dhāraṇā* (concentration) of different types. Leading sages perform the *Aṣṭāṅga* (eight-limbed) observance for the sake of Brahman. They are—*Āsana* (posture), *Prāṇarodha* (restraint of breath), *Pratyāhāra* (withdrawal of the senses), *Dhāraṇā* (concentration), *Dhyāna* (meditation), *Samādhi* (trance, ecstasy), *Yama* (restraint) and *Niyama* (observance).

26. Those who strictly adhere to the injunctions of the Vedas, perform holy rites only for the sake of Brahman. They are free from desires and sins. They perform the holy rites dedicating the fruit thereof to the greatest soul.

27. Those of pure rites and observances resort to the holy centres of Gaṅgā etc. in order to wipe off their sinful actions and to know the supreme soul.

28-29. That Brahman is the greatest. It is pure. It has neither beginning nor end. It is free from ailments. It is eternal and omnipresent. It is steady like the summit of a mountain. It is devoid of deception. It pervades all sense organs but is imperceivable. It is devoid of sense-organs that are the creations of Prakṛti. It is undeflected by *Dik* (Space) and *Kāla* (Time) etc. It is eternal. It is pure consciousness. It is unchanging.

30-31. The whole universe is super-imposed on it like the serpent on a piece of cord[1] and hence appears so. Brahman is devoid of aberrations. If pondered well, foam, bubble and wave will be found not different at all from water; similarly considered the universe too is not at all different from Brahman.

32. The Nigamas (Vedas) declare, 'Everything is Brahman There is no multiplicity'. It is from Brahman that the crores of Brahmāṇḍas (Cosmic Eggs) are created and dissolved.

---

1. This *Adhyāsavāda* shows that this chapter was written in the post-Śaṅkara period. See v. 39 below.

33. The dissolution and creation of all the worlds depend upon the *Unmeṣa* (opening) and *Nimeṣa* (closing) of Brahman.[1] The great Śakti (the divine goddess of power) is stationed with the support of Brahman.

34. The universe is in it. It originates from Brahman. It is Brahman itself. It is due to the ignorance of Brahman that the universe appears. When Brahman is realised there is no universe.

35. The universe is explained as *Asatya* (unreal), *Jaḍa* (insentient), *Duḥkha* (cause of misery) and *Avastu* (unreal, unsubstantial). The opposite of it is *Saccidānandamūrti*—the embodiment of existence, knowledge and bliss.

36. It is called *Viśva* when the individual soul is in the wakeful state. It is remembered as *Taijasa* when the individual is in a state of dream. It is called *Prājña* when the individual soul is in the state of dreamless slumber.[2] It persists in all the states.

37. It is the eye of eyes. It is the ear of ears. It is the *Tvac* (skin, i.e. organ of touch) of all *Tvacs*. It is the tongue of tongues. They consider it the Prāṇa (vital breath) of Prāṇas.

38. Human beings are incapable of knowing precisely and attaining it by means of intellect, worldly knowledge, vital breath or physical activity for ever.

39. Just as snake (is misconceived as such) in the rope, mirage as water in the desert, and blueness in the sky is superimposed due to ignorance, so also the non-existing universe is superimposed on Brahman and hence it simply appears to exist.

40. The vast sky appears to be different inasmuch as it is restricted by jars etc. Similarly the Jīva is the restricted form of the all-pervading soul, restricted through the *kārya* (product e.g. the physical body).

---

1. A partial quotation from Vasugupta's *Spanda-Kārikā* 1, but attributes this creation and destruction of the Universe to Śiva's Parā Śakti—an attempt to adapt a *Trika Śaiva* concept and adopt it in *Kevalādvaita*.

2. The terms Taijasa, Prājña etc. used here are of Upaniṣadic antiquity (*vide* Māṇḍūkya Up. 9, 10 and 11).

41. The whole Cosmic Egg is an incomparably superb painting drawn on Brahman as if on a wall by the Māyā (Illusion) of wonderful activities possessing diverse Guṇas.

42. That imperishable Brahman is conclusively arrived at by the Vedic and Upaniṣadic passages and principles. Brahman is beyond those who rush after it. It is beyond the words of those who try to explain it.

43. There is nothing greater than the *Akṣara* (indestructible Brahman). That is the Acme. That is the great goal. So it is explained in the Vedas, when (they are) closely pondered over.

44-52. I have heard this from the Vedas with whose help he became cognisable. Also that Lord Kṛṣṇa is that supreme man (Puruṣa).[1] He is abiding in the form of Ātman in that *Akṣara Ātman* (imperishable soul). He is of the form of the mass of Bliss, the embodiment of *Ānanda* (bliss and felicity). He takes interest in divine sports in the midst of the cowherdesses. He is embellished with a crown decorated with peacock plumes and studded with shining gems. He shines with the two earrings having the brilliance of lightning. His eyes beautiful like the Khañjarīṭa (birds) move up to (are longish up to) the ears. He indulges in dalliance with the beloved cowherdesses in every flower-grove. He wears a divine yellow garment. He has smeared himself with sandal paste. He fascinates the cowherdesses with the notes of his flute sprinkled with the nectar oozing out of his lips. He is the *Cidānanda* (the bliss of knowledge). He suppresses the arrogance of Anaṅga (Cupid) (by means of his beauty). He is a past-master in the arts of love of crores of Kāmas. He is as pure as the rays of crores of Moons. Bees and deer surround him. Round his neck with three lines a diamond necklace shines with beads interspersed. To control cows from straying away, he runs about here and there on the high banks of Yamunā in the jungle of Tamāla trees and trees of Kadamba, Campaka, Aśoka and Pārijāta that appear very beautiful. It (the forest) is full of the chirping sounds of cuckoos, parrots, doves and peacocks. He is particularly fond of sporting with Rādhā.

---

1. Verses 44-55 show the influence of the Rādhā-Kṛṣṇa cult or Bhāgavatism.

53. He sports in the world called Goloka which is Brahman itself, the *Cit* alone, free from difference and Guṇas. I have heard it so.

54. There is nothing greater than He as mentioned in Nigamas and Āgamas. Still the Vedas say that he is beyond and greater than *Akṣara*.

55. The lord who is the resident of Goloka is called greater than *Akṣara*. Who is this always spoken by the Vedas as beyond even that ?

56. How is the special meaning, that which is indicated by the words of the Vedas to be known? Is the text of the Veda to be interpreted otherwise as it implies more than recorded in words (?)

57. Vyāsa, the son of Satyavatī, became doubtful as to the meaning of the Śruti. He pondered over it for a long time. He could not understand it precisely.

Sūta said:

58. Even after deliberating (long) the sage did not arrive at the decisive meaning of the Vedic passage. The Veda is Nārāyaṇa himself, where even great sages (poets) become confounded.

59. Still he underwent great distress of the heart. Then he thought: 'Whom shall I approach ? What shall I do ?

60-62. I do not see anyone in this world who is omniscient and who sees everything.' After not knowing anyone in the world who could clear his doubts he went to a cave in Meru and performed a great penance. There was a beautiful forest there. Although there was blinding darkness within, the rocks shed a golden brilliance everywhere.

63-66. The forest was resonant with the chirping sounds of the birds among the groves of the different trees and creepers. It was devoid of the sufferings due to hunger, thirst, fear, anger, distress and dejection. Ponds and tanks beautified with lotuses abounded there. Their banks were set with golden slabs on which the birds moved about. It was served by the winds wafting the fragrance from the lotuses. It was devoid of beasts of prey. It was frequented by animals having auspicious nature. The place was devoid of crowds of people. It was embellished with pleasing groves of divine creepers. The chirping sounds of parrots, doves and intoxicated cuckoos were very pleasing.

67. The pollen dust particles rose up and rendered all the quarters fragrant. The divine golden cave of very great splendour was there (in such a forest).

68. The sage entered that cave. After attaining full control over his mind, posture and urge for food, he meditated on the four Vedas with great concentration.

69-73. Even as he was meditating, three hundred years passed and then the four Vedas of beautiful appearance[1] stood in front of him. Their eyes were resplendent like the petals of the lotus. Their heads were embellished with matted hair like coronets. Sacred Kuśa grass was held in the fists of their lotus-like hands. Their shoulders were adorned with deer skin. The splendour of their mouths was heightened by means of the sixteen *Svara* (vowel) sounds intersprsed with *Praṇava* (Om). Their hands with five fingers to each were constituted by the letters of the guttural and the palatal classes of consonants. Their right legs were constituted by the labial class consonants and the left legs consisted of the letters of the dental. The sides of their belly were constituted of intermediate and last consonants (of each group). The letter *Na* constituted their navels. Their backs were refulgent (The letters ending with *Ka* constituted their backs). The letter *Ma* was their stomach. The letters *Ya, Ra, La* and *Va* were their tied up hair (tresses). *Agnibīja* (the seed-like Mantra of Agni) shone in their right shoulders. The *Dharā* (*Bīja*) (the seed-like Mantra of the earth) was their neck and the Bhṛta (? Mantra) shone on their (left) shoulders.

74. Their joints consisted of the *Antaḥstha* (semi-vowel) letters. They were throbbing with *Vaikharī* speech. He saw (the city of) Mathurā marked in their lotus-like hearts.

75. Indeed that is the holy centre of the manifestation of Lord Hari himself. He saw (the holy place) Kāśī in the middle

1. A beautiful yet significant description of the personality of the Vedas. The vision of seven holy cities, important or major sacrifices, four sacred fires on their person is interesting as it shows the attritude of the author to synthesize Purāṇic and Vedic traditions.

of their eyebrows. He saw the city of Māyā (Haridvāra) stationed in a mystical plexus at the posterior part of the body.

76. He saw the city of Kāñcī in the region of their penis; the city of Avantī in the navel region; the city of Dvārakā in the region of the neck and the city of Prayāga in the region of Prāṇa (vital air).

77. To their left and right flowed the rivers Gaṅgā and Yamunā. In the middle flowed the river Sarasvatī itself. The holy centre of Gayā was in the facial region.

78. The excellent holy centre of Prabhāsa was in the middle of the neck and the chin. He saw the hermitage of Badaryāśrama in their Brahmarandhra (cerebral aperture).

79. The holy seats of Paundravardhana (Pandua) (Malda District) and Nepāla were seen in the two eyes. The seat named Pūrṇagiri was seen on the forehead.

80. The holy seat (Pīṭha) of Mathurā was seen in the neck. The seat of Kāñcī was stationed in the hips. The Pīṭha of Jālandhara was seen in the region of the breasts.

81. The Pīṭha called Bhṛgu was in the region of the ears; the city of Ayodhyā was in the cup of the nose. The holy centre Brāhmya was stationed in the cerebral aperture; the holy centre Śaiva was in the partition on the crown of the head.

82. The holy centre Śākta was situated on the tip of the tongue. The holy Vaiṣṇava centre was in the lotus of the heart; the holy centre of the Sun was situated in the region of the eyes and all Bauddha (Buddhistic) holy centres were stationed in the shadows.

83. He saw the Sautrāmaṇi Yajña in the region of the neck; the Paśubandha in the chest. He saw the Vājapeya sacrifice in the region of the buttocks and the Agnihotra in the mouth (? face).

84. He saw Aśvamedha in the region of the buttocks and Naramedha (human sacrifice) in the belly. He saw Rājasūya in the region of the head and Āvasathya in the lower lip.

85-86. He saw Dakṣiṇāgni on the upper lip and the Gārhapatya (fire) in the mouth. The *Havya* was in the ears. He saw the different Mantras stationed in the bodily hair. He saw the Vedas severally revered and honoured by the Purāṇas, Nyāyas,

Saṁhitās and Tantra texts like a great king served by his attendants. He saw the Vedas who blessed the people through holy rites, perfect knowledge and Upāsanās (modes of worship).

87. They had the divine brilliance of Brahman; they were blazing like the descending (rays of) the Sun and the shooting flames of fire. They had the appearance of crores of Moons (put together). On seeing them, the sage Kṛṣṇa (Dvaipāyana) became greatly struck with wonder.

88. He got up suddenly and prostrated himself (before them), while saying repeatedly: "I am contented. I have achieved my object (in life).

89. Since, O holy Sires, you have been visible to me, my birth is fruitful today. My mind is satisfied. My life (longevity) has become fruitful today.

90. Whatever there is whether worldly or divine, whatever is worth knowing whether past, present or future is not unknown to you.

91. You all are not the mere instructors of the path of action. Even if you show the path of action, it is only to restrict the haphazard actions of those who are passionate.

92. Your words of injunction and prohibition regarding the status of Brahman and the unreality of the universe are not based on attachment which is unreal. They are binding as the injunctions and prohibitions (?)

93. Hence the objects such as heaven etc. mentioned by yourselves have been censured by you, saying that they are of a perishable nature, while the truth is being explained by you, the benefactors of the worlds.

94. By teaching the path of action and the path of knowledge to different individuals according to their capacity and eligibility, the world has certainly been saved by you whose person is constituted of the revealed word of the supreme Brahman.

95. Hence I would like to ask you, should you be kind and merciful (towards me). With regard to those whose minds are filled with desires only, the fruit ordained for their rites is Svarga (heaven).

96. To those men who have dedicated their minds and souls to Īśa (the Lord), the fruit of the action performed is the

purification of the mind. Thereafter they attain perfect knowledge and subsequently salvation.

97. Salvation is the identity with Brahman which is Existence, Knowledge and Bliss. When it is realized whatever is done or left undone, everything comes to an end.

98. It is unattached. It is the firmament of knowledge of the nature of wisdom unobscured by Māyā. It is free from desire. It is steady (immovable), pure and devoid of Guṇas. It is proclaimed to be all-pervading.

99. When products (the created beings, the world) are being destroyed, Brahman (the unchangeable) does not perish, just as the Sun retains its splendour while the whole world becomes plunged in blinding darkness.

100. It is with the brilliance of the *Sattā* (the existent Brahman) that the universe is illuminated, in the same way as a piece of iron is ignited by the solar crystal or Araṇi produces fire.

101. It manifests in the form of *Jīva* (the individual soul), Īśvara (godhead) etc. and lo ! in the form of the universe too ! When everything is dissolved the firm, motionless Brahman alone remains.

102. This has been decided by you and undoubtedly it must be so. Still I have a desire to know something and have a doubt in my mind.

103. Is there anything greater than this or not ? O blessed ones, please tell it, as you have the vision of reality.

104. The listening to that alone shall be conducive to the success and fruitfulness of my life."

When Vyāsa, the sinless son of Satyavatī, said thus the Nigama (Vedas) exclaimed 'very good, quite right', and replied to him:

Vedas said:

105. Very well, O highly intelligent one. You are Viṣṇu, the Ātman of all embodied ones. Though unborn, you take up birth and desire to bless the worlds.

106. Otherwise why should you be fettered by the worldly Karmans? It does not affect you. You are untouched for ever by the divine Māyā that hides perfect knowledge.

107-108. You take up forms according to your own will and you withdraw the same at your own will. Only matters accepted by us have been revealed by you in the Purāṇas, Itihāsa (Mahābhārata) and the (Brahma) Sūtras in various ways. The imperishable Brahman is supreme, the cause (source) of all causes.

109-110. Like the fragrance of a flower or its taste (juice) it is the Ātman of the Ātman. Know that it is the ultimate form. This has been experienced by us when the dissolution pertaining to Prakṛti took place. It is that which is beyond the *Akṣara* (the indestructible). It is the supreme *Rasa* alone. It is beyond all words of expression. We are of the forms of words and hence incompetent to express it specifically.

CHAPTER FORTYTHREE

The Greatness of Gayā[1]

Vāyu said:

1. Henceforth I shall explain the excellent greatness of Gayā[2] on hearing which one is absolved of all sins. There is no doubt in this.

---

1. This is a *Sthala-Purāṇa* glorifying the sacredness of Gayā. It has a tenuous relation with the Vā. as it comes after the *Phala Śruti* etc. showing the completion of the Vā. P. Gayā, as a sacred place, was famous in pre-Buddhist times as Aurṇavābha's mention of Samārohaṇa, Viṣṇupada and Gayāśiras (all sacred spots at Gayā) as the three steps of Trivikrama, in RV. I. 22.17, is recorded by Yāska (*Nirukta* 12.19). We have *Gayā Māhātmya* in Mbh. Vana. Chs. 84-95, Garuḍa Chs. 82-86, AP Chs. 114-116, KP II.35, NP Uttarabhāga 44-47. A number of verses are common in the works. It shows that probably there must have been an ancient independent *Sthala-Purāṇa* called *Gayā Māhātmya* which was the source of the different Gayā Māhātmyas in these works.

2. The name indicates that it must have been the site of the hermitage or capital of King Gaya. A pious king Gaya, the son of king Samudravijaya of Rājagṛha, the eleventh Cakravartin as mentioned in *Uttarādhyayana Sūtra* a work of Śvetāmbara Jaina Āgama. Buddha's visits to Gayāsisa (Gayāśirṣa) and hermitage of Kāśyapa at Gayā are recorded in the Pāli canon (*Mahā-*

Sūta said :

2. Once upon a time, the celestial sage Nārada was accompanied by Sanaka and other blessed sages. Bowing duly to Sanatkumāra, he enquired thus:

Nārada enquired:

3. O Sanatkumāra, please recount to me that holy place which is the most excellent of all excellent sacred places and which saves all living beings who read about it or listen to it.

Sanatkumāra replied:

4. I shall recount the holy and excellent sacred centre which saves all by means of (performance of) *Śrāddha* and other holy rites. Listen to the description of the holy place Gayā which is superior to all other holy centres in the whole of the country.

5. Gaya, the Asura, performed penance. He was requested (to offer his body) for the performance of a sacrifice by god Brahmā. Dharma placed a slab of stone on his (Gaya's) head, when he offered (his body).

6. There Brahmā performed a sacrifice. In order to keep the demon Gaya steady and immovable day and night (for ever), Gadādhara (the mace-wielder Viṣṇu) too stayed there assuming the form of the (river) Phalgu and other sacred places, along with prominent Brāhmaṇas, god Brahmā and other Devas.

7. After concluding his sacrifice, Brahmā granted houses etc. to the Brāhmaṇas. He had performed the sacrifice at Gayā in the beginning of the Śveta Vārāhakalpa.

8. The holy centre became famous by the name Gayā after (the demon) Gaya. This holy centre is liked by god

---

vagga I.21.1 (also Aśvaghoṣa's *Buddhacarita* XII. 87-88, XVII.8). This king Gaya is not the same Gaya, the Vedic Seer of RV. X. 63 and 64 as his father's name was Plati.

Gaya belonged to the ancient Asura clan. We need not associate evil with the Asura clan, as we have very pious yet powerful Asura kings Prahlāda, Bali, Bāṇa. Even Lord Kṛṣṇa was an Asura by his mother's side (S.K. Chatterji—*Selected Writings*).

Brahmā. All manes (*Pitṛs*) afraid of falling into hell, desire for sons.

9. 'The son who goes to Gayā will be our saviour'. On seeing their sons reaching Gayā, the Pitṛs become overjoyed. (They say) 'Even by touching its waters with his feet, what is it that he cannot give us?'

10. If the son goes to Gayā and offers balls of rice (to the Pitṛs) they will realise the benefit of (their) having such a son. If the son remains there for three fortnights, he sanctifies his family till the seventh generation. If that is not possible, let him stay there for fifteen days, or seven nights or (at least) three nights.

11. Sins accumulated during the long period of a Mahā Kalpa perish on reaching Gayā. One should offer balls of rice to the Pitṛs and others. He can even offer the Piṇḍas to himself, but without including gingelly seeds in that case.

12. By performing the Śrāddha at Gayā, all the sins such as those resulting from Brāhmaṇa-slaughter, addiction to wine, stealing (gold), intercourse with the wife of the preceptor and those due to the association with those sinners, perish completely.

13. Whether it is by one's own son or another's son, if the Piṇḍa is offered in one's name anywhere on the ground at Gayā at any time, one is transported to the eternal Brahman.

14. There are four modes of attaining liberation, viz. (1) through the knowledge of Brahman, (2) through performance of Śrāddha at Gayā, (3) (by) death in a cowshed, and (4) through residence at Kurukṣetra.[1]

15. If the son goes to Gayā, of what avail is the knowledge of Brahman; what is the necessity of dying in a cowshed; and what is the need for a residence at Kurukṣetra?

16-17. The real devotee may offer Piṇḍas at Gayā at any time. It should not be discarded during the intercalary month, or on one's birthday or when Jupiter and Venus are set, or when Jupiter is in the Zodiac of Siṁha (Leo). If by ill-luck or inadvertence or when one is struck or wounded (one is un-

1. Cf. NP. II (Uttara) 44.30; AP, 115.5-6.

able to perform the Śrāddha at the proper time), one is eligible to perform afterwards the Śrāddha and other rites. He thereby attains Brahmaloka.

18. Even the opportunity to go to Gayā once or to offer Piṇḍa even once is very rare to achieve. What then, if one is able to stay in it for ever?

19. If accidentally one dies in this holy centre which confers salvation even upon Brahmā and others, one attains salvation in the same manner as through the realisation of Brahman. There is no doubt about tthis.

20. In order to redeem the Pitṛs who might have died due to wormbites etc., one should be wise enough to make all efforts to perform Śrāddha at Gayā.

21. One should honour and propitiate with *Havyas* and *Kavyas* (offerings) the Brāhmaṇas who had been assigned the right of receiving those things by Brahmā himself. If they are pleased, all the Pitṛs and Devas will be pleased.

22. Except in the case of the holy centres of Kurukṣetra, Viśālā, Virajā and Gayā in all the holy centres, it has been ordained that the devotees should shave off their head and observe fast.

23. A Bhikṣu (a recluse) need not offer balls of rice after going to Gayā. It is enough if he shows his staff. After placing his staff at the feet (the footprint) of Viṣṇu he becomes liberated along with all his forefathers.[1]

24. Really the staff-bearing ascetic (Sannyāsin) does not incur sins or acquire merits. Hence he renounces all activities and meditates on Viṣṇu with noble thoughts.

25. One may renounce all Karmans but should not forswear the Vedas. He should shave his head outside the limits of the holy centre to the east, west, south or north.

26. The area of the sacred place of Gayā, as declared by Brahmā, is two and a half krośas (1 krośa = 5 km.), that of the holy centre Gayā is five krośas and that of Gayāśiras (Headland of Gayā) is one krośa.[2]

---

1. Cf. NP. II. 45.31.
2. Cf. NP. II.44.16; AP. 115.42

27. Whatever holy places there are in the three worlds are present within[1] (the area of Gayāśiras). A person who performs Śrāddha to the Pitṛs in the holy centre of Gayā becomes free from indebtedness to them.

28. He who performs Śrāddha at Gayāśiras uplifts a hundred generations in his family. The moment one starts on his pilgrimage to Gayā, every step that he takes (on his journey of Gayā) constitutes a flight of steps leading to Svarga to his Pitṛs (ancestors).

29. At every step taken (by the son) in his journey towards Gayā, the fruit of Aśvamedha is certainly acquired by him. There is no doubt in this.

30-32. Piṇḍas in Gayā are offered by means of milk pudding, *Carus* (cooked rice soaked in ghee), *Saktu* (flour of fried grains), *Piṣṭaka*, rice grains, roots etc. Powdered gingelly seeds, lumps of jaggery with ghee or mere curds, any foodstuff mixed with honey, oilcake with jaggery, raw sugar and ghee, if offered to the Pitṛs yield everlasting benefits. Or worship is performed and any seasonal fruit is offered as food or Haviṣya food is also offered as mentioned by the sages.

33. On one side are all the articles of offering such as clothes and things sweetened with tasty honey. On the other side is the sacred water from the Phalgutīrtha brought after meditating on the lotus-like feet of Gadādhara (i.e. Both these are at par with each other).

34. The procedure of the Śrāddhas in the holy centres is this: Seat is offered to Piṇḍas; Piṇḍas are offered, then *Avanejana* rite is performed (water is ritualistically sprinkled on the Darbha grass); Dakṣiṇā is then offered and then the *Annasaṁkalpa* (ritualistic verbal utterance of one's intention of offering food).

35. In the Śrāddhas performed in the holy centres, there is no ritualistic invocation to Pitṛs. As there is no defilement through seeing (i.e. on being seen by others) there is no screening of the sides. Intelligent persons should perform Śrāddha with due sympathy.

36. In other places, the Pitṛs if and when invoked at the

1, This is the claim of all *Sthalas* even of lesser importance such as those of Karavira, Pandharpur.

proper time, go there. But they always stay in the holy centre. Hence there is no (need of any) invocation.

37. By a person desirous of fruits and performing *Śrāddhas* in the holy centres all the rites must always be performed after eschewing lust, anger and covetousness.

38. One who observes celibacy, sleeps on the bare ground, takes food only once a day, speaks only the truth, remains always pure and is always engaged in the welfare of all living beings, attains the fruits of visiting the holy centres.

39. A self-possessed man visiting holy centres must at the outset eschew heresy. A person who does everything urged by lust, should be known as a heretic.

40. Just as the knowers of Brahman engaged in the meditation of Brahman with single-minded attention attain the knowable object, so also the self-possessed persons performing the holy rites in the holy centres enter Brahman named Pareśa (the supreme lord).

41. The river Vaitaraṇī which is famous in all the three worlds, has descended into the holy centre of Gayā for saving Pitṛs. One who takes the sacred bath in the Vaitaraṇī and gifts away cows uplifts three times seven (i.e. twentyone) generations.

42. The devotee should go to the Akṣayavaṭa (the eternal holy fig tree) and propitiate the Brāhmaṇas there. One who propitiates the Brāhmaṇas who had been granted the right of staying there by god Brahmā (shall attain the fruit thereof). If they (those Brāhmaṇas) are pleased all the Devas and the Pitṛs will be pleased.

43. There is no spot anywhere in Gayā where there is no holy centre.[1] It has the *Sānnidhya* (presence) of all holy centres. Hence the sacred place of Gayā is the most excellent holy centre.

44. It is a rare achievement that cannot be had anywhere else in the three worlds if one could offer balls of rice at Gayā when the Sun is in the Zodiacs of *Mīna*, *Meṣa*, *Kanyā*, *Dhanus* and *Kumbha*.

---

1. Cf. AP. 116.28.

45. Similarly rare is the opportunity, very rare indeed in the three worlds, to perform Śrāddha at Gayā when the Sun is in the Zodiac *Makara* and also at the times of the eclipses of the Sun and the Moon.

46. The fruit that one achieves by offering balls of rice at Gayā, cannot be described by me even in hundreds of crores of Kalpas.

CHAPTER FORTYFOUR

*The Glory of Gayā : The Story of Gayāsura**

Nārada enquired:

1. How was Gayāsura (Demon Gaya) born? What was his power? What was his nature? How did he perform the penance? How did he acquire purity of the body?

Sanatkumāra replied:

2. Brahmā, the grandfather of the worlds, was born of the umbilical lotus of Viṣṇu. Formerly, at the instance of lord Viṣṇu, he created the subjects.

3. Formerly he created the Asuras (Demons) through a demoniac inclination. Through a benevolent disposition of mind he created the Devas of gentle minds.

4. Demon Gaya possessed the greatest strength and exploit among Asuras. His height is remembered to be one hundred and twentyfive Yojanas.

*According to Rajendralal Mitra, the story of Gayāsura is an allegory of the vanquishing of Buddhism by Brahmanism (*Bodha-Gaya* pp. 14-18). O. Malley thought it to be an amalgamation of Brahmanism and popular demonolatry which preceded Brahmanism (JASB LXXII. iii. 7, 1904). B.M. Barua regards, this as an invention to impress the sanctity of the Gayā range of hills (*Gayā and Buddha Gayā*, 1934). I agree with B. M. Barua as, while editing the *Karavīra Māhātmya*, a Sthalapurāṇa of Kolhapur, I found similar creation of stories to justify and glorify some rites etc. of Mahālakṣmī (*vide* Intro. to *Karavīra-Māhātmya*, pp. 19-29, Pub. Shivaji University, Kolhapur, 1980). I find the same claim in the *Sthala Purāṇas* of Pandharpur, Tirupathi.

5. His girth was sixty Yojanas. He is remembered as the most excellent of all the devotees of Viṣṇu. He performed a very terrible penance on the excellent mountain Kolāhala (Brahmayoni hill including Muṇḍapṛṣṭha at Gayā).

6. He remained steady for many thousand years without breathing. Scorched by his fiery penance, Devas were greatly agitated.

7. Devas went to Brahmaloka and spoke to Pitāmaha (god Brahmā), "O Lord, save us from demon Gaya". Then Brahmā spoke to the Devas:

8. "O Devas, we shall go to god Śaṅkara." Brahmā and others went to Śiva. At Kailāsa, they bowed to him and said, "O Lord, save us from the great demon".

9. Śaṁbhu spoke to Brahmā and others: "We shall seek refuge in Hari, in the ocean of milk. He is the lord of all Devas. He will do something conducive to our welfare". Brahmā, Śiva and the Devas bowed to Viṣṇu and eulogised him.

The Devas said:

10. Om! Obeisance to Viṣṇu, the lord of all, the all-powerful, the radiant, the victorious and the devourer (destroyer) of Rākṣasas and others.

11. Hail to the sustainer of all these (worlds). Bow to him who leads the Yogins beyond (the ocean of worldly existence). Obeisance to the ever-increasing, the Infinite. Hail to the resplendent one.

Sanatkumāra said:

12. On being eulogised thus, Vāsudeva granted vision unto the Suras (i.e. manifested himself in front of them). "O Devas, wherefore have you all come?" On being asked thus by Viṣṇu the Devas said to him:

13. "O Lord, save us from the danger of demon Gaya". Hari said, "May Brahmā and others go near that Daitya. I shall also come there".

14. Seated on Garuḍa, Keśava started in order to grant a boon to Gayāsura. All the Devas seated themselves on their respective excellent vehicles and proceeded.

15. Vāsudeva and others spoke to him: "O demon Gaya, what for is this penance being performed by you? We have all arrived here fully satisfied (with your penance). Mention the boon (you wish to have)."

Gayāsura said:

16-18. O Devas, Brahmā, Viṣṇu and Maheśvara, if you are pleased, may I be ever holier than these: than all the Devas, and Brāhmaṇas, than all the Yajñas, holy rivers and mountains; than all the Devas; than all the sages; than even the unchanging Śiva; than all the Mantras; than all the lords of Devas; than all the Yogins; than all the renouncers; than all the *Karmins* (the performers of holy rites); than all the *Dharmins* (pious ones); than all the holy *Jñānins* (wise ones and knowers).

19. "May you be pure and holy". After saying this to the Daitya, the Devas went to heaven. After seeing and touching the Daitya, all people went to Hari's city (i.e. Vaikuṇṭha).

20. All the three worlds became vacant. The whole of the city of Yama became void. Thereafter, Yama went to Brahmaloka along with Indra and others.

21. All the Devas displaced by Gayāsura spoke to Brahmā: "O Pitāmaha, please take back the authority which has been given by you (to us)."

22-23. Then Brahmā spoke to the Devas: "We shall go to the immutable Viṣṇu". Brahmā and others said to Viṣṇu: "Since the Asura has been granted the boon by you, all the people have been going to heaven by merely looking at him. All the three worlds have become void." On being informed thus by the Devas, Vāsudeva spoke thus to god Brahmā:

24. "Go and request the demon thus, 'Give your body for the purpose of Yajña'." Urged by Viṣṇu, Brahmā went there accompanied by the Suras and saw the great Asura.

25. On seeing Brahmā along with the Devas, the demon Gaya stood up and duly and devoutly worshipped them.

Gayāsura said:

26. My birth has become fruitful today. My penance has

become fruitful today, since Brahmā has come as my guest. Everything is obtained by me today.

27. O Yogin, O knower of all the ancillaries of Yoga, O master of all the worlds, O father, O preceptor, O Brahmā, I shall carry out the work for which you have come.

Brahmā said :

28. All the holy centres of the earth seen by me while wandering over it, are not as pure as your body, for the purpose of Yajña.

29. Holiness of the body has been attained by you, thanks to the grace of Viṣṇu. Hence, O Asura, give unto me your pure body for the purpose of Yajña.

Gayāsura said :

30. O lord of Devas, I am blessed since my body is being asked for by you. If you perform Yāga (sacrifice) over my body the Pitṛs in my family shall be contented.

31. It was by you alone that this body was created. It was by you that it was rendered holy and pure. The Yāga should necessarily take place for the benefit of everyone.

32. After saying thus, during the Śveta Kalpa, the demon Gaya fell on the ground in a south-western direction on the mountain Kolāhala.[1]

33. Keeping his head in the north and the feet in the south, the Daitya (lay there). After collecting together all the requisites, Brahmā mentally created the Ṛtviks.

34-39. They were: Agniśarman, Amṛta, Śaunaka, Yañjali, Mṛdu, Kumuthi, Vedakauṇḍilya, Hārīta, Kāśyapa, Kṛpa, Garga, Kauśika, Vasiṣṭha, the unchanging sage Bhārgava, Vṛddha Parāśara, Kaṇva, Māṇḍavya, Śrutikevala, Śveta, Sutāla, Damana, Suhotra, Kaṅka, Laukākṣi of huge mighty arms, Jaigīṣavya, the Brāhmaṇa Dadhipañcamukha, Ṛṣabha, Karka, Kātyāyana, Gobhila the sage of great fierce rites, Supālaka, Gautama, Vedaśirovrata, Jaṭāmālin, Avyagra, Cāṭuhāsa the terrible, Ātreya,

1. The Brahmayoni hill in Gayā, including the hill called Muṇḍapṛṣṭha which contains the impressions of Gadādhara's feet—De 201.

Aṅgiras, Aupamanyu of great holy rites, Gokarṇa, Guhāvāsa, Śikhaṇḍin and Umāvrata.

40. After creating these and other leading Brāhmaṇas, god Brahmā, the grandfather of the worlds, performed the Yāga on the body of Gayāsura.

41-42. Agniśarmā, without wasting his penance, created these five fires from his mouth : Dakṣiṇāgni, Gārhapatya, Āhavanīya, Satya and Āvasathya. O celestial sage, the Yajñas are founded on these. To stabilise the Yajña, he gave Dakṣiṇā to the Brāhmaṇas.

43. After performing the Pūrṇāhuti and taking the ablution of Avabhṛtha, Brahmā caused the sacrificial post to be brought along with the Suras and fixed it.

44. The auspicious post was fixed in the Brahmasaras which is the most excellent of all lakes. Shaken and surprised, Brahmā spoke to Dharmarāja:

45. "There is a slab of stone in your house. Without hesitation bring it here at my behest and fix it on the head of the Daitya."

46. On hearing it, Yama placed the slab on the head of the demon to keep him steady. Even when the slab was placed, the demon shook along with the slab.

47. He spoke to Rudra and other Devas, "O Devas, you all stand steady on the slab". They said "Yes" and stood there (on it).

48. The Devas pressed the slab with their feet (?) and noted that still the demon quaked. Then the distressed Brahmā went to Viṣṇu who was lying down in the ocean of milk. Bowing down and honouring the lord, he eulogised him.

Brahmā said :

49. O Lord, O sovereign of the cosmic egg, I bow down to the lord of the worlds, the goal of persons possessing glory, the granter of worldly pleasures and salvation.

50. Viṣvaksena spoke to Viṣṇu, "O Lord, the lotus-born deity eulogises you". Hari said, "You bring him". Urged by Viṣṇu, he brought him. Hari spoke to Aja (Brahmā), "Tell me why you have come?"

Brahmā said :

51-52. O Lord of Devas, when the Yāga was performed the demon Gaya moved even when the slab of stone of the form of the Devas was placed on his head. Even when Rudra and other Devas were stationed (over it) there, the demon quaked, O Mādhava, be pleased to make it steady now.

53. On hearing the words of Brahmā, lord Hari pulled out a *Mūrti* (physical body/idol) from his person and gave it to Brahmā to stop the restless quaking (of the demon).

54. Bringing the idol with him, Brahmā placed it on the slab of stone. Still the demon quaked, on seeing which, he (Brahmā) invoked the lord again.

55. Viṣṇu came from the ocean of milk and stationed himself on the slab, with the name of Janārdana and Puṇḍarīka. The primordial Gadādhara (wielder of mace) himself stood there to steady the slab, for stabilising (Gaya or his body).

56-57. For stabilising (Gaya or his body), Brahmā divided himself into five, viz. *Prapitāmaha* (Great-grandfather), *Pitāmaha* (Grandfather), the master of Phalgu, Kedāra and Kanakeśvara. Brahmā as Vināyaka stood there in the form of an elephant. The Sun divided himself into three: Gayāditya, Uttarārka and Dakṣiṇārka.

58. Lakṣmī stood there in the name of Sītā, Gaurī in the name of Maṅgalā and Sarasvatī stationed herself in the forms of the three, viz. Gāyatrī, Sāvitrī, and Trisandhyā.

59. Indra, Bṛhaspati, Pūṣan, the eight Vasus of great strength, Viśvedevas, the two Aśvinī Devas, Maruts, the leader of the universe and Devas along with the Yakṣas, serpents, and Gandharvas remained there accompanied by their respective *Śaktis* (powers).

60. Since the Daitya was made steady by the primordial club and Hari stood there, he is famous as Ādi-Gadādhara.[1]

61. Gayāsura spoke to the Devas, "Why have I been deceived ? The pure body was given unto Brahmā by me for the purpose of Yajña. Would not have I been steady at the sheer instance of Viṣṇu ?

1. Etymology quoted in *TSS* (*Tristhalīsetu*), p. 338.

62. Why have I been harassed by Suras and Hari by means of the club ? May Devas be delighted for ever now that I have been tortured."

63. Gadādhara and others were pleased. They all simultaneously spoke to Gayāsura, "Speak out (choose) a boon. We are all very delighted". Gayāsura then spoke to Devas:

64. "As long as the earth lasts, as long as the mountains, the Moon, the Sun and the stars remain, may Viṣṇu, Brahmā and Maheśvara stand on the slab along with all other Devas. Let the holy centre be named after me.

65. The holy centre of Gayā shall extend to five krośas and Gayaśiras to one krośa. Amidst them may all the holy centres grant welfare unto all men.

66. By taking ablution etc. and performing Tarpaṇa one should offer balls of rice. Then it is more fruitful. That man becomes a great soul and uplifts a thousand members of his family.

67. All of you, stay (here) for ever in manifest and unmanifest forms. May Gadādhara himself be the destroyer of all sins.

68. May those on whose behalf the Śrāddha has been performed and Piṇḍas offered, go to Brahmaloka. May the sins due to Brāhmaṇa slaughter etc. of those who report to this holy centre perish.

69. May all the holy centres in heaven, firmament and the earth such as Naimiṣa, Puṣkara, Gaṅgā, Prayāga, Avimuktaka and others come here regularly, O Suras, and yield welfare unto all men.

70. O hosts of Devas, of what avail is much talk. Unless one of you Devas stand (on this slab), I too will not be steady. This is the condition. Let it be strictly observed."

71. On hearing the words of Gayāsura, Viṣṇu and other Suras spoke, "All that you have requested for shall undoubtedly be granted.

72. After worshipping our feet (all the devotees) will attain the great goal." When the boons were granted to him by Devas, the Daitya became delighted and remained steady.

73-76. When Devas stood steady, the urborn deity (Brahmā) gave unto Brāhmaṇas fifty-five villages and the holy centre of Gayā extending to five krośas. He built divine houses endowed with all necessities of life and gave *Kāmadhenu* (wish-yielding divine cow), *Kalpavṛkṣa* (Kalpa-tree) and Pārijāta and other trees also were given. A great river of milk, many streams of ghee, exudations of honey, streams of honey, lakes rich in curds etc., a lake of gold, many mountains of cooked food etc. were given. Brahmā created different items of food and fruits and gave them all to the Brāhmaṇas. While giving these things, Aja said, "O leading Brāhmaṇas, do not beg of others".

77-78. After giving away all these things and bowing to Ādigadādhara Brahmā went to Brahmaloka. The Brāhmaṇas of Gayā officiated as priests of Dharma in his sacrifice at Dharmāraṇya and later begged him (for Dakṣiṇā). Out of covetousness they took monetary and other gifts at the sacrifice of Dharma. Brahmā came there and cursed the Brāhmaṇas.[1]

79-81. "O Brāhmaṇas even when everything had been given by me, you coveted for more. Hence you will always be burdened with debts. The river shall flow with water only (and not milk). The mountains of foodstuffs will turn into those of rocks. All the rivers shall flow with water and your houses will be of mud. Kāmadhenu and the Kalpa-tree will come back to my own region." Cursed thus by Brahmā all those Brāhmaṇas imploringly said to the Unborn deity:

82. "O lord, everything that had been given by you has gone off due to your curse. May you be kind enough to assign something for our livelihood".

83. On hearing those words, the sympathetic Brahmā spoke thus to the Brāhmaṇas: "As long as the Moon and the Sun shine, you will be maintaining your livelihood by means of (the earning at the) holy centres.

84. Those meritorious persons who perform Śrāddhas in Gayā will attain Brahmaloka. I will also always be considered worshipped by those who worship you."

85-86. The stomach of the Daitya is overlapped by the mountain Viraja, the righteous. Near the well that forms its

1. The story is repeated in NP. II.44.16-18, AP. 114.36-38.

umbilical cavity, goddess Virajā is stationed. One who offers Piṇḍa etc. shall uplift twenty-one generations. His (the demon's) feet had been made steady by the mountain Mahendra. A man who offers balls of rice there uplifts seven generations.

CHAPTER FORTYFIVE

Gayāmāhātmya (*Contd.*): *The Story of the Śilā*

Nārada said:

1. What is the origin of that slab whereby Gayāsura was kept steady and submissive? What is its form? What is its greatness? Please mention its name.

Sanatkumāra said:

2. There was once a highly refulgent person named Dharma. He had mastered all sacred lore. His wife Viśvarūpā was devoted to the service of her husband.

3. A daughter of great qualities and endowed with all the auspicious characteristics like Lakṣmī was born of her to Dharma. She was the chaste girl named Dharmavratā.

4-5. Whatever good qualities there are in the three worlds, were present in her. Dharma searched for a befitting bridegroom to Dharmavratā in all the three worlds, but in vain. Then he told her, "Perform a penance for the sake of attaining a bridegroom". She said, "So be it", and went to the forest.

6. That girl performed a very severe penance which could not be performed by anyone. She subsisted only on the air and spent ten thousand Yugas in that Śveta Kalpa.

7. During the course of his wandering over the earth, the mental son of Brahmā, well known by the name of Marīci, saw that jewel of a girl.

8. To that girl who was endowed with beauty and youth and who was engaged in the greatest penance, Marīci asked, "Tell me who you are and to whom you belong.

9. O timid lady, of excellent vows, you are a fascinating one by this beauty of yours. I am the son of Brahmā, well-known as Marīci. I have mastered the Vedas."

10. On hearing the words of Marīci, the girl replied to the sage, "I am the daughter of Dharma. My name is Dharmavratā. I am endowed with penance.

11. O leading Brāhmaṇa, I am performing this great penance for the wooing of a good husband". Marīci thereupon spoke to Dharmavratā lovingly:

12. "O woman of auspicious rites, by merely looking at me, you will become a great chaste lady. I am roaming day and night on the earth, only with a desire to meet with a chaste lady.

13. If you have become a Pativratā, I shall resort to you Come unto me as your bridegroom. There is no other girl in the world like you, and you will never have another bridegroom equal to me.

14. Hence O Dharmavratā, be my lawfully wedded wife now". Dharmavratā thereupon told the sage, "O sage of good rites, request Dharma (for my hand)."

15. On hearing those words, he went to Dharma. Dharma saw the (prospective) bridegroom like a mass of refulgence. He bowed to him and honoured him with the offer of seat and materials of worship.

16. On being asked "Why have you come ?" Marīci replied to Dharma, "While roaming over the whole earth for the sake of a (marriageable) girl, your excellent daughter has been seen by me. Give that daughter unto me. You will have welfare resulting therefrom."

17. After honouring him with Arghya etc., Dharma said to him, "So be it". He brought Dharmavratā there and gave her to Marīci.

18. He granted him boons as well. He fulfilled the promise made. The Brāhmaṇa (Marīci) took her to his hermitage along with Agnihotra (sacred fire).

19. The sage sported in her company like Viṣṇu with Śrī or Śaṁbhu with Pārvatī or Brahmā with Sarasvatī.

20. Marīci begot of her a hundred sons comparable even

with Viṣṇu. Once Marīci went to the forest for the sake of flowers and fruits and returned (very tired).

21. As he was tired, he told thus to his chaste wife, "After taking food massage my feet, even as I lie down on the couch".

22. Dharmavratā said, "So be it". As the sage lay down on his bed, she rubbed his feet with ghee and began to massage them with eagerness.

23-24. Even as the sage was becoming sleepy Brahmā came to that place. She was placed in a dilemma, "Shall I continue to massage the feet or honour the Jagadguru (the preceptor of the world)." Then deciding to honour him, as he was Guru of Gurus, she stood up.

25. She offered *Arghya*, *Pādya* etc. and worshipped Brahmā. Brahmā took rest on a couch after due worship.

26. In the meantime, the husband got up from his bed. Unable to see Dharmavratā, the Brāhmaṇa became infuriated and cursed her.

27. "Abandoning the massage of my feet and thereby disobeying my behest, you have gone elsewhere. Hence you will be consumed by this fire of curse. Be a slab of stone."

28. On being cursed by her husband, she spoke to Marīci in a great fury, "While you were sleeping, Brahmā, your father and preceptor, arrived here.

29-30. It was your duty to have got up and worshipped your father. O sage, strictly adhering to pious activities (as a wife), I carried out your duty. Hence I am guiltless. Still I have been cursed by you. So I too curse you. O husband, you will have that curse undoubtedly from Mahādeva."

31-32. On seeing her husband agitated, she too became distressed. She went to Prajāpati and bowed to him, as he was lying down. She kindled the fire *Gārhapatya* with fuel and stood in its middle. There she performed a very terrible penance. Similarly Marīci who too had been cursed, performed a terrible penance.

33. Indra and others who were distressed due to the penance of Marīci sought refuge in Hari.

34. They spoke to Hari who was sleeping in the ocean of milk: "O Hari, we are extremely distressed due to the penance

of the chaste lady and the sage. O Keśava, save the three worlds."

35. On hearing the words of Indra and others, Viṣṇu went up to Dharmavratā. In the meantime, Aja (Brahmā) woke up. The Devas including Keśava, spoke to Dharmavratā who was in the middle of the fire:

36. "O chaste lady, who has the capacity to perform penance in the middle of the fire? But that has been achieved by you. It is really a thing that terrifies all worlds.

37. O knower of Dharmas, choose any boon that you desire from us". On hearing the words of Viṣṇu and others, Dharmavratā spoke to the Devas:

38. "I am unable to turn back the curse of my husband even with all my power. Let that curse given by Marīci to me recede."

39-41. On hearing the words of Dharmavratā, the Devas spoke to her again, "O daughter of Dharma, of pious rites, this curse has been given to you by a great sage. It cannot be nullified by Devas and Brāhmaṇas. Hence choose any other boon, so that the Dharma proclaimed by the Vedas will be established in the three worlds, O lady of auspicious vows". On hearing the words of Devas, Dhamavratā spoke to the Devas:

42. "O immortal gods, if you are not able to redeem me from the curse of my husband, please grant me an excellent boon like this.

43. I shall then become a slab of stone which will be the most auspicious and the holiest in the whole of the Cosmic Egg. I shall be more sanctifying than rivers, lakes, Devas etc.

44. I shall be holier than the sages, ascetics, the chief of Devas and others. Let all those Liṅgas in the three worlds, whether manifest or unmanifest, abide for ever on my body in the form of a holy place.

45. Let all the holy centres, the chiefs of the constellations, all the Devas and the Devīs (goddesses) and the sages stand by (on me).

46-47. Brahmā, Viṣṇu and Rudra shall mark their footprints on me. The five fires and Kumāra and others be stationed in their multiforms. The Devas are stationed in their embodied and unembodied forms as well as through their foot-prints. They are stationed on the earth over the slab in the form of idols, within the dimension of a krośa.

48. All the people will become purified on seeing that slab which is the destroyer of all great sins. The performer of Śraddhas becoming pure, will be authorised in the holy rites and will attain Brahmaloka.

49. Let all those who after taking their baths in all the sacred waters stationed on the rocky slab, perform Tarpaṇa and then the Śrāddha along with the offerings of Piṇḍa attain Brahmaloka.

50-51. Let the visible holy centre of Gadādhara be the most excellent of all excellent holy centres. May those who stay there or die there go to the region of Brahmā. Let the holy centres of Vārāṇasī and Prayāga stay there with the name of Puruṣottama. Let the holy centres named Gaṅgāsāgara stay in the holy spot of Phalgu. The holiest of spots is presided over by Gadādhara. By performing Śrāddha of dead persons, Pitṛs will attain salvation.

52. May *Jarāyujas* (viviparous beings), *Aṇḍajas* (oviparous), *Svedajas* (sweat-born beings) or *Udbhids* (vegetable kingdom) attain the form of Viṣṇu after abandoning their bodies on the slab.

53. Just as all Yajñas become completely accomplished when Hari is worshipped, so also let the Śrāddha, Tarpaṇa and ablution be everlasting here.

54. Let those who perform the Japas of the mantras of the leading Suras on my body become Siddhas and the masters of Siddhis ere long.

55. It is certain that a man who performs Śrāddha etc. uplifts thousand Pitṛs of his family including himself and leads them to Viṣṇuloka, the region of Viṣṇu.

56. O leading Suras, whatever excellent (sacred) rivers there are such as Gaṅgā etc., whatever auspicious eddies there are whether oceans, or important lakes such as Mānasa etc., let them be conducive to salvation of the persons who perform Śrāddhas.

57-60. Let the Devatās go in their embodied forms in some places and in other places let them not go; Viṣṇu is one and single; but he is glorified by learned men as having three *Mūrtis* (physical forms). Let the sages and all the groups of Gandharvas stand on the slab of stone along with the Devas and all the holy centres. The Śilā (slab of stone) shall be called *Sarvadeva-svarūpa* (having the form of all the Devas). Let it (the (slab of stone) stay as long as the Cosmic Egg lasts. Those who perform Japa and penance on my physical body in the form of Rocky Slab, shall also be permitted to perform Homa in the fire. May it be eternal. Let the Śrāddha be eternal, so also be the Japas, Homas and the penances. Let them stay on me in the form of huge mountain".

61-62. On hearing the words of the chaste lady, the Devas spoke to her, "Undoubtedly whatever has been requested by you shall take place. When you remain steady on the head of Gayāsura we shall stay there in the form of footprints and remain there steadily." After giving the evidence, of having granted the boon, the Devas vanished there itself.

CHAPTER FORTYSIX

Gayāmāhātmya (Contd.) : Śilā-tīrtha and Other Sacred Spots

Sanatkumāra said :

1. O Nārada, listen. I shall recount the greatness of the slab of rock, that confers salvation. Devas and the prominent sages sing of the greatness of the slab.

2. That rocky slab situated on the earth, has the forms of Devas. It is highly sanctifying. The wonderful Śilātīrtha[1] is well known in the three worlds.

---

1. Śilā Tīrtha, the same as Muṇḍapṛṣṭha, as the Śilā was placed on the back of the (shaven) head of Gaya (v.12 below, also TSS, p. 337). It has the combined sanctity of itself and that of the sacred head of Gaya (v.8 below). The area of Śilā or the head of Gayāsura is 3 Sq. Kms.

3. On touching it, all the people in the worlds went to Hari's city (Vaikuṇṭha). When the three worlds became void, Yama's city became empty thereby.

4. Accompanied by Indra and others Yama went to Brahmā and reported (to him) the wonderful event, "O Pitāmaha, take back this staff of office as well as the assignment offered to me as Yama (the controller of the world)."

5. Brahmā then said to Yama, "Keep it in your house". Advised by Brahmā, Dharmarāja retained the slab in his house.

6. Yama continued to carry out his duty, viz. the chastisement etc. of the sinners. Thus the weighty slab became well known in the universe.

7. The slab having the forms and features of Devas is on a par with Brahmā, Viṣṇu, lord Maheśvara and Meru, in the whole of the Cosmic Egg.

8. Since it was held (laid) on the head of Gayāsura due to its heaviness, the happy combination of two holy things is the bestower of salvation on Pitṛs.

Sacred Places Connected with Śilā

Part of the Śilā	*Covered by* (Verse Nos.)	*Other details*
Middle (Belly)	Mt. Ādipāla (68)	
Middle Region	Mt. Nāga (26)	
Foot	Mt. Prabhāsa (13)	Its contact with the Phalgu Rāma tīrtha (17).
Protruding	(1) Preta-Śilā (15)	
Toe	(2) Prabhāseśa (14)	
Left Leg	Preta-Parvata (70)	
Left foot	Mt. Abhyudyantaka (42)	
Right-hand side	Mt. Kunda (35-36)	
	Mt. Bhasma Kūṭa (56)	
	Mt. Udyantaka (46)	
Left hand	Mt. Vāditraka (44)	
	Mt. Gṛdhrakūṭa	
Muṇḍapṛṣṭha	The main base of the slab	

Vidyārthi (p.6) in the tabular statement of locational and functional elaboration of the sacred centre at Gayā includes temples of Rāma and Śiva, Yama's sacred centre and the famous tree (of spirits) under Rāma-Śilā (hill-top cluster), and Śiva, Gaṇeśa, Brahma Kuṇḍa and Phalgu under Rāmaśilā (foot-hill cluster) while Pretaśilā, Pretabhavānī, Viṣṇu, Rāma-kuṇḍa, Kāka-bali under Preta Śilā cluster.

9. The unborn deity (Brahmā) performed *Hayamedha* (horse sacrifice) on the combination of the two holy things. On seeing Viṣṇu etc. who came to receive their due shares (in the sacrifice), the slab requested :

10. "All of you take the vow of standing on the slab (for ever) to enable Pitṛs to attain liberation". Saying "So be it" Viṣṇu and other Devas stood on the *Śilā* (the slab of rock).

11. In accordance with their previous promise, Devas stayed on the Śilā in embodied and unembodied forms either through their idols of stone or footprints.

12. Since the *Śilā* was stationed on the top of the tonsured head of the Daitya, it was called Muṇḍapṛṣṭhādri. It is the bestower of Brahmaloka upon Pitṛs.

13. The foot of the *Śilā* is concealed by the mountain Prabhāsa. It is called Prabhāsa because it is illuminated by Bhāskara (the Sun-god).

14. *Śilāṅguṣṭha* (the thumb of the *Śilā*) has come out of Prabhāsa by piercing through it. The lord presiding over *Aṅguṣṭha* section is glorified as Prabhāseśa.

15. A portion of the *Śilāṅguṣṭha* is remembered as *Pretaśilā* (the Rock of the Dead). If Piṇḍas are offered to the dead on this rock, the dead man becomes free from the state of a goblin.

16. A devotee should perform his ablution at the place where the Prabhāsa mountain meets the great river. Rāma had his bath here in the company of the gentle lady (i.e. Sītā). Hence this is remembered as 'Rāmatīrtha'.

17. Here Rāma was requested by the great river, "O Rāma, take your bath (in my waters)." Since then it became well known in the three worlds as 'Rāmatīrtha'.

18. Mantra—"Let all those evil sins committed by me in my hundred and odd former births, become destroyed due to my ablution in Rāmatīrtha."

19. A man who takes his bath repeating this Mantra and performs Śrāddha and offers Piṇḍas in Rāmatīrtha, goes to Viṣṇuloka. (When the great river requested him), Rāma, the elder brother of Bharata, said, "So be it" and stayed here accompanied by Sītā.

20. If a devotee repeats this Mantra—"O Rāma, O

Rāma of mighty long arms, O the bestower of fearlessness on Devas, I bow unto you, the lord Devas. Let my sin become destroyed":

21. If the devotee takes his bath repeating this Mantra and performs the *Śrāddha* along with the offering of *Piṇḍas*, his Pitṛs become released from the state of a ghost and attain *Pitṛtva* (the state of Pitṛhood).

22. Mantra—"O lord of Devas, you are the waters. You are the lord of the luminaries. O lord, destroy my sins committed mentally, verbally and physically".

23. After bowing to the lord of Prabhāsa, one should go unto the refulgent Śiva. After making obeisance to Śaṁbhu, one should perform the oblation to Yama.

24-25. When Rāma had gone to the forest, Bharata came to this mountain and performed the offerings of Piṇḍa etc. to the Pitṛs. The lord (Bharata) installed the idols of Rāma, Sītā, Lakṣmaṇa and the sages. In the holy hermitage of Bharata, the foot-print of Mataṅga is seen by all men. It is always surrounded by highly meritorious men.

26. It is established as a model for people. It contains the essentials of piety. One who performs *Śrāddha* in *Mataṅgapāda* enables all the Pitṛs to cross the ocean of existence (*saṁsāra*).

27. A man who takes bath in Rāmatīrtha and worships Sītā and bows down to Rāmeśvara is not reborn as an embodied being.

28. The middle region of the *Śilā* is again covered by a mountain. It was urged by Dharmarāja by saying "*Na Gaccha*—Do not go". Hence it is called *Naga* (mountain).

29. "Yamarāja and Dharmarāja attempted to make (Gayāsura) steady. I give *Bali* (oblation) unto them for the sake of liberation of (my) ancestors.

30. There are two dogs of dark and variegated colour. They are born of the family of Vaivasvata (i.e. of Yama). I am giving *Bali* unto them. May they refrain from violence.

31. May the crows stationed in east, west, north-west-south and south-west accept the balls of rice offered by me (on the ground).

32. O strong one, you are Yama; you are Yama's messenger. You are a crow. Eating the oblations, destroy the sins committed during the seven births."

33. When Rāma went to the forest, Bharata came to this mountain. After offering the Piṇḍas etc. to the Pitṛs, Rāmeśa was installed by him here.

34. After the bath and the worship of Rāmeśa accompanied by Rāma and Sītā, one should perform *Śrāddha* with the offerings of *Piṇḍas*. Such a pious soul shall go to Viṣṇu's abode along with the Pitṛs and hundreds of the members of his family.

35-36. On the right-hand side of the *Śilā*, the Kuṇḍaparvata (mountain) is established. Various deities are installed there. Timirāditya, Īśāna, Bharga—these are the forms of Maheśvara. The Vahni, two Varuṇas and the four Rudras yield liberation unto the Pitṛs. After going to the hermitage of Bharata, the devotee should bow to them and worship them.

37. He is liberated from all major sins as well as minor ones along with his Pitṛs. O celestial sage, a man can take bath anywhere in the hermitage of Bharata. If he performs a *Śrāddha* etc. the fruit thereof is not lost even after a Kalpa.

38. Really the *Śrāddha* performed anywhere in Gayā is never perishing. Still they say that the Japas, Homas and penances and anything offered (as religious gift) at Bharata's hermitage are of infinite nature.

39. There are four idols of Ravi (the Sun-god) in the forms of the four Yugas. On being seen, touched and worshipped, they bestow salvation on the Pitṛs.

40. There are two deities, viz. Muktivāmana and Tāraka Brahman. These deities are the boats for those who are overwhelmed by the ocean of worldly existence. Brahman is *Tāraka* (that which enables one to cross the ocean of Saṁsāra) of all people dead and alive.

41. He who sees Trivikrama, Puruṣottama and Brahmā becomes a pious soul and attains the greatest goal along with the Pitṛs.

42. At the left foot of the *Śilā* there is the mountain Abhyudyantaka established. A devotee who offers Piṇḍas there, leads his Pitṛs to Brahmapura.

43. Brahmā performed his sacrifice along with Suras near the Naimiṣa forest. That Tīrtha is called *Mukhyatīrtha* (the chief of holy waters). Devas are stationed at its feet.

44. O Nārada, the excellent among the sages, whatever inauspicious deeds there may be, perish in the three *Padas* (spots) in those holy centres.

45. The Naimiṣa forest is holy and resorted to by meritorious persons such as Vyāsa, Śuka, Paila, Kaṇva, Vedhas, Śiva, Hari.

46. By their mere sight, a man is liberated from all sins. On the right-hand side of the *Śilā*, there is the Udyantaka mountain.

Some variants (Pāṭhāntara Verses)—additional verses after verse 46.

1-2. This mountain is established. One who offers Piṇḍas there leads Pitṛs to the city of god Brahmā. Kuṇḍa and Udyantaka were created by him by means of his penance. Brahmā stayed there along with Sāvitrī and Kumāra (i.e. Sanatkumāra).

3. Hāhā and Hūhū and the others made the sound of music. The mountains Kuṇḍa and Udyantaka were full of songs and the sound of musical instruments.

4. It is here that the holy sage Agastya performed an austere penance. From Brahmā, he received the boon of greatness rarely achieved on the earth. He secured Lopāmudrā as his wife and the great goal (Mokṣa) to his Pitṛs.

5. At midday the devotees should take their bath and worship Sāvitrī. The Brāhmaṇa will become a master of the Vedas and very rich for a crore of births (?)

6. By taking ablution in the Agastya Pada and by offering Piṇḍas there, one becomes a pious soul and attains Brahmaloka along with the Pitṛs. He is worshipped even by the heaven-dwellers.

7. A man who enters Brahmayoni and comes out attains the greatest Brahman. He is liberated from the miseries of wombs (i.e. rebirth).

8. A man who bows to Gayākumāra attains Brāhmaṇa-hood. One who performs ablution in Somakuṇḍa leads the Pitṛs to Somaloka (Lunar world).

9. The oblation to the crows at the *Kākaśilā* (the slab of crows) is conducive to freedom from indebtedness. After bowing to Svargadvāreśvara, one attains Brahmapura through heaven.

10. One who offers Piṇḍas at Vyomagaṅgā becomes free from impurities and leads the Pitṛs to heaven. There is a heap of *Bhasma* at the right-hand side of the *Śilā*. O Nārada, the devotee should take bath with this *Bhasma* from the mountain called *Bhasmakūṭādri*.

11. Prapitāmaha (Brahmā) is stationed on the *Vaṭa* as Vaṭeśvara (Lord of the holy banyan tree). One who offers Piṇḍas at the holy Mataṅgapada leads the Pitṛs to heaven.

12-13. Ahead of it is Rukmiṇī Kuṇḍa and to the west is the river Kapilā. Kapileśa is on the banks of the river. On the new moon day, one should take bath in Kapilā and worship Kapileśa. If he performs *Śrāddha* in Māheśīkuṇḍa, he shall attain heaven.

14-15. Gaurī, under the name of Maṅgalā there, grants all types of prosperity and glory. Janārdana is near the *Bhasmakūṭa*. One who offers Piṇḍas in his hand, with mantras, if for oneself and without gingelly seeds, in the left hand, if for others and mixed with curds for those who are alive—all these attain Viṣṇu-loka.

16. Mantra—"O Janārdana, this Piṇḍa is offered by me in your hand; give it unto him who dies in Gayāśīrṣa".

17. Mantra—"This Piṇḍa has been given, O Janārdana, in your hand. At Gayāśīrṣa this must be given to me when I am dead".

18-19. O Janārdana, obeisance unto you. Hail to you of the form of the Pitṛs. O Lord of Pitṛs, obeisance to you. Bow to you, O cause of salvation, O Janārdana, O lord of Lakṣmī, you assume the form of the Pitṛs at Gayā yourself. Obeisance be to you, O bestower of salvation on the Pitṛs.

20. After meditating on Puṇḍarīkākṣa (Viṣṇu) one becomes released from the three forms of indebtedness. Certainly people attain heaven after worshipping Puṇḍarīkākṣa.

21. Bhīma knelt on his left knee and bowed to Janārdana. After performing *Śrāddha* along with the offerings of Piṇḍa, he attained Viṣṇuloka along with his brothers.

22-24. On the right foot of the *Śilā*, the mountain Pretakūṭa[1] is held by Dharmarāja with both of his feet. He kicked it off with his feet on account of the weight of sins. In the forest of *Kara-grahaṇa*, many have stayed behind (unliberated) in the form of departed souls (ghosts). They are the cause of obstacles. The Tīrtha confers salvation on the Pitṛs through the performance of Śrāddha etc.

25. *Pretakūṭa* attained sacredness due to the contact of the *Śilā*. Devas are stationed in the form of footprints on *Pretakūṭa*. After performing Śrāddha etc. there, one should get the Pitṛs released from ghost-hood.

26. O Brāhmaṇa, those who have the terrible forms of a ghost near the Śilā wander over the earth and in Yama's world.

27. On the holy head of Gayāsura which is devoid of ghosts etc., Brahmā and other Devas are stationed and he attains sacredness.

28. Among Kīkaṭas (southern Magadha) Gayā is the holiest. Rājavana and Rājagṛha are holy. The hermitage of Cyavana is holy. The river is many times holy (than the rest).

29. Hemadaṇḍa and the mountain Hemakūṭa are in Vaikuṇṭha. One who performs Śrāddha and offers Piṇḍas etc. there leads the Pitṛs to Brahmapura.

30. On the right foot of the Śilā, the mountain *Gṛdhrakūṭa* is held by Dharmarāja in order to stabilise (Gaya). It is very holy.

31-32. Sages performed their penance there in the form of Gṛdhras (vultures) and attained liberation. Hence this is called Gṛdhrakūṭa. Gṛdhreśvara is stationed there. A man who sees Gṛdhreśvara attains Śambhu's region. After bowing down to Gṛdhravaṭa one shall achieve one's desire and attain heaven.

---

1. Pretakūṭa, Gṛdhrakūṭa, Bhasmakūṭa etc. are the tops of hillocks near Gayā.

33. He who offers Piṇḍas in the Gṛdhraguhā (vulture-cave) attains Śivaloka. There is the Māheśvarī Dhārā (the current of Maheśvara). He who offers Piṇḍas there, leads the Pitṛs to heaven.

34. There is a lake called Mūlakṣetra. He who offers Piṇḍas there, attains Brahmaloka. After visiting Śiva he attains freedom from indebtedness and salvation from sins. He attains Śiva himself after visualizing Śiva.

35. The middle of the *Śilā* (the belly portion) is overlapped (covered) by the mountain Ādipāla. It is here that Vighneśa, the destroyer of obstacles, stands in the form of an elephant. He who offers Piṇḍas at the umbilical region (of the god) leads his Pitṛs to Brahmapura.

36. On the hips (i.e. ridges) of the mountain Muṇḍapṛṣṭha, there was a big forest of Devadāru trees. One shall destroy one's sins by seeing the mountain Aravinda on Muṇḍapṛṣṭha.

37. A certain sage performed penance here in the form of a *Krauñca* (heron). The mountain was marked by his feet. Hence it is called *Krauñcapāda.*

38. One who takes bath there in the water reservoir, leads three generations to heaven. Lakṣmīśa (Viṣṇu) is stationed on the Śilā in the manifest and unmanifest forms along with Devas. Hence the *Śilā* is full of Devas.

[End of Addl. Verses]

47. That mountain was brought by the noble-souled Agastya. Brahmā and Hara performed a fierce penance there.

48. There is the excellent Kuṇḍa (Pool) of Agastya which is of a very rare excellence in the three worlds. It was here that the eight sages achieved *Siddhi* after performing penance. They attained final beatitude. After bowing to the eight sages in the Kuṇḍa, the pilgrim will be able to lead the Pitṛs to Brahmā's city.

49. O celestial sage, an auspicious prominent mountain was established on the left hand of the *Śilā*. It is always resounding with the sounds of musical instruments and divine symphony. It is called mountain *Vāditraka.*

50. Even today Vidyādharas, accompanied by hosts of Gandharvas and Apsaras-s sing divine songs in chorus.

51. Mohana, Sunītha, Śailūja, Mohanottama, Parvata,

Nārada, Dhyānī, Saṅgītī, Puṣpadantaka, Hāhā, Hūhū and others perform musical concert.

52. Similarly the Gandharva named Citraratha surrounded by all the Gandharvas, sings sweet songs of great festivities on the mountain.

53. Hence that mountain is resorted to by Devas for ever even today. Hara, the lord of Devas, is desirous of applying *Bhasma* all over the body like an unguent.

54. Rudra accompanied by Pārvatī rejoices on that mountain resonant with music. He is worshipped as he is the greatest goal of the Pitṛs. He should be meditated upon.

55. The greatest Ātman (Deity) in Gayā is either the lord of the cows or Gadādhara (the wielder of the mace). O sage, thanks to the worship of Rudra, the Māyā pertaining to Viṣṇu becomes quelled.

56. On the right-hand side of the *Śilā*, the mountain Bhasmakūṭa is held by Dharmarāja. Agastya stays there with his wife.

57-58. One who takes bath at the spot of Agastya and offers Piṇḍas, goes to Brahmaloka. It was from Brahmā that he secured the excellent boon of greatness in the world, Lopāmudrā as wife and the highest goal (liberation) to his forefathers. There, on seeing Agastyeśvara, one is absolved of the sin of Brāhmaṇa-slaughter.

59. On seeing Agastya along with his wife, one leads the Pitṛs to Brahmapura. Daṇḍin performed a penance on the mountain south of Sītādri.

60-61. There is a *Vaṭa* (banyan tree) called Vaṭeśvara. Prapitāmaha (god Brahmā) is stationed there. Beyond that is Rukmiṇīkuṇḍa. To the west of it is the river Kapilā. Kapileśa is on the banks of the river. When the New Moon and Monday coincide with each other, a devout man must take bath in Kapilā and worship the lord of Kapilā. If after that, Śrāddha is performed and Piṇḍas are offered the Pitṛs shall attain salvation.

62. There is a current of fire coming from the excellent mountain. There is the pool called Sārasvata Kuṇḍa. It has been created by Sarasvatī.

63. Lord Śukra stayed there with his sons Saṇḍa, Amarka and others. O excellent sage, a man who performs Śrāddha and offers Piṇḍa etc. in the various spots at the feet of the eminent sages, enables the Pitṛs to cross (the ocean of worldly existence).

64. On the left-hand side of the *Śilā* there stands the mountain Gṛdhrakūṭa. The great sages assuming the form of cranes performed penance there and became Siddhas.

65. Hence the mountain is called Gṛdhrakūṭa. The deity Gṛdhreśvara is stationed there. A man who visits and bows to Gṛdhreśvara shall achieve the region of Śaṁbhu.

66. He who offers Piṇḍas on Gṛdhrakūṭa and in the cave, attains Śivaloka. One who bows to the *Vaṭa* (the banyan tree) on Gṛdhrakūṭa attains all his desires and goes to heaven.

67. On seeing Śiva, one attains freedom from indebtedness, release from sins, and goes unto Śiva. There is a Śūlakṣetra (shrine of the trident) there. One who offers Piṇḍas there, leads the Pitṛs to heaven.

68. The centre of the Śilā is overlapped by the mountain Ādipāla. Vighneśa, the destroyer of obstacles, stays there is the form of an elephant. On visiting him a devotee is freed from obstacles. He leads the Pitṛs to Brahmapura.

69. There was a forest of Devadāru trees on the ridge of the mountain Muṇḍapṛṣṭha. After visiting the mountains Muṇḍapṛṣṭha and Aravindādri, one quells all sins. He who offers Piṇḍas in the umbilical region of Gayā called Suṣumnā (like the nerve Suṣumnā in human body) leads his Pitṛs to heaven.

70. On the left leg of the *Śilā*, the mountain Pretaparvata was established by Dharmarāja. The mountain is called Pretaśilā because of its impurity due to sins.

71. The mountain was kicked off to a great distance. Pretakūṭa was freed from sins and attained sanctity due to the contact with the Śilā.

72. There is a pool called Pretakuṇḍa there. Devas are stationed at its foot. Performing Śrāddha etc. in the Kuṇḍa, one shall relieve the Pitṛs of goblinhood.

73. There are many of the ghosts staying separately and causing obstacles to those men who perform Śrāddha etc. for the sake of the liberation of Pitṛs. The ghosts assume the form of archers and catch hold of the hands (of the pilgrims).

74. There is a rock on Muṇḍapṛṣṭha where Mahādeva stays. On seeing it all people become relieved of heinous and lesser sins.

75. Gayāśiras is holy and devoid of all sins. It is devoid of ghosts etc. Hence it is highly sanctifying and excellent.

76. In the Kīkaṭa land (i. e. the territories comprising southern Bihar) Gayā is the holiest centre. The Rājagṛha forest is also holy. The hermitage of Cyavana is another holy spot. The river Punaḥpunā (?) is also holy.

77. There are other holy spots, viz. Vaikuṇṭha, Lohadaṇḍa, Gṛdhrakūṭa and Sonaka. By performing *Śrāddha* etc. here, a pilgrim leads all the Pitṛs to Brahmapura.

78. Assuming the form of a heron, a sage performed penance on the ridge of Muṇḍapṛṣṭha. Since the mountain is marked by the foot-prints of the heron, it is remembered as Krauñcapāda.

79. One who takes bath in the water reservoir there, shall lead the entire family to heaven. An oblation offered to crows on the rock Kākaśilā, is conducive to relief from indebtedness.

80. The two sages Lomaśa and Lomaharṣaṇa performed a great penance on the ridge of Muṇḍapṛṣṭha. Both of them attained Siddhi of the highest magnitude.

81-85. Many excellent rivers had been invoked by Lomaśa[1], viz. Mahānadī, Śarāvatī, Vetravatī, Candrabhāgā, Sarasvatī, Kāverī, Sindhuvīrā, the excellent river Candana, Vāsiṣṭhī, Sarayū, Gaṅgā, Yamunā, Gaṇḍakī, Indirā, Mahāvaitaraṇī, Nikṣarā that originates from heaven, Alakanandā, the northern river called Kanakā, Kauśikī, Brahmadā, all these are the absolvers of everyone's sin. The two rivers Kṛṣṇavalvā and Carmavatī are the bestowers of salvation. They were called the most excellent of all rivers by Lomaharṣa daringly. O excellent sage, by means of the power of his penance, Narmadā also was invoked by him. He who takes bath in any of these rivers and offers Piṇḍas leads his Pitṛs to heaven.

---

1. Like other Sthala-purāṇas, this text claims all important rivers in India to be present at Gayā. Small streams and streamlets are supposed to represent big rivers like Gaṅgā, Yamunā, Kāverī etc.

86. A man who enters the holy spot Brahmayoni and comes out of it, attains the greatest Brahman freed from the distress of wombs (i.e. re-birth).

87. A man who bathes in the Puṣkariṇī (holy pond) Nikṣarā and performs Śrāddha etc. on the divine Krauñcapada regularly for three days, leads his Pitṛs even if they were Pañcapāpins (those guilty of the five heinous sins) to heaven.

88. Janārdana stays in *Bhasmakūṭa*. He who offers Piṇḍas in his hands whether for himself or for others—if it is for one's own self it must be without gingelly seeds (and be offered) with the sacred thread in the *Savya* (hanging from the left shoulder) position; and if for those who are alive, it must be mixed with curds—all these go to Viṣṇuloka (Vaikuṇṭha).

89. Mantra: "O Janārdana, the Piṇḍa that I offer in your hand, may please be given by you to that person for whom I have given it to thee now. It be given to him after he is dead, O lord."

90. Mantra: "O Janārdana, this Piṇḍa is given into your hand by me. When I reach the end of my time (when I am dead) this must be given to me at Gayāśiras.[1]

91. O Janārdana, obeisance to you. Bow to you, granter of liberation to the Pitṛs. O lord of Pitṛs, obeisance to you. Hail to you in the form of Pitṛs."

92. In Gayā, Janārdana assumed the form of Pitṛs himself. On visiting that Puṇḍarīkākṣa (lotus-eyed god Viṣṇu) one is released from three-fold indebtedness.

93. "O Puṇḍarīkākṣa, obeisance to you, O releaser from the three-fold indebtedness. O Lakṣmīkānta (Lord of Lakṣmī), obeisance to you, be the granter of liberation to the Pitṛs."

94. Kneeling on his left knee, Bhīma bowed to Janārdana. After performing the *Śrāddha* along with the offerings of *Piṇḍas*, he attained Brahmaloka in the company of his brothers. He became a pious soul and uplifted a hundred forefathers in his family.

1. Cf. NP. II.47.63b-65.

95. On the *Śilā*, the lord of Lakṣmī stays both in the manifest form as well as in the unmanifest form, along with Devas. Hence the *Śilā* is *Devamayī* (full of Devas).

CHAPTER FORTYSEVEN

Gayāmāhātmya (*Contd.*) : *The Glory of Ādigadādhara*

Nārada enquired:

1. How did the primordial Gadādhara (wielder of the mace) stay in the manifest form? How did he stay both as manifest and unmanifest?

2. How did the mace (Gadā) originate and how did he come to be known as Ādigadādhara? How did the Gadālola spot become so (sanctifying) as to wipe off all sins.

Sanatkumāra replied:

3. There was an Asura named Gada whose body was very hard and adamantine. By performing a very terrible penance he secured boons from Brahmā. When he was requested, he gave up to Brahmā the bones of his body which is very difficult to part with.

4. Urged by Brahmā, Viśvakarmā made the wonderful club (out of it). He turned the bone of the demon in the lathe that could crush even *Vajra* (thunderbolt) and kept it in the heaven itself.

5. After a great deal of time, in the Svāyaṁbhuva Manvantara, the demon Heti, the son of Brahmā, performed a very terrible penance.*

6-7. For a hundred thousand divine years he subsisted only on the air. Then looking up, he stood on his toes with hands raised up. Then he stood on a single foot for a long time taking in only air or dry leaves. Brahmā and others were pleased by

*. For the Story of Heti cf AP. 114.26-27 and NP. II (i.e. uttara) 47.9-16.

his penance. He chose the boons from them, the bestowers of the boons.

8. "I should become very mighty. I cannot be killed by Devas, Daityas, or human beings with any kind of *Śastra* or *Astra* (ordinary weapons and miraculous missiles). I should not be killed by the discus and other weapons of Kṛṣṇa (Viṣṇu), Īśāna and others".

9. Saying "So be it", they vanished. Heti conquered Devas and began to rule as Indra. Brahmā, Hara and others became afraid (of him).

10. They sought refuge in Hari. They told him, "Kill Heti". Hari said to them, "O Suras, this Heti cannot be killed by Devas or Asuras.

11. Give a great weapon unto me whereby I can kill that Heti". When told thus, Devas gave the (bone) club to Hari.

12. At the outset he held that (bone) club, so he was called, "Gadādhara" by Devas. After striking Heti with his (bone) club, he went to heaven along with Devas.

13. In order to steady the rocky slab of Gayāsuraśiras, he went there armed with this Gadā to stabilise the Śilā. Hence he is called Ādigadādhara.[1]

14-17. Ādigadādhara is manifest in the form of *Śilās*[2] (rocky slabs and mountains). Through Muṇḍapṛṣṭha mountain, Prabhāsa mountain, the mountains Udyanta, Gītanāda, Bhasmakūṭa, Gṛdhrakūṭa, Pretakūṭa, Ādipāla and Aravindaka, Pañcaloka, Saptaloka, Vaikuṇṭha, Lohadaṇḍaka, Krauñcapāda, Akṣayavaṭa, Phalgutīrtha, Madhuśravā, Dadhikulyā, Madhukulyā, the great river Devikā and Vaitaraṇī etc. Ādigadādhara becomes manifest.

1. This etymology does not explain the term '*Ādi*' in Ādigadādhara.

2. Near Gayā there is a chain of sacred but rocky hillocks and their tops are called Bhasmakūṭa, Gṛdhrakūṭa etc. Gayāśiras consists of this chain of hillocks extending to about two miles.

This spot was well-known before the Buddha, as we find the record of the Buddha's visit to Gayāsisa (Pali for Gayāsīrṣa) in the *Aṅguttara Nikāya* Vol. IV, p. 302.

18-20. The following are manifest-cum-unmanifest[1]: Viṣṇu's Pada (footprint), Rudrapada, the excellent Pada of Brahman, Kāśyapa's Pada, which is divine as well as wherein two hands have come out, the *Padas* of the five fires, the prominent *Padas* of Indra and Agastya and the *Padas* of Ravi, Kārtikeya, Krauñca and Mataṅga. In all the Liṅgas the primordial Gadādhara, the glorious and manifest Gadādhara, abides in manifest-cum-unmanifest form.

21-25. The primordial Gadādhara is stationed[2] as Gāyatrī, Sāvitrī, Sandhyā, Sarasvatī, Gayāditya, Uttarārka, Dakṣiṇārka, Naimiṣa, Śvetārka, Gaṇanātha, the eight Vasus, the leading sages, the eleven Rudras, the Seven Sages, Somanātha, Siddheśa, Kapardīśa, Vināyaka, Nārāyaṇa, Mahālakṣmī, Brahmā, Śrīpuruṣottama, Mārkaṇḍeyeśa, Kautīśa, Aṅgireśa, Pitāmaha, Janārdana, Maṅgalā, the excellent Puṇḍarīkākṣa etc. (these are the various shrines and deities in Gayā). When the Rākṣasa Heti was killed Viṣṇu went back to his city.

26. When the Asura was rendered motionless by Brahmā in the company of Rudra and others, Vedhas (god Brahmā) who was overjoyed eulogised Ādyagadāpāṇi (the primordial wielder of the club) (as follows):

Brahmā said:

27. I bow unto Gadādhara who is the bestower of boons, from whom Times (Death's) blemishes have receded, who is stationed in Gayā, whose attributes are well known, who possesses many attributes, who is present in the cavity (of the heart), who is in the white-coloured house of the excellent mountain and who is worshipped by all the Gaṇas (groups).

28. I bow unto Gadādhara, who bestows prosperity on the day, who grants prosperity on the hosts of Devas, who grants royal glory even to Bhava (Śiva), whose glory tears down Daityas, who bestows glory in the Kali age and whose glory

---

1. The various *Padas* (footprints) of gods and sages at which Piṇḍas are to be offered are the manifest-cum-unmanifest forms of Ādigadādhara. The idols are the manifest forms, unmanifest in Phalgu (TSS 365).

2. These are various deities and shrines at Gayā. The presence of Gadādhara is thus claimed everywhere in Gayā.

suppresses the impurities of the Kali age. He bestows affluence on those who seek refuge.

29. I bow unto him who is both steady and unsteady, who is eulogised regularly by masterly persons, who possesses wonderfully desirable features, who is very firm, who is both present and not present in the traditions, who presides over flourishing persons, who cannot be approached by those who commit sins, who has his own abode and whose spiritual lineage and eulogy is great.

30. I perpetually bow to the supreme eternal Lord Hari, who is incorporeal, who has no sense organs, who has no birth, who is decorated on *Sūryavedi*[1] (altar of the Sun), to Gadādhara who is devoid of sound and face.

31. I bow unto Gadādhara who is present in the heart, who is faster than the mind, who is beyond the reach of the mind, who is always without a second, who is eulogised by learned men in the Vedāntas, who is *Cidātmaka* (pure consciousness) and who is beyond the causes present in Kali.

Sanatkumāra said:

32. The primordial wielder of the club, on being eulogised thus by Brahmā along with Devas said, "You choose the boon" and Brahmā spoke to him :

33. "We will not stay on the rock of divine nature and features without you. We will stay here for ever along with you who have the manifest form."

34. "So be it", said Gadādhara and stayed there along with Śrī for the protection of the worlds and for the salvation of the people. The manifest form Puṇḍarīkākṣa (Viṣṇu) is well known as Janārdana.

35. The primordial and eternal form that is incomprehensible even to the Vedas, is very clear and manifest in the Śvetakalpa, will become unmanifest in the Vārāhakalpa although it had become manifest before.

36. There is no doubt in this that he will be clearly manifest in Gayāśiras for the emancipation of the worlds and the protection of the Devas.

1. Refers to the sacred cluster of the Sūrya temple—Vidyarthi p. 6.

37. Those who visit lord Ādigadādhara and pray to him devoutly, will become free from the ailments of leprosy etc. and will attain Hari's abode.

38. Those who regularly and devoutly visit lord Ādigadādhara will attain wealth, foodgrain, longevity and good health.

39. Men who bow unto Ādigadādhara with great devotion and faith achieve good qualities, fame and happiness, wives, sons and grandsons. They attain Brahmapura. They will enjoy the fruits of a heap of meritorious action.

40. By offering scents, one will be rich in fragrance; by offering flowers, he attains good fortune; by offering sweet incense, he attains a kingdom and illumination through lamps.

41. By gifting flags, he becomes free from sins; by undertaking pilgrimage, he attains Brahmaloka. He who performs a Śrāddha and offers Piṇḍas, leads his Pitṛs to Viṣṇu.

42. Those who bow to Ādigadādhara with great faith and eulogise him and worship him, lead their Pitṛs to Mādhava, Even Śiva eulogised Ādigadādhara with great pleasure.

Śiva said :

43. I bow to Ādigadādhara who though unmanifest, becomes manifest in the form of Muṇḍapṛṣṭha etc. and the holy centre Phalgutīrtha etc.

44. I bow down to Ādigadādhara who is both manifest and unmanifest in the forms of Padas and Mukhaliṅgas etc.

45. I bow down to Ādigadādhara who is born naturally on Muṇḍapṛṣṭha and who is of unmanifest nature in the form of Janārdana.

46. I bow down to Gadādhara who is stationed in the Śilā of divine features, who is worshipped by Brahmā and other Suras and who is honoured by Devas.

47. I bow down to Ādigadādhara on seeing, touching, worshipping and bowing down to whom people attain Brahmaloka.

48. I bow down to Ādigadādhara who is the sole cause of *Mahat* etc. that is manifest and who is of the unmanifest form.

49. I bow down to Ādigadādhara who is devoid of physical body, sense organs, mind, intellect, vital airs and ego and who is free from wakeful and dreaming states.

50. I bow down to Ādigadādhara who is free from the eternal and the non-eternal (state), who is truth, bliss and the unchanging state, the fourth one, the luminous Ātman.

Sanatkumāra said :

51. Eulogised thus by Maheśa, Ādigadādhara became delighted. That lord stationed himself on the slab along with Brahmā and other Devas.

52. Those who eulogise and worship Lord Ādigadādhara who is stationed on the mountain Muṇḍapṛṣṭha shall attain Brahmaloka.

53. He who seeks piety shall attain piety; he who seeks love shall secure love and he who seeks salvation shall get salvation.

54. Even a barren lady gets a son who will be a master of Vedas and their Aṅgas (ancillaries). A king attains victory; a Śūdra too shall attain happiness.

55. By worshipping Ādigadādhara, a person who seeks sons gets sons. Everything that is desired by the mind is obtained through worship etc. of Hari.

CHAPTER FORTYEIGHT

Procedure of the Pilgrimage to Gayā

Sanatkumāra said :

1. O Nārada, listen. I shall recount the (procedure of) pilgrimage to Gayā which yields salvation. Redemption for those who perform Śrāddha has been sung by Brahmā earlier.

2-4. If one makes preparations for going to Gayā,[1] one should duly perform Śrāddha and circumambulate the village, dressed only in loin cloth like a pilgrim. He should then go to the next village and partake of the remainder of the Śrād-

1. Verses 2-5 deal with preliminaries before starting on pilgrimage to Gayā.

dha. Thereafter, he should go on foot everyday. He must avoid taking monetary gifts. He who abstains from taking monetary gifts, who is contented, who is invariably pure and who is devoid of arrogance enjoys the fruit of the pilgrimage to the holy centres.

5. He whose hands and feet are controlled, the mind is restrained and who possesses learning, penance and fame, attains the fruit of the pilgrimage to the holy centre.

6. At the entrance to Gayā to the east is the great river Phalgu. After digging upwater (in the river bed), he should take his bath in the pure water.[1]

7. After performing the Tarpaṇa of Devas and others and after performing the Śrāddha in accordance with the injunctions, one should recite the Vedic passage belonging to one's own branch but need not perform *Arghyapradāna* (offering of *Arghya*) and Āvāhana (invocation).

8. On the next day he should with all (bodily and mental) purity go to Pretaparvata.[2] The intelligent pilgrim should thereafter take bath in Brahmakuṇḍa and perform Tarpaṇa of Devas and others.

9. With all purity, he should perform the Śrāddha for those who are Sapiṇḍas (having the similar Piṇḍas i.e. near kinsmen) on the Pretaparvata. The intelligent pilgrim should face the southern direction and wear the sacred thread as *Prācināviti* (from the right shoulder across the chest and passed under the left arm.)

10-12. "The fire with Kavyabāla (?), Soma, Yama, Aryamā, the Pitṛ-god, like Agniṣvāttas, the Barhiṣads and the Somapās may (please) come; you are the deities of the Pitṛs. O blessed deities, my Pitṛs are protected by you. Those kindred relations born in the family are to be offered the ball of rice. I

1. Verses 6-7 deal with the 1st day of the Yātrā. Vā.P. prescribes only bath in Phalgu, Śrāddha and recitation of one's Veda. TSS. (p.352) prescribes visit to Pretaśilā and Śrāddha on that very day after Śrāddha at Phalgu.

2. The rites on the 2nd day: Visit to Pretaparvata, bath in Brahmakuṇḍa, Śrāddha, offering of Piṇḍas first to one's paternal anscetors (vv. 23-25) and to other relatives—a long list of which is given in vv.33-55. The list shows the breadth of outlook of the ancients.

have come to Gayā for that purpose. Let them all attain perpetual contentment by means of this Śrāddha."

13-14. After saying this and performing Ācamana, the pilgrim should perform Prāṇāyāma with effort, in order to obtain Brahmaloka which is devoid of *Punarāvṛtti* (a return to Saṁsāra again). After performing the Śrāddha duly in this manner, he, should invoke the Pitṛs and worship them with the mantras. Then he should offer the balls of rice.

15-16. In the holy centre, on the Pretaśilā etc. the place must first be washed with *Pañcagavya* separately while their *mantras* are being recited. Then the deities must be worshipped with offerings of *Caru* soaked in ghee. So long as the gingelly seeds are taken by the pilgrim in the holy rites of the Pitṛs, Asuras run off from the place of holy rites like deer afraid of lion.

17. The Śrāddha of the mother[1] should be performed separately during the Aṣṭakas (i.e. the 8th day of the three months on which the Pitṛs are to be propitiated), during the Vṛddhi (increase) days and on the day of the death at Gayā. On other occasions the Śrāddha should be performed along with that of her husband (i.e. one's father).

18. During Vṛddhi Śrāddha, that of the mother should be performed first. But at Gayā that of the father should be performed first. The Śrāddha is begun with the offerings of *Pādya* at the outset and the proper laying of the Kuśa grass with the tips pointing to the south to the father etc. The remaining part of the Śrāddha is to be performed as mentioned in the respective *Gṛhya Sūtras*.

19. In the case of Sapiṇḍas, the Darbha grass is duly spread and the water with gingelly seeds is offered once and the Śrāddha is performed on their southern side.

20. The water libation is offered with the sacred water of the Pitṛs holding it in the hollow of one's palms. He should then offer the *Akṣayya* (inexhaustible) Piṇḍa with a fistful of powdered fried grain. The other kinsmen are then to be invoked in the Kuśa grass by means of the waters with gingelly seeds.

1. The special Śrāddha for one's mother is prescribed during the Aṣṭakas and in Vṛddhi Śrāddha.

21. May all those Devas, sages, Pitṛs and human beings, mothers and maternal grandfathers and others beginning with Brahmā and ending with a blade of grass, be propitiated by this water libation.

22. May this be the water libation along with gingelly seeds to all those crores of past (members of) families, residing in the seven continents beginning with Brahmā and ending with the earth.

23-24. A ball of rice has been offered by me to all these: father, grandfather, great-grandfather, mother, grandmother, great-grandmother, maternal grandfather, his father and his grandfather. May that Piṇḍa be of everlasting benefit.

25-27. At Gayāśiras the Piṇḍa offered is of the size of a first or that of the green emblic myrobalan fruit or that of the leaf of the Śamī tree. The devotee shall uplift seven Gotras and a hundred families. The Gotras—seven in number—are those of the father, mother, one's wife (before marriage), one's sister (after marriage), one's daughter (after marriage), and those of the father's sisters and mother's sisters. The hundred and one families are as follows: father and his twentyfour ancestors, mother and her twenty ancestors, wife and her sixteen ancestors, twelve ancestors of the sister's husband, eleven ancestors of the son-in-law, seven ancestors of the husband of the sister of one's father and eight ancestors of the husband of mother's sister.

28. There is no invocation in a *Tīrthaśrāddha* nor is screen erected shutting off the quarters. There is no defect due to the viewing of others. Clever people should not perform the *Tīrtha-śrāddha* out of pity.

29. This following is the procedure in the *Tīrtha Śrāddhas*: providing seat of the Piṇḍas, offering of the Piṇḍas, *Avanejana* (ritualistic sprinkling with the Darbha grass), monetary gifts and the *Annasaṁkalpa* (ritualistic expression of one's intention in preparing food).

30. Mantra: "I invoke all those members of our family who are dead and who have no other way of salvation. I shall

invoke them on the Darbha grass, with water libations along with gingelly seeds.

31. I invoke all those persons in the family of our kinsmen who are dead and who have no other way of salvation. I shall invoke them on the Darbha grass with water libations along with gingelly seeds".

32. Thus the pilgrim should meditate on the Darbhas, repeat these mantras with the offering of water libations along with gingelly seeds, invoke and worship the Pitṛs and offer the Piṇḍas in due order.

33. "I am offering this Piṇḍa in order to uplift those persons of our family who are dead and who have no other means of salvation.

34. I am offering this Piṇḍa in order to emancipate those persons of our maternal grandfather's family who are dead and who have no other means of salvation.

35. I am offering this Piṇḍa for the uplift of those persons belonging to the family of our kinsmen who are dead and who have no other means of salvation.

36. I am offering this Piṇḍa for the uplift of those persons who (died) before cutting teeth and those who were afflicted even while in the womb.

37. I am offering this Piṇḍa to those persons who were duly cremated and who were not those who were struck dead by lightning or by robbers.

38. I am offering this Piṇḍa to those who died in the forest fire, to those who were killed by lions and tigers and those who were slain by horned and fanged (beasts of prey).

39. I am offering to those who died by getting hanged, who were killed by poison or by weapons and those who have committed suicide.

4 I am offering this Piṇḍa to those who died of hunger, thirst in the forest path, and to those who were killed by goblins, ghosts and other evil spirits.

41. I am offering this Piṇḍa for the upliftment of those persons who have fallen into the hells called Raurava, Andhatāmisra and Kālasūtra.

42. I am offering this Piṇḍa for the emancipation of those

persons who have fallen into the terrible hells of Asipatravana or Kumbhīpāka.

43. I am offering this Piṇḍa for the uplift of those persons who are stationed in the various abodes of torture and those who have gone to the world of ghosts.

44. I am offering this Piṇḍa for the uplift of those persons who are stationed in the various abodes of torture and those who have been taken away by Yama's attendants.

45. I am offering this Piṇḍa for the uplift of all those persons who are stationed in any of the hells or abodes of torture.

46. I am offering this Piṇḍa to those who are born in the animal wombs or as birds, worms, insects or reptiles or even as trees.

47. I am offering this Piṇḍa to those persons who are transmigrating into the thousands of other lives as a result of their own actions and to whom the human birth has become a rarity.

48. I am offering the Piṇḍa to those Pitṛs who are stationed in heaven, firmament or on the earth and to those kinsmen etc. who have not been cremated duly after death.

49. May all those Pitṛs of mine be propitiated through this Piṇḍa for ever, those Pitṛs who exist in the form of ghosts.

50. This Piṇḍa has been offered by me to those who may or may not have been my kinsmen in this birth but who were my kinsmen in the other births. May it be of everlasting benefit reaching unto them.

51-53. This Piṇḍa has been offered by me to all those who are dead in my father's family, to those who are dead in my mother's family, to those kinsmen, elders, fathers-in-law or other relatives who are dead, to such of those in my family as had neither sons nor wives and hence had been deprived of Piṇḍa offerings, to those who had been defaulters in the holy rites, to those who were born blind, to those who had been lame, to those who had hideous forms, to those who had been prematurely born, to all persons of my family known and unknown. To all those the Piṇḍa has been offered by me. May it be of everlasting benefit in reaching unto them.

54-55. I am offering this Piṇḍa with *Svadhā* to all these: Those who are born in my father's family ever since the days of god Brahmā; those who are born in my mother's family; those who had been my servants in both these families; to those attendants and dependents, to the friends, disciples, animals, trees, birds seen or not seen, those who had rendered help unto me; those who had been in contact with me in my previous births".

56. With these Mantras the pilgrim should offer the Piṇḍas to the women too, beginning with mother. In that case he should make necessary changes in the substantives and adjectives making them conform to the feminine gender.

57. Whether in one's own Gotra or in the other man's Gotra, the offering of the Piṇḍas, the performance of Śrāddhas and the water libation is futile if done separately.

58. He should put the gingelly seeds in the vessel of Piṇḍas and fill it with holy water. He should perform the *Parisecana* rite thrice for all the Piṇḍas and conclude the rite by prostrating himself (before them).

59. After ritualistically dismissing the Pitṛs, he should perform *Ācamana* and express these words to Suras as witnesses. "May these Devas, Brahmā, Īśāna and others be my witnesses. After coming to Gayā the redemption of my Pitṛs has been effected by me.

60. O Lord Gadādhara, I have come to Gayā for the performance of the rites of the Pitṛs.[1] O Lord, you alone are the witness thereof. I have become free from the threefold indebtedness".

61. O Nārada, the offering of Piṇḍas in all the places should be like this alone. Beginning with the Preta mountain, he should do it in all the holy spots in due order.

62. Thereafter, O celestial sage, he should throw powdered fried grains mixed with gingelly seeds on the Pretaparvata, anticlockwise and facing the south.

1. To request the supreme deity of Gayā to stand witness to one's visit may appear funny to some, but that denotes the living faith of the pilgrim in Gadādhara.

63. Mantra: "May all those Pitṛs of mine be propitiated by means of these powdered fried grains mixed with gingelly seeds, those Pitṛs who exist in the form of ghosts.

64-65. May all the mobile and immobile beings beginning with Brahmā and ending with a blade of grass be propitiated by means of the libation offered by me." O Nārada, his Pitṛs shall be released from ghosthood. Thanks to his greatness, this ghosthood will never recur in his family.

66. In Gāyaśiras the rocky slab Pretaśilā is well known for its efficacy in bringing salvation. Ādigadādhara is stationed in the form of the holy centre, Mantra etc.

CHAPTER FORTYNINE

The Procedure of Pilgrimage at Gayā (Continued)

Sanatkumāra said:

1-3. At the outset, I shall mention the procedure for holy rites in the five holy centres[1] in the Uttara (Northern) Mānasa.[2] The pilgrim should perform Ācamana and sprinkle water over his head. Then he should go to the Uttaramānasa and perform

---

1. On the third day *Pañcatīrthī* rites are to be observed. The five Tīrthas are Uttaramānasa, Udīcitīrtha, Kanakhala, Dakṣiṇamānasa and Phalgu. TSS (p. 360) clarifies that five baths in a day or bath in each of them is not necessary. Phalgutīrth is Gayāśiras. The real Kanakhala is near Hardwar. Here the tank is supposed to represent that Himalayan Tīrtha.

2. As I stated elsewhere, these *Sthala Purāṇas* claim all the sacred spots in the three worlds as being present in their locality. The real Uttara Mānasa is a twin-lake of Payoda and Puṇḍarīka. It is modern Karakul in northern Pamirs (AGP.70), while Southern Mānasa is the twin take Mānasa-sarovara and Rākṣasa Tāla of the Kailāsa range. But this Purāṇa claims two ponds at Gayā as representing those two magnificent lakes.

The Uttara-mānasa tank is now a neglected 'filthy and weedy tank' (Vidyarthi 21). Even Dakṣiṇa Mānasa, Kanakhala and Udīcī Tīrtha are partially neglected (Vidyarthi, p. 19, Table 3).

the holy ablution repeating the following Mantra: "I am taking the holy bath in Uttaramānasa for the purity of the soul and for the achievement of Sūryaloka (the region of the Sun-god) etc. and for the salvation of the Pitṛs". After propitiating Devas and others he should perform Śrāddha along with the offer of Piṇḍas.

4. Indeed the lake Mānasa is here. Hence it is called Uttaramānasa. The devotee shall bow to the Sun and worship him. He will lead the Pitṛs to the solar sphere.

5. "Obeisance to the lord and sustainer (Sun) who assumes the forms of the Moon, Mars, Mercury, Jupiter, Venus, Saturn, Rāhu and Ketu."

6. From Uttaramānasa, the pilgrim should go to the Southern Mānasa,[1] duly observing the rite of silence This is called Udīcītīrtha (the Northern Holy Centre). An Audīcya (Northern) holy centre is conducive to salvation. A man who takes the holy bath here goes to heaven along with his physical body.

7. The holy centre Kanakhala which is well known in the three worlds is there. One taking bath there, shines like gold. The man attains sanctity.

8. The holy centre of Dakṣiṇamānasa is on the south of it. Hence Kanakhala is well known as an excellent holy centre.

9. These are three holy spots in the Southern Mānasa. The devotee should take his bath therein duly and perform the Śrāddhas severally.

10. "I am performing my holy ablution in the Dakṣiṇa Mānasa for the purification of the Ātman, for the achievement of the solar world etc. and for the salvation of the Pitrs.

11. O Divākara (Sun), I am taking my holy bath here in Dakṣiṇamānasa for the sake of freedom from the torture of the sins of Brāhmaṇa-slaughter etc.

12. I bow down to the Sun-god for the propitiation and redemption of the Pitṛs and for the increase of sons, grandsons, wealth, prosperity, longevity and health".

---

1. Dakṣiṇa Mānasa is divided into three separate Tīrthas: the northern part is the Udīcī Tīrtha, the middle is Kanakhala and the southern part is Southern Mānasa—TSS 359.

13. With this Mantra the pilgrim should perform the holy ablution, worship and Śrāddha with the offering of Piṇḍas. After bowing silently to the Sun, he shall repeat this Mantra.

14. Thereafter the pilgrim should go to the holy centre Phalgutīrtha[1] which is the most excellent of all the Tīrthas. It yields salvation perpetually to those who perform Śrāddha of Pitṛs there.

15. Viṣṇu on being requested by Brahmā formerly, became Phalguka (the river Phalgu?). When its dust particles were consecrated in the Dakṣiṇāgni, it came to be known as Phalgutīrthaka.

16. There the wish-yielding cow, viz. the earth bears fruits in the form of water through Phalgu. It is within (underground hence unseen).

17. All the holy centres in all the three worlds come over to Phalgutīrtha to take their bath along with Suras.

18. Gaṅgā is the water oozing out from the foot of Viṣṇu. But Phalgu is the primordial Gadādhara himself. He assumes the liquid form himself. Hence they call it more sacred than Gaṅgā.

19. Even he who performs a thousand times thousand horse sacrifices does not attain that fruit which one attains in Phalgutīrtha.

20. "I perform the ablution in the waters of Viṣṇu, in Phalgutīrtha with due respect, in order to secure Viṣṇuloka for the Pitṛs and for the realisation of worldly pleasures and salvation".

21. The man (the pilgrim) should take bath and perform Tarpaṇa and Śrāddha in Phalgutīrtha in the manner it has been mentioned in his own Sūtra (i.e. Gṛhyasūtra he follows) with due offerings of Piṇḍas. He shall then bow down to Pitāmaha.

22. "Obeisance to lord Śiva, Īśa, the (great) Puruṣa, to Aghoravāmadeva, Sadyojāta and Śaṁbhu".

---

1. Phalgutīrtha is Gayāśiras and its boundaries as given in vv. 28-29, from Nāgakūṭa to Gṛdhrakūṭa, from there to Yūpa and upto Uttara-mānasa. It is beneath the mountain Muṇḍapṛṣṭha-AP. 115-25-26 and G.P.I.83. 4 differ.

23. After taking bath in Phalgutīrtha and visiting lord Gadādhara, the man (the pilgrim) shall redeem his own soul, ten generations of the past and ten generations of the future.

24-25. After bowing to Lord Gadādhara, one should worship by means of this Mantra: "Om, obeisance to Vāsudeva. Obeisance to Saṅkarṣaṇa, to Pradyumna, to Aniruddha, to Śrīdhara, to Viṣṇu". After performing the ablution in the "five holy centres", the pilgrim shall lead the Pitṛs to Brahmaloka.

26. Futile indeed is the *Śrāddha* of that person who does not bathe the mace-bearing deity by means of *Pañcāmṛta* nor embellishes it with flowers, garments etc.

27. From the Nāgakūṭa mountain to Gṛdhrakūṭa, from there to *Yūpa* and from there upto Uttaramānasa—This is mentioned as Gayāśiras. It is otherwise called Phalgutīrtha.

28. The excellent Phalgutīrtha is beneath the mountain Muṇḍapṛṣṭha. All the Pitṛs shall attain salvation by means of the performance of Śrāddha etc.

29. Thus the procedure of the first day has been explained.

The Second Day:

On the second day[1] the pilgrim should go to the Dharmāraṇya since it was here that Dharma performed the *Yajña.*

30. O Nārada, he who performs ablutions, *Tarpaṇa* and *Śrāddha* in the Mataṅgavāpī (the tank of Mataṅga) obtains Brahmaloka by going to Dharmāraṇya.

31-32. After going to Mataṅgavāpī the pilgrim should bow down to Mataṅgeśa and repeat this Mantras: "May the deities be the authority and may the guardians of the quarters be the witnesses (to the fact that) I had come to this Mataṅgavāpī and the redemption of the Pitṛs has been effected by me".

At the outset he should perform the Śrāddha etc. at the well (called) Brahmatīrtha.

33. (He who performs the Śrāddha etc.) in between that well and the sacrificial post, enables all the Pitṛs to cross the (ocean of existence). After bowing down to Dharma and Dharmeśvara, he should bow down to the tree of Mahābodhi (the great enlightenment).

1. The second day of Pañca Tīrthī Yātrā is the 4th day from entrance at Gayā. NP.II.45.103-104, AP. 115.34-37 mention these very Tīrthas on the 'second day'.

34. "Obeisance to you the king of Aśvatthas (holy fig trees), of the form of Brahmā, Viṣṇu and Śiva, the tree of enlightenment (*Bodhidruma*)[1] for the performers (of Śrāddha etc.) and the redeemer of the Pitṛs.

Additional Verses

1. Repeated obeisance to the Aśvattha (the holy fig tree), the tree with tremulous leaves, the cause of permanent stabilisation. Obeisance to Yajña, the Bodhisattva.

2. O Pippala, you are the eleventh among Rudras. You are the fire among Vasus; you are Nārāyaṇa among Devas. You are the king of trees.

3. O Aśvattha, king of trees since Nārāyaṇa stays in you perpetually, you are the most auspicious of all trees; you are blessed for ever; you are the destroyer of evil dreams.

4. I bow down to Hari who has assumed the form of a tree, who is in the form of the Aśvattha tree, who is the lord Puṇḍarīkākṣa (Viṣṇu) wielding Śaṅkha, Cakra and Gadā.

[End of Addl. Verses]

35. As a result of seeing and touching you, may our kinsmen, of our family or our mother's family who have been in distress, attain perpetual stay in heaven.

36. O king of trees! After coming to Gayā, the three debts have been repaid by me. Thanks to your grace, I have been relieved from the great sin. I have been released from the ocean of worldly existence."

The Third Day:

37. On the third day[2] the pilgrim—the son—should duly take bath in Brahmasaras and perform Śrāddha with the offering of Piṇḍas repeating the Mantra thereof.

---

1. The Bodhidruma where the Buddha evolved *Pratītyasamutpāda*, became a place of Śrāddha! It, however, shows that the Buddha was completely Brahmanised by the time of this Purāṇa.

2. The 3rd day of Pañcatīrthī is the 5th day from entering Gayā. Some of the rites mentioned here are found in *AP*. 115. 35-40 and *NP*. II. 46.

38. "I am performing the ablution in this holy Tīrtha for the relief from the three debts". (Śrāddha performed) in the middle of *Kūpa* (well) and *Yūpa* (the sacrificial post) shall lead the Pitṛs to Brahmaloka".

39. This Yūpa (sacrificial post) was raised by Brahmā after performing the sacrifice. After performing this Śrāddha in Brahmasaras, he redeems all the Pitṛs.

40. After circumambulating the Yūpa, one attains the fruit of Vājapeya sacrifice. After bowing down to Brahmā, he will lead the Pitṛs to Brahmaloka.

41. "Obeisance be to Brahmā, the unborn, the causal form of the birth etc. of this universe. Repeated bows to the redeemer of the devotees and the Pitṛs."

42. The Mango trees growing near the place called *Gopracara* were planted by Brahmā. Merely by watering them, one shall enable the Pitṛs to attain salvation.

43. Mantra : "For the cause of the salvation of the Pitṛs, I am watering the mango tree that has come up from the Brahmasaras and which is of the forms of Brahmā and Viṣṇu".

44. "(Like a Sage) I with the tips of my hands am touching the water pot and the Kuśa grass. I am offering water at the root of the Mango tree. The Mango tree is watered and the Pitṛs are propitiated. One action alone has become famous as serving two purposes."

45-46. Then, with a controlled mind, the pilgrim should offer the oblation[1] to Yama with the Mantra: "Yamarāja and Dharmarāja have been engaged in the work of stabilising (demon Gaya). I am offering oblation to both of them for the cause of the liberation of the Pitṛs".

O Nārada, thereafter the pilgrim should offer oblations to the dogs, repeating the following Mantra :

47. "There are two dogs born of the family of Vaivasvata (Yama). They are dark and variegated in colour. I am offering oblation to them. May they protect me for ever, on the path".

---

1. V. 45 is the Mantra for Yamabali, v. 46 for *Śva-bali* (Bali to Dogs) and v. 47 is for *Kākabali* (Bali to Crows). The pilgrim is to take a bath (in Brahmasaras thereof)— TSS 362-363.

48-49. O Nārada, thereafter the pilgrim should offer oblation to the crows repeating the following Mantra : "May the crows from the quarters of Indra (i.e. East), Varuṇa (West), Vāyu (North-west), Yama (South) and Nirṛti (South-west) accept the Piṇḍa placed on the ground."

The Fourth Day:

On the Fourth Day,[1] the pilgrim should perform the rites of ablution etc. in Phalgutīrtha.

50. Then the pilgrim should perform Śrāddha at the foot (of Viṣṇu) in Gayāśiras along with the offering of Piṇḍas. The real Gayāśiras is within the limit of Phalgutīrtha.

51. Nāga, Janārdana, Brahmayūpa and Uttaramānasa—these delimit the holy spot called Gayāśiras. It is also called Phalgutīrtha.

52. That area of Phalgutīrtha extending from the seat of Pitāmaha upto Uttaramānasa should be known as difficult of access, rare even to Devas.

53. The real Gayāśiras extends from Krauñcapāda up to Phalgutīrtha. Since this is the face of Gayāsura, the Śrāddha performed here is of everlasting benefit.

54. The region below the mountain Muṇḍapṛṣṭha too constitutes Phalgutīrtha. It is here that the primordial Gadādhara is stationed in both manifest and unmanifest forms.

55. The foot-prints of Viṣṇu and others are there conducive to the liberation of the Pitṛs. This Viṣṇupada (the foot-print of Viṣṇu) is divine and destructive of sins at its very sight.

56-58. By touching and worshipping it sins are dispelled. Whatever is given unto the Pitṛs becomes *Akṣaya* (of inexhaustible benefit). By performing the *Śrāddha* along with the *Piṇḍa* offerings one leads a thousand members of one's family to the divine foot of Viṣṇu which is auspicious and infinite. By performing *Śrāddha* at the foot of Rudra, a man takes a hundred

1. The 4th day of Pañcatīrthī is the 6th day from entry into Gayā. TSS. 366 tells us that there is no separate Śrāddha on Gayāśiras apart from the Śrāddhas at Viṣṇupada and other *Padas*. Gayāśiras is the holiest spot at Gayā. It extends from Krauñcapada to Phalgu Tīrtha (v. 53).

members of his family including himself to Śiva's city. Similarly a pilgrim performing the *Śrāddha* etc. at the foot of Brahmapada leads hundred members of his family to Brahmaloka.

59. A person performing *Śrāddha* at the footprints of Kāśyapa leads his Pitṛs to Brahmaloka. A person performing Śrāddha at the footprint of Dakṣiṇāgni leads Pitṛs to Brahmapura.

60. One who performs Śrāddha at the foot (print) of Gārhapatya attains the fruit of Vājapeya. After performing Śrāddha at Āhavanīya, one attains the benefit of a horse-sacrifice.

61. By performing Śrāddha at the foot of (fire called) Sabhya one attains the benefit of Jyotiṣṭoma. He who performs Śrāddha at the foot of Avasathya leads Pitṛs to Brahmapura.

62. Performing Śrāddha at Śakra's foot leads Pitṛs to Indraloka. One who performs Śrāddha at Agastya's foot leads Pitṛs to Brahmapura.

63. He who performs Śrāddha at Krauñcapāda and Mātaṅgapāda leads Pitṛs to Brahmaloka. He who performs Śrāddha at the foot of the Sun-god leads even the perpetrators of five great sins to the city of Arka.

64. He who performs Śrāddha at the foot of Kārtikeya leads the Pitṛs to Śivaloka. He who performs Śrāddha at the foot of Gaṇeśa leads the Pitṛs to Rudraloka.

65. One who performs Tarpaṇa rites in the holy spot Gajakarṇa leads his Pitṛs to the resplendent heaven. One who performs Śrāddha at the feet of other deities leads the Pitṛs to Brahmapura.

66. Among all the footprints, those of Kāśyapa, Viṣṇu, Rudra and Brahmā are glorified as the most excellent of all.

67. At the beginning and at the conclusion one of them is remembered. O Nārada, it is conducive to the welfare of the performer of the Śrāddha.

68. Formerly sage Bhāradvāja performed Śrāddha at the divine feet of Kāśyapa and began to offer Piṇḍas to the Pitṛs and others.[1]

---

1. In order to emphasize that Piṇḍas are to be offered at the footprints and not in the hands of the dead ancestor even if he come in person,

69. Two hands, one white and the other black, came out jutting out of the foot (of Kāśyapa). On seeing the two (projected) hands, the sage was overwhelmed with doubts.

70-71. Then the great sage asked his mother Śāntā: "O mother, is the Piṇḍa to be offered to the white hand or to the black hand, at the divine foot-print of Kāśyapa? you know father (hence) say."

Śāntā said:

"O Bhāradvāja of great intellect, give the Piṇḍa unto the black one."

72. Then Bhāradvāja attempted to give the Piṇḍa to the black one. Then the white one, remaining invisible said, "You are my legitimate bosom son."

73. The black one said, "The field is mine (i.e. the wife). Hence give the Piṇḍa to me." Then the *Svairiṇī* (wanton woman) said that the Piṇḍas are to be given both to *Kṣetrin* (the husband) and the *Bījin* (the procreator).

74. Bhāradvāja thereupon placed the Piṇḍa at the foot of Kāśyapa. Both of them went to Brahmaloka by means of an aerial chariot to which a swan was yoked.

75. Rāma attempted to offer the Piṇḍas at the sacrifice at the foot of Rudra. His father Daśaratha came there from heaven stretching his hand.

76. Rāma did not offer the Piṇḍa unto the hand. Then he placed the Piṇḍa at the foot of Rudra. Daśaratha spoke to Rāma who was afraid of transgressing the injunctions of the sacred texts:

77. "O Son, I have been redeemed by you. I shall attain Rudraloka. If the Piṇḍa had been given (deposited) unto the hand, I would not have attained heaven.

78-79. You will rule over the kingdom for a long time and protect Brāhmaṇas and other subjects. After performing Yajñas with due Dakṣiṇā, you will go to Viṣṇuloka along with all the citizens of Ayodhyā and (including) even germs and insects."

---

the stories of Bhāradvāja, Rāma, Bhīṣma are given in vv. 68-82. These stories are given in NP.II.46.29-45.

After saying this Daśaratha went to Rudraloka.

80-81. Bhīṣma invoked his Pitṛ (father) at the excellent Viṣṇupada and performed the Śrāddha. When he attempted to offer the Piṇḍas to the Pitṛs, both the hands of his father Śantanu came out of Gayāśiras. Bhīṣma did not offer the Piṇḍas into the hands. He placed them at the foot-print of Viṣṇu.

82. The delighted Śantanu said: "You are definite about the meaning of the sacred text. May you have the vision extending to the three times (past, present and future). In the end, may Viṣṇu be your goal.

83-88a. You will have death at your will". After saying this he attained salvation.

By worshipping Kanakeśa, Kedāra, Narasiṁha, and Vāmana in the northern path, one shall redeem all the Pitṛs.

If Piṇḍas are offered at Gayāśiras invoking their name, persons (who are thus invoked if) they are in the hell, will go to heaven and those that are (already) in heaven, attain liberation (from Saṁsāra).

If anyone were to offer Piṇḍas of the size of Śamī leaf at Gayāśiras or were he to offer fruits, roots etc. he shall lead the Pitṛs to heaven.

By performing Śrāddha along with the Piṇḍa, he will lead his Pitṛs to the worlds of those deities, Viṣṇu etc. at whose feet he performs the Śrāddhas. Everywhere the mountain Muṇḍapṛṣṭha has been clearly marked by these footprints.

88b-89. All the Pitṛs will attain Brahmaloka, free from ailments. The head of the Asura Heti was split into two. Then the Gadā was washed in this Tīrtha. Hence it is conducive to liberation. It is called *Gadālola.*[1] It is the most excellent of all excellent Tīrthas.

90. Since the Gadā of Hari was washed in that great Tīrtha, it was called Gadālola. "I am taking my bath for the realisation of Siddhis. I shall attain the imperishable *Pada* (station)."

The Fifth Day:

91. On the fifth day[2] the pilgrim shall take his bath in the

1. TSS. 366 tell us that Gadālola is in the stream Phalgu.

2. The 5th day of Pañcatīrthī is the 7th day from entering Gayā. On this day one should perform Bath and Śrāddha at Akṣayavaṭa, honour

holy Tīrtha Gadālola and perform the Śrāddha along with the offerings of Piṇḍas. He will (thereby) lead the Pitṛs, and himself to Brahmaloka.

92. The devotee shall propitiate the Brāhmaṇas who had been originally assigned the duties at Gayā by god Brahmā. He should propitiate them by means of Havyas, Kavyas etc. If they are satisfied, all the deities along with the Pitṛs are propitiated

93. If the Śrāddha at Akṣayavaṭa is performed with great care and effort, with cooked rice alone, the pilgrim will lead the Pitṛs to the indestructible and eternal Brahmaloka.

94. If a single Brāhmaṇa is fed near that Vaṭavṛkṣa (banyan tree) with vegetables or even with water, it is as fruitful as feeding a crore (of Brāhmaṇas).

95. Sixteen types of gifts should be made to the priest at Gayātīrtha after honouring him and offering him clothes, scents etc. in the company of one's sons.

96-99. Whatever is given at the Vaṭa tree at Gayātīrtha to the Pitṛs will be Akṣaya (indestructible). By seeing, bowing to and worshipping Vaṭeśa with calm and composed mind, the pilgrim will lead his Pitṛs to the indestructible and eternal Brahmaloka.

Whatever is offered to the Pitṛs at Gayā, Dharmapṛṣṭha and Brahmasaras and at the Vaṭa at Gayāśīrṣa is Akṣaya (inexhaustible). Obeisance unto that *Yogaśāyin* (one slumbering in Yoga sleep) who has assumed the form of an infant boy and who sleeps on the top of the Vaṭa tree in that vast sheet of cosmic waters.

100. Obeisance to the Akṣayavaṭa which is a weapon severing the tree of worldly existence, which removes all the sins and which gives the imperishable Brahman.

---

the Gayāwal Brāhmaṇas with offerings and food and get their blessing and worship Prapitāmaha. Cf. AP. 115. 71-73.

Thus the Gayā Yātrā is completed within seven days. Śrāddha at Preta Śilā is the 1st rite and that at Akṣayavaṭa is the last rite culminating in the blessing of the Gayāwal—the Brāhmaṇa privileged by god Brahmā in this matter.

There are slight differences in the order of Tīrthas to be visited in AP and NP but TSS follows our Text (Vā.P.).

In the Kali age, people are the followers of Maheśvara. Hence Gadādhara has assumed the form of a Liṅga.

I bow down to that Prapitāmaha.

CHAPTER FIFTY

The Glory of Gayā

Sanatkumāra said:

1. The king Gaya, performed a Yajña[1] wherein Dakṣiṇā was offered and much food was cooked. It is impossible to calculate the number of articles made use of in it.

2-4. At Gayā there were twentyfive mountains of cooked food and other articles. The Brāhmaṇas who were well-honoured in the different lands, praise it like this: "No one did like this before. No one will (can) do like this in future. The monetary gifts (in gold) coins offered were innumerable like the sand particles in the world and the stars in the sky. Formerly no one has done like this. No one will be doing like this in future."

5. The Brāhmaṇas who were well propitiated and honoured well in the different lands, praised it. Viṣṇu and others (gods) who were pleased spoke to Gaya, "Mention the boon you wish to choose."

6. Gaya requested them, "May those Brāhmaṇas who were formerly cursed by Brahmā, become sanctified. Let them be honoured in the sacrifices."

7-9. For the performance of Gayāśrāddha there were Brāhmaṇas of fourteen Gotras. Even Brahmā himself has to carry

---

1. Verses 1-11a give the story of King Gaya's munificent sacrifice. The object of the story is to inform that Brāhmaṇas who were cursed by Brahmā for their greed were absolved of that curse. Verses 7-9 state the names of the 14 Brāhmaṇas—which are the Gotras of present-day Gayāwals. Out of these 11 are Mādhyandins, 2 Sāmavedins and only one Ṛgvedin (follower of Āśvalāyana Sūtra). (Vidyarthi, Appendix IV, p. 145)

out their behests. They were : Gautama, Kāśyapa, Kautsa, Kauśika, Kaṇva, Bhāradvāja, Uśanas, Vātsya, Parāśara, Haritkumāra, Māṇḍavya, Lokākṣi the greatest in the world, Vasiṣṭha and Ātreya. These were the names of the Gotras.

10. May this city be known as Gayā after my name. Let it be as renowned as the city of god Brahmā." The Suras said, "May this be so". After granting the boon they vanished.

11. After enjoying various pleasures Gaya attained the great Viṣṇuloka.

There was a king named Viśāla,[1] in the city called Viśālā. He had no sons. He spoke to the Brāhmaṇas thus:

12. "How can I beget sons etc.?" The Brāhmaṇas said to Vīśāla, "You will have everything by offering Piṇḍas at Gayā."

13-14. Viśāla offered Piṇḍas at Gayāśīrṣa and begot sons. He saw in the sky three persons white, red and black in colour. He then asked, "Who are you?" One of them, the white one, said to Viśāla, "I, the white-one, am your father. I have come here from Indra's world.

15. O Son, my father is this red one. He had slain a Brāhmaṇa. He was a sinner. This black one is your grandfather by whom many sages had been killed.

16-17. They had fallen into the hell called Āvīci. They have been liberated by your offer of Piṇḍas. O destroyer of enemies, you offered the water libation saying, "I shall propitiate my Pitṛs, Pitāmahas and Prapitāmahas". O excellent one, as a result thereof and in view of your above statement, we have come here simultaneously.

Pāṭhāntara (Additional verses)

1. All of us have been liberated by you. We shall go to the imperishable heavenly abode. Accompanied by you, the good son, all of us shall go to Brahmaloka.

---

1. Verses 11b-20a give the story of the childless King Viśāla, how by performing Śrāddha and Piṇḍadāna at Gayā he got a son and promoted his father, grandfather and great-grandfather (though sinners) to Brahmaloka. Story repeated in AP. 115.54-59 and NP.II-44.26-42; GP.I.84-34-39.

2. You shall be endowed with sons and grandsons. You will rule over the kingdom and then go to heaven. Becoming satiated with the pleasures thereof, you shall attain salvation.

[End of addl. verses]

18. O son, liberation has been effected by you. We shall go to the excellent heaven. In this manner the excellent liberation of the Pitṛs must be effected by all sons.

19. You will rule over the kingdom for a long time. You will enjoy the rarest of pleasures. You will perform Yajñas with suitable Dakṣiṇās and go to Viṣṇu's city (Vaikuṇṭha) thereafter."

20. The king who secured the boon thus ruled over the kingdom and went to heaven. The king of ghosts[1] attained heaven along with the other ghosts, thanks to Gayāśrāddha.

21-23. In order to secure his liberation, a certain ghost spoke thus to a certain merchant: "Please offer Piṇḍa in my name at Gayāśiras in order to secure for me release from my ghosthood. Take (all) my wealth. Taking all the wealth to meet theexpenses connected with the Gayāśrāddha. I have given you five-sixteenth part of my wealth (as your remuneration). I have mentioned my name (etc.) in the proper manner."

24. The man went to Gayā along with his kinsmen and offered Piṇḍas to the king of ghosts at Gayāśīrṣa. It was only after that, that he offered the Piṇḍas to his own Pitṛs.

25. The ghost was liberated from ghosthood. The merchant came back to his house. Thus is the holy centre of Gaya, of Śaṁbhu, Viṣṇu and Ravi.

26. The pilgrim should observe fast in the holy centre of Gāyatrī, on the banks of the great river Phalgu (Mahānadī). After taking bath, in front of Gāyatrī, one should perform *Prātaḥ-Sandhyā* (Sandhyā prayer to be perfromed at dawn).

27-28. By performing the Śrāddha along with the offering of the Piṇḍas, the pilgrim shall lead his family to the state of being favourabler to the Brāhmaṇas. After taking the holy dip

1. Verses 20b-25 tell how a ghost attained heaven when at his request (and for consideration of some property) an unrelated merchant offered piṇḍas at Gayā.

This story is also found in NP.II.44.44-50 and in AP. 115.60-63, GP I.84 32-33.

in the Samuditatīrtha (in the holy centre mentioned) in front of Sāvitrī and performing *Sandhyā* at the midday junction, the pilgrim leads hundred members of his family to heaven. Then with a desire for the liberation of the Pitṛs, he should offer the Piṇḍas unto them.

29. After taking bath duly in the holy water called Prācīsarasvatī and performing the Sandhyā-prayer in the evening the pilgrim shall lead the Pitṛs to Viṣṇuloka.

30-32. A person who has incurred sin due to negligence of performing Sandhyā (prayer to be performed during the twilight period e.g. dawn and dusk) in many births becomes liberated by performing Sandhyā on three occasions in the holy centre Lelihāna, in Viśālā as well as in the hermitage of Bharata.

A person who takes holy ablution and offers Piṇḍas on the ridge of the mountain Muṇḍa (Pṛṣṭha) marked by footprints and near Gadādhara, in the holy centre Ākāśagaṅgā and in those called Girikarṇamukhas, leads hundred members of his family to Brahmaloka. He who takes bath in the celestial river Vaitaraṇī leads his Pitṛs to heaven.

33-37. A person who takes bath and makes gifts of cows in Vaitaraṇī, uplifts twentyone generations. O Nārada (I repeat it three times to emphasize that it is true) it is true that he who takes bath in Vaitaraṇī redeems twentyone generations; they say so; there is no doubt in this. The river Vaitaraṇī which is well known in the three worlds has descended down into Gayākṣetra for the redemption of Pitṛs. A person who performs Śrāddha in (on the bank of) the Godāvarī, Vaitaraṇī, Yamunā and in the celestial river (i.e. Gaṅgā) in the holy centre *Gopracāra*, leads his Pitṛs to heaven. A person who offers Piṇḍas in Puṣkariṇī, in Ghṛtakulyā and Madhukulyā, in the Koṭitīrtha pertaining to Rukmiṇī leads his Pitṛs to heaven by observing fast for three nights and visiting the sacred waters.

38-39. By not giving gold or kine, a man becomes indigent. A man who takes ablutions in Ghṛtakulyā, Madhukulyā, Devikā, Mahānadī (Phalgu) and in the celebrated place of meeting of Śilā (called) Madhusravā,[1] attains the benefit of ten thousand Aśvamedhas.

40. After performing the Śrāddha along with the offering of Piṇḍas, the man uplifts a hundred generations in his family and leads them to Viṣṇuloka.

41. One who offers Piṇḍas in Daśāśvamedha, Haṁsatīrtha, Amarakaṇṭaka, Koṭitīrtha and Rukmakuṇḍa leads his Pitṛs to heaven.

42-43. By taking bath in Vaitaraṇī, Ghṛtakulyā, Madhukulyā and Koṭitīrtha and visiting Kotīśvara, the pilgrim becomes a rich Brāhmaṇa and a master of all the Vedas for a crore of births. Bowing to Mārkaṇḍeyeśa and Koṭīśa he shall be the redeemer of his Pitṛs.

44. Formerly Śaṅkara sported secretly with Pārvatī[2] in the forest called Rukmapārijātavana for ten thousand Yugas.

45. Marīci went to this Pārijātavana for gathering fruits and flowers. He was seen by Maheśa. Since he had become the cause of the obstruction of his (Śiva's) pleasure he was cursed by Maheśa.

46. "You shall become miserable." This was the curse. Afraid of him, Marīci eulogised Śiva. The delighted Śambhu spoke to him, "Choose an excellent boon".

47. Marīci spoke to Śaṅkara, "May I have the absolution from the curse". "At Gayā you will have the liberation", spoken thus by Śiva, he went to Gayā.

48. Marīci who had been cursed by Īśvara formerly attained *Kṛṣṇatva* (blackness of complexion). Seated on a rock, he performed a penance very difficult for anyone else to perform.

49. By means of a terrible penance, that Brāhmaṇa attained *Śuklatā* (whiteness of complexion). Hari spoke to Marīci, "O son, choose a boon".

50. Marīci said to Mādhava, "When you are satisfied, what is inaccessible? I have been relieved from the curse of Hara. May this rock be sacred.

1. Verses 26-43 describe other sacred spots at Gayā such as Gāyatrītīrtha, Prācī-Sarasvatī Tīrth, Viśālā, Lelihāna and Bharata's hermitage (30-32), Muṇḍapṛṣṭha, Ākāśagaṅgā (26-32), Vaitaraṇī (33-37) and others.

2. Verses 44-51 tell how Marici was absolved of the curse of Śiva by performing penance at Gayā.

51. May it be conducive to the salvation of the Pitṛs". Saying "So be it" he (Hari) went to heaven. A man approaching Puṣkariṇī of the heaven-dwellers becomes pure.

52. Whatever is offered to the Pitṛs here becomes inexhaustible. He who takes bath there, goes to heaven with his own physical body.

53. He shakes off his sin like a serpent casting off its slough. That forest of clusters of lotuses is holy and is resorted to by meritorious persons.

54. The slab of Pāṇḍu (Pāṇḍuśilā) is there.[1] If Śrāddha is performed (at Pāṇḍuśilā), it becomes inexhaustible. O sage, once Yudhiṣṭhira went there to perform Śrāddha.

55. At that time he was requested by Pāṇḍu, "Give the Piṇḍa into my hand." Avoiding the hand, he placed the Piṇḍa on the rock.

56-58. By the offer of the Piṇḍa on the rock, Vyāsa's son (i.e. Pāṇḍu) was delighted. He granted this boon to his son: "Rule over the kingdom on the surface of the earth. May the kingdom flourish perfectly and devoid of thorns (trouble-makers). O son, you are my saviour. Go unto heaven surrounded by your brothers and along with your physical boby. Lead those in the hell to heaven after purifying them by means of your vision alone". Saying this, Pāṇḍu attained the eternal immutable region.

59. All the four types of living beings, viz. *Udbhijjas* (plants), *Svedajas* (sweat-born germs), *Aṇḍajas* (egg-born birds) and *Jarāyujas* (womb-born animals) who approach Madhusravā shall go to the city of heaven after death.

60. By performing Śrāddha in Daśāśvamedhika and Haṁsatīrtha one goes to heaven. By bowing to Daśāśvamedha and Haṁsa, one goes to Śivapura.

61. By performing Śrāddha in the hermitage of Bharata one leads the Pitṛs to the abode of Brahmā. One who performs Śrāddha at the footprint of Mataṅga leads the Pitṛs to Brahmaloka.

1. Verses 54-58 state how Yudhiṣṭhira deposited the Piṇḍa at the Śilā, not in the hand of Pāṇḍu though he appeared personally.

62-63. After churning the fire within the Śamī tree in the company of Viṣṇu and others, Vidhi (Brahmā) secured the Tīrtha for the purpose of Yajña. It is well known in the three worlds. That Tīrtha named Makha (sacrifice) yields salvation unto the Pitṛs. One who takes bath, performs the Tarpaṇa rites and offers Piṇḍas shall attain salvation.

64. After bowing to Aṅgāraka (Mars) and Īśvara (Śiva) at the *Saṅgama* (confluence), the pilgrim leads the Pitṛs to heaven. By offering Piṇḍas at Gayakūṭa one derives the benefit of Aśvamedha.

65. After bowing to Bhasmanatha at Bhasmakūṭa, one shall redeem and uplift the Pitṛs. One who performs ablutions at Saṅgama, shall be relieved of sins and he becomes liberated.

66-67. The excellent sage Vasiṣṭha performed the sacrifice called Aśvamedha. Śambhu who came out of the *Iṣṭi* (sacrifice) said to Vasiṣṭha, "Choose a boon". Vasiṣṭha too then replied, "O Śiva, if you are pleased with me, O lord of Devas, you stay here (alone)." Saying "So be it", Śiva stayed there.

68. One who offers Piṇḍas at the footprints of Kāmadhenu in Dhenukāraṇya after bathing, bowing down and worshipping them, leads the Pitṛs to Brahmaloka.

69. By taking bath and performing Śrāddha etc. at Kardamāla, holy centre in Gayānābhi, near the ridge of the mountain Muṇḍapṛṣṭha, one is absolved of debts to his Pitṛs.

70. One shall worship (the deities) Phalgu, Caṇḍī, Śmaśānākṣī, Maṅgalā and others. By means of *Vṛṣotsarga* (letting loose a bull calf) one shall uplift twentyone generations of his family.

71-74. The deities and the sages who have conquered their sense organs are stationed here and there (in Gayā). Meditating on the primordial Gadādhara and offering Piṇḍas etc., one uplifts a hundred generations in his family and leads the Pitṛs to Brahmaloka. The six Gayās,[1] viz. Gayā-gaya (Gayāgaja), Gayā-

1. This enumerates the Six Gayās where worship and Piṇḍa-dāna lead to *mukti*. Gayāgaya may be Gayāgaja. If so, Kāṇe thinks it may a referenee to the pillar with a figure of an elephant near Gadādhara temple—HD IV Foot Note 150a. This verse is found in NP. II. 47. 39-40.

ditya, Gāyatrī, Gadādhara, Gayā and the demon Gaya—are the bestowers of salvation.

A man who reads this holy narrative of Gayā continuously and listens to it with faith attains the greatest goal. A man who teaches the anecdote of Gayā to the Brāhmaṇas (or who causes Brāhmaṇas to read it) is meritorious.

75-79. Gayāśrāddha is performed by him. Certainly it is done. He who studies the glory of Gayā with purity of mind has actually performed Rājasūya and Aśvamedha. O Nārada, Goddess of fortune, Lakṣmī, will stay delightedly in the house of the person who writes this book or worships it or causes others to write it.

If this book containing this holy anecdote remains in the house, there is no fear due to serpents, fires or robbers there.

If anyone reads this glory of Gayā at the time of *Śrāddha*, it will be considered by Pitṛs on a par with Gayāśrāddha even if it is against strict injunctions in the Śāstras.

O Sage, if anyone knows, hears or reads the anecdote of Gayā, all the Tīrthas of the three worlds are visited by him.

Sūta said:

80. Sanatkumāra thus narrated the holy story with devotion to the leading sage. He then bade farewell to the preceptor in music (i.e. to Nārada) and went to his own hermitage surrounded by holy forests.

INDEX

Abbreviations

c — capital
h — husband
k — king
l — lake
mt — mountain
n — name
p — page, pp. — pages

r — river
s — son
v — verse, vv. — verses
w — wife
Explanation:
Abhra—I (Part I). 51 (Chapter 51). 27 (verse no. 27)